BUILDING INTERACTIVE SYSTEMS: PRINCIPLES FOR HUMAN-COMPUTER INTERACTION

Dan R. Olsen, Jr.

COURSE TECHNOLOGY
CENGAGE Learning

Australia • Brazil • Japan • Korea • Mexico • Singapore • Spain • United Kingdom • United States

COURSE TECHNOLOGY
CENGAGE Learning™

Building Interactive Systems: Principles for Human-Computer Interaction
Dan R. Olsen, Jr.

Executive Editor: Marie Lee

Acquisitions Editor: Amy Jollymore

Senior Product Manager: Alyssa Pratt

Editorial Assistant: Julia Leroux-Lindsey

Marketing Manager: Bryant Chrzan

Senior Content Project Manager: Jill Braiewa

Art Director: Marissa Falco

Cover Designer: Curio Press

Cover Illustration: Veer, Inc.

Compositor: GEX Publishing Services

Manuscript Quality Assurance Project Leader: Chris Scriver

Quality Assurance Reviewers: John Freitas, Serge Palladino, Danielle Shaw, Teresa Storch, Susan Whalen

Copy Editor: Karen Annett

Proofreader: Kim Kosmatka

Indexer: Rich Carlson

For product information and technology assistance, contact us at **Cengage Learning Customer & Sales Support, 1-800-354-9706**

For permission to use material from this text or product, submit all requests online at **www.cengage.com/permissions** Further permissions questions can be emailed to **permissionrequest@cengage.com**

ISBN-13: 978-1-4239-0248-5

ISBN-10: 1-4239-0248-3

Course Technology
25 Thomson Place
Boston, MA 02210
USA

Cengage Learning is a leading provider of customized learning solutions with office locations around the globe, including Singapore, the United Kingdom, Australia, Mexico, Brazil, and Japan. Locate your local office at: **international.cengage.com/region**

Cengage Learning products are represented in Canada by Nelson Education, Ltd.

To learn more about Course Technology, visit **www.cengage.com/coursetechnology**

Purchase any of our products at your local college store or at our preferred online store **www.ichapters.com**

Printed in the United States of America
1 2 3 4 5 6 7 15 14 13 12 11 10 09

CONTENTS

CHAPTER 2

Drawing   15

CHAPTER 3

Event Handling   43

CHAPTER 6

Multiple View Models   141

CHAPTER 7

Abstract Model Widgets   153

CHAPTER 8

Look and Feel   173

CHAPTER 9

Interface Design Tools   187

CHAPTER 11

Input Syntax Specification   221

CHAPTER 12

2D Geometry   243

CHAPTER 13

Geometric Transformations   271

CHAPTER 14

Interacting with Geometry   291

CHAPTER 15

COLOR PLATE   A-1

CHAPTER 16

Undo, Scripts, and Versions   327

CHAPTER 17

Distributed and Collaborative Interaction   341

C H A P T E R   1 8

CHAPTER 19

Digital Ink   383

CHAPTER 25

Functional Design   527

CHAPTER 26

Evaluating Interaction   543

APPENDIX A

Mathematics and Algorithms for Interactive Systems   557

PREFACE

This text, *Building Interactive Systems: Principles for Human-Computer Interaction*, is designed for a two-semester computer science sequence in the technologies that underlie user-interface programming. Building innovative user interfaces requires a number of diverse skills. Many texts discuss the design process, software, and the user interface, and many texts cover usability testing of the resulting application. Texts on visual design also exist. All of these skills and the texts that explore them are critical to great interactive applications. However, these are all dependent upon the technical skills of the programmers who support them. This text is for the training of programmers in the software architecture and mathematical skills they will need for building the interactive systems of the next century.

Chapters 1–17 and 25 are intended for a first semester course in interactive applications. The focus of these chapters is on the Model-View-Controller architecture and its guiding role in laying out the structure of an application. Chapter topics include basic 2D graphics, event handling and widget architecture, layout algorithms, and the management of multiple views of the same data. A second theme in the book is the impact of human physiology on user-interface design. The properties of the eye, vision system, and muscle control are used to address the design of the look and feel. The reader is introduced to notation systems to aid in the design of event-handling techniques. These notations facilitate the exploration of alternative input techniques before committing to code.

There is also an extensive section on 2D geometry. One of the barriers faced by user-interface programmers is their relatively weak knowledge of geometry. This lack of skill forces them to reject design proposals from artists that require more than trivial geometry. The goal is to push programmers over this knowledge hump so that they can be more supportive of designers and more creative in the kinds of user interfaces that they can implement.

This section also covers the software architecture requirements for more advanced capabilities in the user interface. The use of command objects facilitates many user-oriented features. However, if an application is constructed without this architecture in mind, features such as undo, macros, change management, and others become unreliable or too expensive to add later. The problems of distributing the user interface across a network are addressed in Chapter 17 along with the software architecture decisions that make this possible.

Chapters 18–24 and 26 are designed for a more advanced course in interactive software. These chapters bring together the latest research ideas in moving beyond desktop interaction. These chapters also present more of the theory of human performance and how it drives the design of new interactive techniques. Topics include alternative text input techniques, digital ink, acceleration of target selection, and alternatives to simple rectangular windows.

Most interactive applications use the screen management architecture described in Chapter 2. However, more powerful processors, graphics cards, and the demands of animation in applications and user interfaces are all changing that approach. Chapter 22 presents a variety of alternative mechanisms for organizing display update software. Chapter 23 shows how the architecture principles of the early parts of the book can inform the special needs of web-based applications.

Chapter 26 covers evaluation of user interfaces from a systems perspective. The student is introduced to a variety of evaluation techniques. However, the traditional usability techniques are left to other texts. The particular focus of this chapter is on the weaknesses of experimental evaluation when designing the large complex systems that characterize today's applications. Approaches are offered for evaluating designs in a more robust and scalable fashion.

Computer Science departments vary widely in their coverage of mathematical principles. There are significant amounts of machine learning used in new interactive techniques. Because of the uneven preparation of students, an extensive appendix is provided that contains all of the mathematics and machine learning background required for the text. For those with a strong mathematics and machine learning background, the text can be read without interruption, focusing on the user-interface software issue. For those without that background, there are numerous references from the body of the text to specific sections of the appendix that provide the needed understanding. Throughout the appendix, algorithms are provided in both mathematical notation and pseudocode wherever appropriate. This allows the reader to absorb the concepts in the form they are most familiar with.

Acknowledgements

Many people contribute their talents to the creation of a book. The following proposal reviewers gave their support to the creation of this text:

- Roger Flynn: University of Pittsburgh
- Saul Greenberg: University of Calgary
- Joseph Konstan: University of Minnesota
- Rani Mikkilineni: Santa Clara University
- Adam Steele: DePaul University

There are also the reviewers of the manuscript, who carefully worked their way through the concepts, algorithms, and notation making corrections and pointing out places for clarification. Their insights were invaluable to the completed text:

- Mark Ackerman: University of Michigan
- John David Dionisio: Loyola Marymount University
- Loren Terveen: University of Minnesota

And, of course, there is Alyssa Pratt, who oversaw the production of the work. There are special thanks due to the valiant copy editors who carefully corrected the details that my eyes never saw.

Of most importance are the researchers in the interactive systems communities whose insight, ideas, and creativity have been documented in these pages; without their efforts over the last 30 years, this book would simply not exist.

CHAPTER 1

Introduction to Interactive Systems

The last part of the twentieth century witnessed an unprecedented growth in computing and information. The resulting explosion of computing innovation has reshaped the modern world, entering homes, businesses, entertainment, and communication. This growth has made computers more accessible and useful. As computing attempts to serve more people in more ways than ever before, the human-computer interface is of critical importance. This book is about the technologies that shape the human-computer interface. The goal is to present not only principles for implementing today's interactive systems, but also to prepare for future models of interaction.

Word processors, spreadsheets, e-mail, and Web browsers are all interactive applications that keep us in touch with each other and provide us with information far beyond what we can handle on our own. Computing can simplify and enrich our lives in so many ways. Cell phones, personal digital assistants (PDAs), music players, and laptops have moved into our way of life. Text messaging has become a serious form of social interaction among teens. All of these require the implementation of interaction systems. These are only the applications that we know. The future holds much more.

To get a grasp on the future of interactive computing, we must look at the forces that drive computing in general. The growth in computing is best characterized by Moore's Law[1], which says that every 18 months computers will be twice as fast and have twice as much memory with no increase in cost. Gordon Moore first stated his law in 1965 and it has been true since then. It is widely believed that although we will eventually reach the barriers of our known physics, this law can continue to hold for two more decades.

This explosive growth, with no increase in cost, continues to radically change the shape and nature of computing. In the late 1960s and early 1970s, computing was characterized by huge machines occupying large, specially air-conditioned rooms and served by specially trained personnel. User interaction was primarily via punched cards with cumbersome, expensive terminal devices being introduced later. In the 1980s, computers began to dominate the desktop and at the turn of the century, a person could carry more computing in a shirt pocket than a 1000-square-foot room once held. A simple way to think of Moore's Law is that computing capacity will increase roughly 10 times in five years and 100 times in 10 years. Thus, the average laptop of the year 2010 will execute approximately 20 billion instructions per second using 20 GB of RAM.

Moore's Law is not the only exponential growth in computing. Growth in disk space has exceeded that of computing power. The number of computers on the Internet has grown even faster. All of these developments bring the power to create, manipulate, and communicate information into the hands of ordinary people. It is a central thesis of this book that computing exists to serve the needs of human beings.

The exponential growth in computing stands in stark contrast to the growth in human capacity to perceive, remember, and express information. The curve describing the change in human capacity over time is flat. Our personal capabilities are not changing. At first, this might be a bit discouraging until you consider how great human capacity really is. The human brain contains several orders of magnitude more memory and computing capacity than the largest computers ever built. When it comes to sophisticated information processing, human beings dominate.

So what, then, are the advantages of computers over people? Computers are more precise. A computer's memory is exact rather than approximate. Computation produces a crisp rather than a fuzzy result. We might use "fuzzy" reasoning in our programs, but the result is always a particular fuzzy value. Computers and their networks assist us in transcending the barriers of time and space. They can perform tasks without us paying attention. Computers can perform the repetitive and boring work without getting tired. In many ways, computers complement rather than replace the capabilities of human beings. The things computers do for us are frequently those things that as humans we enjoy the least or perform poorly. The human-computing team forms a powerful combination in seeking solutions to problems.

To understand the future of interactive systems, a more interesting curve is the inverse of Moore's Law. If, instead of holding cost constant, we hold computing capacity constant and look at the change of price, the cost of a unit of computing is cut in half every 18 months or is 100 times cheaper in 10 years. It is this inverse law that brought us the personal computer and the PDA. In the year 2008, a computer that can perform speech recognition cost $700. In the year 2018, speech recognition will be a $7 part that can be included in virtually any device.

The inverse of Moore's Law is very important when we consider the future of interactive systems. For both human and economic reasons, the dominant model for interacting with a computer is seated at a desk with a screen, keyboard, and mouse. For the recent past, the desktop computer is the most economical compromise between the capabilities of computers and the physical/perceptual capabilities of human beings. When powerful computing costs $7, the economic balance between humans and computing will shift just as powerfully as when the room-size computers arrived on the desktop. We can already see this trend toward embedding computing into the way people live, work, and play. As of this writing, the number of cell phones (which are computers) far exceeds the number of personal computers. Cell phones are so inexpensive that they are given away as promotions to attract phone system customers. The number of smart phones or PDAs being sold has now exceeded the number of laptops sold.

Computers will be everywhere. Interactive devices will be everywhere. At the end of the twentieth century, we witnessed a transformation from each computer served by hundreds of people to each person served by their own computer. This transition will occur again with each person served by hundreds of computers. This will radically change the way in which people interact with technology. In particular, interactive computers must blend into the physical situations in which people live and work. Interacting in a car is very different from interacting on the trading floor of a stock exchange, which is different from the needs of a mechanic repairing a computer-controlled engine, which contrasts with a search-and-rescue worker on an earthquake site. The computer must adapt to people rather than the other way around. In this book, we consider not only the dominant forms of interaction, as they exist today, but also those principles that will carry us into the next decade.

HUMANS AS PART OF INFORMATION-PROCESSING SYSTEMS

In most human-computer teams, the role of the computer is to remember, manipulate, find, and communicate information. The handling of information is what a computer does best. Consider the diagram of the Internet shown in Figure 1.1. This is the most common view of the Internet with servers, workstations, and people on the outside with the network in the middle forming the connective tissue that holds it all together.

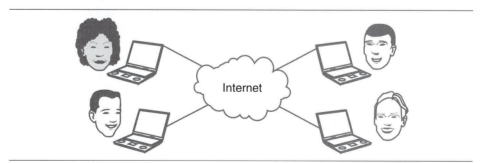

Figure 1.1 – Network-centric view of the Internet

However, if we consider the Internet as a massive information-processing engine, it looks more like Figure 1.2. The network and its computers form the conduits that connect people together. This is more reflective of the modern business and social world. When someone decides to buy a laptop, they will access the Web site of a vendor and decide what configuration they want. They will communicate that decision to some staff member who will check the budget and communicate the order to a purchasing agent. The purchasing agent will recheck the budget and send a purchase order to the vendor. The original client will get anxious about the delay and contact staff, who will contact purchasing, who will contact the vendor. In the meantime, the vendor has sent the order to manufacturing, which starts to assemble the computer and gives it to the delivery service. The message comes back to the client that it is being delivered and a tracking number can be used to find the state of the delivery. This entire process is a network of information transactions. From this view, the network appears as shown in Figure 1.2.

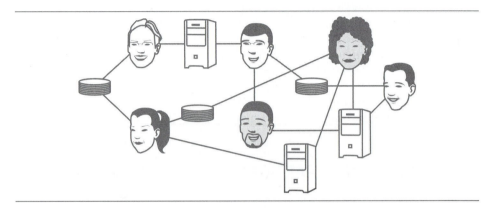

Figure 1.2 – Human-centric view of the Internet

The nodes of the network are human, with computing devices as the connections. We frequently think about the speed of the network in terms of bits transferred. However, in a human-centric network it is the human throughput, not the network that constrains the speed of the process. The human-computer interface is a key bottleneck to these transactions. As we look to the future, increasing the effectiveness of the human-computer interface will do as much or more for information processing as increasing the speed of computers and networks.

This book presents the whole of interactive technology rather than simply the design of interactive software for a screen/keyboard/mouse. The principles are frequently the same among the various modes of interaction. This book focuses particularly on the tools and technologies that make up an interactive system. A fundamental thesis of this book is that tools and technology drive what is possible. The economics of software development dictate rapid development time. This forces many products to pursue well-trodden interface designs because those are the tools that come readily to hand. Programmers, when pressed, tend toward the skills that they know. The goal of this book is to provide a solid background in a variety of interactive technologies that cover the whole range of human activity.

Though the coverage of all of human activity sounds like a huge task, it is actually limited by the number of ways in which humans can perceive and express information. This book uses the set of human capabilities accompanied by a set of basic information-processing tasks as an overarching outline.

ARCHITECTURE OF INTERACTIVE SYSTEMS

Regardless of the form it might take, all human-computer interaction has an architecture like that shown in Figure 1.3. It all begins with a *model* of the information to be manipulated. This information can serve a variety of purposes. It might be relatively static information, such as a diagram or a document that changes only when the user requests a change. The information might also be a representation of an ongoing process, such as the state of a robot, the stock market, or an online auction where independent events constantly change the information. Regardless of the mode of interaction (pictures, speech, pressure on the skin, and so on), the software must present the current state of its information model to the user. This presentation is called the *view*. Not only must the view present the state of the model, but it must also update its presentation in response to model changes from the user or some other activity. In some view architectures, this update is handled automatically.

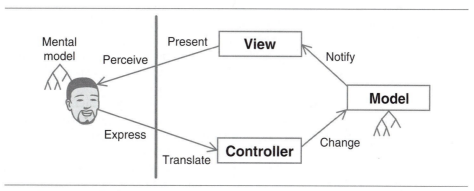

Figure 1.3 – Model of interaction

When the information is presented, the user must *perceive* that presentation and form a mental model of the application's state. This leads to the problem described by Don Norman as the "Gulf of Evaluation"[2]. A gulf of evaluation occurs when the user misinterprets the presentation and forms a mental model that is inconsistent with the actual model of the application. This gulf can arise for a variety of reasons. The user might be distracted, poorly trained, or just not paying attention. On the other hand, the presentation might be poor, the form of presentation might be inadequate for the information to be communicated, or the model might be too complex for the problem the user is trying to solve. The user will make decisions and take action based on his or her mental model of the application's state. If the mental model is incorrect, the user will make incorrect decisions on what to do next.

Based on his or her mental model, a user will formulate a plan of action and *express* some desire to the application. The software must understand what is being expressed and translate that expression into changes to the underlying model. These changes might do a variety of things. In a simple document-editing task, the model changes are simply modifications to the document. In a robot-control task, the change of information might be to modify the direction the robot should travel. In the majority of human-computer interaction, the user expresses or modifies some information, which the computer then uses to guide its own future behavior. It is the *controller* that must understand the user's expression. The controller must translate the user's input into model changes. For example, a word processor's controller translates the Backspace key into a deletion of a character in the document. Frequently, the translation is much more complicated than simple key mapping. For example, speech or handwriting recognition might be part of the input translation.

It is currently impossible to write a controller that can understand all possible forms of human expression and translate them accurately into correct model changes. Human beings themselves cannot do it for all forms of expression with any reliability. Any controller can only understand a limited set of human expressions. Therefore, Don Norman's "Gulf of Execution" arises. This is where the human has formulated a plan for a desired change but has difficulty translating that plan into an expression the controller can understand. This can occur either because the human wants to do something that the program cannot do or because the human cannot remember or figure out the necessary expression.

This discussion has used the general terms present, perceive, express, and translate. The reason for this generality is the wide range of human and computer capabilities that can be used for these activities. Take, as an example, a simple temperature control. The model consists of three integers: Max, Min, and Temp. Figure 1.4 shows a slider bar on a screen being used to present a temperature control. The view draws a picture of the slider bar and the user perceives the slider to be halfway between the maximum and the minimum. Note that the user's mental model is not exactly the same as the actual model. If the user feels a little cool and wants to make the room warmer, this presentation might be enough. However, the user might be confused about what Max and Min are and might move the slider too high. This would be a gulf of evaluation problem (does not know Max and Min) that can cause a gulf of execution problem (does not know how far to move the slider). This can be improved by having the view present the actual values for Max, Min, and Temp. However, for other uses of a slider, this additional information might unnecessarily clutter the interface. Resolving such design questions requires thoughtful consideration of the users and their goals.

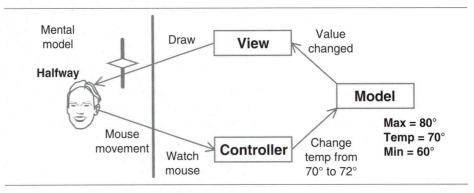

Figure 1.4 – Graphical temperature control

The user uses the mouse to press down over the slider, drag the mouse up, and then release. The controller receives the mouse-down, mouse-movement, and mouse-up events and in cooperation with the view concludes that the user wants to change Temp from 70° to 72°. The controller calls the model to make this change and the model notifies the view of the change. The view then redraws the slider to reflect this new value. This translate-change-notify-present cycle is fundamental to all interaction.

You could modify Figure 1.4 to the one in Figure 1.5. In this case, the user has called his or her home automation system from a cell phone and the interface now uses speech instead of graphics as its interactive medium. The view is implemented differently because instead of drawing its version of the model, it translates it into a sentence, which is passed to a text-to-speech engine, which then speaks the view information to the user. The mental model is different because the user hears the exact temperature. The user expresses herself in a sentence, which a speech recognizer must interpret and the controller must translate into a change to the Temp value. The model notifies the view and the new temperature is spoken to the user. The architecture is the same. Only the mode of presentation and translation has changed.

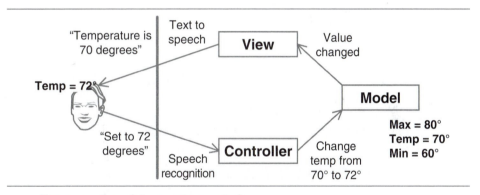

Figure 1.5 – Speech temperature control

In a home of the future, you could place a little statue of an elf on the kitchen windowsill as shown in Figure 1.6. A camera mounted in the ceiling would watch the position of the elf (as well as many other things in the kitchen). To make the room warmer, you move the elf to the right; to make it colder, you move the elf to the left. The interactive loop now becomes that shown in Figure 1.7. The view does nothing because the physical position of the elf is the feedback to the user. The user interacts with the system by moving a physical object in the real world (the elf). The camera system watching the room detects the change of the elf's position. The controller interprets the new position as a change to the model. The only effect is to notify the heater to turn up the temperature. There is no need to notify the view of anything.

These three examples—slider, speech, and the magic elf—all demonstrate the model-view-controller architecture that pervades interactive computing. They also demonstrate the wide range of ways in which people might interact with computers.

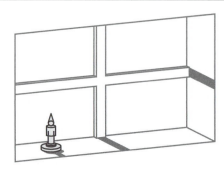

Figure 1.6 – The temperature elf

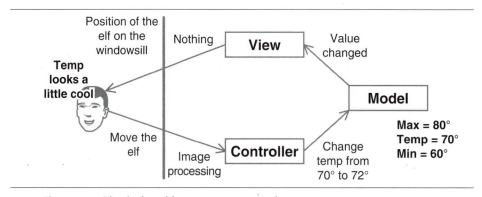

Figure 1.7 – Physical world temperature control

FORMS OF PRESENTATION

Now that we have a software architecture around which we can discuss user interfaces, we must also consider the human aspects of the problem. Only a brief overview of the human issues is given here. We need to understand how our software can present information to users and how users can express their desires to the computer. Chapter 8 provides a more detailed discussion of how human physiology impacts the user interface.

At first, the task of addressing all forms of human-computer interaction might seem daunting until you consider the limitations on human abilities to interact. Humans perceive and express information in fixed ways. For the purposes of interacting with information, only the visual, audio, and tactile (touch) senses have sufficient bandwidth and precision to be useful as an interactive medium.

Vision is the highest bandwidth channel for humans to receive information. The information bandwidth of the two eyes exceeds all other senses by at least an order of magnitude. The most important interactive consideration is the spatial resolution of the eye. Human vision has about a 90-degree field of view. However, the resolution is not uniform across that area. Most of our visual acuity is in the macula at the center of the retina. The macula also contains most of the color vision. Our peripheral vision is low resolution and mostly gray scale. We compensate for this by rapid eye movement to focus the macula on the regions of interest. This accounts for the time it takes to visually scan a page. This also accounts for many of the visual design principles that are discussed in later chapters.

Audio is the second highest bandwidth information channel. Audio bandwidth is much lower than visual and we have much less control over it. With audio, we need not pay attention to receive input. Conversely, we find audio hard to ignore. Audio is also a transient medium. Unlike vision, where the eyes can rapidly go back and review any part of an image that was not understood, there is no audio playback function in the real world. Consequently, we must experience audio as it happens. Listening as compared with looking can be slow and tedious.

Speech is a very special form of audio presentation because it uses words and language. Although the audio channel has very low bandwidth, speech conveys a large amount of information by exploiting shared experiences. When someone says the word "puppy," very few bits of audio are transmitted, but the word invokes in the hearer a large store of visual, tactile, and emotional information associated with puppies. This is both an advantage and a disadvantage. The advantage is the communication leverage that we gain and the disadvantage is the differences in experience between the speaker and the hearer. The speaker might be thinking of warm, soft, and cute, whereas the hearer might be remembering teeth marks on the furniture and unpleasant wet spots on the carpet.

As humans, we do receive information through the sense of touch. The bandwidth, however, is much lower than audio and our precision is very poor. Tactile presentation devices do exist, but they are relatively expensive and have limited ability to communicate a sense of touch for arbitrary objects.

FORMS OF EXPRESSION

To complete the interactive cycle, the user must express his or her desires to the computer in some fashion. The highest bandwidth human expression is voice. This can be speech or other sounds. A second form of expression is pointing or gesturing. This can take place either on a surface such as a screen, on a piece of paper, or in the 3D physical world. A rather specialized form of expression is the keyboard. This form is effective only because of widespread training of the workforce. Without the training, typing is a rather unnatural form of expression. With such training, keyboards are currently the most accurate way for humans to communicate words to machines. A last form of human expression is the movement of various body parts or the movement of physical objects. An example of this is the conductor of an orchestra who communicates tempo and dynamics through her hands and baton. Human beings do have a sense of smell and taste, and experimental devices for digitally generating smell are being explored. Currently, however, no effective systems have been built using these two senses, and these senses are not considered further in this text.

A key problem with human expression to machines is the accuracy of that expression. There is a mismatch between what humans can communicate and what computers can understand. Speech recognition by computers has error problems. Current computer vision cannot accurately recognize sign language used by the deaf. One of the key reasons that we still use typing as a means of input to computers is that we can trust the computer to accurately receive the message.

There is also a mismatch between the accuracy of expression required by a computer and the accuracy with which people express themselves. Suppose when working on a project a user says, "That is such a pain!" In a human-human setting, this is entirely appropriate. It communicates feelings of disgust and frustration. Other people rarely attempt to clarify what "That" really is and they do not ask what hurts. In this situation, disambiguating the references is not important to what is being communicated. That is not to say that this phrase has no meaning or importance. Sensing a companion's frustration will change the way we interact with them in the near future. Today's computers cannot handle such vague communications. They must either attempt to understand this phrase or ignore it completely. Our computer applications do not carry a "sense of the mood."

The speed and accuracy of human expression largely depends on training, voluntary muscle control, and the ratio of muscle mass to body part being manipulated. Our eye muscles are fast and accurate, but most of their motion is semivoluntary, flitting rapidly from point to point, controlled mostly by attention management rather than conscious will. The fingers are very good because they are small compared with the large muscle mass in the forearms. The wrist and hand have much larger size than fingers, yet are controlled by muscles of roughly the same size. Interaction through the wrist and hand is slower and less accurate than the fingers. It is easy to do handwriting with a pen (fingers) and almost impossible with a mouse (wrist). This rough analysis of physical dexterity, which also extends to other body parts, is sufficient for most of our interactive designs.

MODELS

The two previous sections discussed ways in which people perceive and express information. However, the design of the user interface does not begin with these surface issues. It begins with the model. The model defines *what* the user interface can accomplish for the user rather than how it is interactively done. In addition to the gulf of evaluation and gulf of execution, designers of user interfaces also face the "modeling gulf." It is not possible to model the entire real world, which has too many details and combinations of details. One of the benefits of a good software design is its focus on the essentials without the clutter of too many details. Every application models only a portion of reality, and, in fact, it only models an abstraction of that. We always leave a great deal of any application out of our model. What we include and what we leave out are critical issues of user-interface design and are of particular importance to programmers as they are the ones who best understand what can be modeled given current technology. The process of creating model designs is called functional design and is discussed in Chapter 18.

At this point, you need to better understand what a model is and how it relates to the rest of your interactive architecture. The model is the information that the user will interactively manipulate and its supporting mechanisms. In the slider example, the model was the minimum, current, and maximum values. Figure 1.8 shows a collection of radio buttons. Their model is the currently selected choice.

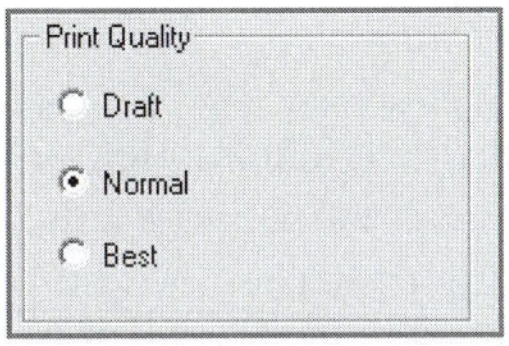

```
public enum PQ
          { DRAFT,
           NORMAL,
           BEST };
private PQ PrintQuality;
public PQ getPrintQuality ()
          { . . . }
public void setPrintQuality(PQ V)
          { . . . }
```

Figure 1.8 – Radio button model

In addition to storing the information to be manipulated, the model must also notify all views of any changes. For this reason, you should never make model variables public—always access them through a method interface, as shown in Figure 1.8. This method interface defines the model. In some architectures (as described in Chapter 2), the changes are handled automatically.

Figure 1.9 shows the game Minesweeper. The model for this game is an array of cells. Each cell is hidden or showing, has a mine or not, and has a flag or not. In addition, there are a number of mines in the field and a number of flags that the user has set. Lastly, there is the state of won, lost, or still playing. The mines, flags, and won/loss values are all read-only because they are computed from the rest of the model and cannot be set directly by the user. The only actions that the controller can take on behalf of the user are to restart the game, set a flag, or show a hidden cell. Minesweeper is also a simple example of the model notification problem. When the user opens a cell, many cells might be uncovered. It is the model's responsibility to do this, not the controller and not the view. Only the model knows how to play the game. When a user, through the controller, requests the opening of a cell, the model must inform the view of all of the cells that have been opened so that the view is correctly updated.

We could easily put a speech-based controller in front of this model that supports commands like "show B-4" to show the cell at row B and column 4. In fact, if we had two controllers, one for the mouse and one for speech that shared the same model, the user could play either by clicking or speaking and the rest of the program would not care.

Figure 1.9 – Minesweeper

Figure 1.10 shows a fragment of a spreadsheet. The model for a spreadsheet is an array of cells (as with Minesweeper), but there is much more information about cells, rows, and columns. Cells have a textual value, but they might also contain a functional expression for that value, a fill color, text color, border information, font style, and font size. A spreadsheet cell actually has many attributes. In addition, the model allows many of these attributes to be set for entire rows or columns. Rows and columns also have heights and widths, which can be absolute or automatically sized from content.

D4	▼		f_x	=B4*C4	
	A	B	C	D	E
1	Name	Wages	Hours per week	Weekly Cost	
2	Phred Gheones	$10.00	40	$400.00	
3	Caren Wriley	$11.50	20	$230.00	
4	Phreda Phancher	$6.75	10	$67.50	
5					
6			Total	$697.50	
7					

Figure 1.10 – Spreadsheet model

In addition to the model information shown in the spreadsheet, the menu and toolbar items of the application correspond to methods on the model that provide a variety of functions, including saving, opening, and printing spreadsheets; cutting and pasting; inserting new functions; sorting; changing the calculation strategy; and so on.

Figure 1.10 also shows two additional views of the model beyond the sheet view. Just above the sheet and below the toolbar are a special view that shows the currently selected cell and a view of the contents (an expression) of the selected cell. When the model changes, all three of these views must be updated to keep the user informed.

SUMMARY

Because the dominant means for humans to receive information is through vision, the graphical user interface is and will remain the primary interactive medium. Consequently, the first half of this book focuses on software principles for building graphical user interfaces. The second half explores interactive technologies for the other human senses and means of expression. All of these provide ways that people can receive and express information.

Although this book focuses primarily on the technology, a basic knowledge of human perception and expression is required to design effective interaction. The goal is not to provide complete coverage of human capacities and usability engineering, but to provide an introduction so as to not leave technology students ignorant of the human issues.

Many software systems have been devised for building interactive applications. Within the limits of this text, we cannot cover them all. However, we do not want to focus on just one. The goal of this text is to present underlying principles for building interactive systems. Because of this, a variety of toolkits and systems are presented in a variety of notations. The goal is to provide a breadth of experiences and understanding. For any reasonable application, the reader will need to acquire specific skills with specific tools. However, it is hoped that this coverage will provide a foundation for learning the next tool and the next tool and the next tool after that.

Because this book is about interactive technology, it relies upon a variety of well-known mathematical concepts and computing algorithms. Some readers will already have an extensive background in computer science and mathematics, which will make the software techniques obvious. Other readers will not have this background. The appendix contains much of the necessary mathematics and algorithms. Portions of the appendix are referenced throughout the book to provide pointers to the necessary algorithms. Algorithms in the appendix contain many references to other parts of the appendix for background concepts and algorithms. Following these dependencies should allow readers to readily learn material that they need without getting bogged down in descriptions of familiar concepts.

EXERCISES

1. Give three examples of future ways for interacting with computers because of the inverse of Moore's Law. Justify why the inverse law will actually make the necessary difference.

2. For an on-screen game of tic-tac-toe (naughts and crosses), describe the following:
    - What is the model for the game?
    - What must the view do?
    - How will the user express their desires and what must the controller do?

3. If the game of tic-tac-toe was implemented only using speech, why would the gulf of evaluation increase? What would the gulf of execution problem be?

4. If a user was going to play tic-tac-toe with the computer using a physical game board with X- and O-shaped blocks, how could you use a camera and a projector to interact with the game? How would the view be different? What would the controller need to do?

5. Select a common interactive application and describe what the model is for that application.

END NOTES

[1] Moore, Gordon E., "Cramming More Components onto Integrated Circuits", *Electronics*, 38(8), 1965.

[2] Norman, Donald A., *The Design of Everyday Things*, Doubleday, 1988.

CHAPTER 2

Drawing

When designing a new interactive application, the place to begin is with the model. However, students of interactive software generally insist on getting something up on the screen as soon as possible. Therefore, this chapter assumes that your model has been designed and implemented and it is now time to create the view. An expanded interactive architecture is shown in Figure 2.1. Most of the implementation of an application's view involves drawing on the screen. This chapter discusses the major concepts in getting pictures drawn on the screen. These are the building blocks for the presentation and it is important to understand how they work.

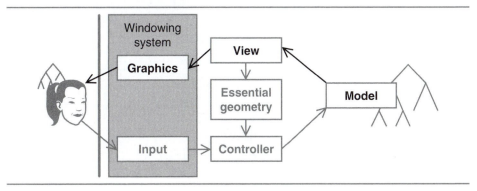

Figure 2.1 – Graphical presentation architecture

On most modern computers, overlapping windows are on the display. This chapter first discusses how these are organized and how they relate to your application code. Because of the demands of overlapping windows, we usually do not directly draw on the screen. Instead, the damage/redraw flow of control is used to make certain that the screen is up to date with the model. This chapter next discusses how applications are generally insulated from the specifics of display or printing devices by a Graphics object. This chapter then discusses the basics of light and color. Knowledge of how the eye sees images is essential throughout this text. This chapter next looks at the various ways in which pictures can be drawn and discusses their strengths and weaknesses, with special attention paid to text as it tends to be more complex. Finally, this chapter looks at an alternative view architecture using a technique called retained graphics. Together, these provide what you need to get pictures on the screen.

Only on the most primitive of devices will the view directly access the screen. Generally, this access is provided by the *windowing system*. The windowing system handles both the drawing from the view and the input to the controller. The input issues as well as their relationship between the view and the controller are discussed in Chapter 3.

The windowing system provides a view with several services. The most obvious is a list of overlapping rectangles called windows, like those shown in Figure 2.2. This list is maintained in a back-to-front ordering so that the topmost windows always obscure any windows that they overlap. Of importance to the view implementation is that the windowing system presents a rectangular region on which the view can draw and insulates the view from all knowledge of the existence of any other application or window. This greatly simplifies the view's drawing problem. In Figure 2.2, the Calculator assumes that it has a full rectangle in which to draw and the windowing system ensures that the Windows Paint window in front is not obscured by the Calculator drawing its lower-left corner.

Figure 2.2 – Windowing system with overlap

Most windowing systems actually provide a *tree of windows* so that the interaction problem can be hierarchically decomposed into pieces. This simplifies both the visual layout and the software architecture. Figure 2.3 shows a simple paint application in a window. This window contains subwindows for the menu, tools, colors, and paint area. Each of these is further decomposed into other rectangular regions.

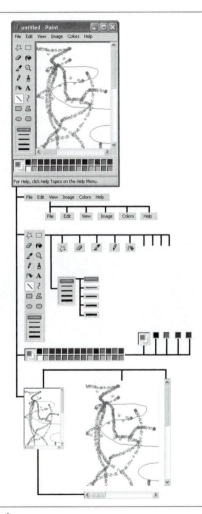

Figure 2.3 – Window tree

Each of these rectangular window regions has an associated *widget* that is responsible for all of the interaction within that rectangle. The widget is the basic unit of interaction. Part of the widget implements the view. One of the annoying characteristics of user-interface software is that there is no uniformity of terms. In some systems, widgets are called controls (Microsoft) and in others, they are called components (Java).

In some cases, the entire widget is called a view even though such views also include controller code. Widget is one of the earliest terms and the one used in this book. Whenever you are learning a new user-interface system, it is very important to find the names for common concepts. The important point here is that your view is provided with a rectangular drawing region that is independent of all other such regions.

REDRAW

Introduction of the overlapping window model for user interfaces created a problem like that shown in Figure 2.4. On the left, the address book window overlaps much of the pinball window. On the right, the address book window has been moved and the outlined section of the pinball window has been revealed. The problem is that this outlined area must be redrawn and only the pinball application knows how to redraw it. However, nothing in the pinball application has caused this condition. Such redraw requests occur when window sizes are increased, when overlapping windows are closed, when a window is brought to the front, and a variety of other conditions. Redrawing the view also arises when the model changes.

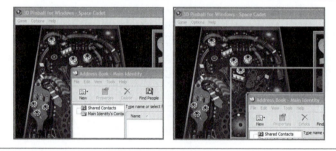

Figure 2.4 – Revealing hidden window space

Because there are so many reasons why a view must redraw itself, a general architectural solution is required. In all modern graphical user interfaces, each widget must implement a redraw(Graphics G) method. The windowing system is responsible for deciding when some region of a window needs to be redrawn and it calls the redraw method each time. The view then only draws when explicitly requested by the windowing system. No other part of the architecture should perform drawing. Every time redraw() is called, it should completely draw the view from the current state of the model. The view has no idea which of the many possible reasons caused the redraw request. In a graphical application, the view consists entirely of the redraw() method and any other methods that it might call. As with other user-interface concepts, redraw() goes by many names, including paint, onPaint, update, draw, or refresh. Every widget class has such a method.

A line-drawing application demonstrates redraw(). The model is an array of lines. For each line, you can access the end points, color, and thickness. The view class must have a pointer to the model so that it can obtain needed information. Figure 2.5 shows the model and view classes for the example. Because there is a widget associated with

```
class DrawModel
{
    int getNumberOfLines() { . . . }
    Point getEndPoint1(int lineIndex) { . . . }
    Point getEndPoint2(int lineIndex) { . . . }
    . . . other model methods . . .
}

class DrawView extends Widget
{
    DrawModel myModel;
    public void redraw(Graphics G)
    {
            for (int i=0;i<myModel.getNumberOfLines();i++)
            {
                    G.drawLine(myModel.getEndPoint1(i),
                        myModel.getEndPoint2(i));
            }
    }
}
```

Figure 2.5 – Redraw method

every window, the windowing system can get the view redrawn whenever necessary and the view always draws the current state of the model.

Accompanying the redraw() method is the concept of *damaging* the screen. In the line-drawing example, some part of the application might change the model by modifying the end point of one of the lines. The display is now inconsistent with the model because the pixels have not changed. The mechanism for handling this is a damage() method defined on Widget. Calling damage() without parameters tells the windowing system that the entire Widget window needs to be redrawn. Usually damage() also accepts a rectangle or more complex region as a parameter. This allows damage() to be more specific about what must be redrawn. However, there might be many changes. The windowing system accumulates a list of the damaged regions and then when the opportunity arises, the windowing system invokes the redraw() method for those regions that have been damaged. This combination of damage() and redraw() is the fundamental mechanism for updating the screen to reflect model changes.

GRAPHICS OBJECT

When redraw is called, it is passed a Graphics object. This is sometimes called a device interface, a device context, a graphics context, a page, a canvas, or a sheet. They are all the same thing, which is a rectangular area on which the redraw() method can paint the data that it needs. The Graphics object provides an abstract interface to the underlying drawing facility. This insulates applications from knowledge of other windows, screen controller hardware, or graphics accelerator cards. The Graphics object defines a set of methods that views can use to draw. The underlying windowing system takes care of all of the interface issues.

The Graphics object architecture provides great software flexibility. The same redraw code can draw to a window on the screen, into an image to be saved, to a special file format from which the drawing can be re-created, to a printer, or over the network to another screen. The redraw() code does not care; it just uses the interface provided.

Because of the history of drawing hardware based on television screen controllers, the coordinate systems for Graphics objects usually have the origin in the upper-left corner with the positive x-axis going to the right and the positive y-axis pointing down. The Quartz system on the Mac OS uses the more traditional coordinate system with the y-axis pointing up.

The Graphics object always has a *clipping region*. This is the region of the coordinate system for which drawing actually occurs. *Clipping* is the process of discarding any drawing that lies outside of the clipping region. This allows you to put code into the redraw() method that ignores what is visible and just draws everything. Clipping then removes anything that should not be redrawn. In Figure 2.4, the clipping region is the outlined shape in the image on the right. By controlling the clipping region, the windowing system keeps all views "playing nice" in their own space.

The presence of the clipping region allows you to optimize your redraw code somewhat. Figure 2.6 shows an alternate implementation of the redraw() method that avoids drawing lines that will be completely discarded because of the clipping region. In this implementation, if the bounding rectangle of the end points does not intersect the clipping region, the line will not be drawn. In this example, the optimization is not much use. With current graphics accelerator, cards, drawing the line is almost as cheap as building the rectangle and computing the intersection. However, in some applications with very complex models, the cost of drawing might well be worth such optimizations. This is particularly true when large sections of the drawing can be ignored following a fast intersection check. The recommended practice, however, is to implement redraw() as a simple complete drawing of the model and then introduce clip region optimization if drawing speed becomes an actual issue. In very many cases, the full draw operation happens faster than the user can see, making optimization a waste of effort and a source of bugs in the code.

```
public void redraw(Graphics G)
{
    Region clip=G.getClipRegion();
    for (int I=0;I<myModel.getNumberOfLines(); I++)
    {
        Point E1=myModel.getEndPoint1(i);
        Point E2=myModel.getEndPoint2(i);
        if (! clip.intersects(new Rectangle(E1,E2) )
        {
            G.drawLine(E1,E2);
        }
    }
}
```

Figure 2.6 – Clipping region drawing optimization

LIGHT AND COLOR

Humans perceive images by sensing light and color. Understanding this tells us how to generate images that appear acceptable to the human eye. The human retina contains *rods* and *cones*. There are about 120 million rods in the eye and they are broadly sensitive to all colors with their best sensitivity being in the blue wavelengths. Because rods are broadly sensitive to most colors, they do not distinguish between colors. Rods provide us with our night vision and our peripheral vision. The cones are sensitive to narrower wavelength bands of light and there are only 6-7 million of them. There are three types of cones: red (64%), green (32%), and blue (2%). The blue cones are more sensitive than the others and their signal is amplified so that all three are sensed in roughly equal proportion. However, because there are very few blue cones, the precision with which we see in blue is much lower[1].

Each type of cone senses a range of light wavelengths around their strongest value. This allows us to see a variety of colors other than red, green, and blue. For example, the wavelength of red light is about 650 nanometers. The wavelength of green is about 510 nanometers. Both of these are sensed by their respective types of cones. Yellow light has a wavelength of about 570 nanometers or close to halfway between red and green. We do not have cones that sense yellow directly. However, because yellow is close to red, the red cones fire and because yellow is close to green, the green cones fire. We sense yellow as a roughly equal firing of red and green.

Color blindness occurs when one of the types of cones is defective. Losing the red cones, for example, does not mean that you cannot see red, but rather that you cannot distinguish red from green or from blue. The red is being sensed by the rods and the other cones but not in a way that can distinguish the red.

Human vision also has a limited *dynamic range*. That is, the rods and cones can only distinguish different levels of color within a limited range of intensities. If the light is too bright, the sensors all fire at maximum value and you just see blinding whiteness. If the light is too dark, you just see blackness. The eye compensates for this to some extent by using its iris to control the amount of light that enters the eye. This increases the range of brightness that you can see, but for a given iris setting, the dynamic range has only so much precision. To prevent eye fatigue, you need a brightness range that does not force frequent iris adjustments. Most graphics screens only support such a range for both ease of use and cost containment.

RGB

All computer displays and all televisions use the RGB or red, green, blue color system for displaying light. Because the human eye can only distinguish red, green, and blue, you can deceive the retina into reporting any color that you want by appropriately mixing red, green, and blue light. The approach in all display systems is to generate spots of red, green, and blue light in a region small enough so that they are not seen as separate spots. This red, green, blue triple is called a *pixel* or picture cell. The density of RGB pixels is called the *spatial resolution* of a display. It generally is expressed as dots per inch (DPI) or in dots per centimeter.

The dynamic range of the eye also has an impact on representing colors. The retina cannot distinguish more than 64 distinct levels of intensity. This is less for some types of cones. For a given iris diameter, only 6 bits are needed to represent all visible light intensities. Because the iris can rapidly adapt within small ranges and for simplicity in computing hardware, 8 bits (256 levels) are typically allocated, which is more than enough to represent all of the colors that can be seen. However, intensities for each of red, green, and blue must be represented for a total of 3 bytes or 24 bits for each visible color.

RGB colors can be expressed in three ways. Display hardware always represents RGB colors as three (generally 8 bit) integers. Thus, red, green, and blue each range from 0 to 255. In some cases, red, green, and blue are represented as real numbers between 0.0 and 1.0. This representation is independent of the number of bits. This is particularly useful when some color representations cheat on the number of bits allocated for blue because humans cannot distinguish levels of blue as easily as other colors. A third color representation uses percentages ranging from 0% to 100% for each primary color.

HSB

The RGB color system is not very convenient for humans to use in selecting desired colors. People generally do not think about how much red, green, or blue they want. They think in terms of light colors, yellow colors, pastel colors, and so forth. The HSB, or *hue*, *saturation*, and *brightness*, system provides a more human-friendly way to express colors. The HSB color system is also sometimes referred to as HSV, or hue, saturation, and *value*. The HSB values are then converted to RGB to control computer displays. The hue corresponds to the primary wavelength or color of the light to be generated. It is expressed as degrees around a color wheel, as shown in Figure 2.7. Yellow, for example, has a hue of 60 or halfway between red and green. Orange is about 30 or halfway between red and yellow. Hue is generally expressed as degrees, but sometimes as a percentage of the way around the color wheel and less frequently as a 0-255 number that is linearly mapped to the distance around the color wheel.

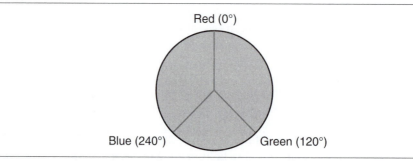

Figure 2.7 – Hue color wheel

Saturation is generally the most confusing to new users of the HSB system. Saturation is the amount of color being displayed, as opposed to the amount of gray or white. For example, the color red has very high saturation; there is no green or blue light involved. The color pink has the same hue as red, but it has lots of green and blue mixed in to give it a more whitish color. Red has high saturation, whereas pink has low saturation. Pastel colors have low saturation. Grayscale images like those produced by ordinary laser printers have zero saturation. There is no color. Saturation is generally represented using 0-1.0, 0%-100%, or as an integer 0-255.

Brightness is the amount of light. Grayscale images are composed exclusively of variations in brightness. Brown, for example, is a low brightness version of orange. Navy blue is a low brightness version of blue. As with saturation, brightness is generally represented using 0-1.0, 0%-100%, or as an integer 0-255.

Using HSB, you independently select the desired hue, such as purple (hue=300 or halfway between blue and red). You can control the brightness to get a bright purple or a deep dark purple. You can also control the saturation to get an intense, highly saturated royal purple or a pale, pastel purple with low saturation.

Conversion to RGB

Conversions from HSB to RGB are generally hard for people to do accurately. However, many systems do not support HSB directly and you must frequently specify RGB values. The best way to do this is to get close to the desired color and then adjust the RGB values to get the desired result—much like you adjust the hot and cold water faucets to get to the right temperature and flow.

Assume that you want the color of a pumpkin. The hue of a pumpkin is orange (30). A pumpkin color has medium-high saturation (70%) and about medium brightness (50%). The brightness varies depending on where you look on the pumpkin. Shadows and shading are primarily controlled using brightness or the total amount of light. The hue of your pumpkin is closest to red, so you set red (your primary color) to be equal to the brightness (red=50%). Your saturation is 70%, so you set blue and green to 70% of the brightness, which is 35% (R=50%, G=35%, B=35%). However, this gives you a red hue rather than an orange hue. To get to more orange (between red and green but mostly red), you raise green to partway between red and the saturation value (R=50%, G=40%, B=35%). If you wanted yellow, you would make red and green equal (R=50%, G=50%, B=35%). In essence, the approach is to make the dominant color (in this case, red) equal to the brightness, make the least dominant color equal to the saturation (based on the brightness), and then adjust the intermediate color to get the right hue.

This is still difficult for most people to do accurately. Therefore, all modern graphical toolkits provide a color-picking widget. The widget for Adobe Photoshop is shown in Figure 2.8. The easiest way to select colors is to spread them out on a surface and have the user select the desired color. Unfortunately, display surfaces are 2D and the color space is 3D. In Figure 2.8, the color choices are laid out with the x-axis being the hue and the y-axis being the saturation. The bar just to the right of the color space controls the brightness. The user can select a desired brightness on this bar and then all possible hues and saturations for that brightness. This particular color picker widget allows users to work in HSB or in RGB. Many only support RGB. However, this is less important because the user primarily is selecting the color that looks right, regardless of the RGB values.

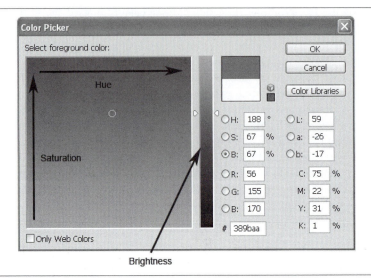

Figure 2.8 – Adobe Photoshop color picker (see color plate)

The algorithms for converting from HSB to RGB and back again are found in Appendix A4.

CMYK

The RGB system is based on producing colors by mixing light. However, when printing or painting, we produce colors by mixing pigment. Pigments work by absorbing some wavelengths of light. Thus, their color is determined not by the light that they generate, but by the light that they take away. RGB is the additive primaries. When adding them together, we get white (all colors). The subtractive primaries—cyan, magenta, and yellow (CMY)—work by absorbing or taking away light. Cyan, for example, is white light with all of the red removed. Magenta removes all of the green, and yellow removes all of the blue. If we mix them all together, we get black because all light has been absorbed. However, most pigments are not exact in the colors that they absorb and frequently do not completely absorb the light that we want. When mixing most CMY pigments, we get muddy dark gray, brown, or green. To get really sharp images, we need very distinct blacks. For that reason, most printing systems introduce a special black pigment to mitigate the pigment-mixing problems. Thus, we have the CMYK, or Cyan, Magenta, Yellow, blacK color system. This is the system used by most printers. You can see this color system in the lower-right corner of Figure 2.8.

Generally, users do not work in CMYK. However, because much of what we do is printed, you should be aware of this complementary color system. Most good visual designers are trained to some extent in the visual arts. People who work in paint and print media are trained using the subtractive primaries appropriate to their medium. Understanding the complementary nature of CMY and RGB is important when communicating with these communities.

Transparency

When drawing on a screen, we always draw in back-to-front order. By drawing in this order, anything in front overlays or obscures whatever is behind. The result is consistent with how we see things in the real world. Sometimes, however, what is in front is partially transparent. In such cases, what we see is light from the object in front as well as some of the light from objects behind. Transparency is a helpful technique in many situations. Many graphics toolkits allow control of the transparency or opacity. Transparency and opacity are complements of each other. Some systems define their controls in terms of transparency and some in terms of opacity.

Transparency is the fraction of the light that should show through from behind the object being drawn. Transparency of 0 shows none of what is behind. The front object is completely opaque. Transparency of 1.0 or 100% means that the object being drawn is completely transparent and all of the light from behind shows through. *Opacity* is 1.0 minus transparency or 100% minus transparency.

To compute transparent color for a particular pixel, we have **B**, which is the color of that pixel in the background, **O**, which is the color of the pixel for the object being drawn, and **T**, which is the transparency of the object being drawn. Based on these three values, we can compute a new pixel color **N=B*T+O*(1.0-T)**. Using this formula, if **T** is 0.0, there is no background color, only object color. If **T** is 1.0, there is no object color. A transparency of 0.5 mixes object and background colors equally. There are other compositing functions besides the one described previously. Duff and Porter[2] defined a set of 12 compositing operators. The one described previously is their A atop B operator.

Many systems specify color as RGBA, where A is for *alpha channel*. The alpha channel is the opacity information. An alpha value of 0 is completely transparent and a value of 1 (or sometimes 255) is completely opaque. In the Mac OS, windows themselves have RGBA defined for every pixel.

Layers

It is sometimes helpful to organize a presentation into layers with each operating independently. The Mac OS Quartz drawing model provides layers explicitly. The idea is that layers are stacked on top of one another and they are drawn in bottom-to-top order. With opaque images, layers are just an organization imposed on the drawing order. However, we frequently want to provide an alpha value of less than 1.0 to an entire layer. One approach is to multiply this alpha value times the alpha values of everything drawn as part of the layer. This is an easy fix but produces inappropriate results by making parts of the layer show through when they should not. To correctly implement layers with transparency, each layer should be rendered separately into an in-memory image buffer. Then, the entire layer image is rendered with the layer's alpha value. The application program need not see this step because the paint() method sees only a Graphics object. It does not care if the Graphics object is a layer image or anything else.

DRAWING MODELS

The basic drawing model for all images is a rectangular array of pixels with each pixel having a color. This is how display screens, printers, and image files are all structured. All drawing models must eventually convert their representations into pixel colors. Three common ways to represent drawings are pixels, strokes, or regions. Many systems and applications move back and forth among these representations depending upon the need.

Pixels

When displaying on a screen, there is always a *frame buffer*. This is a piece of memory that contains a rectangular array of pixel values. These pixel values are used to determine the color of each spot on the screen. Changing the pixel values changes the screen. On good displays, this change occurs within $1/60^{th}$ of a second. Slower update rates introduce flicker in the display and cause eye fatigue.

Frame buffers have two basic forms. A full-color frame buffer stores 24 bits (one byte each for red, green, and blue) for each pixel. This allows colors to be defined independently for each pixel. This provides for the most realistic images, but is more expensive in terms of space and time to update the frame buffer. Some frame buffers use *indexed color*. In an indexed-color representation, each pixel has 8 bits (or sometimes fewer). The pixel value is not a color but an index into a table of colors (see Figure 2.9). The *color lookup table* is an array of 256 entries, each of which has 24 bits of color information stored. Indexed-color representations take one-third as many bytes to store (1 byte per pixel rather than 3) and are three times faster in copying material from one part of the buffer to another, as when a window is dragged across the screen. However, indexed-color representations can only have 256 colors visible at a time. The GIF image format uses indexed color in its representation. For many applications, this is fine; however, for realistic images, this is insufficient. Some indexed-color schemes go beyond 256 elements in the table.

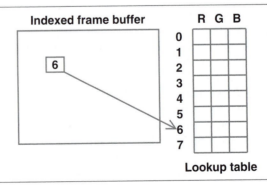

Figure 2.9 – Indexed-color images

The quality of a drawn image is determined both by its *spatial resolution* and its *color resolution*. Spatial resolution is measured in the number of dots per inch or pixels per centimeter. The higher the spatial resolution, the more crisp and smooth the image looks. However, there are limits to useful spatial resolution. At some point, the spatial resolution of the retina limits the perceived spatial resolution of an image. Remember that the relationship between image spatial resolution and retina resolution depends upon the distance between the image and the eye. An image that is half as far away must have twice the spatial resolution to appear to have the same quality. Perceived color resolution is not dependent upon distance.

Various systems exploit the spatial/color trade-off. This is particularly true when printing. Printers generally have the ability to place ink on a spot or not. They generally do not have the ability to vary the intensity or transparency of the ink. However, it is much easier for a printer to print finer spots than the eye can see. Printers use this ability to provide the perception of color resolution. By printing spots of various sizes, they control how much ink is shown versus how much background paper. Computer screens generally have limited spatial resolution both because of display technology and memory limitations. However, such screens easily produce all of the colors that a human can see. Such screens can compensate for lack of spatial resolution by using shades of color to produce more smoothly appearing shapes.

Stroke Drawing Models

All drawing on a computer is a process of determining the color for each of the pixels in a displayed or printed image. However, with the exception of pointillist painters such as Georges Seurat, most of us do not want to draw one pixel at a time. Much of the drawing that we do on a computer is composed of simple geometric shapes or strokes, as shown in Figure 2.10. These are lines, circles, ellipses, and curves. These shapes have the advantage of being simple to specify and somewhat resolution independent. A line has four parameters (X1,Y1, X2,Y2), which are the coordinates of its end points. A circle has a center and a radius. Ellipses have bounding rectangles. Text-string drawing is also generally included in the stroke model. Most drawing interfaces provided by graphical toolkits are based on the stroke model. In addition to the geometry of strokes, other properties must be specified, such as color, width, and patterns, such as dashes, dots, or cross-hatching. The Graphics object is predominantly stroke

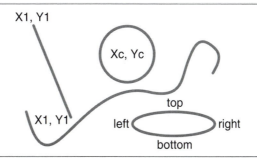

Figure 2.10 – Stroke drawing

based. The hardware/software implementation under the Graphics object handles the conversion from strokes to pixels.

Region Models

Strokes, however, are a geometric myth. A theoretic line is not useful to us because it is infinitely thin. We need a line that has thickness so that we can see it and we need to vary that thickness to create various weights of lines. The reality is that all strokes actually define regions of pixels. It is convenient to think about a line being one pixel wide, but this causes many problems. The first is when printing. A line one pixel wide might appear well on the screen, but when printed, one pixel wide on a 600 dots per inch printer appears very faint and thin. As shown in Figure 2.11, a line is actually a polygonal region. Representing the line as a polygonal region explicitly accounts for its width. The region-defined line is now resolution independent. If a device has more dots per inch, more pixels lie inside of the line's region and the edges of the line are smoother. The same occurs for all of the other stroke representations. They are most accurately represented by converting them to regions. However, we retain the stroke model because specifying the end points and width of a line is much simpler than specifying its polygonal region. We leave it up to the underlying graphics software to make the conversion from stroke representations to regions.

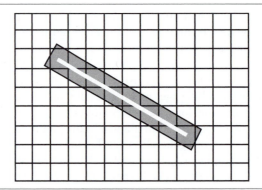

Figure 2.11 – Region representation of a line

The limitations of the stroke model became very clear when the first laser printers were produced. The very high resolutions of laser printers made simple strokes appear ugly. Similar problems occurred with text. To accommodate this, PostScript[3], which is the language of many laser printers, uses a region model for all of its drawing. PostScript also supports drawing images directly using the pixel model.

Regions are represented by their borders, and in most systems, the borders are connected segments of straight lines and cubic (polynomials of degree 3) curves. The geometry of cubic curves is discussed more in Chapter 12. As shown in Figure 2.12, a wide variety of shapes, including circles, text characters, and blobs, can be represented in this form.

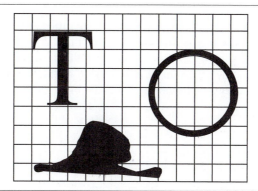

Figure 2.12 – Region shapes

All region models must eventually be reduced to pixels. This gives rise to "the jaggies" or *aliasing*. If we take our line region from Figure 2.11 and convert it to pixels by coloring all pixels that are more than 50% covered by the line region, "the jaggies" appear, as shown in Figure 2.13 because pixels do not match up cleanly with region boundaries. The term aliasing comes from signal processing, where signals that are sampled at too low of a resolution take on the appearance of completely different signals. In this case, the signal is a shape and it starts to look funny.

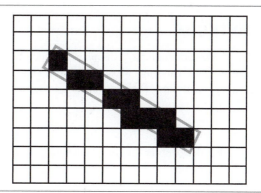

Figure 2.13 – Aliasing of a region

The ultimate solution is to use more pixels so that the jagged edges become so fine that the eye can no longer distinguish them. This is the approach that quality printers use. Unless a person gets very close or uses a magnifying glass, the edges appear smooth because the spatial resolution is higher than the perceived resolution. The alternative solution used in many on-screen drawing applications is called *antialiasing*.

It works by using shades of gray or shades of color to approximate the partially included pixels. The amount of color is modified according to how much of the pixel is covered by the region. We use the percent of pixel coverage as an opacity value. The result is as shown in Figure 2.14. At a distance, the shaded pixels make the edges appear smoother. The antialiased version of the line looks straighter and more like a line rather than a blobby bunch of boxes even though the spatial resolution is the same for both.

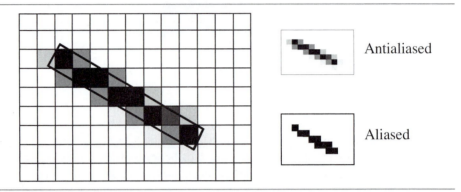

Figure 2.14 – Antialiased regions

DRAW METHODS

Using pixels, strokes, or regions, a `Graphics` object must provide a set of methods that the view can use for drawing. Most `Graphics` class designs separate their drawing methods into path drawing, region drawing, image drawing, and text.

Paths

The simplest path drawing is the line. Lines have two end points (X1,Y1) and (X2,Y2). However, there are three basic styles for drawing lines. Older systems such as the Microsoft Foundation Classes use two calls to draw a line: `MoveTo(X1,Y1)` and `LineTo(X2,Y2)`. This model is based on the old pen plotter interfaces where a `MoveTo()` would move the plotter head to a new location with the pen up and a `LineTo()` would move the plotter head with the pen down. Newer APIs, such as Java and C#, use a single `drawLine(X1,Y1, X2,Y2)` method. A third approach is to provide a superclass of data objects called shapes. There is then a single `draw()` method that takes a shape as its only argument. Shapes contain all of the geometric information for drawing. The purpose of the shape approach is to provide a simple way for saving geometry information in the model of a drawing application.

There is more to drawing a line than its geometry. There are properties of the line such as its color, thickness, transparency, style (such as dashed or dotted), and a variety of others. One approach is to add all of these parameters to the `drawLine()`

method. However, this would be very painful to use because we usually draw many lines in the same style. Various graphics APIs specify drawing properties in two ways.

In the *current settings* approach, the Graphics object stores attributes for various drawing settings. Such graphics objects provide set and get methods, such as setColor() and getColor(). When a line is drawn, only its geometry is specified as parameters to the method. The remaining information is drawn from the current settings of the Graphics object. Figure 2.15 shows how to draw red and blue lines using Java's Graphics object.

```
public void paint (Graphics g)
{
    g.setColor(Color.BLUE);
    g.drawLine(10,12,35,14);
    g.setColor(new Color(1.0,0.5,0.5)) // red with medium saturation
    g.drawLine(45,14,20,13);
}
```

Figure 2.15 – Drawing lines using current settings in Java/Graphics

An alternative approach to nongeometric information is the concept of a *pen*. A pen is an object that contains all of the nongeometric information about how to draw a path shape. All path drawing methods such as drawLine() have a pen object as a parameter. By packaging all of the information into a single object, there is only one additional parameter. The code is also easier to read because it is clear from the parameters what is actually being drawn. Figure 2.16 shows an example of drawing lines in C# using the pen approach.

```
protected override void onPaint(PaintEventArgs e)
{
    Graphics g = e.Graphics;
    Pen bluePen = new Pen(Color.Blue,1); // color and width
    g.drawLine(bluePen, 10, 12, 35, 14);
    Pen redPen = new Pen(Color.FromArgb(255,128,128),1); // color and width
    g.drawLIne(redPen, 45, 14, 20, 13);
}
```

Figure 2.16 – Drawing lines using pen objects in C#

In many cases, you want to draw a series of lines that are connected together. This can be done with multiple calls to drawLine() and in many cases this is perfectly acceptable. However, when you consider that lines with width greater than one pixel are actually regions, problems arise when joining lines together. To deal with this problem, most APIs provide a polyline drawing method that takes an array of points rather than just two and connects them all together smoothly. Figure 2.17 shows a pair of lines drawn independently and as a polyline. The polyline on top is joined smoothly because the software knows that they are joined when drawn in a single call. When drawn using separate drawLine() calls, the software does not know they should be joined and simply squares off the end of each line.

Figure 2.17 – Polylines versus separate lines

Lines, of course, are not the only path shapes that can be drawn. Virtually all graphics systems provide a drawRectangle() method. Rectangles are specified either by their bounds (top, left, bottom, right) or by the upper-left corner and size (top, left, width, height).

Almost all systems draw ellipses whose axes are aligned with the x- and y-axes of the Graphics object. Ellipse geometry is specified by a bounding rectangle. Circles are drawn as a square ellipse. Most systems also provide for elliptical arcs or portions of an ellipse. Arc geometry is specified by providing the bounding rectangle of the ellipse plus the starting angle (generally in degrees) with zero being vertical and then specifying the angle of the arc. Positive arc angles go clockwise from the start angle and negative angles go counterclockwise.

Most systems also provide a mechanism for drawing curves using cubic polynomials. However, cubic polynomials are a painful user interface for specifying curve geometry. Chapter 12 provides a more extensive treatment of how curves are specified and drawn. The simplest way to specify a curve is to provide a list of points through which the curve must pass. This can be thought of as a smooth polyline. The geometry information to draw such curves is identical to polylines. In addition, polylines can be closed to form polygons and curves can also be closed to form blobby paths, as shown in Figure 2.18. Closed paths implicitly connect their first and last point.

Figure 2.18 – Polygons and curves

Regions

Drawings are not simply made up of lines. The next most important class of drawing primitives is the filled region. Any closed shape, such as a rectangle, ellipse, polygon, or closed curve, can define a filled shape. For all of these shapes, most drawing systems provide draw methods and fill methods. For example, drawRect() draws the lines around the border of the rectangle. The corresponding fillRect() method fills in the area of the rectangle. Figure 2.19 shows the code in C# to draw a variety of shapes. Figure 2.20 shows the results. Following C#'s approach to bundling properties, all of the property information for a filled shape is gathered into a Brush object. The equivalent Java/Graphics code uses methods to set the current fill properties. Note that filling a shape and then drawing a shape with a different color creates a bordered version of the shape.

```
Graphics g = e.Graphics;
Brush grayBrush = new SolidBrush(Color.Gray);
Pen blackWidePen = new Pen(Color.Black,6);
Pen blackSkinnyPen = new Pen(Color.Black,2);
Brush lightGrayBrush = new SolidBrush(Color.LightGray);
g.FillRectangle(grayBrush,10,10,600,200);
g.DrawRectangle(blackWidePen,10,10,600,200);
Brush whiteBrush = new SolidBrush(Color.White);
g.FillEllipse(whiteBrush,10,10,600,200);
g.FillPie(lightGrayBrush,10,10,600,200,30,-60);
g.DrawPie(blackSkinnyPen,10,10,600,200,30,-60);
g.DrawEllipse(blackWidePen,10,10,600,200);
g.DrawLine(blackWidePen,310,40,310,180);
```

Figure 2.19 – C# code for drawing shapes

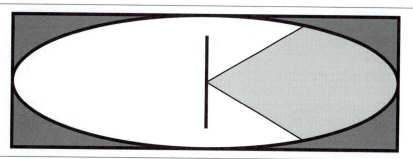

Figure 2.20 – Sample drawing

A region can be filled in a variety of ways. These include various colors, patterns, transparency, gradients in shading, and others. These nongeometric attributes for filling regions are handled similarly to the information for paths.

Image Drawing

The last picture drawing methods are those that draw images. These have become increasingly important in enhancing the visual appeal of graphical applications. Images are easy to create using a variety of painting tools. Many image representations use RGBA for their colors, which means that pixels can be transparent or translucent. The end result is that artistic effects are very simple to add by using previously painted images. Much of the visual appeal of many Web pages comes from the effective use of images. The HTML drawing model is quite primitive, but images make up the difference quite nicely.

Modern interactive toolkits provide some easy mechanisms for loading images from files or across the Web into some `Image` object. The `Graphics` object then provides methods for drawing those images. The simplest drawing methods take an image and the x, y position for the upper-left corner of the image. Many systems allow the programmer to specify a rectangle on the `Graphics` object where the drawing is to appear and possibly a rectangle in the image from which pixels are to be drawn. A scaling and stretching of the image is performed to make the two rectangles conform.

Java has complicated its image-drawing model somewhat to support Web programming. Because images can be slow to load over the Internet, Java provides a facility for drawing images asynchronously as the information arrives. This is nice for Web applet development because it allows the images to gradually appear rather than making the user wait for the entire image. However, Java applies this model to all image drawing. Therefore, every image to be drawn must be managed asynchronously regardless of whether it is necessary. Reading a good Java book is essential to correct image drawing.

TEXT DRAWING

Drawing text is special because of the variety of information to be specified and the ways in which drawing systems handle how text is to be drawn. There are three basic parameters to drawing text: the string, the font, and the geometry. For text that uses all one font, the drawing is quite easy. Most `Graphics` objects provide a `drawString(String, X, Y)` method. This draws the specified string of text at the specified *anchor point* using the current font setting.

Specifying the font usually involves the size of the text, the font family, and the style information. The size of text is usually specified in points. A point is 1/72 of an inch. A font size of 12 pt. with normal spacing produces 6 lines of text per inch. Points are a term held over from the printing press industry. With many different output devices of many resolutions, the scale-independent point measure dominates over pixels in specifying text size.

Font Family

When a user selects a font, he is actually selecting a font family. This defines how the characters are actually drawn. On most systems, a font family is an array of character shapes indexed by character code (ASCII or Unicode). On older systems, the character shape was defined as a 2D array of bits with a 1 signifying where a pixel should be drawn and a 0 signifying not to draw. This strategy was very efficient and produced good results for the low-resolution displays then in use. However, with the advent of laser printing, large fonts, and high-resolution screens, the pixel approach was not adequate. Modern font systems such as TrueType/OpenType or PostScript use regions bounded by lines and cubic curves. The region representation is scalable to any resolution with good, clear results. Changing fonts allows for many styles of script to be implemented. It also allows for the script of many different languages and writing systems, as discussed in Chapter 10 on internationalization.

Font families are divided into monospaced and proportionally spaced, and also into serifed and sans serifed. In a monospaced font, every character is exactly the same width. This mimics the old typewriter and text terminal technology. Monospaced fonts are also easier to specify alignment by adding spaces. This paragraph is set using a proportionally spaced font where each character has a different width. Proportional spacing is easier to read and more efficient in its use of screen space.

This paragraph is set using a serifed font. At the bottom of each character, there are serifs or "little feet." The effect of this is to create the illusion of a continuous line across the page at the baseline of the text. The macula of our eye (where character recognition occurs) is very small. The tracking of our eyes as we read is handled by the low-resolution periphery of our retina. The serif aids in following along close lines of text. However, with larger headings or in posters, the cleaner look of a sans serif font without the clutter is frequently preferred.

Graphics objects generally only provide two style options: bold and italic. If a font family only contains normal font characters, bold and italic characters can be automatically created from the region shapes by scaling and skewing the shape. Many font families, however, provide separate character shapes for bold and italic. Many user applications provide other styles, such as superscript, subscript, underline, shadowed, or strikethrough. Generally, these are not provided in the Graphics object interface because they are easy to produce by combining features already present. Some systems, such as the Mac OS, do provide them.

Text Metrics

Drawing text requires that the programmer pay attention to the size of the text to place it correctly. Figure 2.21 shows the basic text measures. The *baseline* is the basic horizontal location for all of the text in the string. The *ascent* is the distance from the baseline to the top of the tallest character in the font. The *descent* is the distance from the baseline to the lowest character. The *leading* is the spacing between lines. It draws its name from the lead spacers placed between lines of type on old printing presses.

There is some variation among graphics systems as to how these measures are used. Traditionally, the anchor point for a piece of text to be drawn was specified at the left end of the baseline and the height was the ascent plus the descent. Leading was up to the programmer and was adjusted by positioning the y-coordinate of the next line's anchor point. Other systems place the anchor point at the upper-left corner of the text's bounding rectangle and define the height to be ascent+descent+leading. This simplifies a lot of text placement chores. Single-spaced text simply starts at some

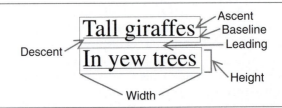

Figure 2.21 – Text metrics

top point and proceeds by adding the height to position the anchor point of the next string. Careful reading of the API of your system is required to get this right.

With monospaced fonts, the width of a string is simply the number of characters times the character width of the font. With proportionally spaced fonts, the width is generally the sum of the widths of the characters in the string. For most drawing systems, a method is provided to calculate the width of a string. There are, however, some subtle details in the sizing of text. As I am typing this paragraph, it is being displayed on my screen using a "Times New Roman" font from Microsoft. When this is printed for you to read, it will probably use a version of the "Times" font prepared by the vendor of the printer on which this page was printed. These fonts will be very similar but not necessarily identical. For the right-justification of this paragraph to work correctly, the size measurement of the strings must be exact, not just sort of, kind of, maybe similar. To accommodate this, every Graphics object provides access to some form of FontMetrics. A FontMetrics object provides information about exact sizing of strings or characters. It is the Graphics object that knows where the text will ultimately be drawn and, thus, can return size information that is appropriate to that output destination.

One variation on proportional spacing is *kerning*. Kerning tries to overlap characters along the x-axis to save space and to produce a more pleasing visual spacing. On the left of Figure 2.22 are two examples of kerning. The upper-left example is the normal kerning provided by Adobe Photoshop. The lower-left example shows even more extreme kerning that appreciably shortens the string. The string on the right is not kerned. It uses the standard proportional font spacing that has each character using its own region on the x-axis. Note that the text on the right seems to be uncomfortably spread out even though there is technically zero space between characters. This is because our eyes see space independent of axis alignment. For interactive use, we generally do not use kerning because it complicates character spacing and also interactive character selection with a mouse. The font metrics are also more complicated because the appropriate spacing is based on character pairs rather than on individual characters. Kerning is, however, widely used in printing where it uses less space (paper) and provides a nicer look to the result.

WAY
WAY   WAY

Figure 2.22 – Kerning

Text Placement

You can specify where a string of text should be drawn in a variety of ways. Most of them are based on an anchor point, which is the x, y position specified in the Graphics method that draws a string. As mentioned earlier, some systems place the anchor point on the baseline of the string and others at the top of the string. Many systems allow an alignment to be specified, generally left, center, or right. These alignments indicate whether the left, center, or right side of the string should be aligned with the anchor point. This simplifies laying out multiple lines of text with a given alignment.

There is a problem, however, with text that is justified on both margins. The standard approach is to calculate the size of each word as a separate string, compute the amount of space on the line, and then distribute the space evenly between the words. Some graphics systems, such as the one associated with C#, allow text to be specified in a bounding rectangle. By specifying a rectangle, the underlying graphics system can provide automatic word wrapping and justification within that rectangle.

Multifont Drawing

Drawing in multiple fonts and multiple sizes, such as in Figure 2.23, is generally done using multiple calls to the drawString() method. Each section of text that has its own font setting is dealt with as a separate draw so that the font information can be specified. This becomes complicated with automatic word wrap or justification drawing. To do the word wrap and justification, the text must be presented all at once. However, a simple text string does not have embedded font information. Some systems have started to provide drawing facilities that support the basic formatting specifications of HTML[4]. This makes multifont drawing quite easy. However, HTML drawing is far from universal among graphics systems.

This has several **Fonts,**
Sizes, *and styles.*

Figure 2.23 – Multifont drawing

Retained Graphics

The preceding discussion has assumed that the application program will update the screen whenever needed through its redraw() method and that changed screen regions will be indicated through the damage() method. A notable alternative to this architecture is the retained graphics or display list architecture.

In very old graphics devices, there was not enough memory to store all of the pixels on the screen. Instead, the presentation was represented by a list of drawing commands and the display hardware would execute these commands fast enough to continuously refresh the screen. This made the stroke drawing model the fundamental hardware display architecture. This architecture had the decided advantage that any modification to the display list would immediately appear on the screen, making animation and dynamic movement of the screen very easy to implement.

The limitations of the stroke drawing model and the advent of inexpensive memory produced the frame buffer hardware architecture that we now use. With that transition, the damage/redraw approach to updating the screen came to dominate. However, in the world of 3D animated graphics, the old architecture was retained because it simplified animation and other 3D operations. It came to be called retained graphics. With increased CPU speed and the desire to include animation in user interfaces, the retained graphics approach is making a comeback. In the dynamic world of 3D computer games, retained graphics is very prominent.

Display Tree

In retained graphics, the Graphics object is replaced with a Drawable class. Each of the drawing methods found on the Graphics object is represented by a subclass of Drawable. For example, Line, Rectangle, and Ellipse would all be subclasses of Drawable and each would have its own redraw() method. The parameters of the method would be represented by fields in the class. The Line class would have x1, y1, x2, y2, and pen fields that would describe how the line was to be drawn.

A special subclass of Drawable is the Group class. This is an ordered list of drawable objects. They are ordered in back-to-front order. The redraw() method for Group objects is to call redraw() on each of the children in turn. Because group objects are themselves drawable, you can create a tree of such drawing primitives. This display tree of drawing objects completely captures the presentation of a view. It is possible for a subtree to appear in multiple places creating a directed acyclic graph (DAG), but without the transformations described in Chapter 13, this just produces a redundant drawing of the same thing. For now, you will use simple trees.

Redrawing the Display Tree

The relationship between the view and the graphics system is modified to that shown in Figure 2.24. The view is given the root of a display tree rather than a Graphics object in which to create its presentation. The view creates its presentation by adding drawable objects to the display tree. When a redraw request comes from the windowing system, the Graphics object is passed to the redraw process rather than to the view. The redraw process paints the screen from the data in the display tree.

When changes are made in the view, the view modifies the display tree to reflect the new presentation. It is up to the underlying redraw process to make certain that this happens effectively. In many respects, this simplifies the view code because it only needs to make the desired changes and can then ignore the whole display update problem. That is left to the built-in redraw process.

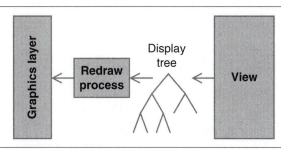

Figure 2.24 – Display tree architecture

The redraw process in one sense is very simple. It just calls the `redraw()` method on the root of the display tree and passes the `Graphics` object. The question, however, is when the redraw process should be invoked. The simplest architecture is the continuous redraw. The redraw process is fired at regular intervals and the display tree is redrawn. If this happens 24 to 30 times per second, the user cannot see the difference. The presentation appears to instantaneously change. In applications like first-person video games, this is an excellent approach because the view is almost certainly changing continuously. In the case of a word processor, however, this is a waste of machine time because for most of those redraws, nothing has changed.

A variation on continuous redraw is the *change flag*. At the root of each display tree is a Boolean flag that indicates if the tree has been changed. Each time any object in the tree is modified, it sets this flag to true. When it is time for the redraw cycle to begin, the change flag is checked. If it is true, the display tree is redrawn and the flag is set to false. If the flag is false, the redraw is not done. This saves extraneous redraws.

An additional variation is that when a drawable element is changed, it damages its old and new positions as in the standard architecture. The windowing system then automatically accumulates the damaged regions and processes them as before. This produces very tight bounds on what must be redrawn but makes the changes more expensive as damage regions are processed. Generally, building up damage regions is faster than actually drawing the primitive objects.

Animation

The retained graphics architecture is particularly amenable to animation effects. Suppose that you want an object to move from one position to another but you want it to move over 2-3 seconds so that the user can follow its path and know where it went. The problem is that there must be many incremental changes over the 2-3 seconds, each drawn slightly differently. Using your standard architecture, you can generate a change to the view every 30th of a second and let the view do a damage/redraw each time. This is a somewhat heavy mechanism and does not scale very well to many simultaneous things happening at once.

What the view can do is provide the redraw process with animation instructions. An animation instruction has the following basic form:

- Object
- Attribute
- Start time
- End time
- Start value
- End value

Each time the redraw process begins, it first looks at each of its animation instructions and the current time. It then updates each attribute of a drawable object as indicated by the current time and then performs the redraw. To create an animation, the view can register its animation instructions and then forget the problem. Using this general form, anything can be animated, such as transparency (make things appear and disappear), color, line width, or position. Everything moves smoothly until it reaches its desired final state.

Animation is frequently nonlinear. In fact, it is more pleasing if the motion starts slowly, speeds up, and then smoothly rather than suddenly stops. Sometimes there is a better physical effect if it overshoots the destination and then settles back to it. These can all be handled by adding an *interpolate function* to the animation instruction so that the redraw process knows what is to be done. There are many more variations to animation control, but most of them work from this same retained graphics basis.

Drawing Efficiencies

Because drawing is no longer part of the application's view but rather embedded in the redraw process and the structure of the display tree, a number of efficiencies can be handled automatically. You will see more of these as you add functionality to your drawing architecture in future chapters.

Double Buffering

One of the first issues that must be addressed is the buffering of the display. Suppose you have a very complicated display tree that takes one-fifth of a second to draw. Because the display tree is drawn back to front, the first thing to be drawn is the background. This means that every one-fifth of a second the presentation disappears from the screen and is replaced by the background and then the rest of the objects appear. This is extremely annoying, especially if the user is not doing anything at the time.

To correct this, virtually all systems support something called *double buffering*. In this technique, there are two images: the one being refreshed onto the screen and the one being redrawn from the display tree. When the redraw process completes a redraw of the display tree, the two image buffers are switched. The old refresh buffer becomes the new redraw buffer and the old redraw buffer becomes the new refresh buffer. This means that at any point in time, the display that the user sees is completely formed rather than only partially drawn. In the retained graphics architecture, this is hidden from the view programmer and happens automatically.

Bounds Checking

Previously, this chapter described an approach where damage rectangles are automatically accumulated for each display tree as changes are made. You can create a special subclass of Group called Clip. In addition to the drawable children of Group, the Clip class has a bounding rectangle to which all of its children are clipped. This ensures that none of the children appear outside of the bounding rectangle. This clipping is enforced automatically by the redraw process. The redraw() method of the Clip class checks its bounding rectangle against the damage region of the Graphics object before drawing. If there is no intersection, the Clip's redraw() method returns without doing anything because there is nothing inside of that subtree that can affect the damaged region. It results in significant time savings when redrawing the display tree.

A variation is an object that automatically recomputes its bounding box from its children any time any of its descendants might change. In this case, clipping is unnecessary because the bounds are always larger than anything drawn inside of that subtree. The advantage to the programmer is that they do not need to manually build code to compute the bounds. In general, a subtree is drawn many more times than it is changed with a net efficiency in the redraw process.

Image Caching

A Clip class can be subclassed by a Cache class. This class maintains an image of the same size as the bounds with each pixel having an R, G, B, and Alpha (opacity) value. Whenever any change occurs in the descendants of this node, the cached image is marked invalid. When redraw() is performed on this node, it first checks to see if the cached image is valid. If it is, that image is drawn to the Graphics object and the subtree nodes are ignored. If it is not valid, it is initialized to pixels that are fully transparent and the subtree's nodes are drawn into this image rather than into the Graphics object. The cached image is then marked as valid and drawn into the Graphics object. It is generally much cheaper to draw the cached image than to perform the pixel conversion required for each drawing primitive. This can result in great drawing efficiencies.

SUMMARY

In the model-view-controller architecture, it is the responsibility of the view to translate some portion of the model into a presentation on the screen. In interactive settings, many different events can create a requirement for the view to be redrawn. Rather than deal with each one individually, every widget (component, view, control, face, or other name) implements a redraw() method (paint, onPaint, refresh) that completely redraws the view from the model. This method is called whenever the windowing system is notified of a need for redrawing.

Drawing generally occurs in a rectangular window and the view assumes that it has complete use of the entire rectangle. All drawing is done through a `Graphics` object (canvas, surface, pane, device context, and so on). The `Graphics` object insulates the view from the underlying hardware or other drawing medium as well as all other visible windows. The `Graphics` object generally provides mechanisms for drawing lines, polylines, ellipses, arcs, curves, polygons, curved boundary regions, and images. Text is also drawn through the `Graphics` object. The drawing of text is also managed by font objects and font metrics to deal with placement and sizing.

The retained graphics architecture can encapsulate many of these issues by representing the presentation as a display tree rather than forcing the view to correctly manage the redraw process. This architecture also allows for animation and many efficiency mechanisms to improve redraw speed.

EXERCISES

1. Take a common interactive application and show how its graphical user interface is decomposed into a window tree.

2. Explain why graphical applications respond to redraw requests rather than just drawing their data on the screen.

3. What is the importance of the `Graphics` object?

4. Write a program that will draw a pedigree chart for a family. Implement this view in a resizable window so that the pedigree chart will grow and shrink as the window is resized.

5. Explain the difference between additive primary colors and subtractive primary colors and in what circumstances we would use each system.

6. Determine the RGB and HSV values for the color of some article of clothing that you are wearing. Use an interactive color selection tool to verify your answer.

7. If printers and screens always draw in pixels, why should we concern ourselves with stroke or region drawing models?

8. Why are monospaced fonts easier to work with than proportional fonts?

9. Why are kerned fonts harder for interactive input?

END NOTES

[1] Kendel, E. R., Schwartz, J. H. and Jessell, T. M, *Principles of Neural Science*, McGraw Hill (2000).

[2] Porter, T. and Duff, T. "Compositing Digital Images," *Computer Graphics* 18(3), (1984) pp 253–259.

[3] Adobe Systems, *PostScript Language Reference*, Addison-Wesley (1999).

[4] http://www.w3.org/MarkUp/

CHAPTER 3

Event Handling

Chapter 2 discussed presenting the model through a windowing system. This chapter addresses the processing of user inputs. The input process is outlined in Figure 3.1. The user generates inputs, which are received by the operating system. In many systems, such as Microsoft Windows, the windowing system is part of the operating system. In others, such as X Windows, the windowing system is separate. Interactive input events are immediately sent to the windowing system, which is responsible for deciding the application, or the part of an application, that is responsible for handling the event. In virtually all cases, this involves selecting a window that should receive the event. The windowing system then notifies the controller of the window's widget. The controller might consult the view's essential geometry to determine how the event maps to the presentation of the model. The controller then makes changes to the model and the model notifies the view of what has changed. The view must then notify the windowing system that it must be redrawn.

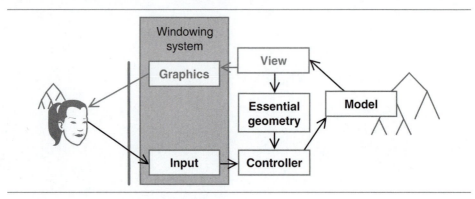

Figure 3.1 – Input event architecture

One of the more difficult aspects of user-interface programming is that there is no true "main program." The traditional "main" only performs initial setup of the user interface. The main program exists in the mind of the user. It is the user who reviews the presentation, considers the problem, and determines an appropriate plan of action. A widget receives events in whatever order the user desires. The software must be constructed to behave reliably no matter which event arrives, even if the event is inappropriate. This chapter covers software architectures that simplify event processing.

Three main issues occur in event handling. The first issue is the process of receiving events from the user and dispatching them to the correct application/window. This process is managed by a *windowing system*, which is the first topic of discussion. The second issue is that, eventually, an event must be associated with the correct code to process the event. This is one of the more complex parts of user-interface code, and there is a long history of ideas for how to make this work. The third issue is the problem of notifying the view and the windowing system of model changes so that the presentation can be correctly redrawn. Although not technically a part of event processing, the relationship between the view and the controller must also be addressed. Because much of the input is mouse actions, the controller needs the view's help in understanding where in the presentation the mouse events have occurred. Each of these issues is addressed in turn.

This chapter covers a wide range of event-handling approaches. This challenging problem has been handled in a variety of ways over the years. This chapter looks at all of the major historical strategies. The reason for this is threefold. First, the more modern event systems are built on the foundations of simpler designs. Understanding these foundations is frequently helpful. Second, an understanding of the entire event process from the simple initial mechanics to the final distribution of an input event to application program code is essential when debugging interactive applications. It is very important to know what is happening to input events. Otherwise, code appears to be invoked by "magic" in strange and wonderful ways. When "magic" is incorrect, it is impossible to debug. A clear understanding of where events are going is necessary to troubleshoot the process. Finally, the historical event mechanisms are regularly resurrected in smaller interactive devices. Currently, cell phones and PDAs use many of the older event mechanisms that have been superseded in desktop applications.

All event handling begins with the windowing system, which must arbitrate which windows and, thus, processes should receive each input event. This chapter first looks at the various styles that windowing systems have used to accomplish this task. This is followed by an overview of the various kinds of input events that might occur and the information that comes with them. The heart of the chapter addresses the problem of how to associate processing code with each event as it is received. These mechanisms are essential to understanding interactive input. Input events are not the only events that can occur in a system. In particular, the model must notify the view of any changes. Getting the view notification wrong is a common source of interactive application bugs. The chapter takes a short look at essential geometry, which is so important in controller implementation. The mathematics for this is discussed in Chapter 12. This chapter then follows input events through the entire event-processing chain to understand how all of the parts fit together. After this exhaustive look at event handling, this chapter then briefly looks at input systems that do not use events at all.

WINDOWING SYSTEM

The windowing system has several responsibilities. The first, as discussed previously, is to provide each view with an independent drawing interface. The second, as discussed in this chapter, is to make certain that the display gets updated to reflect any change to the model. Third, is to receive input events from the operating system, and, finally, to dispatch those events to the appropriate widgets.

A primary purpose of an operating system is to allow many applications to safely share computing resources. This is exactly the role of the windowing system. Its responsibility is to share screen space and input devices among many applications while providing each application with its own private world in which to function. The role of the windowing system in sharing screen space among windows was discussed in Chapter 2. This chapter looks at how input events are associated with windows.

Input Event Dispatch

When the windowing system receives an input event, it must dispatch that event to a particular window. The four common strategies are bottom-up, top-down, bubble-out, and focused. As shown in Figure 3.2, windowing systems are generally organized around a window tree. This tree controls much of how input events are handled. Many input events are associated with the mouse or pen. The location of the mouse is frequently used to identify the desired window. In the bottom-up dispatch strategy, the event is directed to the lowest, frontmost window in the tree that contains the mouse location. This approach dispatches the event to the window that the user perceives as directly under the mouse location. For example, clicking on the black square in the color palette of Figure 3.2 sends the mouse-pressed event directly to that black square's window and, thus, to its widget. Choosing the lowest item in the tree dispatches the event to its most specific meaning and choosing the frontmost window chooses the one that the user can see.

In some cases, the lowest window might not want the event. For example, the palette implementation might prefer to handle input events at the palette level so that selected colors can be highlighted and previously selected colors can be unhighlighted. It might just be simpler to manage it all at that level. In the bottom-up dispatch strategy, the lowest window gets the event, but if it does not need it, the event is promoted up the tree until a window is found that can use it.

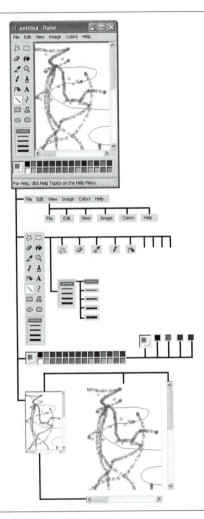

Figure 3.2 – Window tree

An alternative dispatch strategy is top-down. The windowing system gives the event to the frontmost window that contains the mouse location and then that window decides how the event will be dispatched. This is very common in object-oriented interaction toolkits. The default implementation for a container widget (one that contains other widgets) is to find the frontmost of its children that contains the mouse location and then forward the event on to that child. This approach proceeds recursively until a widget is found that can use the input event. Using inheritance, a Widget class can implement the top-down strategy while allowing subclasses to override that strategy if desired.

The default implementation of the top-down strategy has the same effect as the bottom-up strategy. The bottom-up strategy does the obvious dispatch, but it might be too restrictive. For example, you might want to display a painting using a paint widget and yet not allow the user to modify it. Rather than reimplementing a view-only version of a paint widget, you can wrap it in a view-only container. The view-only container forwards various drawing and resizing events while discarding any mouse or keyboard events. The top-down strategy gives the application software more control of what happens. In the bottom-up strategy, the only way to disable inputs on widgets is to modify them individually. Chapter 9 shows how to use top-down event handling to simplify the development of interactive design environments.

The top-down strategy is also more amenable to creating test cases for interactive systems. An interactive application could be wrapped in an event-logging widget that logs every event that it receives and then forwards them to its child widget. Later during testing, the event-logging widget can read the log and play back the events to its child widgets as if they had been received from the user.

Some systems do not have a clear nesting of windows, and groups of interactive objects are not arranged into rectangular regions. In this case, mouse events should be directed at specific graphical objects. This is frequently the case when retained graphics are used, as discussed in Chapter 2. In such situations, a bubble-out event dispatch is used. The tree is traversed as in the top-down approach, but the bounding rectangles are hints rather than guarantees that something will be selected. As the tree of graphical objects is traversed, each graphical primitive is matched against the mouse/pen location using the algorithms in Chapter 12. Objects are checked in the opposite order from their drawing so that frontmost items are checked first. If a hit is detected, the traversal algorithm unwinds up the tree, firing any events that are found on any node of the tree. The object that was hit is attached to the event so that its ancestors up the tree can know what was selected and take appropriate action. Events are fired as the process "bubbles up" from the selected item. This is the event mechanism used in Adobe Flash.

Focus

Many input events, such as mouse button presses or mouse movements, are directed to the correct widget using the location of the mouse. This provides straightforward interaction directly with a particular widget. However, there is no intrinsic screen location associated with the keyboard. The windowing system must determine which window/widget should receive the event when a keyboard button is pressed. In older systems, the mouse location was associated with key events and the events were dispatched just like mouse events. For the user, this meant placing the mouse over whatever location was to receive the keystrokes. This approach was particularly painful when filling in forms. Rather than moving from field to field with a Tab key, the user's hand had to leave the keyboard and move the mouse.

Key Focus

Modern graphics systems use the concept of *key focus*. The windowing system keeps a pointer to the widget that currently has the key focus. Whenever a keyboard event occurs, the windowing system forwards that event directly to the widget that has the focus regardless of where the mouse is located. Handling the key focus involves requesting the focus, losing the focus, receiving the focus, and tab order.

A widget acquires the key focus by requesting it using a `getKeyFocus()` method. For example, when a text box receives a `mouseDown` event, it would use the mouse location to determine where to insert text and would call `getKeyFocus()` to make certain it receives future keyboard events. In virtually all object-oriented user-interface systems, the request for focus is a method defined on the widget. In C#, it is the `Focus()` method. In Java, it is the `requestFocus()` method. In Visual C++, it is `SetFocus()`. In PalmOS, it is `FrmSetFocus()`.

In most cases, widgets that have the key focus show a caret or flashing bar to indicate where text will be inserted. In some systems, buttons or other widgets take the key focus and generate an action event when the Enter key is pressed while they have focus. When these other widgets have focus, they need to display this by highlighting themselves in a special way.

When focus is transferred to a new widget, the widget that originally had the focus must be notified so that it can remove its insertion point or highlight. All systems have events that notify when focus has been lost. These work through the standard event mechanism for each toolkit. Overcome by the love of a pun, some systems, such as JavaScript, use the term "blur" for losing the focus.

When typing, it is very helpful to be able to use the Tab or arrow keys to move from one widget to another. This means that a widget can receive key focus without receiving a mouse event. The Tab input was received by the widget that previously had the focus. The reason for this is that Tab should not always force a transfer of key focus. Focus transfer upon a Tab key would be particularly irritating in a word processor because word processors use the tab. Therefore, the widget that has the focus must decide to yield it. The first problem is "yield the focus to whom?" In the very limited PalmOS, each widget makes its own decision. In Java, container widgets define a *focus cycle*, which is a default order for traversing widgets (usually left to right, top to bottom). A widget, such as a label, can set a property that indicates that it should not receive the focus. In addition, widgets can set a property that explicitly designates some other widget as the next widget in the focus cycle. In C#, each widget has a `TabStop` and `TabIndex` property. `TabStop` must be true for the widget to receive focus. `TabIndex` is a number that indicates the order in which widgets should receive the focus.

A final issue with keyboard focus is the accelerator keys. These are special keys generally associated with menu items or buttons. Their purpose is to provide efficient access to the actions of those items without moving the hands from the keyboard. In most systems, accelerator keys are specially handled before the widget receives any keyboard events.

Mouse Focus

Sometimes widgets also need to request the mouse focus. Figure 3.3 shows a horizontal scroll bar with the path of the mouse shown between mouse-down and mouse-up. Notice that the mouse regularly leaves the scroll bar window. People are rarely very good at following a skinny space without going outside. To alleviate this problem, the scroll bar requests the mouse focus at mouse-down. It then receives all mouse events regardless of whether they are in the scroll bar window. This allows the user to be a little sloppy and still do what they want. When mouse-up occurs, the mouse focus is released. In many scroll bar implementations, the mouse focus is also released if the mouse strays too far from the scroll bar. Mouse focus can also be useful to drawing or painting widgets that do not want to lose the mouse while painting very near the edge.

Figure 3.3 – Scroll bar mouse drift

Receiving Events

Input events from the user arrive whenever the user decides to cause them. They are generated whenever the user does something with an input device. The software, however, might not be ready to receive them. One of the functions of the operating system is to process the device interrupts and place the inputs onto an event queue. The windowing system removes events from the queue and dispatches them to the appropriate window/widget. In early systems, each application or each window would have an event queue and the application software would remove events from the queue one at a time to process those events.

In addition to the asynchronous input events, a variety of other events can be generated by other portions of the software. These include requests to redraw the presentation, notification of window changes, focus change events, and sometimes timing events. Most systems send these software events through the same event-processing mechanism as the input events. Thus, the application programmer has a uniform model for handling all of the many things that might occur.

In most cases, the application programmer is not concerned about event queues or interrupt handlers. The exceptions, however, are when the interactivity needs are pushing the limits of the processor. This occurs in applications like speech, digital ink, and virtual reality. With speech and digital ink, the inputs must be sampled fast enough that no data is lost. Even on today's machines, this can be an important consideration. To get this right, you might require operating system help. The problem with virtual reality is that the input, model, redraw loop must be fast enough to prevent motion sickness. This is still a very tight loop for most systems and not very tolerant of delay.

INPUT EVENTS

Input events generally carry three pieces of information: the event type, the location of the mouse or pen when the event occurred, and some modifier button information. The modifier information includes which mouse/pen buttons are currently pressed and whether Control, Shift, Alt, or Command keys are also pressed at the same time. In many cases, most of the modifier information is ignored. In other cases, the modifiers are used to distinguish the user's meaning. For example, the right and left mouse buttons have well-defined purposes in the Microsoft environment and it matters which has been pressed.

Every event has an *event type*. This is a system-defined list of integer constants that specifies the kind of event. Most event/code binding is based on event type. The following section describes the most common events. However, every input event system varies in the types of events generated and certainly in their names.

Button Events

The primitive button events are `mouseDown` and `mouseUp`. These are generated whenever a mouse button goes down or up. Some systems augment these with software events such as `click` and `doubleClick`. The `click` event is generated when a `mouseDown` and `mouseUp` event occur at the same location in a very short time. The `doubleClick` event is generated when there are two clicks within a specified time. The button events are still generated, but for many situations the click events are simpler for the application to work with. When the system generates `doubleClick`, it can check the user preferences for the time delay that should be used on `doubleClick`. This is important for accessibility for people with motor impairments. In pen-based systems, "hover" events can sometimes indicate when the pen is very close to the tablet surface but not pressed against the surface. Hovering can be used for a variety of user-interface purposes[1].

Mouse Movement

There are also events for mouse motion. The `mouseMove` event is generated whenever the mouse location changes. Because this can happen a lot with no particular meaning, many systems allow these events to be disabled so that they do not produce unnecessary overhead. A system might also provide a `mouseDrag` event, which is a `mouseMove` event that is automatically enabled whenever one of the mouse buttons is down. This captures the most common situation for using `mouseMove`. Some systems also provide `mouseEnter` and `mouseExit` events for when the mouse enters or leaves the window.

Keyboard

All systems provide a simple `keyInput` event that occurs when a key is pressed. The modifiers such as Control, Shift, or Caps Lock are generally processed automatically to produce an *input character*. Thus, the input character would already be capitalized or converted to a control character. Sometimes, however, this is not sufficient. Specialized handling might be required for a particular application. Most `keyInput` events also supply the actual character pressed. In addition, many systems provide a key map code that identifies the actual key pressed on the keyboard. This is important for software mapping of character input to specialized translation of characters.

In addition to the key map codes, the program can generally inquire after all of the key codes that are currently pressed. This supports even more complex mappings, including special "chording" inputs that involve multiple simultaneous keys. `keyPressed` and `keyRelease` events are also available for more specific keyboard handling. For most purposes, the simple `keyInput` event is sufficient.

Window Events

Every interactive system has a windowing system that is responsible for the sharing of screen, drawing, and input device resources. Virtually every system also has a *window manager*. The window manager is the user interface that allows the user to resize, select, drag, open, close, and iconify windows. On most systems, the window manager handles the title bar of the window, including all of those buttons and the resizing controls. Window management is separate from the application code so that it is uniform across all applications that the user is working with. Microsoft Windows integrates its window manager with its windowing system. In X Windows the window manager is a separate application that the user can readily change to suit personal preferences. Java Swing provides a special `JDesktopPane` widget that can serve as a platform-independent window manager for a variety of applications.

Regardless of the window manager being used, the application needs to know what is happening to the window. For this purpose, the window manager can generate events such as `windowOpen`, `windowClose`, `windowResize`, or `windowIconify`. Because these events are dependent on the window manager, there are many differences in what events are provided and exactly when they are generated. The goal is to inform the application program of anything that might have happened to the window. Many programs ignore most of these events depending on their needs. A most important event is the `redraw` event that notifies the application when a window needs to be drawn.

Other Inputs

The input events described previously correspond to the standard screen-keyboard-mouse device configuration. There are other inputs and more complex models. Chapter 17 discusses distributing the interaction so that multiple people can participate in an application. When there are multiple parties involved, each input event must be tagged with some identifier of the participant who generated the event. If persons A and B are both working on an application, the event stream might be "mouseDown(A), mouseMove(A), mouseDown(B), mouseMove(B), mouseMove(A), mouseMove(B), mouseUp(A), mouseMove(B), mouseUp(B)." These interleaved events are problematic. This question is not addressed in this chapter, but it is a consideration that can arise.

Pen inputs also provide some challenging differences. In many situations, a pen is made to look like a mouse to the underlying application. However, this is not always sufficient. Many pens have tilt and pressure information that can be very helpful to some applications. The pen tip switch is frequently mapped to a mouse button for use with existing applications, but the mapping is not exact. A stylus that is completely passive has no buttons. Points simply begin appearing and then stop appearing when the stylus is lifted. These pen issues are addressed in Chapter 20.

Also discussed in Chapter 20 are gesture inputs. These, along with voice and camera-based techniques, use a recognizer step to convert raw input into a more manageable event. However, recognizers are frequently probabilistic and are not certain as to the correct classification. Dealing with the questions of "it might be this input, or it might be that" complicates event handling.

Some new interactive spaces, such as touch surfaces upon which several people can interact, also have the property of multiple touches. Unlike a mouse, which has a single input point, users have up to ten fingers that they can use as inputs. A number of systems exploit two input points from a given user, frequently one for each hand. These multitouch issues also complicate input handling.

This chapter focuses on the screen-keyboard-mouse approach because of its dominance and because many of the other techniques have been mapped into it. The other problem with these additional input models is that they have not been unified in any way so that tools can be built around them. The screen-keyboard-mouse approach is the only one with mature techniques and tools. Hopefully this will change in the future.

EVENT/CODE BINDING

After the windowing system has decided on the appropriate window to receive the event, we require a mechanism for binding that event to some code that will process the event. On slower machines, efficiency was the dominant issue. With processors over 1 GHz in speed, this is not as serious as it once was. We would also like our event/code binding model to work well with user-interface design tools. Ultimately, we want to design user interfaces by drawing most of the layout. The challenge comes when trying to associate a layout design with the code to process the events. User-interface design tools are discussed more in Chapter 9, but they do have a bearing on how we associate events with code. The programming language that we are using also has a bearing on this binding. We want the binding strategy to be smoothly supported by the language so that errors are detected and the compiler can do much of the work for us. Finally, we need to address the problem of complexity. Many events and notifications are generated in an interactive application. We need a mechanism that can handle all of them without swamping the programmer in unnecessary detail.

The discussion in this section follows a historical path through the various event-handling mechanisms. In various forms, all of these approaches are present in various interactive devices today. Many of the later approaches involve smoothly integrating earlier approaches into a programming language. This historical trend also shows a shift of focus from the code efficiency dictated by slow computers to the complexity management required by large applications. Particular attention is paid to how object-oriented languages have implemented event dispatching.

Event Queue and Type Selection

The early Macintosh used a very primitive event-handling mechanism. As shown in Figure 3.4, the programmer was responsible for the event loop and the event/code binding was handled by a switch statement on the event type. This is a very efficient event-handling mechanism and is still used in small devices with limited speed and space for code.

```
public void main()
{
        perform any setup of widgets including layout, setting of properties and
        assignment to container widgets.

        while (not time to quit )
        {      Event evnt = getInputEventFromSystem()
               switch ( evnt.type )
               {
               case MOUSEDOWN: . . .
               case MOUSEUP: . . .
               . . . . .
               }
        }
}
```

Figure 3.4 – Main event loop and switch

Window Event Tables

The next step forward in event handling was the GIGO/Canvas[2] system developed by David Rosenthal and eventually delivered on all Sun workstations. This model relies on the ability of the C programming language to manage pointers to procedures. The entire event strategy is built around the tree of windows (which would later become your tree of widgets). An example is shown in Figure 3.5. All events in GIGO carried the current mouse position with them (even keyboard events). Each event also had a type. The windowing system would navigate the window tree looking for the lowest, frontmost window in the tree whose bounds contained the mouse position. Each window then had a table of procedure pointers indexed by event type. The windowing system would index this table and invoke the procedure whose address was stored there. The main program is changed to that in Figure 3.6.

The algorithm goes down the tree recursively searching windows in front-to-back order. In this way, the frontmost window is always selected. When a window is found that has no children or the event is not inside of one of the children, the event table is indexed to find the correct event-handling procedure. The heart of the event handling, then, is the setting up of the event table when creating a window. The GIGO system also introduced the concept of bottom-up event promotion. When setting up the event table for a window, all events for which there is no event-handling procedure are initialized to a special procedure that forwards events on to the container of the window. Thus, any unused events would propagate back up the window tree until some container is found that can handle the event.

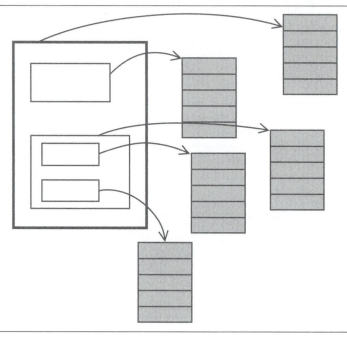

Figure 3.5 – GIGO event tables

```
public void main()
{
        initialize the windows and for each window create a procedure pointer
        table to handle any events that should be sent to that window
        while (not time to quit)
        {     Event evnt=getInputEventFromSystem()
              handleWindowEvent(rootWindow, evnt);
        }
}
public void handleWindowEvent( Window curWindow, Event evnt)
{
        foreach Window CW in curWindow.children in front to back order
        {     if( CW.bounds.contains(evnt.mouseLocation))
              {     handleWindowEvent(CW,evnt);
                    return;
              }
        }
        invoke procedure at curWindow.eventTable[evnt.type];
}
```

Figure 3.6 – Main event loop using event tables

The event-table approach is simple to implement, efficient, and removes the event loop from the application programmer. One of the deficiencies of this approach is that procedure pointers are difficult to debug. It is also very easy to introduce programmer errors and become completely lost as to how a particular event is to be handled. A second problem is that this technique does not work well with interface-design environments. The addresses of event-handling procedures are not known at design time and really make little sense to designers anyway. This makes binding a window and event to an unknown address impossible for a design tool.

Callback Event Handling

To simplify the interface-design process, many toolkits for X Windows used the notion of callbacks[3,4]. As part of the initialization, the programmer registers any event-handling procedure address with a descriptive string name. Each window has properties for its various events and other code needs. These properties contain the names of procedures to call. When a window is initialized, the system looks up all of the callback names in the Registry and retrieves the procedure address for each callback. The windowing system can now use the procedure address as in event tables. If, however, no such callback exists, a clearly understood error can be generated. Design tools could now use the callback names in their designs, leaving the binding between the names and the procedure addresses until run time. This approach also solved the problem of many different kinds of events because each widget would have properties for the kinds of events it could generate without paying attention to what all other widgets might need.

WindowProc Event Handling

At the very heart of the Microsoft Windows event-handling system is the fact that every window has a *window proc*. This is the address of the procedure that handles events for that window. This is a simplification of the event table process. Instead of a table of procedures, there is just one. The `windowProc` generally contains a `switch` statement as in the original Macintosh main program. The difference is that each `switch` statement is unique to a particular type of window rather than handling all possible types. This approach is more modular than primitive switch statements and as easy to implement as event tables. However, this approach is very opaque to user-interface design tools.

Inheritance Event Handling

The Smalltalk-80 system reintroduced object-oriented programming and began the process of establishing object-oriented languages as the preferred mechanism for handling interactive events[5]. This is the basis for event handling in most current user-interface toolkits. The windowing system and other parts of the interactive environment must be capable of dealing with any widget at any time. Therefore, all widgets must share a common interface so that tools working with widgets need not know about their implementation. In inheritance event handling, a `Widget` class has a method for each type of input event. A sample `Widget` class is shown in Figure 3.7.

```
public class Widget
{
    methods and members for Bounds

    public void mousePressed(int x, int y, int buttonNumber)
    {    default behavior  }
    public void mouseReleased(int x, int y, int buttonNumber)
    {    default behavior  }
    public void mouseMoved(int x, int y)
    {    default behavior  }
    public void keyPressed(char c, int x, int y, int modifiers)
    {    default behavior  }
    public void windowClosed()
    {    default behavior  }
    public void redraw(Graphics toDraw)
    {    default behavior  }

    and a host of other event methods

}
```

Figure 3.7 – Base Widget class

These event methods can be organized in a variety of ways. When learning a new toolkit, it is very important to find the class that corresponds to Widget and study its event-handling methods to see how the input events are managed. In Figure 3.7, all of the mouse events are separated into different methods as was done in Smalltalk. In other systems, all mouse events are collected together in a single method processMouseEvent(). Various mouse events are differentiated by looking at the MouseEvent parameter. Default method behavior might be to report the event to the widget's parent. This would mirror the GIGO default behavior. Other default implementations forward events to the children. This automatic forwarding, as part of the default behavior, provides a top-down implementation of the bottom-up dispatch strategy.

Creating new widgets such as buttons or scroll bars involves creating a new class that is a subclass of Widget or some other widget class and then overriding the desired input event methods. By overriding mouseDown(), a scroll bar implementation can provide code to locate what part of the scroll bar the mouse is in and decide how to change the scroll bar appropriately. Overriding mouseMove() would allow the scroll bar to drag the thumb back and forth to perform the scrolling. Of course, overriding redraw() is imperative for any new widget because redraw() is where a widget generates its unique appearance.

The Object-Oriented Event Loop

Using object-oriented techniques, you can associate an object that is a subclass of Widget with every window in the window tree. In many implementations, the window tree is integrated directly with the widget tree rather than having them separate. When the windowing system receives a mouse event, key event, window event, or some other input, it invokes the appropriate method on the root widget of the window. That widget's method either handles the event, or passes it on to the appropriate child widget.

The event loop is so simplified that in systems such as Java or C# the event loop is completely hidden from the programmer. After the windows are set up with their widgets, the event loop just runs, dispatching events to the appropriate window widgets.

Implementation of Inheritance Event Handling

An important concept in object-oriented event handling is in how an event method invocation is associated with the right code to handle that event. In Smalltalk, each object had a reference to a class definition and each method had a name. When a method named M was invoked on an object of class C, the class C was queried to see if it had a method named M. If it did not, C's superclass was queried and so on up the class tree until the method was found or a failure occurred. This simple mechanism allowed subclasses to override event methods and provide code to handle the event in the unique manner required by the widget. It also allowed the windowing system to have a pointer to an object and send it the event mouseDown without knowing the object's class or what code would handle the mouseDown event. The problem with the Smalltalk message/method binding was that it was very inefficient. To invoke a method, a search for the right method must be conducted. To make it more efficient, after a class/method pair was associated with a particular implementation, it could be cached in a hash table. The hash table was faster than the search but orders of magnitude slower than a simple procedure call. This was not acceptable for interactive input.

C++ introduced a more efficient method invocation mechanism[6]. These were called virtual methods. Every C++ class has a virtual table of addresses of procedures that implement each virtual method. Every virtual method of a class has a unique index in the virtual table where the appropriate procedure address is stored. To illustrate how this would work, let's consider the class and method definitions in Figure 3.8.

```
class C
{      public void M1()
       {      declare bankruptcy
}
       public void M2()
       {      sell all stocks }
}
class D extends C
{      public void M3()
       {      pay taxes }
       public void M2()
       {      buy bonds }
}
public main()
{      C  aCObj = new C();
       D  aDObj = new D();
       aCObj.M2();
       aDObj.M2();
       aCObj = aDObj;
       aCObj.M2();
}
```

Figure 3.8 – Class declarations with inheritance and override

In the main routine in Figure 3.8, the first invocation of aCObj.M2() will "sell all stocks." The invocation of aDObj.M2() will "buy bonds." The code then assigns aDObj to the variable aCObj. In object-oriented programming, this is appropriate because D is a subclass of C. The second invocation of aCObj.M2() should cause the program to "buy bonds" rather than "sell all stocks" because a different class of object has been assigned to aCObj. Virtual tables make this association work efficiently. Figure 3.9 shows how the virtual tables would look for the class declarations in Figure 3.8. As you will see, virtual tables are identical to the event tables created for GIGO/Canvas. The only difference is that the programming language manages the addresses, tables, parameter passing, type checking, and debugger information so that the mechanism is seamless and easy to program.

Note that each method has its own index in the virtual table and that subclasses share those same indices. Class D did not declare a method M1 so it inherited C's version of M1 at the same index. Class D declared its own version of M2, but placed it at the same index that class C used for M2. Class D created a new method, M3, which got its own index beyond those defined by class C. Whenever code is generated for aCObj.M2(), the underlying code is actually aCObj.virtualTable[2](aCObj). Thus when aCObj actually contains an object of class D, the code to "buy bonds" is executed because that is the procedure address at index 2 of that object's virtual table. Note that the implicit first parameter of a method is the object to which it was applied.

The virtual method invocation mechanism is slightly slower than a simple procedure call but very much faster than Smalltalk's implementation. This is the method mechanism used by C++, Java, and C#.

Virtual table for class C

> 0: Pointer to C's descriptor
> 1: address of M1 to "declare bankruptcy"
> 2: address of M2 to "sell all stocks"

Virtual table for class D

> 0: Pointer to D's descriptor
> 1: address of M1 to "declare bankruptcy"
> 2: **address of M2 to "buy bonds"**
> 3: address of M3 to "pay taxes"

Figure 3.9 – Virtual tables

Listeners

The event models described so far are concerned with the simple user events that can be generated from input devices. There are not very many of these and they are quite easy to handle with the mechanisms described previously. However, many kinds of events can occur in an interactive application. There are additional events from the windowing system such as when windows are opened, closed, hidden, iconified, made active, made inactive, and so on. All of these are indirectly generated events. They are frequently caused by the user, yet filtered and processed by other software to generate new information. The operating system can also generate events such as devices being activated, files being changed, or floppy disks being ejected. Widgets themselves generate events. A scroll bar can process input device events and then eventually generate an event that says that the value of the scroll bar has changed. Software using the scroll bar does not want to see the input events, but does want to be notified when the scroll bar changes. When event-based programming became the norm for handling input events, it was clear that this process could also handle all of these other kinds of events. The event-handling load went from 10 to 15 events to thousands in large operating systems. The event-management mechanisms described previously could not effectively handle all of this. It became extremely confusing to the programmers and not very efficient in terms of memory. When there are thousands of events, the virtual table for each new class is very large.

In addition to the many kinds of events, there is also the problem that the object that should handle an event is not necessarily associated with the window that received or generated the event. Sometimes it is the model rather than the view or controller that should receive the event. Sometimes all of the events from a group of widgets are collected together and handled in one place. It is also a problem to create a new subclass every time a new event must be handled.

Advanced user-interface toolkits use a listener model for handling events. This is an evolution of the inheritance model but without the problems of scaling to thousands of events. To understand how Java/Swing's listener model works, you must first understand the implementation of Java interfaces. Using class inheritance as an event model, you can define a class `Widget` that has all of the methods that a windowing system needs to know about widgets to draw them and send them events. You then can create various subclasses of `Widget` that implement these methods in various ways. Polymorphism in object-oriented languages allows any object to be used wherever a superclass of that object is acceptable. This supports the need for a common mechanism to access all subclasses of `Widget`. The problem is that the object that you want to handle a particular event is sometimes not a subclass of `Widget`.

Implementation of the Java Interface
The Java interface mechanism simply defines a set of methods that an interface must implement without requiring that the class that implements those methods be part of any particular class hierarchy. Consider the code fragment shown in Figure 3.10.

```
interface Kid
{      public run();
       public jump();
}
interface Human
{      public eat();
}
class Wiggly implements Kid, Human
{      public run()
       {      runs around erratically  }
       public jump()
       {      jumps up and down 10 times }
       public eat()
       {      eats lots of candy  }
}
class Goat implements Kid
{      public run()
       {      runs on four legs }
       public jump()
       {      jumps over fences  }
}

public main()
{
1)     Kid someKid = new Wiggly();
2)     someKid.run();
3)     someKid = new Goat()
4)     someKid.run();
}
```

Figure 3.10 – Use of interfaces

Note that in Figure 3.10 the class Wiggly implements two different interfaces, Kid and Human. A class can implement as many interfaces as it wants provided that it defines all of the methods required by the interfaces it claims to implement. Statement 2 of the main routine someKid.run() causes a Wiggly to "run around erratically." In statement 4, the same someKid.run() causes a Goat to "run on four legs."

To implement the interface mechanism, you first define a virtual table for each interface definition. Then for each class C that implements interface I, you define a virtual table CasI, or a table in interface I format that contains the appropriate methods for class C. When you declare a variable using an interface rather than a class or type name, that variable has two parts: (1) a pointer to the object assigned to the variable, and (2) a pointer to the virtual table that is appropriate for the object's class and the variable's interface. Figure 3.11 shows the value of someKid at statement 2 of Figure 3.10 and later at statement 4. The implementation of someKid.run() is now someKid.virtualTable[0](someKid.obj). This approach is relatively efficient and extremely flexible. You can now declare an interface for any capability that you desire. Any class can declare that it implements any interface and can be used wherever the interface is used without the constraint of inheritance.

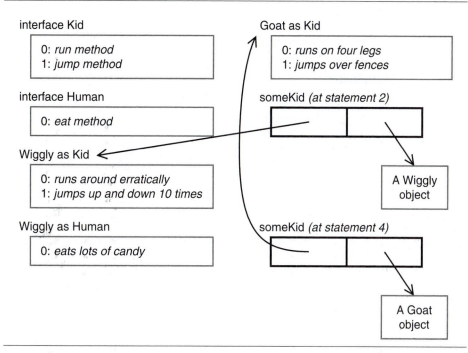

interface Kid

0: *run method* 1: *jump method*

interface Human

0: *eat method*

Wiggly as Kid

0: *runs around erratically* 1: *jumps up and down 10 times*

Wiggly as Human

0: *eats lots of candy*

Goat as Kid

0: *runs on four legs* 1: *jumps over fences*

someKid *(at statement 2)*

A Wiggly
object

someKid *(at statement 4)*

A Goat
object

Figure 3.11 – Virtual tables for interfaces

Listener Class Structure

The idea of listeners is that there are objects that can produce events (generators) and objects that want to be notified of events (listeners). With each event, there is almost always some information object that describes the event. For example, a Swing JButton generates ActionEvents whenever the button is pressed. In many cases, you will want to implement special widgets that will be reused in many places. For example, a sound mixer application might need a special kind of slider bar that will be used in many places for various adjustments. Such a widget will need to generate events that notify other parts of the application when the widget has changed.

As an example of event generation, the Button class in Figure 3.12 defines the interface ActionListener that has one method actionPerformed(ActionEvent). All of the classes defined for the Button listening structure are shown in Figure 3.12.

```
class ActionEvent
{      information about the action event }
interface ActionListener
{      public void actionPerformed(ActionEvent e); }

class Button
{      lots of other methods and fields
       ....
       private Vector actionListenerList;
       public void addActionListener(ActionListener listener)
       {      actionListenerList.add(listener); }
       public void removeActionListener(ActionListener listener)
       {      actionListenerList.remove(listener); }
       protected void sendActionEvent(ActionEvent e)
       {      for (I=0;I<actionListenerList.size();I++)
              {    ActionListener listen=(ActionListener)
                   actionListenerList.get(I);
                   listen.actionPerformed(e);
              }
       }
       ......
}
```

Figure 3.12 – Listener implementation

The listener mechanism in Figure 3.12 uses Java's Vector class, which allows an arbitrary number of objects to be added, removed, and retrieved. The ActionEvent class contains information about the event. An ActionEvent might contain the type of event (if there is any) and possibly the widget that generated the event. If you were processing mouse events, you would create the MouseEvent class that would contain the mouse location at the time of the event, which mouse buttons are pressed, as well as the settings for the Shift, Control, and Alt keys. The event class is the carrier for the event information. You next implement a listener interface for your event. For action events, this is the ActionListener interface with only one method. Some listeners have more than one method. For example, the ContainerListener has a method for when objects are added to the container and one for when they are removed. The Button class has two methods addActionListener and removeActionListener for adding and removing listeners to the button. This add/remove pattern is used whenever a Java/Swing class can generate events.

The protected sendActionEvent method is also a good practice for implementing view notification. This method is used inside of the JButton implementation whenever an action event should be sent. This method loops through all of the listeners and sends the event to each in turn. Packaging up this loop in one method simplifies the maintenance of the rest of the code.

In summary, to create a generator for event Evt, you should do the following:

- Create an Evt class to contain information about the event.

- Create an EvtListener interface that contains all of the methods associated with this listener structure.

- Create a private member of your generator class that can hold all of the listeners for the event.

- Create the add*EvtListener*(EvtListener) and remove*EvtListener*(EvtListener) methods to allow others to add and remove listeners.

- Create private methods to send events, which will loop through the listeners invoking each of their event methods.

  To create a listener that can receive *Evt* events, you should do the following:

- Implement the *EvtListener* interface.

- Add the object to the event generator using add*EvtListener*().

As an example, the Swing toolkit assumes that the standard way to receive mouse events is via a mouse listener. The default implementation of the inherited method processMouseEvent() is to loop through all of the mouse event listeners, sending the event on to each of them.

The advantages of the listener model are first that all of the various types of methods are separated rather than all being forced through the same mechanism. Therefore, you need only listen to the events of interest without considering all of the other events that might be generated. Second, any number of objects of any type can listen to a particular set of events from a particular event-generating object. This provides great flexibility. Finally, listeners provide the mechanism that you need to set up the model view controller architecture. This is discussed later in this chapter and again in Chapter 6 on shared model architectures.

Delegate Event Model

Several problems occur with the Java listener model for event handling. The first is that many events still need to go through the same channel. For example, Figure 3.13 shows two scroll bars. Each generates an AdjustmentEvent. The text widget in the center needs to scroll itself whenever these events occur. The text widget can implement AdjustmentListener and add itself as a listener to both scroll bars. However, the vertical and the horizontal scroll bars both call the same listener method. The listener method can sort out which scroll bar generated a particular listener call, but it is awkward. It would be better to have a separate method for each scroll bar because they have separate behaviors.

Figure 3.13 – Scrolled window

A second problem is that listeners frequently only care about a particular method in a particular context. Implementing a multimethod listener interface is still a somewhat heavy solution to set up a communication link. Java has answered this problem with the concepts of *adapters* and *anonymous classes*. Adapters are classes that implement dummy versions of all of the methods of an interface. Anonymous classes are special subclasses that can be created in place with only a few methods being specified. Using anonymous classes with adapters allows programmers to define isolated, special-purpose methods, but it is somewhat clumsy. Finally, a third, minor problem is that every event-generating class creates listener interfaces, add/remove methods, listener list-handling code, and internal methods for looping through all of the registered listeners.

C# has handled all of these issues with *delegates*. A delegate is very similar to the procedure address mechanism found in C except that it is better adapted to an object-oriented language model and is completely type checked for code reliability. Using delegates allows you to reconsider the button example. The code for buttons to generate action events is shown in Figure 3.14.

```
public class ActionEvent
{    information about the action event }
public delegate void ActionEventHandler(ActionEvent evt);
public class Button
{    lots of other methods and fields
        ....
    public ActionEventHandler actionPerformed;
        ....
    Public void processMouseEvent(MouseEvent mevt)
    {    if (evt.mouseIsUp())
            {        actionPerformed(new ActionEvent(some stuff));
                . . .
            }
    }
}
public class BunchOfButtons
{
    public BunchOfButtons()
    {    Button myDelete = new Button("Delete");
        myDelete.actionPerformed = this.myDeleteAction;
        myDelete.actionPerformed += this.myCancelAction;
        Button myCancel = new Button("Cancel");
        myCancel.actionPerformed = this.myCancelAction;
    }
    private void myDeleteAction(ActionEvent evt)
    {    perform the delete action }

    private void myCancelAction(ActionEvent evt)
    {    perform the cancel action }

}
```

Figure 3.14 – Use of delegates

In this example, the class `Button`, which generates the action events, simply declares a delegate type (`ActionEventHandler`) that describes the parameters and return type of the desired delegate. The `Button` also provides a public variable (`actionPerformed`) of type `ActionEventHandler`. As you see in the `processMouseEvent()` method, the button code treats a delegate variable (`actionPerformed`) as if it were a method and just calls it. The looping through all registered delegates is all handled automatically. The class `BunchOfButtons` declares as many buttons as it wants. It associates whatever methods it wants with each of the buttons that it has declared. For some reason in this example, the programmer wants to attach both the `myDeleteAction()` and the `myCancelAction()` to the Delete button. The Cancel button only receives the `myCancelAction()` as a delegate. In many ways, the delegate mechanism is like the old callback mechanism except that it is explicitly supported and checked by the programming language. The += operator performs just like the `addListener()` methods and the −= operator performs just like the `removeListener()` methods. The difference is that individual methods are added rather than whole classes with specially declared interface definitions. The delegate mechanism is much lighter weight than the listener mechanism. It should be pointed out that when there are many related methods, the interface/listener mechanism is still available in C#.

Every variable that is declared to be a delegate can contain a list of (object, method) pairs. The += and −= operators simply add or remove pairs from the list. The syntax *object.method* defines the pair to be added. The compiler can verify that the method to be added conforms to the parameter interface defined when the delegate type was declared. When a delegate is invoked, the generated code simply loops through each of the (object, method) pairs invoking the method on the object and passing in the parameters supplied with the invocation. This is a very simple, very direct mechanism for attaching code to an event generator.

Reflection

Many languages such as C#, Java, and Objective-C provide a mechanism called reflection. Reflection provides language structures and libraries that allow objects, classes, and methods to be discovered and used at run time. Sometimes this is also called introspection[7]. Every object has a `getClass()` method that returns information about the class of the object. A `Class` object, which describes a class, typically has methods for finding all of the methods for that class. In particular, it is possible to find a method by its name and parameter types. Having found a `Method` object, the method can be invoked dynamically.

Using reflection, you can take any object and the name of a method. You can then write code that will find the `Class` of the object, locate a `Method` of the correct name, and invoke that method. You can also save the `Method` object and save future costs of looking for it by name. This is very similar to the original callback model. The difference is that the reflection mechanism and the compiler handle the registration of methods and their names. In addition, everything is completely type checked to prevent errors. The reflection mechanism allows interface design tools to (1) look at the methods defined by a given object class and provide designers with a menu of acceptable choices, and (2) save the method name in the user-interface design where it can be retrieved at run time and used to locate an appropriate `Method` object. Reflection is a very important part of the development of user-interface design tools, as discussed in Chapter 9.

Interpreted Expressions

The last event/code binding mechanism is the interpreted expression. This was first introduced in Henry Lieberman's EZWin system[8]. In EZWin, each event was associated with a Lisp S-expression. In Lisp, an S-expression is simply a list structure to which `eval()` has been applied. The EZWin interface design tool simply allowed the designer to enter a Lisp expression for any event. When the event occurred, the expression was evaluated.

Interpreted expressions are also used in HTML/JavaScript's event handling[9]. Each interactive widget is defined as an HTML tag. For each event that the widget can generate, an attribute is defined such as `onClick` or `onChange`. The attribute contains a text string that is a JavaScript expression. Whenever the event occurs, the Web browser extracts the event's string and interprets the expression using any currently defined JavaScript methods.

The interpreted expression event model is particularly well suited for applications where the user interfaces can be modified by the user at run time. The macro facility of the EMACS text editor is simply Lisp. Spreadsheets are built around user-specified expressions and animation systems such as Macromedia have scripting languages like Lingo[10].

MODEL/VIEW NOTIFICATION

Up to this point, the user has generated an input event and the windowing system has directed that event to the controller of some window. The controller has consulted the essential geometry and has decided on a change to the model. Now you need to complete the interactive cycle. The controller interfaces with the model by invoking one or more of the model's public methods. The model is then responsible for changing itself and notifying its view of the changes. The view is responsible for notifying the windowing system of the portions of the screen that must be redrawn. This notification process is a key piece of the model-view-controller architecture.

Notification from the Model

To illustrate how the notification works, you can use a simple application to draw lines. The model for this application is shown in Figure 3.15. This model provides enough methods for the controller to manipulate the content of the model. You could just make `linesToDraw` publicly visible and let the controller modify the array directly. Making the variable public would prevent the notification techniques that you need. If the variable is public, changes could be made without the view being notified. Using private variables along with get and set methods allows you to notify the view of any change to the model.

```
public class LineDrawModel
{
        private Line [] linesToDraw;
        public int addLine( int x1, int y1, int x2, int y2) // add line and return its index
        { . . . . }
        public void moveLine(int index, int newX1, int newY1, int newX2, int newY2)
        { . . . . }
        public void deleteLine(int index)
        { . . . . }
        public int nLines() { return linesToDraw.length; }
        public Line getLine(int index) // return a line from the model
}
public class Line { int x1, int y1, int x2, int y2 }
```

Figure 3.15 – LineDrawModel

Whenever the controller calls the methods on the model, the model needs to notify the view that changes have been made. To do this, you can create a "listener" interface that defines all of the ways in which the model might change, which listeners will need to know about. For each kind of notification, there is a method in the listener interface. For this simple model, you can use the interface shown in Figure 3.16. The lineWillChange() method is called whenever a single line is modified. The modelHasChanged() method is called when more extensive changes have been made. Any object that wants to be notified of changes to a LineDrawModel should implement the LineDrawListener interface. This interface definition defines the notification protocol.

```
public interface LineDrawListener
{
        public void lineWillChange( int index, int newX1, int newY1, int newX2, int newY2);
            // a particular line will change.
            // Assumes that the old line is still in the model
        public void modelHasChanged();
            // a major change has occurred to the whole model
}
```

Figure 3.16 – Model listener interface

Figure 3.17 shows a new version of the model that includes the notification mechanism. The LineDrawModel has been modified in several ways. First, the private member listeners has been added along with two methods, addListener() and removeListener(). This is the mechanism that the view will use to register itself with the model and receive notification of any changes to the model. This registration is not restricted to views. Any object that implements LineDrawListener can register using addListener(). Note that any number of listeners can be added to this model. Any object that needs to know about changes to the model can listen.

```
public class LineDrawModel
{
        private Line [] linesToDraw;
        public int addLine( int x1, int y1, int x2, int y2) // add line and return its index
        {       notifyLineWillChange(linesToDraw.length,x1,y1,x2,y2);
                . . . code to add the line . . .
        }
        public void moveLine(int index, int newX1, int newY1, int newX2, int newY2)
        {       notifyLineWillChange(index,newX1, newY1, newX2, newY2);
                . . . code to change the line . . .
        }
        public void deleteLine(int index)
        {       . . . code to delete the line . . .
                notifyModelHasChanged();
        }

        private Vector listeners;
        public void addListener(LineDrawListener newListener)
        {       listeners.add(newListener); }
        public void removeListener(LineDrawListener listener)
        {       listeners.remove(listener); }

        private void notifyLineWillChange( int index, int newX1,
        int newY1, int newX2, int newY2)
        {       for each LineDrawListener listen in listeners
                        listen.lineWillChange(index, newX1, newY1, newX2, newY2);
        }
        private void notifyModelHasChanged()
        {       for each LineDrawListener listen in listeners
                        listen.modelHasChanged();
        }
        . . . other methods . . .
}
```

Figure 3.17 – Adding listeners to LineDrawModel

In addition to the registration methods, there are also the private methods `notifyLineWillChange()` and `notifyModelHasChanged()`. By convention, these are named the same as the notification methods in `LineDrawListener`. These methods loop through the registered listeners and invoke the corresponding method on each listener. This separates the listener notification code from the rest of the model so that it can be maintained. It is very important that this code work correctly because in more complex applications, many notifications are doing many things. This is not a good place to have a bug.

The last modification is to actually perform the notification. The public `addLine()`, `moveLine()`, and `deleteLine()` methods have been modified to call the notification methods. These methods also illustrate some subtleties in designing notifications. Note that `notifyLineWillChange()` is called before the line is added or modified and that the new position of the line is passed as parameters. When you look at the view's implementation of the notifications, you will see that the view needs both the old position of the line and its new position. By convention, the notification is called with the new information while the old information is still stored in the model. This is a common change notification idiom called *prenotification*. That is also why the notification method is named `lineWillChange()`. When a line is deleted, the model moves all lines at a higher index down to fill in the gap. For listeners that care about the line numbering, this is a problem. Because so many lines change because of this, the `deleteLine()` method calls `notifyModelHasChanged()` after the change is complete. Designing notifications is a combination of capturing the changes to the model as well as understanding the needs of those objects being notified.

View Handling of Notification

Up until now, the view was only concerned with responding to calls to its `redraw()` method. The view must also handle notifications from the model of any changes to the model. Figure 3.18 shows an implementation of `LineDrawView` that provides for the notification. This class extends `Widget` because it will be attached to a window for interaction. This class implements `LineDrawListener` so that it can be notified of changes to a `LineDrawModel`.

The `LineDrawView` constructor takes a `LineDrawModel` as a parameter. There is no point in having a view that does not have a model to present. This constructor does two things: saves the model pointer so that the model can be accessed by the view and registers with the model using its `addListener()` method. This makes the necessary connections between the view and the model so that they can communicate.

```
public class LineDrawView extends Widget implements LineDrawListener
{
      private LineDrawModel myModel;
      public LineDrawView(LineDrawModel model)
      {    myModel=model;
           myModel.addListener(this);
      }
      public void redraw(Graphics g)
      {    for (int i=0;i<myModel.nLines();i++)
           {    Line line=myModel.getLine(i);
                g.drawLine(line.x1,line.y1, line.x2, line.y2 );
           }
      }
      public void lineWillChange( int index, int newX1, int newY1, int newX2, int newY2)
      {    Line line=myModel.getLine(index);
           if (line!=null)
           {    Rectangle oldRegion=new Rectangle(line.x1, line.y1,
                     line.x2-line.x1+1, line.y2-line.y1+1;
                this.damage(oldRegion);
           }
           Rectangle newRegion=new Rectangle(newX1,newY1,
                newX2-newX1+1, newY2-newY1+1);
           this.damage(newRegion);
      }
      public void modelHasChanged()
      {
           this.damage();
      }
}
```

Figure 3.18 – View with model change notification

The lineWillChange() and modelHasChanged() methods implement the notification. The lineWillChange() method is called whenever an individual line has changed. This might be when a new line has been added or when an existing line has moved. Whenever a change is made by a view, the windowing system must be notified of the region of the screen affected by the change. In most object-oriented systems, the Widget or Component class will have a method for such notification. For this Widget class, you call the method damage(). It is sometimes called repaint(), update(), or redraw(). There is a great deal of confusion in this naming because some systems call their damage() method by the same name that others use for their redraw(). The damage() method comes in two forms. The simplest has no parameters and reports the entire widget rectangle as damaged. It is also possible to report only a rectangular piece of the widget as damaged.

When the view invokes damage(), the windowing system is notified of the damaged screen rectangle and remembers it. Generally, windowing systems collect damaged regions until input event processing is complete, merge the damaged regions where possible, and then call redraw() on the windows that display the damaged region. You do not want the view to start drawing whenever a change occurs for a variety of reasons. The window might not be visible when model changes occur. The damaged region might not be visible. Many changes might result from some user input. Changing the contents of a spreadsheet cell can cause many other cells to recalculate and change their values. The view simply reports the damaged regions and relies on the windowing system to call `redraw()` whenever appropriate.

In many cases, the view is so simple to draw that `damage()` of the entire widget is used. This is guaranteed to make certain that everything gets drawn. If the presentation is more complex, the view should be more specific about what part of the presentation needs to be updated. A good rule is to first damage everything and then add more specific techniques if there are performance problems. In this example, the `modelHasChanged()` method damages the entire widget because the whole model is affected. In a small application like this one, damaging the entire widget works fine.

Because situations regularly occur where damaging everything is too slow, we will work through another example of how to be more specific. Figure 3.19 shows a line drawn over a rectangle. The old position of the line is gray and the new position is black. Simply damaging the rectangle around the new line position leaves the result shown in Figure 3.20. A correct implementation damages both the old position and the new position. The `lineWillChange()` method in Figure 3.18 looks for the old position of the line in the model and damages its rectangle. It then takes the new position from the notification parameters and damages that rectangle.

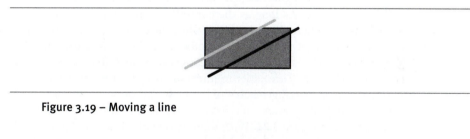

Figure 3.19 – Moving a line

Figure 3.20 – Damage new without damaging old

ESSENTIAL GEOMETRY

You now have a model that can generate change notifications, a view that can receive notifications and notify the windowing systems of regions that need to be refreshed, and a mechanism for the windowing system to redraw any portion of the presentation. You also have a mechanism for the controller to receive input events. You now need a connection between the view and the controller.

The binding between input events and the program fragment that should handle the event is generally based on event type. This is because the set of input events is standard across all applications and processing a small, fixed set of types is computationally simple. However, event type alone is not enough in virtually all graphical applications.

Consider the scroll bar shown in Figure 3.21. The scroll bar has five distinct regions. When a `mouseDown` event is received, the action to be taken differs based on where the event occurred. For the scroll bar, the five regions constitute most of the "essential geometry" shown in Figure 3.21. The other piece of the essential geometry is the mapping between the position of the drag region and the current value of the scroll bar.

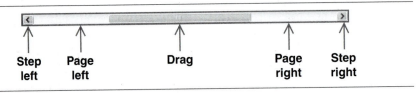

Figure 3.21 – Scroll bar

The scroll bar's controller is responsible for translating input events into changes to the model. Beyond the essential geometry, the controller does not care what the scroll bar looks like. As long as the controller knows which region was selected and how to map the drag region to a model value, the controller is satisfied. The view needs to know where all of these regions are because the view is responsible for drawing them. A basic goal of clean software architecture is to define concepts in only one part of the code where they are easier to understand and maintain. Therefore, we leave the computation of essential geometry to the view and provide the controller with a clean interface to that information. In the case of the scroll bar, the essential geometry might be that shown in Figure 3.22. With these two methods and the enumeration, the controller has everything that it needs to know about the scroll bar's view.

```
enum ScrollRegion { stepLeft, pageLeft, drag, pageRight, stepRight }

ScrollRegion mouseRegion( Point mouseLocation) { . . . }
int mouseToCurValue( Point mouseLocation) { . . . }
```

Figure 3.22 – Scroll bar essential geometry

By separating out the essential geometry, you simplify the testing and debugging of the user interface. One of the serious problems with building user interfaces is that regression testing is difficult. It is relatively easy to write regression tests that verify when the essential geometry is working correctly. It is also easy to instrument the essential geometry methods to print out the mouse point translations as they occur. This simplifies debugging of the interface. It is also very helpful to think through the essential geometry issues before trying to write the controller code. Figure 3.23 shows four different views of a vertical scroll bar[11]. Each has quite a different look and yet all would share the same essential geometry interface to the controller.

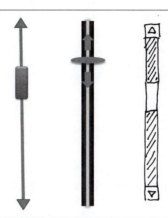

Figure 3.23 – Different scroll bar views

Essential geometry has no precise definition other than information that will map mouse position into some meaningful concept in the model or the behavior of the controller. For example, the essential geometry of the Minesweeper game in Figure 3.24 maps mouse location to the row and column of the selected game cell.

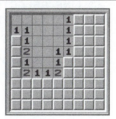

Figure 3.24 – Minesweeper essential geometry

The essential geometry of the text box shown in Figure 3.25 maps the mouse position to the correct insertion point (an index) in the text string. In the case of the HTML viewer in Figure 3.26, this can be more complicated. The essential geometry might map the mouse position to a character position as with the text box or it might map the mouse position to a pathname in the HTML domain object model (DOM). In either case, the HTML essential geometry is greatly complicated by the many font changes that are possible and by the somewhat complex meaning of what a "delete" key might mean in terms of updating and balancing HTML tags. A very careful design of the essential geometry of HTML editing is important to getting everything to work correctly.

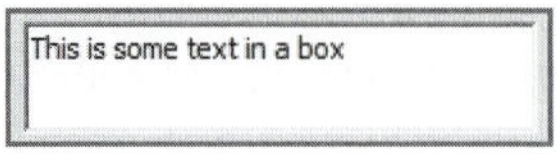

This is some text in a box

Figure 3.25 – Text box essential geometry

Augmenting shared personal calendars
Proceedings of the 15th annual ACM symposium on User interface software and technology
Joe Tullio , Jeremy Goecks , Elizabeth D. Mynatt , David H. Nguyen

Figure 3.26 – HTML essential geometry

For the `LineDrawView` from Figure 3.18, the essential geometry is that the mouse is either near a line to be selected or it is in open space. You might implement this with the `nearestLine()` method shown in Figure 3.27.

```
public class LineDrawView extends Widget implements LineDrawListener
{
     private LineDrawModel myModel;
     public LineDrawView(LineDrawModel model) { . . . }
     public void redraw(Graphics g) { . . . }
     public void lineWillChange( int index, int newX1, int newY1, int newX2, int newY2)
     { . . . }
     public void modelHasChanged() { . . . }
     private const int NO_LINE_SELECTED = -1;
     private int nearestLine(Point mouseLoc)
     {    for (int i=0;i<myModel.nLines();i++)
          {
               if ( mouseLoc is near to myModel.getLine(i) )
                    return int;
          }
          return NO_LINE_SELECTED;
     }
}
```

Figure 3.27 – Drawing essential geometry

Implementing Essential Geometry

The implementation of essential geometry can be as simple as comparing a mouse point with a set of rectangles, as with the scroll bar in Figure 3.21. This simple rectangle approach is very common in a wide variety of situations. In other cases, such as a drawing program, more complex geometry is required. The mathematics of the most common problems is discussed in Chapter 12.

The retained graphics architecture described in Chapter 2 can provide significant help in the computation of essential geometry. In the retained graphics approach, a tree or DAG of drawing primitives is managed as a representation of the current presentation. In modern systems, these primitives are represented as objects in an object-oriented language. In addition to the `draw()` method that will draw each primitive, there can be an `isHit()` method that accepts a mouse point and then returns true if the point is sufficiently close to or inside the draw primitive. The `isHit()` method is implemented by the retained graphics system and relieves the application programmer of any geometry calculations. Each part of the essential geometry of a presentation can be associated with some subtree of the retained graphics. This makes essential geometry very easy. This use of retained graphics to compute essential geometry is found in systems like Adobe Flash and in the Document Object Model (DOM) of many Web browsers. This architecture greatly simplifies the construction of new controllers.

CONTROLLER IMPLEMENTATION

Given a model with public methods, a notification mechanism for model changes, and a view that can notify the windowing system of damaged regions and redraw whenever necessary, you can now work through a complete controller implementation. When model-view-controller was first introduced with Smalltalk[12], the controller was implemented as a separate class. It was recognized that for many different kinds of widgets the controller code would be the same even though the view might be very different. This idea is captured in Myers' definition of Interactors[13]. However, most implementations of model-view-controller combine the view and the controller in the same class. Although they are in the same class, it helps to discuss them separately and work out their relationships before diving into the code.

Figure 3.28 shows the controller implemented using Java's version of the inherited event-handling model. For drawing lines, you will process mouse-down, mouse-up, and mouse-move events. For simplicity, this example ignores line selection and deletion. Java collects many of its mouse events into a single `processMouseEvent()` method. This means that you must sort out the exact event by checking the event ID. The mouse movement is handled in a separate `processMouseMotionEvent()` method. For efficiency reasons, Java requires that the desired events be enabled. If an event is not enabled, its corresponding method is never called. The enabling is handled in the constructor code.

```java
public class LineDrawView extends Component implements LineDrawListener
{
    private LineDrawModel myModel;
    public LineDrawView(LineDrawModel model)
    {    ... other setup ...
        enableEvents(AWTEvent.MOUSE_EVENT_MASK +
            AWTEvent.MOUSE_MOTION_EVENT_MASK);
        creatingLine=false;
    }
    ... other methods ...
    private int activeLineIdx;
    private boolean creatingLine;
    private int startX, startY;
    public void processMouseEvent(MouseEvent evt)
    {
        if (evt.getID() == MouseEvent.MOUSE_PRESSED)
        {    // the mouse has just been pressed
            creatingLine=true;
            startX=evt.getX();          // get the mouse location
            startY=evt.getY();
            activeLineIdx=myModel.addLine(startX,startY,startX,startY);
        }
        else if (evt.getID() == MouseEvent.MOUSE_RELEASED)
        {    // the mouse has just been released
            creatingLine=false;
            myModel.moveLine(activeLineIdx,startX,startY,
            evt.getX(),evt.getY());
        }
    }

    public void processMouseMotionEvent(MouseEvent evt)
    {
        if (creatingLine)
        {    myModel.moveLine(activeLineIdx,startX,startY,
            evt.getX(),evt.getY());
        }
    }
}
```

Figure 3.28 – Java inherited controller

When the mouse is pressed, we save its starting location in startX and startY. We ask the model to create a new line and we remember its index. As the mouse motion events occur, we tell the model that the line has moved. Finally, when the mouse is released, we move the line one last time. Notice that we need the field creatingLine to remember when we are creating a line. Many mouse movement events can occur without any buttons being pressed. We do not want to move the line whenever we receive a mouse motion event. One of the challenges of interactive programming is that each event is independent and a single task can involve many events. The controller code must keep track of the state between events. Chapter 11 discusses this problem in much more detail and provides notation to help you get the controller code to work correctly.

Java also provides a listener model for handling mouse events. In fact, the default implementations of processMouseEvent() and processMouseMotionEvent() actually invoke the listener event mechanism. Figure 3.29 shows the same controller implemented using Java's listener event handling.

```java
public class LineDrawView extends Component implements LineDrawListener,
        MouseListener, MouseMotionListener
{
    private LineDrawModel myModel;
    public LineDrawView(LineDrawModel model)
    {    . . . other setup . . .
        addMouseListener(this);
        addMouseMotionListener(this);
    }
    . . . other methods . . .
    private int activeLineIdx;
    private boolean creatingLine;
    private int startX, startY;
    public void mousePressed(MouseEvent evt)
    {    // the mouse has just been pressed
        creatingLine=true;
        startX=evt.getX();    // get the mouse location
        startY=evt.getY();
        activeLineIdx=myModel.addLine(startX,startY,startX,startY);
    }
    public void mouseReleased(MouseEvent evt)
    {    // the mouse has just been released
        creatingLine=false;
        myModel.moveLine(activeLineIdx,startX,startY,
        evt.getX(),evt.getY());
    }
    public void mouseClicked(MouseEvent evt) { }
    public void mouseEntered(MouseEvent evt) { }
    public void mouseExited(MouseEvent evt) { }

    public void mouseDragged(MouseEvent evt) { }
    public void mouseMoved(MouseEvent evt)
    {
        if (creatingLine)
        {    myModel.moveLine(activeLineIdx,startX,startY,evt.getX(),
         evt.getY());
        }
    }
}
```

Figure 3.29 – Java listener controller

The LineDrawView class now must implement MouseListener and MouseMotionListener. These are the listener interfaces for the two types of events. The MouseListener interface defines the methods mousePressed() and mouseReleased(), which you use to handle those two events. In addition, the MouseListener interface also defines mouseClicked(), mouseEntered(), and mouseExited(). Because the class said it would implement the MouseListener interface, you must provide methods for all of them even though you do not care about the last three. The MouseMotionListener interface defines two methods. You can ignore mouseDragged() and implement mouseMoved() to move the line on every mouse move while creatingLine. In Figure 3.28, the mouse events were handled directly by over-riding processMouseEvent() and processMouseMotionEvent(). In Figure 3.29, the controller is added as a listener and the default implementations of these two methods are used to call the listener methods instead.

Implementing the listener interface is not enough. You also must register as a listener. This is a little confusing because the LineDrawView must actually register with itself. However, the event-handling mechanism notifies any registered object. It does not care what that object is. In the LineDrawView constructor, you add the object as a mouse listener and a mouse motion listener.

As a final example, Figure 3.30 shows a C# implementation of the same controller using delegates. In the constructor, the event-handling methods are individually added to their respective delegates in the constructor. The superclass is Panel, which is the appropriate Widget class for this particular situation.

```
public class LineDrawView : Panel
{     private LineDrawModel myModel;
      public LineDrawView(LineDrawModel model)
      {    . . . . other code . . .
           this.MouseDown+=new MouseEventHandler(this.myMouseDown);
           this.MouseMove+= new MouseEventHandler(this.myMouseMove);
           this.MouseUp+= new MouseEventHandler(this.myMouseUp);
      }
      private int activeLineIdx;
      private boolean creatingLine;
      private int startX, startY;
      public void myMouseDown(MouseEventArgs e)
      {    // the mouse has just been pressed
           creatingLine=true;
           startX=e.X;     // get the mouse location
           startY=e.Y;
           activeLineIdx=myModel.addLine(startX,startY,startX,startY);
      }
      public void myMouseUp(MouseEventArgs e)
      {    // the mouse has just been released
           creatingLine=false;
           myModel.moveLine(activeLineIdx,startX,startY,e.X, e.Y);
      }
      public void myMouseMove(MouseEventArgs e)
      {
           if (creatingLine)
           {      myModel.moveLine(activeLineIdx,startX,startY,eX,eY);
           }
      }
}
```

Figure 3.30 – C# delegate event handling

SUMMARY

As a review, let's work through the entire event-handling/notification mechanism using the sample drawing application. Let us assume that the user has started drawing a new line by pressing the mouse button over the start point and is now holding down the button and dragging the mouse. With each movement of the mouse, the following occurs:

- A mouse-move event is generated by the operating system and passed to the windowing system.

- The windowing system uses one of the event dispatch mechanisms (bottom-up, top-down, or focused) to locate the window that should receive the event.

- The event is passed to the controller associated with the selected window using one of the event-handling mechanisms (event table, call-back, object-inheritance, and so forth).

- The controller receives the event (in this example of drawing, no essential geometry is required) and calls the model's `moveLine()` method.

- The `moveLine()` method invokes the `lineWillChange()` method on all registered listeners. In this simple application, only the view is listening.

- The view's `lineWillChange()` method invokes `damage()` on the old and the new position of the line using the information in the model and the parameters that it received.

- The windowing system receives the `damage()` notifications and remembers the damaged regions.

- The windowing system returns to the view. The view returns to the model.

- The model now updates its data to the new line position and returns to the controller.

- The controller returns to the windowing system.

- The windowing system checks for any damaged regions and calls the view's `redraw()` method on those regions.

- The view's `redraw()` method consults the values stored in the model and redraws the damaged regions by making calls on the `Graphics` object passed to the `redraw()` method. The view then returns to the windowing system.

- The windowing system determines that all damaged regions have been redrawn and it waits for the operating system to send a new event.

A great deal happens as a result of a simple mouse movement. However, because of the model-view-controller architecture, each piece of the architecture has a relatively simple task to perform. By using an organizing architecture for all of these tasks, the complexity of the implementation is substantially reduced.

POLLED INPUT

This chapter has focused heavily on the event model for processing inputs. Among desktop and PDA applications, this is by far the dominant mechanism for managing user input. It is not, however, the only approach. In gaming applications or in other software that has a continuous animation structure, a polled approach is more prevalent. In gaming and in animation applications, there is an assumption of continuous update to the display, as described in the retained graphics discussion in Chapter 2.

Because the display is continuously updated, view notification is modified in one of two ways. If the view is drawn directly from the model, no view notification is required. The redraw() method is invoked 10–30 times per second and the new model values are immediately reflected on the screen. If the retained graphics approach is used, the model notifies the view, which changes the retained graphics tree and, thus, updates the screen. In either case, the notifications are simplified.

With the assumption that the screen must be continually redrawn, many such applications poll the input devices before the redraw starts. A structure containing the state of the input devices, along with the Graphics object, is then passed through the widget tree. As each node in the widget tree is asked to draw itself, it first modifies its model to reflect the current inputs. This unifies the drawing strategy with the input-processing strategy in a single mechanism. This approach, however, is very wasteful for applications that are not continually changing their presentations.

EXERCISES

1. What is the difference between a windowing system and a window manager?

2. Why are windowing systems frequently tied closely to the operating system?

3. What is the difference in purpose between key focus and mouse focus?

4. Read the API for some interactive toolkit and describe which mechanism it is using for binding events to code.

5. How is the window event table similar to the inheritance model for event handling?

6. Callbacks associate string names with code to be executed. How does this simplify building tools for visually designing user interfaces?

7. Compare the strengths and weaknesses of listeners versus delegates.

8. Select a graphical user interface and describe the notifications that the view should receive from the model.

9. For your selected graphical user interface, describe all of the steps and notifications that must occur from the time an event is received until the entire screen has been correctly updated.

10. What is the essential geometry of the game tic-tac-toe?

END NOTES

1   Bezerianos, A. and Balakrishnan, R., "The Vacuum: Facilitating the Manipulation of Distant Objects", SIGCHI *Conference on Human Factors in Computing Systems* (*CHI '05*), ACM Press, New York, NY, (2005), pp 361–370.

2   Rosenthal, D.S.H., "Managing Graphical Resources", *Computer Graphics* 17(1), ACM, 1983, pp 38–45.

3   Scheifler, R. W. and Gettys, J., "The X window system," *ACM Trans. Graph*, 5, 2 (Apr. 1986), pp 79–109.

4   Asente, P. J. and Swick, R. R., *X Window System Toolkit: The Complete Programmer's Guide and Specification*, Butterworth-Heinemann, (Oct 1990).

5   Goldberg, A. and Robson, D., *Smalltalk-80: the language and its implementation*, Addison-Wesley Longman Publishing Co., Inc., (1983).

6   Stroustrup, Bjarne, *The C++ Programming Language*, Addison-Wesley, (2000).

7   Bracha, G. and Ungar, D., "Mirrors: Design Principles for Meta-level Facilities of Object-oriented Programming Languages," *Conference on Object-Oriented Programming, Systems, Languages, and Applications* (*OOPSLA '04*), ACM Press, New York, NY, (2004), pp 331–344.

8   Lieberman, Henry, "There's More to Menu Systems than Meets the Screen," *Computer Graphics* 19(3), (1985), pp 181–189.

9   Flanagan, D., *JavaScript: The Definitive Guide*, O'Reilly Media, (2001).

10 Macromedia, Inc., *Macromedia Interactive: Lingo for Director 5*, Macromedia, (1997).

11 Hudson, S. E. and Tanaka, K., "Providing Visually Rich Resizable Images for User Interface Components," *Symposium on User interface Software and Technology* (*UIST '00*), ACM Press, New York, NY, pp 227–235.

12 Goldberg, A., *SMALLTALK-80: the interactive programming environment*, Addison-Wesley Longman Publishing Co., Inc., (1984).

13 Myers, B. A., "A New Model for Handling Input," *ACM Trans. Inf. Syst.* 8, 3 (Jul. 1990), pp 289–320.

CHAPTER 4

Widgets

In 1981, Xerox introduced the Star[1]. This computer boasted a graphical user interface where users could interact with their information directly on the screen using a mouse and a keyboard. Though many parts of these ideas had occurred earlier, the Star is heralded as the trendsetter for the workstations we know today. In 1983, Apple introduced the Lisa with similar capabilities. The Lisa was costly and slow. However, during the 1984 NFL Super Bowl, Apple introduced the Macintosh, which forever changed the way people interact with their computers. Graphical user interfaces were now affordable for everyone.

A unique aspect of these computers was their software architecture. Not only did they support graphical interaction, but they also provided a software toolkit of reusable interactive components. In 1984, MIT formed Project Athena, which developed X Windows. Project Athena also provided a toolkit of reusable pieces of interaction called "widgets"[2]. The Athena widgets provided reusable interaction for the UNIX world. This chapter explores how widgets work and how they simplify the creation of graphical user interfaces.

Many different widget toolkits are available in the world. Some are built around operating systems such as Microsoft Windows or Apple's OS X. Many are built around the unique capabilities of languages such as Java's Swing[3] toolkit or the components that come with C#[4]. There are also toolkits for specialized hardware such as personal digital assistants (PDAs)[5] or tablet computers. Despite this diversity, a number of ideas are common across almost all of these systems. This chapter discusses these general ideas. Between the time of writing this chapter and its publication, there will be at least one new widget toolkit introduced by someone for some reason. Therefore, this chapter focuses on the central ideas and leaves it up to the reader to learn the specifics of a particular implementation.

Prebuilt widgets fall into three categories: simple widgets, container widgets, and abstract model widgets. This chapter discusses the first two categories, and Chapter 7 covers the abstract model widgets. The simple widgets are a modification of the model-view-controller architecture where the model, view, and controller are all packaged in a single class, as shown in Figure 4.1. The reason for this is that the model is not sufficiently complex to justify a separate class. The models for most widgets are single values, such as a number, text string, Boolean value, or list of choices. The advantage of such simple widgets is that the programmer does not need to implement them, their look and feel becomes standardized across all applications, and most of their design choices are based on changing properties, such as colors, fonts, and sizes. Interface design based on changing properties rather than writing code makes it possible to create the interface design tools, which is discussed in Chapter 9.

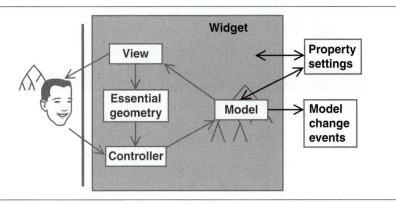

Figure 4.1 – Widget architecture

When using a widget, you must give it a position on the screen, set its properties, and arrange to bind its model change events to the appropriate application code. Chapter 5 discusses the layout problem (positioning widgets). The model change events historically were handled using the callback strategy. This allowed textual callback names to be specified as part of a widget's properties. This transitioned to the object inheritance model and quickly outgrew that model with the number of events to be handled and the number of classes that must be declared to handle those events. Most modern widget toolkits use either the listener or delegate models described in Chapter 3. Some interactive design tools, such as forms layout tools in database systems or Web design tools, use the interpretive language or reflection event-handling strategies.

Figure 4.2 shows a dialog box design consisting of a variety of widgets. These widgets are arranged in the usual tree. At the top level, a container widget holds the General tab and the Print and Cancel buttons. The General tab has three container widgets: the Select Printer group, the Page Range group, and the Copies group. Each of these then contains other widgets. The widget tree reflects the window tree. Each widget has its own window to manage and provides its own view and controller to interact through that window.

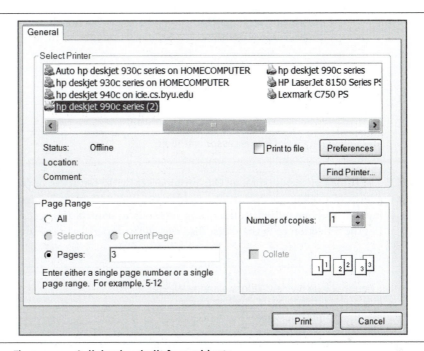

Figure 4.2 – A dialog box built from widgets

The setting of widget properties is fundamental to widget-based interface design. The most important property that is common to all widgets is the Bounds property. This is the rectangular area that the widget is to use as its window. The coordinates of the Bounds are almost always defined relative to the coordinates of the widget's container. This allows a container to be moved around while all of its children remain in their relative positions within the container.

There are two styles for getting and setting properties. These depend on whether the programming language supports field accessors. Java does not have field accessors. Therefore, you might use two separate methods and the get/set naming convention shown in Figure 4.3. This pattern of using two methods with the get/set naming convention is used by interface design tools to discover the properties of a widget. You need to ensure property access through methods because when a property is changed, the view must be notified. This notification is internal to the widget class, but it still must be handled. In the case of changing the Bounds, the layout algorithm (Chapter 5) must be invoked.

```
public class myNewWidget extends Widget
{
        private Rectangle myBounds;
        public Rectangle getBounds() {  return myBounds; }
        public void setBounds(Rectangle newBounds)
        {
                . . . . view notification code . . .
                myBounds=newBounds;
        }
}
```

Figure 4.3 – Get/set accessor methods

Some languages, such as C#, provide explicitly for accessors to fields. Figure 4.4 shows an example of such field accessors. This provides fieldlike access (`myWidget.bounds`) with underlying methods to control the access. This also simplifies the reflection code that must discover such properties in the interface design tools.

```
public class myNewWidget extends Widget
{
        private Rectangle myBounds;
        public Rectangle bounds
        {
                set {    . . . view notification code . . .
                        myBounds=value;
                }
                get {    return myBounds; }
        }
}
```

Figure 4.4 – C# field accessors

The sections that follow look at many kinds of widgets. Generally, such widgets are characterized by the following:

- The model information that they manipulate
- The properties that the programmer/designer can set to control the behavior or appearance
- The events that the widget generates

This chapter first looks at simple widgets that have a single value as their model and provide the basis of any widget toolkit. Next, this chapter looks at container widgets. These provide mechanisms for grouping other widgets together to create more complex user interfaces. An important class of widgets includes those created for a particular application. These form the heart of most user-interface implementation efforts. Finally, this chapter looks at how these widgets can be collected together to form a higher-level model-view-controller architecture for your application.

SIMPLE WIDGETS

An early concept in the development of interactive systems was the notion of *logical input devices*. A logical input device is defined by its function and its interface. The actual implementation on the screen is separate. This is an important design concept because it supports exploring various styles of interaction without changing the way in which they interact with the underlying model. Rapid interchange of interactive style is very important to the process of creating interactive designs that work effectively. For example, we can define the logical device "button" that simply generates an event when it is pressed. Figure 4.5 shows several possible implementations of a logical button. A single button concept can be an icon on a toolbar, a physical keyboard button, a menu item, a control sequence such as Ctrl+P, or a picture of a button on a screen. Although each is implemented very differently, they all have the same relationship to the model, which is "do this thing." Most widget sets are organized around the model for each widget. For each kind of model, there is a corresponding widget. Using such a widget set, application models can be represented interactively.

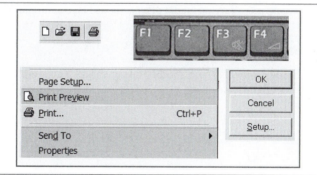

Figure 4.5 – Implementations of logical buttons

The button widgets shown in Figure 4.5 do not really have a model. Their purpose is to generate events. In most toolkits, all of these types of buttons generate the same `ActionEvent`. This makes the application software independent of the kind of button that produced the event.

The simple widgets are grouped by the models that they handle. The following sections look at information or style widgets used to dress up the interfaces. These are followed by Boolean and choice widgets that provide selections. Text widgets are an important group for a variety of purposes. In addition, many variations of widgets exist for interacting with numbers. Finally, several special-purpose widgets that are found in most toolkits are explored.

Information and Style Widgets

The simplest widgets are those that provide information or style. The most notable examples are labels and images. A label provides a piece of text that does not interact in any way. It just shows its text. Image widgets similarly show whatever image is associated with them. Image widgets are very useful in creating widely varying styles to attract attention or to set a mood. For example, Figure 4.6 shows two different "skins" for the Windows Media Player. The logical behavior of all the different skins is the same; the stylistic differences are provided by the images that some artist has drawn, into which the various control widgets have been embedded. The usual properties for style or information widgets are label text, images, font, text color, and background color.

Figure 4.6 – Varying media player "skins" (see color plate)

Boolean Widgets

Most widgets display and modify some value. The simplest are the Boolean widgets. The most common forms are the check box and the toggle button, which are shown in Figure 4.7.

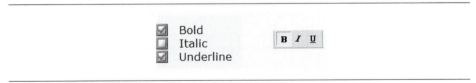

Figure 4.7 – Boolean widgets

There is some variation in how check boxes are organized. In some systems, a label is associated with the check box. In other systems, the check box is implemented by itself with a label widget placed next to it to provide the information. The two-widget approach simplifies the implementation while providing flexibility. However, in practice designers do not vary much from the standard box/label style. Packaging them together is simpler for most programmers. In many user interface style guides, clicking the label should behave the same as clicking the check box. This is easier for the user to click with the mouse. When the label and check box act together, including both in the same widget is a good idea. When a check box includes a label, a property is frequently available to define where the label should be placed.

These generate an event whenever their model changes state. They share most of the properties of the label widgets. Some toolkits have a choice of styles for the state indicator. Other toolkits have trueImage and falseImage properties that allow the designer to provide any two images to represent the state of the widget. These images can be applied to the entire button as on the right of Figure 4.7 or just to the indicator box as on the left. The use of images allows for wide stylistic variation without changing the implementation.

Choice from a List

A very common and highly flexible interactive technique is to select one or more choices from a list of alternatives. Several issues influence the interactive style of such widgets. Is it possible to select one choice or many? The most common case is one. Are there relatively few choices or many choices? Is the list of choices dynamic and can change with time? Figure 4.8 shows a variety of choice widgets.

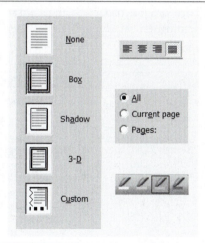

Figure 4.8 – Fixed-choice widgets

All of the widgets shown in Figure 4.8 are implemented using a standard technique. Each choice has two images (selected/not selected) and an optional text label. Again, the image/label technique pushes widget design into the realm of artists rather than programmers. The classic radio button style shown in the middle right was made popular by the Macintosh. Historically, this style of choice is called a radio button because of its similarity to the station selector buttons on old car radios. This style is used when the number of choices is small and fixed.

Conceptually, the model for a choice widget is a single variable that can take on multiple values. Depending on the system, these choice values are usually strings or integers. A single model value is shared among the choice widgets in a group. Each choice has a specific constant value associated with it. When the shared variable has the same value as a choice widget, that choice is shown as selected; otherwise, it is shown as not selected.

A group of single choices is generally not treated as a single widget. Rather, each button is created as a widget of its own and then groups of them are linked together. This strategy allows for wide variations in layout of the choices, including columns, rows, tables, or others. These individual widgets must be grouped together in mutually exclusive groups. In JavaScript, this is done by having several widgets share the same name. In C#, all radio buttons placed on a form are mutually exclusive. Each button has a checked property that specifies which of the buttons is the selected one. In addition, a special container widget called a GroupBox handles mutual exclusion for radio buttons on a finer scale than the whole window. In Java, a special class called ButtonGroup manages the shared variable that controls which of its members is selected. Unlike GroupBox, a ButtonGroup is not a widget. It is an invisible object that ties together radio buttons.

The widgets shown in Figure 4.9 have the ability to handle more choices than can fit on the screen at one time. The widget on the right is a Microsoft ComboBox. The two on the left are variants of Java/Swing's JList widget. These widgets are also special because the program can dynamically change the set of choices.

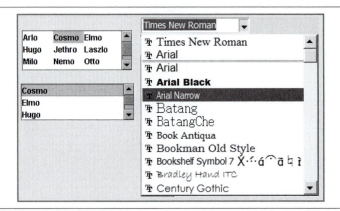

Figure 4.9 – Large choice lists

The properties of choice widgets include the appearance properties found on labels. Images to indicate choice and properties to indicate how choices should be laid out might be available. When many choices are possible, a property is available to indicate how many should be shown at once. This sets the size of the scroll region for the widgets, as shown in Figure 4.9.

The model for choice widgets has a list of choices and a selected item or items. Selection is represented as an index into the list of choices. Such choice lists can frequently handle multiple selections. Some implementations allow for a range of selections represented with a start and end index. Others allow for multiple ranges. The most common technique, however, is the single selection.

Text

The text box is one of the most commonly used widgets. Its model, of course, is a string of text. In addition, some implementations expose the start and end of the selection when the user has selected some region of the text in the box. Text boxes come in multiline and single-line variants. In Java/Swing, the JTextField is single line and the JTextArea is multiline. In C#, the JTextBox has an attribute that can switch the same widget between multiline and single-line modes. Multiline text boxes also have properties that control word wrapping and alignment.

In many cases, text boxes are used to represent numbers or numbers with specific units, as shown in Figure 4.10. Text should be restricted in its format in a wide variety of ways. To support this, some such widgets provide a *formatter* object that can be set as a property of such text boxes. When the user changes the text in the box, the formatter is sent the new string. The formatter then accepts the string, rejects the string, or modifies it to conform. Most toolkits that support formatted text provide a wide variety of prebuilt formatter classes, for such items as percentages, decimals, measurements, dates, times, and IP addresses.

Figure 4.10 – Formatted text boxes

Some toolkits provide text boxes that can handle formatted text, such as bold, italic, and font changes. Java/Swing provides the JEditorPane that can edit HTML. C# provides much of the functionality of the Microsoft Internet Explorer Web browser as a widget.

Text widgets generate events when the text changes. In addition, they generate events when the selection changes. For example, an application could provide a dictionary widget that shows the definition of any selected word. This dictionary could listen to selection change events from a text box and change its definition whenever the selected text changes.

Number Widgets

A variety of widgets exist for specifying or displaying numbers. Figure 4.11 shows several such widgets. The number widgets generally have a maximum, minimum, and current value. The user controls the current value. The properties of such widgets control the color, font, and sometimes the orientation (vertical/horizontal). These widgets generate events whenever the number they control is changed. There are some differences as to how often change events are generated. One style might generate an event every time the slider moves. Others might generate a change event only when the drag of the slider is complete. Generating an event on every change allows other information to change continuously, such as the text box to the right of the bottom widget in Figure 4.11. However, this generates many events. Some widget sets provide a property to control when change events are generated. Others provide two different events: one for incremental changes and another for the final change.

Figure 4.11 – Number widgets

Special Values

Widgets have been developed for a variety of special values. Some of these are provided as built-in parts of a toolkit, whereas others are developed for special purposes. Common built-in widgets include a color picker (Figure 4.12), selecting where to save a file (Figure 4.13), selecting a date from a calendar (Figure 4.14), and selecting a time of day (Figure 4.15).

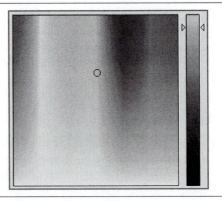

Figure 4.12 – Color selection widget (see color plate)

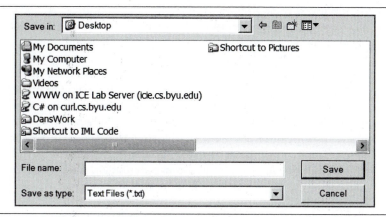

Figure 4.13 – File save widget

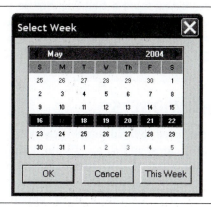

Figure 4.14 – Calendar widget

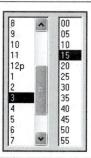

Figure 4.15 – Time selection widget

Many of these widgets are used in a *modal* fashion. A modal dialog is one where only a particular kind of interaction is possible. For example, when trying to select a color, all other parts of an application are disabled and do not accept input. The reason for this is control of the dialog. The user might have specified that the foreground color should be changed. The dialog cannot proceed until the user specifies the new color. In situations where the application needs a value to proceed, a modal dialog is required. However, you could embed the color selection widget in the interface so that it is always visible. Whenever the user changes the selected color, the model is updated appropriately. This would be a *modeless* dialog because the user is not required to change the color before proceeding. This can be freely done at any time. However, if the application has foreground color, background color, and text color, putting all three color pickers on the screen would be a waste of screen space. Instead, you could put color icons that show the current selection for each such color and then launch a modal dialog whenever the user specifies a change. In most cases, the switch from modeless (preferred) to modal (more restrictive) is dictated by the need to conserve screen space. The modal approach can also simplify the implementation of the user interface. If you need a filename before proceeding to save an application's model, it is easier to block the rest of the user interface while the file selection widget is active and then continue processing the save operation. Such requests for user parameters to a command frequently use the modal approach.

CONTAINER WIDGETS

The widgets discussed so far all support the editing of simple values of words, strings, numbers, colors, dates, and so on. To build realistic interfaces, you need to collect such simple values together to form more complex models. The container widgets serve the same function in the user interface as a `struct` in C or as an object with member fields in Java. A variety of such container widgets are available. A container widget's model is a list of other widgets. Container widgets generally do not generate events. That is delegated to the widgets that actually have values. The sections toward the end of this chapter show how container widgets can serve as collectors of events and provide controllers at a higher level of abstraction. The common container widgets are menus, forms, tabs, and toolbars.

Menus

A menu is one of the simplest widget collections. All of the items in a menu are stacked up either vertically or horizontally, as shown in Figure 4.16. For user-interface consistency, menus are handled in the same way across a given operating system. This is so that users always know how to find the commands that they need for any new application. Generally, menus are composed of buttons that perform actions, open modal dialogs, or open other menus. Sometimes, check boxes or radio buttons are found in menus.

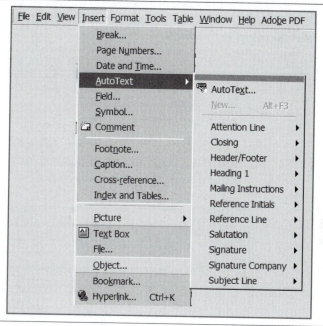

Figure 4.16 – Menu container

Panes/Forms

Another common form of container widget is the pane or form. The term pane comes from the panes in a window. Widgets are laid out on a 2D surface just like a paper form, as shown in Figure 4.17. Handling widget layout in a pane can become complex when the user can change the size of the pane. Chapter 5 discusses these layout questions in more detail.

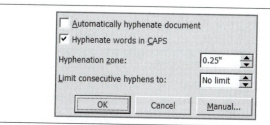

Figure 4.17 – Simple pane of widgets

Panes can also be nested within other panes, as shown in Figure 4.18. This figure also shows that panes can have borders with labels for the group of widgets collected together by the pane. Each pane has a collection of widgets that can be any possible widget, including other panes. This provides trees of widgets and supports tree models where the shape of the tree is fixed. For more dynamic trees, use the abstract model widgets described in Chapter 7.

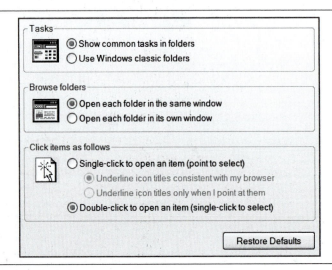

Figure 4.18 – Nested panes

Tabs

Collecting widgets together in panes can take up a lot of screen space. There are frequently more controls than can possibly fit. One solution to the screen space problem is to use a tab container. Just as with a pane, a tab container widget contains several child widgets, each with an associated name. The user is provided with a set of tabs to select which widget should be visible at any time. Figure 4.19 shows a simple row of tabs for selecting widgets. Figure 4.20 shows multiple rows of tabs where there are many choices.

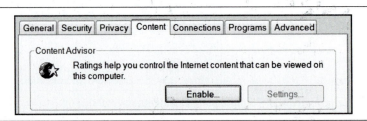

Figure 4.19 – Simple tabbed pane

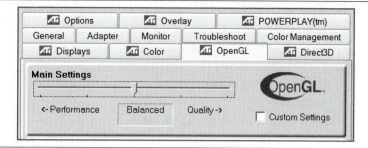

Figure 4.20 – Multirow tabs

Toolbars

Another common container for simple widgets is the toolbar. It has the advantage of arranging a variety of simple widgets along the top or bottom of a window in a way that is easy to access and yet takes up very little screen space, as shown in Figure 4.21. The success of a toolbar depends upon having widgets that are frequently used and whose purpose can be conveyed in very little screen space.

Figure 4.21 – Toolbar

APPLICATION WIDGETS

Beyond the built-in widgets provided with most user-interface toolkits, there are almost always widgets that the programmer must create to perform application-specific tasks. For example, a word processor would have many check box, button, combo box, and text widgets around the periphery of the window. However, most of the window will be occupied by the document and its text. This interaction is the heart of the word processor and must be implemented especially for this application. Almost all interactive programs have one or more key widgets that are specially constructed for that application. The implementation of these widgets use the techniques discussed in Chapters 2 and 3.

MODEL-VIEW-CONTROLLER WITH WIDGETS

Though each simple widget has its own model, view, and controller, you will need to map these to the needs of your application. To create an application using preexisting widgets, you must address the following issues:

- Build a model for the user interface with a change notification/listener mechanism.

- Create the tree of widgets (both prebuilt and application specific) that will define the view.

- Implement the view code to handle model change notifications and change widget properties so that the new information will appear.

- Create a controller by attaching listeners to any prebuilt widgets so that changes made by the user can be propagated to the model. This controller gets its events from other widgets rather than directly from the input devices.

- Resolve notification race conditions.

Suppose you have a simple application for managing member lists for your soccer team. Each player would have information like that shown in Figure 4.22.

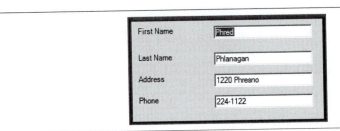

Figure 4.22 – Team member form

The model for the user interface in Figure 4.22 is the Java class shown in Figure 4.23. As with our previous models, this one must implement a notification mechanism so that the view can determine when the model has changed. Because this is a rather simple model, you can use the listener interface shown in Figure 4.24.

```
public class TeamMember
{
            public String getFirstName() { . . . }
            public void setFirstName(String firstName) { . . . }
            public String getLastName() { . . . }
            public void setLastName(String lastName) { . . . }
            public String getAddress() { . . . }
            public void setAddress(String address) { . . . }
            public String getPhone() { . . . }
            public void setPhone(String phone) { . . . }

            public void addTeamMemberListener(TeamMemberListener listener) { . . . }
            public void removeTeamMemberListener(TeamMemberListener listener) { . . . }
}
```

Figure 4.23 – Java model for team member

```
public interface TeamMemberListener
{           public void changed();
}
```

Figure 4.24 – TeamMemberListener

A view for your team member model is a panel container that contains four panel containers. Each of the four contains a label and a text box. The implementation of the view implementation in Figure 4.25 is simplified to ignore layout specifications. Layout is covered in Chapter 5. In this case, TeamMemberView extends JPanel, which is a Java/Swing container widget. By extending the container, you can set up your other widgets as well as the event handling. Figure 4.25 shows how you might set up your TeamMemberView widgets. The setup all occurs in the constructors. The TeamMemberView's constructor creates LabeledText widgets and adds them to itself. JPanel does not know about any widgets that it contains until they are added. The add() method adds widgets into the widget tree where they can be drawn and receive events. Just creating a widget is not enough. It must be added into the widget tree. TeamMemberView also saves each of the LabeledText widgets in a local variable where you can refer to them later. There is a widget for each piece of model information.

```
public class TeamMemberView extends JPanel implements TeamMemberListener
{
        private TeamMember myModel;

        private LabeledText firstName;
        private LabeledText lastName;
        private LabeledText address;
        private LabeledText phone;
        public TeamMemberView(TeamMember model)
        {       myModel=model;
                myModel.addTeamMemberListener(this);

                firstName=new LabeledText("First Name");
                this.add(firstName);
                lastName=new LabeledText("Last Name");
                this.add(lastName);
                address=new LabeledText("Address");
                this.add(address);
                phone=new LabeledText("Phone");
                this.add(phone);
        }
        private class LabeledText extends JPanel
        {
                private JTextField textField;
                public LabeledText(String label)
                {       this.add(new JLabel(label));
                        textField = new JTextField();
                        this.add(textField);

                }
        }
}
```

Figure 4.25 – Widget setup

The LabeledText is a private class that is implemented as another subclass of JPanel. In its constructor, add a label widget, with the appropriate label text and a JTextField widget that will contain the information. Remember the JTextField is a private member that you can use later.

In some introductory texts, the TeamMemberView class would actually contain the fields for the model without the separate class for TeamMember. For simple applications, this is adequate. If, however, a team member's name is also shown in a list of names in another widget, this would not be acceptable. Whenever model information might appear in more than one view, it must be in its own class. This is discussed in more detail in Chapter 6. It is frequently the case that programmers will integrate the model and view into one class because it is simple and the notification problems are avoided. Little interfaces tend to grow up into bigger interfaces as software develops. The need for a list of team member names might come later in the evolution of the product. It is also a good idea to separate the model from the view so that the view can be readily changed by designers without impacting the deeper model implementation. It is good practice to build the MVC pattern from the beginning so that the user interface can adapt with product needs. The simple all-in-one class approach just does not scale well.

Figure 4.25 has set up the view. However, the model change notification and the controller are missing. Figure 4.26 shows `TeamMemberView` with the change notification added. `TeamMemberView` implements the `changed()` method required by `TeamMemberListener`. In this method, it extracts information from the model and then notifies each `LabeledText` widget that its text has changed by calling `LabeledText.setText()`. The `LabeledText` widget in turn calls `setText()` on its own `textField` widget. Java/Swing in its `JTextField` implementation calls `damage()` so that the windowing system knows that the text will be redrawn. `JTextField` also implements the `redraw()`. All the code needs to do is give the new string the text field widget.

```java
public class TeamMemberView extends JPanel implements TeamMemberListener
{
        private TeamMember myModel;

        private LabeledText firstName;
        private LabeledText lastName;
        private LabeledText address;
        private LabeledText phone;
        public TeamMemberView(TeamMember model)
        {       ...}
        private class LabeledText extends JPanel
        {
                private JTextField textField;
                public LabeledText(String label)
                {       ...}
                public void setText(String newText)
                {       textField.setText(newText); }
        }
        public void changed()
        {       firstName.setText(myModel.getFirstName());
                lastName.setText(myModel.getLastName());
                address.setText(myModel.getAddress());
                phone.setText(myModel.getPhone());
        }
}
```

Figure 4.26 – Model change notification

You now need to add controller code to the `TeamMemberView`. However, you do not handle mouse events. That is done by the prebuilt widgets. You need to handle the events produced when the user types new text into a text box. In Java/Swing, the `JTextBox` produces an `ActionEvent` whenever its text is changed. You want the `TeamMemberView` to receive such events so you have it implement the `ActionListener` interface, as shown in Figure 4.27. In `TeamMemberView`'s constructor, add it as a listener to each `LabeledText` widget. The `LabeledText` widget in turn adds the listener to its `textField` box because that is the widget that will generate the events.

```
public class TeamMemberView extends JPanel
                implements TeamMemberListener, ActionListener
{
        private TeamMember myModel;

        private LabeledText firstName;
        private LabeledText lastName;
        private LabeledText address;
        private LabeledText phone;
        public TeamMemberView(TeamMember model)
        {       ... other setup code ...
                firstName.addListener(this);
                lastName.addListener(this);
                address.addListener(this);
                phone.addListener(this);

        }
        private class LabeledText extends JPanel
        {
                private JTextField textField;
                ... other methods ...
                public void addListener(ActionListener listener)
                {       textField.addActionListener(listener); }
                public String getText()
                {       return textField.getText(); }

        }
        ... other methods ...
        public void actionPerformed(ActionEvent e)
        {       myModel.setFirstName(firstName.getText());
                myModel.setLastName(lastName.getText());
                myModel.setAddress(address.getText());
                myModel.setPhone(phone.getText());

        }

}
```

Figure 4.27 – Listening to events

The `ActionListener` interface requires an `actionPerformed()` method that will be called whenever the user changes text in a `JTextField`. The `actionPerformed()` method gets the text from each `LabeledText` widget (which gets it from their `textField`) and uses that text to set the various fields on the model. Thus, whenever the user enters any text, the action event is generated. Because `TeamMemberView` is a listener on all of those events, its `actionPerformed()` method is called to get the information out of the text widgets and send it to the model.

This is a good point to review the various event-handling strategies discussed in Chapter 3. If you were using the inheritance event-handling strategy, you would need to make subclasses of `JTextField` to handle the action events. This is awkward for two reasons: You do not want to make all of those subclasses and it is `TeamMemberView` that wants to handle the events because `TeamMemberView` has the model. The listener event mechanism used in Figure 4.27 allows the `TeamMemberView` (which is not in any way related to the implementation of `JTextField`) to receive and handle the events in a way that is appropriate to the model.

This example also shows a deficiency of the listener model. Any change to any `JTextField` generates the same call to `actionPerformed()`. In the `ActionEvent` parameter, you could find out which text box generated the event, but they all come through the same `actionPerformed()` method. It would be better to have a separate event method associated with `firstName`, `lastName`, `address`, and `phone`. Each of these methods would change only the model field that needed to be changed. The delegate event-handling strategy found in C#, Objective-C, JavaScript, and other languages does exactly this.

Notification Race Conditions

There is one final problem with notification race conditions. If the user enters some text in the Last Name field, an `actionPerformed()` is called on the view. The `actionPerformed()` calls `setFirstName()` on the model (Figure 4.27), which, in turn, notifies all views listening to the model that the model has changed. Because the view is listening to the model, its `changed()` method (Figure 4.26) is called. The `changed()` method calls `setText()`, which changes the text in the `JTextField`. In many widget implementations, events are generated whenever the widget model changes, no matter who changed the model. `JTextField` is one such widget. Changing its text generates an `actionPerformed()`, which changes the model, which notifies the view, which changes the text, which generates `actionPerformed()`, and so on.

These race conditions happen frequently in user interfaces because of the inherent loop of mutual notifications. You need to be aware of these possibilities and block the loop when necessary. Figure 4.28 shows one mechanism to handle the problem. A private flag `activeAction` is initialized to false. This indicates when we are already handling an action event. If `actionPerformed()` is called when it has already been called previously, it simply returns and blocks the loop. If it is not currently active, it sets `activeAction`, does its business, and then clears the flag. It is very important to understand the conditions under which prebuilt widgets generate events. Frequently, this is not documented clearly and can only be discovered by experimentation with the code.

```
public class TeamMemberView extends JPanel
                implements TeamMemberListener, ActionListener
{
        private boolean activeAction;
        public TeamMemberView(TeamMember model)
        {       . . . other setup code . . .
                activeAction=false;
        }
        private class LabeledText extends JPanel
        {       . . . }
        . . . other methods . . .
        public void actionPerformed(ActionEvent e)
        {       if (activeAction) return;
                activeAction=true;
                myModel.setFirstName(firstName.getText());
                myModel.setLastName(lastName.getText());
                myModel.setAddress(address.getText());
                myModel.setPhone(phone.getText());
                activeAction=false;

        }
}
```

Figure 4.28 – Blocking race conditions

SUMMARY

Prebuilt widgets greatly simplify the development of user interfaces by standardizing the look and feel of the interface and eliminating the need to write and debug relatively complex code. Widgets also move much of the user-interface design problem from coding of graphics and mouse events to the selection and setting of properties.

With the exception of the information and style widgets, all prebuilt widgets generate events. It is normal to have some container widget collect those events and handle the interface between the view and the model. The events from the simple widgets are translated into changes to the model. Model change notifications are translated by the view into changes to widget model properties.

Various toolkits use one or more of the event-handling strategies described in Chapter 3. Any of the object-oriented techniques are in wide use. The delegate strategy is the simplest for stitching widgets together into more complex applications. Events generated by prebuilt widgets can produce notification race conditions that must be handled by the programmer.

EXERCISES

1. How does a toolkit of widgets help to enforce a common look and feel on graphical applications?

2. Implement a contact manager application using a common widget set. Each person should have a name, address, phone number, and category. Use a table widget to create a list of contacts with a text box for searching for a particular name. Use form, label, and text widgets to enter new contacts. Use a bank of radio buttons to select a category from a small list. Modify your application to use a drop-down list for a larger set of categories.

3. Why are widget properties accessed through methods rather than just exposing the appropriate fields?

4. If each widget handles its own mouse and keyboard input events, then what does an application's controller use for inputs?

5. In a user interface built entirely of widgets, what is the purpose of notification methods received by the view from the model? If they no longer damage a region of the screen (the widgets do that), what do they do?

END NOTES

[1] Bewley, W. L., Roberts, T. L., Schroit, D., and Verplank, W. L., "Human Factors Testing in the Design of Xerox's 8010 'Star' Office Workstation," *Human Factors in Computing Systems (CHI '83)*, ACM Press, New York, NY, (1983), pp 72-77.

[2] McCormack, J. and Asente, P., "An Overview of the X Toolkit," *Symposium on User interface Software (UIST '88)*, ACM Press, New York, NY, (1988), pp 46-55.

[3] Zukowski, J., *The Definitive Guide to Java Swing*, Apress, (2005).

[4] MacDonald, M., *User Interfaces in C#: Windows Forms and Custom Controls*, Apress, (2002).

[5] McKeehan, J. and Rhodes, N., *Palm OS Programming: The Developer's Guide*, O'Reilly Media, (2001).

CHAPTER 5

Layout and Constraints

Chapter 4 discussed how user interfaces can be assembled from previously built widgets. Chapter 4 deferred the issue of the placement of those widgets on the screen. When a user drags or resizes windows and other objects, the positions and possibly orientation of other graphical objects must be kept consistent. Widgets must be repositioned, connecting lines between objects must stay connected, alignments must be preserved, and so forth. Keeping objects geometrically consistent is a fundamental problem. When the objects are widgets, it is called a layout problem. When the objects are other things, it is called a constraint problem.

Consider the widgets shown in Figure 5.1. When the window changes size, a variety of things happen. The scroll bars and color palette remain a constant distance from the right and bottom edges. When there is not enough room for the menu bar, it changes itself to two lines. When the menu bar occupies two lines, it causes the painting and the tool palette to move down to make room for the second menu line. When there is not enough room for the line width selector, it gets clipped off of the bottom. When the window gets narrower, the paint region in the middle changes size. When the paint window changes size, the scroll bars change the size of their sliders. All of these things work together so that the user interface retains visual consistency. This chapter addresses these kinds of issues. This chapter first discusses widget layout. It next looks at constraints, which are a more general model for maintaining visual and interactive consistency.

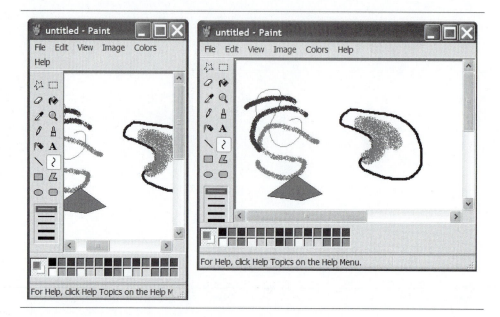

Figure 5.1 – Widgets move when windows are resized

LAYOUT

Figure 5.1 demonstrates most of the problems that must be addressed by a layout system. When you use windowed applications, you assume all widgets move appropriately. However, this movement must be programmed to behave correctly. The layout problem is complicated by the fact that most people really want to design layouts by drawing them. Since Bill Buxton's MenuLay[1] system was published in 1983, it has been clear that drawing widgets and their layouts is preferable to programming the layouts in many cases. Layout models, therefore, are constrained by whether you want to program them or draw them. If you want to draw layouts, you must consider the user interface for doing so. The three most popular layout algorithms are fixed position, edge-anchored, and variable intrinsic size.

For each style of layout, three issues must be dealt with: (1) the information that must be stored with the widgets from which the layout can be computed, (2) the algorithm for computing the layout, and (3) the method the interface designer will use to specify the layout—either interactively or programmatically.

Fixed-Position Layout

The simplest layout mechanism is to assign every widget a fixed rectangle whose coordinates are relative to the rectangle of its parent widget. Figure 5.2 shows a dialog box that uses a fixed layout. All of the widgets are of a fixed size and there are a fixed number of them. There is no reason to resize this dialog box and, therefore, a fixed layout is entirely appropriate.

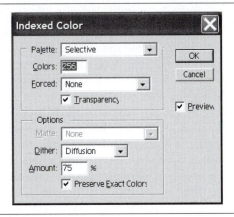

Figure 5.2 – Fixed-size dialog box

The data required is simply a rectangle for each widget and the layout algorithm is very straightforward. Because each child has its desired bounds determined relative to its container widget, the container widget simply sets the child's bounds location (left, top) to be its own location plus the desired child's location. The child's size is unchanged from its desires. This allows a container widget to be moved around and all of its children will stay in position relative to the container. The recursive nature of the algorithm repositions the children's children. The algorithm is shown in Figure 5.3.

```
public class Widget
{
        ....other fields and methods....
        public Rectangle desiredBounds;
        public void doLayout(Rectangle newBounds)
        {      setBounds(newBounds);
               foreach child widget C
               {      Rectangle newChildBounds=
                             new Rectangle(newBounds.left+C.desiredBounds.left,
                                    newBounds.Top+C.desiredBounds.top,
                                    C.desiredBounds.width, C.desiredBounds.height);
                      C.doLayout(newChildBounds);
               }
        }
}
```

Figure 5.3 – Fixed-layout algorithm

The advantages of fixed layout are a simple algorithm, minimal data, and a very simple model to specify. When designing programmatically, you just need to construct a rectangle with the desired location and size, set desiredBounds, and then add the widget to its container. Figure 5.4 shows an interface design being drawn interactively. The designer positions and resizes each widget to create a complete design. Designing an interface with fixed layout is as simple as drawing in a variety of other applications. A final advantage is that the model is trivial to understand and all widgets stay exactly where the designer has placed them. This model was used in Apple's HyperCard[2] and early versions of Visual Basic. The primary disadvantage is that it does not handle resizable windows. If the window gets smaller, widgets are simply clipped or not displayed. If the window gets bigger, all of the widgets stay in the upper-left corner of the container and waste the additional space. In cases like Figure 5.2, this is fine but for the paint program in Figure 5.1, fixed layout would be unacceptable. In a toolkit that uses fixed layout, the problems of Figure 5.1 would need to be handled by special code in response to window resize events. The edge-anchored and variable intrinsic size layout algorithms attempt to eliminate the programmer's need to write such code.

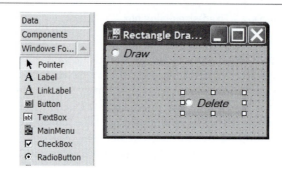

Figure 5.4 – Drawing widget layouts

Edge-Anchored Layout

The fixed-layout algorithm can be expanded to accommodate most of the common resizing needs. Note that in Figure 5.1 most of the layout issues involve keeping widgets collected around the edge of the pane with the central space occupied by the primary paint area. You can accommodate this behavior by modifying the widgets so that their edges can be anchored to the edges of their container's rectangle. This form of layout was first introduced by Cardelli[3]. One of its more popular current uses is in Visual C#, Visual Basic, and Mac OS X.

Using the C# form of edge-anchored layout, each widget has coordinates for left, right, top, and bottom. The interpretation of these depends upon the Boolean values anchorLeft, anchorRight, anchorTop, and anchorBottom. In addition, the widget has a desiredWidth and desiredHeight. The algorithms for the x- and y-axes are independent and identical so this section only describes how the layout in x works.

The core idea is that an edge is either anchored or not. If an edge is anchored, it is a fixed distance away from the corresponding container edge. If only one edge is anchored, the desired width is used to determine the location of the other edge. If neither edge is anchored, the left value is used to compute a proportional distance between the container edges and the desired width is used for the other edge. If both edges are anchored, they follow their respective edges. The algorithm is shown in Figure 5.5.

```
public class Widget
{
        . . . . other fields and methods . . .
        public Rectangle bounds;
        public int left, right, top, bottom;
        public boolean anchorLeft, anchorRight, anchorTop, anchorBottom;
        public int width, height;
        public const int MAXSIZE=4096;
        public void doLayout( Rectangle newBounds)
        {
            bounds=newBounds;
            for each child widget C
            {       Rectangle childBounds=new Rectangle();
                    if (C.anchorLeft)
                    {       childBounds.left=newBounds.left+C.left;
                            if (C.anchorRight)
                            {   childBounds.right=newBounds.right-C.right; }
                            else
                            {   childBounds.right=childBounds.left+C.width; }
                    }
                    else if (C.anchorRight) // right is anchored left is not
                    {       childBounds.right=newBounds.right-C.right;
                            childBounds.left=childBounds.right-C.width;
                    }
                    else // neither edge is anchored
                    {       childBounds.left = newBounds.width*C.left/MAXSIZE;
                            childBounds.right=childBounds.left+C.width;
                    }
                    . . . . perform similar computation for Y . . . .
                    C.doLayout(childBounds);
            }
        }
}
```

Figure 5.5 – Edge-anchored layout algorithm

This algorithm involves a few key ideas. The first is that a widget never does its own layout, nor does it use the anchor or location information. The widget's container does all of that. When a widget receives a `doLayout()` call, it accepts the bounds information and then performs layout on its children if it has any. Normally, `left` and `right` are the number of pixels from their respective edges. If one edge is unanchored, the width/height is used to compute its position from the other anchored edge. If both edges are unanchored, `left` is used to store a fractional value. Because `left` is an integer, `left/MAXSIZE` is used as the fractional value. For example, if `left==MAXSIZE/2`, `width*left/MAXSIZE` is `width*(MAXSIZE/2)/MAXSIZE` or `width/2`. This horizontally centers the widget. Most layout problems can be handled with this mechanism. Setting `left` to 0 places the widget at the far left.

To lay out a widget, a programmer sets the various member fields and adds the widget to its container. The container then makes certain that the widget's bounds are placed in the correct position. Interactively, you need a user interface to specify the values. For the most part, the user interface is the same as that shown in Figure 5.4. The user draws out the bounding rectangle for the widget and then moves it around to the correct place on the form. Visual Studio provides a special editor for the anchors. Two examples of this are shown in Figure 5.6. The anchor editor on the left is the default and shows the widget anchored to the top and left. This is exactly the same behavior as the fixed-layout algorithm. The editor on the right is only anchored to the left edge with the vertical position of the widget to be proportional between the top and bottom.

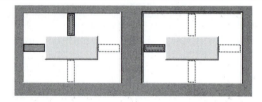

Figure 5.6 – Anchor editors

Figure 5.7 shows an interface design with the form at two different sizes. The button is using the anchors shown on the left in Figure 5.6 and the text box is using the anchors shown on the right.

Revisiting the paint application shown in Figure 5.1, you could lay out the pane with the paint area and its scroll bars using anchors to all edges. This would allow room for the menu bar above and the palettes below and to the left. The paint area essentially grows with the window itself. The vertical scroll bar would be anchored top, bottom, and right to the paint area pane. Its left edge would be determined by the width of the scroll bar.

The layout mechanism in Mac OS X is very similar but more precise in its specification. Figure 5.8 shows widget placements using "struts" and "springs." A strut (straight line) is a fixed distance. A spring (coil) is a proportional distance. By specifying a strut/spring for the interior for the widget, this form makes clear what should happen to the size of the widget. The size behavior is inferred in the C# specification.

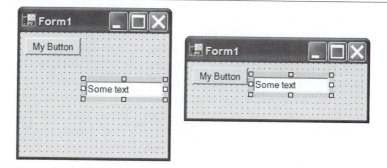

Figure 5.7 – Resizing with anchors

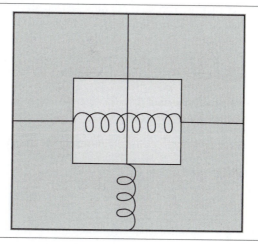

Figure 5.8 – Struts and springs

Variable Intrinsic Size Layout

The fixed-position and edge-anchored layout presume that the designer wants to manually position the widgets. Many times, this is not the case. In many situations, you might want to create a list or other group of widgets and have them position themselves in an appropriate way. A good example is a menu. You add items to the list and the items all position themselves in the list and the width of the menu is automatically determined. You are not required to manually design the menu—it just works. Another example is when changing an interface from English to German or English to Kanji (Japanese ideographic writing). German words are in general longer than English words. This means that many labels need to get larger, which forces changes in the layout. Using the two previous mechanisms, the layout would need to be redrawn by the designer. Ideographic languages cause similar layout distortions. Inserting or removing items from a list would also cause the interface layout to be redesigned. In these cases, you might prefer a layout model that handles these automatically.

The variable intrinsic size layout is designed to automatically adapt the layout to changes in interface content. The idea is that each widget knows how much screen space it can reasonably use (intrinsic size) and each container has a plan for how to allocate screen space based on the needs of its children. By recursively arranging containers with various layout plans, you can produce a wide variety of designs that automatically adjust to their content.

This layout model was first developed Donald Knuth in his T_EX^4 system for laying out mathematical formulas. This layout strategy was adapted to user interfaces by Linton, Vlissides, and Calder in their InterViews[5] system. Its most popular current use is in the Java user-interface architecture. A restricted form of this algorithm is used in HTML <table> tags.

Basic Layout Algorithm

The variable intrinsic size layout algorithm is based on two recursive passes. The first pass requests each widget to report its desired size. The second pass sets the widget bounds. The general algorithm is shown in Figure 5.9.

```
public void doLayout(Rectangle newBounds)
{
        foreach child widget C
        {    ask for desired size of C }

        based on desired sizes and newBounds, decide where each child should go

        foreach child widget C
        {    C.doLayout( new bounds for C); }
}
```

Figure 5.9 – Generic layout algorithm

Most modern intrinsic size layouts ask a widget for its minimum size (the smallest dimensions that it can effectively use), its desired size (the dimensions that would work best for this widget), and its maximum size (the largest dimensions that it can effectively use). These size values are determined by the nature of each widget and, if it is a container, by the sizes of its children. This is done by adding the methods in Figure 5.10 to the Widget class. Each class of widget must implement these three methods in its own way.

Sizes of Simple Widgets

Figure 5.11 shows a button widget with various properties of the widget identified. The marginWidth and bevelWidth are usually properties set by the designer. The label width depends upon the actual text of the label and its font. There is usually a margin height property that is not shown. The label height is also computed from the label's font. Based on these values, you can implement the size methods for a button, as shown in Figure 5.12.

```
public class Dimension
{       public int width;
        public int height;
}

public class Widget
{
        . . . other methods and fields . . .
        public Dimension getMinSize() { . . . }
        public Dimension getDesiredSize() { . . . }
}
```

Figure 5.10 – Abstract methods to report desired sizes

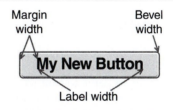

Figure 5.11 – Button size parameters

```
public class Button
{       . . . other methods and fields . . .
        public Dimension getMinSize()
        {       int minWidth = bevelWidth*2+font.getLength(labelText);
                int minHeight = bevelWidth*2+font.getHeight();
                return new Dimension(minWidth,minHeight);
        }
        public Dimension getDesiredSize()
        {       int desWidth = bevelWidth*2+marginWidth*2+font.getLength(labelText);
                int minHeight=bevelWidth*2+marginHeight*2+font.getHeight();
                return new Dimension(desWidth,desHeight)
        }
        public Dimension getMaxSize()
        {       return getDesiredSize(); }
}
```

Figure 5.12 – Desired size methods for an example button

For the minimum size, dispense with the margins around the text so that the button can be as small as possible. The bevel space is needed to show whether the button has been pressed or not. Of course, the button label is necessary so that the user will know the button's purpose. The desired size adds in the margins so the button looks better. Note that the maximum size is the same as the desired size. It is not necessary to give the button more screen space.

Figure 5.13 shows a horizontal scroll bar. The scroll bar has different size needs from the button. Its height is fixed so its minimum, desired, and maximum height are all the same constant. Its minimum width is `arrowWidth*2+sliderWidth*2`. This is just enough to show all of the controls with a little room to move the slider. Its desired width might be `arrowWidth*2+sliderWidth*5`, which would provide more room to scroll. Its maximum width is some constant `MAXSIZE` because the scroll bar wants as much horizontal space as it can get.

Figure 5.13 – Scroll bar

The paint region in Figure 5.1 might specify a modest 20 × 20 as its minimum to give just enough space to paint a small icon. For its desired size, it might report the size of a modest screen at 400 × 400. For its maximum size, it wants as much screen space as it can get, so it reports `MAXSIZE` × `MAXSIZE`. This allows the paint region to grow and shrink as the window is resized.

Just because a widget has expressed a minimum or maximum size does not mean that its container will not violate those requests. A widget must be prepared to deal with whatever bounds it is given. For example, if a button is too small, it might truncate its text or use a smaller font. If the button bounds are larger than the button's maximum size, it might draw its bevel around the entire bounds and center its text.

Simple Container Layouts

So far, this chapter has discussed the size requirements of widgets that have no children. You can actually build designs by collecting widgets together in containers. The simplest containers are the vertical and horizontal stack. In InterViews and Java, these are referred to as Box widgets. The menu in Figure 5.14 is an example of a vertical stack and the toolbar in Figure 5.15 is an example of a horizontal stack. Figure 5.16 shows a schematic of a horizontal stack. This can be used to illustrate the layout of a stack.

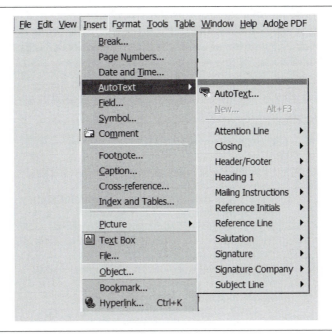

Figure 5.14 – Menu layout

Figure 5.15 – Toolbar layout

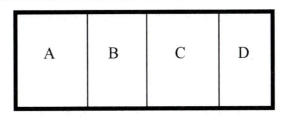

Figure 5.16 – Horizontal stack

The size methods for this stack can be implemented as follows. The width is the sum of the children's widths and the height is the maximum of their heights. By exchanging width and height, you can implement a vertical stack. The algorithms for the intrinsic sizes of a horizontal stack are shown in Figure 5.17.

```
public class HorizontalStack
{
        public Dimension getMinSize()
        {       int minWidth=0;
                int minHeight=0;
                foreach child widget C
                {       Dimension childSize = C.getMinSize();
                        minWidth += childSize.width;
                        if (minHeight<childSize.height)
                        {               minHeight=childSize.height; }
                }
                return new Dimension(minWidth,minHeight);
        }
        public Dimension getDesiredSize()
        {       similar to getMinSize using C.getDesiredSize() }
        public Dimension getMaxSize()
        {       similar to getMinSize using C.getMaxSize() }
}
```

Figure 5.17 – Size reporting for a horizontal stack

The doLayout() method for a horizontal stack has a number of cases depending on the bounds the stack receives. It is common when a new window is opened to request the desired size of the root widget and allocate that as the window size. However, there might not be enough screen space for a window that big. The way in which space is allocated among the children depends on whether the width is less than min, greater than min but less than desired, greater than desired but less than max, or greater than max. The idea of the algorithm is to give each child as much as possible and then divide up the remainder proportionally among the children according to their requests. The layout algorithm for a horizontal stack is shown in Figure 5.18.

```
public class HorizontalStack
{
        . . . the other methods and fields . . .
        public void doLayout(Rectangle newBounds)
        {     Dimension min = getMinSize();
              Dimension desired = getDesiredSize();
              Dimension max = getMaxSize();

              If (min.width>=newBounds.width)
              {     // give all children their minimum and let them be clipped
                    int childLeft=newBounds.left;
                    foreach child widget C
                    {     Rectangle childBounds = new Rectangle();
                          childBounds.top=newBounds.top;
                          childBounds.height=newBounds.height;
                          childBounds.left=childLeft;
                          childBounds.width= C.getMinSize().width;
                          childLeft+=childBounds.width;
                          C.doLayout(childBounds);
                    }
              }
              else if (desired.width>=newBounds.width)
              {     // give min to all and proportional on what is available for desired
                    int desiredMargin = desired.width-min.width;
                    float fraction= (float)(newBounds.width-min.width)/desiredMargin;
                    int childLeft=newBounds.left;
                    foreach child widget C
                    {     Rectangle childBounds=new Rectangle();
                          childBounds.top=newBounds.top;
                          childBounds.height=newBounds.height;
                          childBounds.left=childLeft;
                          int minWidth=C.getMinSize().width;
                          int desWidth=C.getDesiredSize().width;
                          childBounds.width=minWidth+(desWidth-minWidth)*fraction;
                          childLeft+=childBounds.width;
                          C.doLayout(childBounds);
                    }
              }
              else
              {     // allocate what remains based on maximum widths
                    int maxMargin = max.width-desired.width;
                    float fraction= (float)(newBounds.width-desired.width)/maxMargin;
                    int childLeft=newBounds.left;
                    foreach child widget C
                    {          . . . Similar code to previous case . . .
                    }
              }
        }
}
```

Figure 5.18 – Layout algorithm for horizontal stack

Using combinations of vertical and horizontal stacks, you can produce a variety of layouts. For example, Figure 5.19 is composed of a horizontal stack that contains a vertical stack of the Palette and Options containers and the vertical stack of OK, Cancel, and Preview widgets. The Options container is a vertical stack. The Dither is actually a horizontal stack of the label "Dither" and a combo box that selects the dither mode.

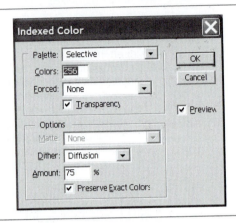

Figure 5.19 – Layout composed of stacks of stacks

One of the problems that has been glossed over in the layout algorithm is the efficiency of computing the desired sizes. The problem is in the recursive use of the algorithm. In Figure 5.19, the window calls the root widget to ask for its desired size. The root widget recursively calls all of its children to compute that size. When the root widget starts to do its layout, it calls the Palette group's desired sizes again. When the Palette group starts its own layout, it calls the Colors group's desired sizes yet again, and, finally, when the Colors group does its layout, it calls desired sizes on the text box. If you count carefully, you'll find that the desired size method on the Colors text box is called at least four times. This is true of almost every widget in Figure 5.19. With a more complex structure, as shown in Figure 5.1, the widgets are called many more times. A second problem is that the size of a window might be changed many times but the desired sizes of the various widgets do not change often. To resolve this, most widget systems cache their desired sizes rather than recompute them. The problem then arises when a widget really does change size. For most such toolkits, an invalidate() method is provided that informs the parent widget that the desired sizes are no longer correct. To accommodate this, the horizontal stack widget's code would change, as shown in Figure 5.20. Note that the invalidate() method not only sets its own sizes to be invalid, but also sends the invalidate() message to its container. The size change might propagate all the way up. Currently, however, Java/Swing does not automatically propagate invalidate() up the tree, which causes interfaces not to change when they might be expected to. This can be remedied by overriding invalidate() in a subclass and calling invalidate() on both the superclass and the parent container.

```
public class HorizontalStack
{
        private Dimension minSize;
        private Dimension desiredSize;
        private Dimension maxSize;
        private boolean sizesAreValid;
        public Dimension getMinSize()
        {     if (sizesAreValid)
                    return minSize;
              int minWidth=0;
              int minHeight=0;
              foreach child widget C
              {     Dimension childSize = C.getMinSize();
                    minWidth += childSize.width;
                    if (minHeight<childSize.height)
                    {    minHeight=childSize.height; }
              }
              sizesAreValid=true;
              return new Dimension(minWidth,minHeight);
        }
        public Dimension getDesiredSize()
        {     similar to getMinSize using C.getDesiredSize() }
        public Dimension getMaxSize()
        {     similar to getMinSize using C.getMaxSize() }
        public void invalidate()
        {     sizesAreValid=false;
              if (myContainer!=null)
                    myContainer.invalidate();
        }
}
```

Figure 5.20 – Desired size code with caching

Spatial Arrangement with Intrinsic Size Layouts

Simple stacks are not generally enough to handle all layout issues. You might want items centered. You might want items grouped at the bottom or top of a list or possibly both. You might want to add extra space, as between the Cancel and Preview widgets shown in Figure 5.19. You can do this with "spreaders" and "spacers." In InterViews they are called "glue" and in Java they are the Box.Filler class. These are special widgets that do no drawing at all. They are invisible. However, they do have minimum, desired, and maximum sizes. For example, suppose you want 5 pixels of space between two widgets in a list. You could create a spacer of 5 pixels, which is a widget whose minimum, desired, and maximum sizes are all 5. You could add this to the list between the two widgets you want to separate. It looks to the layout algorithm like it is a widget and gets allocated the 5 pixels, thus creating the space, but otherwise it does nothing.

If you want to push all widgets to the top of a list as on the right side of Figure 5.19, you can end the list with a spreader widget that reports a very small minimum and desired size but reports a very large maximum height. All of the other widgets would get their desired sizes, but the spreader, because of its large maximum height, would take everything else and, thus, push the other widgets up to the top. Putting the spreader first in the list would push everything to the bottom. You can center a widget horizontally by putting spreaders with large but equal maximum widths on both sides of the widget to be centered. They would compete equally for space and, thus, move the widget to the center. Changing the relative magnitudes of their maximum widths could adjust the widget off of center if desired. The use of spreaders and spacers is effective but not very intuitive for new designers.

Layout Managers

In the original InterViews system, container widgets carried their own layout algorithms. Thus, you used a `HorizontalStack` or `VerticalStack` widget as a container to perform the desired layout. The problem with this is that container widgets are frequently the place where the view/controller code is placed. It is inconvenient to change the class of the container whenever it is desired to change the layout. Java handled this by creating the concept of *layout managers*. Layout managers are separate objects that handle a particular style of layout. The desired layout for a container now becomes a property that can be set rather than a change to the class hierarchy. All container widgets inherit the same standard layout code. The approach is shown in Figure 5.21.

Note that setting the layout manager also calls `invalidate()` so that all of the sizes are recalculated and all of the containers of this widget will know that their sizes are also invalid and need recomputation. `LayoutManager` is implemented as an interface so that a variety of objects can serve as layout managers. Note that all of the `LayoutManager` methods have an additional parameter for the container being laid out. This is so that the layout manager will have access to the children of the container to actually do the layout.

```
public interface LayoutManager
{
        public Dimension getMinSize(Widget containerWidget);
        public Dimension getDesiredSize(Widget containerWidget);
        public Dimension getMaxSize(Widget containerWidget);
        public void doLayout(Rectangle newBounds, Widget containerWidget);
}
public class Widget
{
        . . . other methods and fields . . .

        private Dimension minSize;
        private Dimension desiredSize;
        private Dimension maxSize;
        private boolean sizesAreValid;

        private LayoutManager myLayout;
        public LayoutManager getLayoutManager() { return myLayout; }
        public void setLayoutManager(LayoutManager newLayout )
        {       myLayout=newLayout;
                invalidate();
        }

        public Dimension getMinSize()
        {       if (sizesAreValid)
                        return minSize;
                minSize=myLayout.getMinSize(this);
                sizesAreValid=true;
        }
        public Dimension getDesiredSize()
        { . . . similar to getMinSize() . . . }
        public Dimension getMaxSize() { . . . similar to getMinSize() . . . }
        public void doLayout(Rectangle newBounds)
        {       myLayout.doLayout(newBounds,this); }
}
```

Figure 5.21 – Layout algorithm with a LayoutManager

The code for laying out vertical and horizontal stacks can now go in special layout manager classes rather than in containers. In addition, other layouts can be created as well. The FlowLayout arranges as many widgets as possible in a horizontal row and then starts a new row as with the menu shown on the left in Figure 5.1. Some layout managers require an additional location property on the child widgets. The location property is a string or other object that gives information about where the child should be placed in its container's layout. One example is the BorderLayout found in Java/Swing. This layout, shown in Figure 5.22, captures the most popular window organization with palettes and buttons around the outside and a large work area in the center. For this layout to work, each child must have a location property of "north," "south," "east," "west," or "center."

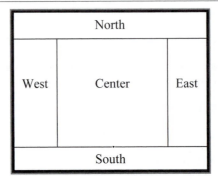

Figure 5.22 – Border layout

Layout Summary

The fixed-position and edge-anchored layouts place widgets by defining a rectangle location for each widget and then possibly tying that rectangle to the edges of its container. These are good for interactive drawing of widget layouts. The variable intrinsic size approach is more dynamic. You define a layout in which the widgets are placed and then let that layout make the choices. This mechanism allows for more extensive changes to be made to the interface content while retaining a reasonable layout for all of the components. However, variable intrinsic size can be frustrating to designers because widgets do not stay in place. They move depending on the needs of other widgets.

CONSTRAINTS

The most common geometric problems in user interfaces are widget layouts. However, there are other kinds of geometry and we need mechanisms that support a consistent model of the geometric relationships between various parts of the model and the view. One such representation system is constraints.

A *constraint system* is a set of equations that relate important variables from the model, view, and controller. A *constraint* is a single equation that relates some of the variables. It is sometimes helpful to separate the *static constraints*, those that must hold all of the time, and the *situation constraints*, those that only hold for the particular problem you are trying to solve. For example, with the scroll bar shown in Figure 5.13, static constraints define how minimum, current, and maximum values relate to the position of the slider. These constraints must always hold. However, when the user is dragging the slider, there are situation constraints on the position of the slider and the minimum and maximum values. There is no constraint on the current value because you want to solve for that value. A different situation is when the max value is changed. You would place situation constraints on the min, max, and current values because you know them. You would not have a constraint on the position of the slider because you would not want that to move. You would also not have a constraint on the mouse position because the mouse is not involved when the max property is set. The following sections look at static and situation constraints in more detail in the examples.

A system of constraints can be *underconstrained*. This is when there are fewer constraints than there are variables. You can generally handle these situations by solving the constraints that you know and then letting the other variables retain the values they had before. A system can be *overconstrained* when there are more equations than variables. It is common to handle this situation by defining constraint priorities. That is, you solve the highest priority constraints first and then ignore any constraints left unresolved.

Sample Constraint Systems

Constraints are best understood in the context of some examples. This section first looks at constraints for performing widget layout and then looks at a scroll bar and a meter dial as representatives of more complicated constraints.

Layout Constraints

The layout constraint problem is usually modeled as a system of constraints with only one situation. That is, the bounds of the layout have been set and you need to compute the placement of the children. Figure 5.23 shows a container widget with three child widgets. Various values have been labeled that will be important to modeling their layout using constraints. In this example, the containing rectangle is called P for parent.

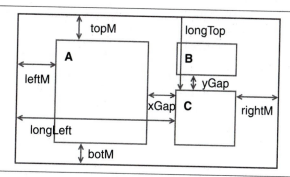

Figure 5.23 – Layout by constraints

The simple, fixed-layout system defines the position of A, B, and C relative to the upper-left corner of P. The system constraints for fixed layout are shown in Figure 5.24.

leftM=10	longLeft=120
topM=7	longTop=40
A.width=100	A.height=150
B.width=60	B.height=25
C.width=60	C.height=120
A.left=P.left+leftM	A.right=A.left+A.width
A.top=P.top+topM	A.bot=A.top+A.height
B.left=P.left+longLeft	B.right=B.left+B.width
B.top=P.top+topM	B.bot=B.top+B.height
C.left=P.left+longLeft	C.right=C.left+C.width
C.top=P.top+longTop	C.bot=C.top+C.height

Figure 5.24 – System constraints for fixed layout

The first two sets of constraints are *design constraints*. These are the values set when the user draws the layout of these three widgets. The situation constraints for this system are constant values for P.left and P.right. Solving this system of constraints is trivial. You simply set the location of P and then evaluate each constraint in the order shown in Figure 5.24. Because there is only one situation, this evaluation order always works. Note that this system of constraints does not use botM, rightM, xGap, or yGap. P.right and P.bot are also ignored. Using fixed layout, you cannot take any of these into consideration.

You can modify this system of constraints to use all of the edges of the bounds. The constraints shown in Figure 5.25 are edge-anchored constraints.

This system of constraints is solved in the same fashion as edge-anchored constraints. You set the value P.left, P.right, P.top, and P.bot and then evaluate in top-to-bottom order. When P changes size, A.bot and C.bot stay a constant distance from the bottom of the parent. In addition, B.right and C.right move as P.right moves.

This is a better layout because it makes use of the size of P, but it is still not what is desired because A is rigid in its width and B is rigid in its height. This also does not have the desired kind of control. What is desired is for B and C to stay a fixed distance from A no matter what the size of A might be. In addition, C should be a fixed distance below B no matter what the size of B. In addition to all of this, the gaps should move proportionally relative to the size of the parent giving each widget its share of the space. One way to do this is with variable intrinsic size layouts. You could put B and C into a vertical stack with a spacer for yGap, then put that stack into a horizontal stack with A and another spacer for xGap. This whole package can be placed in other stacks with other spacers for leftM, topM, rightM, and botM.

This combination of stacks and spacers works, but it seems counterintuitive. Figure 5.26 shows a system of constraints that accomplishes the same thing. The widths and heights of A, B, and C are now used to compute two new variables xProp

leftM=10   longLeft=120
topM=7   longTop=40
rightM=12   **botM=7**

A.width=100   A.height=150
B.width=60   B.height=25
C.width=60   C.height=120

A.left=P.left+leftM   A.right=A.left+A.width
A.top=P.top+topM   A.bot=**P.bot-botM**

B.left=P.left+longLeft   B.right=**P.right-rightM**
B.top=P.top+topM   B.bot=B.top+B.height

C.left=P.left+longLeft   C.right=**P.right-rightM**
C.top=P.top+longTop   C.bot=**P.bot-botM**

Figure 5.25 – System constraints for edge-anchored layout

and yProp, which are the fractional distance of A.right between the horizontal edges and the fractional distance of B.bot between the vertical edges. These, in conjunction with xGap and yGap, define the layout. As P gets wider, A.right moves proportionally to the right and widgets B and C stay a constant distance away. The design is manipulated by changing the constants for the various gaps and margins.

leftM=10   **xGap=10**
topM=7   **yGap=5**
rightM=12   botM=7

A.width=100   A.height=150
B.width=60   B.height=25
C.width=60   C.height=125

xProp=(leftM+A.width)/(leftM+A.width+xGap+B.width+rightM)
yProp=(topM+B.height)/(topM+B.height+yGap+C.height+botM)

A.left=P.left+leftM   A.right=**xProp*P.width**
A.top=P.top+topM   A.bot=P.bot-botM

B.left=A.right+xGap   B.right=P.right-rightM
B.top=P.top+topM   B.bot=**yProp*P.height**

C.left=**A.right+xGap**   C.right=P.right-rightM
C.top=**B.bot+yGap**   C.bot=P.bot-botM

Figure 5.26 – Extended layout constraints

Constraints such as these are very powerful in providing explicit control over layout positions. However, they are problematic as a design tool. The difficulty lies in presenting an interactive layout tool that provides clear control over the constraints. Luca Cardelli proposed a mechanism for drawing layout constraints similar to those shown in Figure 5.26. In his system, each widget was drawn into position inside of a parent widget. Each edge of a widget had a *constraint handle*, represented as a small circle. If the user left the constraint handle undefined, that edge was placed proportionally between the corresponding edges of the parent. The proportion was determined by where the edge had been drawn in the design. The constraint handle could also be connected to any edge of any other widget. This would create a constant distance constraint between those edges. Figure 5.27 shows a Cardelli-style design that is consistent with the constraints shown in Figure 5.26. Since the Cardelli work, there have been systems such as Apogee[6] that allow designers to define invisible guidelines similar to what draftsmen do to create alignments. Apogee also introduced *maximum constraints* that use the maximum values of other constraints. This allows consistent alignments relative to widgets of varying sizes. Other systems introduced squiggly lines to represent spring or spreader style constraints that expand to fill whatever space is available. All of these systems resolve to a set of constraint equations like those discussed previously in this chapter.

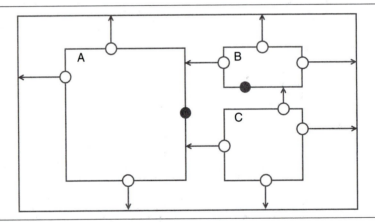

Figure 5.27 – Layout design with Cardelli constraints

Interactive Constraints

In layout constraint systems, the size and location of the parent rectangle are specified as the only situation constraints and all other positions are directly or indirectly derived from those values using other constraints. There are, however, interactive constraints that connect the geometry of a widget's view and controller to the values in the widget's model. Changing parts of the model or dragging parts of the geometry all cause updates to occur. The system constraints preserve the consistency and the situation constraints define what is known for a particular interactive task.

As a first example, consider the scroll bar shown in Figure 5.28. There is an enclosing rectangle for the scroll bar called P and three rectangular regions within the scroll bar called L, S, and R. In addition, three variables are defined: leftBnd, sliderPos, and rightBnd. In the constraints, other variables will be defined to simplify their creation. The goal of a scroll bar is to present and manipulate a model. The model for the scroll bar is shown in Figure 5.29. This particular scroll bar is intended to scroll a window across a larger region. So that the width of the slider reflects the width of the window, the windowWidth value is added to the model to represent how much of the area between min and max is actually being displayed.

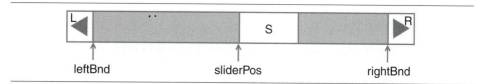

Figure 5.28 – Scroll bar geometry

Scroll bar model
        int min;
        int windowLeft;
        int max;
        int windowWidth;

Figure 5.29 – Scroll bar model

The system constraints for the scroll bar are shown in Figure 5.30. A most common situation for this set of constraints is when the model is known and P is known. From this information, you need to compute the geometry of the view. This would occur whenever there is a model change or whenever essential geometry is required. Formally, you would represent this situation by providing constant constraints for all of the known values. In Figure 5.30, the known constant variables are set in boldface.

By looking carefully at Figure 5.30, you will see that by evaluating these constraints from top to bottom, each constraint has only one unknown variable, given the constant constraints of the situation and previously computed variables. This is, then, a simple constraint solution process, with a challenge on the last constraint. This is not a simple assignment. This constraint specifies the relationship between the slider position and the windowLeft position. In the constant model situation, you would solve for S.left because all other variables will be known when you reach this constraint.

L.left=**P.left**
L.top=**P.top**
L.right=**P.left+P.height**   *// makes L square*
L.bot=**P.bot**

R.right=**P.right**
R.top=**P.top**
R.left=**P.right-P.height**   *// makes R square*
R.bot=**P.bot**

windowLeftRange=**max-min-windowWidth**
     // window moves between min and max but the left does not move all the way to max

leftBnd=L.right+1
rightBnd=R.left-1

S.width = (**windowWidth***(rightBnd-leftBnd)/(**max-min**))
                         // compute slider width proportional to window width
S.top=**P.top**
S.bot=**P.bot**
sliderLeftRange=rightBnd-leftBnd-S.width
(S.left-leftBnd)/(rightBnd-leftBnd-S.width) = (**windowLeft-min**)
     /(**max-min-windowWidth**)

Figure 5.30 – System constraints for scroll bar

When the user drags the slider using the mouse, the final constraint is in a different situation. The s.left is known because of the mouse position. The windowLeft is not known because you need to compute that value from the mouse position. In the slider dragging situation, you solve for windowLeft rather than s.left. The system constraints are the same and retain the relationships across all situations. The difference is in the situation constraints that provide our initial constants.

A geometrically more complicated widget is shown in Figure 5.31. Here, you have a meter whose needle shows a cur value between min and max, with min being displayed to the left and max to the right. The other variables are the points C, where the center is, N, where the needle meets the edge of the meter, M, where the mouse is dragging the meter needle, R, where the max point of the meter arc should be, and L, which is a construction point you will need.

In this widget, many of the variables are points and, in some cases, the constraints are defined as equations on points. Note that a point is really two variables and an equation involving points is actually two equations, one for x and one for y. Figure 5.32 shows a possible set of system constraints for the meter widget. The constraints in Figure 5.32 are designed to mathematically capture the relationships among all of the points and the model. They were not necessarily designed to evaluate the constraints for any particular situation. These constraints are also not all linear.

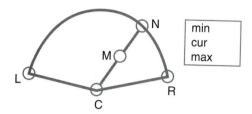

Figure 5.31 – Meter widget geometry

1. radius = sqrt((R.x-C.x)2+(R.y-C.y)2)
   // establish L, N and R at same distance from C
2. radius = sqrt((L.x-C.x)2+(L.y-C.y)2)
3. radius = sqrt((N.x-C.x)2+(N.y-C.y)2)
4. L.y = R.y

5. (M.x-C.x)/(N.x-C.x) = (M.y-C.y)/(N.y-C.y)
   // establish colinarity of C, M and N

6. cos(angleR)=(R.x-C.x)/radius
7. cos(angleL)=(L.x-C.x)/radius
8. cos(angleN)=(N.x-C.x)/radius

9. (cur-min)/(max-min) = (angleN-angleL)/(angleR-angleL)
   // relate model to geometry

Figure 5.32 – System constraints for meter widget

The first situation is where the model, C, and R are known. What you need is the necessary information to draw the meter. To do this, you need to compute point N to draw the needle as well as radius, angleR, and angleL to draw the meter arc. You can start with the situation constraints that give constant values to min, cur, max, C.x, C.y, R.x, and R.y.

- Constraint 1 can give you radius from C and R.
- Constraint 4 can give you the value of L.y.
- Solve constraint 2 for L.x.
- Solve constraint 6 for angleR.
- Solve constraint 7 for angleL.
- Solve constraint 9 for angleN.
- Solve constraint 8 for N.x.
- Solve constraint 3 for N.y.

For this situation, an algorithm known as the propagation of known states[7] is used. This algorithm provides an ordering to the constraints so only one variable must be solved for each constraint. Given the situation constraints, several variables are automatically known. You search the list for a constraint that has exactly one unknown variable, solve the constraint for that variable, add the solved constraint to the list of solutions, and then mark the solved variable as known and continue. This algorithm stops when there are no remaining constraints with exactly one unknown variable. If there are still unknown variables, either the system is underconstrained or simultaneous solutions are required. In this particular system, you avoided solving for the intersection of the needle line equation and the arc, which would have involved simultaneous equation solutions. The constraint system in Figure 5.32 is underconstrained because M cannot be solved. However, M is not needed in this situation and, therefore, we do not care.

A second situation for the meter widget is when min, max, C, R, and M are known. This occurs when you use the mouse to set the needle position and, thus, change the value of cur.

- Solve constraint 1 for radius.
- Solve constraint 4 for L.y.
- Solve constraint 2 for L.x.
- Solve constraint 7 for angleL.
- Solve constraint 6 for angleR.
- Simultaneously solve constraints 3 and 5 for point N.
- Solve constraint 8 for angleN.
- Solve constraint 9 for cur.

This situation demonstrates the need to solve simultaneous equations and some of the challenges of working with constraints. You could have escaped the simultaneous equation problem by adding constraints that tied M to the model rather than to N. The mouse input situation could then have been solved by simple propagation of known states.

This example has also ignored the situation where there are multiple solutions to a constraint. Constraints 1–3 are quadratic and might have zero, one, or two solutions. A simple technique in the case of multiple solutions is to choose the solution closest to the previous value of the variable. This works in many cases because interaction is generally incremental, but not in all cases. Another alternative is to add inequality constraints that restrict possible solutions.

Constraint Solution Techniques

The preceding section showed how constraints can be used to model the relationships between widgets and portions of a view. A set of constraints is not the same as executable code that you can put into widgets. At one level, you can use the constraints as a design tool and then write code from the constraints. This is a useful exercise when there is a tight relationship between geometry and the model because it is very easy to get these issues incorrect and produce a hideous tangle of code. Some researchers have pursued the creation of constraint systems with automatic techniques for solving them.

You can use one of three major techniques for solving systems of constraints. First, the iterative techniques are derived from numerical analysis and optimization theory. These techniques are sometimes used for graph layout problems but are generally too slow for use as an integral part of most user interfaces. However, increasing processor speed might remove that barrier. Second, the symbolic equation solvers use techniques from programs like MatLab[8], Maple[9], and Mathematica[10]. These applications are designed as automatic aids for mathematicians, but most have the nice property of generating C or Java code from their resulting solutions. They can be useful in developing a solution by hand for a particular widget design problem. Finally, the function ordering techniques are much more computationally tractable for user-interface work.

In user-interface work, the goal is usually to convert the constraints of a particular situation into a sequence of program statements that will compute the solution. This problem has two parts. The first is to solve a particular constraint for a particular variable. The second is to plan or order the constraints so that all variables except the one being solved for are known before a constraint is evaluated.

One-Way Constraints

A popular set of constraints are the one-way constraints. In such systems, every constraint has the form `y=f(x1,x2,. . .)`. Such a constraint maps directly to an assignment statement. Figure 5.25 is an example of a one-way constraint system. With such a system of constraints, you only need to order them so that for each constraint all of the arguments `(x1,x2,. . .)` have been computed before the constraint is evaluated. Because one-way constraints are already in the form of an assignment statement, there is no automatic algebra to be performed. One-way constraints are the basis for spreadsheets. The early spreadsheet systems used the fixed-point algorithm to iterate over all constraints until there is no change. This is simple to implement but not very efficient. The propagation of known states algorithm described earlier produces an efficient solution to a set of one-way constraints.

One-way constraints are also found in attribute grammars[11] from compiler theory. Attribute grammars are designed to propagate semantic information through the parse tree of a program fragment.

Incremental One-Way Constraints

There is also an efficient algorithm for incremental evaluation of one-way constraints. In interactive settings, generally one or two variables are changed. It would be better to have an efficient algorithm for evaluating only those constraints that must be evaluated to be consistent with the change. In the simple constraint systems discussed previously, this is not an issue, but in more complex systems involving hundreds to thousands of objects with many interconnecting constraints, this can be a serious issue.

A simple incremental algorithm is recursive evaluation of all affected constraints. Figure 5.33 shows an algorithm to update all necessary constraints when some variable C is changed. When a variable is changed, all constraints that use that variable are changed and they must be updated also. This updating propagates recursively until all changes have been recomputed.

```
{      . . .
     updateVariable(C);
}
public void updateVariable(Variable V)
{
     For each constraint C where V appears as an argument
     {
          C.evaluate();
          updateVariable(C.result);
     }
}
```

Figure 5.33 – Simple incremental constraint evaluation

This recursive incremental evaluation has serious problems. If some variable is used in multiple constraints and those results are then used in multiple constraints, a given constraint might be evaluated many times based on all of the ways in which values could have changed. There might also be partial evaluations because some of the argument changes will propagate later through different paths. In the extreme, this algorithm will evaluate a constraint an exponential number of times.

A more efficient algorithm is based on an incremental attribute flow algorithm[12]. In this algorithm, shown in Figure 5.34, every variable has a value and a Boolean "known" flag to identify that this variable has a known value. Using this flag, a more efficient two-pass algorithm can be designed that computes only the necessary constraints and only computes them once. Figure 5.34 shows a revised algorithm for updating variable C. This algorithm first propagates the "unknown" state through the constraint system to mark all variables to be changed as unknown. The pass that updates the variables only updates a variable if all arguments are known. Thus, the actual evaluation of a constraint is put off until it has all changes, not just the first one.

Hudson[13] observed that in user interfaces, the existence of scrolling, zooming, and other techniques means that only a fraction of the geometry of many widgets is on display at any one time. Rather than recompute all constraints affected by a change, you should only recompute those that are actually visible. This created a "push-pull" algorithm where the model would "push" changes through the system, as in Figure 5.34, while the view would "pull" visible values. This algorithm is shown in Figure 5.35.

```
{     . . .
      markUnknown(C);
      assign new value to C
      updateVariable(C);
}
public void markUnknown(Variable V)
{
      if (!V.known) return
      V.known=false;
      For each constraint C where V appears as an argument
      {     markUnknown(C.result); }
}
public void updateVariable(Variable V)
{
      V.known=true;
      For each constraint C where V appears as an argument
      {     if (for all arguments A of C, A.known is true and C.known is false)
            {
                  C.evaluate();
                  updateVariable(C.result);
            }
      }
}
```

Figure 5.34 – Efficient incremental constraint evaluation

```
{     . . .
      markUnknown(C);
      assign new value to C
      For each visible variable V
      {     computeValue(V); }
}
public void markUnKnown( Variable V)
{     . . . as in figure 5.34 . . }
public void computeValue(Variable V)
{
      if (V.known) return;
      C=the constraint that will compute V;
      For each argument A of C
      {     computeValue(A); }
      C.evaluate();
      V.known=true;
}
```

Figure 5.35 – "Push-pull" incremental constraint evaluation

The "push" part of the algorithm in markUnknown() marks all changes as unknown. However, the "pull" part in computeValue() only recomputes values as they are actually needed. Values that are not needed are not computed and remain marked as unknown. The "push" does not reenter those constraints because they are already unknown and they will never be visited again until there is some need. When scrolling or some other change of the view causes new values to be exposed, the view should call computeValue() on them. If they have been changed, the new values are computed. If they have not, nothing is done. This is a very efficient model for managing update of change.

Multiway Constraints

The biggest disadvantage of one-way constraints is that they are one way while interaction is inherently two way. Sometimes, the model changes and the view must update and sometimes the controller changes the geometry of the view and the model must update. One-way constraints do not capture these multidirectional changes.

Figure 5.36 shows a constraint taken from Figure 5.32 that describes the relationship between the angle of the meter needle and the model variables. Algebraically, you could solve for any of the variables in this constraint. However, you do not want to code up an algebra solver and you really only need two solutions. You need to solve for angleN when the model has changed and you need to move the needle and for cur when the needle has moved and you want to update the model. Figure 5.36 shows the general constraint augmented with two one-way constraints. Each of these is identical to the original constraint. In different situations, different variables are known and either of these two variants can be computed. This example used a human algebra solver to provide something that the propagation of known states algorithm can readily use.

(cur-min)/(max-min) = (angleN-angleL)/(angleR-angleL)

cur=min+(max-min)*(angleN-angleL)/(angler-angleL)
angleN=angleL+(angleR-angleL)*(cur-min)/(max-min)

Figure 5.36 – Using multiple one-way constraints

Simultaneous Constraints

Most of the work involving simultaneous constraints uses iterative solutions. Borning[14] reports a very efficient algorithm using linear programming to solve a variety of interactive problems. Juno[15] constructed many geometric relationships using the standard constraints from compass/straightedge geometry. This work showed a variety of relationships with iterative numerical solving. Olsen and Allan[16] observed that most simultaneous equations involved the intersection of pairs of geometric equations. In Figure 5.31, the simultaneous constraints solve for point N, given the line of the needle and the circle of the meter boundary. All possible intersections of lines and circles were solved by hand and encoded. The propagation of known states algorithm was extended so that when no constraints were available with a single unknown variable, a pair of constraints with a shared point was found and the simultaneous solution was selected from the set of presolved solutions. This created a tool for designing a variety of geometric widgets by drawing their view and their constraints.

Constraint Summary

Constraints are equations that define the relationship between geometric entities in a view, mouse inputs in the controller, and model information. They provide a mathematical basis for many layout mechanisms as well as a representation of a variety of view/model problems. Solving a system of constraints involves finding a set of variable values for which all of the constraint equations are true. Very general numeric solutions are available, but they are generally too slow for interactive use. The propagation of known states algorithm works from known values looking for constraints that have exactly one unknown variable, solving for that variable, and adding the solution to the list of solutions. This produces a presolved set of assignment statements that are readily translated into code.

The simplest constraint systems use functional or one-way constraints. Here, the constraint equations are already solved, however, for only one variable. Solving the constraint system involves ordering the constraint evaluation so that all arguments are known before they are required. The one-way constraints also have an incremental solution that minimizes the number of constraints that must be evaluated in response to a small change in variable values. By specifying more than one solution for a constraint, the propagation of known states algorithm can be extended to the multiway constraints required for interaction.

EXERCISES

1. Why is it so easy to build an interactive tool that can do fixed-position layouts?

2. Why is an edge-anchored layout easier to build into an interactive tool than a variable intrinsic size layout?

3. Originally, variable intrinsic size layouts had only vertical stacks and horizontal stacks as their compositing mechanism. Why would the alignments in the layout in Figure 5.37 be problematic using only these two mechanisms?

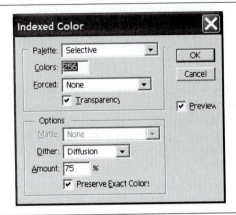

Figure 5.37

4. Why is it important to cache the sizes when computing desired sizes for a variable intrinsic size layout?

5. Suppose you created a new layout for variable intrinsic size that is a resizable grid. The rows and the columns of this grid are sized according to the widgets placed in the various cells of the grid. Give an algorithm for computing the desired width and height of such a grid.

END NOTES

[1] Buxton, W., M.R. Lamb, D. Sherman, and K.C. Smith, "Towards a Comprehensive User Interface Management System," *Computer Graphics* 17(3), (July 1983): pp 35-42.

[2] Goodman, D., *The Complete HyperCard Handbook*, New York: Bantam Books, 1987.

[3] Cardelli, L., "Building User Interfaces by Direct Manipulation," *ACM SIGGRAPH Symposium on User Interface Software*, (October 1988): pp 152–166.

[4] Knuth, D., *The TeXbook*, Reading, MA: Addison-Wesley, 1984.

[5] Linton, M.A., J.M. Vlissides, and P.R. Calder, "Composing User Interfaces with InterViews," *IEEE Computer* 22(2), (February 1989): pp 8–22.

[6] Hudson, S.E., "Graphical Specification of Flexible User Interface Displays," *User Interface Software and Technology (UIST 89)*, (1989): pp 105–114.

[7] Borning, A., and R. Duisberg, "Constraint-based Tools for Building User Interfaces," *ACM Trans. Graph* 5, 4, (October 1986): pp 345–374.

[8] Palm, W., and W.J. Palm, *Introduction to MATLAB 7 for Engineers*, New York: McGraw-Hill, 2003.

[9] Heck, A., *Introduction to Maple*, New York: Springer, 2003.

[10] Wolfram, S., *The Mathematica Book*, Champaign, Illinois: Wolfram Media, 2003.

[11] Aho, A.V., R. Sethi, and J.D. Ullman, *Compilers: Principles, Techniques, and Tools*, New York: Addison-Wesley, 1986.

[12] Reps, T., T. Teitelbaum, and A. Demers, "Incremental Context-Dependent Analysis for Language-Based Editors," *ACM Trans. Program. Lang. Syst.* 5, 3 (July 1983): pp 449–477.

[13] Hudson, S.E., "Incremental Attribute Evaluation: A Flexible Algorithm for Lazy Update," *ACM Trans. Program. Lang. Syst.* 13, 3 (July 1991): pp 315–341.

[14] Badros, G.J., A. Borning, and P.J. Stuckey, "The Cassowary Linear Arithmetic Constraint Solving Algorithm," *ACM Trans. Comput.-Hum. Interact.* 8, 4 (December 2001): pp 267–306.

[15] Nelson, G., "Juno, A Constraint-based Graphics System," *Computer Graphics and Interactive Techniques (SIGGRAPH '85),* (July 1985): pp 235-243.

[16] Olsen, D.R., and K. Allan., "Creating Interactive Techniques by Symbolically Solving Geometric Constraints," *User Interface Software and Technology (UIST '90),* (August 1990): pp 102–107.

CHAPTER 6

Multiple View Models

Chapters 3 and 4 looked at how the controller makes changes to the model, the model notifies the view, and the view notifies the windowing system of damaged regions. The windowing system calls the view to redraw damaged portions of the display image from the current state of the model. You looked at the model-view-controller architecture from the point of view of a single model, single view, and single controller. However, the MVC architecture is more general than that.

Many situations have many different kinds of views associated with a given model. Figure 6.1 shows the split screen feature in Microsoft Word. Any edits in the lower window, where the selection is shown, are also seen in the upper window. Many times, this split screen feature is used to present different parts of a document. In such a case, the changes in one view are not seen in the other. However, the user is allowed to position the split views any way he wants and our software must work correctly regardless of the positioning.

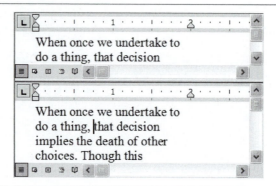

When once we undertake to
do a thing, that decision

When once we undertake to
do a thing, that decision
implies the death of other
choices. Though this

Figure 6.1 – Word with split view

Figure 6.2 shows a Microsoft Excel spreadsheet with a split view. This allows items in a shopping list to be viewed in the upper window while the total is shown in the lower window. Although these two views are presenting different parts of the spreadsheet, changing the price of socks in the upper view changes the total in the lower view. This example also demonstrates the sharing of selection among the views. A cell in the lower view is selected, but the column selection is shared between the upper and lower views. Figure 6.2 also demonstrates small helper views that are tied to the same model. The "B8" seen in the upper left is an independent view of the currently selected cell. It must be updated whenever a different cell or range of cells is selected. The upper right of Figure 6.2 shows the actual contents of the selected cell. This might include formulas or other information. This is a different view of the same cell contents.

B8		f_x	15	
	A	B	C	D
1	Socks	$ 5.00		
2	Shoes	$ 50.00		
3	Shirts	$ 25.00		
8	Potatoes	$ 15.00		
9	**Total**	**$142.00**		
10				

Sheet1 / Shee

Figure 6.2 – Excel split windows

Figure 6.3 shows two views from Adobe Photoshop of a middle-aged woman's cheek. The view on the left is the original image with a region of the cheek selected. The view on the right is showing a filter of that region and how it will look after the filter has been applied.

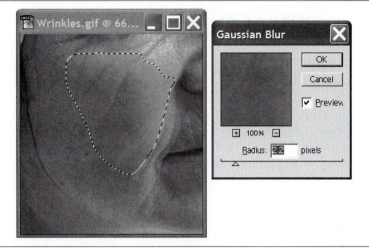

Figure 6.3 – Photoshop filter views (see color plate)

A more extensive use of multiple views is shown in Figure 6.4. This shows an art piece being developed in Adobe Photoshop. The image is higher resolution and size than the display screen and it consists of many different layers used to construct the final image. The artist must be able to manipulate all of these facilities while retaining a sense of the final result.

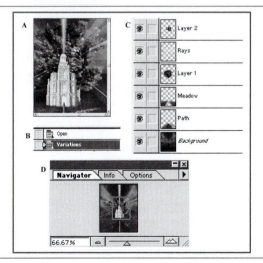

Figure 6.4 – Photoshop image model windows (see color plate)

View A shows the resulting image with all of the current settings. The user can paint directly in this view. View B shows a history of all of the changes to the model. By selecting items in this history, the artist can change the appearance of the picture to reflect only the changes made up to that point. The change history is also a part of the model. View C shows all of the layers from which the picture is composed. Each layer shows a thumbnail of that layer's image. These thumbnails are fully live views of their respective portions of the picture's model. Clicking on the eyeball icon of a layer in view C causes the contents of that layer to disappear from the composite image in view A. Selecting a layer from view C dictates the layer in view A where paint should be placed. Finally, view D shows a navigator view, which displays the entire picture as well as a rectangle showing the current pan and zoom used by view A. Moving the rectangle in D changes the image in A.

REVIEW OF MODEL-VIEW-CONTROLLER

In each of these examples, there are complex relationships among multiple views of the same model. What is needed is a software architecture that makes all of these complexities work together without programmers needing to deal with all of the interrelationships. The model-view-controller architecture provides just that mechanism.

Chapter 3 describes the following steps for implementing model-view-controller:

- Implement the model as a class with public methods for the controller to change the model and for the view to get access to model information.

- Define a listener interface with methods for reporting all model changes to any other object that might need to be aware.

- Implement `addlistener()` and `removelistener()` methods in the model so that listeners can register themselves.

- For each method M in the listener interface, implement a `notifyM()` method in the model that will loop through all listener objects L and call the corresponding $L.M()$ method on each.

- Have the view implement the listener interface and call `damage()` on any screen regions affected by each change method.

- Register the view with the model using the `addlistener()` method.

Most of what is necessary to implement interfaces like those in Figures 6.1 through 6.4 are found in these six steps. These examples point to three different techniques in the use of multiple views: (1) differing views for multiple purposes, (2) multiple views with differing view controls, and (3) views with synchronized selection. Most of the differences in software architecture lie in deciding what information goes into the model and what information is retained in the view/controller.

The differing views such as in Figure 6.4 are handled by several view classes that implement the model's listener interface and are all registered with the model. Each makes its own changes to the model and responds to changes made by it or other views. To make the relationships in Figure 6.4 work correctly, the model must contain more than an image. It must contain an image change history, the current pan/zoom rectangle and the image layers. All of this information is shared among the various views with each view/controller manipulating and presenting various parts of that information.

Figure 6.2 points out a special problem that is easily handled by model-view-controller. When a change is made to cell B2, the spreadsheet model recalculates and causes cell B9 to change value. Cells B2 and B9 are displayed by different views. Attempting to synchronize directly across the two split views creates a tangled web of notifications. However, having the model report changes on any cell that it changes during recomputation creates a relatively simple solution that always works correctly. Both the upper and the lower views receive change notifications for cells B2 and B9. The upper view damages a small rectangle for cell B2 and ignores the change from cell B9. The lower view damages the rectangle associated with cell B9 and ignores the notification from cell B2. However, if the upper view was larger so that cell B9 appeared there also, it would damage both cells B2 and B9 because it receives both notifications.

MULTIPLE VIEWS WITH DIFFERING VIEW CONTROLS

Figure 6.1 shows the split window feature of Word. The splitter pane is a type of widget with a horizontal or vertical line across the middle; the widget controller allows the user to drag this line to adjust the relative size of the split windows. In Figure 6.1, each of the views is an identical class. Each of them is registered as a listener on the same document model, as shown in Figure 6.5. At a given time, at most one of these widgets can have the key focus and receive keyboard input. Each widget keeps a flag indicating whether it has key focus and where the text insertion point should be. This information is independent of the model. When one of the windows is selected, it requests the key focus and the previous window is notified that it has lost key focus. In this example, the focus and selection point are maintained independently in each view; only the content of the document is shared in the model.

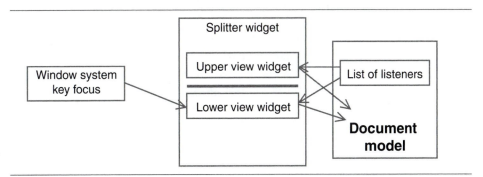

Figure 6.5 – Multiple view listening

Each of the document views in Figure 6.1 also has its own scroll position. This allows them to be positioned independently. By not sharing scroll position in the model, the user can work in two places in the same document at the same time.

In the example shown in Figure 6.1, a splitter widget is used to organize the two views. This is not necessary, in general. If the application would allow the document to be opened in more than one window, the architecture from Figure 6.5 would allow virtually any application to edit and view in multiple places at the same time. However, the MVC model listener architecture must be built in from the beginning. Many applications, including Word, do not allow an arbitrary number of windows to be open on the same model, and, thus, a useful feature is lost.

SYNCHRONIZED SELECTION

There are many situations where similar views should work together. Figure 6.6 again shows the split windows of an Excel spreadsheet. In this application, the selected cell is shared by both views in the model. The horizontal scroll position is also shared by both views. Each view has its own vertical scroll position.

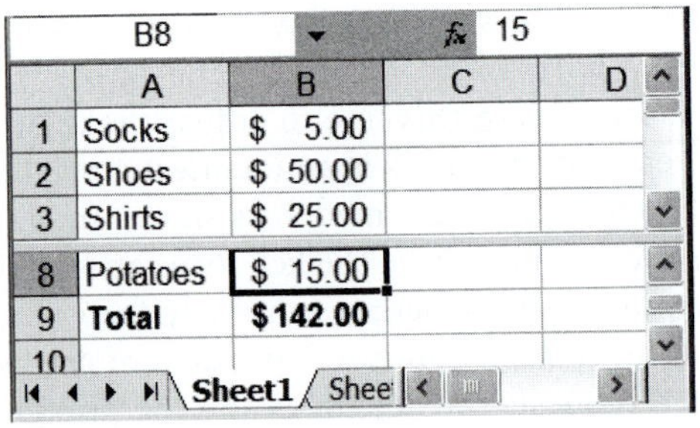

Figure 6.6 – Synchronized spreadsheet views

By placing the selected cell or range of cells into the model, both views share the selection information. Thus, the upper view, which has the column headers, can display the selected column for both views and the lower view can display the selected row as well as the actual selected cell. Sharing the horizontal scroll position in the model allows both views to display aligned columns. For a spreadsheet application, this makes a lot of sense because people tend to organize their information into columns.

A similar situation occurs in Figure 6.7 with the Photoshop drawing and navigator views. Both of these views share the same drawing model and both draw in virtually the same fashion. In addition, the model for the drawing contains the current pan/zoom region of the drawing being viewed. However, each view interprets this information differently. The drawing (left) uses the pan/zoom information of the model to draw only that region of the model at the specified resolution. The navigator view (right) always draws the entire drawing and then shows the zoom information as the red rectangle on the drawing and in the zoom-factor widgets at the bottom. Dragging the rectangle in the navigator scrolls the drawing and scrolling the drawing moves the rectangle in the navigator. This works because the rectangle information is stored in the model that they both share and, thus, both are notified of changes to the viewed region.

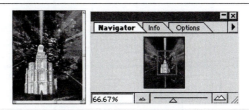

Figure 6.7 – Shared zoom and navigation

Figure 6.8 shows a common list/item pattern for synchronized selection. The e-mail reader has a list of e-mail messages from a mail folder. One of the messages is selected. When one is selected, the message view shows the content to the selected message. Placing the selected message information in the model allows both views to synchronize on what is to be displayed.

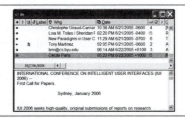

Figure 6.8 – Collection/Item synchronization

Figure 6.9 shows a widget arrangement that is common in 3D applications. A single model object is shown in all three views. Each view shows a different top, front, or side perspective on the object. Simultaneously showing all views aids the users in getting a sense of the 3D shape.

The user is pointing at a location in the front view using the mouse. This specifies x- and y-coordinates, but not a z value. However, the selection point is shared by all three views. The other two views show lines rather than points because that is the projection of the user's selection into each of the other views. Each view renders the selection in its own way, but all views share the same selection information.

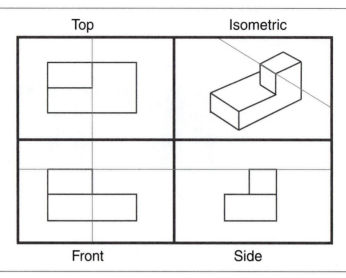

Figure 6.9 – Synchronized 3D position

In the upper right of Figure 6.9 is an isometric view of the same model. You now have a design decision. Do you synchronize the selection information of all four views or do you allow the isometric view to handle selection in its own way? Suppose for some reason that you want the selection of the top and isometric views to be synchronized and the front and side views to be synchronized independently. You cannot do this by putting the selection information into the model because there are four views and two sets of selection information.

What you need is an architecture like that shown in Figure 6.10. In this figure, selection has been separated from the model into selection objects. These selection objects are treated like models in that they have public methods for the controller and they have listeners. Each view is now listening to both a model and a selection model for changes. Note that the selection objects also listen to the object model. Deletion or addition of objects to the model might change the selection and the selection objects must update themselves accordingly.

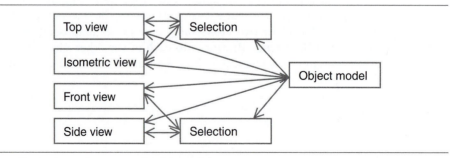

Figure 6.10 – Separate selection models

A pass-through variation on the selection-model architecture is shown in Figure 6.11. In this case, the views only listen to the selections. The selection objects are responsible for propagating model changes through to the views. This simplifies the interconnections and the definition of what is actually shared between views.

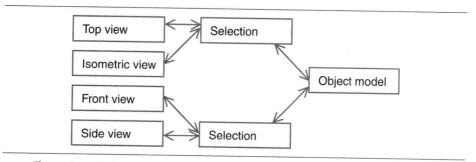

Figure 6.11 – Selection pass-through model access

In the pass-through architecture, the selection listener interface should extend the model listener interface. This allows selection listeners to receive model changes in addition to the selection changes. The selection objects, in general, receive model changes and propagate them directly to their own listeners. Thus, the model changes come straight through. In some cases, the selection might want to modify itself in response to model changes. In those cases, the selection is modified and both the selection change and model change are sent on. The selection object also mirrors and forwards the model change method calls from the controller.

MANAGING MODEL PERSISTENCE

A last issue is the problem of saving the model when changes have been made. You might open a second view on a document to make changes to a different part of the document and then close that view. The original view is still open. It would be very annoying for the model to ask the user to save the contents every time a view is closed. One way to handle this is to add a method to the model to report the number of listeners registered with the model. When a view is closed and this is the last listener, a dialog box can be displayed to ask if the model should be saved. The problem with this is that there are many kinds of listeners. In Figure 6.2, four views are listening to the model. Closing that window closes all of them as a group.

One solution is to have only the container window registered as a listener on the model and have it forward all of the change messages to each of its views. In this case, the approach of watching the listener count works just fine. The architecture for this is shown in Figure 6.12.

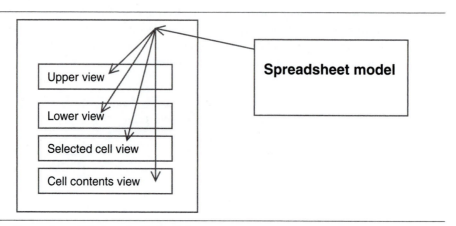

Figure 6.12 – Window dispatch of change messages

A different solution is to add the code in Figure 6.13 to the model. When a window (which might have a group of views) is opened and references the model, it calls openWindow(). When that window closes, it calls closeWindow() but only actually closes if the result is true. This allows the user to select Cancel in response to the request to save the model.

```
public class MyModel
{
    private boolean unsavedChanges=false;

    . . .
        many other fields and methods
        any methods that change the model will set unsavedChanges to true
        any methods that save the model will set unsavedChanges to false
    . . .

    private int windowCount=0;
    public void openWindow()
    {     windowCount ++; }
    public boolean closeWindow()
    {
      if (!unsavedChanges)
          return true;
      int rslt = pop up model save box with options (Save,Discard,Cancel);
      switch(rslt)
      {
      case SAVE:
          save the model
          return true;
      case DISCARD:  return true;
      case CANCEL:   return false;
      }
    }
}
```

Figure 6.13 – Model saving

SUMMARY

Views need to synchronize with each other in a variety of ways. The listener mechanism on a model that is shared by those views is the primary mechanism for such synchronization. It allows each view to be implemented independently and yet stay consistent with each other. A key design decision is whether viewing and selection information is to be shared. For independent view/selection, the information goes in the view class. For shared view/selection, such information goes in the model. For more complex relationships, the selection information can be separated from the model with its own listener/notification mechanism that is either independent of the model or passes the model information through to its own listeners.

EXERCISES

1. What is the key architectural component in the MVC that makes multiple views of the same model actually work and stay synchronized?

2. Modify a previous program so that it can open multiple views and keep them updated.

3. In a multiple view implementation, why might you want to retain selection information in the view/controller rather than place it in the model? What interactive benefit would you gain from this approach?

4. What is the advantage of putting selection information in its own independent model object?

CHAPTER 7

Abstract Model Widgets

The use of a toolkit of prebuilt widgets has greatly improved the development of user interfaces. Widget toolkits provide consistency to the user interface, more reliable implementation, easier design, and more rapid development. However, the widgets discussed so far are limited in the kinds of interfaces that they can construct. This chapter looks at a widget architecture that supports more complex interactions.

Figure 7.1 shows the classic model-view-controller architecture with the view and the controller implemented together in a single view class and the model as a separate class. Chapter 6 showed how this separation allows for many kinds of synchronization and other relationships among views.

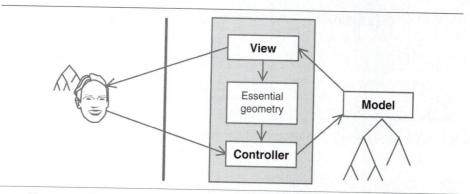

Figure 7.1 – Classic model-view-controller architecture

Figure 7.2 shows the standard widget architecture. For the widgets discussed so far, the model is simple (integer, string, Boolean) and is incorporated into the `Widget` class itself. Other software interacts with the widget by getting and setting properties of the widget and by responding to model change events.

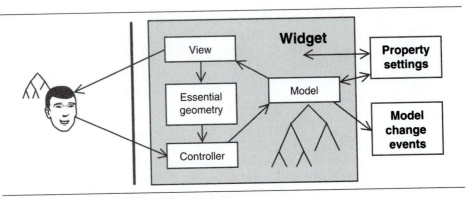

Figure 7.2 – Standard widget architecture

The standard widget architecture works very well for simple models. In addition, you might want to use more complex models. Tables and trees are examples of complex behavior that could be shared across many applications. You would want prebuilt widgets for these cases because they occur so often, but the simple model architecture in Figure 7.2 does not work on such large models. For these situations, you can adopt an architecture like that shown in Figure 7.3.

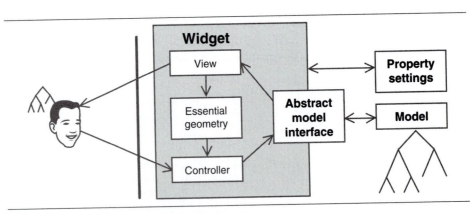

Figure 7.3 – Abstract model architecture

Abstract model widgets have property settings as in the standard widget architecture, yet the model is external to the widget as in the classic model-view-controller architecture. The model is represented to the widget as an interface that defines the methods that a model must have. You can then plug any number of models into this widget as long as they conform to the widget's model interface. A number of large-scale widgets can be defined in this way. To understand this architecture, this section reviews three examples of such widgets and how they relate to their models. They are a tree widget, a table widget, and a generalized drawing widget.

In designing abstract model widgets, look for a common form of interaction and study what is the same about all instances and what is different. Take the things that are the same and build them into the widget. Take the things that are different and put them either in properties or in the model. This same/difference analysis is used in each of the following three examples.

The architectural key to these kinds of widgets is in the interface to the model. In languages like Java or C#, the widget designers create an interface type that specifies all of the methods that the model must provide. A common technique is to also create an *adaptor* class that implements all of the methods and provides default behavior for them. To use these widgets on a given model, the model must implement the methods of the interface or must inherit the adaptor class as its superclass and then override only those methods that are necessary. In older object-oriented languages such as C++ that do not have interfaces, the widget defines a superclass for the abstract model. To use the widget, the programmer creates a subclass of the abstract model class.

In many situations, the model already exists or must be placed somewhere else in the class inheritance tree. In such situations, the programmer creates a *translator* class. The translator class accepts the model in its constructor and then implements all of the widget model methods, passing them on to the appropriate model methods. This forms a translation between the existing model and the needs of the widget's model interface. This architecture is shown in Figure 7.4.

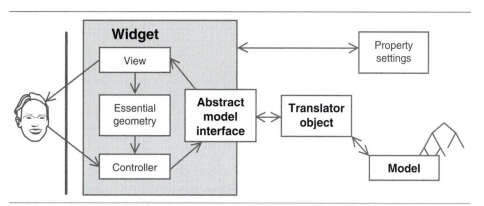

Figure 7.4 – Translator object for the widget/model interface

There are many possible examples of abstract model widgets. These include editors for trees where the tree is too large for inclusion in the widget. Another example is tables of data. In addition, in generalized drawing widgets, objects can be dragged around a surface but the objects being represented can vary widely. For example, the interactive techniques for dragging lines, rectangles, and circles around a drawing surface are virtually identical to the interactive techniques for laying out buttons and scroll bars in an interface design. You could construct an abstract model widget to generalize this interaction. You could create a widget that shows data as a bar graph. Using the abstract model widget architecture, you could generalize the bar graph so that it can present data from any model.

TREE WIDGET

One of the common ways for people to organize information and objects is in trees. This allows you to group things by similarity, topic, location, or a variety of other purposes. Because trees occur so often in applications, you want to do only one implementation of the user interface. Dragging, dropping, opening, and closing of tree nodes can all be programmed only one time and provide a consistent interactive behavior for these tasks. To design a tree widget, this section first looks at several examples of trees in user interfaces.

Figure 7.5 shows trees from four different applications: (A) file folders from the Windows file explorer, (B) bookmarks tree from the Firefox Web browser, (C) Package Explorer from the Eclipse Java development tool, and (D) mail boxes from the Eudora e-mail reader.

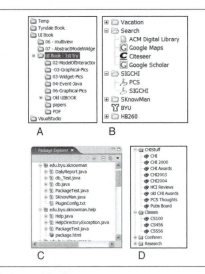

Figure 7.5 – Sample tree widgets

First, look at how they are all the same. When there are many things in common, there is an advantage to building a widget that shares and reuses the commonality. The similarities are as follows:

•   They all represent a tree as an indented outline using the same layout.

•   Every node of the tree has a textual name and one or two icons. Containers have two icons, one for open and one for closed.

- They all use little plus/minus boxes to open/close the container.

- Clicking on the name allows the user to change the name of any of the nodes.

    Now look at how they are different. The differences are as follows:

- Containers have variable numbers of children arranged in varying depths in the tree.

- Every node has a different name.

- There are different icons for different applications and for different items within those applications.

- Three of the four examples use faint gray lines to indicate which nodes are siblings. One example (A) does not.

- Example B uses a different font and size of font.

    The similarities are built in to the widget. The differences are built in to the properties and in to the abstract model. The properties that this widget provides might be as follows:

- Font face, size, and style

- Boolean to display sibling lines

- Number of pixels to indent at each level

    The abstract model comes in two parts. The first is the model itself that this widget will manipulate and the second is the notification mechanism for the widget to learn about model changes. The model itself can be defined around the TreeNode interface shown in Figure 7.6.

```
public interface TreeNode
{
    int numberOfChildren(); // how many children nodes are there. Zero for leaf nodes
    TreeNode getChild(int childIdx);      // get one of this node's children
    Image getIcon();                 // gets the primary icon for this node
    Image getOpenIcon();             // if this is a container this returns the icon for when it is open
    String getName();                // gets the name of this node
    void setName(String name);       // changes the name of this node
}
```

Figure 7.6 – Abstract TreeNode model

    This interface provides all of the information the widget needs to know about the tree. With this interface, the widget can recursively tour the tree. The widget must also know about changes to the tree. Because changes can occur at any point in the tree, you need to notify the widget as to where the change occurred. Because each container provides access to its children by an index, you can locate any node in the tree with a *path* or sequence of indices that leads from the root of the tree to the desired node.

This is represented using Java's generic template notation `List<int>`. The `TreeWidget` class needs to implement the methods shown in Figure 7.7.

```
public class TreeWidget extends Widget
{
    public void nodeChanged(List<int> pathToChangedNode){ . . . }
    public void nodeToInsert(List<int> insertLocation) { . . . }
    public void nodeToDelete(List<int> deleteLocation) { . . . }
}
```

Figure 7.7 – Widget notification of model change

The tree model is not complete because it needs a mechanism to register the widget with the model. It also needs methods that let the widget make changes to the model. The `TreeRoot` class in Figure 7.8 provides the necessary methods for this purpose.

```
public interface TreeRoot
{
    public TreeNode root;
    public void addListenerWidget(TreeWidget widget);
    public void removeListenerWidget(TreeWidget widget);
    public void deleteNode(List<int> deleteLocation);
    public void moveNode(List<int> fromLocation, List<int> toLocation);
    public void changeName(List<int> nodeToChange, String newName);
}
```

Figure 7.8 – `TreeRoot` access

As an example, you can use this widget to provide the file explorer interface from Figure 7.5(A). The file explorer is an example of a model that you are not allowed to modify. Microsoft provides the API to access the file system and is not going to allow the source code to be viewed. For this, you need three translator classes. You can create a `FileRoot` class that implements `TreeRoot`. This class can have a constructor that accepts a pathname for the root folder. You need a `TreeFolder` class and a `TreeFile` class to interface to folders and files, respectively. Both of these must implement the `TreeNode` interface. A `TreeFolder` would find out the number of files and folders that it contains and report them as children. Using the file system API, the `TreeFolder` class creates `TreeFolder` or `TreeFile` classes for the folders and files that it contains. Creating these classes to access the file system is much simpler than implementing the tree widget. The entire file system is obviously too large to copy into the tree widget model. The abstract interface technique provides the advantage of prebuilt widgets on models that are too large for replication within the widget.

Varying the Widget

After you have an abstract model interface for a tree, you can plug many different models into the tree widget. It is also possible to create many kinds of tree widgets that all work from the same model. Each widget would have a different way of viewing the tree but share the same underlying tree. Robertson, Mackinlay, and Card's cone tree representation[1] is three dimensional with the subtrees rotating into position. The model interface is the same as what has been shown here, but the presentation and manipulation of the tree is very different. Cone trees use 3D presentation to give a spatial sense of the whole tree and its contents. Hyperbolic trees from Lamping and Rao[2], where the nodes of a tree are laid out on a hyperbolic plane is also a possible widget for this model. In hyperbolic geometry, the circumference of a circle grows exponentially with its radius. This maps naturally to tree layouts, where the number of nodes to be displayed grows exponentially with tree depth.

In some tree models, properties other than the name are to be presented. A variety of displays have a "size" property of each tree node to be presented. The "size" can be many things. It can be the number of bytes allocated to files and folders, the total sales volume of an organization, or just the number of items in the tree. To accommodate such widgets, you only need to augment the abstract model from Figure 7.6 with a getSize() method. Some tree widgets display data as actual fruit trees and other more abstract three-dimensional shapes. The point is that the abstract tree model forms an interface between many different data models and many different ways to present those models as a tree.

TABLE WIDGET

Figures 7.9 through 7.12 show various uses of a table widget. Each is from a different application, yet all have a similar presentation and interaction techniques. You can implement all of these using the same design approach and architectural structure used for the tree widget.

Name ▲	Size	Type	Date Modified
📁 06 - multiview		File Folder	6/22/2005 6:55 AM
📁 07 - AbstractModelWidgets		File Folder	6/24/2005 7:30 AM
📁 UI Book - 1st try		File Folder	6/9/2005 7:51 AM
📄 01-Introduction.doc	376 KB	Microsoft W...	6/21/2005 7:32 AM
📄 02-Drawing.doc	1,319 KB	Microsoft W...	6/21/2005 7:31 AM
📄 03-Events.doc	423 KB	Microsoft W...	6/21/2005 7:30 AM
📄 04-Widgets.doc	331 KB	Microsoft W...	6/21/2005 7:29 AM
📄 05-Layout.doc	367 KB	Microsoft W...	6/21/2005 7:27 AM
📄 06-MultiView Models.doc	1,161 KB	Microsoft W...	6/22/2005 7:55 AM
📄 07-AbstractModelWidgets.doc	1,477 KB	Microsoft W...	7/6/2005 10:00 AM
📄 A-mathAndAlgorithms.doc	830 KB	Microsoft W...	5/6/2005 8:36 AM
📄 PlanForProgress.xls	23 KB	Microsoft Ex...	7/6/2005 10:00 AM

Figure 7.9 – Microsoft file table

Message	Plug-in	Date
Argument not valid	org.eclipse.ui	2005-06-08 13:50:4...
Unhandled event loop exception	org.eclipse.ui	2005-06-08 13:50:4...
80020009: The SourceSafe datat org.vssplugin		2005-06-07 17:54:2...
80020009: The SourceSafe datat org.eclipse.team.core		2005-06-07 17:54:2...
80020009: The SourceSafe datat org.vssplugin		2005-06-07 17:54:2...

Figure 7.10 – Eclipse error log

●	◇	⬚	⬚ Label	⬚ Who	⬚ Date		⬚	⬚	⌐	⊏ Subject
●				James Sollami	01:28 AM 6/17/2005 +0000	2				Re: About getting your
●		⬚		Patrick Baudisch	06:26 PM 6/17/2005 -0700	13				UIST 2005 procedings
●		⬚		Mindy Varkevisser	11:28 AM 6/20/2005 -0600	3				[Faculty] Tuition/Insura
●				Quinn Snell	01:13 PM 6/20/2005 -0600	20				[Faculty] Fwd: marylou
●				Lisa M. Tolles / Sheridan F	02:20 PM 6/21/2005 -0400	15				Re: UIST 2005 proced
●		⬚		Jeffrey Clement	09:11 AM 6/23/2005 -0600	2				sentence and paragra
●				Patrick Baudisch	02:41 PM 6/28/2005 -0700	5				RE: Supporting intersp

Figure 7.11 – Eudora mail message list

Title	∠ Artist	Album	Rating
Early In The Morning	Peter, Paul & Mary	Peter, Paul an...	★★★☆☆
500 Miles	Peter, Paul & Mary	Peter, Paul an...	★★★★☆
Sorrow	Peter, Paul & Mary	Peter, Paul an...	★★★★☆
This Train	Peter, Paul & Mary	Peter, Paul an...	★★★★☆
Bamboo	Peter, Paul & Mary	Peter, Paul an...	★★★★★
It's Raiing	Peter, Paul & Mary	Peter, Paul an...	★★★★☆

Figure 7.12 – Music list

You can begin by identifying the similarities. Without a large degree of similarity, there is no point in trying to design a general-purpose widget. However, these widgets do have many things in common:

- There is a fixed set of columns each with a title and/or possibly an icon.
- There are an arbitrary number of rows that will probably require scrolling.
- Every cell of the table has a string and/or an icon for its content. If the icon and string occur together, the icon is first.
- Rows can be sorted based on any of the column contents.

- Rows can be selected and that selection used elsewhere. The use of selection is not shown in these figures. Selecting a song in Figure 7.12 plays that song. Selecting a message in Figure 7.11 displays the contents of the message.

- It is possible, though not visible in the figures, to hide or show columns and to resize their width.

You should also identify the differences that you must capture in the abstract model and in the properties:

- Although the number of columns is fixed, there are varying numbers of columns between applications.

- Columns have different names, icons, and widths.

- The contents of rows and cells are all different.

- There are differences in font and background color.

The key to the table widget is the communication between the widget and the model both to retrieve and change model information as well as to be notified of changes to the model. In most situations, the table is used primarily for viewing information rather than editing it. However, selected rows can be deleted and frequently, cell string contents can be edited and changed. More complex manipulations of the table model are generally handled by other widgets and then notifications forwarded to the widget. The model-view-controller architecture automatically handles the cooperation between the table widget and other widgets by means of the shared model.

Table Model

A possible abstract model for a table widget is shown in Figure 7.13. As usual, you need a mechanism to register listeners. The widget needs to know how many rows there are and needs descriptors for the columns. These descriptors provide information about the name, icon, width, and justification of the column. The name and width can be interactively changed, so you need to provide methods to tell the model when that happens. A column also has a columnID that you can use to identify the column to the model when manipulating cells.

```
public interface TableModel
{
    public void addTableListener(TableListener listener);
    public void removeTableListener(TableListener listener);
    public int nRows();  // returns the number of rows
    public TableColumn [] getColumns(); // returns descriptors for all of the columns
    public String getCellString(int rowIndex, int columnID);
    public void setCellString(int rowIndex, int columnID,
    String newCellValue);
    public Image getCellIcon(int rowIndex, int columnID);
    public void selectRow(int rowIndex); // notifies the model when a row is selected
    public void deleteRow(int rowIndex);
}
public enum ColumnJustify{LEFT, CENTER, RIGHT}
public interface TableColumn
{
    public int columnID();
    public ColumnJustify justification();
    public String getColumnName();
    public void setColumnName(String newName);
    public Image getColumnIcon();
    public int getColumnWidth();
    public void setColumnWidth(int widthInPixels);
    public boolean isReadOnly();
}
```

Figure 7.13 – Abstract model for Table widget

If a cell has an icon but no string (as in the Rating column in Figure 7.12), a null is returned by getCellString(). If there is a string with no icon, as in most of the columns, the getCellIcon() method returns null.

Sorting of rows can be handled without the assistance of the model by using the string value for the cells. This provides great functionality without any effort in the model. The model simply provides data.

Notification Interface

Figure 7.7 integrated the notification methods into the TreeWidget class. This simplified the architecture. For TableWidget, you need to define a TableListener interface for notification. The difference in the approaches lies in whether you believe that there will be other classes of objects that will be interested in receiving notifications. The sample TableListener interface is shown in Figure 7.14. This interface provides for notification at various levels of granularity. The listeners and models can then decide for themselves how they want to deal with the changes. A simple model would just call tableChanged() on every change. For small table models, this would be just fine. For very large models, this might cause efficiency problems. In a large model, most rows would not be visible and, therefore, changes to those rows would not affect the presentation.

```
public interface TableListener
{
    public void cellToChange(int rowIndex, int columnID, String newCellValue);
    public void rowChanged(int rowIndex);
    public void rowsToDelete(int firstRowIndex, int nRowsToDelete);
    public void rowsInserted(int firstRowIndex, int nRowsInserted);
    public void columnDescChanged(int columnID);
    public void tableChanged();
}
```

Figure 7.14 – `TableListener` **interface**

Table Properties

The `Table` widget also needs properties. A possible set of properties would be header font, cell font, background color, and alternating line background color. The alternating line background color would handle the effect in Figure 7.12 that highlights rows with slightly different colors. You might also need column properties. Figure 7.13 shows column justification as part of the model. The column justification generally does not change very often. Its behavior is more like a property where it is set at the initialization of the widget and rarely modified. The justification property was placed in the model because the model already had column descriptors.

Information that varies among widget instances can appear in the model or in the properties of the widget. The decision about where they should appear depends on two issues: how frequently the information changes as a natural part of the interaction and whether the information should normally be set in code or by an interface design environment. Information that normally is established at widget initialization should probably be a widget property. Information that is frequently modified by the end user should be in the model. Information to be specified at design time should probably be a widget property that is available to the interface design environment.

In the case of the `Table` widget, the width of a column is changed interactively by the user by dragging column borders. The justification of a column is generally not modified by end users. The justification is generally specified at design time. These facts would lead us to place column justification and possibly column color, border, and font in properties. However, as you will see in Chapter 9 on interface design environments, single value properties are easier to deal with than multiple complex properties such as multiple column descriptors each with several property values. Ultimately, the decision on whether column justification should be part of the model or a property will probably rest upon the capabilities of the target interface design environment. This issue is revisited in Chapter 9.

Varying the Table Widget

Because tables are such a common technique for representing lists of information and because they map naturally to the results from relational databases, there have been many extensions and variations. The key idea, however, is that the abstract model interface remains essentially unchanged.

Most of the variations in the table widget attempt to address very large tables where very little of the information in the table will fit on the screen. The very early Table Lens[3] used a focus + context technique. In this technique, selected rows, columns, or cells are given more prominence than the others. The user is able to select items that they want to see more clearly. These are expanded and the others are reduced. Figure 7.15 shows the modified table layout when cells G4 and H5 are selected for emphasis.

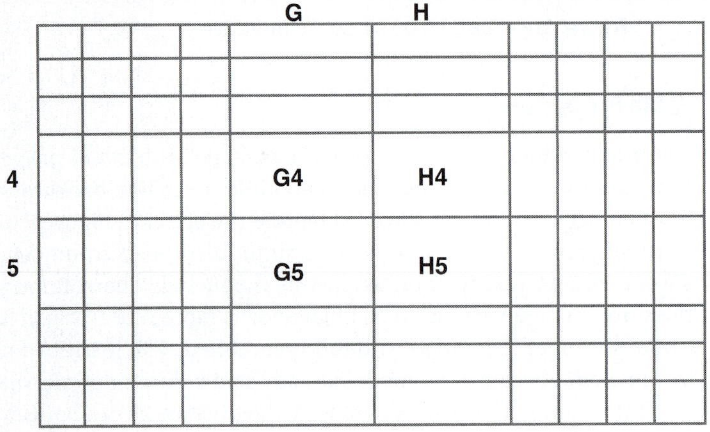

Figure 7.15 – Table Lens focus technique

A major challenge is dealing with cell contents that need to be shrunk down to make room for the focus cells. Rao and Card addressed this by identifying those columns that contained numeric rather than textual information. You can do this by adding a column property that indicates numeric columns. Their brief form of numeric information is a bar indicating the size of the value relative to the maximum value for that column. An alternative presentation is a dot indicating the position of the value in the range of possible values for a column. Shrunken textual cells are simply shown in gray. Again, the table model interface forms the basis of many different table views.

DRAWING WIDGET

Trees and tables have relatively simple abstract models and relatively straightforward interaction techniques. This section now considers a more complex widget inspired by the Workspaces architecture[4]. Figure 7.16 shows two applications; one of them is for drawing and the other is for laying out widgets in a user-interface design. Although these two applications have very different purposes, they have very similar interactive behavior.

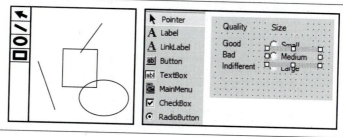

Figure 7.16 – Drawing widgets

First consider how these two applications are similar. The similarities lie in the way that they interact with objects. This particular type of widget has rather complicated interactive behavior. Separating the behavior out into a widget simplifies the creation of complex applications.

- The model is fundamentally a list of objects to be drawn on a surface.
- A menu of objects can be selected and placed in the drawing area.
- Creating new objects uses the same event sequence and interactive behavior. There are three forms: click to place an item, down-drag-up to create two control points, and placement of multiple control points.
- Selection works by clicking on objects, shift-clicking to select multiple objects, and rubberbanding rectangles to select a group of objects.
- Objects can be dragged around the draw area.
- Objects are manipulated by dragging control points and those control points are displayed in a similar way.
- Deleting objects is the same.

The obvious differences are as follows:

- The set of objects to be created is very different as is their appearance in the menu.
- How each object is drawn and how each relates to its control points are different.
- The geometry for selecting objects differs.

Drawing Model

The model for a drawing object is quite simple. However, the model is special because, ultimately, the model is the presentation. One of the ways in which objects in the drawing model differ is in the way that they draw themselves and in the way that they handle their geometry. Selecting a circle is very different from selecting a line or selecting a scroll bar. Because of this fuzzy relationship between the model and the presentation, this section spends more time on how the widget itself is constructed.

The model for a drawing is simply a sequence of drawing objects that can be painted in order and a list of possible classes for drawing objects. Figure 7.17 shows a possible interface for a DrawingModel.

```
public interface DrawingModel
{
    public void addDrawingListener( DrawingListener listener);
    public void removeDrawingListener(DrawingListener listener);

    public int nDrawingObjects();
    public DrawingObject getDrawingObject(int index);

    public void deleteDrawingObject(int index);
    public void addDrawingObject(DrawingObject newObject);

    public int nDrawingClasses();
    public DrawingClass getDrawingClass(int index);
}

public interface DrawingObject
{
    public void redraw(Graphics g);
    public boolean isSelected(Point mousePoint);
    public Rectangle getBounds();

    public int nControlPoints();
    public Point getControlPoint(int index);
    public void setControlPoint(int index, Point newPoint);
    public void addControlPoint(Point newPoint);
    public void move(int dX, int dY);
}

public enum InputSyntax{SINGLEPOINT, DRAGPOINT, MULTIPOINT}
public interface DrawingClass
{
    public Image getIcon();
    public String getName();
    public DrawingObject createNew();
    public InputSyntax getSyntax();
}
```

Figure 7.17 – Drawing model

The DrawingModel itself consists of only three parts: the registration of listeners, the list of drawing objects with means for deleting and adding them, and a list of object classes that can be created. A DrawingObject needs a means for drawing itself to a Graphics object (redraw), support for selection (isSelected and getBounds), and mechanisms for manipulating control points. The DrawingClass contains the necessary information to create the menu and to create new objects.

There are six basic tasks that a widget must perform. These tasks depend on whether the widget is in object creation mode (when one of the object classes is selected in the menu) or in selection mode (when the pointer is selected in the menu). In addition to the model, the most important data item retained by the widget is a list of indices of those objects that are currently selected. Much of the interaction is based on the currently selected object set. For this simple drawing widget, the tasks are as follows:

- Redraw the drawing from the model.
- Create new objects on the drawing surface.
- Select objects.
- Drag objects around.
- Drag control points.
- Delete objects.

This section now addresses each of these tasks in turn and shows how the widget can do them using the abstract model. Redrawing consists of drawing the objects and then drawing the control points of any selected objects. This algorithm is shown in Figure 7.18.

```
public class DrawingWidget
{   private DrawingModel myModel;
    private int[] selectedObjects;
    . . . .
    public void redraw(Graphics g)
    {   for (int i=0;i<myModel.nDrawingObjects();i++)
        {   myModel.getDrawingObject(i).redraw(g);
        }
        for (int i=0;i<selectedObjects.length; i++)
        {
            DrawingObject so=myModel.getDrawingObject(i);
            for (int cp=0;cp<so.nControlPoints();cp++)
            {   Point p=so.getControlPoint(cp);
                draw control point at point p
            }
        }
    }
}
```

Figure 7.18 – Redraw for DrawingWidget

The redraw code is not very complicated because the DrawingObject implementations do most of the work.

Creating New Drawing Objects

Before you can create new objects, you need to build the menu of objects that you are offering to the user. The `DrawingModel`'s `nDrawingClasses()` and `getDrawingClass()` methods give you the information that you need. For each `DrawingClass`, the `getIcon()` and `getName()` methods give you the information that you need to fill the menu.

One of the important things about this abstract model architecture is that it is readily extended. Even if you never reuse the `DrawingWidget` for more than one application, the architecture still has significant advantages because it allows the design to grow over time. For a company to make money over the long term, it must improve its product so that it can sell new versions. This economic drive for a new version leads to new features. If you built your drawing application with all of the objects hard-coded into the widget, adding new kinds of objects would be difficult because the code must be changed in so many places. With this architecture, you simply add another class to the model and implement a new `DrawingObject`. You will see the importance of such extensibility in Chapter 8 on interface design environments.

To create a new object, the user selects an item from the object menu and then uses the mouse in the drawing area to show where the object is to be created. There are three kinds of input syntax depending on the geometry of the object to be placed. These three types of input syntax are captured in the `InputSyntax` enumeration in Figure 7.17. The fact that input syntax (the sequence of mouse events) is frequently the same across many widgets was the primary reason that the view and the controller were separated in the original MVC architecture. Myers describes a number of such general syntax models. The three used here are simplifications of some of his interactors[5]. The details of how to design input syntax is discussed in more detail in Chapter 11.

The syntax for these three creation techniques is spread over the mouse-down, mouse-move, and mouse-up event-handling methods. Each method must choose its behavior based on the currently selected drawing class's input syntax.

Single Click

Some drawing objects, like locations on a map, locating a text string, or special marks only have a single point. Figure 7.19 shows how this would be handled. Positioning the object is all done by setting its zero control point. The drawing object is responsible for getting itself drawn in the right position. This syntax allows the user to place an object and move it into position in a single motion.

```
DrawingObject newObj;
on mouse down
    DrawingClass dc = object class selected in the menu;
    newObj = dc.createNew();
    newObj.setControlPoint(0, current mouse position);
    myModel.addDrawingObject(do);
on mouse move
    newObj.setControlPoint(0, current mouse position);
on mouse up
    newObj.setContolPoint(0, current mouse position);
```

Figure 7.19 – Single-click input syntax

Two Point Drag

Many objects such as lines, rectangles, ellipses, and widgets require two points for their initial geometry. They may have other control points later to allow many ways to resize or manipulate the object, but they all use the mouse-down, drag, mouse-up sequence to specify two points. Figure 7.20 shows how this might be done.

```
DrawingObject newObj;
on mouse down
    DrawingClass dc = object class selected in the menu;
    newObj = dc.createNew();
    newObj.setControlPoint(0, current mouse position);
    newObj.setControlPoint(1, current mouse position);
    myModel.addDrawingObject(do);
on mouse move
    newObj.setControlPoint(1, current mouse position);
on mouse up
    newObj.setControlPoint(1, current mouse position);
```

Figure 7.20 – Two point drag input syntax

Multipoint Input

Multiple input points are required to create polylines with many segments, polygons, and curves. For these, there is a first click to identify point zero and then successive clicks to create new points. The process terminates when a click occurs on the first point (to close the shape) or on the last point (to end a polyline or curve).

Selecting Objects

Using the abstract model, the selection of objects is a simple loop. It is the individual drawing objects that must work out the geometry issues in their isSelected() method. Figure 7.21 shows selection with a single point. Note that the loop operates backward so that the top item under the mouse (the last one drawn) is selected first.

```
public class DrawingWidget
{   public DrawingModel myModel;
    public int selectObject(Point selectPoint)
    {
        for (int i=myModel.nDrawingObjects()-1;i>=0;i--)
        {
            DrawingObject do=myModel.getDrawingObject(i);
            if (do.isSelected(selectPoint) )
                return i;
        }
        return -1; // no selection
    }
    . . . .
}
```

Figure 7.21 – Single-point selection

Similarly, Figure 7.22 shows selection with a rectangle.

```
public class DrawingWidget
{
    . . .
    public IndexList selectObjects(Rectangle select)
    {
        IndexList result= empty list of object indices;
        for (int i=0;i<myModel.nDrawingObjects();i++)
        {
            DrawingObject do=myModel.getDrawingObject(i);
            if (do.getBounds().isInsideOf(select))
                result.add(i);
        }
        return result;
    }
}
```

Figure 7.22 – Rectangle selection

Other Tasks

Dragging objects is simply a matter of looping through the list of selected objects and calling the move( ) method for each one. To drag a control point, the widget loops through the selected objects and through each of their control points to find the object and point for dragging. After this is known, dragging is performed by changing that control point each time the mouse moves. Deleting objects involves looping through the selected objects from highest to lowest index and deleting each one. The order is important so that early deletions do not change the index for later selected objects.

Most of these tasks are embedded in the three event methods for mouse-down, mouse-move, and mouse-up. Sorting out which is active and when each should be performed can become complicated. It must be thought through carefully. Chapter 11 covers design techniques for working out these complexities.

SUMMARY

This chapter worked through a software architecture for widgets where the details of the model are not known. It defines an abstraction of the model using one or more interface definitions. This interface defines what you need to know about the model for the widget to function correctly. Based on the abstract model, you can build a powerful widget. To reuse the widget, the developer must only implement the model or adapter classes that map the abstract model to the actual model. This takes much less time and is more reliable than building the user interface from scratch. Even in cases where a widget will only be used once, the techniques of abstract models can be used to enhance the extensibility of the application.

EXERCISES

1. In designing a new widget using the abstract model architecture, how would you decide whether a piece of information should be a property of the widget or should be something to put in the abstract interface?

2. Why do implementations that use abstract model widgets frequently have translator objects between the widget and the real model?

3. Suppose that you want to build a widget that would draw and edit network diagrams like those in Figure 7.23. The nodes can be virtually anything (computers, airports, employees); the arcs can be such things as network connections, flight paths, or reporting relationships. Given that you want such a widget, what would an abstract model be?

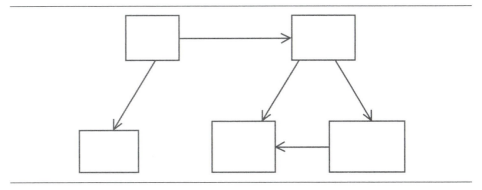

Figure 7.23 – Network diagrams

END NOTES

[1] Robertson, G. G., J. D. Mackinlay, and S. K. Card. "Cone Trees: Animated 3D Visualizations of Hierarchical Information." *Human Factors in Computing Systems (CHI '91).* (March 1991): 189-194.

[2] Lamping, J., and R. Rao. "Laying Out and Visualizing Large Trees Using a Hyperbolic Space." *User Interface Software and Technology (UIST '94)* (November 1994): 13-14.

[3] Rao, R., and S.K. Card. "The Table Lens: Merging Graphical and Symbolic Representations in an Interactive Focus + Context Visualization for Tabular Information." *Human Factors in Computing Systems (CHI '94)* (April 1994): 318–322.

[4] Olsen, D.R., T.G. McNeill, and D.C. Mitchell. "Workspaces: An Architecture for Editing Collections of Objects." *Human Factors in Computing Systems (CHI '92)* (May 1992): 267–272.

[5] Myers, B. A. "A New Model for Handling Input." *ACM Trans. Inf. Syst.* 8, 3 (July 1990): 289–320.

CHAPTER 8

Look and Feel

When the Apple Macintosh was first released, the terms "look" and "feel" entered computing culture. Though Apple did not invent these terms, they made them real for the computing public. The Macintosh enshrined the concept of a common look and feel across all applications as they had done in the Xerox Star. The purpose of a common look and feel across all applications is to simplify usability of an interface [1].

In particular, a consistent look and feel reduces the learning of a new interface. This consistency aids learning in two ways. If an application is internally consistent (has a consistent look and feel across the application), then learning one feature also teaches the user how to access many other features. If different features have different interactive mechanisms, then each must be learned independently. External consistency (features work the same across all or many applications) also aids learning because users can reuse knowledge that they gained on other applications and need not learn yet another approach.

External and internal consistency also aid in remembering how to use an application's interface. Most computer users have two to three applications that they use regularly and many more that they use occasionally. Even within a user's primary applications, some features are used infrequently. A consistent look and feel aids a user in rapidly remembering and reusing these features.

A consistent look and feel is also important to the effectiveness of an interface. This chapter discusses some physiological reasons why consistency increases speed and effectiveness of use. This chapter first addresses what it means to be consistent and what kinds of consistency are important. It then discusses the look of an interface, which is implemented in the view. Finally, this chapter discusses the interactive feel, which is implemented in the controller. This chapter is only a cursory overview of visual design issues. A few pages are not adequate to acquire good visual design expertise. Technical people are encouraged to collaborate with designers when constructing interfaces with a pleasing look.

CONSISTENCY

Before launching into the issues of look and feel, we need to attend to the meaning of consistency. Grudin has argued clearly that trivial notions of consistency can actually damage the usability of an application[2]. He provides a compelling example of where knives should be stored in a home. Consistency would dictate that all knives should be stored together so that whenever you want a knife, you know right where to find it. However, carving knives are frequently stored in a block stand within easy reach and where their edges are protected. The good silver knives are stored in a special box in the same place as the china and crystal. Putty knives are stored in the garage with the other tools. His primary point is that consistency should be consistency of use rather than consistency of thing.

To translate these ideas into user interfaces, consider the process of selecting a file to open. Applications should use the same mechanisms for finding files in all parts of the program. Using one technique in one place and another in a different place would be inconsistent. However, we must consider the use of those files. If a user needs to select images (which are stored in files), you can provide a file open dialog box to select them. However, the standard file open dialog box uses filenames, sizes, and types to select files. Users frequently select images by what they look like. Although you might want to allow images to be selected using the file dialog box, this new use might imply that selection from small thumbnail images would be more appropriate. If you decide to provide a special image selection technique, that technique should be available wherever images are selected and not just in some places.

LOOK

Designing the "look" of an interface primarily involves the view. Designing the look is best done visually before any code is written. Java and C# might be helpful in designing a model, but they are terrible tools for developing a look. Designing a look is not completely independent of the "feel" implemented by the controller. How an object is displayed has a lot to do with how we interact with that object. Displaying line segments in a drawing where they can be selected and their endpoints can be dragged around is very different from displaying line segments in a table showing each of the four coordinate values of the two endpoints. The first view shows you how the resulting drawing will appear and the second gives you exact control of coordinates. Which of the two is appropriate depends very much on the task at hand.

Before discussing principles of visual design, this section first reviews the physiology of the eye and vision system. It then shows how these concepts influence visual consistency of a look. Next, this section discusses the concept of affordances and how they influence the look of an application, followed by visual design concepts and how they can be used to draw the user's attention to what is most important.

Physiology of the Eye

It is helpful when designing a look to understand some basic principles of how the eye functions. Our primary goal with a design is to overcome the gulf of evaluation by bringing as much useful information to the user through their eyes as rapidly as possible. Sight sensing begins with the retina where we find two types of sensors: rods and cones. Rods are sensitive to a broad spectrum of light and, therefore, have no ability to discriminate among colors. Rods are particularly sensitive to dim light and provide high amplification. Cones are of three types, each sensitive to red, green, or blue. Based on the particular type of cone that is stimulated, we sense a different primary color. The absence of appropriate pigment in a particular type of cone will produce color blindness where someone cannot distinguish one of the primary colors. The ratio of rods to cones[3] is about 20 to 1. The numbers of various types of cones are not uniform. The distribution of cones is red (64 percent), green (32 percent), and blue (2 percent). Though there are very few blue cones, they are more sensitive and have higher amplification. Their lack of numbers does, however, reduce the ability to sense fine detail.

The rods and cones are not uniformly distributed across the retina. There is a region in the center of the retina where most of the cones are concentrated. This is called the macula. Within the macula, there is an even more concentrated region called the fovea. This small portion of the retina is where "reading vision" occurs. To understand this effect, focus your eyes on one word in the middle of a paragraph on this page. Without moving your eyes, attempt to read words in the neighborhood of your focus word. We feel that we see the world in high resolution because we can rapidly move our eyes so that the fovea is focused on the area of interest. In reality, we have relatively low resolution perception of most of what we see at a particular instant. This is one of the reasons photography is never as "real" as being there. If we are present in person, we can focus on whatever we desire and see it in high resolution. With many photographs, they are either highly focused on a particular thing providing high resolution but no ability to look around or they are wide with low resolution providing little ability to study what we want.

Another property of the distribution of rods and cones is that the rods are generally scattered around the periphery (outside the macula), whereas the cones are concentrated in the fovea. This means that our peripheral vision is mostly gray scale rather than color. Even though the ratio of rods to cones is 20 to 1, the ratio of the peripheral area to macular area is much higher than that. This produces the low resolution of peripheral vision.

We exploit the differences between the periphery and the macula by rapid eye movement. This allows us to rapidly focus the fovea wherever we want. However, this movement is not continuous. The eye moves in saccades or periods of move and stop, move and stop. Each saccade takes about 200 milliseconds or five times per second. The periphery and the fovea work together in controlling eye movement. Because of the periphery, the eye muscle control system knows where to move to focus on some item detected in the periphery. The periphery also helps in maintaining context and alignment of images as the fovea jumps around.

The structure of the visual process in the brain is also important. A major component of visual understanding is edge detection. One of the first stages in the visual cortex of the brain is to detect the location, orientation, and strength of edges. The dependence upon edges in our understanding of an image is why line drawings or cartoon sketches are just as recognizable to us as the original image. Texture recognition is closely related to edge detection. These are primary visual mechanisms for segmenting an image into meaningful parts. A related process is the periphery's ability to detect motion. To protect ourselves from danger, reflex processes translate detection of unexpected motion into a flinch or jump with very little cognitive effort. This keeps us safe from falling or flying objects but makes it very difficult to ignore objects that are flashing or jumping.

Visual Consistency

One of the most time-consuming parts of using an interface is finding the needed controls or visual objects. Detailed study of labels or icons requires that the fovea be focused on them and the fovea can only be moved five times per second. The word processor used to write this chapter has approximately 100 icons or widgets available on the screen. This does not count pull-down menu items. To scan each of them with your fovea as fast as possible would require at least 20 seconds. To achieve rapid visual use of an interface, you must have faster means for locating items than a foveal scan.

A most important mechanism for rapidly scanning a display is to place items in a consistent location. Using the visual periphery as an alignment mechanism, the eye can rapidly switch to a known location in one to three saccades. Very common items, such as New Document, Open, Save, and Print, are always located in the same position and you can find them without scanning. Using the same icons for the same concepts also improves scan time. The low resolution periphery can rapidly locate regions that are consistent with the desired shape and allow saccades to only jump to those visual locations rather than saccade to each icon trying to understand it. The consistent look of a toolbar, as shown in Figure 8.1, also helps the visual scan. The blended look has a nice appeal and the strong dark line that it forms allows the low resolution periphery of the retina to guide a rapid scan of the toolbar.

Figure 8.2 shows the same interface fragment only blurred and gray scale as the periphery would see it. Note that you can readily find the window title, menu bar, and icons. The consistent look of the drop-down combo boxes for style and font are

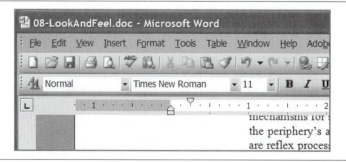

Figure 8.1 – Consistent icons and toolbars

Figure 8.2 – Peripheral view of an interface

easily identified in the blurred peripheral image. The icons for Bold and Italic are also distinctively recognized by someone familiar with the application. However, without a consistent interface look, such recognition in the periphery would be impossible.

Affordances

One of the key ideas popularized by Don Norman[4] is the concept of affordances. An affordance is something that leads you to know how to interact with an object. Nobody needs training on which end of a hammer to hold. The wrong end simply does not lend itself to holding. A good example of an affordance is the door bar shown in Figure 8.3. This bar only presses on one side of the door, which is the side that can be opened. Many commercial door mechanisms have a bar that crosses the entire width of the door with a uniform look all the way across. The user is left to guess which side of the door will actually open. Pressing on the hinge side does nothing. The partial bar has a good affordance (doing the obvious thing makes it work) and the full bar has a poor affordance (guess which side to press).

Figure 8.3 – Affordance of a door opening bar

Many of the early visual designs of user interfaces drew their affordances from physical objects. Buttons have a three-dimensional look that makes them visually protrude from the surface of the interface, whereas labels are given a flat look that makes them appear painted onto the surface. Scroll bars have little traction marks like physical sliders to provide the look of something that can be moved with a finger.

Realistic ties to the physical world might not be effective. User interfaces that looked like rooms with documents lying on tables and pictures of real file cabinets were never widely accepted. These highly realistic affordances did not succeed for three reasons. The first is that the physical behavior did not translate well to screen behavior. For example, there is no "pull" action on a screen that maps well to pulling open a drawer. The user might see a drawer and yet suffer a gulf of execution problem by not knowing what input events will open a drawer on the screen. The second problem is the visual scan. It is frequently much easier for the visual periphery to scan for a simple stylized shape than a more complex realistic shape. Finally, the realistic views tend to take more screen real estate, which is generally scarce.

The most common form of affordance today is consistency with other interfaces. If a widget looks like the other scroll bars or buttons that the user has seen, users are likely to know how to use it. If it looks like other widgets yet behaves very differently, this can be a negative affordance. The goal is to design a look that most users will understand how to use because it looks like other things that they have seen and behaves in a similar fashion. One very useful affordance is when items react visually when the mouse passes over them. This indicates to the user that such items are active and will respond to input.

Much of the work on affordances and the look of user interfaces was done when very few people had ever used a graphical user interface. It is now difficult to imagine a college student who has not used such an interface. The original graphical interfaces drew their affordances from the physical world that their users were familiar with. Today's users are as familiar with the digital world as they are with a physical one. The affordances for new designs can be drawn from different sources.

Visual Design of Attention

Scanning a large screen to locate necessary items can be time consuming and the look should be designed to minimize that time. To do this, we can use concepts from visual design that help draw visual attention to those things that are most important.

The most important visual attention concept is the reading scan order. Being taught to read defines a natural order for perusing a page. Among European languages, the scan pattern is left to right, top to bottom. Thus, the first place that a reader of a European language looks is at the upper-left corner and then across the top. For European language users, that is where the most important information and controls should be placed to be found most quickly. The last place that such users will look is the lower-right corner. However, Hebrew and Arabic speakers read right to left, top to bottom. The scan order is thus, right to left. Among some Asian languages, the scan of a line of text is vertical right to left. Schools spend a lot of time teaching people to read and our visual design should use that training rather than fight against it.

An obvious rule of attention is that larger items attract more attention than smaller items. That is why section headings and titles are generally larger and/or thicker than normal text. It makes it easy to scan through the main points. Figure 8.4 shows a blurred region of text as the retina's periphery would see it. Note that the section heading is readily identified. This means that the eye can find the heading in a single saccade using the peripheral information to target the correct location. Care should be taken in overusing size. If the size of the text becomes larger than the foveal region, it becomes harder to read rather than easier. The user must move away from the text to read it comfortably.

Figure 8.4 – Periphery view of a heading

A third attention principle involves texture. The edge-detecting visual process is drawn to textured areas as more interesting than smooth-toned areas. Surrounding active objects with smooth "white space" sets them off and makes them easier to find. Adding lots of borders and decorations draws attention away from the important information. White space leads the eye toward the interesting information. This principle is generally violated in two ways. The first is to put borders around items rather than using empty space to set them off. The result is a busy look that makes it difficult to find important information. Borders should only be used when really needed and should be lower contrast than the key information. The second mistake is the excessive use of textured backgrounds. This is a particular problem in Web page design. The background texture interferes with the important information. Figure 8.5 shows a text segment with a heavy texture behind it. Not only does the texture draw attention away from the text, it also makes it much harder to read because the texture edges distract from the character edges.

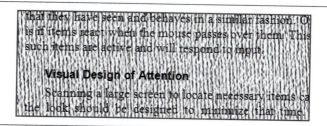

Figure 8.5 – Textured background

The next attention principle is contrast and light. The eye is drawn to high contrasts and to light regions in preference to dark regions. The contrast comes from the edge-detection process of the visual system. High contrast produces strong edges from which shapes are recognized. The preference for light comes from the retina's function as a light detector. The use of contrast also guides the use of color. Color is best used as a highlight of colored versus not colored or high versus low saturation. Color is less effective to encode information, although it can be used as such. A colored area in an otherwise desaturated gray area will draw some attention. However, remember that the periphery is basically gray scale in its sensing. Color saturation should never be used alone to highlight a region. There must also be a difference in brightness. Contrast in the brightness channel accommodates the retina's periphery as well as color-blind users. Figure 8.6 shows a text message printed blue on red and illustrates two visual issues. The first, shown on the right, is that the periphery with little color sensing would have trouble even finding the text because of poor contrast. The second is that the text is in blue, which has the fewest of all sensors in the eye. Because there is no contrast in brightness, the rods cannot help at all and because there is high saturation, the green cones are useless also. Contrast should first be ensured on the brightness axis so that the rods can help. Second, contrast should be ensured on the saturation scale so that all of the cones are involved. Contrast in hue alone has poor visual value.

Figure 8.6 – Poor color contrast (see color plate)

Presentation of State

The look must clearly present the state of the widget. In most cases, the visual look presents enabled/disabled, active/inactive, and an echo of the current state of the widget.

A widget is enabled if it is currently appropriate for that widget to accept input. Figure 8.7 shows both enabled and disabled menu items. You could simply remove all disabled items from the menu, but this causes other problems. If a user is searching for an item and it is missing, they might search the entire user interface, including the menu structure, looking for something they know that they have seen before. This is very frustrating. If, however, they see the item but see that it is disabled, they at least know what is going on. A very frustrating feature of most user interfaces is that disabled items do not show ToolTips that explain why the item is disabled and what can be done about it. This creates a serious gulf of execution problem because the user is confused about what will enable the desired item.

A second problem is visual consistency. Removing an item from the interface generally causes other items to move around in the interface. Users get very good at remembering where they last saw an item. If the removal of another item causes a change of position, this can be very confusing.

For these reasons, we disable widgets that are temporarily inappropriate rather than removing them. The disabled look should generally display with less attention attraction than the enabled look. It is very common to show a disabled state using lower contrast than the enabled look. In Figure 8.7, the disabled items are labeled in gray (lower contrast) rather than in black. This makes it easy to visually skip over them while still being able to identify what they are.

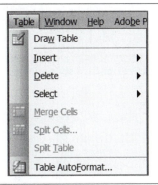

Figure 8.7 – Enabled and disabled menu items

A widget should also indicate whether it is active or inactive. A widget is active generally when it currently has the mouse or the key focus. When the mouse moves over a widget and the widget's look changes from inactive to active, the user is then aware that this is something that can receive input. Figure 8.8 shows a toolbar where the icon under the mouse is shown with a highlighted background and a ToolTip (active state) while the other icons have no such highlight (inactive). Figure 8.9 shows a list of style names with the one under the mouse displayed with a border and an indicator for a pull-down menu. The other items are shown only as names.

The echo of a widget displays the state of the widget in a form that is readily perceived by the user. An appropriate echo depends on the purpose of the widget. Figure 8.10 shows two versions of a vertical scroll bar, one showing the current value and one without. When using a scroll bar to pan around an image, the actual number of the current value is generally not helpful. The relative position in the image is the most important information and, thus, we would use the version on the left. However, if scrolling through a program listing where line numbers are important, the scroll bar echo on the right might be more appropriate. We should carefully design a look that clearly echoes the information that is most necessary for the task at hand.

Figure 8.8 – Active/inactive toolbar icons

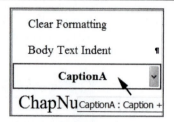

Figure 8.9 – Active/inactive style choices

Figure 8.10 – Two scroll bar echoes

FEEL

The feel of an interface defines how it interactively behaves. In particular, it specifies the design of the controller. A consistent feel is even more important than a consistent look. Figure 8.11 shows three different styles for a scroll bar. The left and middle variants show a similar appearance to most scroll bars, although they are drawn differently from the look of most toolkits. The one on the right has a somewhat different look in that the step arrows are attached to the slider rather than fixed at the ends. However, most users when seeing one of these will recognize it as a scroll bar and will know how to try to use it. Clicking on the arrows steps the bar. Dragging the slider moves to a new position. Clicking in the empty space pages the scroll bar up or down.

Figure 8.11 – Scroll variations

A first-time user would try these techniques because they are consistent with the ways that scroll bars behave on all major computer systems. However, there is nothing about the look of these scroll bars that says that they must work in this way. We could design our controller so that the slider does not drag at all but is moved by clicking the left mouse button for page down and the right mouse button for page up. We could redefine clicking in the empty space as moving the slider directly to that position rather than paging up or down. We could define right-click in the empty space to go directly to the clicked position with left-click performing a page operation. We could also define right-click to open a small text box where we type the value rather than clicking and dragging to get there.

All of these controller behaviors are consistent with the three looks in Figure 8.11, but they all would be extremely confusing to the average computer user. Before the Macintosh became popular with its uniform look and feel, each individual program created its own scroll bar behavior. This created a huge gulf of execution because the feel of an interface is invisible, leaving the user to guess at the appropriate inputs for manipulating a widget. Users can sort out the differences in look in Figure 8.11 with a little thought. Users have no recourse in discovering a new feel. Because of this, it is extremely important that the feel be consistent where possible across applications.

A consistent feel is also important to the *perceived safety* of the interface. One facet of an easily learned interface design is that the user can discover most of the features by exploring the interface rather than by reading the manual or help pages. To foster such exploration, the user must feel safe in the interface. This perception of safety is fostered by predictability of behavior. If the user performs some action, they should have confidence in what might possibly happen. This confidence and predictability not only simplifies learning but also increases speed of use because the user is not burdened with guarding against mistakes. If the feel is not consistent within an application and across applications, the user must slow down and be more careful.

When the Macintosh was introduced, it popularized the pull-down menu. The feel for such menus was to perform mouse-down on the menu header at which point the menu would appear. The user would then drag the mouse (holding down the button) until the desired menu item was highlighted and then release the button to select the item. Macintosh users became very comfortable with this feel. When Windows was first introduced, the menu bar looked similar to the Macintosh but the feel consisted of clicking on the menu header, moving the mouse with the button up, and then clicking on the desired item. When Macintosh users attempted to use Windows systems, there was chaos. Macintosh users would push down the mouse button causing the menu to appear. However, when dragging the mouse down to select an item, the menu would disappear as soon as the mouse left the menu header button. This "peek-a-boo" menu behavior was very disconcerting to Mac users moving to Windows. Microsoft recognized the problem and released a new menu implementation that worked with both the original Windows feel and the dragging feel of the Macintosh. They very much wanted ex-Mac users to feel comfortable on their system. Conversely, Macintosh menus now support the Windows menu feel so that Windows users will be comfortable moving to the Mac.

There are occasions when an application has some new concept that does not generally exist in other applications and a new interactive technique must be designed. In those situations, the feel should be consistent within the application and the developers must shoulder the burden of training users in the new technique.

For graphical user interfaces, a small handful of mouse behaviors make up the majority of interactive inputs. Although there is a very wide variety of mouse behaviors, there is a very small set of common ones. This alphabet of behaviors is as follows:

- *Click*—Mouse-button-down and then up with minimal mouse movement. This is always used to cause an action to occur or to select an object.

- *Double-click*—Two clicks in rapid succession with minimum mouse movement. Most systems allow users to set the time and movement constants to adjust for the dexterity limitations of various users. Applications should use these systemwide control settings rather than circumvent them. Double-click is normally used to "open" the object being referenced to show more information about it. It is also used to indicate selection of a larger region, such as a whole word in a document.

- *Right-click*—A click with the alternate (usually the right) mouse button. This brings up a menu of commands that can be applied to the object being clicked.

- *Drag*—A mouse-down followed by extended mouse movement followed by mouse-up. This has a variety of uses: moving an object, selecting a region or set of objects, or creating an object. Usually the goal is to provide a start point and an end point for some action. The normal technique is to echo what the action would be if the mouse-up occurred at the current mouse move position.

The fact that there are a limited number of very common mouse behaviors led the designers of model-view-controller to separate the controller into its own class so that the code could be reused. However, the simplicity of these behaviors and the complexity of integrating them smoothly with the view has led to the integration of the controller with the view into a single class.

SUMMARY

The look and feel of an interface define its appeal, usability, and learnability. The perceptual structure of the visual system dictates several principles to guide the look. Consistency of both the look and the feel is important for the learnability and usability of most applications. Being consistent with other applications in the same environment can greatly simplify the user experience. Consistent feel is extremely important because the feel is invisible to the user.

EXERCISES

1. When doing the visual design of a new interface, how can you test the ability of users to use their periphery to scan the design and find important items?

2. Physiologically, why do we care if it is easy for the periphery to scan an interface?

3. How does a consistent visual "look" help with the periphery scan for items of interest?

4. When we are looking for affordances that will visually help users know what to do, where might designers look to find them?

5. In terms of visual processes, why are decorations that have no information a problem in a user-interface design?

6. What is not a good color to use for text and why?

7. Why is changing the "feel" of an interface more problematic than changing the "look"?

END NOTES

[1] Polson, P. "The Consequences of Consistent and Inconsistent User Interfaces." *Cognitive Science and its Applications for Human-Computer Interaction*. Hillsdale, NJ: Lawrence Erlbaum, 1988.

[2] Grudin, J. "The Case Against User Interface Consistency." *Commun. ACM* 32, 10 (October 1989): 1164–1173.

[3] Kandel, E.R., J.H. Schwartz, and T.M. Jessell. *Principles of Neural Science*. New York: McGraw Hill, 2000.

[4] Norman, D.A. *The Design of Everyday Things*. New York: Doubleday Business, 2002.

CHAPTER 9

Interface Design Tools

Graphical user interfaces are inherently visual in their appeal and in their use. The way the interface looks has a lot to do with how well users can find what they need and effectively accomplish their goals. A user interface frequently conveys the personality of its user base or the company that created it. A user interface might be conservative, spartan, frilly, soft, aggressive, hip, cool, or efficient. Very few programmers have the skills or the interest to make these differentiations in the interface. The visual organization of the interface has much less to do with model-view-controller and everything to do with the culture and habits of the intended user community. Programmers rarely have the time or inclination to become involved enough in the user community to make such design decisions.

Up to this point, you have built up a set of tools and techniques for programmers to create user interfaces. This chapter addresses the tools that empower designers and artists. These professionals possess significant and important skills, but programming is generally not among them. Interface design tools (IDT) have been developed to support the visual skills of other professionals in the design process. Some use interface design environments to describe such tools, but the term IDE has been co-opted for integrated design environments, which are interactive tools that support the entire program development process. This chapter is only concerned with those parts that design the graphical user interface.

Though the goal is to support artists and designers as part of the user-interface development process, most of this chapter is concerned with the software architecture to create such tools. This architecture is complicated by the fact that the interface design tool is a program that is written and supported by a completely different group of people than those who are creating user interfaces. Usually they are in completely different companies and their software is mutually opaque. The IDT developers cannot know about all of the possible user interfaces to be built and all of the new widgets that will be created for use in those interfaces. On the other hand, the applications developers cannot be expected to look into or modify the interface design tools. Most IDTs are built around a *plug-in* architecture, which is a dynamic variant of the abstract model architecture discussed in Chapter 7.

In addition to the abstract model interfaces, you need reflection or introspection[1]. Reflection is the ability at run time to find out information about the program currently running. SmallTalk and other interpreted languages had good reflection capabilities. Until Java and C# were developed, most compiled programming languages did not have good reflection capabilities and, thus, several mechanisms were developed to allow the programmers to provide the run-time information. However, programming languages with good reflection capabilities allow for a much simpler programming model than those that do not. Microsoft attempted to provide reflection-like capabilities with their COM and ActiveX libraries. These approaches are much more cumbersome than language-based reflection. Most of this chapter assumes the presence of reflection. Where appropriate, the historical alternatives are briefly discussed.

The key reflection features needed are (1) the ability to create an object of some class whose name is not known until run time, (2) the ability to explore the set of methods defined on any object of any class, and (3) the ability to select and invoke a method whose identity is not known until run time. Optionally, it is helpful if programmers can add information to their classes and methods that can be retrieved through the reflection mechanism. This is known as annotation.

The important issues in creating an interface design tool are creating the user interface visual layout, managing the properties associated with widgets, and, finally, establishing the binding between the user-interface design and the code that implements the interface.

LAYOUT DESIGN

The most prominent feature of an IDT is the interactive design of user-interface layouts. The nature of the IDT is strongly influenced by the layout-management mechanism of the underlying widget toolkit (see Chapter 5). The first published IDT was Buxton's MenuLay[2], similar to Figure 9.1. The system had a means for creating sketches of objects drawn with a pen and assembling these sketches into a palette, as shown across the bottom of Figure 9.1. The user could then select sketches from the palette, drag them onto the user interface, and attach callback names to them. Although the sketching tools were crude and the binding of events to callbacks was very simplistic, this tool formed the inspiration for Apple HyperCard[3] and later Microsoft Visual Basic[4]. In many ways, layout design tools have not changed in 20 years. The paradigm is still the selection of objects and placing them in the design.

The overwhelming advantage is that it is far easier to drag an object into a visually pleasing position than it is to change integer numbers in source code, recompile, and then view the result.

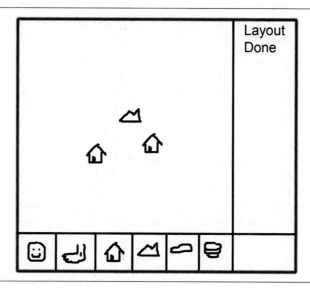

Figure 9.1 – Early screen layout tool

Almost immediately, the simple "place it here" style was replaced by drawing a rectangle into which the object should be placed. This provides the fixed-position layout design from Chapter 5. Fixed-position layouts were great when screens were small and there was generally only one window open on the screen at a time.

The initial problem is to incorporate a layout model with the interactive design metaphor. This section briefly discusses how edge-anchored layouts and variable intrinsic size work with interactive tools. The next problem is to work with live widgets in the design tool. The inputs for design are different from the inputs for interaction and the widget model must deal with this issue. The last problem of a layout tool is finding and presenting a set of widgets that are not known at the time the IDT is implemented. This is key to the extensibility of IDT tools.

Edge-Anchored Layouts

With the advent of many windows with variable size, fixed layout was just not adequate. The MIKE[5] system introduced dynamic coordinates. These are essentially the edge-anchored layout mechanism found in C# and modern Visual Basic. C# uses the layout design tool to specify a rectangle for a widget's placement and then uses the anchor property editor shown in Figure 9.2 to establish the connection to the edges. A similar mechanism was used in NeXTStep and has continued into Mac OS X.

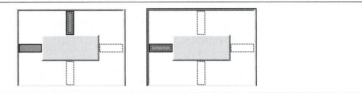

Figure 9.2 – Visual Studio .NET anchor property editor

MIKE took a different approach to the edge-anchored user interface. MIKE divided the screen into nine regions, as shown in Figure 9.3. When the user draws out the rectangle for a widget, its anchor properties are inferred from where the rectangle edges fall. For example, widget A would be of fixed width with both edges anchored to the left edge of the window. Widget A has its top anchored to the top and its bottom anchored to the bottom so that it will grow vertically with the window. Widget B has its edges anchored a fixed distance from the windows edges. It will grow and shrink with the window. Widget C will have a fixed vertical size anchored to the bottom of the window. Its left edge is anchored, but its right edge will stay about 70% of the distance between the window's left and right edges. The key idea is that anchors occur near the edges and can be directly inferred from where the widget is drawn. The combination of the MIKE and C# approaches would be a very effective layout design tool.

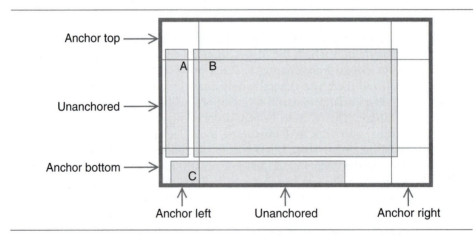

Figure 9.3 – Inferring anchors

Variable Intrinsic Size Layouts

Interactive layout design with intrinsic size is much more difficult. Layout design tools such as Jigloo from CloudGarden[6] or NetBeans from Sun[7] are available. These tools do not have the same ease of use because their model is not geometric. The model for variable intrinsic size is a tree of widgets with layout managers and minimum, preferred, and maximum sizes. These layouts are more naturally designed programmatically.

The tools that do exist for interactive design of intrinsic size layouts face two difficulties. The first is that designers expect widgets to stay approximately where they are put. However, it is the layout manager and preferred size, not the original widget placement that controls layout. This conflict of control can be very frustrating to designers. It is also difficult for those who create the tools because designers specify placements and the tool must do the "nearest appropriate thing." This can lead to combinations of settings that can create bizarre behaviors.

The most successful systems in interactively building layouts with variable intrinsic size have been the Web authoring tools such as Adobe Dreamweaver. The layout of a Web page is generally a flow layout that reflects the layout of text in a document. The `<table>` tag in HTML provides a quite general two-dimensional variation on stack layouts. One of the things that helps in using variable intrinsic size for Web page layout is that the layout goals are different. With an application window, the idea is to effectively use as much of the window space as possible. In this approach, the widgets tend to be greedy and somewhat annoying in their use of space when only a few widgets are on the screen. A Web page is assumed to be potentially infinite in height. The layout goal, then, is to effectively use a finite amount of that space. The widgets tend to not be greedy and, thus, are better behaved during design time.

A second difficulty is in visually interacting with the widget tree. Intrinsic size layouts are very tree oriented. Layouts are produced by combining various primitive layout schemes to produce the desired result. However, the structure of the tree is invisible and ambiguous on the screen. Figure 9.4 shows a fragment of a Microsoft Word window. If this had been created using variable intrinsic size, its tree structure would be that shown in Figure 9.5. The problem lies in the fact that the "Word window", "Menus and toolbars", "Menu bar" and "File" menu headers all have the same geometric position for their top edge. The left edge of "Menus and toolbars" is completely occupied by the left edges of "Menu bar", "Toolbar 1" and "Toolbar 2". There is no unambiguous way to select its left edge. Because of the way that nested widgets are used to create layouts, a container might frequently have all of its space filled by its child widgets, leaving no point that can be used to select the parent widget. There are various ways around this problem, but they all break the smooth feeling of interactively laying out widgets. Many interactive tools resolve this problem by adding new, special-purpose layout managers that mimic fixed-position and edge-anchored layout models.

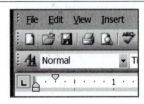

Figure 9.4 – Toolbars and menus

Word window

Menus and toolbars				
Menu bar	File	Edit	View	Insert
Toolbar 1	File group	Print group	. . . .	
Toolbar 2	Front selector		. . . .	

Document widget

Figure 9.5 – Menus and toolbars widget tree

Drawing-Based Interfaces

Most of this chapter is concerned with tools that arrange and utilize rectangular widgets that are arranged in trees. However, a different class of applications is arising around free-form drawings as the basic unit of interaction. Adobe Flash is one of the leaders followed by Java-FX and Microsoft's XAML/Silverlight initiatives. The interface paradigm is a set of drawing primitives or groups of drawing primitives. Event-handling mechanisms are then attached to pieces of drawings to then be invoked when input events such as mouse-down or mouse-over occur relative to those drawings. In such user interfaces, there is no automatic layout mechanism; however, the following discussions about properties and event handling still apply.

Drawing with Live Widgets

The layout of drawn icons and text labels is still an important part of user-interface design, but in modern systems, it is the layout of widgets that is most important. Figure 9.6 shows two widgets being positioned using Visual Studio. These two widgets have had various properties set to change their color and font. The layout design tool must support any widget that has been added to the configuration, including widgets never seen by the implementers of the design tool. This means that live widget implementation must be used by the design tool so that the user will see how the interface will actually appear. There is a problem when trying to design with live widgets. When the user places the mouse on the Delete radio button to drag it to a new location, the live widget will receive the mouse-down event and begin selecting itself to be set. This is not what you want. What you want is to drag the widget.

The solution to this problem is found in the top-down event-handling strategy from Chapter 3. In the top-down strategy, the event is first passed to the interface design tool, which can choose whether to pass the event on to its child widget. In the case of paint or resize events, the design tool passes them on to the child widgets so that they will appear as they should. With mouse events, however, the design tool retains those events for its own user-interface needs. The child widgets being moved around the screen receive instructions to change their bounds but never any mouse events. Attention to the event-handling strategy of the widget system takes care of the problem.

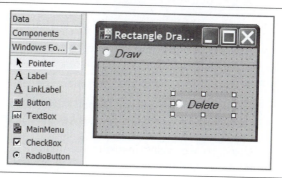

Figure 9.6 – Laying out live widgets

Finding All of the Widgets

Suppose you want your interface design tool to handle new widgets that the tool builders have never seen and use them as easily as the original widget set. Chapter 7 showed how an IDT might be implemented using an abstract drawing widget. This approach, however, requires that the model know about all object classes at compile time. This is not acceptable for an extensible IDT.

Using reflection, you can replace the model's list of classes with a text file that contains a list of class names for subclasses of Widget. The reflection capabilities of Java or C# allow for new instances of these widgets to be dynamically created from their names. Because all widgets have a bounds() and a repaint() method, the IDT has all of the access it needs to position and display any widget. Figure 9.7 shows sample Java code for retrieving a widget given a class name.

```
Widget getNewWidget(String widgetClassName)
{
    try
    {    Class widgetClass=Class.forName(widgetClassName);
         Object obj = widgetClass.newInstance();
         return (Widget)obj;
    } catch (Exception E)
    {    System.out.println(widgetClassName+" is not a Widget class");
         return null;
    }
}
```

Figure 9.7 – Creating a widget from a class name in Java

The C# equivalent shown in Figure 9.8 is slightly more complicated. The Type class instead of the Class class is used. From the Type class, you retrieve a ConstructorInfo object from which an instance of the class can be created.

```
Widget getNewWidget(String widgetClassName)
{
    try
    {    Type
         widgetType=Type.GetType(widgetClassName);
         ConstructorInfo constInfo=widgetType.GetConstructor(Type.EmptyTypes);
         Object constArgs[]=new constArgs[0];
         Object obj = constInfo.Invoke(constArgs);
         return (Widget)obj;
    } catch (Exception E)
    {    return null; }
}
```

Figure 9.8 – C# construction of new widgets

There still remains the problem of the menu of widgets on the left side of Figure 9.6. You can take several approaches to this problem. A simple approach is to give the Widget class two methods getMenuName() and getMenuIcon(). A new widget implementation would provide the needed information through these methods. A second approach is to augment your configuration file so that each widget class name is accompanied by the menu name and the name of a file containing the desired icon.

A third approach for providing this information is to use a reflection technique called annotation. In C#, these are referred to as attributes. Annotations or attributes are pieces of data that can be attached to declarations in the source code and bound at compile time to the reflection information. Using attributes, you can attach the menu name and menu icon information to the Widget class. Figure 9.9 shows how this is done in C#. A special class `WidgetInfo` is defined as a subclass of `Attribute`. It is given members and a constructor to store the information. When the class `MySpecialWidget` is defined, it is preceded by the attribute declaration that provides the menu name and menu icon information. In the `widgetMenuName()` method, this information is retrieved from the `Type` information of a widget so that it can be used to display the menu.

```
public class WidgetInfo : Attribute
{
    public String menuName;
    public String menuIconFileName;
    public WidgetInfo(string mName, String mIconFile)
    {   menuName=mName;
        menuIconFileName=mIconFile;
    }
}

[ WidgetInfo("My Special Widget", "icons\special.gif") ]
public class MySpecialWidget : Widget
{ .... }

public String widgetMenuName(Widget aWidget)
{
    Attribute [] attributes = Attribute.GetCustomAttributes(aWidget.GetType());
    foreach (Attribute attr in attributes)
    {   if (attr is WidgetInfo)
        { return ((WidgetInfo)attr).menuName; }
    }
    return aWidget.GetType().GetFullName();
}
```

Figure 9.9 – Annotating widgets in C#

Microsoft's Expression Blend tool for designing Silverlight or WPF applications uses a special superclass for all user-defined widgets. The reflection mechanism of C# then allows Expression Blend to find such tools and add them to a menu of possible widgets.

Many IDTs, such as Adobe Flash, do not automatically find user-defined widgets. Flash has the concept of libraries in which designers can place units of interaction that include drawings and associated event code. The designer can then add new items to a library or can import items from existing libraries. The designer then explicitly tells the tool about the set of widget-like units. The reason for these differences is that tools like Flash did not begin as user-interface design tools. Flash and Dreamweaver began as tools for creating media artifacts, such as animations and Web documents. Only later did they acquire interactive features, and their connection to programming language concepts, such as reflection, type checking, and abstraction, has come more slowly.

PROPERTIES

There is much more to designing an interface than positioning widgets in a layout. A simple button has foreground color, background color, text color, font sizes and styles, border styles, border widths, the text to be displayed in the button, any icon on the button, text for a ToolTip to explain the button, whether there should be a different icon displayed when the button is pressed, and a variety of other pieces of information. These are all called properties and they are a key part of the interface design. When designing a widget, you should cast as many of the design decisions into properties rather than in special code. Setting of properties is essentially a process of making choices rather than writing code.

As with layout interaction, the property setting interface must be able to deal with the properties of widgets that were not known when the IDT was created. The ability for the IDT to discover newly implemented properties is important. This is further complicated by the fact that new properties might have new data types. Specifying such property values also complicates the IDT architecture. When a design is complete and all of the properties are set, there must be some means for saving that design in the IDT and then loading it at run time when the application is executed. This is primarily a property-saving problem. Lastly, the properties allow an interface design to be localized to a variety of cultures and languages. This is discussed more extensively in Chapter 10, but its implementation foundation is discussed here.

Figure 9.10 shows the Jigloo[8] interface design tool for Java/Swing. A radio button is selected and some of its properties are shown at the bottom of the window. The foreground property is selected and a color editor has been opened to allow the user to select a color by looking at choices rather than typing RGB values. A variety of kinds of properties are available, including Booleans, fonts, colors, lists of choices, icon filenames, and integer numbers. An IDT must be able to adapt to whatever properties a widget might have and allow the user to edit those properties.

Access to properties was introduced in Chapter 4. Some languages like C# provide field accessors that allow properties to be defined as fields with two hidden get and set methods to control access to that field. Java has no such mechanism, so it uses the following pattern method pairs:

```
type getPropertyName();

void setPropertyName(typeNewValue);
```

Either of these two mechanisms can be handled using reflection. The Java Class class has a method called getMethods() that returns an array of Method objects. Method objects reveal the name, return type, and argument types of the method. It is quite easy to write the code necessary to detect property method pairs. Using the Method objects, you can also write code to invoke the methods to get their property values and to change their property values. Getting property names and their values, you can construct the property list shown in Figure 9.10. The property values can be displayed using the toString() method defined on all Java objects. A similar technique is possible in C# by using a Type object to retrieve all public fields of a Widget. The property list is then built in a similar way.

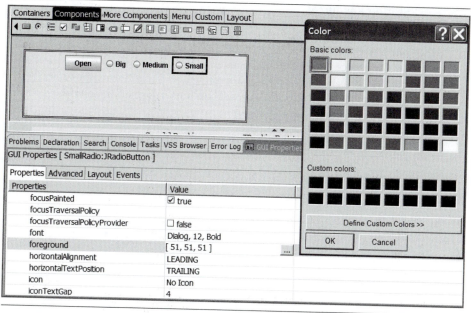

Figure 9.10 – Jigloo properties for a radio button

With this approach to editing properties, four problems arise. The first problem is parsing property values typed in by a user. The second problem occurs when the property names are defined for the consumption of programmers rather than designers. The third problem occurs when a property is intended for software use, but not to be exposed to the designer interface. The final problem is the use of the special editors such as the color editor on the foreground property.

Systems like ActiveX and Java Beans resolve these problems by creating special libraries that associate descriptive information with widget definitions. Java Beans provides methods that use reflection to access properties, but allows the programmer to add other information.

A better solution is to use the annotation facility. For a method or field to be included as a widget property, you can require a WidgetProperty annotation that includes the public name of the property. This resolves both the naming and the interactive access problems. A StringParse annotation can name a method that will translate a string into an appropriate property value. A PropertyEditor annotation can name the class of a widget that can edit a property's value and produce a new value.

This approach should again be contrasted with tools like Flash and Dreamweaver that began as media editing tools rather than user-interface design tools. Dreamweaver, for example, is closely tied to the HTML standard, which has no concept of abstraction or widget development. The HTML standard defines the set of objects that can appear in a document and the set of valid properties that those objects can have. Flash is not subject to an external standards body, but it has similar characteristics. There are a fixed number of graphical object types and they have a fixed number of properties each with a clearly defined type. Unlike the general IDT, these tools have complete knowledge of the properties that they must manage. The property set is fixed at tool creation time.

Storing Resources

The preceding section discussed how tools can be built that know about widgets and can provide a designer with an interactive way to create a new user interface. After a user interface has been designed, the IDT needs a way to save the design and make the design available as part of a deployed application. An interface design tool has a model that it is editing. This model contains information about how the user interface is to be structured. This is different from the model that the user interface is to manipulate. Figure 9.11 shows a user-interface design in progress. The model for the application being designed is shown in Figure 9.12. The model that the IDT is working on is shown in Figure 9.13. The application will be editing information about dogs while the IDT is editing information about widgets.

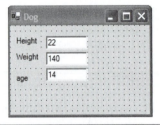

Figure 9.11 – User interface being designed

```
public class Dog
{
        int heightInches;
        int weightPounds;
        int ageMonths;
}
```

Figure 9.12 – Dog model

As with any other interactive application, the IDT must have a means for saving its model. This is complicated by the fact that the interface design must be connected to the application that implements the user interface. This can be done in several ways. One of the earliest mechanisms for resource storage used text files consisting of property names and property values. Generally, there was one line per property. This gets a little complicated when there are many designs that make up an application's user interface. The X Toolkit[9] designed for X Windows[10] created a hierarchical

```
public class Form extends Widget
{
      WidgetDescriptor [] widgets;
      String title;
      Color background;
      Color foreground;
      . . . .
}
public WidgetDescriptor
{
      String widgetClass;
      Rectangle bounds;
      int edgeAnchors;
      WidgetProperty [] properties;
      . . . .
}
public WidgetProperty
{
      String propertyName;
      Object propertyValue;
}
```

Figure 9.13 – IDT model

property naming system to resolve the problem. When a user interface is initialized, the property files are read to provide the settings for the widgets.

A problem with this approach is that the property resource files get separated from the code files. The problem is not a design or development-time separation, which is a good thing. The problem is in what is delivered as an application. If a deployed application is a single file with all of its resources and code bundled together, it is easier to manage, install, and support. If the resources and the code are in separate files, they can get inadvertently detached from each other. This makes application installations more easily damaged and requires more support expertise. Without the resources created by the IDT, the application has no information about how to structure the interface. The earlier Apple Macintosh solution avoided this resource-code separation by creating special modifications to the file system. Every file on a Mac had a data fork and a resource fork. The data fork is the traditional stream of bytes that you expect from a file. The resource fork consisted of zero or more resources. Every resource had a resource type (4 bytes), a resource ID (4 bytes), and a value that could be any number of bytes. The operating system provided a Resource Manager to retrieve resources by ID. Within an application, every resource was given an ID and this was used to retrieve the bytes associated with the resource. The type provided information on how to edit the resource. Code fragments were also resources. An executable file consisted entirely of resources.

When the Mac moved away from its old operating system to the UNIX-based NeXT operating system, it inherited the .nib file structure. NIB (NeXT Interface Builder) files contain all of the resources necessary to build a user interface. The abandonment of the resource fork in favor of .nib files produced the same detachment problem. The Mac resolves this through *bundles*. A bundle is a folder or directory much like in any operating system. Inside a bundle is a hierarchy of files including user-interface resources. The Mac user interface to the file system treats bundles as special and makes them opaque to normal users. Files do exist in the bundle but they only get separated if someone writes special code to separate them.

The Microsoft .NET initiative created the notion of an *assembly*. An assembly gathers together all of the code and resources associated with an application. An assembly extends the programming language concepts of linker entry points to find other information besides code in the assembly.

In a number of modern IDTs, however, the mechanism for storing resources is code. Many IDTs are integrated with an IDE (Integrated Development Environment) such as Visual Studio or Eclipse. Because of this integration, the text editor for editing code and the IDT for editing interface designs are now combined into one tool. Figure 9.14 shows an interface being designed in Visual Studio. Figure 9.15 shows the C# declarations and constructor that are automatically generated when creating this form. A special method InitializeComponent() is added to the constructor automatically. Figure 9.16 shows some of the code automatically generated by the IDT in the InitializeComponent() method.

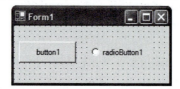

Figure 9.14 – User-interface design

The button and radio button widgets are added as private variables of the Form1 class. This allows them to be readily found and accessed by both the application software and the IDT. Because of the way that the code is generated, it is just as easy for the IDT to find the widgets in this class file as it is in most resource files. The most complex parts of the generated code are found in InitializeComponent().

```
public class Form1 : System.Windows.Forms.Form
{    private System.Windows.Forms.Button button1;
     private System.Windows.Forms.RadioButton radioButton1;
     /// <summary>
     /// Required designer variable.
     /// </summary>
     private System.ComponentModel.Container components = null;

     public Form1()
     {
     //
     // Required for Windows Form Designer support
     //
     InitializeComponent();

     //
     // TODO: Add any constructor code after
         InitializeComponent call
     //
     }
     . . . .
}
```

Figure 9.15 – C# constructor code for a form

```
#region Windows Form Designer generated code
    /// <summary>
    /// Required method for Designer support - do not modify
    /// the contents of this method with the code editor.
    /// </summary>
    private void InitializeComponent()
    {
      this.button1 = new System.Windows.Forms.Button();
      this.radioButton1 = new System.Windows.Forms.RadioButton();
      this.SuspendLayout();
      //
      // button1
      //
      this.button1.Location = new System.Drawing.Point(8, 24);
      this.button1.Name = "button1";
      this.button1.Size = new System.Drawing.Size(88, 32);
      this.button1.TabIndex = 0;
      this.button1.Text = "button1";
      //
      // radioButton1
      //
      this.radioButton1.Location = new System.Drawing.Point(120, 24);
      this.radioButton1.Name = "radioButton1";
      this.radioButton1.Size = new System.Drawing.Size(96, 32);
      this.radioButton1.TabIndex = 1;
      this.radioButton1.Text = "radioButton1";
      //
      // Form1
      //
      this.AutoScaleBaseSize = new System.Drawing.Size(5, 13);
      this.ClientSize = new System.Drawing.Size(240, 86);
      this.Controls.AddRange(new System.Windows.Forms.Control[] {
        this.radioButton1,
        this.button1});
      this.Name = "Form1";
      this.Text = "Form1";
      this.ResumeLayout(false);

    }
#endregion
```

Figure 9.16 – InitializeComponent()

Every property specified in the IDT is encoded in `InitializeComponent()` as an assignment statement. As such, it is very easy to parse out the property values when the design is reloaded. Changing a property involves extracting the code from the file between `#region` and `#endregion`, generating a new version of `InitializeComponent()` and inserting the newly generated code back into place.

Visual Studio .NET is quite clean in the way its IDT connects with the code. Many such approaches are not as clean. The generated code is rather fragile and user modifications to the code can cause major damage from which the IDT might not be able to cleanly recover.

Globalization

One of the important purposes for resources is globalization of the user interface. Globalizing a user interface makes it possible to restructure the interface for a specific culture or language. By separating user-interface information into resources, you can localize the interface to a particular culture by modifying the resources rather than the code. The Eclipse IDE is very helpful in this regard by providing the "Externalize Strings" feature that locates all string literals and assists the programmer in changing those literals to resource references. The Visual Studio approach makes localization a little harder because the resource information is embedded in code. Localization teams can use Visual Studio to modify the resources visually, but these teams are now more intimately involved in the actual code. Globalization is discussed in more detail in Chapter 10.

BINDING EVENTS TO CODE

Manipulating properties is not enough when designing the user interface. Eventually, the interaction must connect with application code. The IDT must support this connection. One of the first attempts was the callback event model. Because every callback was associated with a string name, the IDT could manage events as string properties. The designer would simply enter the name of the desired callback into the associated property.

A second approach used in EZWin[11] and JavaScript is to use an interpreted language for the user-interface implementation. If the underlying language is interpreted, then event handlers are text properties that have expressions in them. Whenever the event occurs, the associated property is evaluated as code.

A common approach in today's IDTs is to generate code. Visual Studio .NET and C# provide good examples. Whenever the radio button in Figure 9.14 is selected, you want some code to be invoked so that other parts of the interface can be notified and updated. Using the reflection capabilities of C#, the IDT has searched for all event declarations in the implementation of `RadioButton`. They are listed in Figure 9.17. Remember that events and delegates are an integral part of the C# language. In addition to finding all of the events, reflection can also find all of the methods in the class whose argument type signature makes them candidates for each type of event. This allows the IDT to generate a list of such methods and place them in a pop-up menu next to the event name. Designers can then simply select acceptable event handlers from a list known to be correct. This was not possible in the old callback model because the set of available callbacks is not known until the application runs and registers them. If there is no appropriate method, the designer can request that a new one be generated, as shown in Figure 9.18. Notice that the IDT generates both the empty method with the correct declaration and the delegate assignment to the CheckedChanged event variable.

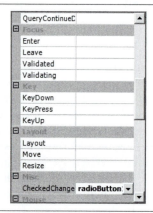

Figure 9.17 – Visual Studio event list for RadioButton

```
private void InitializeComponent()
{
    . . .
    this.radioButton1.Text = "radioButton1";
    this.radioButton1.CheckedChanged +=
        new System.EventHandler(this.radioButton1_CheckedChanged);
    . . .
}

private void radioButton1_CheckedChanged(object sender, System.EventArgs e)
{
    // event code goes here
}
```

Figure 9.18 – C# automatic generating of event handlers

SUMMARY

Many aspects of a user interface design are visual. As such it is difficult to represent those design elements in code. Many times the interface designers are not programmers, but their special expertise is essential. Interface Design Environments provide tools that support visual specification and review of interactive designs in ways that are better suited to the problem and the skills of those involved. The layout model selected for a user interface design is strongly affected by the needs of a visual environment. Edge-anchored layouts are generally easier to manipulate visually than variable-intrinsic sized layouts.

When performing visual layout it is essential that the widgets appear as close as possible to their actual appearance in use. Using top-down event dispatching the redraw and resize events can be used for a widget while capturing the input events for use by the IDE.

Programming languages that support reflection are a great boost to the implementation of IDEs. Reflection simplifies the location of all widget classes in the code so that they can be used to populate a visible palette of tools. Reflection is also useful for identifying properties of widgets so that IDEs can visually edit the properties. The addition of annotation facilities to reflection models makes it easy to integrate visual information such as icons, colors and external names to be used in the IDE's user interface.

The most challenging part of IDE design is the connection between visual information and the code that must implement the controller and model. Reflection is very helpful here. Code generation has also been successful in tools like Eclipse or Visual studio where the IDE is integrated into the tools used to edit and debug code.

EXERCISES

1. Why do edge-anchored layouts form a good compromise between variable intrinsic size layouts when you are trying to build a visual widget positioning tool?

2. How does the top-down event dispatching model described in Chapter 3 help to create a widget layout tool that uses live widget implementations?

3. How is C# different from Java in the way widget properties are handled?

4. When an IDE is showing the properties of a widget, what can it do to handle the editing of property types that the IDE has never seen before?

5. What are some of the IDE architecture choices that keep resources such as colors and widget positions from getting separated from the code?

6. Why is it so hard for an IDE to make the connection between widgets and the code that actually handles the model?

END NOTES

[1] Kiczales, G., J. des Rivières, and D. G. Bobrow. *The Art of Metaobject Protocol*. Cambridge: MIT Press, 1991.

[2] Buxton, W., M. R. Lamb, D. Sherman, and K. C. Smith. "Towards a Comprehensive User Interface Management System." *Computer Graphics and Interactive Techniques (SIGGRAPH '83)*, ACM, (July1983): 35–42.

[3] Goodman, D. The Complete Hypercard 2.2 Handbook. iUniverse, 1998.

[4] Microsoft Visual Basic .Net Standard 2003. Redmond: Microsoft Software, 2003.

[5] Olsen, D. R. "MIKE: the Menu Interaction Kontrol Environment." *ACM Trans*. Graph 5, 4 (October 1986): 318–344.

[6] http://cloudgarden.com/jigloo/

[7] Boudreau, T., J. Glick, S. Greene, J. Woehr, and V. Spurlin. *NetBeans: The Definitive Guide*. Cambridge: O'Reilly Media, Inc., 2002.

[8] http://cloudgarden.com/jigloo/

[9] McCormack, J., and P. Asente. "An Overview of the X Toolkit." *User Interface Software (UIST '88)* (January 1988): 46–55.

[10] Scheifler, R. W., and J. Gettys. "The X Window System." ACM Trans. Graph 5, 2 (April 1986): 79–109.

[11] Lieberman, H. "There's More to Menu Systems Than Meets the Screen." *Computer Graphics and Interactive Techniques (SIGGRAPH '85)*, (July 1985): 181–189.

CHAPTER 10

Internationalization

Most of the people in the world are not North Americans or even European. Though English is the dominant language of trade, most people speak another language. Because human-computer interaction is designed to serve people, the creation of culture- and language-specific user interfaces is very important. This chapter does not cover all of the possible ways that a culture or language can impact software design, but it does cover the major ones. In some discussions of this topic, internationalization is abbreviated as "I18N."

When working on any software that deals with humans, you must consider the language and culture of the people involved. The gulf of evaluation occurs when the user translates information on the screen into an inappropriate mental model. That translation occurs in the context of the user's language and culture. When creating an interactive consumer product, the user-interface designer must consider how the product will be used in Canada, France, China, and any number of other places. In some specialized cases, such as international flight and NATO military operations, the organization has purposely established language/culture standards that are uniform regardless of geographic or ethnic boundaries and, thus, internationalization might not be an issue. For virtually every other interface project, consideration of international issues is essential.

Internationalization itself is a misnomer when developing software. What you want is a *globalized* implementation for our user interface. A globalized interface is one that is prepared to be easily *localized* to a particular language and culture. A major issue in localization is adapting to the language. Not only do different languages have different words but they vary widely in how words are assembled into phrases and concepts. This can pose a challenge.

Language also impacts screen layout. For cultures that read European languages, the most important information should be placed at the top and left of the screen. This is because European languages are read from left to right and top to bottom. Because of the reading order, this is the way European users naturally scan a screen, whether reading or not. In languages such as Arabic or Hebrew, the reading order is from right to left. Chinese is frequently written vertically. Language-imposed reading order trains literate users to scan a page in a particular way. Attention to this scan order can impact the usability of the interface. One of the advantages of variable intrinsic sized layouts is that logically organized rather than spatially organized layouts can be rapidly modified to produce new language-adapted layouts.

Language, however, is not the only issue. There is wide diversity in the expression of common concepts, such as money, dates, times, and numbers. The meaning of color is very culture dependent. The pervasiveness of traffic signals has defined the meaning of green (go), yellow (caution), and red (stop). You cannot necessarily extend these concepts into green being good or red being a warning. For those with cultural antecedents in Rome, purple is the imperial color, whereas in China, it is yellow. Symbols and icons are very different in many cultures.

Globalization of an application involves *externalizing* any information that is culture or language dependent. Externalizing information moves it out of the code and into resources. After the information is moved into resources, culture specialists can localize the interface by modifying those resources rather than modifying the code. The architecture imposed by interface design tools (Chapter 9) greatly facilitates our ability to globalize and localize our user interfaces.

Figure 10.1 shows a list of culturally dependent items that must be externalized. Most of these can be moved into resources and then localized quite easily. The most complex problems involve language, which is the topic for most of this chapter.

Messages and alerts	Labels on user interface components
Help text	Sounds
Colors	Icons and symbols
Dates	Times
Numbers	Currencies
Measurements	Phone numbers
Honorifics and personal titles	Postal addresses
Page layout	

Figure 10.1 – Items requiring localization

Many complexities and subtleties are involved in localizing a user interface to a particular culture. The best that can be done in this chapter is to highlight the issues, leaving the reader to work out the details for a particular application implemented in a particular graphical toolkit. The following issues are discussed:

- Locales and resources

- Character encodings and input

- Numbers, currency, and measurements
- Dates and times
- Formatting compound strings
- Sorting

LOCALES

Many modern programming languages come with standard libraries for supporting internationalization. Most of these revolve around the notion of a *locale*. A locale specification consists of a language and a country. Optionally, a locale can have a variant code if the language and country are not sufficiently specific. In C#, locales are handled by the CultureInfo class and in Java by the Locale class.

Figure 10.2 shows an excerpt of the ISO 639 standard for language abbreviations and Figure 10.3 shows an excerpt of the ISO 3166 standard for country abbreviations. These standard abbreviations are rarely violated, although the API of most locale systems does not require that these abbreviations be used. Note also that the abbreviations are derived from that language's own term for itself, not the English word for that language. The country codes have two-letter, three-letter, and numeric variants. In locales, the alphabetic forms are generally used.

az Azerbaijani	ba Bashkir	be Byelorussian
bg Bulgarian	bh Bihari	bi Bislama
bn Bengali; Bangla	bo Tibetan	br Breton
ca Catalan	co Corsican	cs Czech
cy Welsh	da Danish	de German

Figure 10.2 – Excerpt from ISO 639 standard language codes

Country	A2	A3	Number
AFGHANISTAN	AF	AFG	004
ALBANIA	AL	ALB	008
ALGERIA	DZ	DZA	012
AMERICAN SAMOA	AS	ASM	016
ANDORRA	AD	AND	020
ANGOLA	AO	AGO	024
ANGUILLA	AI	AIA	660

Figure 10.3 – Excerpt from ISO 3166 country codes

A locale is a grouping of resources tuned to a particular language and culture. In systems such as Java or .NET, the locale also provides many of the services for handling money, numbers, dates, and times. These come with a large number of predefined locales for these concepts. Figure 10.4 shows the Java code for obtaining a list of currently installed locales. This is useful if the application can dynamically change locale. The user can be presented with a list of locales and select one.

```
static public void main(String[] args)
{
    Locale list[] = DateFormat.getAvailableLocales();
    for (int i = 0; i < list.length; i++)
    {
        System.out.println(list[i].toString());
    }
}
```

Figure 10.4 – Java code to list available locales

Most systems implement locales by bundling resources and associating them with locale names. Some of the resources are the properties set by the IDT when creating the user interface. In addition, other kinds of resources are available for such things as messages, help text, conversion factors, and string formats. Resources are grouped together in *resource bundles*. A resource bundle is a group of conceptually related resources. For example, several resources are associated with the toolbar shown in Figure 10.5. These resources are the icons, colors (background and highlight), ToolTip text, and ToolTip font. These resources could be collected into a resource bundle called ToolBar.

Figure 10.5 – A sample toolbar

Resources are simply bindings between string names and some object. In many cases, the objects themselves are text strings. For icons, you could have the names of files where the icon images are stored, for colors the RGB values, and font names can also be given as text. If all of the resources are text strings, a simple file like that shown in Figure 10.6 would suffice to represent the resources. Most of the string, font, and color properties specified using the IDT should be tied to resources. Distances between buttons might not be culture specific, but the labels on those buttons will be.

\# this is a comment for the file that provides resources to the ToolBar resource bundle
Background = 200,200,255
HighlightColor = 255, 255, 200
NewFileIcon = NewFileIcon.gif
NewFileDisabledIcon = DisabledNewFile.gif
NewFileTip = "Create New File"
. . . .

Figure 10.6 – Resource bundle file fragment

You could place this text into a file called `ToolBar.properties` (using the Java convention). To localize this user interface into French, you could create a new file called `ToolBar_fr.properties`. In this new file, you would translate all of the ToolTips into French. If some of the ToolTips contained words used primarily in Quebec you could create a `Toolbar_fr_CA.properties` file with those terms unique to French-speaking Canadians. In a Chinese or Arabic resource bundle, you would use a different icon for the toolbar button in Figure 10.5 that contains the text "ABC."

To obtain a bundle of resources, the programmer provides the name of the resource bundle ("Toolbar") and a locale. Most systems also provide for a current locale setting as the default. If the current locale is `fr` (French) and `CA` (Canada), you could retrieve the `ToolBar` bundle and it would look for `ToolBar_fr_CA.properties`. Most such systems provide an inheritance mechanism so that common resources need not be repeated. When asking a bundle for the resource "NewFileIcon," it would first look in the following files in order:

- `ToolBar_fr_CA.properties`
- `ToolBar_fr.properties`
- `ToolBar.properties`

For most locales, the icons will remain the same, but the ToolTips text will change with the various languages. Therefore, the `Toolbar_fr` bundle would only contain definitions for ToolTips text and not for icons. The `Toolbar_fr_CA` bundle would only contain colloquialisms found in Quebec and inherit the rest of the text from standard French.

In some cases, resources are not easily represented as text. Good examples are the conversions between various calendar systems. These must use algorithms to do the conversions. You would like to associate a `Calendar` object with each locale. Java handles this using reflection. A class can be defined for a resource bundle that extends `ListResourceBundle`. This class must provide the `getContents()` method that returns a mapping between resource names and objects. When searching for a resource in the bundle `ToolBar_fr_CA`, Java first looks for a class (using reflection) named `ToolBar_fr_CA` that extends `ListResourceBundle`. If it does not find the class or does not find the named resource in that class, it then looks in `ToolBar_fr_CA.properties`. The full search path for a resource, then, is as follows:

- `ToolBar_fr_CA.class`

- `ToolBar_fr_CA.properties`

- `ToolBar_fr.class`

- `ToolBar_fr.properties`

- `ToolBar.class`

- `ToolBar.properties`

Note that a resource can be anything. If it is text, placing it in a resource file simplifies the localization process. However, the reflection mechanism makes any kind of resource possible. The externalization process is one of factoring all culture-specific concepts out of the code and into resources where localization teams can define new values for particular locales.

UNICODE

In the beginning of computing, everything was based on American English and character encodings were defined by American computer manufacturers. The standard for text for many years has been ASCII (American Standard Code for Information Interchange). By its very name, it is obviously not very international. The reason for its wide usage has been the dominance of the U.S. computing industry and the fact that, historically, programming languages are ASCII-only. This has dictated that ASCII be the language of software. However, ASCII can never successfully be the language of commerce—too many cultures and peoples are involved.

There have been a variety of encodings for international character sets. Most of them have been dominated by the desire to conserve disk and memory space. With the advent of cheap RAM and disk space, the size of text files and strings has become irrelevant. Fundamentally, the question revolves around how many bits can be devoted to a single character. ASCII and its Latin extension (to include European accents, umlauts, and other marks) fit a character into 1 byte, which is very convenient. The Unicode[1] standard broke that barrier by allocating 16 and then 32 bits per character. The Unicode Standard, Version 4.0 contains definitions for 96,447 characters, including all European, Middle Eastern, and many Asian scripts. Virtually all of the commonly used scripts fit in the first 64K code points and, thus, fit in 2 bytes. The Unicode Standard refers to this as the Basic Multilingual Plane (BMP). Conveniently, the ASCII code occupies the first 128 code points and, therefore, the ASCII value and the Unicode value for a character are identical. In Unicode, each writing system is allocated a range of values for their characters.

There are several ways for encoding Unicode in strings and in files. The UTF-8 encoding focuses on the dominance of ASCII and preserving file size. Because ASCII occupies only 128 code points (7 bits), the high-order bit is available. With ASCII characters, the high-order bit is always zero. In UTF-8, a high-order bit of 1 indicates that some other character ranges are being specified. The UTF-8 encoding uses from 1 to 4 bytes to encode any of the Unicode characters. The advantage of UTF-8 is that ASCII files automatically conform without modification. The disadvantage is the variable length of the character codes. HTML generally uses UTF-8.

The Unicode BMP occupies only 16 bits. Based on this, the UTF-16 encoding allocates virtually all of the BMP into 16 bits with special codes to indicate when an extra 16-bit word is required to encode the remainder of the 95K+ characters in Unicode. Java supports only the first 2 bytes of the UTF-16 encoding. This guarantees that every character is exactly 16 bits long. It does not encode the entire Unicode standard but does handle all of the BMP. The 16-bit restriction allows for a wide degree of internationalization without incurring the computational costs of variable-length character sets.

In addition, a UTF-32 encoding exists that requires exactly 4 bytes per character. This encodes the entire Unicode standard in a fixed character size, but uses four times as much space as ASCII.

Working with Unicode Characters

You regularly use many basic operations on characters in ASCII. For example, in ASCII, white space is any character less than or equal to a space. This is only true in European languages. The concepts of white space, word breaks, sentences, and punctuation vary among writing systems. The Java `Character` class and the C# `Char` class provide methods to perform a variety of Unicode compliant tests, including the following:

- `isDigit()`
- `isLetter()`
- `isLetterOrDigit()`
- `isLowerCase()`
- `isUpperCase()`
- `isSpace()`

Using these methods produces reliable international results that are way too cumbersome to maintain on your own. When programming for an international audience, be very careful about incorporating any character code arithmetic or numeric comparisons. The familiar numeric tricks for working with ASCII do not translate to Unicode.

A major problem when interacting with characters is their direction of writing. European languages are read left to right, top to bottom. Many languages, such as Arabic and Hebrew, are read right to left, top to bottom. Some Asian languages read top to bottom, right to left. These issues make international text editing somewhat problematic. Even more complicating are bidirectional languages. Arabic and Hebrew both write their numbers left to right rather than right to left. Such mixed directionality makes it quite complicated. Apple has attempted to address this problem with their Text Services Manager that encodes all of the editing of text so as to provide a common implementation of international editing and display. There is not room here to do more than note the problem.

Fonts

The Unicode standard only associates characters with numeric codes, not with the visual form or shape of the character. A font associates character codes with *glyphs*. A glyph is a picture of a character to be drawn on the screen. Though Java, C#, and most Web browsers have Unicode support built into them, most users do not have fonts to display all possible Unicode characters. Without an appropriate font, the character can be stored, but not seen appropriately. Fonts exist for all of the major character sets and are generally installed on a given computer. Your software should have a mechanism for checking to see if appropriate fonts are installed for the specified locale.

Character Input

Interaction, of course, involves not only presentation, but also input. In phonetic languages such as English, French, or Russian, a small number of characters are available and a keyboard is easily designed. At the system level, a keyboard produces a key code that associates a unique number with each key. The key codes are translated into characters in coordination with various Shift keys. To move from one language to another, the keyboard key caps are changed to show the new letters and the translation from key code to letter is changed.

The input problem is more serious when using ideographic writing systems. Kanji, for example, can contain up to 50,000 symbols. Obviously, one key per character is not going to work. A variety of typing techniques exist for such writing systems. The Tsangchi system for Chinese characters uses a keyboard of 24 symbols that can be composed together to form a single ideographic character. In Japanese, two other writing phonetic systems, Hiragana and Katakana, each have 46 characters. Some text-entry systems have users type using the phonetic system and then translate into the ideographic characters.

The good news is that user-interface programmers are generally immune from the character-input problem. The major operating systems and computer manufacturers have already dealt with this problem. Recognize that in modern systems the text input events come in Unicode characters that have already been translated by the input device drivers installed on the computer.

NUMBERS, CURRENCY, AND MEASUREMENTS

Fortunately, most of the world's commerce represents numbers using the basic 10 digits. These are referred to as "Arabic numbers" because they were designed by Arab scholars. However, they are not the symbols used in the Arabic language. Virtually every language has alternate words for the numbers and most writing systems have their own symbols for the 10 digits. However, in the world of commerce, the familiar 10 is almost universally used.

The punctuation of numbers, however, varies among cultures. In the United States, you write "95,241.23," whereas in Europe the same number is written as "95.241,23." The number system is the same, but the punctuation is different. Most software libraries that support internationalization provide a class for formatting numbers. The locale object will yield a number formatter object that has methods appropriate for that locale. Many systems offer special custom formatting of numbers.

The uniformity of base-10 numbers throughout the world of commerce simplifies our internationalization problem. This uniformity breaks down when looking at speech interfaces. People rarely speak in digits. You generally have language forms for numbers such as "three thousand two hundred fifty-four point seven five." These language forms for numbers vary widely with language and must be accounted for in spoken language interfaces. Outside of speech interfaces, many programming language APIs provide a mechanism for formatting numbers with desired punctuation. Those formats are frequently text strings in some special formatting language, such as "$99,999.99" for formatting American decimal numbers. The format string can be placed in an external resource so that appropriate numeric display can be specified for some locale.

Currency

Currency is a common number form that is very important in international computing. Again, the pressures of international commerce have already assisted us in localizing our interfaces. The international monetary system requires that money be quoted as a decimal number for some unit of currency. In the United States, this is dollars; in Japan, it is yen; in Europe, it is euros; and in the U.K., it is pounds. The international monetary system does not recognize nickels, shillings, guineas, pence, or pieces of eight. Though a particular culture might use various locally significant pieces of money, when currency is quoted on virtually all computers, it is a decimal number quoted in a particular unit of currency.

Many cultures have a specific symbol for their currency such as $ (dollars), £ (pounds), € (euros), or ¥ (yen). These symbols can become rather confusing when there are many currencies involved. This is also a problem when multiple countries have their own monetary system yet share the same name for their currency. To resolve this, there are standard, three-character symbols for particular currencies. For example, $ could be replaced by USD (U.S. dollars), CAD (Canadian dollars), or AUD (Australian dollars).

Conversion among currencies is simply a matter of multiplying by a conversion factor. These conversion factors are not constant, due to fluctuations in international markets. The conversion factor is also slightly different depending on the direction the money is flowing. This is due to markets moving money in and out of currencies and the handling charges of those providing the exchange. Thus, currency conversion is generally handled by special-purpose software. User interfaces only format the amount correctly and let other software manage the conversion process.

When programming with money, the amount and currency should both be stored. Formatting money for external display or parsing can be handled as with numbers plus the currency indicator. When and how to perform currency conversions will depend upon the business purpose of the user interface.

Measurements

Measurements are another specialized form of number that varies among cultures. Many numbers such as American and European clothing sizes are not numerically convertible. For a user interface, these are not a problem because they are directly associated with what is being sold. You need only quote them as text.

Other measurements are convertible and those conversions are constant. Thus, a user interface can readily support a variety of such measurements. As with currency, most measurement systems can be represented as a single unit. The metric system for length uses the meter as its basic unit. The English system (not used by the English) uses feet. There is a constant conversion factor between feet and meters of approximately 0.3048. The simple multiplier conversion works well with three exceptions. The first is for measurement systems for which no standard zero point was known, as in temperature. Until absolute zero was discovered, the Fahrenheit and Celsius systems arbitrarily picked a zero point. For such conversions, a multiply and a constant offset will handle the conversion. There are some measurement systems, such as the Richter scale for earthquake strength, that are logarithmic rather than linear.

An additional complication is colloquial fractional units. Prime examples are feet and inches for length and pounds and ounces for weight. In many such systems, the subunits are not decimal multiples but use other units such as 12 inches to the foot, 3 feet to the yard, 16 ounces to the pound, and 2000 pounds to the ton. Fortunately, most of the world has adopted the metric system for most measures. This eliminates the need for conversions and greatly simplifies everything for computer applications. However, the world's largest economy (the United States) is still mired in a colloquial system already abandoned by its creators (the English). Fortunately, most colloquial systems have simple numeric conversions among their subunits that are not difficult to program. The lack of difficulty to program them has not led to standard libraries for their conversion because there is no simple straightforward conversion system that unifies them all. Heavy sigh.

When programming an international user interface that involves measurement, you should first pick some standard unit of measure for internal representation, such as meters or liters. Then, you should write or obtain a standard library that has a function to convert the standard unit into a string as indicated by a specification of the external units. You also need a function that will take a string and a unit specification and translate into the standard units. The translation can be specified as conversion constants or in code as desired. Your program also needs a resource that allows localization to select the desired external units.

DATE AND TIME

Dates and times are very important units because people in technically developed societies organize their lives around them. Dates and times are simply different units for the same measure of time since some starting point. You commonly think about dates and times as being different, but this is only when you consider our daytime activities. An activity might start at 11:00 p.m. today and end at 1:00 a.m. tomorrow. You cannot exclude dates from the specification of these times.

The standard international unit of time is the second, with smaller units such as milliseconds, microseconds, and nanoseconds being decimal fractions of a second. Larger units, unfortunately, use 60 seconds to the minute, 60 minutes to the hour, and 24 hours to the day (approximately). You also need to differentiate between times and durations. Seconds are actually a unit of duration or the amount of time that has passed between two events. When you ask, "What time is it?" the answer is quoted in the duration since some fixed point. When you quote a time of 10:30 p.m., you mean 22 hours and 30 minutes past midnight today. This evolves, then, to the questions of midnight where and is it political midnight or astronomical midnight?

For computing use, time and dates are generally stored as the number of milliseconds since some epoch. There are variations on when the epoch starts. Many computers use 1960 because no good timekeeping computers existed before then. Others use 1900 because it naturally subsumes the twentieth century and beyond. The Macintosh used 1904 as its epoch base. Whatever the epoch used, the conversion among them is trivial and not part of the user interface. There is also the question of where on the Earth that epoch started. Because of England's domination of the sea during the great years of exploration, the base location is the Royal Observatory at Greenwich, England. Originally, this was called Greenwich Mean Time (GMT). To break its cultural association, it is now called Universal Time Coordinated (UTC). Because the solar day is not absolutely $24 \times 60 \times 60$ seconds long, systems of leap seconds have been created to keep time synchronized with the sun.

Time zones are represented as offsets from UTC. Most time zones are defined as constant hour offsets, but there are other offsets. Newfoundland is offset on a 30-minute boundary and Nepal is on a 45-minute boundary. The simple answer is that UTC time can be converted to or from any other time zone by adding a constant number of minutes.

More recently, the Swiss watch company, Swatch, has created Internet time.[2] This divides the solar day into 1000 "beats" and uses Biel, Switzerland (the headquarters of Swatch) as the base meridian. This defines a universal time all over the world that is absolutely synchronized with the sun.

The textual representation of the time of day varies from culture to culture. The two common variants are AM/PM and the 24-hour clock. There are also variations in punctuation. A locale object can provide the appropriate formatting for a culture.

When defining a user interface around time, an internal time standard for the software should be adopted. Based on that, many programming language APIs have a mechanism for formatting and parsing time strings. Use this rather than hard-coding your own. Time zones are a very special problem. The question is which time zone should you use? If I am flying to France next week and I have a meeting at noon on Wednesday, is that noon my time or noon in Paris? I create the appointment entry in my office in Provo but I would not be happy if the notification went off at 5:00 in the morning in Paris. The problem is that time zones are fixed and well known. Present and future places of a user are not known and must be carefully considered when designing an international user interface.

Calendars

Calendars are very complicated things. Most calendars were created to represent the order of astronomical events. Years are based on revolutions around the sun, months are based on revolutions of the moon, and days are based on rotations of the Earth. Unfortunately for computer software, none of these revolutions are integer multiples of each other. Calendars based on days get out of sync with years, thus the introduction of leap years, which periodically add days to the year. Lunar months are radically out of sync with years. This leads to the modern European calendar with months of varying lengths or traditional Hebrew calendars that periodically add a 13th month to resynchronize the months with the year.

Calendars are very important culturally. Because observance of the heavens is a part of so many religions, their religious observances are strongly related to astronomical periods and events. This religious connection leads to strong cultural connections to calendars. Various cultures also define quite different zero points for their calendars. The Christian, Hebrew, Arabic, Chinese, and Japanese years are quite different because of the event on which they base the start of their counting.

In many cultures, work is organized around weeks. The combination of Jewish, Christian, and Islamic cultures have established the seven-day week. However, the French Republican Calendar established the 10-day week. This was discarded by Napoleon because nobody wanted to work nine days without a day off.

Internationally, the Gregorian calendar (decreed by Pope Gregory XIII in 1582) is the common form for communication. The Gregorian calendar is a correction of the Julian, established by Julius Caesar in 45 BC (note the Christian reference BC to a Roman calendar). The Gregorian calendar, like the metric system, provides a common basis for international trade. The Gregorian calendar's strong religious and cultural basis does not make it the common calendar of everyday life for much of the world's populations. Even where the Gregorian calendar is the cultural norm, each language has its own words for the days of the week and months of the year.

In dealing with dates in localized software, it is appropriate to use the Gregorian calendar in most situations provided the locale is used to translate the names to the appropriate language. Some systems provide a `Calendar` class for modeling other calendars, handling date conversions to and from those calendars, and formatting date representations appropriately. There does not yet seem to be any standard for such facilities.

COMPOUND STRING FORMATTING

The most difficult problem when localizing a piece of software is the compound string. Suppose, for example, you have a small database with the names of people and the number of apples that they each bought. You might write a program that generates the message "Mary bought 4 apples," where Mary and 4 are values drawn from the database. Many Web-based systems do exactly this when translating data into Web pages. The first obvious problem is that "bought" and "apples" need to be changed when moving to a new language. Suppose, however, that the database has the value 1 for

George. The appropriate string would be "George bought 1 apple." Notice that "apples" has changed to "apple" to create a correct sentence in English.

A naïve approach to the compound string problem is to create a "bought" resource and an "apples" resource in a resource bundle. The code might then read as follows:

```
message=name+getResource("bought")+number+getResource("apples");
```

The resources would handle the translation. Our example for George showed that even in English, the output is awkward. Many languages have more complex number and gender associations between words as well as wide variations in word order. The problem is to dynamically generate a phrase that is semantically consistent with the target language.

One technique that is used to resolve this problem is the macro resource. You might create a resource "AppleSales" that contains the following string:

```
"<name> bought <number> apples"
```

The localization library would provide a mechanism for generating a full string by substituting the name and number into the resource string. The advantage of this approach is that when localizing the message, the entire phrase can be translated rather than just words at a time. Localization libraries also provide mechanisms for selecting different translations depending on the numbers involved. Even with these facilities, it can be hard to get correct message generation that works in all languages. The message macro resource technique does provide a way to generate understandable messages in most languages even if the syntax is slightly awkward in some cases. These macro substitution mechanisms are found in many APIs and operating systems. The correct macro pattern for a given locale should be stored in a resource to allow localization.

SORTING

Sorting is a very important component of a user interface because it is the primary mechanism for people to search through long lists. Most computer science students learned that sorting is done by comparing characters and putting them in numerical order based on their ASCII code. This is great for teaching a first programming course, but it fails even for English because of upper- and lowercase letters. The additional characters from the ISO Latin encoding for European characters are completely out of their sort order and Unicode is only mildly based on an appropriate sort order. The complexity of sort order is much worse in ideographic languages such as Chinese.

For user-interface development, the answer is the Collator class. This can be obtained from a locale object and provides a method for comparing two Unicode strings to establish their sort order. Trying to encode sort order on your own is an exercise in pain. In those cases where there is no available locale specification, most Collator classes provide a mechanism for adding explicit rules for character precedence. This can adapt your sort order to a new language. When writing any text-sorting algorithm, always use the Collator class or its equivalent rather than coding your own comparison algorithm.

SUMMARY

Internationalizing an interface involves designing it so that it can be easily localized to a particular language and culture. The primary mechanism for doing this is to externalize information into resources and resource bundles. These pull culture-specific information out of the code and into resources where they can be easily edited by language/culture experts. Careful attention must be paid to the following:

• Character sets

• Icons

• Colors

• Messages both simple and compound

• Numbers

• Dates and times

Other subtle complexities might arise in particular cultures. It is always a trade-off between localization effort and expected return from more careful attention to a particular culture.

EXERCISES

1. What is the difference between internationalization, globalization, and localization?

2. Take a small user interface and do the following:

   a. Identify a set of resource bundles in which the parts of the user interface needing globalization can be grouped.

   b. Identify all of the resources that would go into each bundle.

   c. Describe how you would efficiently organize the locales for United States, France, English Canada, and Quebec so that duplication of resources is minimized.

3. Describe how you would organize your code so that the user can select the locale that they want to use.

4. Why is sorting Unicode characters a problem?

5. Why are simple resource files not sufficient for taking care of date issues?

6. Why is it so hard to internationalize compound strings?

END NOTES

[1] www.unicode.org

[2] www.timeanddate.com/time/internettime.html

CHAPTER 11

Input Syntax Specification

Chapter 8 discussed the role of consistent look and feel. Tools like interaction design environments and other user-interface layout tools are excellent for working through the look of an interface. Even paper and pencil or drawing on a whiteboard are excellent techniques for a design team to work through how a new user interface should look. This helps many design teams to understand clearly what they are trying to implement in their view. The design of the feel, the sequence of inputs through which a user causes an action, is much more problematic because it is not visual. The legal sequences of user inputs coupled with the actions to be taken as a result of those inputs is called the *input* syntax. This syntax is implemented in the controller. Implementing the controller code is difficult and requires tools and notations of its own.

For many widgets such as buttons, radio boxes, and check buttons, the input syntax is trivial. When the mouse goes down, the button on the screen looks pressed; when the mouse goes up, the button pops out while some programmatic action is executed. Even a button is not as trivial as it looks. What happens if the mouse moves outside of the button's rectangle before the mouse is released? What happens if the mouse moves into the button while the mouse is already down? The on-screen button is one of the simplest of all input sequences, but there are still issues that are not immediately obvious and must be worked out.

When moving beyond simple button interaction to the file folder view shown in Figure 11.1, many more complex issues arise. If the mouse hovers over a file for a period of time, the ToolTip window should be shown. If the mouse clicks, the file or folder should be selected. If the mouse double-clicks, the file should be opened, if possible. If the mouse clicks and then clicks again at some later time, the title of the file/folder should be presented for editing and renaming. If keyboard events occur, they should be ignored except when the syntax is in name editing mode. If Enter is pressed, the file should be renamed, unless there is a problem with the name, in which case the user should be notified and the renaming aborted. The event sequence mouse-down, mouse-move, mouse-up generally means that the file or folder is engaged in a drag-and-drop sequence to move it to a different location in the folder hierarchy. However, if the interface is in file rename mode, that same sequence selects a portion of the name for deletion. These complexities grow in drawing or visualization environments where the simple click-and-drag techniques take on different meanings in a variety of situations.

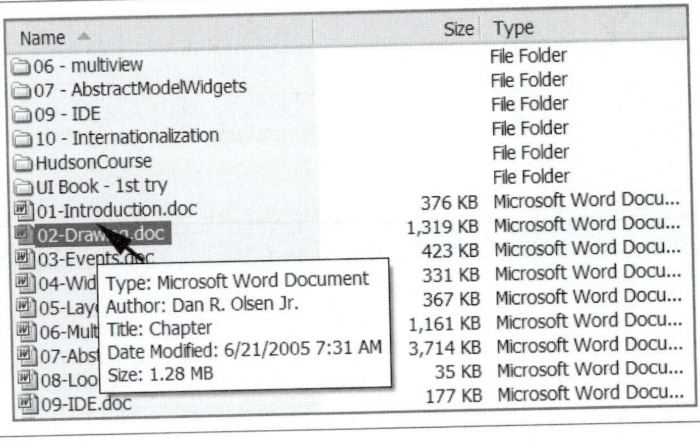

Name ▲	Size	Type
06 - multiview		File Folder
07 - AbstractModelWidgets		File Folder
09 - IDE		File Folder
10 - Internationalization		File Folder
HudsonCourse		File Folder
UI Book - 1st try		File Folder
01-Introduction.doc	376 KB	Microsoft Word Docu...
02-Drawing.doc	1,319 KB	Microsoft Word Docu...
03-Events.doc	423 KB	Microsoft Word Docu...
04-Wid	331 KB	Microsoft Word Docu...
05-Lay	367 KB	Microsoft Word Docu...
06-Mult	1,161 KB	Microsoft Word Docu...
07-Abs	3,714 KB	Microsoft Word Docu...
08-Loo	35 KB	Microsoft Word Docu...
09-IDE.doc	177 KB	Microsoft Word Docu...

Type: Microsoft Word Document
Author: Dan R. Olsen Jr.
Title: Chapter
Date Modified: 6/21/2005 7:31 AM
Size: 1.28 MB

Figure 11.1 – Interacting with a file view

At first, you might be inclined to resolve these issues in a series of prototypes. The problem is that the complexities of the code can frequently produce a prototype that has the right feel but nobody any longer knows what it actually does. The patches upon patches have buried the true behavior beyond recognition. The value of pencil and paper for designing the look of an interface lies in the fact that it can be readily understood and openly discussed by all members of the design team. This is not true of 400 lines of C++ code. It is even less true of that same 400 lines scattered throughout the event handlers of Visual Basic.

Programs are a poor mechanism for designing input syntax for three reasons. The first reason is that the code is generally scattered among many different event-handling methods. For example, the file drag-and-drop sequence must be divided among the mouseUp, mouseMove, mouseEnter, mouseExit, and mouseUp event-handler methods. Following a coherent trail of action becomes rather difficult. The second reason is that code is not expressively dense. That is, a 400-line implementation of an input syntax is very difficult to read, understand, or discuss. Only 10 percent to 20 percent is visible at any one time. For a group design effort, the syntax design must fit on a whiteboard so that all can see and comment. The third reason is that when the syntax is scattered among so many methods, it is difficult to reliably change during the ebb and flow of a design process. What we need is a compact, easily expressed, easily modified notation for capturing input syntax design. That is the subject of this chapter.

This chapter looks at three such notations. The first are mouse event diagrams that capture a single input task involving the mouse. The second are state machine diagrams. These have long been used for syntax design, yet they have serious practical drawbacks. The final notation in this chapter is Propositional Production Systems that have the same expressive power as state machines without most of the problems.

MOUSE EVENT DIAGRAMS

In most cases, a task can be characterized by user-caused events, the path of the mouse, the state of the mouse buttons, and the screen objects beneath the mouse. Figure 11.2 shows a mouse event diagram for the simple pressing of an on-screen push button. The events are identified on the path by letters and then described underneath the diagram. The mouse buttons are shown white when that button is up and dark when that button is down. While the button is down and the mouse is dragging, the path is shown with a thicker line.

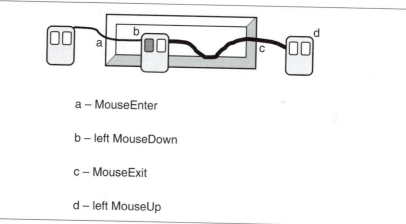

a – MouseEnter

b – left MouseDown

c – MouseExit

d – left MouseUp

Figure 11.2 – Mouse event diagram for a push button

The condition being described in Figure 11.2 is where the mouse button goes down inside the screen button and then is moved outside of the screen button while the left button is still down and then released outside of the button. This is not the traditional click behavior, but it must be addressed in a good button syntax design. The problem with the presentation in Figure 11.2 is that it does not show what should happen to the screen button while all of this is going on. Figure 11.3 shows a modified version of Figure 11.2 with the state of the button being presented at every event. This visual depiction at each event gives us a clear picture over time of what is to happen to the screen button during this sequence.

Some interactive tasks do not lend themselves as well to this presentation because multiple events happen in a particular place, such as clicking on this button. These can be handled by showing multiple event letters in the same position and then describing what should happen at each. The important issue is that a diagram like this clearly and briefly shows what should be happening during this interactive task.

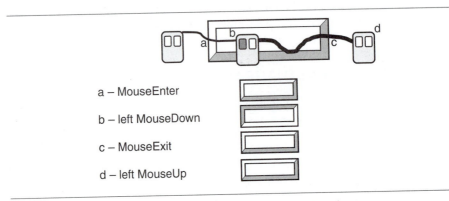

Figure 11.3 – Events augmented with widget presentation changes

Figure 11.4 shows a slightly more complicated task where the user is dragging the slider of a scroll bar. When the mouse enters the scroll bar, the slider lightens to show that it is active. When the mouse goes down on the slider, its border gets thicker to show that it is being moved. As the mouse leaves and reenters the region of the scroll bar, the slider stays active and moves with it. When the mouse is released, the slider reduces its border but stays light to show that it is responding to the mouse location.

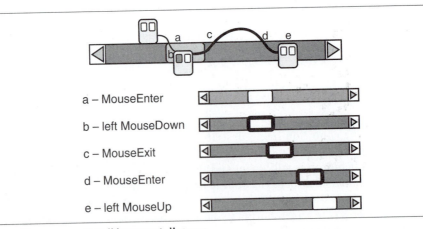

Figure 11.4 – Scroll bar event diagram

If this diagram had been drawn on a whiteboard during a design meeting, it would be very easy to discuss the behavior and whether it is appropriate. Perhaps some added texture would be appropriate rather than the thickened border. Perhaps the body of the scroll bar should lighten rather than the slider to show that the scroll bar is active. The point is that all of these options can easily be discussed, modified, remodified, modified again, and, finally, documented in a way that everyone clearly understands.

For any particular widget, many such tasks must be developed. For example, for the scroll bar, tasks for clicking in the arrows, clicking in the body, and holding down the mouse in the arrows must be developed. You might want a different highlight when the mouse enters the body rather than the slider or an arrow. Using diagrams for each of these tasks, you can easily design and document all of these alternatives.

STATE REPRESENTATIONS OF SYNTAX

The mouse event diagrams are suitable for outlining a single interactive task. A real widget design will have many such tasks. However, the widget implementation must combine all of those tasks into the same event-handling code. The event handling for push buttons and scroll bars is quite simple in comparison to many interactive tasks.

Figure 11.5 shows a screen capture of the drawing facility in Microsoft Word. When the mouse goes down, many different things could happen. If it goes down on the dot at the end of the control handle on the rectangle, a rotation action begins. If it goes down on any of the corner or side dots, a resizing action begins. If it goes down in an open space, (depending upon the current menu selections) a selection or the creation of a new object begins. If it goes down on the black arrow, the rectangle is unselected, the arrow is selected, and a drag of the arrow might or might not begin depending on how far the mouse moves. There are very many interactive tasks, with all of their behavior embedded in the mouseDown( ), mouseMove( ), and mouseUp( ) event methods.

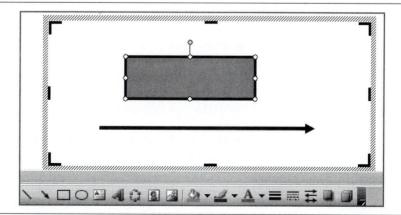

Figure 11.5–Drawing program

One of the first attempts to address this event complexity was through state machines[1] and state machine diagrams[2]. Figure 11.6 shows a diagram for the interactive behavior of the screen button design in Figure 11.3. The circles are states and the transitions are *event/action* pairs. When an event is received that corresponds to a transition from the current state, the action for that transition is taken and the current state becomes the new state at the other end of the transition.

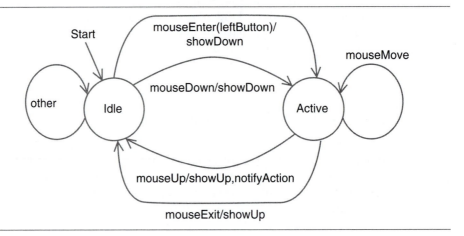

Figure 11.6 – State machine diagram

The state machine diagram in Figure 11.6 illustrates both the advantages and disadvantages of this notation. It is quite easy to follow what events are acceptable and what actions should be taken on those events. Such diagrams are also relatively easy to translate into code. Each widget has a data member called `state` and there is an enumerated type for all of the states. Within each method is a `switch` statement on the `state` variable and another on the input type to select the correct transition for that input event. In each case of the switch, the transition action is performed and `state` is set to the value for the next state. The problems are primarily ones of scale. If the number of states + transitions gets larger than 20–30, a single page is not sufficient to hold the information. In many situations, the state machine is not a planar graph, which means that it is not possible to draw the diagram without transitions crossing each other. This makes it very complicated to read such a diagram.

An additional problem is the creation of tools for manipulating the diagrams. Systems like Microsoft Visio[3] that can edit connected diagrams can help, but the tools are still rather uncomfortable.

A final problem with state machine diagrams is their expressive power. The problem lies in many of the combinations and repetition required to adapt the finite state machine to diverse syntax design needs. There have been a variety of adaptations, including the use of context free grammars[4] and parser generation technology[5]. None of these has done extremely well. The problem is that they do not sufficiently represent the intrinsic parallelism found in many syntax specifications. In many cases, a variety of things need to be specified but the order is only important in short chunks and a user might interleave their activities in many ways. A highly ordered syntax is difficult for users to learn because they must map their intentions onto the prescribed order of the syntax. This leads to a serious gulf of execution problem.

To illustrate this difficulty, consider the problem of entering eight pieces of information (A through H) each exactly once but in any order. To get this right, the syntax description must preserve whether each piece of information has been received. Thus, for each input you need one bit (received or not) in your state. For all eight inputs, you need 8 bits. This is a trivial amount of memory, but the problem is difficult to express in a state machine diagram because there are 2^8 or 256 states. Consider trying to scale Figure 11.6 up to 256 circles with a similar number of labeled arrows. The problem is that whether or not input B has been received is completely independent of whether any other input has been received, yet the state diagram approach forces the designer to consider all possible combinations.

PROPOSITIONAL PRODUCTION SYSTEMS

Propositional Production Systems (PPS)[6] are an alternative representation of finite state machines. In formal language theory, they still belong to the same finite state category in the Chomsky hierarchy. However, they can express many problems in a linear number of statements rather than the exponential number that we saw with state diagrams. They are also edited using any text editor and much more spatially compact so that more of the syntax fits on a whiteboard, piece of paper, or computer screen. Because a PPS is still a finite state machine, it is also computationally tractable for performing automatic analysis. It is easy to design algorithms that automatically prove[7] statements such as "it is always possible to request help," "action Z will never be performed without the user first entering a valid password," or "action P can always be reached in less than five steps from any point in the syntax." Because of these properties, this text uses PPS as the notation for syntax design. In most cases, the primary value of the PPS notation is to work out syntax designs in a more understandable and modifiable form than code.

Field Definition

One of the key concepts in a PPS is that the state space is divided up into fields. Each field has two or more conditions. Within a field, the conditions are mutually exclusive (the field can only hold one value at a time) but different fields are independent of each other. Formally, some state dependencies cannot be conveniently represented, but they rarely occur in practice. Figure 11.7 shows the field definition for the previous eight-input problem. There are only eight fields and 16 conditions rather than the 256 states required in state diagrams. In this machine, the conditions Ayes and Ano cannot hold at the same time but they are independent of all other conditions.

A { Ayes, Ano }
B (Byes, Bno }
C { Cyes, Cno }
D { Dyes, Dno }
E { Eyes, Eno }
F { Fyes, Fno }
G { Gyes, Gno }
H { Hyes, Hno }

Figure 11.7 – PPS fields for the eight-input problem

For convenience, we define a variety of types of fields with their conditions to actually model interactive syntax. This book uses a notation standard for each type of condition. It helps in reading the syntax specification and in translating the specification into code. The types of fields are as follows:

- Input events (* before the condition name)

    {*mouseDown, *mouseUp, *mouseMove}

- Input modifiers (* after the condition name)

    LeftMouse{leftUp*, leftDown* }
    RightMouse {rightUp*, rightDown*}
    ControlKey {controlUp*, controlDown*}
    ShiftKey {shiftUp*, shiftDown* }

- State information to be remembered

    SliderDisplay { sliderInactive, sliderActive }
    ButtonState { buttonUp, buttonDepressed }
    MouseDragging { idle, dragging }

- Query fields (? before name)

    Password {?validPassword, ?noPassword }
    ScrollPos {?stepUp, ?pageUp, ?slider, ?pageDwn, ?stepDwn }

- Actions (! before name, sometimes there are parameters)

    {!drawButtonUp, !drawButtonDown}
    {!notifyButtonAction}
    {!increment(amount), !decrement(amount), !scroll(newPos) }

Only one input event field is available because only one event can be received by an application at a time. This is where you list all of the input events that are relevant for a particular widget. The input modifiers are arranged in separate fields because they are independent of each other. It is possible to press the right mouse button while holding down the Shift key and at the same time ignore whether the Control key is pressed. Input modifiers are separated from input events because modifiers by themselves do not cause actions to occur. In many cases, you must know the modifier state so that you can take the correct action when one is required.

Most of the control of the interactive syntax is encoded in state fields. State fields can represent many different things. It is up to the syntax designer to decide how various pieces of information can be modeled. The examples later in the chapter show how these are used.

Query fields are special in that their conditions are not remembered but, rather, are the result of some other code. For example, it is not possible to encode all of the possible passwords in a PPS. It is far simpler to create a piece of code that looks up the password and determines if it is valid. You can define a method `Password()` that returns `validPassword` or `noPassword`. You can use the returned condition to then control the behavior of your controller implementation. Essential geometry is represented using query fields.

Action fields are placeholders for pieces of code to be executed. They can be grouped into fields because many actions are mutually exclusive. For example, you do not want to increment the scroll bar at the same time you are decrementing it. Actions are where the model methods are invoked. Frequently, you'll need to provide parameters and you'll generally handle this informally in the notation.

Productions

The syntax of a PPS is encoded in a set of productions rather than in state transitions. Each production has a left-hand side (antecedent) and a right-hand side (consequent). If all of the conditions in the antecedent hold, the consequent is asserted. Input events, input modifiers, and query conditions can only occur in the antecedent because they cannot be changed by the controller. Actions can only occur in the consequent. A PPS consists of multiple productions and all productions with matching antecedents fire at once. This is to prevent race conditions where one production can change the conditions for a later production. This parallel firing policy requires some care when converting a PPS into code, as discussed later. Sample rules might include the following:

```
*mouseUp, shiftDown*, selectClick -> !addSelect, selectModeIdle
*mouseUp, shiftUp*, selectClick -> !newSelect, selectModeIdle
```

These two productions only fire when the `mouseUp` event has occurred and the state of the controller is `selectClick`. They differentiate their behavior based on whether the Shift key is pressed.

SCROLL BAR SYNTAX EXAMPLE

The first step in defining a PPS specification is to identify the interactive tasks that the widget must accomplish. For the scroll bar example in Figure 11.4, the following can be identified:

1. Click in the left arrow to step left.
2. Click in the right arrow to step right.
3. Click in the left body area to page left.
4. Click in the right body area to page right.
5. Drag the slider to scroll.

Based on these tasks, you can identify a set of fields that have information you'll need in your syntax. Figure 11.8 shows a field with all of the events you will receive from the mouse, a query field for the essential geometry, and a `state` field that remembers what you are doing from event to event. To know the right thing to do on mouse-up, you must remember what you were doing on mouse-down. The actions have been grouped into two different fields, each handling a different set of issues. The `Model` field handles the actual changes to the model, whereas the `Feedback` field handles highlighting the scroll bar to provide user feedback. These actions are separated because between the groups they are not mutually exclusive. Some rules might perform a model action at the same time that they perform a feedback action, which is just fine. You do not, however, want to `!pageLeft` and `!pageRight` at the same time. Putting these two actions in the same field specifies that they are mutually exclusive.

```
Input {*mouseDown, *mouseMove, *mouseUp }
    // events we will receive as the mouse moves
State { idle, steppingLeft, steppingRight, pagingLeft, pagingRight, dragging }
    // remembers what the controller is doing from one event to another
EssentialGeometry { ?leftArrow, ?rightArrow, ?leftBody,?rightBody, ?slider }
    // query field that identifies which of the 5 regions the mouse is in at the current time.
Model { !stepLeft, !stepRight, !pageLeft, !pageRight, !dragStart, !dragEnd, !dragScroll }
    // action methods that actually do the various things that a scroll bar should do
Feedback { !sliderActive, !leftArrowActive, !rightArrowActive, !bodyActive, !allPassive }
    // action methods to handle highlighting the slider
```

Figure 11.8 – Fields for scroll bar PPS

You can build up your set of production rules by looking at each task in turn. Tasks 1–4 involve simple clicking in regions. You can handle these with the rules in Figure 11.9. Each task has two rules, one for mouse-down and one for mouse-up. Each rule works with the `State` and `EssentialGeometry` fields to decide what should be done.

---

1. *mouseDown, idle, ?leftArrow -> steppingLeft, !leftArrowActive
2. *mouseUp, steppingLeft -> idle, !allPassive, !stepLeft
3. *mouseDown, idle, ?rightArrow -> steppingRight, !rightArrowActive
4. *mouseUp, steppingRight -> idle, !allPassive, !stepRight
5. *mouseDown, idle, ?leftBody -> pagingLeft, !bodyActive
6. *mouseUp, pagingLeft -> idle, !allPassive, !pageLeft
7. *mouseDown, idle, ?rightBody -> pagingRight, !bodyActive
8. *mouseUp, pagingRight -> !allPassive, !pageRight

Figure 11.9 – Production rules for tasks 1–4

Rule 1 in Figure 11.9 specifies that when the `mouseDown` event occurs, the `State` field is in its `idle` condition and the mouse location is in the `leftArrow` region, the `State` field should be changed to `steppingLeft` and the `leftArrowActive` action (usually a method) should be called. Similarly, rule 2 in Figure 11.9 specifies that when the `mouseUp` event is received and the `State` field is in the `steppingLeft` condition, the `State` field should be returned to `idle` and the `allPassive` and `stepLeft` actions should be called. Each rule can be read as an "if-then" sentence. You will see later that the "if-then" reading does not directly translate into code in the same way.

Looking at your rules, you realize that you are not accounting for mouse movement in these tasks. The design team discussion might be:

"What happens on mouse move?"

"No problem, these are all clicking tasks."

"Yes, but what if the mouse moves out of the left arrow before mouse-up?"

"Well, I guess we should unhighlight the arrow."

"And what happens if the mouse movement goes completely outside of the scroll bar rectangle?"

"We would still unhighlight the arrow."

"But what if the mouse is still down and the mouse is moved back?"

"I think the arrow becomes active again."

"That doesn't feel like a click task to me."

The advantage here is that you can have a discussion about eight rules and five fields in a way that is not possible with several pages of code. Having discussed the alternatives, the input field is changed to that shown in Figure 11.10 and the production rules are changed to those shown in Figure 11.11. Notice in rules 2, 5, 8, 11, and 13 of Figure 11.11, the "~" is added to indicate that the condition must not hold for the rule to fire. This is simpler than a separate rule for each of the other conditions. You will need to remember this case, however, when you translate into code. Rule 13 handles all of the mouse-exit issues.

Input {*mouseDown, *mouseMove, *mouseUp, **mouseExit**}
// events we will receive as the mouse moves

Figure 11.10 – Modified input field

1. *mouseDown, idle, ?leftArrow -> steppingLeft, !leftArrowActive
2. ***mouseMove, steppingLeft, ~?leftArrow -> !allPassive, idle**
3. *mouseUp, steppingLeft -> idle, !allPassive, !stepLeft
4. *mouseDown, idle, ?rightArrow -> steppingRight, !rightArrowActive
5. ***mouseMove, steppingRight, ~?rightArrow -> !allPassive, idle**
6. *mouseUp, steppingRight -> idle, !allPassive, !stepRight
7. *mouseDown, idle, ?leftBody -> pagingLeft, !bodyActive
8. ***mouseMove, pagingLeft, ~?leftBody -> !allPassive, idle**
9. *mouseUp, pagingLeft -> idle, !allPassive, !pageLeft
10. *mouseDown, idle, ?rightBody -> pagingRight, !bodyActive
11. ***mouseMove, pagingRight, ~?rightBody -> !allPassive, idle**
12. *mouseUp, pagingRight -> !allPassive, !pageRight
13. ***mouseExit ~idle -> !allPassive idle**

Figure 11.11 – Updated rules to handle mouse movement

Task 5, where the slider is being dragged, has still not been addressed. We can address that task with the rules in Figure 11.12. While discussing these rules, it is discovered that the mouse focus, in case the user strays outside the box, needs to be handled. The additional action field shown in Figure 11.13 takes care of this.

14. *mouseDown, idle, ?slider -> !sliderActive, dragging, !dragStart(mousePoint), !getMouseFocus
15. *mouseMove, dragging -> !dragScroll(mousePoint)
16. *mouseUp, dragging -> !dragEnd(mousePoint), idle, !releaseMouseFocus

Figure 11.12 – Additional rules to handle mouse dragging

Focus {!getMouseFocus, !releaseMouseFocus }

Figure 11.13 – Additional action field to handle mouse focus

We now have a PPS that we believe captures the entire controller syntax for a scroll bar. Before jumping into code, we want to first check our PPS to see if it is functioning correctly. We do this by working through each of our interactive tasks for which we created mouse event diagrams. We want to see if our PPS does the right thing for each of these tasks. In Figure 11.14, we work through our event diagram identifying what will happen to the state variables, what rules will fire, and what actions will be taken.

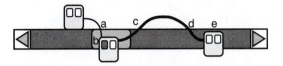

```
start – State{idle}
a – *mouseEnter – no rule fires, nothing happens
b – *mouseDown – rule 14 fires, !sliderActive, State{dragging}
        !dragStart(mousePoint), !getMouseFocus
* – *mouseMove – rule 18 repeatedly fires calling !dragScroll()
c – *mouseExit – rule 13 fires and does the wrong thing –
            we correct rule 13 to those shown in Figure 11.15 and now
            no rule fires, which is correct
d – *mouseEnter – no rule fires, nothing happens
e – *mouseUp – rule 19 fires, !dragEnd, State{idle},
            !releaseMouseFocus
```

Figure 11.14 – Working through PPS with mouse event diagram

As we are working through the rules on this interactive task, we find that rule 13 is too general in that it shuts down the scroll bar even though we have the mouse focus. We, therefore, replace rule 13 with rules 13–16 in Figure 11.15 and continue our work. We also realize from our mouse event diagram that we need to account for the fact that only the left mouse button should trigger any of the actions. We add an additional input field to create the final field list shown in Figure 11.16 and we update the rules to account for the button information, as shown in Figure 11.15.

1. *mouseDown, idle, **leftDown***, ?leftArrow -> steppingLeft, !leftArrowActive
2. *mouseMove, steppingLeft, ~?leftArrow -> !allPassive, idle
3. *mouseUp, **leftUp***, steppingLeft -> idle, !allPassive, !stepLeft
4. *mouseDown, idle, **leftDown***, ?rightArrow -> steppingRight !rightArrowActive
5. *mouseMove, steppingRight, ~?rightArrow -> !allPassive, idle
6. *mouseUp, **leftUp***, steppingRight -> idle, !allPassive, !stepRight
7. *mouseDown, idle, **leftDown***,?leftBody -> pagingLeft, !bodyActive
8. *mouseMove, pagingLeft, ~?leftBody -> !allPassive, idle
9. *mouseUp, **leftUp***, pagingLeft -> idle, !allPassive, !pageLeft
10. *mouseDown, idle, **leftDown***, ?rightBody -> pagingRight, !bodyActive
11. *mouseMove, pagingRight, ~?rightBody -> !allPassive, idle
12. *mouseUp, **leftUp***, pagingRight -> !allPassive, !pageRight
13. ***mouseExit steppingLeft -> !allPassive idle**
14. ***mouseExit steppingRight -> !allPassive idle**
15. ***mouseExit pagingLeft -> !allPassive idle**
16. ***mouseExit pagingRight -> !allPassive idle**
17. *mouseDown, **leftDown***, idle, ?slider -> !sliderActive, dragging,
        !dragStart(mousePoint), !getMouseFocus
18. *mouseMove, dragging -> !dragScroll(mousePoint)
19. *mouseUp, **leftUp***, dragging -> !dragEnd(mousePoint), idle, !releaseMouseFocus

Figure 11.15 – Revised production rules

Input {*mouseDown, *mouseMove, *mouseUp }
    // events we will receive as the mouse moves
LeftButton {leftDown*, leftUp* }
    // state of the left mouse button
State { idle, steppingLeft, steppingRight, pagingLeft, pagingRight, dragging }
    // remembers what the controller is doing from one event to another
EssentialGeometry { ?leftArrow, ?rightArrow, ?leftBody, ?rightBody, ?slider }
    // query field that identifies which of the 5 regions the mouse
    // is in at the current time.
Model { !stepLeft, !stepRight, !pageLeft, !pageRight, !dragStart, !dragEnd, !dragScroll }
    // action methods that actually do the various things that a scroll bar should do
Feedback { !sliderActive, !leftArrowActive, !rightArrowActive, !bodyActive, !allPassive }
    // action methods to handle highlighting the slider
Focus {!getMouseFocus, !releaseMouseFocus }
    // manage the mouse focus

Figure 11.16 – Revised PPS fields for scroll bar

TRANSLATING PPS INTO CODE

Having gone through the design process, we now have a PPS specification in Figures 11.15 and 11.16 that we believe accounts for everything that our scroll bar's controller will need and we have corrected several design and specification errors. We are now ready to translate the PPS into controller code. In this step, it is important to follow a principled process step-by-step so that we accurately translate the rules into code. We might also find additional errors in the specification as we go through this process and find rules that are in conflict with each other.

In translating a PPS into code, we are assuming that the controller is part of a view class. The controller is implemented primarily as event-handling methods on such a class.

Encoding of Fields

The first step is to translate all of the fields into code. The input events are translated into event-handler methods. There is one such method for each of the input events used in the PPS. The naming of these methods will depend upon the toolkit platform on which the controller is being built. The input modifiers are not directly encoded in the class. It is normal for every input event method to have a parameter that contains the event information, including the mouse location and the state of various buttons. There are methods on such event objects for determining the state of the Control or Shift keys, for example. Where those input conditions occur in the production rules, we will replace them with code appropriate to the underlying platform.

State fields are very important because they are our memory from event to event. For every state field, we create an enumeration of all of the conditions for that field and a data member of that type. Figure 11.17 shows Java code for our scroll bar's state field. Note that many controller designs will have more than one state field. Our scroll bar only required one for its implementation. The data member `state` has also been initialized to `IDLE` as its starting state.

```
private enum State { IDLE, STEPPING_LEFT, STEPPING_RIGHT,
        PAGING_LEFT, PAGING_RIGHT, DRAGGING }
private State state = IDLE;
```

Figure 11.17 – Implementing the state field

Query fields also have an enumerated type, but their values are dynamically computed rather than stored in a variable. Figure 11.18 shows how our scroll bar's `EssentialGeometry` field is implemented.

```
private enum EssentialGeometry{ LEFT_ARROW, RIGHT_ARROW, LEFT_BODY, RIGHT_BODY, SLIDER };
private EssentialGeometry essentialGeometry (int mouseX, mouseY)
{
        . . . . code to determine which region of the scroll bar
        has been selected . . .
}
```

Figure 11.18 – Implementing the EssentialGeometry query field

The action fields and their conditions are implemented as a method for each action condition. These methods will be invoked whenever they appear in a rule that is to fire.

To tidy up the PPS, the fields must be ordered in the sequence that they are to be checked. The first fields should be the input events followed by the input modifier fields. This is because the first task is to identify the user's input. Second, comes the state fields. It is helpful to place the most discriminatory fields first. These are the ones that are most frequently used to decide what action to take. This is a judgment call on the part of the designer. After the state fields come the query fields. These are placed later because they involve more complex code than simple field checking and should only be called when necessary. Last, are the action fields because they are invoked after everything else. The order is:

- Input fields
- Input modifier fields
- State fields in most used to least used order
- Query fields
- Action fields

It is helpful to get in the habit of using this order from the beginning, as was done in Figure 11.16.

Reordering Rules

During the design phase, rules were arranged in the order that made sense while working through the interactive tasks. This ordering is not appropriate for the code because the code is organized by input event method rather than by interactive task. The antecedents (left side) should be in the same order as the fields. These two reorderings will greatly simplify the step-by-step construction of code that accurately implements the PPS. The reordered rules for the scroll bar are found in Figure 11.19.

1. *mouseDown, leftDown*, idle, ?leftArrow -> steppingLeft, !leftArrowActive
2. *mouseDown, leftDown*, idle, ?rightArrow -> steppingRight, !rightArrowActive
3. *mouseDown, leftDown*, idle,?leftBody -> pagingLeft, !bodyActive
4. *mouseDown, leftDown*, idle,?rightBody -> pagingRight, !bodyActive
5. *mouseDown, leftDown*, idle, ?slider -> !sliderActive, dragging,
        !dragStart(mousePoint), !getMouseFocus

6. *mouseMove, steppingLeft, ~?leftArrow -> !allPassive, idle
7. *mouseMove, steppingRight, ~?rightArrow -> !allPassive, idle
8. *mouseMove, pagingLeft, ~?leftBody -> !allPassive, idle
9. *mouseMove, pagingRight, ~?rightBody -> !allPassive, idle
10. *mouseMove, dragging -> !dragScroll(mousePoint)

11. *mouseUp, leftUp*, steppingLeft -> idle, !allPassive, !stepLeft
12. *mouseUp, leftUp*, steppingRight -> idle, !allPassive, !stepRight
13. *mouseUp, leftUp*, pagingLeft -> idle, !allPassive, !pageLeft
14. *mouseUp, leftUp*, pagingRight -> !allPassive, !pageRight
15. *mouseUp, leftUp*, dragging -> !dragEnd(mousePoint), idle, !releaseMouseFocus

16. *mouseExit steppingLeft -> !allPassive idle
17. *mouseExit steppingRight -> !allPassive idle
18. *mouseExit pagingLeft -> !allPassive idle
19. *mouseExit pagingRight -> !allPassive idle

Figure 11.19 – Reordered scroll bar rules

Grouping Rules into Event Methods

This reordering of the rules places all of the rules for a given input method together and they can be grouped accordingly. From all over the design, all of the rules that might fire on a *mouseDown or *mouseExit event gathered together. We can now start building our event method implementations, as shown in Figure 11.20. Each rule is grouped into an event method by number. It is a waste to recopy the rules because we will be making continuous changes to these methods as our process proceeds. Remember that the names of these methods and their parameters are determined by the toolkit's event-handling protocol. For example, some systems group mouse events into the same input event and distinguish up or down by the button modifiers.

```
public void mouseDown (MouseEvent e)
{   // rules 1, 2, 3, 4, 5
}
public void mouseMove (MouseMoveEvent e)
{   // rules 6, 7, 8, 9, 10
}
public void mouseUp(MouseEvent e)
{   // rules 11, 12, 13, 14, 15
}
public void mouseExit(MouseEvent e)
{   // rules 16, 17, 18, 19
}
```

Figure 11.20 – Event-handler methods with their PPS rules

Translating the Antecedent Tests

Within each method are several rules. The antecedents of the rules must be translated into tests using `if` or `switch` statements. Start first with the `mouseDown()` event. The first condition of every rule is `*leftDown`. this is translated into an `if` test, as shown in Figure 11.21. The code is not drawn from any particular toolkit and would be similar in most toolkits.

```
public void mouseDown(MouseEvent e)
{
    if (e.leftButtonState == BUTTON_DOWN)
    {   // rules 1, 2, 3, 4, 5
    }
}
```

Figure 11.21 – Translating the *leftDown input

All of rules 1–5, are conditioned on the state being `idle`. Translate the `mouseDown()` method as shown in Figure 11.22. Note that just because all rules have the same condition we cannot ignore that condition because there is the implicit alternative to take no action. Note also that by ordering the fields and then reordering the antecedents in the same order, we have simplified our translation process.

```
public void mouseDown(MouseEvent e)
{
  if (e.leftButtonState == BUTTON_DOWN)
  {
    if (state == IDLE)
    {  // rules 1, 2, 3, 4, 5
    }
  }
}
```

Figure 11.22 – Translating the state field

The next field to consider in the `mouseDown()` method is the `essentialGeometry()` query field. Because there are many alternatives in this case, the best option is a `switch` statement, as shown in Figure 11.23.

```
public void mouseDown(MouseEvent e)
{
   if (e.leftButtonState == BUTTON_DOWN)
   {
      if (state == IDLE)
      {
         switch( essentialGeometry(e.mouseX, e.mouseY) )
         {
         case LEFT_ARROW: // rule 1
                 break;
         case RIGHT_ARROW: // rule 2
                 break;
         case LEFT_BODY: // rule 3
                 break;
         case RIGHT_BODY: // rule 4
                 break;
         case SLIDER: // rule 5
                 break;
         }
      }
   }
}
```

Figure 11.23 – Translating the essentialGeometry field

We now have every rule for `mouseDown()` in its own group by itself. Therefore, we know that only that rule can fire and we are free to translate its consequent into action code. In some situations, we might have exhausted all of the antecedent conditions and still have more than one rule in the group. At this point, we check the consequents of each rule to see if they are in conflict. Two consequents are in conflict if they contain two different conditions for the same field. We cannot assert two mutually exclusive conditions. If there is a conflict, there is an error in our specification and we need to figure out what it is and correct it. This is a major reason to pursue a careful step-by-step translation so that we flush out all such problems. If there are no conflicts, we can translate the consequents of the rules in any order we choose.

Our consequent should only contain state conditions or action conditions. State conditions are translated as assignments and action conditions are translated as method calls. This is shown for mouseDown() in Figure 11.24.

```
public void mouseDown(MouseEvent e)
{
    if (e.leftButtonState == BUTTON_DOWN)
    {
        if (state == IDLE)
        {
            switch( essentialGeometry(e.mouseX, e.mouseY) )
            {
            case LEFT_ARROW: // rule 1
                state=STEPPING_LEFT;
                leftArrowActive();
                break;
            case RIGHT_ARROW: // rule 2
                state=STEPPING_RIGHT;
                rightArrowActive();
                break;
            case LEFT_BODY: // rule 3
                state=PAGING_LEFT;
                bodyActive();
                break;
            case RIGHT_BODY: // rule 4
                state=PAGING_RIGHT;
                bodyActive();
                break;
            case SLIDER: // rule 5
                sliderActive();
                state=DRAGGING;
                dragStart(e.mouseX, e.mouseY);
                getMouseFocus();
                break;
            }
        }
    }
}
```

Figure 11.24 – Translating the rule consequents

One case that might arise while translating antecedents is: When within a group of rules, some rules mention a particular field and some rules do not. Using a field in a test is designed to separate groups of rules into subgroups. If a rule does not mention a field being used for a decision, it must be duplicated into all subgroups derived from that field.

SUMMARY

To build the feel of a new widget into the controller, we need a notation that lets us conveniently discuss and analyze our design before translating it into code. Mouse event diagrams are a useful means for working through sequences of events that might occur in particular interactive tasks. They capture not only the event sequence, but also the changes to the visual appearance as events are received. State machines have been used historically to capture valid event sequences, but they have problems in scaling up to realistic problems. Propositional Production Systems provide a convenient notation for capturing and analyzing input event and action handling. There is a straightforward technique for translating a PPS into working controller code.

EXERCISES

1. Given a drawing program such as Visio, Adobe Illustrator, or pictures in Word, create a mouse event diagram for drawing a new line.

2. For the game Minesweeper, create a full mouse event diagram (with pictures for the states) for the task of selecting a cell.

3. Write a PPS for handling cell selection and its appropriate responses in Minesweeper.

4. What is the advantage of the PPS notation over simple state machines?

5. Develop a PPS specification for a text box. Include selections of a single point, a range of characters, normal text keys, as well as Backspace and left/right arrows. Be sure to address essential geometry and semantic actions.

6. Translate the following PPS into appropriate code.

```
input {*md,*mm,*mu}
check { ?hit, ?miss }
status { idle, seeking, working }
control { !append, !delete, !reorder}
active { first, last }

first *md ?hit -> seeking
first *md ?miss -> working
first *mm -> last !reorder
last seeking *mu -> !delete
last idle *mm -> !append first
```

END NOTES

[1] Jacob, Robert J. K. "Using Formal Specifications in the Design of a Human-computer Interface." *Communications of the ACM* v.26 n.4 (April 1983): 259–264.

[2] Newman, W.M. "A System for Interactive Graphical Programming." *Spring Joint Computer Conference*. AFIPS Press (May 1968).

[3] Walker, M. H., and N. Eaton. *Microsoft Office Visio 2003 Inside Out*. Redmond: Microsoft Press, 2003.

[4] Hanau, P. R., and D. R. Lenorovitz. "Prototyping and Simulation Tools for User/Computer Dialogue Design." *Computer Graphics and Interactive Techniques (SIGGRAPH '80)* (July 1980): 271–278.

[5] Olsen, D. R., and E. P. Dempsey. "SYNGRAPH: A Graphical User Interface Generator." *Computer Graphics and Interactive Techniques (SIGGRAPH '83)* (July 1983): 43–50.

[6] Olsen, D. R. "Propositional Production Systems for Dialog Description." *Human Factors in Computing System (CHI '90)* (March 1990): 57–64.

[7] Olsen, D. R., A. F. Monk, and M. B. Curry. "Algorithms for Automatic Dialogue Analysis Using Propositional Production Systems." *Human Computer Interaction* 10 (1995): 39–78.

CHAPTER 12

2D Geometry

Up to this point, this book has treated the view and the controller separately by speaking of "essential geometry" that links the two. The controller calls the view's essential geometry method(s) to determine what object the controller should manipulate and how. For the scroll bar example in Chapter 11, the essential geometry consisted of checking the mouse against five rectangles. In many applications, the essential geometry is not so simple. This chapter works through the necessary mathematics for dealing with geometric questions in most two-dimensional graphics interfaces. Chapter 13 addresses geometric transformations, which are a powerful model for a variety of interactive manipulations. Chapter 14 looks at interactive techniques based on these geometric concepts.

Many user-interface programmers cripple themselves by not understanding computational geometry. As this chapter shows, the mathematics and the code for a wide variety of geometric problems are not very difficult. It is primarily just algebra and trigonometry and only rarely is a little differential calculus required. Avoiding the geometry leads to user interfaces that are all rectangles. It is not that the geometry is hard or that people like rectangles. It is just that programmers avoided learning the necessary mathematics. These next three chapters should provide most of what is necessary for current graphical user interfaces.

To understand the geometry discussions in this book, a basic knowledge of linear algebra is required. The basic concepts are presented in this chapter. More detailed discussions are found in the appendix (A1.1 and A1.2). The appendix also contains code for all of the operations. Following the discussion of basic matrix algebra, this chapter then looks at the kinds of geometric problems that arise in interactive programs. All of the geometry problems in this chapter are solutions of either implicit or parametric equations. The differences between these two are discussed. Lastly, this chapter works through lines, circles, ellipses, rectangles, cubic curves, and polygons, deriving solutions for the geometric problems of interaction.

BASIC MATRIX ALGEBRA

Before addressing the geometry issues, you must review some basic matrix algebra. Those already familiar with linear algebra can skip this section. Most of this book only uses real matrices and the linear algebra discussion is confined to those cases. The most rudimentary structure is the vector, which is a one-dimensional array of real numbers. Vectors are written as column matrices or just as a letter, as in Figure 12.1. For 2D problems, vectors will have two or three elements as needed. On occasion a row vector is needed, which is represented as the transpose of the column vector (A^T).

$$\mathbf{A} = \begin{bmatrix} u \\ v \\ w \end{bmatrix} \quad \mathbf{A}^T = \begin{bmatrix} u & v & w \end{bmatrix}$$

Figure 12.1 – Vectors and their transpose

A vector is a degenerate case of a matrix, which is a two-dimensional array of real numbers. Many matrices are square, but they need not be. A matrix also has a transpose, as shown in Figure 12.2. The transpose is constructed simply by exchanging the rows and columns for each item in the matrix. Any element of a matrix M is referenced as $M_{r,c}$. For example, $M_{1,2}$ from Figure 12.2 would be q. Note that the matrix indices start at 1 rather than the 0 used in most programming languages.

$$M = \begin{bmatrix} p & q \\ r & s \\ t & u \end{bmatrix} \quad M^T = \begin{bmatrix} p & r & t \\ q & s & u \end{bmatrix}$$

Figure 12.2 – Matrices and their transpose

In this chapter, matrices are frequently constructed from row or column vectors. This is true when building the geometry matrix for various spline forms and when constructing representations for simultaneous equations. Figure 12.3 shows matrices constructed from two vectors.

$$A = \begin{bmatrix} c \\ d \\ e \end{bmatrix} \qquad B = \begin{bmatrix} f \\ g \\ h \end{bmatrix} \qquad S = [A\ B] = \begin{bmatrix} c & f \\ d & g \\ e & h \end{bmatrix}$$

$$T = \begin{bmatrix} A^T \\ B^T \end{bmatrix} = \begin{bmatrix} c & d & e \\ f & g & h \end{bmatrix} = S^T$$

Figure 12.3 – Matrices from vectors

If you have an n by m matrix S and an m by p matrix T, you can compute the matrix product of S and T to produce an n by p matrix result. The definition of matrix product is shown in Figure 12.4.

$$S \bullet T = P \text{ such that } P_{r,c} = \sum_{i=1}^{m} S_{r,i} \bullet T_{i,c}$$

$$S \bullet T = \begin{bmatrix} c & f \\ d & g \\ e & h \end{bmatrix} \bullet \begin{bmatrix} j & k & p \\ q & r & u \end{bmatrix} = \begin{bmatrix} (cj+fq) & (ck+fr) & (cp+fu) \\ (dj+gq) & (dk+gr) & (dp+gu) \\ (ej+hq) & (ek+hr) & (ep+hu) \end{bmatrix}$$

Figure 12.4 – Matrix multiply

Figure 12.4 shows the most common matrix multiply for 2D geometry. The more general matrix multiplication algorithm is found in appendix A1.2b. A special case of matrix multiply, called the dot product, is the product of two vectors of equal dimension. The result is a scalar real number, as shown in Figure 12.5.

$$A \bullet B = A^T \bullet B = \begin{bmatrix} c & d & e \end{bmatrix} \bullet \begin{bmatrix} f \\ g \\ h \end{bmatrix} = cf + dg + eh$$

Figure 12.5 – Vector dot product

There is a square (same number of rows and columns) identity matrix I that is all zeros except for ones down the diagonal. The identity matrix is defined as $I \bullet A = A \bullet I$ for any matrix A. Matrix multiplication is associative but not commutative. This is shown in Figure 12.6.

$$A \bullet (B \bullet C) = (A \bullet B) \bullet C$$

however

$$A \bullet B \neq B \bullet A$$

Figure 12.6 – Associative but not commutative

For many square matrices M there exists an inverse matrix M^{-1}, such that $M \cdot M^{-1} = I$ and $M^{-1} \cdot M = I$. There is not always an inverse for a square matrix, but where one exists you can use it to solve many problems. The algorithm for computing the inverse of a matrix is given in appendix A1.2e.

The preceding set of matrix algebra operations is sufficient for most of the geometry to be discussed in the next three chapters. A good grounding in linear algebra beyond what is given here can be very helpful in many applications.

GEOMETRIC PROBLEMS FOR USER-INTERFACE WORK

For a given geometric shape, seven basic problems might arise in user interfaces:

- Scan conversion
- Constructing a shape from a set of points
- Distance between a shape and a point
- Nearest point on a shape
- Intersection of two shapes
- Bounding box
- Inside or outside of a shape

Scan conversion is an algorithm for deciding which pixels on a screen or in an image correspond to some geometrically described shape. It is assumed that your underlying Graphics object has code to solve this problem and it is not discussed further here. The algorithms can be found in most good graphics texts[1].

Your next interactive task is to construct or change a shape by manipulating points. Virtually all 2D interaction consists of manipulating points with a mouse or pen and then inferring the change to some shape from the new point set. The simplest case is manipulating a line by its two end points.

Computing the distance between a shape and a point is critical for selecting geometric objects on the screen. Users do not want to exactly hit a line with the mouse, they want to hit close to it and have the computer figure it out. Computing the distance between a shape and a point is critical to determining when a mouse position is close enough for selection.

In Figure 12.7, a user is trying to draw a line that ends exactly on a circle. The mouse position, however, is not exactly on the circle—it is near the circle. Again, the user does not want to hit the circle exactly because that takes time and distracts from the task. They want the computer to "snap" the mouse point to the nearest point on the circle. For such snapping operations, you need to compute the nearest point on some shape from some mouse or pen point. Frequently, the distance to a shape is determined by computing the nearest point and then computing the distance between the two points.

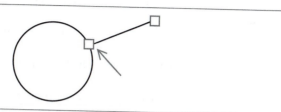

Figure 12.7 – Snapping to the nearest point on a shape

In some situations, you will need to intersect two shapes. Shape intersection allows you to construct a point that meets some criteria rather than forcing the user to interactively approximate such a point.

Selecting shapes can be computationally expensive. This is particularly true when there are thousands of shapes on the screen and you must compare them all with the mouse position. It is sometimes faster to compute a bounding box around the shape and test the bounding box against the mouse point. If the mouse point is outside of the bounding box, you need not spend any more time on that shape. Checking a bounding box against a point involves only four compares, which is very efficient. What you need, then, is an efficient mechanism for computing the bounding box.

When you have closed shapes such as in Figure 12.8, you need to determine whether a mouse point is inside or outside of a shape. Inside/outside is the basic selection mechanism for closed shapes.

Figure 12.8 – Inside or outside of a closed shape

FORMS OF EQUATIONS AND THEIR SOLUTIONS

To represent geometric shapes, this chapter uses two forms of equation: implicit and parametric. The implicit form in 2D is an equation of the form $f(x, y)=0$. An example is the equation of a 2D line, which is $ax+by+c=0$. Implicit equations have the property of dividing the space into two half-spaces $f(x, y) > 0$ and $f(x, y) < 0$. For several shapes, this is useful for separating inside and outside. For some shapes, $f(x, y)$ is the distance between $[x\ y]$ and the shape. Given the implicit equations of two shapes, you have two equations and two unknowns, which can be solved algebraically to produce the intersection point.

Geometric shapes are also represented with parametric equations. In parametric equations, there is an additional parameter t that can be any real number. For example, a line is represented by $x = at + b$ and $y = ct + d$. For a variety of finite shapes, you constrain t to the range 0.0 to 1.0. In 2D, there are two equations $x = g(t)$ and $y = h(t)$. Using these two equations, you can pick any real value of t and get a point $[x\ y]$. Parametric equations can represent shapes for which the implicit form is awkward and they also are the basis for many blending functions.

Parametric equations also have a general form for computing the nearest point on a shape to some point $[x\ y]$. Given two parametric equations and some parameter value t, the distance is $dist(x, y, t) = \sqrt{(g(t) - x)^2 + (h(t) - y)^2}$. Using calculus, you can replace $g(t)$ and $h(t)$ with the parametric equations for the shape, take the first derivative with respect to t, set it equal to zero, and solve. You can simplify matters by throwing away the square root because minimizing the square produces the same answer.

For some geometric forms, the calculus approach is problematic because of the need to solve polynomial equations of degree 4 or higher. In this case, remember that in a user interface, any answer within a pixel or two is good enough because the user cannot do any better on their own. A simple recursive algorithm will produce an answer that is close enough for interactive work. Assuming that the parameter t lies in some range (usually 0.0 to 1.0), you can slice that range into small parts and find the nearest point. You can then take the values of t on either side of that nearest point and create a new much smaller range and try again recursively. The algorithm stops when the end points of the range are less than one pixel apart. This algorithm is shown in Figure 12.9 and works for virtually any parametric shape. This algorithm is guaranteed to converge. However, there is a possibility that it might converge to a local rather than true minimum. However, chopping the shape into 10 regions prevents such problems for all but the most bizarre shapes.

```
public Point nearestPoint(Point p, float lowerT, float upperT)
{
      int N=10; // any integer in this range is fine
      float inc = (upperT-lowerT)/N;
      Point lowP = computePoint(lowerT);
      Point hiP=computePoint(upperT);
      if ( dist(lowP, hiP)<1.0 ) return lowP; // close enough for pixel resolution

      float nearT = lowerT;
      Point nearP=lowP;
      float nearD = dist(nearP,p);

      for (float t=lowerT+inc; t<=upperT; t=t+inc)
      {
            Point tp=computePoint(t);
            if (dist(tp,p)<nearD)
            {
                  nearD=dist(tp,p);
                  nearT=t;
                  nearP=tp;
            }
      }
      float newLow=nearT-inc;
      if (newLow<lowerT) newLow=lowerT;
      float newHi=nearT+inc;
      if (newHi>upperT) newHi=upperT;
      return nearestPoint(p,newLow, newHi);
}
private float dist(Point a, Point b)
{     // returns the square of the distance, which is acceptable for minimization of distance
      float dx=a.x-b.x;
      float dy=a.y-b.y;
      return dx*dx+dy*dy;
}
private Point computePoint(float t)
{
      Point rslt;
      rslt.x=g(t);          // X component of the parametric equation
      rslt.y=h(t);          // Y component of the parametric equation
      return rslt;
}
```

Figure 12.9 – Nearest point on a parametric shape

GEOMETRIC SHAPES

Using the matrix tools, as well as implicit and parametric forms, you can now describe a set of useful geometric shapes and address each of the interactive tasks for each shape. The following shapes are considered:

- Points and vectors
- Lines
- Circles and ellipses
- Cubic curves
- Rectangles
- Polygons
- Curvilinear shapes

Points and Vectors

In some sense, points are trivial in that they have an X and a Y in 2-space. However, to simplify their use with matrix algebra, points are frequently represented in *homogeneous coordinates*, where each point is a triple [x y 1]. The constant 1 proves useful in many equations and in the geometric transformations of Chapter 13. It is also sometimes helpful to represent vectors as well as points. A vector has a direction and a magnitude and is frequently represented by two components [dx dy]. A vector has no position. For example, northwest at 50 kph has a direction (northwest) and a magnitude (50 kph) and is the same no matter where in the city you are driving. It can be represented as [$-50\sqrt{2}, 50\sqrt{2}$]. Vectors are frequently represented in homogeneous coordinates as [x y 0]. The zero multiplier eliminates position information (irrelevant for vectors) in many of your equations. A vector is frequently constructed by the difference between two points. Given two points $A=[$ p q 1 $]$ and $B=[$ r s 1 $]$, their difference $A-B$ would be the vector $V=[$ $p-r$ $q-s$ 0 $]$.

Homogeneous coordinates convert two-dimensional points and vectors into three-dimensional ones by adding a 1 for points (with position) and a 0 for vectors (without position). The homogeneous representation simplifies the use of matrices to perform linear transformations. You see this later in the discussion of cubic curves and in Chapter 13 where geometric transformations are discussed.

Lines

Lines are the next simplest geometric shape. A line is constructed from two end points, as shown in Figure 12.10, which also shows the parametric representation for a line. The bounding box for a line is simply the minimum and maximum X and Y components of the end points.

Figure 12.11 shows the vector algebra equivalent of the parametric representation. Subtracting point A from point B, produces a vector along the line that has the same length as the distance between A and B. The parameter t adjusts how much of that vector is added to point A. If t is 0.0, the result is simply point A. If t is 1.0, the resulting point is point B. Various values of t between 0.0 and 1.0 produce all of the points on the line that lie between point *A* and point *B*. Other values of *t* produce other points on the infinite line. It is a nice property of the parametric form that bounding *t* directly defines a finite line segment.

$$x = A.x + t(B.x - A.x)$$

$$y = A.y + t(B.y - A.y)$$

Figure 12.10 – Parametric equation of a line

$$L = A + t(B - A)$$

Figure 12.11 – Vector equation for a parametric line

Figure 12.12 shows how to solve for the nearest point *L* to some mouse point *M*. You formulate the square of the distance between *L* and *M*, take the first derivative with respect to *t*, set the derivative equal to zero, solve for *t*, and substitute *t* back into the original equation of the line to produce a function for *L*. The equation in Figure 12.12 is cheaper than the iterative solution in Figure 12.9.

$$\text{dist}^2(L,M) = |L - M|^2 = (L.x - M.x)^2 + (L.y - M.y)^2$$

$$\text{dist}^2(L,M) = (A.x + t(B.x - A.x) - M.x)^2 + (A.y + t(B.y - A.y) - M.y)^2$$

$$\frac{d\text{dist}^2}{dt} = 2\,(A.x + t(B.x - A.x) - M.x)(B.x - A.x) + 2(A.y + t(B.y - A.y) - M.y)(B.y - A.y)$$

$$0 = t\left[(B.x - A.x)^2 + (B.y - A.y)^2\right] + (A.x - M.x)(B.x - A.x) + (A.y - M.y)(B.y - A.y)$$

$$t = \frac{-(A.x - M.x)(B.x - A.x) - (A.y - M.y)(B.y - A.y)}{(B.x - A.x)^2 + (B.y - A.y)^2}$$

$$L = A + t(B - A) = A + \left[\frac{-(A.x - M.x)(B.x - A.x) - (A.y - M.y)(B.y - A.y)}{(B.x - A.x)^2 + (B.y - A.y)^2}\right](B - A)$$

Figure 12.12 – Nearest point L, on a parametric line, to point M

Knowing the nearest point *L* to the point *M*, you can compute the distance of *M* to the line.

Given parametric equations for two lines, you can solve for their intersection simply by setting them equal to each other and solving for their two parameters, as shown in Figure 12.13. Note that the vector equation of a line is actually two equations (one for X and one for Y) so there are two equations and two unknowns (s and t) with a simple algebraic solution.

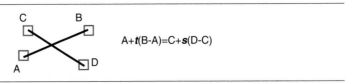

Figure 12.13 – Intersecting two parametric lines

Implicit Form of a Line

The implicit equation for a line is any point $[\,x\ y\,]$ such that $ax+by+c=0$ for three real coefficients a, b, and c. This equation can also be represented in vector form using homogeneous coordinates $[a\ b\ c]\bullet[x\ y\ 1]=0$. The equation of a line in 2D is a special case of the hyperplane equation in N-space. The hyperplane equation has many uses in dividing spaces. A most important property of the hyperplane equation of a 2D line is that the vector $[\,a\ b\,]$ is a normal vector to the line or perpendicular to the line. You can normalize the equation of the line so that the normal vector is a unit vector (length 1). The normalized formulation is shown in Figure 12.14.

$$\frac{a}{\sqrt{a^2+b^2}}x+\frac{b}{\sqrt{a^2+b^2}}y+\frac{c}{\sqrt{a^2+b^2}}=0$$

Figure 12.14 – Normalized implicit equation of a line

Note that there are an infinite number of coefficients a, b, and c that can represent the same line. Multiplying a set of coefficients by any nonzero real number produces another set of coefficients that describes the same line. This is a problem when trying to construct an implicit equation for a line given two points, because you end up with two equations (one for each point) and three unknowns (a, b, and c).

To construct the implicit equation, you first take advantage of the fact that $[\,a\ b\,]$ is known to be a vector perpendicular to the line. You also know that (B-A) is a vector along the line. What is needed is a vector perpendicular to (B-A). For any vector $[\,u\ v\,]$, there is a perpendicular vector $[\,-v\ u\,]$. Using this, you can construct the implicit equation for a line containing two points A and B, as shown in Figure 12.15.

$$a = B.y - A.y$$

$$b = -(B.x - A.x) = A.x - B.x$$

$$ax + by + c = (B.y - A.y)x + (A.x - B.x)y + c = 0$$

$$(B.y - A.y)x + (A.x - B.x)y = -c$$

$$(B.y - A.y)A.x + (A.x - B.x)A.y = -c$$

$$(B.y - A.y)x + (A.x - B.x)y - (B.y - A.y)A.x - (A.x - B.x)A.y = 0$$

Figure 12.15 – Implicit equation of a line

If you have a normalized equation of a line, as shown in Figure 12.14, the normal vector is of length 1. One of the properties of a normalized implicit equation is that it is really a function for the distance from the line. Figure 12.16 shows a function for the distance from a mouse point M to a line.

$$dist(M, a, b, c) = \frac{a}{\sqrt{a^2 + b^2}} M.x + \frac{b}{\sqrt{a^2 + b^2}} M.y + \frac{c}{\sqrt{a^2 + b^2}}$$

Figure 12.16 – Distance from M to the line a,b,c

You can compute a point L on the line that is nearest to mouse point M using similar techniques. You have two unknowns ($L.x$ and $L.y$) and two equations (the equation of the line and the first derivative of the distance). However, there is an advantage to the parametric solution to the nearest point problem. Lines are infinite. The implicit equation gives you a nearest point on the line but does not directly tell you if the point is on the line segment. The parametric solution in Figure 12.12 gives you a value for t that can be used to determine if the nearest point is actually on the line segment that is desired. Therefore, you use the parametric rather than implicit form for nearest point problems.

Circles/Ellipses

Circles and ellipses are discussed together because a circle is just a special case of an ellipse. This section only discusses ellipses whose axes are aligned with the x- and y-axes. This is the most common interactive form for an ellipse. Rotated ellipses that are not axis aligned are dealt with more easily using the scale and rotation transformations described in Chapter 13.

A circle is best described either as a center point with a radius or as a center point and some point on the diameter of the circle, as shown in Figure 12.17. The center/radius form is more comfortable mathematically, but the two-point form is easier to manipulate interactively.

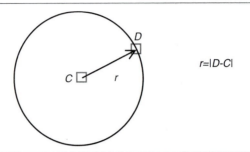

Figure 12.17 – Circle constructed from two points

The implicit equation of a circle is constructed by asserting that the distance between any point [x y] and the center C must be equal to the radius of the circle. The implicit equation is shown in Figure 12.18. Figure 12.18 also shows the squared formulation that asserts the same thing, but removes the redundant square root. The final formulation divides the equation by r^2 to provide an alternative formulation that will be used later with ellipses.

$$\sqrt{(x-C.x)^2+(y-C.y)^2}-r=0$$
$$(x-C.x)^2+(y-C.y)^2-r^2=0$$
$$\left(\frac{x-C.x}{r}\right)^2+\left(\frac{y-C.y}{r}\right)^2-1=0$$

Figure 12.18 – Implicit equation of a circle

Distance from a mouse point M to a circle with an implicit equation can be handled in the same way as lines. The first formulation of the implicit equation is actually a distance from the shape formulation, as shown in Figure 12.19.

$$dist(M,C,r)=\sqrt{(M.x-C.x)^2+(M.y-C.y)^2}-r$$

Figure 12.19 – Distance from a point M to a circle C,r

The nearest point on a circle is only slightly more complicated. As shown in Figure 12.20, the nearest point N is along the vector M - C but is only the distance r away from the center. To find N, compute M - C, normalize it to a unit vector, multiply it by r to make it the right length, and then add it to C to find the point N.

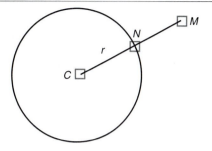

$$N = C + r\left(\frac{M - C}{|M - C|}\right)$$

Figure 12.20 – Nearest point *N* to *M* on circle *C, r*

The circle is your first shape that has an inside and an outside. The implicit form of the circle gives you the inside condition shown in Figure 12.21. If the distance to the diameter is less than zero, the point is inside of the circle.

$$\left(\frac{M.x - C.x}{r}\right)^2 + \left(\frac{M.y - C.y}{r}\right)^2 - 1 \le 0$$

Figure 12.21 – Inside test for a point *M* and a circle *C, r*

Parametric Form

The parametric form of a circle is based on trigonometry. Your parameter *t* is the angle (in radians) around the circle. Using this, you can describe the circle by the equations shown in Figure 12.22.

$$x = r \cdot \cos(2\pi t) + C.x$$

$$y = r \cdot \sin(2\pi t) + C.y$$

Figure 12.22 – Parametric form of a circle

The parameter *t* is multiplied by 2π so that as *t* ranges from 0.0 to 1.0, the angle ranges from 0.0 to 2π radians. This preserves your convention of parameters that range from 0.0 to 1.0.

Finding the nearest point on the circle is best solved by the technique shown in Figure 12.20, which uses neither the implicit nor the parametric form. However, it is frequently useful to determine the parameter *t* at the nearest point *N*. This can be used for interactively defining arc segments. The tangent of the angle is easily computed using the x and y components of M-C. However, if $M.x\text{-}C.x$ is zero, the tangent is infinite. Fortunately, most trigonometry libraries provide an *arctan2* function that computes the arctangent directly without the division. This rather directly gives a value for t, as shown in Figure 12.23.

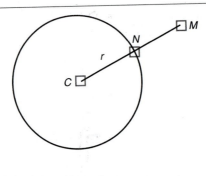

$$\tan(2\pi t)=\frac{M.y-C.y}{M.x-C.x}$$

$$2\pi t = \tan^{-1}\left(\frac{M.y-C.y}{M.x-C.x}\right)$$

$$2\pi t = \arctan2\left(M.y-C.y, M.x-C.x\right)$$

$$t = \frac{\arctan2\left(M.y-C.y, M.x-C.x\right)}{2\pi}$$

Figure 12.23 – Nearest point

The parametric form of a circle is quite convenient for intersections with lines or other circles simply by equating the x and y equations to produce two equations and the two unknown parameters for the two shapes. The parametric form is not useful for determining inside/outside.

Ellipses
As mentioned earlier, a circle is a special case of an ellipse. Most interactive graphics use ellipses that are aligned with the x- and y-axes. Normally, such ellipses are interactively constructed in terms of a bounding rectangle for the ellipse, as shown in Figure 12.24. The user has specified point D (where the mouse went down) and point U (where the mouse went up). From these, compute the center C and the two radii a and b. The bounding box for an ellipse is computed by addition/subtraction or the radii from the center. In many cases, it is the bounding box that is retained as the representation of the ellipse.

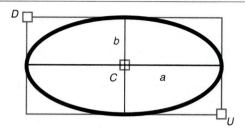

$$C = \frac{D+U}{2} \quad a = \frac{U.x - D.x}{2} \quad b = \frac{U.y - D.y}{2}$$

Figure 12.24 – Coefficients of an ellipse C, a, b from two points U, D

In this formulation, an ellipse is the same as a circle except that the radius in x is different from the radius in y. By taking the implicit equation of a circle found in Figure 12.18, you can derive an implicit equation for the ellipse shown in Figure 12.25. Using a similar technique, convert the parametric equation for a circle from Figure 12.22 into the parametric equations for the ellipse shown in Figure 12.26.

$$\left(\frac{x - C.x}{a}\right)^2 + \left(\frac{y - C.y}{b}\right)^2 - 1 = 0$$

Figure 12.25 – Implicit equation for an axis-aligned ellipse C, a, b

$$x = a \cdot \cos(2\pi t) + C.x$$
$$y = b \cdot \sin(2\pi t) + C.y$$

Figure 12.26 – Parametric equations for an axis-aligned ellipse C, a, b

The simple angle tricks for computing the nearest point and distance to the shape used for circles will not work on ellipses. The best solution is to use the general numeric technique for parametric shapes shown in Figure 12.9. This produces the parameter t of the nearest point from which the nearest point and the closest distance are easily computed. The implicit form of an ellipse does easily produce an inside test, as shown in Figure 12.27.

$$\left(\frac{x - C.x}{a}\right)^2 + \left(\frac{y - C.y}{b}\right)^2 - 1 \leq 0$$

Figure 12.27 – Inside test for an axis-aligned ellipse C, a, b

Arcs

It is common to desire an arc, which is only a portion of a circle or ellipse. Arcs are easily represented using parametric equations and placing bounds on the parameter t. When considering an arc, however, there is the problem of the zero angle, which is the same as the angle 2π. Thus, the point for parameter 0.0 is the same as the point for parameter 1.0. This is a problem when an arc that extends through the zero angle is desired, as shown in Figure 12.28. The points S and E might define two possible arcs U and V. This is easily handled by recognizing that sin and cos are periodic and you can use parameter values larger than 1.0. You can define V using the bounds for t of 0.125 to 0.875. You can cross the zero angle for arc U with the bounds 0.875 to 1.125.

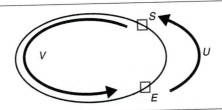

Figure 12.28 – Parameterization of arcs

Rectangles

Rectangles are one of the simplest closed shapes. They are represented by $minx$, $miny$, $maxx$, and $maxy$. Finding the distance to an edge is simply a matter of comparing the corresponding coordinate of the mouse point with the edges and taking the smallest distance. Finding the nearest point is equally trivial. Rectangles are generally constructed aligned with the axes, as with ellipses, and they are created interactively in the same manner as an ellipse, as shown in Figure 12.24. The inside test checks the point for larger than both minimums and less than both maximums.

Curves

The simple shapes of lines, circles, ellipses, and rectangles are generally not interesting enough for many needs. For creating arbitrary curved shapes such as those found in Figure 12.29, you use curves defined by cubic polynomials that are connected together piecewise to form a particular shape.

Figure 12.29 – Curved shapes

A quadratic polynomial (degree 2) can only have one bend. A cubic polynomial (degree 3) can only have up to two bends. However, the shapes in Figure 12.29 have many bends. Using higher-degree polynomials will allow for more bends in the shape. However, higher-degree polynomials are very difficult to manage and specify interactively. Instead, you use many cubic polynomials and stick them together end-to-end to form a more complex shape. The shapes in Figure 12.29 consist of 10–20 cubic curves stitched together.

Quadratic polynomials have the very nice property that many geometric problems can be solved using the quadratic equation. Cubic polynomials do not have this property. However, because shapes are constructed by piecing together many curves, you want a representation that will easily blend between pieces. Figure 12.30 shows two thick curves that you want to blend together smoothly with the thin curve. There is no way to blend these two curves with only one bend (quadratic); however, you can blend any two curves with two bends (cubic), as shown. The cubic curve is the lowest degree polynomial that will smoothly blend two arbitrary curves. That is why the cubic polynomial is the most common representation for curved shapes.

Figure 12.30 – Blending curves with cubic polynomials

Although there are implicit representations for cubic curves, they are not as easy to work with interactively; therefore, you will only concern yourself with parametric representations. The parametric representation of a cubic curve is shown in Figure 12.31 along with its matrix representation.

$$x = at^3 + bt^2 + ct + d$$
$$y = et^3 + ft^2 + gt + h$$

$$\begin{bmatrix} a & b & c & d \\ e & f & g & h \end{bmatrix} \bullet \begin{bmatrix} t^3 \\ t^2 \\ t \\ 1 \end{bmatrix} = \begin{bmatrix} x \\ y \end{bmatrix}$$

$$C \bullet \begin{bmatrix} t^3 \\ t^2 \\ t \\ 1 \end{bmatrix} = \begin{bmatrix} x \\ y \end{bmatrix}$$

Figure 12.31 – Parametric equations for cubic curves

The coefficients a through h are formed into the *coefficient matrix C*. The coefficient matrix forms a compact representation for the cubic curve. As with other shapes, the cubic curve is actually infinite in length. Only the part of the curve where the value of t lies between 0.0 and 1.0 is actually used in practice. Though the coefficient matrix C is a nice mathematical representation, it is an extremely poor interactive representation of a curve. No human can reliably specify a curve by manipulating the coefficients. This chapter discusses three forms of *spline* that accept a set of four control points and produce a coefficient matrix for a cubic curve. Each of these forms has different handles for how users control the shape of a curve.

As a mathematical representation, the cubic polynomial is quite convenient. To find the nearest point on a curve, use the iterative solution shown in Figure 12.9. Because there are up to two inflection points in a cubic curve, there are local minima to the nearest point problem. That is why the algorithm in Figure 12.9 sets the number of slices to higher than two. Using 10 or more initial slices of the parameter range ensures that the true minimum will be found in all but the most violently distorted curves, which very rarely occur in practice. With a nearest point solution, you also can get the distance to the shape. Intersections are also handled using the standard parametric form. However, because cubic polynomials are involved, the solution is generally solved numerically rather than algebraically.

To compute the bounding box of a curve, you must compute the maxima and minima in both X and Y. The first derivative with respect to the parameter t of a cubic polynomial is always a quadratic polynomial that can be solved using the quadratic equation to give zero, one, or two values of t for each of the equations for X and Y. Any solutions for t that are outside the range 0.0 to 1.0 are discarded. The maxima and minima values of t from the X equation are added to the x-coordinates of the curve end points to give two to four values. Take the largest and smallest of these as the right and left edge of your bounding box. Do the same in Y for the top and bottom edges. This gives the smallest bounding box on the curve. For some spline formulations, there are cheaper ways to compute a bounding box, but it is not always the tightest bounding box.

Continuity

Because curved shapes are created by piecing together a series of cubic polynomial curves, ensuring continuity at the joints is very important. In working with cubic curves, you consider C(0), C(1), and C(2) continuity. C(0) continuity between curves S and T holds if the ending point (parameter $s = 1.0$) of S and the starting point (parameter $t = 0.0$) of T are the same point. C(0) means that the zeroth derivatives are the same. This gives a curve with no gap at the joint, but there might be a sharp corner. C(1) continuity holds when the first derivatives of the two curves are the same at the shared point. C(1) gives a curve that is "smooth" across the joint with no sharp corner. In most interactive situations, C(1) continuity is sufficient. However, in some design situations, C(2) continuity is required. C(2) continuity holds if the second derivatives are the same at the joint point. You also assume that C(2) continuity implies C(1) and C(1) implies C(0). There are no formulations of cubic curves that can ensure C(3) or higher; therefore, they are not considered.

Spline Formulations

As mentioned earlier, the coefficient matrix has good mathematical properties but a terrible user interface. What is wanted is a set of control points that can be manipulated interactively by the user and then a mechanism for converting those control points into a coefficient matrix. This can be accomplished by decomposing the coefficient matrix C into two matrices, the *geometry matrix G* and the *spline matrix S*, as shown in Figure 12.32. As shown, the geometry matrix is constructed from four points *P0* through *P3*. These are your control points. The spline matrix S is a constant matrix for each form of spline. Each form of spline uses a different arrangement of the four control points to accomplish different purposes. There are spline formulations that do not use points, but this text will not consider them because they do not map as directly to a user interface. Create a cubic curve, by populating the geometry matrix with the positions of four control points and then multiply by the appropriate spline matrix. This produces the eight coefficients in the coefficient matrix and thus a parametric representation of a cubic curve. The interesting work is in selecting the correct spline formulation for a given problem.

$$G \cdot S = C$$

$$G \cdot S \cdot \begin{bmatrix} t^3 \\ t^2 \\ t \\ 1 \end{bmatrix} = \begin{bmatrix} P0 & P1 & P2 & P3 \end{bmatrix} \cdot S \cdot \begin{bmatrix} t^3 \\ t^2 \\ t \\ 1 \end{bmatrix} = \begin{bmatrix} x \\ y \end{bmatrix}$$

Figure 12.32 – Decomposition of the coefficient matrix of a cubic curve

Bezier

The Bezier spline geometry consists of two end points (*P0, P3*) and two additional interior control points (*P1, P2*), as shown in Figure 12.33. The interior control points are defined such that the vector *P1-P0* is tangent to the curve at *P0* and the vector *P3-P2* is tangent to the curve at *P3*.

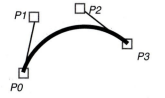

Figure 12.33 – Bezier control points

The Bezier curve has the most flexible interactive controls of the three forms to be discussed. The end points and their tangents are easily manipulated by moving the four control points. Increasing and decreasing the distance between an interior control point and its corresponding end point also controls the shape of the curve. Figure 12.34 shows *P2* at various positions along the same line. This changes the shape of the curve by increasing or decreasing the "influence" of the tangent vector at *P3*.

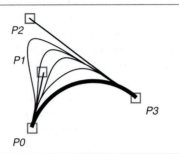

Figure 12.34 – Extending Bezier control points

Two Bezier curves *A* and *B* will have C(0) continuity if *A3* and *B0* are the same point. C(1) continuity is also easy to achieve by C(0) continuity and by *A2*, *A3*, *B0*, and *B1* all being collinear, as shown in Figure 12.35. Many user interfaces will maintain this relationship automatically. When a user moves *A2*, the end points *A3* and *B0* stay in position, but *B1* is automatically repositioned to maintain collinearity and to maintain the distance between *B0* and *B1*. It is only possible for two Bezier curves to have C(2) continuity in very special cases.

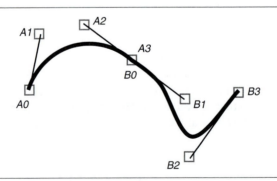

Figure 12.35 – C(0) and C(1) continuity in Bezier curves

Bezier curves also have the convex-hull property, which is that the *convex hull* of the control points is guaranteed to contain all of the points on the curve segment from 0.0 to 1.0. The convex hull of a set of points is the smallest polygon that contains all of the points in the set. Computing the convex hull is not of interest, but taking the maximums and minimums in X and Y of the four control points produces a bounding box that contains the convex hull of the polygon. The convex-hull property produces a cheaply computed bounding box for the curve. Because of their flexibility, many graphics packages use

Bezier control points rather than the coefficient matrix as their representation for drawing cubic curves. The Bezier representation also has a very efficient algorithm for scan-converting cubic curves that avoids repeated evaluation of the cubic polynomial and, thus, increases drawing speed. The constant spline matrix **Bz** is shown in Figure 12.36.

$$[P0 \quad P1 \quad P2 \quad P3] \bullet Bz \bullet \begin{bmatrix} t^3 \\ t^2 \\ t \\ 1 \end{bmatrix} = \begin{bmatrix} x \\ y \end{bmatrix}$$

$$\begin{bmatrix} P0.x & P1.x & P2.x & P3.x \\ P0.y & P1.y & P2.y & P3.y \end{bmatrix} \bullet \begin{bmatrix} -1 & 3 & -3 & 1 \\ 3 & -6 & 3 & 0 \\ -3 & 3 & 0 & 0 \\ 1 & 0 & 0 & 0 \end{bmatrix} \bullet \begin{bmatrix} t^3 \\ t^2 \\ t \\ 1 \end{bmatrix} = \begin{bmatrix} x \\ y \end{bmatrix}$$

Figure 12.36 – The Bezier spline matrix

B-Spline

Your second spline organizes its points in a very different way. The control points are arranged in sequences with the control points of individual curves sharing control points with their neighbors. Curve segments drawn from the sequence of control points automatically have C(0) through C(2) continuity. The B-spline is very useful in this regard because with a minimum of user effort, high continuity of the curve is achieved. Figure 12.37 shows such a curve composed of four curve segments and seven control points. Note, however, that with B-splines, the curves do not necessarily pass through the control points.

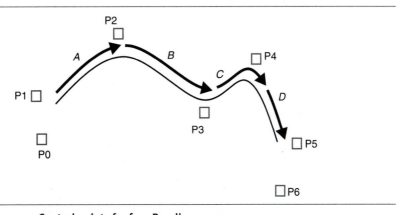

Figure 12.37 – Control points for four B-spline curves

Given a sequence of control points like that shown in Figure 12.37, the geometry for a particular curve is defined relative to its start point at *Pi*. For example, curve *B* is defined relative to *P2* (*i=2*). Note also that there are two control points (*P0* and *P6*) that extend beyond the ends of the curve. These control the direction at the ends of the curve. The reason that the continuity comes automatically is because adjacent curves share control points. In Figure 12.37, the points for *A* are [*P0 P1 P2 P3*] and the points for *B* are [*P1 P2 P3 P4*]. These two adjacent curves have three control points in common. The full geometry matrix for a B-spline curve along with the B-spline matrix **Bs** is shown in Figure 12.38.

$$
\begin{bmatrix} P_{i-1} & P_i & P_{i+1} & P_{i+2} \end{bmatrix} \bullet Bs \bullet \begin{bmatrix} t^3 \\ t^2 \\ t \\ 1 \end{bmatrix} = \begin{bmatrix} x \\ y \end{bmatrix}
$$

$$
\begin{bmatrix} P_{i-1} & P_i & P_{i+1} & P_{i+2} \end{bmatrix} \bullet \frac{1}{6} \begin{bmatrix} -1 & 3 & -3 & 1 \\ 3 & -6 & 0 & 4 \\ -3 & 3 & 3 & 1 \\ 1 & 0 & 0 & 0 \end{bmatrix} \bullet \begin{bmatrix} t^3 \\ t^2 \\ t \\ 1 \end{bmatrix} = \begin{bmatrix} x \\ y \end{bmatrix}
$$

Figure 12.38 – Matrix for B-spline curve

As with the Bezier spline, the B-spline has the convex-hull property. You, thus, can compute a bounding box for a curve segment directly from the control points. It is important to note that this bounding box is not a tight bound. The points of the curve are inside of the box, but the box is generally larger than the curve. All of the other interactive geometry problems are solved by computing the coefficient matrix from the geometry matrix and then solving directly in the parametric form of the curve.

The B-spline uses a sequence of points to produce a sequence of curves that are automatically C(2) continuous. The sequence of points from which overlapping sets of control points are drawn is interactively more efficient than the Bezier because there are fewer controls for the user to manipulate. However, the B-spline does not pass through the control points. This makes the B-spline harder to control for a particular task. It is more difficult to get the curve to go exactly where you want it to go.

Catmull-Rom

The Catmull-Rom spline sets up its geometry matrix in a way similar to the B-spline in that it uses overlapping sets of control points from a sequence of points. The Catmull-Rom spline does pass through every control point. This makes it an excellent choice for interactive curves, as shown in Figure 12.39. The Catmull-Rom is automatically C(0) and C(1) continuous. It does not have the convex-hull property. To find a bounding box of a Catmull-Rom curve segment, you must convert it to one of the other representations. Figure 12.40 shows the matrix **Cr** for the Catmull-Rom spline.

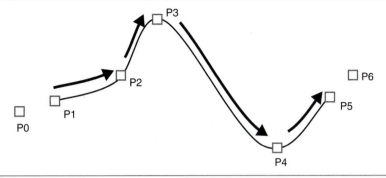

Figure 12.39 – Catmull-Rom control points

$$\begin{bmatrix} P_{i-1} & P_i & P_{i+1} & P_{i+2} \end{bmatrix} \cdot Cr \cdot \begin{bmatrix} t^3 \\ t^2 \\ t \\ 1 \end{bmatrix} = \begin{bmatrix} x \\ y \end{bmatrix}$$

$$\begin{bmatrix} P_{i-1} & P_i & P_{i+1} & P_{i+2} \end{bmatrix} \cdot \frac{1}{2} \begin{bmatrix} -1 & 2 & -1 & 0 \\ 3 & -5 & 0 & 2 \\ -3 & 4 & 1 & 0 \\ 1 & -1 & 0 & 0 \end{bmatrix} \cdot \begin{bmatrix} t^3 \\ t^2 \\ t \\ 1 \end{bmatrix} = \begin{bmatrix} x \\ y \end{bmatrix}$$

Figure 12.40 – Spline matrix for Catmull-Rom spline

Conversion Between Spline Forms

All three of the curve forms that have been discussed are simply different controls for the same formulation of cubic curves. They are different ways of converting control points into polynomial coefficients. In fact, any curve represented by a coefficient matrix can be converted into any of the three geometry matrices. Because all of the forms represent the same polynomials, you can convert the geometry matrix of one form of spline into the geometry matrix of any other. Figure 12.41 shows how to convert a Catmull-Rom G_{cr} into a Bezier G_{bz}. This, for example, would allow us to compute a bounding box for a Catmull-Rom spline or draw a Catmull-Rom spline using a graphics package that only supports Bezier curves.

$$G_{cr} \bullet Cr = C$$

$$G_{bz} \bullet Bz = C$$

$$G_{cr} \bullet Cr = G_{bz} \bullet Bz$$

$$G_{cr} \bullet Cr \bullet Bz^{-1} = G_{bz} \bullet Bz \bullet Bz^{-1}$$

$$G_{cr} \bullet Cr \bullet Bz^{-1} = G_{bz}$$

Figure 12.41 – Converting Catmull-Rom to Bezier

Because both splines compute the same coefficient matrix, set them equal to each other, multiply both sides by the inverse of the Bezier matrix Bz and you get a function that will compute Bezier geometry from Catmull-Rom geometry. A similar technique will convert any curve into any other.

It is very important to note that the continuity properties are not changed by these conversions. Converting Catmull-Rom to B-spline will not introduce C(2) continuity. The curve itself does not change. Given two adjoining Catmull-Rom splines A and B, you can convert them into two B-splines A' and B'. However, the splines A' and B' do not share any control points; therefore, there are no additional continuity guarantees. Constructing two curves using overlapping control points is not the same as constructing them from other representations.

Polygons

One of the most important closed shapes is the polygon. Polygons are represented by a sequence of vertex points and it is assumed that adjacent vertex points are connected by a straight line. Nearest point and distance to the polygon border problems are solved using each of the line segments and taking the smallest distance. The bounding box is defined by the maximums and minimums of the vertex points in X and Y. The most challenging problem is to determine whether a point is inside or outside of the polygon. The approach, as shown in Figure 12.42, is to intersect a horizontal line that passes through the point M with all of the edges of the polygon. This produces a set of intersection points. Count the number of intersection points whose x-coordinate is less than $M.x$. If the number of points to the left (less than) is odd, the point is inside the polygon. If it is even, M is outside. The idea is that if you start from outside of the polygon, each time you cross a boundary, you transition from outside to inside, inside to outside, and so on.

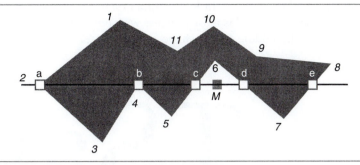

Figure 12.42 – Inside/outside test on a polygon

Figure 12.42 shows an odd number of intersection points (*a*, *b*, and *c*) to the left of *M*. An odd number indicates that *M* should be inside of the polygon when obviously it is outside. The problem is that points *a* and *b* actually represent two intersection points each because they are each on two line segments (1-2,2-3 and 3-4,4-5). However, they each represent a different case. In the case of point *a*, the horizontal line entered the shape and, thus, had only one inside/outside transition. At point *b*, the horizontal line transitions outside and then right back inside and, thus, should be treated as two transitions.

A problem occurs when the horizontal line passes through one of the vertices of the polygon. These vertices fall into two cases. In the first case, the sign of the change in Y is the same for both line segments on the vertex. For example, the sign of change in Y for 1-2 is negative and for 2-3 it is also negative. Therefore, this vertex should only be counted once. The same is true for vertex 9, where the change in Y for 8-9 is positive and for 9-10 is positive. The other case is where the change in Y reverses at the vertex. Vertex 4, has a positive change in Y for 3-4 and a negative change for 4-5. In this case, the vertex should be counted twice. For vertex 7, the change in Y reverses from negative (6-7) to positive (7-8). If the horizontal line passes through vertex 7, count it twice.

With careful checking of the vertices, the inside/outside test is an easy algorithm for determining whether a polygon has been selected. It is almost always more efficient to first check to see if point *M* is inside of the bounding box of the polygon. For most polygons on the screen, the point *M* is outside and the bounding box check can avoid the more costly analysis of the intersection points.

Curvilinear Enclosed Shapes

Polygons are somewhat restrictive in the kinds of shapes that they can represent. For most graphics packages, the most general shape is the curvilinear shape. Essentially, it is like a polygon except that the edges need not be only lines, they can be any cubic polynomial. Note that lines are degenerate cubic polynomials with zero coefficients for t^3 and t^2. Curvilinear shapes form the basis for most typeface systems. Looking closely at the letter "T" in Figure 12.43, you see 12 straight lines filled in by four curves. The letter "S" is mostly curves with only six straight lines. The letter "a" has a hole in the middle of the shape and the letter "i" is composed of two separate shapes.

TSai

Figure 12.43 – Curvilinear shapes for Times-Roman letters

Curvilinear shapes are treated in much the same as polygons. For nearest point, each edge (curved or linear) is considered separately and the closest is the result. Selection, however, can be a problem because a given cubic curve can have up to two inflection points that might or might not create local minima/maxima in Y. Figure 12.44 shows the issues that must be addressed in adapting the inside/outside test to shapes with cubic curved edges. The blob shape is defined by control points 1 through 10 shown as black squares.

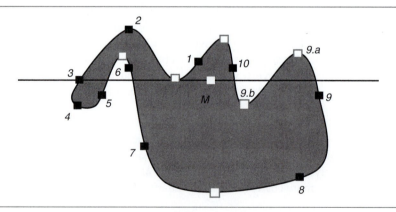

Figure 12.44 – Inside/outside on curved shapes

The same problems occur in curved shapes as in polygons when the horizontal test line goes through the end points of two adjoining curves (vertex 3). You can solve those problems using the same techniques as you used with polygons. The cubic curves offer two additional problems not found in polygons. The first is that a cubic curve might intersect a line up to three times (curve 9-10). The second is that local minima and maxima might intersect the line (curve 1-2).

Your first step is to break each curved edge that actually crosses the line at its minima and maxima. Finding the minima and maxima of the curve relative to Y is easy. Take the first derivative of the Y component of the curve equation, set it equal to zero, and apply the quadratic equation. This produces up to two values of the parameter t where maxima or minima are located. Discard any solutions that do not lie between 0.0 and 1.0 because they are outside of your curve segment. These maxima and minima are shown by the hollow squares in Figure 12.44. You now have subsegments of curves that are monotonic in Y. Being monotonic in Y, there is at most one intersection with the line in each subsegment. Consider, for example, the subsegments (9-9.a, 9.a-9.b, and 9.b-10). A subsegment of a curve is defined by a range of t that is smaller than 0.0 to 1.0.

For each curve or subsegment of a curve, you can now test to see if the end points lie on opposite sides of your test line. If both end points of a curve segment lie on the same side of your line, there can be no intersection of that curve segment with the line. You can do this test because you have placed segment end points at all the maxima and minima so there are no intermediate intersections. For segments that do straddle the test line, you can iteratively solve for the value of t whose Y component is equal to $M.y$. This algorithm is similar to that shown in Figure 12.9. If the line passes through a maxima or minima, always count it twice as with similar cases for polygons. You now can count the intersection points to the left of $M.x$ to determine odd/even for inside/outside.

SUMMARY

You now have a set of primitive shapes that you can use to draw a variety of model presentations. You also have a set of mathematical tools for manipulating and selecting those shapes.

EXERCISES

1. If most of your shapes are not rectangular, why is computing the bounding box important? Based on this answer, why is a loose bounding box usually just as good?

2. Describe how to use a parametric representation of a shape to produce answers that are good enough for interactive use.

3. What is the difference between a point and a geometric vector?

4. How does normalizing the implicit equation of a line help us to find the distance between some point and that line?

5. Given the implicit equation of a line, how do you find a vector perpendicular to that line?

6.   Write an interactive program that will place a set of lines, ellipses, and cubic curves on the screen. Use the geometry in this chapter to report when a mouse click is within three pixels of one of the shapes.

7.   Why do you use arctan2 in computing angles rather than arctangent?

8.   Why are cubic polynomials used rather than the simpler quadratic polynomials when creating curves?

9.   Why is C(1) continuity easier to achieve for Catmull-Rom and B-spline than it is for Bezier curves?

10.   Why do you care about the convex-hull property when interactively working with curves?

11.   When performing the inside/outside test on a shape with curved edges, why do you need to solve for the minimum and maximum points?

END NOTE

[1] Foley, J.S., A. van Dam, S. K. Feiner, and J. F. Hughes. *Computer Graphics: Principles and Practice*. New York: Addison-Wesley, 1995.

CHAPTER 13

Geometric Transformations

Chapter 12 discussed a variety of geometric shapes. In many instances, such shapes by themselves are not sufficient. You might want to move them around, make them bigger or smaller, rotate them, flip them different ways, display them on the screen, and assemble them into more complex shapes.

Many applications on current workstations are implemented using rectangles aligned with the x- and y-axes. This has been the convention because the original computers were not powerful enough nor the graphics cards crisp enough to do anything else. That has changed and continues to change. Displays on a desk or tabletop frequently allow windows to be rotated to any orientation acceptable to the computer. New interactive techniques that animate objects as they move across the screen are not axis aligned. In addition, in many applications, objects must change shape, position, and orientation. This chapter describes the basic matrix operations that allow you to do all of these things using a few simple concepts combined in a variety of ways. Only the mathematical notation is used in the body of the chapter. Implementations for all of these operations can be found in Appendix A1.2.

Most of what you want to do with your shapes can be composed of three basic transforms: translate, scale, and rotate. These three and all of their possible combinations are part of a general class of linear transforms.

Translate

Translation is the transform that moves shapes around. A translation has two parameters D_x and D_y, which are the distance to move the object in X and Y respectively. The equations for this transform are shown in Figure 13.1.

$$trans(D_x, D_y)$$

$$X' = X + D_x$$
$$Y' = Y + D_y$$

Figure 13.1 – Translation equations

Scale

Scaling is the transformation that changes the size of shapes. Scaling has two parameters S_x and S_y. These are scale factors that are multiplied times X and Y respectively to change size. The scaling equations are shown in Figure 13.2.

$$scale(S_x, S_y)$$

$$X' = X \cdot S_x$$
$$Y' = Y \cdot S_y$$

Figure 13.2 – Scaling equations

Scale factors that are greater than 1.0 make an object larger. Scale factors between 0.0 and 1.0 make an object smaller. Negative scale factors reflect an object across the axes. Figure 13.3 shows examples that transform the rectangles on the left into the rectangles on the right.

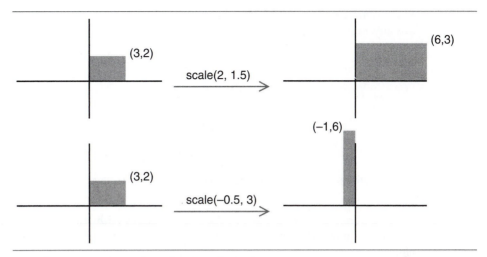

Figure 13.3 – Sample scaling transformations

All scaling transformations are relative to the origin. That is, only the origin point stays fixed. Any points that are not at the origin will move as a result of scaling. Figure 13.4 shows what happens to shapes not at the origin when scaling is applied. The object got twice as big, but also moved twice as far away from the origin.

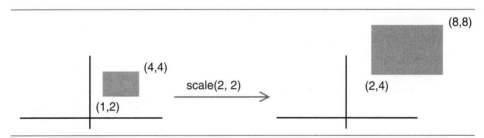

Figure 13.4 – Scaling not at the origin

A common mistake when using the scaling transformation occurs when you do not want the size to change, but the scaling transformation has been programmed as part of the transformation sequence. The temptation is to use *scale(0,0)* for a null transformation. Unfortunately, this transforms the entire shape into a single point at the origin. In most applications, this appears as a single black pixel in the upper-left corner of the window. The correct scaling when no scaling is desired is *scale(1,1)*.

Rotate
The final transformation is rotation. Rotation is defined by a counterclockwise angle from the positive x-axis. This is generally in radians. The rotation equations are shown in Figure 13.5. Sometimes, rotation is specified not as an angle, but as the sine and cosine of the angle ($rot(sin_A, cos_A)$). In many interactive problems, you can more

easily compute the sine and cosine than you can the angle and the equations do not actually need the angle.

$$rot(A)$$

$$X' = \cos(A)X - \sin(A)Y$$
$$Y' = \sin(A)X + \cos(A)Y$$

Figure 13.5 – Rotation equations

Rotation is always centered at the origin. Just as with scaling, objects not at the origin will move when rotation is applied. This is shown in the sample rotations in Figure 13.6.

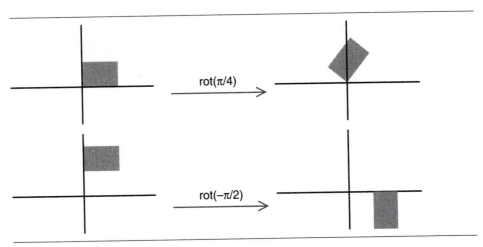

Figure 13.6 – Sample rotations

Matrix Transformations

The three basic transforms by themselves are not very interesting. You also need to build up complex transforms when you put many shapes together to form complex objects. To accommodate this, you need a more flexible model of transformations than the equations themselves. All of the three basic transformations are special cases of the more general linear transformations shown in Figure 13.7. Using homogeneous coordinates for the points, Figure 13.8 represents all of the transformations as a matrix.

$$X' = aX + bY + c$$
$$Y' = dX + eY + f$$

$$trans(D_x, D_y) \rightarrow \begin{array}{l} X' = 1X + 0Y + D_x \\ Y' = 0X + 1Y + D_y \end{array}$$

$$scale(S_x, S_y) \rightarrow \begin{array}{l} X' = S_x X + 0Y + 0 \\ Y' = 0X + S_y Y + 0 \end{array}$$

$$rot(A) \rightarrow \begin{array}{l} X' = \cos(A)X - \sin(A)Y + 0 \\ Y' = \sin(A)X + \cos(A)Y + 0 \end{array}$$

Figure 13.7 – General linear transform

$$\begin{array}{l} X' = aX + bY + c \\ Y' = dX + eY + f \end{array} \Rightarrow \begin{bmatrix} X' \\ Y' \\ 1 \end{bmatrix} = \begin{bmatrix} a & b & c \\ d & e & f \\ 0 & 0 & 1 \end{bmatrix} \cdot \begin{bmatrix} X \\ Y \\ 1 \end{bmatrix}$$

Figure 13.8 – Matrix form for homogeneous linear transforms

Using the matrix form of the general linear transform, you can produce a matrix representation for each of the three primitive transformations. The matrix forms for each transformation are shown in Figure 13.9.

$$trans(D_x, D_y) = \begin{bmatrix} 1 & 0 & D_x \\ 0 & 1 & D_y \\ 0 & 0 & 1 \end{bmatrix}$$

$$scale(S_x, S_y) = \begin{bmatrix} S_x & 0 & 0 \\ 0 & S_y & 0 \\ 0 & 0 & 1 \end{bmatrix}$$

$$rot(A) = \begin{bmatrix} \cos(A) & -\sin(A) & 0 \\ \sin(A) & \cos(A) & 0 \\ 0 & 0 & 1 \end{bmatrix}$$

Figure 13.9 – Matrix representations for translate, scale, rotate

Careful examination of these matrices shows that the third column of the matrix contains only the translation component of the transformation. For scale and rotate, these coefficients are zeros. The 1 as the third coordinate of a homogeneous point is multiplied by these, which adds in the translation constants. Remember that vectors have direction (rotation) and magnitude (scale) but no position (translation). This is the reason that we represent vectors as [X Y 0]. The zero homogeneous coordinate discards the translation information (multiply by zero) while retaining changes in orientation and magnitude.

Concatenation

The real value of the matrix representation comes in the ability to concatenate together a sequence of transformations. Suppose that you want to scale an object to a new size, rotate the object, and then move it to some location. The steps for this are shown in Figure 13.10. These steps can be collected together into a single expression. Using the associative property of matrix multiplication, you can replace the three steps by multiplying together all of the matrices to produce a single transformation matrix. Applying this single matrix to all of the points in an object is the same as applying each of the individual matrices in turn. This is much more efficient and much easier than working out the algebra of all of the steps by hand.

Any sequence of matrix transformations can be collapsed into a single matrix using matrix multiplication. However, the order is important. Matrix multiply is associative but not commutative. Consider the shape in Figure 13.11. In the first case, it is scaled and then rotated, as shown in the top pair. In the second case, it is rotated and then scaled. The results are not at all the same. Note also that the order of transformations is read from right to left, not from left to right. In Figure 13.10, the shape is scaled, rotated, and then translated. The algorithm for matrix multiply is given in Appendix A1.2b.

This book does not frequently use the matrices in discussions of transformations. Instead, this chapter uses a sequence of transformation functions, such as *trans*(14,16) • *rotate*(–0.3) • *scale*(0.1,2.4). It is important to remember how multiplication of a transformation times a point actually works. Because of the matrix algebra, transformation sequences are read in right-to-left rather than left-to-right order. In the example, the object will first be scaled, then rotated, then translated.

$$\begin{bmatrix} S_x & 0 & 0 \\ 0 & S_y & 0 \\ 0 & 0 & 1 \end{bmatrix} \bullet \begin{bmatrix} X \\ Y \\ 1 \end{bmatrix} = \begin{bmatrix} X_1 \\ Y_1 \\ 1 \end{bmatrix}$$

$$\begin{bmatrix} \cos(A) & -\sin(A) & 0 \\ \sin(A) & \cos(A) & 0 \\ 0 & 0 & 1 \end{bmatrix} \bullet \begin{bmatrix} X_1 \\ Y_1 \\ 1 \end{bmatrix} = \begin{bmatrix} X_2 \\ Y_2 \\ 1 \end{bmatrix}$$

$$\begin{bmatrix} 1 & 0 & D_x \\ 0 & 1 & D_y \\ 0 & 0 & 1 \end{bmatrix} \bullet \begin{bmatrix} X_2 \\ Y_2 \\ 1 \end{bmatrix} = \begin{bmatrix} X_{final} \\ Y_{final} \\ 1 \end{bmatrix}$$

$$trans(D_x, D_y) \bullet \left(rot(A) \bullet \left(scale\left(S_x, S_y\right) \bullet \begin{bmatrix} X \\ Y \\ 1 \end{bmatrix} \right) \right) = \begin{bmatrix} X_{final} \\ Y_{final} \\ 1 \end{bmatrix}$$

$$\left(trans(D_x, D_y) \bullet rot(A) \bullet scale(S_x, S_y) \right) \bullet \begin{bmatrix} X \\ Y \\ 1 \end{bmatrix} = \begin{bmatrix} X_{final} \\ Y_{final} \\ 1 \end{bmatrix}$$

$$M \bullet \begin{bmatrix} X \\ Y \\ 1 \end{bmatrix} = \begin{bmatrix} X_{final} \\ Y_{final} \\ 1 \end{bmatrix}$$

Figure 13.10 – Concatenation of matrix transformations

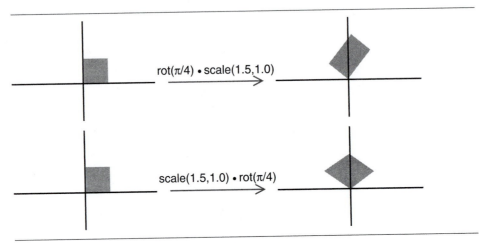

$$rot(\pi/4) \bullet scale(1.5, 1.0)$$

$$scale(1.5, 1.0) \bullet rot(\pi/4)$$

Figure 13.11 – Importance of transformation order

Inverse Matrices

It is very important in interactive applications to be able to compute an inverse of a transformation or sequence of transformations. Mapping an object onto a display might involve transformation M. Mapping a mouse point that occurs in display coordinates back to the object requires the transformation M^{-1}.

The inverses of the basic three transformations are quite straightforward and are shown in Figure 13.12. The inverse of any sequence of transformations is the individual inverses in the opposite order. Sometimes, however, you just have the matrix M and want the inverse. The general matrix inverse algorithm is given in Appendix A1.2e. Only square matrices have inverses and not all square matrices have an inverse. However, any matrix built up from the basic three will have an inverse as long as scaling by zero is not one of the transformations.

$$trans(D_x, D_y)^{-1} = trans(-D_x, -D_y)$$

$$scale(S_x, S_y)^{-1} = scale\left(\frac{1}{S_x}, \frac{1}{S_y}\right)$$

$$rot(A)^{-1} = rot(-A)$$

$$(A \bullet B \bullet C)^{-1} = C^{-1} \bullet B^{-1} \bullet A^{-1}$$

Figure 13.12 – Inverses of transformations

Transformation about an Arbitrary Point

One of the problems discussed earlier with scaling and rotation transformations is that they always occur about the origin. This is frequently not very helpful. For example, suppose you have a picture of a car and want to rotate the wheels; you want them to rotate about their axles and not about the origin, which would move them completely away from the car.

With concatenation of transformations and inverses of transformations, you can now operate about any point $[C_x,C_y]$. The technique is to move the point to the origin, do the rotation or scaling, and then put it back. Figure 13.13 shows how to rotate about a point. Remember that the transformation sequence reads from right to left. Translating by $-C_x,-C_y$ moves that point to the origin. You then do the rotate and then translate the origin back to $[C_x,C_y]$. The same can be done for scaling. This is a special case of a general geometric technique that is heavily used in Chapter 14. You transform the problem to an easier problem (in this case, at the origin), do the operation that you need to do, and then using the inverse transformations, you put the problem back in its original state.

$$trans(C_x,C_y) \bullet rot(A) \bullet trans(-C_x,-C_y) \bullet \begin{bmatrix} X \\ Y \\ 1 \end{bmatrix}$$

Figure 13.13 – Rotation about a point $[C_x,C_y]$

Generalized Three-Point Transform

In some cases, you will have three points, A, B, and C, that you want to transform to three new points, A', B', and C'. If points A, B, and C are not collinear, you can compute a general transformation matrix M that will accomplish the goal. Using each of the points as columns in a matrix, you can formulate the problem as shown at the top of Figure 13.14. If you call the matrix of points A, B, and C the *From* matrix and call the matrix of A', B', and C' the *To* matrix, you can easily compute the desired matrix M as shown. You might use this as a general transformation technique where three points on an object are dragged to three new positions and an appropriate transform is needed.

$$M \bullet [A\ B\ C] = [A'\ B'\ C']$$
$$M \bullet From = To$$
$$M \bullet From \bullet From^{-1} = To \bullet From^{-1}$$
$$M \bullet To = From^{-1}$$

Figure 13.14 – General transform from three points to three new points

Shape Transforms

Up to this point, this chapter has discussed transforming vectors and points. However, what you really want is to transform shapes. Before addressing each of the shapes, you need to consider the concept of closure of a shape representation under a particular transformation. A shape representation is closed under a transformation if the transformation yields a shape with the same type of representation. This is best explained by examples.

Because all of your transformations are linear, the set of lines is closed under any linear transformation. If you take the end points of a line segment and transform them with any linear transformation, the resulting end points define a line segment that contains the transformation of any of the original points on the line segment. Thus, the set of line shapes is closed under any linear transformation.

Circles are closed for translation. Moving any circle to another place produces a circle. Circles are closed under rotation. Rotate a circle and you still have a circle. Circles are closed under uniform scaling ($S_x = S_y$). The result is a circle of a different size. Circles are not closed under nonuniform scaling; the result is an ellipse. Fortunately, the result is an axis-aligned ellipse, which is why axis-aligned ellipses are used rather than circles as the basic shape primitive. However, axis-aligned ellipses are not closed under rotation. Rotating an ellipse off of the axes produces an ellipse that cannot be represented simply by its bounding rectangle.

Axis-aligned rectangles of the kind that are commonly used are not closed under rotation. The Xmax, Xmin, Ymax, and Ymin representation of a rectangle cannot be rotated without producing a different shape representation. When a rectangle is rotated to tip up on its corner, the values Xmax, Xmin, Ymax, and Ymin no longer represent the shape correctly. However, if rotation is excluded, transforming the upper-left and lower-right points of a rectangle produce a new correct rectangle. For rectangles, you can solve this problem by using the corner points as your representation. In reality, this means representing your rectangle as a polygon. Transforming the points of a polygon produces a new and correct polygon.

Cubic curves have very nice transformation properties. Consider a curve with coefficient matrix C that is to be transformed by matrix M. You want a new curve such that each point on the original curve will be transformed by M. This is shown in Figure 13.15. To transform the curve, you need only multiply the coefficient matrix by M to produce a new coefficient matrix. By the same reasoning, you can transform any spline to a new spline of the same type by multiplying the geometry matrix by M. The set of cubic curves is closed under any linear transform.

A polygon consists of a list of vertices connected by straight lines. By transforming the vertices, you transform the polygon and all of its edges. If you want to transform a rectangle, convert it to a four-vertex polygon and transform. You lose the efficiency properties of rectangles but the shape is preserved. Because curvilinear shapes consist of vertices and control points connected by lines or cubic curves, you simply transform the vertices and control points to produce a new shape. With the exception of rectangles and ellipses, you can transform any shape by simply transforming its control points. Many systems, such as PostScript and PDF, model virtually all shapes using piecewise cubic curves because they are closed under all linear transforms and form a uniform model of virtually anything.

$$C \cdot \begin{bmatrix} t^3 \\ t^2 \\ t \\ 1 \end{bmatrix} = \begin{bmatrix} X \\ Y \\ 1 \end{bmatrix}$$

$$(M \cdot C) \cdot \begin{bmatrix} t^3 \\ t^2 \\ t \\ 1 \end{bmatrix} = M \cdot \begin{bmatrix} X \\ Y \\ 1 \end{bmatrix}$$

$$C_{new} \cdot \begin{bmatrix} t^3 \\ t^2 \\ t \\ 1 \end{bmatrix} = M \cdot \begin{bmatrix} X \\ Y \\ 1 \end{bmatrix}$$

Figure 13.15 – Transforming a cubic curve

Viewing Transforms

You now have mechanisms for transforming shapes in arbitrary ways by composing sequences of linear transformations. You now need to deal with the problems of coordinate systems. In an interactive application, many possible coordinate systems are generally related to each other by linear transformations. For an interactive program to work correctly, you must understand the coordinate system in which your points are defined and make certain that you have all points in the same coordinate system when you are working on them. Figure 13.16 shows a diagram of most of the coordinate systems found in interactive applications.

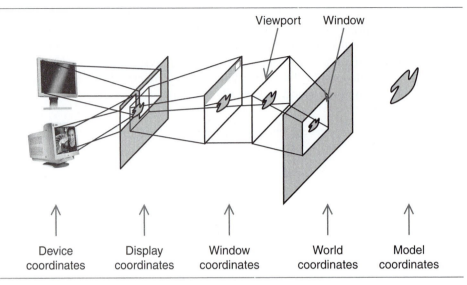

Viewport   Window

Device   Display   Window   World   Model
coordinates   coordinates   coordinates   coordinates   coordinates

Figure 13.16 – Coordinate systems

Model coordinates are the coordinates in which objects are defined. These can be anything. They can be parsecs, nanometers, rods, or angstroms. It is whatever is appropriate for the model. There is a *modeling transformation* that will transform points from model coordinates to *world coordinates*. There might be many model objects in an application and, thus, many modeling transformations to bring each model into world coordinates. The modeling transformation can be built up hierarchically with models being transformed into other models and so on until they are transformed to world coordinates. Hierarchic model transforms are discussed in the next section.

World coordinates are a single 2D surface onto which all objects to be presented are transformed. Onto this surface, you can place a rectangle called the *window*. This is a different window from the one that is normally seen on the screen. The world of computer graphics evolved somewhat differently from graphical user interfaces and they use the same words for different concepts. The purpose of the window is to select the region of the world that is to be displayed. The window is defined in world coordinates. World coordinates are defined in any units suitable to the application.

On the screen window (the one familiar to interactive users) is another rectangle called the *viewport*. The viewport shows where the selected portion of the world is to be displayed. The viewport also specifies the clipping of the world objects to be drawn. The viewport is defined in screen *window coordinates*. The transformation from the world window to the viewport is called the *viewing transformation*. Window coordinates are defined in pixels.

From the window coordinates, where the viewport is defined, there is a transformation into *display coordinates*. Display coordinates are a uniform coordinate system for all of the display devices connected to a workstation. In your example, two screens have been mapped into display coordinates side by side. Screen window positions are defined in display coordinates. This allows the user to move windows anywhere without regard to the boundaries between various display devices. Display coordinates are always in pixels.

From display coordinates, there is a transformation to actual *device coordinates*. Device coordinates are always in pixels. The mapping from display coordinates to device coordinates is generally hidden from the programmer. Most software defines itself in terms of display coordinates but at times more information is needed. For example, it is useful to know where display device boundaries are located in display coordinates. It is not very user-friendly to pop up a menu right across the boundary between two display devices. Because displays are frequently not the same size, there are often undisplayable gaps in display coordinates. Popping up a window into one of these undisplayable gaps is not good form.

On occasion when printing or when doing very precise work on a screen, you might need to work in *physical coordinates*. Physical coordinates are the actual physicals sizes of displayed or printed objects. You might, for example, need a shape that is actually 1.2 inches high. This is independent of the number of pixels required to display the shape. When displaying on the screen, you generally do not have access to the transform between physical coordinates and device coordinates. However, with most printers, you specify drawing in physical coordinates and rely upon the printer to perform the appropriate transformation.

When you are interacting, you need to know exactly what coordinates you are working in. Generally, mouse points are received in window coordinates. The objects you are manipulating are in model coordinates. Before you can do any manipulation, you must have the mouse points and the object points together in the same coordinate system. Sometimes when moving windows around or dragging between windows, you will work in display coordinates because you are outside of or independent of a particular screen window. It is very important to understand the coordinates that you are working in and the coordinates of all parts of the interaction.

Because all of these transformations are linear transformations, you can represent them in a matrix. You can compute a single matrix that transforms points in model coordinates all the way to device coordinates in a single matrix multiply.

Windowing

The viewing transformation, as discussed earlier, maps a portion of world coordinates into a viewport in screen window coordinates. This can be expressed in a variety of ways. This section looks at the two most popular. The first technique is windowing. This is where a rectangular window in world coordinates is mapped to a rectangular viewport in screen window coordinates. The specification of the problem is shown in Figure 13.17. This would occur when a drawing or document is too large to fit on the screen. The window is the section of the drawing or document to be displayed. The viewport is the section of the windowing system's window (confusing conflict of terms) where the information is to appear.

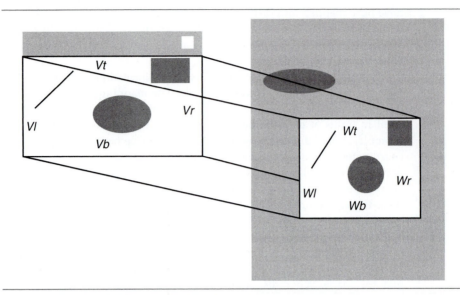

Figure 13.17 – Window viewing transformation

Using this representation of the transformation, the programmer can pan across the world by moving the window. Moving the window to the left causes the objects in the viewport to scroll right. Enlarging the window is the same as zooming out, and shrinking the window zooms in. As shown in Figure 13.17, the window and the viewport need not have the same aspect ratio. This can produce various scaling effects.

Using the viewport and window parameters shown in Figure 13.17, you can develop the transformation sequence shown in Figure 13.18. This first moves the upper-left corner of the window to the origin. It then scales the window size to the viewport size and then translates the origin to the upper-left corner of the viewport. Note that you could have used any point in the window (center, lower-left, and so on) as long as you use the same point on the viewport.

$$trans(Vl, Vt) \bullet scale\left(\frac{Vr-Vl}{Wr-Wl}, \frac{Vb-Vt}{Wb-Wt}\right) \bullet trans(-Wl, -Wt) \bullet \begin{bmatrix} X_{window} \\ Y_{window} \\ 1 \end{bmatrix} = \begin{bmatrix} X_{viewport} \\ Y_{viewport} \\ 1 \end{bmatrix}$$

Figure 13.18 – Matrix for windowing transform

If there is a modeling transform M that transforms an object from model coordinates to world coordinates, you can include it, as shown in Figure 13.19. Using the associative property, you can multiply the modeling transformation and the viewing transformation together into one transformation matrix.

$$M \cdot \begin{bmatrix} X_{model} \\ Y_{model} \\ 1 \end{bmatrix} = \begin{bmatrix} X_{world} \\ Y_{world} \\ 1 \end{bmatrix}$$

$$trans(Vl, Vt) \cdot scale\left(\frac{Vr - Vl}{Wr - Wl}, \frac{Vb - Vt}{Wb - Wt}\right) \cdot trans(-Wl, -Wt) \cdot M \cdot \begin{bmatrix} X_{model} \\ Y_{model} \\ 1 \end{bmatrix} = \begin{bmatrix} X_{viewport} \\ Y_{viewport} \\ 1 \end{bmatrix}$$

Figure 13.19 – Combining modeling and viewing

Point and Zoom

One of the problems with the windowing transformation is that a change of aspect ratio is possible in the scaling. This is a flexible model but it provides the user with one more control than is normally desired. An alternative model for the viewing transformation is "point and zoom." The user specifies a point in the world (WC) that should map to the center of the viewport (VC) and a zoom or magnification factor. To simplify the user interface, the zoom factor (Z) is frequently represented as a percentage. Using this representation, the transformation is shown in Figure 13.20. The window center is moved to the origin, the zoom factor is applied, and then the origin is moved to the viewport center. Notice that the scale factor is the same in both X and Y, which prevents aspect distortion.

$$trans(VC_x, VC_y) \cdot scale\left(\frac{Z}{100}, \frac{Z}{100}\right) \cdot trans(-WC_x, -WC_y) \cdot \begin{bmatrix} X_{window} \\ Y_{window} \\ 1 \end{bmatrix} = \begin{bmatrix} X_{viewport} \\ Y_{viewport} \\ 1 \end{bmatrix}$$

Figure 13.20 – Point and zoom viewing transformation

Hierarchic Models

It is sometimes the case that models are built from parts, which themselves may be built from parts. For example, a neighborhood might be built from several houses (which in cheap retirement communities look all alike). Each house is built from doors, windows, chimneys, and so on. The door is built of a frame, window, and knob. There are model objects and model instances. In a door, there is an instance of a knob. In a house, there are one or more instances of the door, and in a neighborhood, there are instances of houses. For each model instance, there is a transformation that maps from the model coordinates to instance coordinates. So, for example, there is a transformation KD from knob coordinates to door coordinates. There is another transformation DH from door coordinates to house coordinates. There are several transformations HN from house coordinates to neighborhood coordinates depending on which house you are drawing. Because this neighborhood is your world coordinates, there is a viewing transformation V from neighborhood coordinates to screen window coordinates. Transforming a knob from its own coordinates involves the sequence shown in Figure 13.21.

$$V \cdot HN \cdot DH \cdot KD \cdot \begin{bmatrix} X_{knob} \\ Y_{knob} \\ 1 \end{bmatrix} = \begin{bmatrix} X_{viewport} \\ Y_{viewport} \\ 1 \end{bmatrix}$$

Figure 13.21 – Transforming a knob into viewport coordinates

To handle this and other transformation tasks, it is common for the Graphics object that is passed to the redraw() method to contain a current transformation (CT). Inside the Graphics object, each draw method first transforms the shape by CT and then draws the shape. When the paint() method is first called, CT is usually initialized to the viewing transformation (V). To manage the current transformation, most Graphics objects have a set of methods like those shown in Figure 13.22. There is usually a class such as Transform that contains a transformation matrix. The Transform class usually has methods for multiplication, inverse, and construction of the basic transformations. The Transform class usually provides direct access to the six coefficients of the transformation matrix.

```
public class Graphics
{    . . . .
     Transform getCurrentTransform()
          // will return the transformation matrix that is the current transformation
     void setCurrentTransform(Transform newTransform)
          // will change the current transformation
     void translate(float dX, float dY)
          // will change the current transform by CT=CT*trans(dX,dY)
     void rotate(float radians)
          // will change the current transform by CT=CT*rot(radians)
     void scale(float sX, float sY)
          // will change the current transform by CT=CT*scale(sX,sY)
     . . . .
}
```

Figure 13.22 – Current transformation methods

With this facility, you can easily construct hierarchic models. What you want is to write methods for each model object that are independent of all other model objects. You do not want to worry about what other parts of the model are doing or what their coordinates might be. This is easily accomplished using the five methods on the Graphics object. The general form for methods to paint an object O is shown in Figure 13.23.

```
public void paintO(Graphic g)
{
        Transform save = g.getCurrentTransform(); // save the current transformation

        set up instance transformation by calling methods on g in the reverse of the order
            in which they are to be applied.

        draw the object by calling methods on g

        g.setCurrentTransform(save); // restore the current transform to what it was before.
}
```

Figure 13.23 – General paint method for a model object

Suppose that your doorknobs come in three sizes, SMALL, MEDIUM, and LARGE, and can be placed anywhere on a door. You can develop a knob design with the origin in the center of the knob. You can then write a paintKnob() method, as shown in Figure 13.24.

```
public enum KnobSize{SMALL, MEDIUM, LARGE};
public void paintKnob(Graphics g, float xLoc, float yLoc, KnobSize size)
{
        Transform save = g.getCurrentTransform();
        g.translate(xLoc, yLoc);

        float s;
        switch (size)
        {
        case KnobSize.SMALL: s=0.75;
        case KnobSize.MEDIUM: s = 1.0;
        case KnobSize.LARGE: s = 1.5;
        }
        g.scale(s, s);

        code to draw the door knob using the Graphics object g

        g.setCurrentTransform(save);
}
```

Figure 13.24 – Paint method for drawing doorknobs

To draw your doorknob, you first want to scale it to the right size and then translate it to the right location. However, in Figures 13.23 and 13.24, these scale() and translate() calls are made in the opposite order. Assume that before paintKnob() is called, the Graphics object has some current transformation T. This might be just the viewing transformation or it might contain transformations that map doors into neighborhoods and then onto the screen or something else. While working with doorknobs, you do not care what this transformation is. That is the problem of other parts of our code. Given the transformation matrix *T*, look at how the current transformation changes as you work through the code (Figure 13.25).

1. at the start	CT=*T*
2. g.translate(dX,dY)	CT=*T**trans(dX,dY)
3. g.scale(s,s)	CT=*T**trans(dX,dY)*scale(s,s)
4. g.*drawsomeshape()*	transform with *T**trans(dX,dY)*scale(s,s)
5. g.setCurrentTransform(save)	CT=*T*

Figure 13.25 – Building up the current transform

When starting the `paintKnob()` method, the current transform is *T*. As the two transformations are called in Steps 2 and 3, they are multiplied onto the right of the current transformation. When you get to Step 4 and want to draw the knob, you multiply your points onto the right of the current transformation, which now (reading from right to left) has the correct scale/translate sequence followed by whatever *T* might do. Lastly, you put the current transformation back the way it was before you exit.

The doorknob might itself have used `screwHead` and `keyHole` model objects in its own model. Calling their methods would cause them to change the current transformation, draw themselves, and put the transformation back. When `screwHead` was manipulating the current transformation, it would have the knob transformation already built into the current transformation that it received.

SUMMARY

You now have a set of matrix operations that allow you to transform objects in a variety of ways. You have a mechanism to concatenate transformations into sequences. You can use these tools to build up models from parts and to transform a portion of your artificial world onto a portion of the screen.

EXERCISES

1. Given the rectangle in Figure 13.26, what would it look like after the transformation sequence *trans(0,2)* • *rotate(45)* • *trans(−1,−2)*?

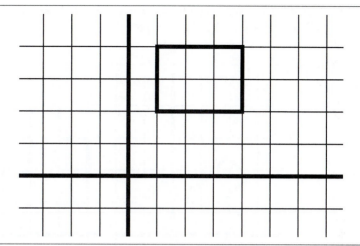

Figure 13.26

2. What is the inverse of the following transformation sequence?
    trans(2,3) • scale(3,1/2) • rotate(150) • trans(1,2)

3. What is the transformation sequence that will make the shape in Figure 13.27
    twice as tall without moving its lower-left corner?

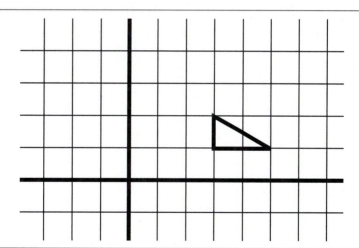

Figure 13.27

4.   What is the transformation sequence that will convert the gray shape in Figure 13.28 into the black shape?

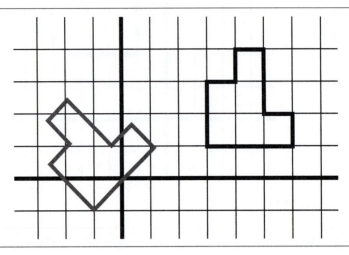

Figure 13.28

CHAPTER 14

Interacting with Geometry

Many applications are not constructed simply of rectangles. House plans, integrated circuits, star charts, simulated paper on a desktop, and many others lay out their information on a two-dimensional plane that is not always aligned with the axes. Given the new power of personal computers and the larger screen sizes, more applications will free themselves of the rigidity of rectangles. This chapter discusses how to interact effectively with the basic interactive shapes and transformations from which a majority of two-dimensional presentations are composed.

This chapter brings together input syntax using PPS, the geometric properties of shapes, and geometric transforms to create a variety of standard interactive techniques. You want a standard set of techniques to create a uniform feel for all of your interactions. This chapter first discusses the choice of coordinates for interaction. It then discusses how to create, select, and manipulate shapes using control points, and, finally, how to interactively express transformations. The PPS notation is used for compactness. For implementation guidance, refer to the section at the end of Chapter 11 that describes translating PPS into code.

INTERACTIVE COORDINATES

Before you can begin, you need to make certain that the shapes you are manipulating and the mouse input points are in the same coordinate system. Most widget packages deliver mouse events with the mouse location in window coordinates. The model could be defined in world coordinates or in a hierarchy of model coordinates.

Window/World Coordinates

If your entire model is represented in world coordinates, you need only worry about the viewing transformation V that transforms points from world to window coordinates. This case arises in most drawing packages, painting of images, word processors, and a number of other applications. With the model in world coordinates and the mouse inputs in window coordinates, you can choose to work in either coordinate system.

Interacting in World Coordinates

If you choose to work in the world coordinates of the model, you need to multiply the mouse input points by V^{-1}. This brings the mouse point into world coordinates and you can work there. The advantage of this approach is that only one transformation of the mouse position is required, and when you are done with any manipulation of geometry, your geometry is already in the world coordinates of the model.

The disadvantage is when you are selecting shapes. You will want to select by being near a shape rather than exactly on it. This is the reason for the distance from a point to a shape calculation. However, that distance needs to be defined in pixels—not in world coordinates. Suppose you decide that 3 pixels is close enough for a selection and you have a zoom factor of 1.0. Transforming the mouse point into world coordinates still leaves the selection distance at 3 pixels. Suppose, however, that the zoom factor is 2.0. A distance of 3 pixels in the world is now 6 pixels on the screen. One of the reasons to zoom in is to get greater precision, but this destroys that advantage. Suppose that the zoom factor is 0.1. This means that a 3-pixel distance in window coordinates becomes a 0.3-pixel distance in world coordinates. Because mouse points are only in pixels, the round-off error might make it impossible to select a shape at all. If your viewing transformation only supports uniform scaling, as with the point and zoom technique, you can transform your selection distance from window to world coordinates by dividing by the zoom factor. Remember that you are transforming a distance, which is neither a point nor a vector. If scaling is nonuniform in X and Y, there is no good way to transform the selection distance from window to world coordinates.

Interacting in Window Coordinates

An alternative is to interact in window coordinates. For this technique, you transform the shapes by V before comparing them with the mouse position. As you manipulate and transform the shapes, first transform them into window coordinates by V, work on them to get a new shape, and then transform them back into world coordinates using V^{-1}. This is a more expensive option because you must transform every shape for selection and manipulation. If any change is made to a shape, it must be transformed back into world coordinates using V^{-1}.

You can also mix the coordinates that you use. For example, you can perform selection in window coordinates where the distance matters and then perform other operations in world coordinates. The choice is up to you (the programmer) so long as both the mouse point and the shape are in the same coordinate system while you are working on them.

Window/Model Interaction

In some cases, the model is composed of many coordinate systems with instance transformations mapping models into the coordinates of other models and then finally into world coordinates. In this case, the choice of coordinate system is more complicated because of the number of coordinates from which you can choose. In the doorknob example, you could interact in any of the following coordinates: window, world/neighborhood, house, door, knob.

You can simplify this problem somewhat by first deciding which object you are interacting with. This is part of the selection problem that will be discussed later. Assuming that you have decided that you are manipulating the door, you really have four choices in which to work: window, world, house, or door. Working in world coordinates is probably the least advantageous because you must transform the mouse into world coordinates (with the same problems discussed previously) and you must also transform the door and all of its instances of other models into world coordinates.

The choice of coordinates is further complicated by the fact that you frequently will be manipulating the instance transformation rather than the object. For example, when you move the door, you are probably changing the transformation from door to house coordinates rather than actually modifying the door. It is easiest to work with this instance transformation of the door in house coordinates. However, if you are moving a piece of decorative molding around on the door, you are actually modifying the model in door coordinates.

Interacting in Window Coordinates

Window coordinates still have the advantage of allowing selection to operate in the coordinate system of the user. They also have the advantage of unifying the problem no matter what the coordinates. To make this work, you must transform the door and all of its instances (such as knobs) into window coordinates. Fortunately, this is the same transformation used when drawing the door. Having manipulated the door in window coordinates, you now must make a decision. Are you changing the door (moving molding) or changing the door's instance transformation? If you are changing the door, the shape is transformed by $DH^{-1} \bullet HN^{-1} \bullet V^{-1}$. If, however, you are changing the instance transformation, you transform the new information by $HN^{-1} \bullet V^{-1}$ and then compute a new DH.

Interacting in Model Coordinates

It is frequently easier when actually manipulating objects to transform the mouse position into the coordinates where the manipulation should occur. With this technique, all of the manipulations in the rest of the chapter can be performed exactly as described. This also reduces the number of points that must be transformed.

A mixed approach is probably best. Selection and snapping a point to the nearest shape are best done in window coordinates where the distances are consistent with what the user perceives. After the selection is done, all manipulating can be performed by transforming the mouse point back into model coordinates and working there. If any snapping to the nearest shape is to be done, this can be done in window coordinates and the new "snapped" mouse points can be transformed back into model coordinates for the shape manipulations.

The remainder of this chapter assumes that the mouse input points and the shape representations are in the same coordinate system. This simplifies the discussions and also makes these techniques independent of whatever coordinate system choices are made. Note that specialized coordinate systems such as polar, latitude/longitude, or logarithmic are not addressed by any of these discussions. They need special application-specific attention.

CREATING SHAPES

The first interactive task is to interactively create the shapes discussed in Chapter 12. In creating shapes, you would like a uniform feel (input syntax) that is easily remembered and reused in a variety of situations. All of the shapes discussed in Chapter 12 can be created in one of two ways: a single mouse drag or sequence of points.

Single Drag Shapes

The syntax for a mouse drag is mouse-down, zero or more mouse moves, and mouse-up. The interactive technique used is called *rubberbanding*. When the mouse goes down, the shape is started at that point and then the shape is continuously drawn after every mouse movement as if the mouse would go up at the current mouse position. This provides the user with continuous feedback of what the shape will be like. This technique works for lines, circles, rectangles, and axis-aligned ellipses. All of these shapes can be defined by two points (down and up).

Figure 14.1 shows a PPS specification for creating such shapes. Figure 14.1 includes the basic three inputs as well as the modifiers for the left mouse button. The Mode field retains the drawing mode selected by the user. This field is set by some other part of the user interface, such as a menu item or palette button. The actions handle the semantics of getting objects drawn on the screen and entered into the model. The state field remembers that you are dragging out a shape. The role of this field is explored in more detail in later sections.

```
Input {*MD,      // mouse down
       *MM,      // mouse move
       *MU}      // mouse up
LeftButton {LD*,     // left down
       LU*}      // left up
Mode { line,     // drawing a line
       rect,     // drawing a rectangle
       ellipse}  // drawing an ellipse
State { idle, dragging }
Actions { !startLine,      // Save the mouse position as the line's starting point.
       !moveLine,       // Redraw the line from the start point to the new mouse position.
       !endLine,        // Add a line to the model from start point to current mouse point.
       !startRect,      // Take the current point as the start of a new rectangle.
       !moveRect,       // Redraw the rectangle to be between the start point
                        // and the current point.
       !endRect,        // Add a rectangle to the model from the start point to the
                        // current mouse point.
       !startEllipse, !moveEllipse, !endEllipse } // similar actions for ellipses

line *MD LD* idle -> !startLine(mX,mY) dragging
         // Start drawing a line when the left mouse button goes down.
line *MM LD* dragging -> !moveLine(mX,mY)
         // Move the line whenever a mouse move occurs while in the dragging state
line *MU LU* dragging -> !endLine(mX,mY) idle
         // When the mouse goes up enter the line in the model and return to idle state

// All of these behave like the line rules except that Mode == rect
rect *MD LD* idle -> !startRect(mX,mY) dragging
rect *MM LD* dragging -> !moveRect (mX,mY)
rect *MU LU* dragging -> !endRect (mX,mY) idle

// All of these behave like the line and rectangle rules except that Mode == ellipse
ellipse *MD LD* idle -> !startEllipse (mX,mY) dragging
ellipse *MM LD* dragging -> !moveEllipse (mX,mY)
ellipse *MU LU* dragging -> !endEllipse (mX,mY) idle
```

Figure 14.1 – PPS for single drag drawing

Multipoint Shapes

A variety of shapes, such as polylines, curves, polygons, closed curves, and curvilinear shapes, require multiple points. The simple down-drag-up sequence is not sufficient. Most systems allow the user to click on a set of points and after each click they construct the shape with the points created so far. It also becomes important to decide if each point is specified on mouse-down or mouse-up. It makes a difference because between mouse-down and mouse-up the user might move. The PPS examples in this chapter use the mouse-down convention and generally ignore mouse-up. Rubberbanding occurs on mouse movement regardless of whether the mouse button is up or not.

In many drawing systems, the question of an open or closed shape is not decided until all of the points are entered. If the last point is near the first point, the shape is closed. If the last point is near the previous point, the shape is terminated as an open polyline or curve rather than a closed shape.

Figure 14.2 shows a PPS that deals with all of these issues. New `Mode` choices for `polyline` and `curve` are added. New actions are added for starting a list of points, moving around, clicking a new vertex point, and ending an open or a closed shape. In addition, the query field `MouseLoc` is added, which provides the information about where the mouse click has occurred relative to the previous points.

```
Input {*MD, *MM, *MU}
LeftButton {LD*, LU*}
Mode { line, rect, ellipse,
      polyline, // drawing a polyline or polygon
      curve,    // drawing an open or closed curve
      }
State { idle,       // waiting for new input from the users
      dragging,     // The user is entering two points by dragging from the first to second.
      points        // The user is entering a whole series of points.
      }
Actions { !startLine, !moveLine,!endLine,
      !startRect, !moveRect, !endRect,
      !startEllipse, !moveEllipse, !endEllipse
      !startPoly,      // Save the first point of a polyline.
      !movePoly,       // Move the last point of a polyline to the current mouse location.
      !clickPoly,      // Record a polyline point at the current mouse location.
      !endPolyLine,    // Enter a polyline into the model using the recorded points.
      !closePolygon,           // Enter a closed polygon into the model using the points.

      // These perform the same functions for curves as the above for polygons.
      !startCurve, !moveCurve, !clickCurve, !endCurve, !closeCurve
      }

// This query field detects whether to create closed or open curves or polylines
MouseLoc { ?nearFirstPoint,    // Mouse point is near the first entered point.
      ?nearPrevPoint,          // Mouse point is near the previous point entered.
      ?farAway }               // Mouse point is not near any points.

      . . . other rules for lines, rectangles and ellipses

polyline *MD LD* idle -> !startPoly(mX, mY) points
      // When the mouse goes down, start a new polyline or polygon.
polyline *MM points -> !movePoly(mX, mY)
      // As the mouse moves echo the line on the screen.
polyline *MD LD* points ?farAway -> !clickPoly(mX, mY)
      // If a left mouse-down is not near previous or first point then record a new point.
polyline *MD LD* points ?nearPrevPoint -> !endPolyLine idle
      // If a left mouse-down is near the previous point then create a polyline.
polyline *MD LD* points ?nearFirstPoint -> !closePolygon idle
      // If a left mouse-down is near the first point then create a closed polygon.

// These do the same for curves as the above rules do for polylines.
curve *MD LD* idle -> !startCurve(mX, mY) points
curve *MM points -> !moveCurve(mX, mY)
curve *MD LD* points ?farAway -> !clickCurve(mX, mY)
curve *MD LD* points ?nearPrevPoint -> !endCurve idle
curve *MD LD* points ?nearFirstPoint -> !closeCurve idle
```

Figure 14.2 – PPS for multipoint shapes

SELECTING SHAPES

Having created a variety of shapes, you also need to be able to select them so that you can change them in various ways. There are four types of selection: single object selection involving just a click to designate the selected object, Shift-clicking for multiple objects, rectangle selection, and lasso selection. The following sections address each of these types of selection in turn.

Click Selection

Simple click selection involves taking the mouse point on mouse-up and comparing it with all objects in the model. The paint() method draws the object in back-to-front order so that the frontmost objects appear on top. The selection method iterates through the objects in front-to-back order and returns the first object that is selected by the point.

To select a path shape such as a line, curve, or edge of a closed shape, use the distance from point to shape methods from Chapter 12. To select filled shapes such as ellipses, rectangles, or polygons, use their inside/outside tests.

Since the first Apple Macintosh, most systems have used Shift-clicking to select multiple objects. If the Shift key is down during a selection, objects are added to the selected set if they are not already in the set or removed if they are already in the selected set. The methods to select from a mouse-point are the same. Figure 14.3 shows a PPS with click selection added to it. A select condition is added to the Mode field to indicate selection rather than creation. The Selection query field indicates if a shape has been hit by the current mouse position. Clicking where there are no shapes causes all selected shapes to be unselected.

```
Input {*MD, *MM, *MU}
LeftButton {LD*, LU*}
ShiftButton {SD*, SU* }
Mode { select,      // This mode indicates that the user wants to select shapes rather than
                    // create a new one.
      line, rect, ellipse, polyline, curve}
State { idle, dragging, points }
Actions { !startLine, !moveLine, !endLine, !startRect, !moveRect, !endRect,
      !startEllipse, !moveEllipse, !endEllipse
      !startPoly, !movePoly, !clickPoly, !endPolyLine, !closePolygon,
      !startCurve, !moveCurve, !clickCurve, !endCurve, !closeCurve,
      !simpleSelect,      // Select the object directly under the current mouse point
      !shiftSelect,       // Add the object under the current mouse point to the other
                          // currently selected objects.
      !deselectAll        // Remove all objects from the selected set.
      }
MouseLoc { ?nearFirstPoint, ?nearPrevPoint, ?farAway }

// This checks the essential geometry to see if an object is under the current point.
Selection{ ?objectSelected, ?noObjectSelected }

select *MU LU* SU* ?objectSelected(O) -> !simpleSelect(O)
      // If the left mouse button goes up while in select mode and the mouse is over
      // the object O, then select only that object.
select *MU LU* SD* ?objectSelected(O) -> !shiftSelect(O)
      // If the left mouse button goes up while the Shift key is down then add the
      // object O to the list of selected objects.
select *MU LU* ?noObjectSelected -> !deselectAll
      // If the left button goes up while in select mode and there are no objects
      // under the mouse location then deselect all objects.

      . . . other rules for lines, rectangles, ellipses, polylines and curves
```

Figure 14.3 – Click and Shift-click selection

Rectangle Selection

One technique for selecting a group of shapes all at once is to drag out a rubberband rectangle around all of the shapes that should belong to the group. After creating the selection rectangle, select all shapes whose tight bounding box (not the loose convex hull bounding box) is completely inside of the selection rectangle. Using the Shift key, you can add or remove elements from the selected set by using clicking or rectangle selection. Some implementations of rectangle selection add any shape whose bounding box intersects the selection rectangle. This makes it easier to select more objects but in practice is harder to control to get exactly the right set. The intersection rather than enclosure approach can also make it simpler to select some things.

Rectangle selection is useful in the presence of hierarchic groups of objects. If the user draws a rectangle around a doorknob, it is clear that the knob rather than the door or the house is being selected. This is much less ambiguous than selection by clicking. The technique is to select the largest object groups that fit completely within the selection rectangle.

Lasso Selection

A problem with rectangle selection is that the set of objects to be selected might not always be selectable by a rectangle. Consider the task of selecting the black shapes and not the gray shapes in Figure 14.4. There is no rectangle that can accomplish this task. The user can, however, draw a "lasso" around the desired shapes and exclude the others as shown. The lasso selection can also be augmented by Shift-select techniques.

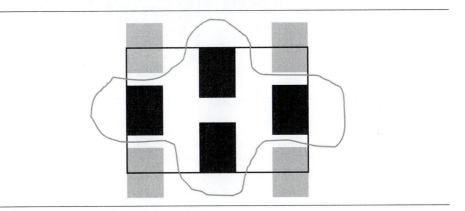

Figure 14.4 – Rectangle and lasso selection

The selection problem is to decide which shapes are inside and outside of the lasso. Lassos are never built from cubic curves, which make the curve inside/outside techniques unusable. One simple technique for lasso selection is to ensure that the entire shape is closed by drawing lines between the mouse movement points when the lasso is drawn as well as a line from the first to last point. You draw the lasso in black into a blank (all white) image. You then perform a black flood fill using a starting point known to be inside of the lasso. This produces a mask of all pixels that are inside of the shape. This is done in any pixel coordinates, but usually screen window coordinates.

Using the mask, shown in Figure 14.5, you must decide which pixels are in or out. There are two techniques for this depending upon your assumptions about user selection. The fastest technique is to take the "principle points" for each shape and check to see if they all fall on a black pixel in the mask. If they do, the shape is selected. For lines, use the end points; for ellipses, the north, east, south, and west points; for curves, the end points and the X/Y maxima and minima; and for rectangles, the corner points.

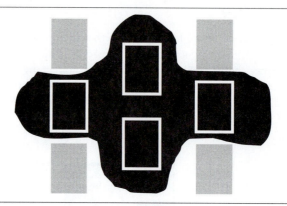

Figure 14.5 – Selection mask

Checking principle points is very fast, but relies upon the assumption that the selection is not crossing shape boundaries in arbitrary ways. In most, but not all, situations, this is a good assumption. An alternative technique is to "draw" each shape into the mask image using the scan-conversion algorithm for that shape. A shape is selected if every point on the shape is drawn into a black mask pixel. For filled shapes, only the boundaries need to be drawn. This pseudodrawing technique gives an exact, pixel-accurate selection.

In most systems, the user must specify whether click, rectangle, or lasso selection is desired. Saund and Lank[1] have proposed that the user need not make such a distinction and that it can be inferred from the movement of the mouse.

- If the mouse goes down and then up without ever moving more than a few pixels from the down point, it is a click.

- If the mouse goes down and then up at some distance from the down point, the selection is a rectangle defined by the down and up point at opposite corners.

- If the mouse moves some distance away from the down point but eventually the up point is near the down point, it is a lasso selection.

The only problem with this technique is providing an appropriate echo while the mouse is moving. Saund and Lank propose that both the lasso and the rectangle be echoed until it is obvious from the mouse movement the approach that is intended. Although both the rectangle and the lasso appear on the screen at the same time, their experience is that the user only watches the shape they are interested in and by the time the selection is complete, the system knows which one to use. All of these selection techniques can be encoded in the PPS, as shown in Figure 14.6. You now must remember the start point, what kind of echo you are doing, and check where the up point is relative to the starting position.

Input {*MD, *MM, *MU}
LeftButton {LD*, LU*}
ShiftButton {SD*, SU* }
Mode { **select**, line, rect, ellipse, polyline, curve}
State { idle, dragging, points,
        clickSelecting,   **// This indicates that a selection has started but it has not**
                                   // yet been determined whether this is a click selection or
                                   // rectangle/lasso selection.
        rectLassoSelecting }
Actions { . . . drawing actions . . .
        !startSelect,   **// Record the current location as a selection point.**
        !clickSelect,   **// Select only the object under the current mouse location.**
        !shiftClickSel,   **// Add the object under the mouse location to the set of**
                                   // selected objects.
        !rectSelect,   **// Using a rectangle from the start point to the current point,**
                                   // select all objects inside of the rectangle.
        !shiftRectSelect,   **// Add all objects inside of the selection rectangle to the**
                                   // selected set.
        !lassoSelect,   **// Using all the points from the start point until the current**
                                   // point to define a lasso region, select all objects in the lasso.
        !shiftLassoSelect,   **// Add all objects inside of the lasso to the selected set.**
        !rectLassoEcho   **// Use current point to update both the rectangle echo and**
                                   // the lasso echo and redisplay both of them.

        }
MouseLoc { ?nearFirstPoint, ?nearPrevPoint, ?farAway }
Selection{ ?objectSelected, ?noObjectSelected }

idle select *MD LD* -> clickSelecting !startSelect(mX,mY)
    // When the left button goes down begin selection without committing to the
    // type of selection.
clickSelecting *MM LD* ?nearFirstPoint -> clickSelecting
    // If the mouse is still near the first point then assume that a click selection is
    // what the user desires.
clickSelecting *MM LD* ?farAway -> rectLassoSelecting !rectLassoEcho
    // If the mouse has moved away from the start point then assume that a
    // rectangle or lasso selection is underway and start both echos.
clickSelecting *MU LU* SU* -> idle !clickSelect
    // If the mouse goes up while still in clickSelecting then do a single point select.
clickSelecting *MU LU* SD* -> idle !shiftClickSel
    // If the Shift key was down add the object to the selected set.
rectLassoSelection *MM LD* -> !rectLassoEcho
    // If the mouse moves while doing a rect and lasso selection then update the
    // echo of both selections with the current mouse point.
rectLassoSelection *MU LU* ?nearFirstPoint SU* -> idle !lassoSelect
    // If the button goes up near the first selection point then the user must have
    // intended a lasso selection. Perform the lasso selection.
rectLassoSelection *MU LU* ?nearFirstPoint SD* -> idle !shiftLassoSelect
    // Perform the lasso selection and add the selected objects to the selected set.
rectLassoSelection *MU LU* ?farAway SU* -> idle !rectSelect
    // If the mouse goes up far away from the first point then the user must have
    // intended a rectangle selection. Perform the rectangle selection.
rectLassoSelection *MU LU* ?farAway SD* -> idle !shiftRectSelect
    // If the Shift key was down then add rectangle selection to the selected set.

    . . . other rules for lines, rectangles, ellipses, polylines and curves

Figure 14.6 − All selection PPS

MANIPULATING CONTROL POINTS

After an object or set of objects has been selected, you must give the user feedback on what is selected. You must also allow the user to manipulate the object. In many systems, both goals are accomplished by displaying a set of control points for the selected object(s), as shown in Figure 14.7. This not only identifies the selected object, but also provides "handles" that the user can use to manipulate the object.

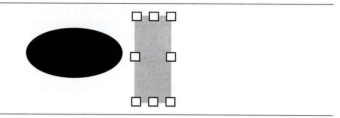

Figure 14.7 – Control points

The manipulation of control points can have a variety of meanings depending upon the shape and the kind of manipulation to be performed. The value of the control-point model is that it is a very concrete way to offer the user an opportunity to change some aspect of the shape. In terms of common look and feel, most computer users believe that by dragging a control point, the selected shape will be changed in some way. This provides an immediate affordance for the user to manipulate the shape.

Because the manipulation of control points is so pervasive and because you have so many meanings for what effect a control point will have, you need to use an abstract-model architecture, as described in Chapter 7. The abstract model allows you to implement any meaning you desire while placing all of the control point manipulation in the widget where it can be reused in many situations. This is accomplished with the interfaces shown in Figure 14.8.

```
public interface ControlPoint
{
      Point getPoint();       // return the control point location in window coordinates
      void setPoint(Point newLoc);    // set the control point location in window coordinates
}
public interface ControlPointModel
{
      ControlPoint [] getSelectedControls();
                  // return all of the control points for selected objects in the model
}
```

Figure 14.8 – Abstract model for control point interaction

The `ControlPointModel` can be implemented by any model. All it does is provide the widget with a list of the control points for the selected objects. It is up to the model to decide what has been selected and what control points should be provided. Based on this interface, the widget can paint all of the model presentation and then ask the model for the list of control points. Using the `getPoint()` method on each point, the widget can draw the control handles over the top of all other model information. The widget also has all of the information that it needs to allow the user to drag the point. The widget then calls `setPoint()` so that the model can do what it wants with the dragged control point.

In many cases, a control point is constrained as to where it can be placed. For example, in Figure 14.7, the control point on the right edge of the rectangle should remain centered vertically between the top and bottom of the rectangle while freely moving horizontally. When the widget controller calls `setPoint()` for this control point, the model can actually place the control point wherever it wants. In this case, the model ignores the *Y* component of the `newLoc`. For this to work correctly, the model should perform a damage on the entire shape and the view should redraw all of the control points from the model. This keeps the presentation consistent with the model rather than with the controller. With control points on the screen, the PPS must be modified to accommodate the dragging of control points. This is shown in Figure 14.9.

```
Input {*MD, *MM, *MU}
LeftButton {LD*, LU*}
ShiftButton {SD*, SU* }
Mode { select, line, rect, ellipse, polyline, curve}
State { idle, dragging, points, clickSelecting, rectLassoSelecting, controlDragging }
Actions { . . . drawing actions . . .
          . . . select actions . . .
    !selectControl,    // Select the control point under the current mouse position.
    !moveControl       // Move the selected control point to the current mouse position.
    }
MouseLoc { ?nearFirstPoint, ?nearPrevPoint, ?farAway }
Selection {?objectSelected, ?noObjectSelected}
Control {?controlSelected, ?noControl }

idle select *MD LD* ?noControl -> clickSelecting !startSelect(mX,mY)
    // If the mouse goes down and the mouse point is not over a control point
    // then start selection as in Figure 14.6.
idle select *MD LD* ?controlSelected(C) -> controlDragging !selectControl(C)
    // If the mouse goes down over a control point then select the control point.
controlDragging *MM LD* -> !moveControl
    // Move the selected control point on mouse-move.
controlDragging *MU LU* -> !moveControl idle
    // On mouse-up move the selected control point to the current point and
    // return to the idle state.

    . . . other rules for selection
    . . . other rules for lines, rectangles, ellipses, polylines and curves
```

Figure 14.9 – Control point dragging

TRANSFORMATIONS

Now that you can create objects, select objects, and change objects, you might want to transform objects using the three basic transformations. With a generic set of interactive techniques for transformations, you have a uniform feel for a large variety of interactive behaviors.

Translation

Interactively expressing a translation is called *dragging* because you are dragging a shape around the screen. In the model, this is generally manipulated in one of three ways. The simplest is that every model object has a position that is changed as a result of dragging. The second way is that the dragging distance (dX, dY) is added to every point of the shape and the new position is encoded in the shape points. The last approach is that there is an instance transformation T for the object and a new transformation is computed as $T=trans(dX,dY)*T$.

What you need is to get (dX, dY) from the mouse position while dragging. One approach is to save the last mouse position *(lX, lY)* and then compute the difference between the current position and the last position. For translation, this generally works. However, for the other transformations, incrementally computing the transformation on each mouse move can have inaccuracy problems because of the accumulation of round-off error. Remember that world coordinates are frequently in floating point and mouse coordinates are always in integers. To eliminate this problem, you should always perform your transformations relative to the mouse-down point rather than relative to the last mouse point.

Interactively, there is a problem because most systems do not require the user to specify "I am going to drag a shape now." In most systems, there is only a "select" mode and the controller must distinguish between click selection, dragging an object, rectangle selection, lasso selection, and control point dragging by watching what the user actually does. This complicates the controller code.

For translation, you must distinguish between click selection and dragging. One of the first techniques is to perform a selection on mouse-down if the mouse is over an object. The selection must be done regardless of whether dragging is intended. You can put off the dragging decision until later. You might want to infer a dragging intention whenever a mouse-move is received. However, most users' hands shake slightly when pressing the mouse button and this might or might not cause a mouse-move event. If you move the object every time the user's hand shakes, there will be frustration. The appropriate technique is to assume clicking until the mouse is no longer near the down point and then assume dragging.

Figure 14.10 shows the PPS that brings together all of the elements of selection and dragging. This has become so complex because you desire the user interface to behave naturally and smoothly to the user with a minimum amount of extra button clicking. When the mouse first goes down, you must consider whether a control point, an object, or nothing is under the mouse and act accordingly. If the mouse is over an object, you must perform the selection or Shift selection on mouse-down so that if you are dragging, the appropriate objects are selected for dragging. The PPS assumes that you are clicking until the mouse moves away from the start point and then you switch to the objDragging state. After entering the objDragging state, the user can move the object back very close to the original point. This technique accommodates hand tremor on clicking while providing for very small movements when desired.

```
Input {*MD, *MM, *MU}
LeftButton {LD*, LU*}
ShiftButton {SD*, SU* }
Mode { select, line, rect, ellipse, polyline, curve}
State { idle, dragging, points, clickSelecting,
        rectLassoSelecting, controlDragging, objDragging }
Actions { . . . drawing actions . . .
     !startSelect, !clickSelect, !shiftClickSel, !rectSelect, !shiftRectSelect,
     !lassoSelect, !shiftLassoSelect, !rectLassoEcho,
     !controlSelected, !moveControl, !moveSelected, !setSelected
     }
MouseLoc { ?nearFirstPoint, ?nearPrevPoint, ?farAway }
Selection{ ?objectSelected, ?noObjectSelected}
Control {?controlSelected, ?noControl }

select idle *MD LD* ?noObjectSelected ?noControl -> rectLassoSelecting !startSelect
       // If no object is selected then start a rectangle or lasso selection
select idle *MD LD* ?controlSelected -> controlDragging !controlSelected
       // If a control point is under the mouse then start dragging that point
select idle *MD LD* SU* ?objectSelected ?noControlSelected -> clickSelecting
          !clickSelect  !startSelect
       // If an object is under the mouse then click select the object
select idle *MD LD* SD* ?objectSelected ?noControlSelected -> clickSelecting
          !shiftClickSelect !startSelect
       // If the Shift key is down then add the object to the selected set.

clickSelecting *MM LD* ?nearFirstPoint -> clickSelecting
       // If the mouse has moved but is still near the first point then stay with click select.
clickSelecting *MM LD* ?farAway -> objDragging !moveObj
       // If the mouse has moved away from the first point then assume translation
clickSelecting *MU LU* SU* -> !clickSelect idle
clickSelecting *MU LU* SD* -> !shiftClickSelect idle

rectLassoSelecting *MM LD* -> !rectLassoEcho
rectLassoSelecting *MU LU* SU* ?nearFirstPoint -> !lassoSelect idle
rectLassoSelecting *MU LU* SD* ?nearFirstPoint -> !shiftlassoSelect idle
rectLassoSelecting *MU LU* SU* ?farAway -> !rectSelect idle
rectLassoSelecting *MU LU* SD* ?farAway -> !shiftRectSelect idle

controlDragging *MM LD* -> !moveControl
controlDragging *MU LU* -> !moveControl idle

objDragging *MM LD* -> !moveSelected
       // Continue dragging the object on each mouse move.
objDragging *MU LU* -> !setSelected idle
       // Move the object to its new location in the model.

       . . . other rules for lines, rectangles, ellipses, polylines and curves
```

Figure 14.10 – Full PPS for select and drag

If you add the actions and rules for shape drawing back into Figure 14.10, you have a complete specification of your controller for interactive manipulating geometry. The remaining techniques in this chapter all rely upon control point manipulation. The resulting PPS fits on a single page and can be studied, discussed, and modified. From this, you can carefully derive the code for the mouseDown(), mouseMove(), and mouseUp() event methods. Notice that in Figure 14.10, the rules are organized according to the tasks that you are trying to accomplish. This helps you think about what you are trying to do while designing. However, the implementation is organized around event methods; you must now use our PPS techniques from Chapter 11 to derive an implementation equivalent to your design.

Scaling

The scaling transformation is used to change the size of objects. The scaling transformation always functions relative to the origin and relative to the x- and y-axes. You learned in Chapter 13 how to scale relative to any point by translating that point to the origin first. You can also scale relative to any axis by rotating that axis to the x-axis first. You need to assemble this geometry together so that you can express scaling using dragging of a few control points. This section discusses three such interactive techniques: rectangle scaling, point scaling, and point-axis scaling.

The most common scaling technique is to bound a shape with a rectangle and use the eight rectangle control points to express a scaling transformation. This is shown in Figure 14.11.

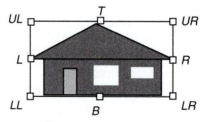

Figure 14.11 – Rectangle scaling controls

For each control point in Figure 14.11, the opposite control point forms its center of scaling. So, for example, if the user grabbed the point *UR* and dragged it to a new position *NUR*, the transformation sequence would be that shown in Figure 14.12. If the user had grabbed *T* and dragged it to *NT*, the transformation sequence would be that shown in Figure 14.13. All of the other control points have similar transformation sequences. There are three main advantages to rectangle scaling: (1) The control points naturally follow selection of the object without introducing any new menu modes, (2) the control points form a natural affordance, and (3) the center of scaling is automatically inferred.

$$trans\left(LL_x, LL_y\right) \bullet scale\left(\frac{NUR_x - LL_x}{UR_x - LL_x}, \frac{NUR_y - LL_y}{UR_y - LL_y}\right) \bullet trans\left(-LL_x, -LL_y\right)$$

Figure 14.12 – Scaling by dragging *UR* to *NUR*

$$trans\left(B_x, B_y\right) \bullet scale\left(1, \frac{NT_y - B_y}{T_y - B_y}\right) \bullet trans\left(-B_x, -B_y\right)$$

Figure 14.13 – Scaling by dragging *T* to *NT*

At times, you will need to grab a corner control point and scale the object, but you will not want to change the object's aspect ratio. You want it bigger or smaller, but still the same shape. For this, you need a transformation that is uniform in X and Y. Such a transformation is shown in Figure 14.14. In Figure 14.14, the axis that has the most change was chosen and both axes were scaled by that amount.

$$S = \begin{cases} \left|(NUR_x - UR_x) > (NUR_y - UR_y)\right| \Rightarrow \dfrac{NUR_x - LL_x}{UR_x - LL_x} \\[2em] \left|(NUR_x - UR_x) \le (NUR_y - UR_y)\right| \Rightarrow \dfrac{NUR_y - LL_y}{UR_y - LL_y} \end{cases}$$

$$trans(LL_x, LL_y) \bullet scale(S, S) \bullet trans(-LL_x, -LL_y)$$

Figure 14.14 – Uniform scaling by dragging *UR* to *NUR*

Suppose in Figure 14.11 that you want to scale your home so that the lower-left corner of the foundation remains in the same location but the right roof/eve point is scaled to a particular position. This is not very realistic for houses but does happen in other situations. To accomplish this task, you want the lower-left foundation point rather than the point *LL* to stay fixed. For this task, you need three points: the center of scaling *C*, a current point *P* on the object, and a new point *NP* for where *P* should end up. All of the dragging techniques only provide two points. Generally, arbitrary scaling is performed by a special "scaling" mode of the interface rather than being integrated with the selection. When a user selects "Scale," they then click on the center of the scaling point followed by dragging point *P* to point *NP*. The resulting transformation sequence is shown in Figure 14.15.

$$trans(C_x, C_y) \bullet scale\left(\frac{NP_x - C_x}{P_x - C_x}, \frac{NP_y - C_y}{P_y - C_y}\right) \bullet trans(-C_x, -C_y)$$

Figure 14.15 – Scaling relative to arbitrary points

These two scaling techniques are still defined relative to the x- and y-axes. Suppose you have the house on the left in Figure 14.16, and you want to make it wider but not taller.

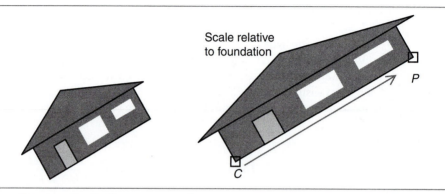

Figure 14.16 – Scaling on a new axis

In this situation, you want scaling only along a particular axis, but the axis is not parallel to the x- or y-axis. You can solve this problem by rotating to the x-axis before scaling and then putting it back. The challenge is computing the angle of rotation. However, remember that you do not need the angle of rotation. What you need are the sine and cosine of that angle. You can compute that directly from points P and C. Note that you first want to rotate by the negative of the angle to get it to the x-axis. Remember that *sin(-A)=-sin(A)* and that *cos(-A)=cos(A)*. This process is complicated by the fact that you want to only scale along the axis C->P, but the user will wiggle the point NP around off of that axis. Therefore, you need to transform P and NP into the new rotated coordinates P and NP before you can compute the scale factor. The transformation matrix T that will perform all of this is shown in Figure 14.17. The steps are shown visually in Figure 14.18.

$$H = \sqrt{(P_x - C_x)^2 + (P_y - C_y)^2}$$

$$SIN = \frac{P_y - C_y}{H} \qquad COS = \frac{P_x - C_x}{H}$$

$$M = rot(-SIN, COS) \cdot trans(-C_x, -C_y)$$

$$P' = M \bullet P \qquad NP' = M \bullet NP$$

$$S = \frac{NP'_x}{P'_x}$$

$$T = M^{-1} \bullet scales(S, 1) \bullet M$$

Figure 14.17 – Scaling of $C{\rightarrow}P$ to NP

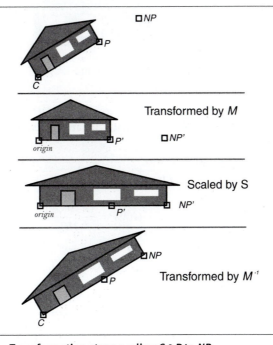

Figure 14.18 – Transformation steps scaling $C{\rightarrow}P$ to NP

Rotation

Rotation, like scaling, needs a center of rotation. Therefore, you will need three points to perform a rotation (*C*, *P*, and *NP*). When the user specifies rotation mode, they then select the object to rotate. You can get the center of rotation from the selection point or from the "center of mass" of the shape. The center of mass is usually calculated as the average of all the points that define the shape. This tends to place the center of rotation near the center of the shape. In some systems, this is displayed as a special control point, as shown in Figure 14.19. Grabbing any point *P* on the shape, the user can specify a rotation by dragging to *NP*. The user can also drag point *C* to change the center of rotation.

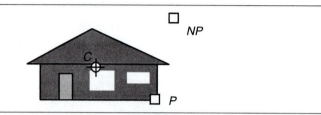

Figure 14.19 – Rotation with three points

To perform this rotation, you rotate point *P* to the *x*-axis and then rotate the *x*-axis to point *NP*. The transformation matrix *T* is derived in Figure 14.20.

$$HP = \sqrt{(P_x - C_x)^2 + (P_y - C_y)^2}$$

$$SINP = \frac{(P_y - C_y)}{HP} \qquad COSP = \frac{(P_x - C_x)}{HP}$$

$$HNP = \sqrt{(NP_x - C_x)^2 + (NP_y - C_y)^2}$$

$$SINNP = \frac{(NP_y - C_y)}{HNP} \qquad COSP = \frac{(NP_x - C_x)}{HNP}$$

$$T = trans(C_x, C_y) \bullet rot(SINNP, COSNP) \bullet rot(-SINP, COSP) \bullet trans(-C_x, -C_y)$$

Figure 14.20 – Rotating from *P* to *NP* about *C*

Nine-Point Transformation Frame

You can interactively accomplish almost all of these transformations using the nine control points shown in Figure 14.21. In this formulation, the object has a natural center that you use as a center of rotation. The center point is not a control point that the user can drag. The object also has a current rotation. As shown, the bounding box frame for scaling is oriented according to the rotation angle. This allows scaling to be expressed relative to the object's natural axes rather than the x- and y-axes. The center of rotation is shown. The extra handle extending above the bounding box is the rotation handle.

All transformations are performed by dragging. Dragging any point on the object translates the object. Dragging any of the nine control points on the rectangular frame scales the object relative to the frame. Dragging the rotation handle rotates the object about its center.

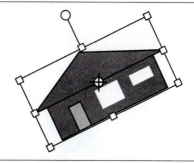

Figure 14.21 – Nine-point transformation frame

SUMMARY

The geometry, transformations, and PPS concepts of previous chapters are brought together in a standard set of interactive techniques. Most of the desired shapes can be created either by a "down-drag-up" technique or by multiple input points. There are also several ways to perform selection. Combining all of these into a single PPS provides a clear description from which the necessary event-handling code can be derived. Each of the three transformations can also be expressed using control points. This chapter provides interactive techniques for all of these operations.

EXERCISES

1. Why would you want to do selection in window coordinates and manipulation of an object in model coordinates?

2. The user wants to draw a curve freehand using all the mouse-move points between mouse-down and mouse-up. Give the PPS that will specify such an interaction.

3. When highlighting a selection using control points, how do you make certain that the control points appear over the top of all other drawings?

4. Figure 14.22 has a house that needs to be placed on a street. Points A and B for the corners of the house are currently known. The mouse goes down on point D and the user drags it to point U, where it is released. You want to rotate the house about point A and make the house wider (but not taller) so that point D will be transformed to point U. Given A, B, D, and U, what is the transformation sequence?

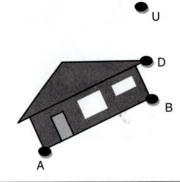

Figure 14.22

END NOTES

[1] Saund, E., and E. Lank. "Stylus Input and Editing Without Prior Selection of Mode." *ACM Symposium on User Interface Software and Technology (UIST '03)* (October 2003): 213–216.

CHAPTER 15

Cut, Copy, Paste, Drag, and Drop

When UNIX introduced the concept of a pipe, which carried information out of one program directly into another program, it fundamentally changed the way people thought about programs. It allowed problems to be solved by piecing together the capabilities of various pieces of code rather than rebuilding from scratch. A similar transition occurred when the Apple Macintosh introduced cut, copy, and paste to the world at large. It suddenly became easy for users to combine the work and interactive capabilities of a number of unrelated programs to create unique solutions.

All of these mechanisms involve the transfer of data from a *source* to a *destination*. In many cases, the source and destination share the same data model in the same program. Examples of this include cutting a paragraph from one part of a document and pasting it into another part, or making many copies of a shape to distribute around a drawing. Throughout most of this discussion, this chapter assumes that the data transfer is between two different programs because that is the most general case. Three issues must be addressed: (1) What is the appropriate data transfer to perform? (2) What is the transfer mechanism? and (3) What should be done with the transferred data? The following sections address each of these in turn.

APPROPRIATE DATA TRANSFER

When the user requests a transfer between source and destination, the applications must determine the kinds of data the source can generate, the kinds of data the destination can receive, and the intent of the user. This requires some communication among programs about data types and possibly some additional input from the user.

For purposes of this discussion, you will use the simple Clipboard model of data transfer, where a source puts information onto the Clipboard (cut or copy) and a destination retrieves information from the Clipboard (paste).

A problem with such transfers arises when the source and destination do not have the same data representation. For example, copying from WordPerfect and pasting into Microsoft PowerPoint can cause a problem. The source and destination must establish a common representation that both can understand.

The simplest mechanism is for the source to generate all of the different forms of data that it can. So when the user requests a copy of a paragraph from WordPerfect, it might place the information on the Clipboard in WordPerfect format, plain text, HTML, and possibly Microsoft Word. By placing all forms that WordPerfect understands onto the Clipboard, any destination programs can then choose for themselves. Similarly, a Web browser might post styled text as HTML, Rich Text Format (RTF), or plain text. The destination application can choose which it wants.

The Macintosh Human Interface Guidelines and all subsequent guidelines have mandated that every source must produce either plain text or an image as one of its formats. Every destination should accept both of these representations. The reason for these requirements is that it virtually guarantees that copy and paste will always work in a form visible to the user. It is very important for usability that users believe that cut/copy/paste will work virtually anywhere. Any information in a graphical user interface can be captured either as text or an image.

Limiting ourselves to just text and images would not be very satisfying. When formatting some text or a drawing, you want that formatting to be retained. When operating in specialized applications, you want all of the information structure to be transferred rather than just a picture.

Types

When placing information on the Clipboard, the source specifies the *type* of each of the clips. In the days before object-oriented programming, this type was a string such as "TEXT". In the very early days, the type name was limited to four characters so that it would fit in a word of memory. To perform a cut or a copy, a program opens the Clipboard and clears out all existing scrap. It then puts as many different types of data in as it wants. With each type of data, there can be a type name and the bytes of content information. By publishing multiple copies of the data in different formats on the Clipboard, the source has made its capabilities available to the destination. By convention, the source should place types of information on the Clipboard in most-preferred to least-preferred order.

To perform a paste, the destination consults the Clipboard for the types of information that it can understand. By looking at the order of the information on the Clipboard, the destination program knows the representations preferred by the source. The text/image requirement ensures that the destination program will usually find something useful.

It is universal for cut/copy/paste that the user interface toolkit will provide access to the Clipboard and a mechanism for a source to place many clips of data on the

Clipboard in various types or data formats. The names for these source mechanisms vary widely but all have the same pattern of:

- Access the Clipboard.
- Clear out existing items.
- Repeatedly add type/content pairs to the Clipboard.
- Close the Clipboard and make it available for use.

Toolkits also provide the destination with mechanisms that will do the following:

- Access the Clipboard.
- Obtain a list of the types or data formats currently available on the Clipboard in the same order as they were added by the source.
- Retrieve a data object using a particular type or data format.

The transport mechanisms and the ways of naming and processing types might vary but these basic strategies are almost universal.

Naming Types

Naming of types is a bit of a challenge because the source and destination must have the same understanding of type names. Apple provided a central registry of type names so that various companies would not accidentally reuse the same names.

Outside of personal computers, the Internet has similar problems with transfer of information via e-mail and Web pages. In an Internet-oriented computing world, the MIME (Multipurpose Internet Mail Extensions) types are commonly used. These are textual names for various kinds of information. MIME type names generally consist of a content type, such as text, image or video, and a subtype such as JPEG, GIF, or TIFF. As with the simple Clipboard type names used by the Macintosh, there is a need to register MIME type names so that their meaning is universally understood. This is handled by the Internet Assigned Numbers Authority (IANA)[1].

With the advent of object-oriented programming, it is frequently desired to pass complex objects between various parts of an application or between cooperating applications. Object-oriented languages that support reflection, such as C# or Java, allow Clipboard entries to use the `Type` or `Class` of the object as a type identifier. In such languages, it is possible just to put an object onto the Clipboard and let the system determine its type. This mechanism allows objects to retain their representations. In Java, for example, the type is sufficient to process the object so long as the other application has that class on its CLASSPATH. In C#, similar things are possible using DLLs and/or assemblies of code. This mechanism is very convenient for integrating programs because programmers can now think exclusively in terms of model objects. However, the `Type` or `Class` mechanisms are confined to transfer among programs using the same language. This is convenient but very restrictive. The more general case is the textual type names and, in particular, the MIME types.

User Intervention

In some cases, the transfer intent is not clear from the source and destination types. Suppose you copy a section of a spreadsheet. Later when pasting that material into another part of the spreadsheet or into a different spreadsheet there are some ambiguities. Are just the visible values of the cells to be pasted or are the formulas for computing the values also to be pasted? When pasting formulas that reference beyond the copied region, what is to be done with those references? Should the format of the source cells be used or the formatting of the destination? These kinds of questions cannot be answered exclusively from type information because all of the options are acceptable to the software. The question is the intent of the user. The user interface convention is for paste to use a default that preserves the most information and then provide a Paste Special option that allows the user to choose from the available possibilities.

MAKING THE CONNECTION

Conceptually, the Clipboard is a shared memory space. The source places items on the Clipboard and the destination rummages through them to find useful information to copy from the Clipboard. However, several issues complicate this model. First are the differences depending on whether an object-oriented programming language, or a lower-level language such as C is assumed. Second is the question of what boundaries exist between source and destination. These include crossing process boundaries, programming language boundaries, and hardware system boundaries. Third, on smaller machines, space for all of the various formats of the same item can be an issue. This is less important than it once was due to larger memories. Fourth is the problem of the time to render an item into all of the various formats that might be useful. If a source renders a copied item into 10 formats, it is rare that more than one will be used in a destination.

The simplest Clipboard mechanism is to serialize the copied or cut objects into all of the possible forms. Serialization is the process of converting a data structure in memory into a serial stream of bytes suitable for some other piece of code to rebuild the data structure from the stream. This is essentially what happens when data is written to a file. Serializing data for each different format makes the Clipboard into a collection of type-named sequences of bytes. This requires the source to generate byte streams in all of the various formats that might be desired. The first improvement on this primitive model was *deferred posting* to the Clipboard. In X Windows, this was accomplished by an application posting itself as the clip source and then responding to any events requesting Clipboard information. Clip contents were not rendered until a particular format was requested. An X Windows application could ask for a list of possible formats before requesting one of the format types to be rendered. Microsoft Windows allowed source programs to post a type with a null pointer to the data. If the destination requests a type for which the pointer is null, the system sends an event to the source program instructing it to render the desired type into the Clipboard where it is then available to the destination.

The advantage of deferred posting is that only formats that are actually used need be generated. The disadvantage is that the source must remember what is on the Clipboard for as long as it owns the Clipboard information. In many cases, the source program has moved on to perform other edits or operations. However, for the Clipboard system to work, it must remember the information. One of the nice features of the Microsoft Windows solution is that the source has either option. It can render all of the types and forget about the Clipboard or it can defer and remember what it needs. A compromise strategy is also possible. The source can render clip information in its native form, post null pointers for all other types, and then, if necessary, render alternative forms from the native information posted on the Clipboard. This has the advantages of deferred posting without the problems of remembering clip information that no longer exists in the source model.

The previous approaches assume that the clip information must be serialized. Serialization means that model objects are rendered into a self-contained stream of bytes. This is required if the source and destination are two different processes with different memory spaces or even more so in the X Windows case where the source and destination might not even be on the same machine. However, a common use of cut/copy/paste is from one place in an application to another place in the same application. It would be helpful just to move the data objects without the serialization step.

Object-Oriented Cut/Copy/Paste

Object-oriented languages can simplify many of the issues in cut/copy/paste. The first step is to wrap the source of Clipboard information in an interface. In C#, this is the IDataObject interface. Java/Swing has the Transferable interface. These interfaces provide methods to find out the types of information available and to get information of a particular type. Any source that conforms to the interface is appropriate. By implementing IDataObject or Transferable, a source has complete freedom to decide how the Clipboard information will be saved and rendered. The methods subsume any event-handling mechanism. The destination need not be concerned with any of these issues. It is presented with an object that conforms to the interface and uses it to get the information that is needed.

A source can create an IDataObject that simply stores the data in process memory. If the destination is in the same process space, pasting is just a copying of objects or pointers to objects. If the destination is in a different process, the Clipboard system presents the destination with an IDataObject that will work through shared memory and the event mechanism to transfer data across process boundaries without either the source or destination needing to know. If the source and destination are on different machines, IDataObject or Transferable proxy objects can handle the communication without either side being involved. This approach allows the source, the destination, and the Clipboard system to all perform their functions relative to a simple interface without much effort on the part of any of them.

A second advantage of object-oriented languages with reflection is the use of language types as the Clipboard types. If the source and destination both share the same language and class definitions, the type naming can simply use the class objects rather than MIME types. This greatly simplifies transferring all kinds of complex objects in a very natural way. The MIME types or similar naming will still be required when information must be transferred to applications written in different languages or possessing different class definitions.

Lastly, reflection-based languages can provide default serialization of objects. Rather than the source application translating its objects into a stream of bytes and the destination parsing those bytes, many languages automatically perform this function using the class object information. In reflection-based languages, every class is known at run time and every field in every class is known also. This allows system developers to write a single method that explores the class information of any object and renders a serialization of that object and any other object that it references. Similarly, a general parse method can be written to reconstruct an object from the stream. This allows source and destination applications to completely ignore everything except posting and getting objects, with the language system taking care of everything else.

There is, however, a warning about automatic serialization. The default automatic mechanisms work by recursively following every pointer to find every part of a complex object. This is particularly a problem in user interfaces. If every model object has listeners to be notified when the model changes, then those listeners are pointers to objects. The automatic serialization will follow those listener pointers to the widgets displaying the model. You rarely want the widgets serialized with the model but it gets worse. Every widget has a pointer to its parent widget. Every parent widget has a pointer to all of its children. Every child widget has a pointer to its model. By implication, serializing a simple model object has the potential of serializing all application data and the entire user interface. This is not a good plan. Most serialization systems have mechanisms for controlling what pointers are followed and what actually gets serialized. With a little attention, this problem can be addressed.

SOURCE/DESTINATION RELATIONSHIP

When an object is copied or cut from a source and placed in a destination, three forms of relationship can be established. The first is that described previously where the data is copied and the relationship to the source is forgotten. The pasted data is now the responsibility of the destination. The second form is where the data is copied in its native form and a link is retained to the source so that the source application can be used to change the data. The third is where a link to the data is what is copied as well as an image of the data's presentation. Whenever the source is changed, the pasted data and the presentation image in the destination are also changed. The first form has already been discussed.

	A	B	C	D	E	F	G
1	**Name**	**Job Type**	**Hours**	**Pay**		**Job Type**	**Wages**
2	Phred Phinster	Manager	40	$800.00		Asst M	$15
3	Joan James	Crew	30	$300.00		Crew	$10
4	Helen Holmes	Asst M	50	$750.00		Manager	$20
5	Kenny Kravitz	Phlunky	10	$ 80.00		Phlunky	$8

Figure 15.1 – Spreadsheet to copy and paste

The second two techniques can be illustrated by copying a portion of a spreadsheet into a word processing document. In the Microsoft world, this is called Object Linking and Embedding (OLE)[2] and has been subsumed into Microsoft's ActiveX. Suppose you have a spreadsheet like that shown in Figure 15.1. You want to copy the shaded region and paste it into a document, as shown in Figure 15.2.

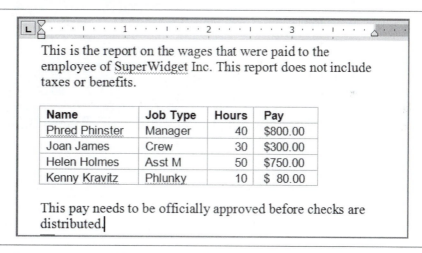

Figure 15.2 – Spreadsheet data pasted into a document

At this point, the data has been pasted into the document and displayed. Pasting a picture of the data would be sufficient for this purpose. However, data tends to change. Suppose that the manager only works 35 hours instead of 40. You could go back to the original spreadsheet, make the change, and then repeat the copy/paste process. However, this would require that the owner of the document could find the spreadsheet.

An alternative is to store the original native spreadsheet data in the document along with the name of the program that manages that data and a picture of the data. For most document uses, the picture is shown. The destination application has no knowledge of how the data is formatted, it just displays the image. When the user double-clicks on the table in the document, it changes, as shown in Figure 15.3. Knowing the application that understands this data, the host has created a window where the data was originally in the document and has launched the source application passing it the data and the window. This allows the source application to edit the data using its own user interface. When the editing is done, the window is deselected, the new data and image replaces the old, and the document returns to normal. This *edit in place* strategy allows a destination, such as a document, to play host to a wide variety of editable information without knowing anything about how those applications function other than the name of the application.

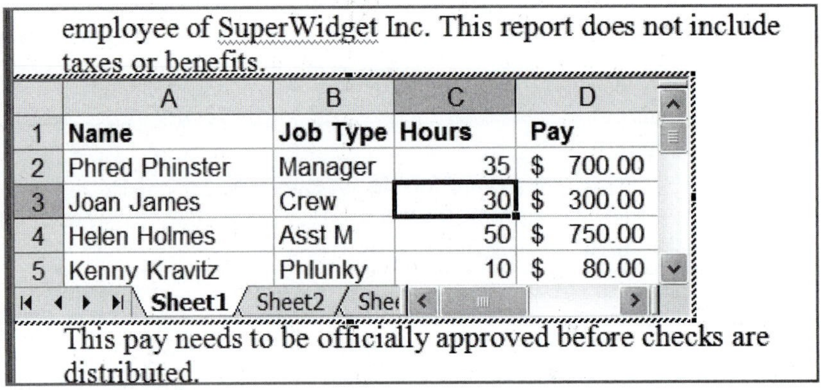

employee of SuperWidget Inc. This report does not include taxes or benefits.

	A	B	C	D
1	Name	Job Type	Hours	Pay
2	Phred Phinster	Manager	35	$ 700.00
3	Joan James	Crew	30	$ 300.00
4	Helen Holmes	Asst M	50	$ 750.00
5	Kenny Kravitz	Phlunky	10	$ 80.00

Sheet1 / Sheet2 / Shee

This pay needs to be officially approved before checks are distributed.

Figure 15.3 – Edit-in-place

When doing pasting in this fashion, there is a question of what should be pasted. Figure 15.4 shows that the table that defines the wages is included in the pasted data even though it does not show in Figure 15.2. Considering the way spreadsheets work, this is important because pay cannot be computed from hours without the wage information. When copying from the spreadsheet, the source must consider the information needed for later editing.

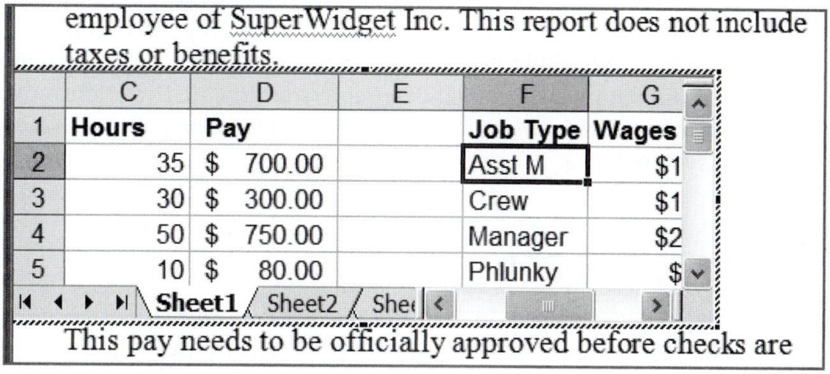

employee of SuperWidget Inc. This report does not include taxes or benefits.

	C	D	E	F	G
1	Hours	Pay		Job Type	Wages
2	35	$ 700.00		Asst M	$1
3	30	$ 300.00		Crew	$1
4	50	$ 750.00		Manager	$2
5	10	$ 80.00		Phlunky	$

⏮ ◀ ▶ ⏭ \ **Sheet1** / Sheet2 / She‹ ‹

This pay needs to be officially approved before checks are

Figure 15.4 – Scrolling the pasted spreadsheet

There is an alternative to edit in place called *edit aside*. In edit aside, the host application opens a new window of its own with its own menus and toolbars. For a source application to support edit-in-place, it must prepare a special view that works well in the embedded situation. Frequently, this involves mixing the source program's menu items with the destination program's menu items to provide the necessary functionality to the interactive user. The edit aside option is much simpler for the source application. The user interface is unchanged. The only thing that is different is saving and loading information from within the destination's paste location rather than a file.

The third source/destination relationship is a link to the original source data. Suppose that the spreadsheet from Figure 15.1 was part of a much larger wages report for all subsidiary companies. You would want the simple document to change whenever the larger report changes. This would involve pasting only an image and a link to the source in the destination. Whenever the source is changed, the destination would follow the link, get the source to generate a new image, and paste that image in. This was pioneered by Apple's Publish and Subscribe facility. The problem with such links is that, like Web page links, they get broken. They also have a problem with robustness. Suppose that the pasted table in Figure 15.2 was implemented as a link and the source application inserted a new column. If the link was defined as C1:F5 and a new column was added, the pasted material is now linked inappropriately. It is possible that the source could remember all published links and update them, but that complicates the source program. Such bookkeeping to support publication also slows down the normal operation of the source program, increasing the latency in its interactive behavior.

Layout of Embedded Information

When pasting embedded information, there is a problem of layout. Suppose that the table in Figure 15.2 were to cross a page boundary. If this were a normal word processor table, an appropriate break could be found at one of the table rows. However, if the pasted table is data from another application, such page break behavior is much more complicated because it requires some negotiation between the destination and source application. Apple's OpenDoc[3] system, which was also supported by IBM and the Object Management Group, attempted to address this problem. Microsoft's OLE, however, assumes that embedded material occupies a rigid rectangular window and does not attempt to accommodate more sophisticated relationships. Because OLE is simpler to create and simpler to use, it made it to market much sooner and was more widely adopted.

DRAG AND DROP

A very popular variant on cut/copy/paste is drag and drop. Drag and drop moves data from a source to a destination but it does not use the conceptual intermediary of a Clipboard. Underneath, many of the data transfer mechanisms are the same, but to the user there are some differences. There are three issues from the user-interface perspective: (1) How do you determine in the user interface when drag and drop has been initiated? (2) How do you provide feedback to the user during dragging? and (3) What does drag and drop actually mean?

Consider the drawing program shown in Figure 15.5. The mouse is over the image and on mouse-down, it will begin some user operation. In the mouse-down event handling, it is unknown whether the user is selecting the image, moving the image around the screen, or dragging the image to another application. In Figure 14.20 in the previous chapter, the PPS shows how to resolve the issue between clicking and dragging. You can resolve the drag-and-drop decision by adding the mouse-exit event (*ME), as shown in Figure 15.6. In the case of the picture, you would probably decide that this is a translation until the user starts to drag outside of the picture boundaries, in which case you would switch to a drag/drop operation. This is shown in the final rule of the PPS in Figure 15.6. When a source does decide, it can offer its data for dragging in much the same way as with putting information on the Clipboard. In Java/Swing, this is done using the same `Transferable` class to encapsulate transferable data. This would be done in the `!startDragAndDrop` action of Figure 15.6.

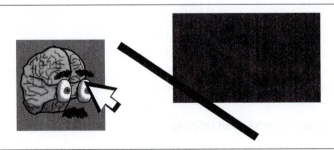

Figure 15.5 – Drag-and-drop image

```
Input {*MD, *MM, *MU, *ME} // New input event for mouse-exit.
LeftButton {LD*, LU*}
ShiftButton {SD*,SU* }
Mode { select, line, rect, ellipse, polyline, curve}
State { idle, dragging, points, clickSelecting,
        rectLassoSelecting, controlDragging, objDragging
    dragAndDrop } // A drag and drop operation is underway.
Actions {  . . . drawing actions . . .
          . . . selection actions (Figure 14.20) . . .
        !startDragAndDrop       // Serialize the selected objects and put them into
                               // whatever form is necessary for droppable information.
                               // Give the drag-and-drop system an icon that represents
                               // what is being dragged.


    }
MouseLoc { ?nearFirstPoint, ?nearPrevPoint, ?farAway }
Selection{ ?objectSelected, ?noObjectSelected}
Control {?controlSelected, ?noControl }


    . . . all of the rules for normal selecting and dragging (Figure 14.20).

objDragging *MM LD* -> !moveSelected
        // Continue dragging the object on each mouse move.
objDragging *MU LU* -> !setSelected idle
        // Move the object to its new location in the model.
objDragging *ME LD* -> !startDragAndDrop dragAndDrop

    . . . other rules for lines, rectangles, ellipses, polylines and curves (Figure 14.2)
```

Figure 15.6 – Full PPS for select and drag

There are three entities that participate interactively in a drag-and-drop operation. The source widget initiates the interaction and must provide feedback to the user about the object being dragged. Potential destination widgets must provide feedback about whether they will accept a drop of a particular data object. Lastly, the drag/drop system must provide feedback about the object being dragged.

The interactive response of the source is generally to show the source component as highlighted. This is relatively straightforward. To handle the feedback by the destination, the Widget interface generally provides events that notify Widgets when there is a drag operation in progress over that widget. In C#, there are the following:

- DragEnter—An object being dragged has just entered the widget.

- DragOver—This is similar to a mouse-move only with drop data attached.

- DragLeave—The dragging object has left this widget.

- DragDrop—The user has released the mouse over this widget to initiate a drop.

In addition, most systems have a flag on a widget to indicate whether that widget will accept drops at all. This allows the drag/drop system to ignore widgets that are not interested. Each of these events includes parameters with information about the mouse location, the source of the data, and the Transferable data container itself.

Flagging a widget as to its acceptance of dropping data allows for a default behavior of showing the "not" cursor over widgets that do not implement drag and drop. The default flag value is negative, which means that if the programmer does nothing, the "not" cursor is automatically present over those widgets. However, when a widget does accept dropped items, the programmer must remember to set the flag or the widget will never receive any of the drag-and-drop events.

There are two common scenarios for the destination. The first is to examine the data on DragEnter to see if any of the information is acceptable. This works much like examining the Clipboard in a paste operation. The destination widget then responds with user feedback on the kind of drop operation it will perform if dropped. In C#, a widget can choose standard feedback options from among Move, Link, Copy, or None. The decision among these is generally based on the data and the mouse button that was pressed. With this simple strategy, the drag/drop system handles all of the feedback, usually by changing the cursor to indicate the operation.

The second approach is that the destination will modify itself in some way to reflect the consequences of the drop if it is performed. Figure 15.7 shows the Eclipse IDE dragging a view around the screen. The mouse cursor at the right has been changed to show where the new view will be placed and the shaded rectangle shows how the existing window space will be split to make room for the new view if it is dropped at that location.

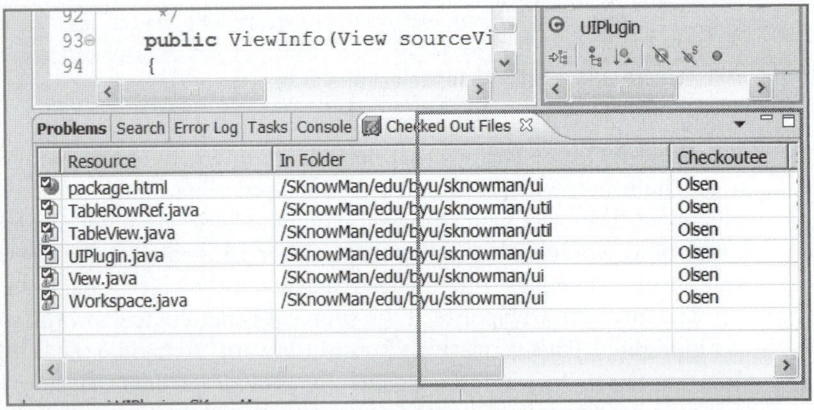

Figure 15.7 – Dragging views around Eclipse

The DragOver event allows the application to update its echo in an appropriate way. Using the Eclipse example in Figure 15.7, the highlight rectangle moves to new positions as the mouse moves to continually show the user where the window being dragged will appear when dropped. The DragOver event is essentially a special mouse-move event with additional information about the data being carried. The DragLeave event is like a mouse-exit. In particular, it allows the destination application to remove any echoes that it has created to show the effect of a drop action. The

`DragDrop` event is much like a paste action. The contents of the drag/drop buffer or `ITransferable` object are added to the destination application's model and all of the appropriate view update notifications are fired.

With cut/copy/paste, it is usually at the source where the ultimate action is decided. For example, a cut removes the data from the source and places it on the Clipboard, whereas a copy makes a duplicate. With drag/drop, it is generally at the destination where the action is decided. This is primarily because in some cases the user expresses an action by the location where the drop is performed. Dropping into a trash can implies a deletion from the source rather than just a copy. Dropping a file onto another folder on the same storage drive implies that the file is to be moved. Dropping it onto a folder on a different drive or network-attached computer implies a copy operation. In some cases, the destination pops up a menu after the drop to allow the user to specify the actual action to be performed. For example, when dragging a file from one part of Windows to another, using the right mouse button, when the button is released a menu pops up asking the user if they want to copy the file to the new location, move the file to the new location, or create a short-cut link from the new location to the original location.

SUMMARY

Cut/copy/paste and drag/drop provide mechanisms for the user to transfer information among applications and across networks. There is always an intermediary such as a Clipboard or `Transferable` object that serves as the container and negotiator between source and destination. The source indicates the data formats that it can deliver and the destination takes what it wants.

EXERCISES

1. Why is a type naming standard so important to the success of cut/copy/paste?
2. How do object-oriented languages help with the problems of appropriate access to a paste buffer?
3. Why is cut/paste simpler within a process than between processes?
4. What must be added to the event structure to support drag and drop?

END NOTES

[1] www.iana.org/
[2] Brockschmidt, Kraig. *Inside Ole*. Redmond, WA: Microsoft Press, 1995.
[3] Apple Computer, Inc. *OpenDoc Cookbook*. Reading, MA: Addison Wesley, 1996.

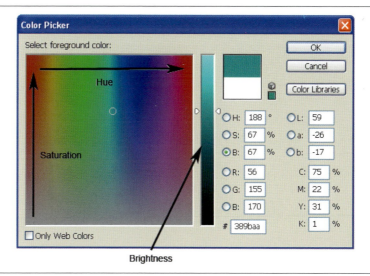

Figure 2.8 – Adobe Photoshop color picker

Figure 4.6 – Varying media player "skins"

Figure 4.12 – Color selection widget

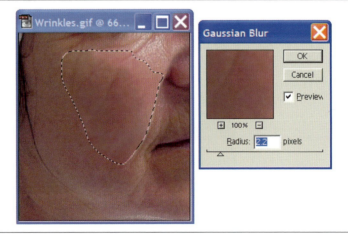

Figure 6.3 – Photoshop filter views

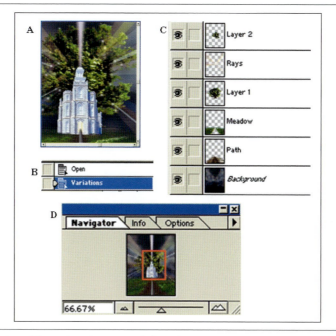

Figure 6.4 – Photoshop image model windows

Figure 8.6 – Poor color contrast

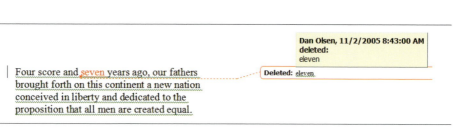

Figure 17.1 – Change tracking in Word

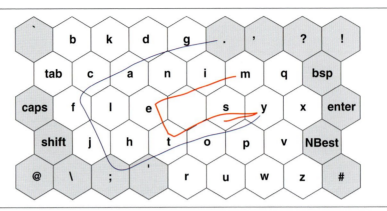

Figure 18.15 – SHARK sokgraph for "system"

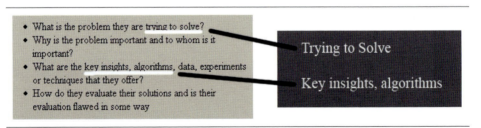

Figure 19.31 – Annotating text

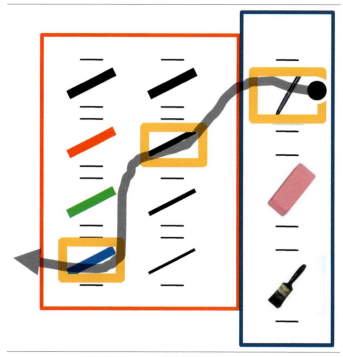

Figure 20.12 – CrossY selection

Figure 24.8 – Image Processing with Crayons

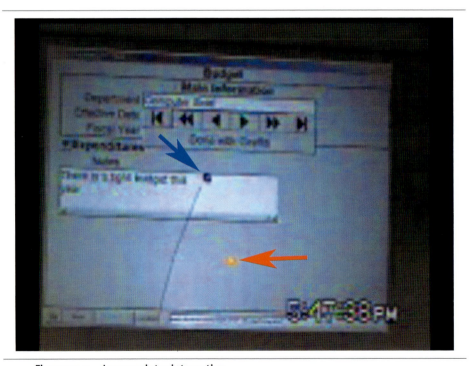

Figure 24.9 – Laser pointer interaction

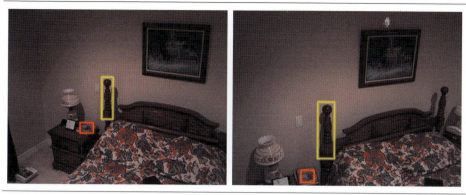

Figure 24.12 – Drawing a Light Widget

Figure 24.13 – Sample picture for separation

CHAPTER 16

Undo, Scripts, and Versions

In 1983, Ben Shneiderman published a paper on the concept of "direct manipulation" [1] where users would stop specifying commands about objects that they could not see but would directly manipulate visual objects on the screen. This was part of the important transition away from command-line interfaces to the graphical user interfaces of today. One of the key claims of direct manipulation is that users would learn primarily by trying manipulations of visual objects rather than by reading extensive manuals. A very important part of learning by trying is perceived safety. A user should be able work in an interface with the confidence that no disastrous thing will happen without warning. The most important feature for such safe exploration is an undo operation that works almost everywhere and in the same way. A second feature is that any operation that cannot be undone must be confirmed by the user before passing the "point of no return."

A common remark by people who are uncomfortable with computers is "I don't want to break it." The fear of permanent loss of information, labor, or the good working order of the system is a major impediment to learning new systems. When a user is asked to march into the unknown of a new application, they want to know if there are "dragons, snakes, bugs, or bears" out there. The answer is usually, "Yes, but undo will kill any that cause problems." That faith in the universal applicability of undo is critical to learning new interfaces.

Undo is also important to efficient use of any application. The existence of an undo means that a user need not plan as carefully before taking an action. If some action leads to a bad place, undo can back out. If there are mistakes caused by working too fast, undo can correct them. Rather than carefully predicting the presence or absence of errors, the user simply speeds ahead and lets the computer show them the result of their actions. If a mistake is made, it can be undone. The basic architecture for supporting undo also provides mechanisms for scripting languages and alternative versions of a work product. Scripting allows users to automate repetitive behaviors so that they need not consume user time. Versioning allows groups of people to work together while controlling their shared work product.

UNDO ISSUES

For undo to be effective, it must be pervasive. The user must know that *every* action can be undone, not just a selected subset. If only a subset of actions is undoable, the user must consider whether the next action is or is not in the set. This defeats the learning and efficiency advantages of undo. However, if undo is to be pervasive, it poses some serious software architecture problems. A modest application might have hundreds of different actions that cause changes to the model. Many applications have thousands and all of them must be reliably undoable whenever the undo action is selected.

You generally view undo as restoring the model to the state it was in before a user action was taken. At first, this might seem like a model-oriented problem; however, some actions might make several changes to the model. For example, a find-and-replace operation might do any number of replacement changes, but the user thinks about them all as one single event. Undoing them one at a time would not be acceptable. Putting a method on the model to perform find-and-replace would support placing all undo facilities on the model, but that is an architectural consideration that requires clear thought. If a single user action is composed either by the model or the controller of several model changes, how do all those changes get collected so that they can be undone?

You must also think of the implications of model changes. For example, when a user changes a cell in a spreadsheet, that change might cause other cells to recompute. Must you save the changes to all of those cells as part of the undo so that they can be restored or can you save only the original cell's change and let the recomputation restore the others? In the find-and-replace command, all changes must be saved. In the spreadsheet, only the source change must be saved. This requires some careful thought when designing an undo facility.

There is also the question of what things must be undoable by an undo operation and which are naturally transient and do not need an undo. For example, does the movement of a scroll bar need to be undone? It is a user action; however, for most users, the easiest undo is to scroll back to the original position. Do selections need to be undone? The model has not changed, but the set of selected objects has changed. Solutions to this issue must answer two questions:

1.   Is there a natural undo as part of the user interface? (scroll back to the original position)

2.   How much user effort would be lost if undo is not present?

A good example of the second question is found in Adobe Photoshop. In most applications, selection is not undoable because it is assumed that the user will simply reselect what is desired and no model information has been lost. In Photoshop, selection of a region of pixels can be very laborious (3-10 minutes) with careful attention to image edges required and some manual dexterity and care. Therefore in Photoshop selection is an undoable operation.

There is also the issue of granularity of the undo. When dragging an ellipse across a drawing, the model is modified every time the mouse moves. The user would not be pleased with an undo operation that undid each individual mouse movement. Repeatedly striking CTRL+Z to watch the "ellipse movie" play backwards will not make any user happy. What is generally wanted is that the ellipse will go back to where it was before being dragged. The path along the way was not important even though it included many model changes. In a text box, an undo might revert the text box contents back to the original text before the user started typing rather than play back the individual character insertions and deletions. In a word processor, this is more problematic. A simple undo model will undo every user command, which is every keystroke. This can be very tedious when the user wants to restore an entire paragraph to what it was before. Other word processors use punctuation, timing pauses, or cursor selection/movement operations to form boundaries for larger-scale undo operations. Granularity of undo requires some careful thought.

Lastly, there is the implementation of the undo command itself. When the user strikes CTRL+Z, the application must undo whichever one of its hundreds to thousands of actions the user did last. Obviously, a giant `switch` statement that encompasses all possible application commands is not going to scale up to large applications. You need a better architectural solution. You need an undo architecture that the generic undo command can use, but whose details are distributed throughout the code and associated with each individual command to be undone.

There are two main architectures for undo. The first is to store a base checkpoint of the model and then to store a series of change records. This is termed *forward undo* because it starts from a known point and reconstructs the model by making changes moving forward in time. There is also *reverse undo* where only the current model is retained and the change records store enough information to convert the current model into the previous model.

BASELINE AND FORWARD UNDO

The forward undo mirrors the patch management strategy found in most source code control systems[2]. These systems store a baseline copy of the model. Each action is then represented by a record of the change that it makes. Starting with the baseline, you can apply the changes in order up to whatever point you desire. To undo the last change, remove it from the change history and rebuild the model from the baseline up to the point just before the change to be undone.

For example, a simple text editor could have two commands:

- Delete *startIndex, endIndex*
- Insert *startIndex, insertString*

These two commands can be used to represent any changes to a text string. A log of these commands constitutes a *patch* or an *edit history* on the original text string. You can augment these two commands with a StartAction command. Before the controller begins modifying the model, it places a StartAction command in the edit log. Thus, if a given controller action makes many modifications to the model, the undo can remove all of them up to the last StartAction. This provides for the undo of complex operations in a natural way.

The action log for forward undo is simply a list of model change commands and their parameters. All that is needed is enough information to repeat the calls to the model change methods in the same order. A simple way to implement action logging is to provide the ActionLog object, as shown in Figure 16.1.

```
public class ActionLog
{
        public void startAction(); // marks the beginning of a controller action
        public void removeLastAction(); // removes all entries back to the last startAction entry
        public void addCommand(int commandID, string parameters);
            // adds a change command to the log
        public replayCommands(Object model);
            // apply each of the commands to the model in order
        public doCommand(Object model, int commandID, string parameters);
            // this must be overridden in a subclass to implement a switch that selects
            // the correct command action, parses the parameters, and calls the method.
}
```

Figure 16.1 – ActionLog for forward undo

You can then take every model change method and add a call to addCommand() at the beginning to log the change being taken. You can also create a subclass of ActionLog and override the doCommand() method with a large switch statement on commandID. This provides the code that will perform the actions by parsing the parameter string and then calling the model method.

This approach is conceptually easy to implement. However, it has three difficulties. The first is that reconstruction of the model through a long series of edits can be inefficient. This is less of a problem with faster machines and the human limits on how many changes human hands can make. The second is that code must be added to every method to correctly log the changes. The third problem is that the doCommand() method becomes the focus of every interactive change in the entire application. This creates serious code management problems.

A minor variant to this architecture is where the addCommand() method is replaced with a doAndAddCommand() method. The doAndAddCommand() method first performs the method and then adds it to the log. The controller then no longer accesses the model directly but through the `ActionLog`. This removes the logging from the model methods and puts it into the controller. It also ensures that the replay will be identical to the original actions because the model actions were performed through the same mechanism.

If your architecture contains an `ActionLog`, it can also be used for a macro recording system and a scripting system. You first augment `ActionLog` to include methods to translate string command names to and from the integer `commandID`s that you use for efficiency. This allows you to represent each command as *commandName parameterString*. You can create a macro recording system that uses a special `ActionLog` to collect all of the actions between the time that recording is turned on and the time that it is turned off. Replaying those actions using the `replayCommands()` method executes the macro. The body of the macro can be saved as a series of command strings for later use. Figure 16.2 shows a small Microsoft Excel spreadsheet. By turning on macro recording, you can record your user-interface actions for bolding a column and computing its sum. Figure 16.3 shows the VBA script created as a macro from your actions.

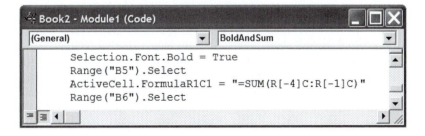

Figure 16.2 – Sample spreadsheet

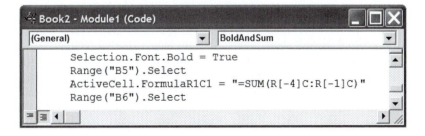

Figure 16.3 – Recorded macro

After you have a mechanism to translate a *command/parameter* string into any action on your model, your interface is now *scriptable*. After your action/macro system is represented in string form, you can edit the macros and scripts. It is now possible to write short programs to augment your interface to do any number of things. A scripting language like the `ActionLog` is quite simplistic but it is a start. The ability to demonstrate a script in the user interface greatly simplifies the learning of such languages. The Macintosh was a leader in providing AppleScript[3] with many of its applications. Microsoft's VBScript and VBA are also examples of such tools[4]. The implementation of the TCL[5] scripting language uses a very similar approach.

Input Event Logging

An alternative to logging model change actions is to log input events. Obviously, all model changes are derived from input events and, thus, a replay of the input events should replay the actions. The attraction of this approach is that there are many fewer input events than there are model actions. There are less than 30 actual input events and even in systems that have hundreds of outside events, the set is fixed and the logging need only be implemented once for all applications. The problem is that the meaning of input events is highly dependent upon the view. Consider, for example, a Web page editor. If the width of the window is changed, the positions of the words move and the meanings of all mouse locations are broken. There are work-arounds for these problems, but they quickly become more complex than logging the model actions. Input event logging has its attractions but generally is not practical.

COMMAND OBJECTS AND BACKUP UNDO

The action log/forward undo model has problems with concentrating all of the interactive command implementations through one `doCommand()` method. It also has problems with its forward approach of recomputing a model from its baseline. A more efficient approach is for undo to restore the model to what it was before the action was taken. This *backward undo* model requires that the application remember enough information to make that restoration. For example, when characters are deleted from a document, the application must remember those characters and where they were in the document so that it can put them back if the undo operation is invoked.

To deal with these issues, Bertram Meyer created *command objects*[6]. The approach is based on the `Command` interface shown in Figure 16.4. Using this interface, you can create a `Command` object class for every model command that you have in your application. Rather than calling a model method, the controller creates the appropriate `Command` object for that action, invokes `doIt()` on the object to have the command performed, and then pushes the command object onto the history stack. An undo operation takes the top item from the history stack and invokes `undo()` to reverse the operation. The reversed object can then be pushed on the redo stack so that if the user requests a redo operation, the controller takes the top command from the redo stack, invokes `doIt()`, and pushes the command back onto the undo stack.

In this approach, each command object class is responsible for remembering the required information for `doIt()` and `undo()` to be performed. The general undo mechanism only needs to know about the `Command` interface.

```
public interface Command
{
        public void doIt();    // execute the command
        public void undo();    // undo the command
}
```

Figure 16.4 – Command object interface

The model shown in Figure 16.5 is for a simple text editor. It includes operations to insert and delete pieces of a string based on the index of the location where the edits are to occur.

```
public class TextModel
{
        public int nCharacters() { .. }    // returns the number of characters in the string
        public String getCharacters(int firstIdx, int lastIdx) { .. }
                // returns the characters stored at firstIdx through lastIdx inclusive.
        public void delete(int firstIdx, int lastIdx) { .. }
                // deletes the characters at firstIdx through lastIdx inclusive.
        public void insert(int firstIdx, String newChars) { .. }
                // inserts newChars into the text so that the first character at newChars will
                // be at firstIdx.
}
```

Figure 16.5 – Text editor model

Figure 16.6 shows the command objects for `delete` and for `insert`. Each has three parts: (1) a constructor that acquires the model and the parameters for the command, (2) a `doIt()` method to perform the command and save any necessary information, and (3) an `undo()` method to restore the model. It is possible to create these command object classes in such a way that the original methods can be made private and accessible only to the objects. This ensures that controller code only uses the undoable approach for making model changes.

Suppose that your controller has a variable called `cursor` that stores the current insertion point for your text editor application. Suppose also that an `undoHistory` object stores previously executed commands. Based on this, you can write the controller's `keyPressed()` method for accepting keyboard input. The method inserts characters, deletes characters on backspace, and performs undo when a CTRL+Z is received. The code for this method is shown in Figure 16.7 and demonstrates how the controller would use command objects to perform actions and to get them undone. You could simplify this code by having the `undoHistory.push()` method perform the `doIt()` before placing the command on the stack.

As was mentioned earlier, some controller actions cause multiple model changes that you might want to undo as a single unit. You can handle this by creating a special `CommandList` class that extends `Command`. This would have an `add(Command)` method

```
public class DeleteCmd implements Command
{       private int firstIdx, lastIdx;
        private String deletedChars;
        private TextModel model;

        public DeleteCmd(TextModel model, int firstIdx, int lastIdx)
        {       deletedChars=null;
                this.model=model;
                this.firstIdx=firstIdx;
                this.lastIdx=lastIdx;
        }
        public void doIt()
        {       deletedChars=model.getCharacters(firstIdx, lastIdx);
                model.delete(firstIdx, lastIdx);
        }
        public void undo()
        {       model.insert(firstIdx,deletedChars);  }
}
public class InsertCmd implements Command
{       private int insertIdx;
        private String insertChars;
        private TextModel model;

        public InsertCmd(TextModel model, int insertIdx, String insertChars)
        {       this.insertIdx=insertIdx;
                this.insertChars=insertChars;
                this.model = model;
        }
        public void doIt()
        {       model.insert(insertIdx,insertChars);  }
        public void undo()
        {       model.delete(insertIdx, insertIdx+insertChars.length()-1);  }
}
```

Figure 16.6 – Command objects for TextModel

that would add command objects to the list. In Java, this list of edit commands is called the `UndoManager`. The `CommandList.doIt()` would perform `doIt()` on each command object in its list in order. The `CommandList.undo()` would perform `undo()` on each command object in reverse order. Using `CommandList`, a controller can collect any number of model changes and then push them on the history stack as one command to be undone.

You could take a similar strategy for a drawing program. You might have command object classes `CreateLine`, `CreateRect`, `CreateEllipse`, and `MoveObject`. Each of the `Create***` classes would accept the input points as constructor parameters. Their `doIt()` methods would create the corresponding objects, add them to the model, and save a model reference to the object. Their `undo()` methods would remove the referenced objects from the model. The `MoveObject` class would take dx and dy and a model object reference o as parameters to its constructor. The `doIt()` method would translate object o by dx and dy. The `undo()` method would translate object o by -dx and -dy.

```
public void keyPressed(Char keyCharacter)
{
    Command cmnd=null;
    if ( isBackspace(keyCharacter) )
    {   cmnd=new DeleteCmd(myModel,cursor,cursor);
        cmnd.doIt();
        undoHistory.push(cmnd);
    }
    else if ( isControlZ(keyCharacter) )
    {   cmnd=undoHistory.pop();
        cmnd.undo();
    }
    else
    {   cmnd=new InsertCmd(myModel,cursor,new String(keyCharacter));
        cmnd.doIt();
        undoHistory.push(cmnd);
    }
}
```

Figure 16.7 – Implementing keyPress() using command objects

Scripting with Command Objects

A scripting system can be built from command objects in much the same way as the action log. You would need to add the method cmndString() to your Command interface. This method converts the command object into a string that can be written to a script file. You would also need to parse the command. When given a command string, you first need to identify which command object class should be instantiated. Remember that the different command behaviors are associated with different classes of objects. A simple technique is to create a hash table that maps command names to object classes. You then would have command strings of the following form:

> *commandName parameters*

To parse a command string, you first extract the command name, look up the appropriate class in the table, and instantiate the correct class of Command object. You need to add a parseParameters() method to Command so that you can pass the remainder of the command line to the object. Parsing the parameters should fill the command object with the information that it needs. You then execute the command by calling doIt(). It is common to have a generic parser that separates the parameters into an array of strings. The parseParameters() method only needs to interpret each parameter's string. This command formulation shares the TCL structure in many ways.

To make parseParameters() work, you need to pass in a reference to all of the models in the application. You also need a mechanism for referencing parts of the model for use as parameters to the commands. Generally, this is done by some kind of path expression such as document.paragraph[7].10-12 to select characters 10 through 12 of the seventh paragraph in the document. The nature of these path expressions varies from application to application. This is a key technique from the Domain Object Model (DOM) used in JavaScript[7]. If every model supports a getPathObject(String path) and a getPathString(Object modelObject) method, then you have what you need. A reference to any object can be obtained by getPathString() and added to the parameter string in cmndString() and when parsed out of the string by parseParameters(), the reference can be used as an argument to getPathObject() to retrieve the desired object. Object paths plus strings and numbers generally provide everything necessary to formulate and parse command strings using the Command object architecture. Figure 16.8 shows an example of how this might be done for the simple insert/delete model.

```
public class DeleteCmd implements Command
{    private int firstIdx, lastIdx;
     private String deletedChars;
     private TextModel model;

     public DeleteCmd(TextModel model, int firstIdx, int lastIdx)
     {    code to build object from parameters }
     public DeleteCmd() { everything to null }
     public void doIt() { ... }
     public void undo() { ... }
     public String cmndString()
     {    return "delete "+model.getPathString()+" "+firstIdx+" "+lastIdx; }
     public void parseParameters(String args[])
     {    model = (TextModel) getPathObject(args[0]);
          firstIdx= Integer.parse(args[1]);
          lastIdx= Integer.parse(args[2]);
     }
}
public class InsertCmd implements Command
{    private int insertIdx;
     private String insertChars;
     private TextModel model;

     public InsertCmd(TextModel model, int insertIdx, String insertChars)
     {    code to build from parameters }
     public InsertCmd() { set everything to null }
     public void doIt() { ... }
     public void undo() { ... }
     public String cmndString()
     {    return "insert "+model.getPathString()+" "+insertIdx+" ""+insertChars+"\""; }
     public void parseParameters(String args[])
     {    model= (TextModel) getPathObject(args[0]);
          insertIdx=Integer.parse(args[1]);
          insertChars=args[2]; // quotes already removed by parameter parser
     }
}
```

Figure 16.8 – Scripting with Command objects

This is not the only way scripting languages can be organized. A command string could start with a path expression and then the object retrieved could have a makeCommand(String commandName) method to produce the desired Command object and attach it to the model. The remaining parameters are then handled as before. This provides a more object-oriented scripting language.

REPRESENTING THE HISTORY

In many applications, the history stack is invisible to the user. All that the user sees is the undo command in the menu or a special key, such as CTRL+Z. With an invisible history, it is difficult to make effective use of a large history stack. The user must remember a desired point in history and accurately return to it. The redo command is helpful here. If, as commands are undone, they are placed on the redo stack, then if the user goes back too far, he can invoke redo to undo the undo. In many applications, it is helpful to show the history stack to the user. Figure 16.9 shows the history stack from Adobe Photoshop.

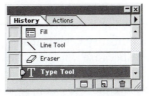

Figure 16.9 – Photoshop history

This kind of history presentation is easily created by adding the getIcon() and getName() methods to Command. In Java, the UndoableEdit interface provides all of these methods. These methods provide for the display of the history stack shown in Figure 16.9. In addition to the standard undo command, the user can select any command in the history stack display. This causes all commands that are later than the selected command to be undone in order. In Photoshop, the undone commands are displayed in gray to show that they are undone. Selecting an undone command causes redo operations up to the point of the selected command. These operations are quite simple to implement given the Command object architecture. The display of the history stack provides a rather friendly way to undo arbitrary amounts of work.

VERSIONING

It is frequently helpful for applications to maintain versions of a model so that changes can be tracked. This is quite common for source code control systems such as CVS[8]. The text editors in Eclipse also keep a Local History version that allows programmers to look at what they have changed. When many people are working on a project or the work is extensive, it is helpful to break it up into *patches* or *versions*. This allows the project to roll back to a previous state where everything was stable. Most versioning systems are based on the forward undo model. A baseline version of the object model is stored and then *patches* are stored that convert the baseline from version to version.

Patches can be constructed in two ways: differencing and history scripting. The differencing approach takes two versions of the model: before and after. A difference() method is applied to this pair to produce a description of how to change the before model into the after model. For source code control, this difference is a list of insert/delete commands. The two versions of the source code are compared and a list of insert/delete edits is generated. If you are using a Command object architecture, this approach can be applied to any model, not just text. Two versions of the model are compared and a list of Command objects is generated that will convert before into after. Using the cmndString() method, you can generate a text file that contains the patch that will convert before into after. You can apply the patch by loading the baseline model and executing the command objects in each patch until the desired version is obtained. All that is needed to implement this differencing form of versioning is a difference() method that can be applied to two versions of the same model. This difference() method is sometimes difficult to implement.

The history scripting approach to versioning saves the history stack as a command script. Producing a desired version involves loading the baseline model and applying the saved history commands to produce the new model. This is much simpler to implement because you just use the existing mechanisms with no need to implement a difference() method. The only drawback is that this might produce less space-efficient scripts. For example, constructing a paragraph by replaying insert commands for every character is not as efficient as recognizing a large insertion and generating one command that does it all. This can be mitigated by some of the history granularity issues described earlier in the chapter. The history approach also remembers all of the intermediate false steps that a user might have gone through to reach the final version. The differencing technique takes a shorter path between versions without replaying the user's uncertainty and explorations. Either differencing or history scripting with command objects can provide versioning capabilities to any application.

For such a versioning mechanism to be really effective, there must be a user interface that clearly shows the differences between two versions by showing the changes made by each of the commands in the patch. This is a more difficult problem than tracking the versions themselves. Such solutions are readily available for text such as programs but not as common for other interactive information.

SUMMARY

If every command that a user generates is tracked, you can undo any of those commands. This creates a safe and more user-friendly environment. The Command object architecture is the most robust for this purpose. After you have begun saving objects for every interactive command, you have enough information to generate a scripting language for that application and a versioning mechanism to support group work.

EXERCISES

1. Why are undo and redo important to the user's speed of use?

2. What are the advantages and disadvantages of the baseline and forward implementation of undo?

3. What are the advantages and disadvantages of using logged input events to implement baseline and forward undo?

4. Why must there be a separate command object class for each command that can be undone?

5. What are the principles you should use in deciding what inputs should be undoable and which should not?

6. Why do command objects lend themselves to the implementation of a scripting language to supplement the user interface?

7. Why is it helpful to have a visual representation of the command history?

8. How can command objects be helpful in managing versions of nontextual work?

END NOTES

[1] Shneiderman, Ben. "Direct Manipulation: A Step Beyond Programming Languages." *IEEE Computer* 16, 8 (August 1983): 57–69.

[2] Berliner, B. "CVS II: Parallelizing Software Development." *Proceedings of the USENIX Winter 1990 Technical Conference* (1990): 341–352.

[3] Neuburg, M. *AppleScript: The Definitive Guide.* Cambridge, MA: O'Reilly Media, 2006.

[4] Barron, D. *The World of Scripting Languages.* Hoboken, NJ: John Wiley & Sons, 2000.

[5] Ousterhout, J. *TCL and the TK Toolkit.* New York: Addison-Wesley, 1994.

[6] Meyer, B. *Object-Oriented Software Construction.* Upper Saddle River, NJ: Prentice-Hall, 1988.

[7] Flanagan, D. *JavaScript: The Definitive Guide.* Cambridge, MA: O'Reilly Media, Inc., 2001.

[8] www.CVSHome.org.

CHAPTER 17

Distributed and Collaborative Interaction

In many cases, the user and the interactive application are on different machines. This requires that the user interface be distributed from where the application is running to where the user is working. This situation occurs frequently when server computing is involved. The days of operators wearing lab coats and occupying the same room with specially air-conditioned, noisy servers are gone. There is no need for humans to work in the same space with large computing. However, to achieve this, the user interface must be distributed from the server to the user's computer. The need for distributing the user interface also arises when providing support to users spread around a company or around the world.

Another reason to distribute the interaction is to support collaboration. People rarely work alone. They are almost always part of a team engaged in a larger enterprise. The ability to share work among team members and to work together is important. In many situations, coworkers are distributed geographically. As computing work has been distributed around the world, the need for groups to collaborate has increased. Research by Kraut et al[1] has shown that a shared view of the work being done is more effective than collaboration solely over the phone or face-to-face video-conferencing. Such a shared view requires the distribution of the user interface among collaborators.

This chapter first discusses the key aspects of collaborative software. This provides a set of criteria for evaluating various strategies for distributing interaction. This is followed by a discussion of the various points in the model-view-controller architecture where distribution can be implemented.

COLLABORATION: A BRIEF INTRODUCTION

Collaborative user interfaces is a very large field with numerous issues, including the sociology of teamwork. This chapter only covers the basic distributed interface techniques that are the foundation of most collaborative systems. For additional reading, the proceedings of the ACM Computer Supportive Cooperative Work (CSCW) conference is an excellent place to start. Before launching into the technology, it is useful to discuss five major issues in collaborative interfaces: types of collaboration, identity, access, awareness, and device consistency.

Types of Collaboration

Much collaborative work is either asynchronous, where various team members work at their own time with no tight coordination with others, and synchronous, where multiple team members are engaged at the same time on the same work product.

A good example of asynchronous collaboration is e-mail. You can send a message, document, spreadsheet, or engineering drawing to a coworker for comments and then move on to other work. The coworker deals with the message when it is appropriate to him or her. Asynchronous collaboration has huge advantages in that resources are not tied down while others are thinking, planning, or obtaining other information and the overhead of synchronizing schedules among multiple people is eliminated.

A good example of synchronous collaboration is a phone call. All of the parties (if it is a conference call) are simultaneously committed and involved. This can provide for a very rapid exchange of information and facilitates reaching a common understanding. Synchronous collaboration in meetings is notorious for wasting some participants' time while others focus on topics that are not universally useful.

Synchronous collaboration at the user interface is characterized by What You See Is What I See (WYSIWIS). The goal is for all participants to see and have access to the same interactive work product as they discuss, modify, and approve whatever work product is under consideration.

Collaboration can also be characterized by the forms of communication. As with operating systems and many other concurrent systems, there are message-based collaboration models and shared data models. As with other systems, these two forms intermingle at various levels of implementation. E-mail and instant messaging are examples of message-based collaboration with e-mail being asynchronous and instant messaging being mostly synchronous. Systems like TeamRooms[2] provide a common place for team information to be stored and various team members work on the information either synchronously or asynchronously as the work requires.

Identity

A very important part of collaboration is the identity of collaborators. This is the heart of the e-mail spam problem where nobody knows for sure who is actually sending a message. An e-mail address provides some measure of confidence about who will receive a message but almost no confidence in who sent it. In more synchronous collaboration, instant messaging systems or collaborative Internet games provide buddy lists and other mechanisms for locating potential collaborators. Identity is a huge problem for collaborative activity, but its solution lies outside of the user-interface architecture and is not addressed here.

Access

After you know who the potential collaborators are, there is the question of how to grant access to the shared work product or user interface. Some people deal with the e-mail spam problem by restricting the set of people who can send messages to them. You might also want to share your network configuration screen with computer support staff, but not the contents of the document that you are editing.

Providing access is a user-interface design problem. Most systems provide access control as a hidden, special configuration option. The average user has only limited awareness of what has been shared and must look several layers deep to determine who can access the shared information. Older computing systems assumed that all users resided on the same machine and that all users were programmers. Such systems provided access to the individual user, a single group to which the user belongs, or to everyone in the world. This means that to share with someone outside of your group, you must share with everyone. This does not in any way reflect the practices of real collaborations.

On shared servers, access was managed on the file level and access privileges were visible in the file system view. Most personal computers were created with the assumption that only one user was on the computer and, therefore, access rights were not important. Most such systems do not show access rights in a consistent and understandable way in spite of the fact that the majority of PCs are connected to the Internet and are involved in worldwide collaborations.

It is also not obvious to the average user what the implications of sharing might be. On some systems, you can share a file with another user, but if the folder containing the file is not also shared, access is not truly granted. This might make sense to the implementers of the operating system but it makes no sense to the average user. A frequent response is to open all folders from the desired file up to the root of the file system so that access is ensured. This usually leads to exposure of many more items than the user intended. The implications of such a move are not visible to the user and, therefore, are the cause of frequent errors. The inheritance of rights is a nice programming concept that confuses many users, leaving them inadvertently exposed or without access. Most operating systems have one or more of these usability problems.

Within a single application, access manifests itself in the issue of *floor control*[3]. When more than one user is accessing an interface, it becomes confusing if all can make changes at the same time. Many multiuser interfaces impose floor control mechanisms whereby only one user can make changes at a time. In a physical meeting, floor control is frequently handled by a moderator who allocates speaking time to each participant or by whoever is at the whiteboard holding the marker. In distributed user interfaces, such social mechanisms are less apparent and sometimes floor control features must be explicitly provided.

A final access problem is the input and output of the interface itself. In a distributed application, both types of information must flow over the network and are, thus, exposed to a variety of snooping techniques. In particular, the presentation might contain private information and the input stream might contain passwords being typed. Mechanisms such as the Secure Sockets Layer (SSL) are important in protecting this data as part of a distributed user interface. One of the major problems with X Windows is its unsecured protocol. At the time of its creation, malicious use of the Internet was not as widespread is it is now.

Consistency Enforcement

When multiple users are working simultaneously on the same work product, a number of asynchrony problems can arise. If one user starts initiating a change and another also starts initiating a change in the same place, the overlap can lead to inconsistent results. This is complicated by latency in the network between the users. There is a large body of literature in distributed systems on schemes for guaranteed consistency. Greenberg and Marwood[4] discuss how the system-level mechanisms for maintaining consistency might or might not be appropriate in an interactive setting. They show how in many situations the inconsistencies might not matter for the problem or the nontechnical communication between users resolves the problems more effectively than cumbersome technical solutions.

An example of when technically correct consistency enforcement might not matter is found in some massively multiplayer games. The very large number of players and the rapidity of game play make the necessary locking mechanisms untenable. The result is that many such games do no locking at all. If my character reaches for the golden ring, it might appear to me that I have it. However, due to network latency, your "grab the ring" command might reach the game server first, at which point the ring appears to pop out of my character's hand and into yours. This is not quite correct, but good enough and the discrepancies feel like a part of the game play.

Awareness

In collaborative work, awareness of who else is working on the same problem and what they are doing is very important. In many cases, it is useful to know what changes they have made. The versioning systems mentioned in Chapter 16 usually retain information about who made the changes. What is also needed is the ability to see in the user interface the places where changes have been made. Figure 17.1 shows change tracking from Microsoft Word. Figure 17.2 shows similar change tracking/awareness in Microsoft Excel. Similar features are found in most source code control systems.

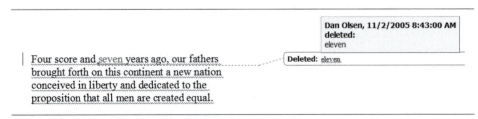

Figure 17.1 – Change tracking in Word (see color plate)

	A	B	C	D	E	F
1	Name	Wage	Hours	Pay		
2						
3	Jane	$ 2.00	10	$20		
4	Michael	$ 1.50				
5	Mary	$ 7.00				
6						
7						
8						

Dan Olsen, 11/2/2005 8:51 AM:
Changed cell B5 from ' $5.00 ' to ' $7.00 '.

Figure 17.2 – Change awareness in Excel

Awareness is particularly important in the user interface because it is additional information that must be handled in the model or in the change history. As can be seen from Figures 17.1 and 17.2, the nature of change awareness must adapt to the presentation of the particular application.

Coupled with awareness is the concept of change approval. In many collaborative applications, the changes are not finalized until others have considered them. A corporate software build process and corresponding source code control processes have this property. Document management systems where the end document is a collaborative effort also have this property. In preparing legislation, there are many changes to a law that have no effect until the final vote.

DEVICE CONSISTENCY

A last issue with distributing interfaces among multiple participants is the consistency of the interactive devices. If two users are interacting with the same application and there are differences between those computers, it becomes a problem for the application to consistently deal with both. Suppose the two computers had slightly different sets of installed fonts. This would make the widths of words slightly different and would make translating mouse clicks into text selection inconsistent. If one computer has a much larger screen than another, compatible window sizes might be impossible, leading to complications in sharing interfaces. There are also problems of installation. One computer might have OpenGL installed for 3D graphics and the other might not. The incompatibility will impact the ability to share interaction.

A more extreme yet very interesting case is when multiple users are on very different devices. Suppose that one user is working on a graphics workstation and the other on a PDA with a correspondingly small screen. The scenario gets more interesting if one user has a screen, but only voice input or perhaps no screen at all as on an older cell phone. These differences make identical interactive styles impossible, yet the desire to collaborate remains. The creation of good interactive architectures that can accomplish this level of sharing is still an open problem.

MVC AND DISTRIBUTION OF THE USER INTERFACE

In the model-view-controller architecture, there are several places where interface distribution can occur. Each has advantages and disadvantages and systems have been built for all of them. Figure 17.3 shows five different distribution schemes and their place in the MVC architecture. Each is discussed in the following sections.

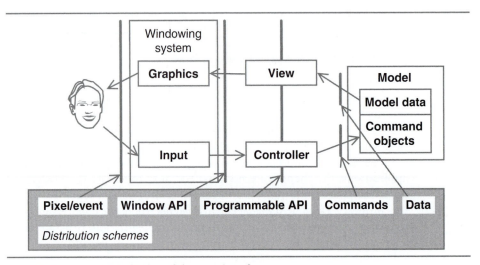

Figure 17.3 – Distribution of the user interface

In all of these schemes, there is a *server* application and one or more interactive *clients*. For simple distribution of the interface for remote access, there is only one client. For collaborative interactions, there might be many clients.

PIXEL/EVENT DISTRIBUTION

The simplest mechanism is the pixel/event distribution scheme. This scheme works at the screen level after the application has done its work. In this approach, there is an interactive application that is operating normally. Special server code is enabled that monitors the pixels on the screen. Whenever changes occur on the screen, the changed pixel regions are captured and sent over the network to each client. At each client, the pixels are painted on the screen. Thus, each client user sees the application exactly the way the user at the server sees it. A common implementation of this is Virtual Network Computing (VNC)[5]. VNC clients and servers generally use the Remote Frame Buffer (RFB) protocol. For a client, there are only two commands: (1) Paint this image at location (x,y) or (2) copy pixels from some rectangle to some other location. The first command is sufficient to perform all client display operations. The copy command provides more network efficiency when objects are dragging or windows are scrolling. Rather than package and send all those pixels, the copy command can reuse pixels that were previously sent.

When input events occur at the server application, they are handled as before. In this distribution approach, the server application is unaware that there are interactive clients. When input events occur at the client, those events are packaged up and sent to the server over the network (generally encrypted). At the server, the events are unpackaged and the server pushes those events to the windowing system as if they had been entered by the user.

Changes to the Screen

A server's display system must capture the pixels from the display and forward changes to those pixels on to the clients. There are three main issues: (1) getting the pixels, (2) determining what has changed, and (3) shipping changes to clients at a rate compatible with network speeds. This architecture is shown in Figure 17.4.

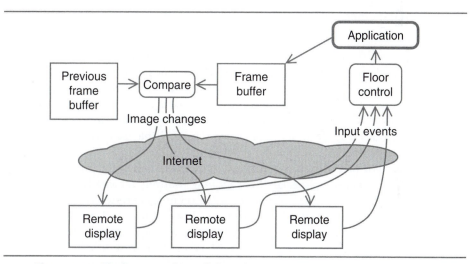

Figure 17.4 – Pixel propagation collaboration

Getting the pixels is easy on most systems. Fundamentally, a display card consists of pixel memory representing the displayed image. This memory can be read to obtain the currently displayed pixels. Most windowing systems provide such a method for screen capture so that server implementations need not know about the details of the display card.

Computing differences is a slightly harder problem. If the server saves a copy of the screen image last sent to the clients, a comparison can be made between the new pixels and the saved image. This comparison produces a set of changed rectangles that can be sent via RFB. This comparison, however, can have a significant cost. If a 1024×1024 window is being shared at 5 frames per second, then 5 megapixels per second must be compared. This can pose a significant load on some computers. This computational load is exacerbated if you try to use copy commands rather than just RFB image painting. Image copy requires a second step of comparing all changed rectangles against the saved image to determine if any of the pixels can be reused in a move command.

The costs of computing differences can be sharply reduced if the windowing system will provide additional assistance. Remember that the interactive loop creates damage() calls for every part of the screen that the application wants updated. If the windowing system provides the necessary hooks to be notified of the damaged regions, there is no need to calculate difference regions by comparison. The damaged regions are the only ones that contain changes.

Network speed is a serious issue when distributing the user interface. Simply sampling the screen based on a timer does not work because it might flood a very slow network channel trying to present many intermediate steps that are not necessary. Many systems wait for a client request before computing the changes. If a client receives a change and then sends a request for the next change, this round-trip effectively meters the network speed. Changes are accumulated and sent only as fast as the network will allow.

Client Input Events

In a simple distributed application with only one client and no actual user at the server, the input event model is trivial. However, if there are multiple users, there is a problem. Suppose that user A presses her mouse button to begin dragging while user B happens to jiggle his mouse. At the application, the event stream would contain a mouse-down from A followed by mouse-move events from B but would not know that they are from separate users. The resulting application actions would be rather chaotic. This interleaving of events from multiple users is almost impossible to interpret correctly.

For pixel-based distribution, the system generally enforces strict floor control. Each client has a special "floor request" button. When a floor request is received by the server, it waits for a good break point (generally when no mouse buttons are pressed), takes control from whoever has it, thus blocking that client from sending input events, and grants the floor to whoever requested it, thus enabling those events. With this mechanism, the underlying application sees only one coherent stream of events. There are a variety of social and technical protocols for requesting and granting of floor control. From an implementation standpoint, the key idea is that the application sees only a consistent input stream regardless of the user generating the inputs.

Awareness

Awareness of what other users are doing can be a problem in these systems. It is tedious for a user to try to watch the entire screen to see where other users are making changes. In multiuser interaction, there are frequently times when no inputs are being generated but the information on the screen is being discussed. To support discussion, some systems provide each user with a telepointer[6]. A telepointer is generally a small icon or colored arrow associated with each user. Each user always has control of his or her telepointer so that they can point to information on the screen. The telepointer can also follow the user's input so that changes are readily visible to other users.

Advantages

The primary advantage of Remote Frame Buffer collaboration is that it works with any application and without the developers of the application knowing that it exists. The clients are very simple to build and require little consistency among participating computers. Implementation of both client and server is also quite straightforward. As network speeds increase, the universal nature of this approach shows great promise.

Disadvantages

The disadvantages revolve around the computing overhead required at the server and the network issues. The computing overhead on the server has been discussed previously. It should be noted that Moore's Law predicts continued increase in the speed of processors but does not increase the number of changing pixels that a user can want. This means that the computing resource issues will probably be solved by Moore's Law.

Networking issues are another problem. First, there is the bandwidth required to ship images over slow connections. With dial-up Internet connections, this can be painfully slow. However, there is not near as much movement in interactive applications as in video, so the bandwidth problems are not as high as the screen size would indicate. Solving the video over the Internet problem will probably solve these distributed interaction problems.

A more serious problem is network latency. The larger the Internet, the more routers, switches, and firewalls a message must go through. Though lots of bandwidth might be available, the time for a message to make the round-trip to the other side of the country might be a second or two. For Web pages, this is not an issue. The problem is in remote interaction. If a remote user grabs the scroll bar and drags it, the mouse-move message must be sent to the server, and the application must process the mouse-move, redraw the scroll bar, and redraw anything else that moved as a result. The image changes must then be sent back to all clients. If the remote user is trying to drag something and the round-trip on each mouse-move is one second, the quality of interaction will be very poor.

A final disadvantage is that all users must interact in lockstep with each other. Users are not free to move to different parts of the workspace when the work might call for it. Users cannot use any of their customizations that adapt the application to their own work style. Distribution across different modes of interaction using pixel-based mechanisms is very difficult because pixels and inputs must be exactly identical for the technique to work.

GRAPHICS PACKAGE LAYER

A second strategy for distributing the user interface is to capture the presentation calls at the graphics layer. As you learned in Chapter 2, drawing is done through a `Graphics` object. The application code does not know what that object does with the information passed to the `Graphics` object. You can distribute the interface by capturing those calls, packaging them up into network messages, and sending them to remote clients. The remote client receives the drawing commands and reproduces them on the client screen, as shown in Figure 17.5. The input events are handled in the same fashion as the pixel distribution approach.

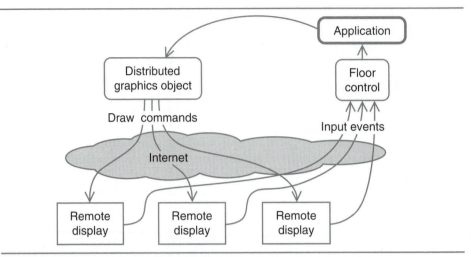

Figure 17.5 – Drawing call distribution

This technique has two advantages. The first is that there is no capture and analysis of screen pixels to locate change regions. This computational load is eliminated. The second advantage is that the graphics calls are generally much more compact than the pixels that they change. This reduces network bandwidth requirements.

This approach was first pioneered by the X Windows[7] system. This system was invented to allow graphical user interfaces for applications running on different computer servers. X Windows did not use the object-oriented Graphics object model. Instead, they provided a procedure library for drawing in windows. This idea was later extended by Hewlett Packard into the SharedX[8] system. In SharedX, the stream of drawing commands can be sent to multiple clients, allowing for multiuser interfaces. X Windows still survives as the windowing system of choice on Linux systems. This graphics package distribution approach is found in Microsoft's remote desktop facility. Because Microsoft controls the API to Windows, it is relatively easy for them to distribute those calls.

Advantages

This strategy has all of the advantages of the pixel-based approach without the computational cost of image differencing and with lower bandwidth requirements. If you have control of the graphics API, this technique is relatively easy to implement.

Disadvantages

With the exception of speed and bandwidth issues, the approach shares most of the disadvantages of the pixel-based approach. Interaction in the presence of network latency is still a problem and all users are locked into a strict WYSIWIS view.

PROGRAMMABLE API

As Figure 17.3 shows, the next approach for distributing the user interface is to create a programmable user-interface layer. This allows portions of the view code and portions of the controller code to be downloaded to the client. The client is then capable of handling many interactive inputs locally without incurring network latency costs as part of a tight interactive loop.

Network latency has long been a problem for distributed interaction. One of the first approaches for dealing with this problem was the *smart terminal*, notably characterized by the IBM 3270. This approach was created in the days of text-only interaction and extremely slow bandwidth. The server would assemble a *screen* of textual information and send it to the terminal for display. Embedded in the screen description were special codes that would indicate which characters could be changed and which could not. The terminal device retained a buffer of all of the characters on the screen and allowed the user to move among the changeable characters making any modifications that the user desired. When the user pressed the Enter key, all of the modified characters were packaged up and shipped back to the server where they could be analyzed.

The key advantage here is that the interaction mostly happened in the terminal and, thus, was very fast and imposed no burden on the server. There was no round-trip over the network to process each user event. In the days of very slow machines and slow disks, there was no swapping in of the server application every time the user provided input. Exploiting the intelligence of the client device has important benefits when distributing the user interface.

Display List Graphics

An early architecture for graphics devices was the vector refresh display[9]. In such displays, the server would provide the graphics device with a *display list*. A display list is a machine-readable list of drawing commands. The display controller would refresh from this list rather than from a frame buffer. Many such systems added matrix transformations to the display list interpreter and many forms of interaction such as dragging, rotating, or scaling were performed by modifying the matrices. A new matrix takes much less bandwidth to transmit than all of a display.

The display list architecture would still have the input/latency problems of the previous distribution schemes. Inputs would be sent to the server and translated into display list/matrix modifications, which were sent back to the client device and then displayed. The Evans and Sutherland PS 300 extended the display list architecture to include *function nets*. Function nets were like hardware-interpreted spreadsheet formulas. Transformations and other display list data could be computed in the display device as functions of inputs and other data. This meant that many interactions could be handled completely in the display processor without involving the server application. By linking the inputs to the display, interaction techniques such as rubber-band rectangles, dragging, or scaling could be done at interactive speeds despite slow processor/graphics communications.

NeWS

As a response to the interactive problems of X Windows, the NeWS[10] (New Windowing System) system was developed, based on PostScript. PostScript[11] was developed by Adobe as a mechanism to reduce the bandwidth requirement for laser printers. The idea behind PostScript was to encode graphics information as Forth[12] programs. Forth is a very efficient interpreted language. The PostScript drawing commands were implemented as procedures called from Forth programs. A PostScript drawing is just a Forth program that executes on the laser printer.

NeWS added input event processing and windowing to the underlying drawing model of PostScript. This allowed interactive applications to be built in PostScript. This not only added the superior drawing model of PostScript, but also opened opportunities in the windowing system. Because the foundation was the language Forth, it was possible to send small Forth programs to the windowing system that could process events and change the screen without going back to the application.

In a networked implementation such as NeWS, interactive techniques that need tight interaction with the user but less integration with the application could be downloaded as code into the remote windowing system. Scroll bars, dragging, highlighting buttons, and a variety of other techniques could be performed in the NeWS server without a network round-trip. NeWS did solve the network latency problem for interactive distribution, but it suffered a variety of other setbacks. At the time, computers were too slow to handle the PostScript drawing model at interactive speeds. Personal computing started to replace terminal/server computing. Programming in Forth is rather painful and highly error-prone, making development of interactive techniques difficult.

WWW Interaction

When the World Wide Web appeared, it created a model of interaction based on HTML. A server would distribute HTML pages to a browser that would allow the user to interact with what he or she saw. Early browsers provided only a "click to follow a link" style of interaction. Early servers mapped URLs directly to some part of the local file system. However, two innovations occurred simultaneously. The first was the inclusion of <form>s in HTML, which would add user inputs to the URL, and the second was the addition of CGI (Common Gateway Interface) to servers. CGI allows Web pages to be generated by programs rather than simply service the contents of the file system. This created a new model of distributed interaction. Server-based applications implemented using CGI would interact with users by generating interactive page descriptions for a standard browser. This allowed applications to distribute their interfaces without needing to install special software on the client. The first truly worldwide distribution of interactivity was born.

A careful look at the forms model of HTML interaction reveals that the style of interaction is identical to the old IBM 3270. Pages of information are sent to the client, the user fills in the changeable parts, and the changes are returned to the server. The only real interactive innovations are that the client is software-, rather than hardware-based, which greatly extends its use and that the formatting/graphics are much more pleasant than the old 3270 block text screens.

The next interactive innovation was the Java applet. Using this mechanism, interactive programs could be embedded in Web pages and downloaded to the client workstation. This achieved the NeWS vision of downloadable interaction. By the time Java appeared in Web browsers, personal computers were fast enough to handle the graphical displays. Java also is a modern object-oriented language rather than a machine-code replacement such as Forth. Consequently, development of applets was much easier.

The most recent development is AJAX or Asynchronous JavaScript and XML. JavaScript was introduced into HTML as a smaller language that could handle simple dynamic formatting of Web page content. JavaScript is tied to Java in name only. Its most notable characteristic is direct access to the Domain Object Model (DOM), which is a tree representation of the HTML page. Using this access, JavaScript code can dynamically modify the HTML being presented to the user. Using event handlers on a variety of HTML tags, JavaScript can embed a high degree of interactivity directly into the page going far beyond the 3270 model of forms interaction.

MODEL SEMANTICS DISTRIBUTION

The next approach for distributing interaction is to place the network between the view/controller and the model, as shown in Figure 17.3. There are many variations on this approach. One such strategy is to provide each interactive client with the application code and then have the server function as a synchronizer of the various models. Because each client has a copy of the application, virtually all of the interaction takes place in the client. This architecture has excellent local performance. This technique is rarely used for distribution of server interfaces to clients because it requires installation of the application on all possible client machines. It is most often used for multiple users to collaborate with each other. Such users are already likely to be using the same application and this facilitates their collaboration.

One such architecture uses the Command objects defined in Chapter 16. Before a command is executed by invoking doIt(), the object is serialized (converted to a byte stream) and sent to all of the other collaborators. The application for each user takes the received command object and invokes doIt(). The model in each case cannot distinguish between command objects received from the controller and those received over the network. The one constraint that this imposes on command objects is that their references to the model must be symbolic rather than by pointers. Obviously, a pointer on one machine will not be valid on another. The same techniques from Chapter 16 that were used by command-object scripting systems will suffice for this purpose.

A related approach was pioneered by Greenberg's GroupKit[13]. GroupKit is based on TCL[14] and TK. The TK graphical toolkit interfaces with its model by means of the TCL scripting language. GroupKit handles much of its distribution of the interface by forwarding the TCL scripts generated by the user interface to all participants in the collaboration. This has an effect similar to the distribution of command objects. In fact, command objects that have been adapted for scripting could use their scripting facilities as their mechanism for serializing and executing distributed commands.

Synchronization

One of the problems with the command or script distribution approach is synchronization of the commands. Take the case of two users editing the string "Hello World". User A has positioned the editing cursor just after the "H" and user B has positioned the cursor just after the "W". Suppose both of them press the Backspace key at the same time. User A's application sends a command to delete the first character of the string. At the same time, user B's application sends a command to delete the seventh character. When user A receives user B's command, it will delete the seventh character giving the result "ello Wrld" because the seventh character (after deleting "H") is the "o" in World. User B will end up with the correct string "ello orld" because its deletion did not confuse the indices of the command from user A. There are a huge variety of such problems that can arise from order confusion in the command stream.

One way to resolve this is to create a collaboration server that manages the ordering of commands. The server's job is to define the command order to which all clients must conform. This means that eventually every machine will have an identical command order and, thus, an identical model. The server defines this order by giving every command that it receives a sequence number. Each client retains the sequence number of the last confirmed command that it received from the server.

When a client performs a command, it assigns that command the next sequence number and sends it to the server. The client also retains the command in a history list just in case the command is rejected. If the server agrees that the received command's sequence number is the next one in order, it confirms the command to the client that created it, adds the command to its server history, distributes the command to all other collaborators, and increments its own command sequence number. If the server already has a command with that sequence number, it rejects the command and notifies the client that created it.

Clients receive commands, confirmations, and rejections from the server. If the client receives a command that matches its next sequence number, it performs the command locally and increments its sequence number. If a client receives a confirmation, it can discard the command or save it for undo purposes. Either way, the client knows that the command was accepted by the server. If the client receives a command rejection from the server, the client undoes all saved commands up to and including the command with the matching sequence number.

This synchronization mechanism allows a client to optimistically move ahead with its interface processing assuming that the server will eventually catch up. If collaborators are talking with each other, the likelihood that command conflicts will occur is low and this optimistic approach will be correct. By being optimistic, the interactivity of the client is not impaired by network latency. The undo capability associated with command objects allows the server to help overly optimistic clients bring themselves into line.

There is one other minor detail to this strategy. With each command, the client must send the sequence number of the last confirmed or forwarded command that it received. This allows the server to know how many commands will need to be discarded as overly optimistic if a command rejection occurs.

The developers of GroupKit determined that social mechanisms and good design of the command set made synchronization errors extremely rare or nonexistent. They, therefore, did not use any synchronization control and relied upon the users to resolve any problems in the unlikely event that they occurred.

DATA LAYER DISTRIBUTION

The last approach shown in Figure 17.3 is distribution at the data layer. This approach has many of the advantages of distribution at the model interface layer. By distributing in the model, latency problems for tight interactions are reduced. By distributing at the data layer, some of the synchronization issues are simplified. Suppose, for example, that a data model consisted of numbers, strings, records, arrays, and trees. This is a small number of concepts that spans a wide number of applications. The protocol for distribution can be uniform across all applications. When one user makes changes to the model, the changes are distributed to the other clients. The other clients modify their models and implicitly update their presentations in response.

This approach was used in the XWeb[15] system. XWeb extended HTTP by adding the CHANGE, SUBSCRIBE, and UNSUBSCRIBE commands to the standard GET and POST commands. The shared XWeb data model was XML. As with the WWW, XML was a communication façade over whatever underlying code was associated with a URL. A client would download XWeb information and make it available to the user interactively. As the user interacted with the client, CHANGE commands were sent back to the site to modify the data. Clients would also SUBSCRIBE to sites with which they were interacting. When another user would use the same site, CHANGE commands would be forwarded to other clients so that they could update their presentation. By building the distribution around an abstract data model, a variety of applications could share the mechanisms without reimplementing them.

XWeb also supported a variety of clients for interacting with XWeb data models. Each client was designed for a particular combination of interactive devices. Thus, the form of the interaction was tailored to the particular devices available. Clients were built for desktops, tablet pens, speech, laser pointers, and whiteboard pens. XWeb interfaces are highly adaptive to the particular devices and situations in ways that are not possible in the other collaborative architectures.

ASYNCHRONOUS COLLABORATION

There is a final type of collaboration that need not directly involve the user-interface architecture. This is when people share the work product, usually outside of the application as with e-mail or Web sites. In this case, each user has a copy of the work product on which they can make changes. Because they are working independently each user has their own copy of the application. Thus the interactive problem appears identical to the single-user case. However, the problems of change consistency and awareness still exist. If you e-mail a document to a collaborator and receive it back changed, you do not want to compare the two documents word for word to see what has changed.

Generally, asynchronous collaboration implementations are built around three concepts: (1) access control, (2) change detection, and (3) conflict resolution. Access control systems were first invented to manage source code for large programming projects. The simplest idea is that a programmer must "check out" a piece of code before making any changes. This is the asynchronous version of floor control. Only one person has the ability to change the work product at any one time. When changes are complete, the code is checked in and everyone on the project can see the changes and possibly check out the code to make their own modifications. This simple "check out for changes" mechanism can be used for any work product that is broken up into separate files.

Change detection is not quite so simple. Suppose someone checks out a piece of code, makes a small change, and then checks it back in. The system build tests fail that night and everyone wants to know "What has changed?" They also want to know "Who did it?" Because source code is made up of simple text files, there are well-known algorithms for comparing two strings of text and identifying the differences. If the text editor has the capability of displaying the differences, the source-code control system is complete and you can quickly find the problem. The key to it all is identifying what changed and presenting the changes in the user interface. This is more complicated for nontext work products. There are not good algorithms for comparing two arbitrary data structures to identify the changes. It is more common to track the changes in the application as they happen. Figures 17.1 and 17.2 show just such change tracking. Such change tracking can be implemented using the `Command` objects techniques of Chapter 16. The presentation of the changes to the user is very much dependent upon the application and how its data is presented.

One of the problems that arises is when two users independently make changes that overlap each other. In the case of the "check out to change" approach for managing access, this cannot happen because only one user can make changes at a time. Sometimes, however, this is too restrictive. Users can be warned of others working on the same product and then allowed to proceed. When they are each done, their respective changes must be resolved into a final version of the product. In many cases, their changes are independent. I make a change to paragraph 3 and you make a change to paragraph 5. There is no conflict and both changes can be accepted. There might still be a problem when I delete a definition from my paragraph and you write a sentence in yours that depends on that definition. This is not a problem that technology can currently solve. Collaborators must just be careful and aware of the changes of others. There is the last case where I change paragraph 5, sentence 2 and you change the same sentence in a different way. The best technical support is to show the user the two conflicting changes and let them decide which will be used. Despite the need for user judgment, this is still great support for collaborative activities that is tedious to perform manually.

SUMMARY

Distributing the interface allows users to work on systems that are remote from where applications are running. Distribution also supports collaboration among users on the same work. There are a variety of points within the application architecture where the distribution mechanism can be placed. Each such location supports a different collection of advantages and disadvantages.

EXERCISES

1. How does floor control simplify the architecture of the user-interface software in a collaborative situation?

2. How does the assumption of device consistency simplify the development of collaborative software?

3. What are the advantages/disadvantages of each?
    a. pixel distribution
    b. graphics interface distribution
    c. programmable clients
    d. model semantics distribution
    e. data layer distribution

4. What is complicated about synchronization of model distribution and how can it be handled?

5. How does data layer distribution simplify the synchronization problem?

END NOTES

[1] Kraut, R. E., M. D. Miller, and J. Siegel. "Collaboration in Performance of Physical Tasks: Effects on Outcomes and Communication." *1996 ACM Conference on Computer Supported Cooperative Work* (*CSCW '96*) (November 1996): 57–66.

[2] Roseman, M., and S. Greenberg. "TeamRooms: Network Places for Collaboration." *ACM Conference on Computer Supported Cooperative Work* (*CSCW '96*) (November 1996): 325–333.

[3] Boyd, J. "Floor Control Policies in Multi-User Applications." *INTERACT '93 and CHI '93 Conference Companion on Human Factors in Computing Systems* (April 1993): 107–108.

[4] Greenberg, S., and D. Marwood. "Real Time Groupware as a Distributed System: Concurrency Control and its Effect on the Interface." *Computer Supported Cooperative Work* (*CSCW '94*) (November 1994): 207–217.

[5] Richardson, T., Q. Stafford-Fraser, K. R. Wood, and A. Hopper. "Virtual Network Computing." *IEEE Internet Computing* Vol. 2, No. 1, (Jan/Feb 1998): 33–38.

[6] Gutwin, C., J. Dyck, and J. Burkitt. "Using Cursor Prediction to Smooth Telepointer Jitter." *International ACM SIGGROUP Conference on Supporting Group Work* (*GROUP '03*) (November 2003): 294–301.

[7] Scheifler, R. W., and J. Gettys. "The X Window System." *ACM Transactions on Graphics*, Vol. 5 (2) (April 1986): 79–109.

[8] Garfinkel, D., P. Gust, M. Lemon, and S. Lowder. "The SharedX Multi-User Interface User's Guide, Version 2.0." HP Research report, no. STL-TM-89-07, Palo Alto, California, 1989.

[9] Newman, W. F., and R. F. Sproull. *Principles of Interactive Computer Graphics* (2nd Ed.). Columbus, Ohio: McGraw-Hill, Inc., 1979.

[10] Gosling, J., D. Rosenthal, and M. Arden. *The NeWS Book*: *An Introduction to the Networked Extensible Window System*. New York: Springer-Verlag, 1989.

[11] Adobe Systems, Inc. *PostScript Language Reference* (*3rd Ed.*). New York: Addison-Wesley Longman Publishing Co., 1999.

[12] Bell, J. R. "Threaded code". *Commun. ACM* 16, 6 (June 1973): 370–372.

[13] Roseman, M., and S. Greenberg. "Building Real-Time Groupware with GroupKit, a Groupware Toolkit." *ACM Trans. Comput.-Hum. Interact.* 3, 1 (March 1996): 66–106.

[14] Ousterhout, J. K. *Tcl and the Tk Toolkit*. New York: Addison-Wesley, 1994.

[15] Olsen, D. R., S. Jefferies, T. Nielsen, W. Moyes, and P. Fredrickson. "Cross-Modal Interaction using XWeb." *User Interface Software and Technology* (*UIST '00*) (November 2002): 191–200.

CHAPTER 18

Text Input

A fundamental component of human thought and communication is language. Language allows knowledge and experience to pass between people in powerful ways. Yes, "a picture is worth a thousand words," but it takes clear and insightful prose to give that picture meaning beyond that snapshot in time. The whole history of scientific and social progress is founded on the power of language to communicate feelings and ideas across time and space. Language is a way for people to communicate connections and associations (sentences and paragraphs) among concepts and ideas (words and phrases).

Because of the importance of language, your computers need the ability to enter text. Text entry is not only for the creation of novels, texts, and letters, but also for more personal communications, such as e-mail or text messaging. Writing systems fall into two broad categories: ideographic and phonetic. In the ideographic systems, such as Chinese characters or Egyptian hieroglyphics, each character represents an entire word, syllable, or idea. Chinese characters are not monolithic pictures. They are generally spatial rather than syntactic compositions of smaller symbols. Ideographic systems are generally more compact in that they communicate more ideas per square inch of display space.

Many modern writing systems are phonetic. In these systems, there are a small number of characters (26 for English) that roughly correspond to sounds. By stringing the characters together, you get a symbolic description of what the word should sound like. However, this phonetic description is not accurate, as any English speaker knows. Languages like Spanish are very phonetic where reading leads almost directly to pronunciation. The accent might be wrong but the pronunciation can be accurately reproduced from the written word. French is less so because in many cases some of the letters are not pronounced at all. English is downright chaotic because it is a hybrid of Celtic, Saxon, Danish, Latin, and French, each contributing its own spelling patterns.

Phonetic writing systems can compose language from a relatively small number of symbols (less than 100). This allows for practical keyboard designs. A keyboard for 10,000 symbols is impossible. Most of this chapter focuses on phonetic writing systems with ideographic approaches being addressed at the end.

Text input systems depend very much upon the physical situation in which the user is attempting to create text. Sitting at a desk, the keyboard is the most rapid way to create the written word. It is far faster for trained people to type than to write by hand. Most people do not always live, work, or play in front of a desk or in a seated position. In particular, mobile computing creates situations that are rarely appropriate for keyboard use. There are two major approaches for text entry without a keyboard: use of a small number of buttons on a small device and use of a pen or stylus on the surface of a tablet. Another issue with mobile text entry is the ability to enter text without looking at the keyboard. Any typing or piano teacher takes great pains to train their students to look at the page, not the input device.

Before launching into a discussion of various input techniques, you must first look at the nature of language. Language is not random combinations of characters. Language has structure. Many text input techniques exploit this structure and you need algorithm models for representing language structure appropriately. Second, you need metrics for comparative evaluation of text input techniques. Following these two foundation sections, keyboard, button, and pen techniques are each discussed in turn. Many pen techniques depend upon recognition of pen gestures. The discussion of recognition techniques is deferred to Chapter 20. Lastly, the special needs of ideographic writing systems are briefly presented.

NATURE OF LANGUAGE

Entering language into a computer is somewhat of an interactive challenge. Obviously, the fastest way to enter language is to speak. The problem is that, so far, computers are only marginally successful at understanding free-form language and do very badly in noisy environments. So far, the only really accurate text entry is through button-based input devices. These are always much slower than people can speak and impose many physical restrictions. Full keyboards do not travel well and are not usable when walking, standing, or during other activities where an appropriate resting surface is not available. This chapter covers many different ways to input text with many proposals as to how to improve the process. Many of the techniques exploit the underlying characteristics of language to provide assistance in text entry. It is helpful to understand basic language models before looking at the various techniques because these models will appear repeatedly in different forms.

For someone educated in a European language, it is generally easy to classify a document as English, French, German, Italian, or Spanish without knowing how to read or speak the language. They all use similar character sets, but the structure of words and the composition of words into sentences is very different among these five. As people, you assemble the letters into sounds (probably incorrectly) and find that they "do not fit your tongue." People say "that sounds Italian" without understanding a word of it. This is because language has structure.

Language structure is very important when people recognize speech because it allows them to disambiguate what is heard based on what can reasonably go together. This structure is what allows people to read bad handwriting. Readers discard interpretations of letters that make no sense in the language (such as "xrtq" in English) and look for alternative interpretations. Readers also consider alternative words based on how well they "fit" in a sentence. The structure of language makes communication more resilient in the presence of small errors. There are two main computational approaches to representing structure in language: syntax and probability.

Syntax

The study of syntax has a very old history in computer science due to its essential role in programming languages. Syntax is based on the idea that there is a *grammar* that defines the set of acceptable inputs in a language. Historically, grammars are defined by automata. Finite-state and context-free are the most common representations. Finite-state and context-free automata have very efficient algorithms for testing an input sequence to see if it is acceptable by a grammar and for extracting structure from the input sequence.

Interactive syntactic systems must be *deterministic*. That is, for a given state of the input and a given input from the user, there is exactly one response/next state. This is important interactively for two reasons: (1) Users are uncomfortable when a computer responds ambiguously and (2) trying all possible combinations is frequently impossible in interactive time. The second issue is fading in importance as computers get faster, but on PDAs and cell phones with limited computing power, it is still a problem.

Any finite-state model can be automatically converted to a deterministic model that recognizes an equivalent[1] set of inputs. This means that every input can be handled in constant time, which is very important for interaction. There is no such deterministic algorithm for all context-free grammars. Therefore, there is no constant time processing for any context-free representation. Deterministic context-free parsers do exist for many kinds of grammars, but most interactive text input uses finite-state models.

A common use of finite-state representations is for encoding a dictionary of possible words. If you know the set of all possible words, then you can use it as a representation of appropriate language structure. A simple algorithm for searching a dictionary for a word W is to compare each word in the dictionary against word W. If there are N words in the dictionary, then the cost of this check is N*length(W). With a large dictionary, that is a problem. However, if you model your dictionary as a grammar for which each word is an acceptable sentence, the dictionary becomes a nondeterministic finite-state grammar. The nondeterminism comes from the fact that given the first input, many words are possible. Because the grammar is finite-state, you can always convert it to a deterministic representation where each input character can be handled in constant time. This makes the dictionary lookup problem of order length(W) regardless of how many items there are in the dictionary. See the appendix A3.2b for an example.

The notion of a grammar for text input is very problematic for interactive text input. People do not spell correctly (violating the dictionary). People do not use correct grammar either accidentally, through ignorance, or on purpose. People continuously invent new words, phrases, and abbreviations. This makes grammars with their precise definitions of what is and is not acceptable rather brittle representations.

Probabilistic Language Models

An alternative way to capture the structure of language is through statistics. For example, the space character and the vowels account for 49.9 percent of all English character usage[2]. Obviously, an input technique that makes spaces and vowels easier to enter does better than a similar technique without such an adjustment.

The most common statistical device for modeling language are *N-grams*. An N-gram is a sequence of N tokens. An N-gram model is the probability of finding each N-gram in some large corpus of text. Sometimes the N-grams are sequences of letters and sometimes sequences of words. Though the data are different, the techniques of analysis are the same. For example, to compute the digram (2-gram) probability of ASCII characters, you can construct a 128×128 table $D[i,j]$ and use it to count the number of character combinations in a large corpus of text such as all back issues of the Wall Street Journal or a collection of 10 million Web pages. You can use this table of counts to compute various probabilities. In many cases, this 128×128 table is restricted to just letters without differentiation of case.

Suppose you are given a digram frequency table D and the user has previously entered the character 'x'. You might then want to compute the probability that 'o' is the next character to be entered using the formula

$$P(o \mid x) = \frac{D[x,o]}{\sum\limits_{i=o}^{127} D[x,i]}$$

Soukoreff and MacKenzie have published the digram frequencies for English letters[2]. These frequencies change, however, depending on the purpose for text. For example, the character frequencies that occur in instant messaging are different from those in the New York Times.

Digrams do not provide a lot of structural information. You can get more structural information using higher values for N. The size of the N-gram table grows as L^N where L is the number of possible tokens and N is the length of each N-gram. For characters, a trigram (3-gram) table easily fits in RAM. For the 10,000 most common words, the trigram table would be 10^{12} or well over a terabyte. In addition to memory costs, a table this size also poses a statistical problem. To get a reasonable sample, you want 10-20 samples per table entry. At five characters per word (in English), this means a corpus of nearly a petabyte.

Fortunately, most linguistic data follow Zipf's Power Law. This says that when items are sorted from most frequent to least frequent they follow a power curve r^{-b} where r is the rank of the item and b is a positive constant near 1.0. Figure 18.1 shows such a power curve. What this tells you is that a few things happen at a very high frequency and this tails off into many very infrequent items. This is consistent with the notion that language has a great deal of structure. There are not actually 10^{12} trigrams in English. The word combination "seven, pig, fluorine" just never occurs in a sentence.

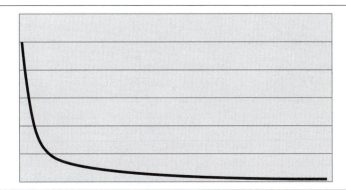

Figure 18.1 – Power curve of item frequency

This structure in the N-gram representation is dealt with in two ways. The first is that for infrequent words, a lower order (N-1)-gram or (N-2)-gram is used. This lets you use the structure information of an N-gram without requiring a huge table[3]. For the frequent combinations like "in the end," you can use trigrams and for less common phrases like "lateral air stabilization," you can use digrams or simple word frequencies. Second, you can use highly sparse representations of your N-gram table so that it actually fits into memory and is usable.

Token frequencies allow predictions about a user's next inputs. These predictions can help optimize input techniques to actual user behavior. An early example of this was Witten's Reactive Keyboard[4] that used letter trigrams to speed the typing of programs where common words like variable and function names occur with high frequency. In this case, the corpus was the program files on which the user was currently working.

EVALUATING TEXT INPUT

The rest of the chapter presents many text entry techniques. When faced with so many alternatives, many people immediately ask, "Which is better?" There are a few key metrics that have been developed for comparing text entry techniques. An overview of these is helpful before diving into the specific approaches. Metrics are a good way to measure progress and should be understood. However, the combination of Situation, Task, and Users (STU) is frequently more important than metric comparisons. People use the buttons on their cell phone rather than a keyboard, not because it is faster or less error-prone but because those 12 buttons are usable in many situations where keyboards do not function.

Evaluation of ways for entering text requires metrics that can compare their performance. The two obvious measures are speed and errors. Good input techniques are those that can enter text as fast as possible with as few errors as possible. The standard for text entry speed is *words per minute*. This is measured as characters per minute divided by the average word length (five characters in English).

Measuring Speed

Measuring speed is problematic because of training effects. There is a huge difference between a beginning typist and a trained touch typist. A new input technique should be evaluated on the speed reached after training and on the amount of practice required to reach proficiency. Expert input speed is measured by having subjects regularly practice the technique until their speed stops increasing. You can then assume that you have reached that subject's maximum speed. Experience with teaching school children to type shows that such speeds are reached after months of practice. Learning is measured as the amount of practice time required to reach this level.

It is difficult and expensive to get a statistically useful number of users to practice a new input technique for long enough to get expert speed measurements. Not only is the time difficult, but many users are not motivated to reach maximum speeds, as evidenced by the number of people who persist in "hunt-and-peck" typing. They know that there is a better technique but what they do now is good enough for their purpose.

To overcome these experimental problems, there are various theoretical measures of text entry speed. These theoretical measures are based on models of user behavior and user motor capabilities. When comparing the theoretical speeds of two input techniques, you can assume that the user's motor capacities are the same between the techniques and the only differences are the techniques themselves. An early model for entry is the Keystroke Level Model (KLM)[5]. This model measures the number of keys that must be pressed to accomplish the goal. For example, on a normal keyboard, the letter 'A' requires two keystrokes: the Shift key and the 'a' key.

The Silfverberg model[6] builds upon KLM by taking into account the positioning of keys and the time required to reach and select one of them. Because of varying distances, the time to reach various keys is different; therefore, Silfverberg takes the probability of various key combinations into account using a digram model. James and Reischel[7] have published data on how these models compare with actual performance.

Speed is not necessarily the primary consideration in a task involving text entry. For example, this chapter contains about 8600 words and I type at about 50 words per minute. This means that actual typing time would be about three hours. However, it took about 20 hours to write this chapter. Text entry is about 15 percent of the total task. Changing my text entry to something twice as fast (not very likely), still only improves my writing task by about 7 percent. That is not a great motivation to learn a new typing technique. However, if I was text messaging this chapter using a phone keypad at about five words per minute, the text entry time would be 30 hours rather than three and I would be very motivated to cut that time in half or better. The context of use is as important as entry speed when evaluating text entry techniques.

Some input techniques use ambiguous entries where each key corresponds to more than one letter. These techniques rely upon probability, dictionaries, and language structure to resolve the ambiguity and eventually select the correct word for entry. One of the measures of such technique is *disambiguation accuracy*. This uses probability to measure the likelihood that the correct word is chosen despite the character level ambiguity. A variant is the measure of the likelihood of the correct selection given a display of the *N* best inputs. These techniques can frequently demonstrate fewer keystrokes than the number of characters in the word.

Measuring Errors

Rapid entry of text is a good thing, but the actual goal is rapid entry of correct text. For this, a measure of user errors is required. The simplest error metric compares the entered string with the desired string and counts the number of differences. This measure has serious problems, as shown in Figure 18.2. With the simple character measure, all of the underlined characters are counted as errors. Simple inspection shows that the only error was an erroneous 'u'.

```
the lazy brown dog ate my lunch

the lazuy brown dog ate my lunch
```

Figure 18.2 – Character-level errors

The problems with simple character comparison can be resolved by computing the Minimal String Distance (MSD) between the desired string and the actual string that was entered. MSD is a special case of the Minimal Edit Distance algorithm where all edit costs are 1. The Minimal Edit Distance algorithm is described in appendix A3.2d. The MSD is a count of the number of edits that must be made to convert one string into the other. In Figure 18.2, the MSD is 1 (remove the 'u'). MSD is a much more accurate measure than simple comparison.

String comparisons like MSD do not account for the effort required to correct an error. For example, the error in Figure 18.2 could be corrected in many ways. If the error is recognized immediately, then a rubout removes it. If the error is not recognized until the end of the word, then the correction might be "rubout, rubout, 'y'" or possibly "left arrow, rubout, right arrow." These kinds of behaviors are accounted for by the Key Strokes Per Character (KSPC) metric. A KSPC of 1.0 means that the entry was correct. Any errors and their corrections cause a higher KSPC. Soukoreff and MacKenzie[8] propose an additional metric that unifies MSD and KSPC. This is expanded by Gong and Tarasewich[9].

Test Data for Measuring Text Input

With all of the metrics for speed, learning, and errors, the text itself matters. MacKenzie and Soukoreff[10] have published phrase sets that can be used as a standard for text entry. However, it has been shown[11] that the words people use when they write are different from spoken words and different still from the words people use when sending text messages on cell phones. It is very important to use a test set that reflects the kinds of phrases that are likely to be used. Drawing test phrases from the Wall Street Journal does not accurately reflect how teens send text messages to each other.

KEYBOARD INPUT

The dominant tool for text input is the keyboard with each letter and number having its own key and a Shift key for changing case. In English, the most popular layout is the Qwerty keyboard that is so named because of the order of the first six letters on the top row. The design of the Qwerty keyboard was dictated by the mechanics of early typewriters and by a lack of ergonomic understanding. With the digital age, the mechanical limitations have long since disappeared.

More efficient key layouts have been proposed. The most common is the Dvorak keyboard shown in Figure 18.3. Dvorak designed his keyboard so that the most common characters are on the home row and thus reduce finger movement. The layout is also designed so that successive keys most probably occur on alternating hands. These innovations make input faster and produce less fatigue.

Figure 18.3 – Dvorak keyboard layout

Using standard Qwerty keyboards, typists can reach 60+ words per minute. As of 2005, the world record[12] is 150 words per minute using the Dvorak keyboard.

An alternative is the stenographer's keyboard used when close-captioning television programs or in court reporting. The stenographer's keyboard is phoneme (sound) rather than character oriented and is chorded (multiple keys pressed at once). For a given syllable, the recorder presses multiple keys simultaneously. For example, the word "cat" is entered by pressing 'K', 'A', and 'T' simultaneously. This allows for much more rapid entry (225 words per minute with training) but does not produce exact text entry. Careful transcription and proofreading is required to produce the final text. Many stenographers cannot read the input of another without effort because the inputs are phonetic and suggestive rather than exact representations of words.

Some keyboards have modified layouts that simplify typing with only one hand. This allows the other hand to work with a mouse or perform some other task. A novel approach to one-handed typing is the Half-Qwerty[13] keyboard. In this keyboard, both the right and left hand portions of the Querty keyboard are mapped on to the same set of keys with a special Shift key to move between the choices. A surprising amount of muscle memory of key locations is transferred between the right and left hands.

BUTTONS

Many devices do not have the physical space required for a full keyboard and many other devices have teeny, tiny keys that are hard for adults to press. One solution to the size problem is to use fewer buttons than the size of the alphabet. There are a large number of methods that have been proposed for generating text input from a small number of buttons. There are techniques that map multiple characters to the same key with various methods for disambiguating what the input should be and various methods for rearranging the character/key binding. Some have proposed chorded systems where the desired character is specified by pressing multiple keys at once. There are techniques for scrolling through character choices and lists that use the layout of letters to define an input sequence.

Much of the effort is focused on the 12-key arrangement found on most telephones (Figure 18.4). The most common technique for text entry is Multitap where the user presses a key multiple times. For example, to enter the word "golf," the user presses 4,6,6,5,5,5,3,3,3. This has the advantage of being very easy to learn. It has the obvious disadvantage of requiring many more keystrokes per character (KSPC) of 1. There is also some remaining ambiguity in the input. For example, the word "cat" requires 2,2,2,2,8. However, this sequence might also mean "bbt" or "act." The problem is using the number 2 for successive letters. This is dealt with in two ways. The first is a timeout at the end of a character, for example 2,2,2,*pause*,2,8. This slows down entry but creates the boundary between "c" and "a." The other alternative is to use a special key to move on to the next character such as 2,2,2,#,2,8. This has been shown to be much faster. Most Multitap systems provide both. Using English character frequencies, MacKenzie et al [14] report that the average KSPC for Multitap is 2.0342.

1	2 abc	3 def
4 ghi	5 jkl	6 mno
7 pqrs	8 tuv	9 wxyz
*	0	#

Figure 18.4 – Telephone text key layout

To resolve the KSPC of 2, the T9 technique was created by Tegic Communications. In this technique, there is a dictionary of words. The keypad is the same as for Multitap but each key is only pressed once. For example, "golf" is 4,6,5,3. This sequence is highly ambiguous until you consider the structure of language. The string "hnke" is a possible interpretation of the input, but does not form an English word. By using the dictionary, much of the ambiguity can be resolved. This is not a complete solution because "cat" and "bat" both use the sequence 2,2,8. The most probable word from the dictionary is shown and then the user can use another key to cycle through other alternatives.

T9 has a KSPC of 1.0072 for English[14], which is very good. The problem is that the user is not sure what word has been entered until the entire word is complete and selected. It is very difficult to detect an entry error without the user doing mental disambiguation as they type. T9 also struggles with words, slang, or abbreviations that are not in the dictionary. Most T9 systems allow for new words to be added (usually with Multitap) but the problem remains.

The LetterWise[14] system addressed the T9 issues by using character N-grams rather than a dictionary. When the user presses a key, the most probable character, given the previous N-1 characters, is displayed. This means that the user sees immediately the character that has been selected. If this character is incorrect, Multitap techniques are used to get at the correct character. This is an extension of the earlier LessTap[15] system that uses only character probabilities. LessTap and LetterWise are not reliant upon words being in the dictionary. MacKenzie et al have reported a KSPC of 1.15 for LetterWise. They also performed actual text entry experiments over many days to address the learning issues. In the first 25-minute session, LetterWise achieved 7.3 words per minute with Multitap generating 7.2 wpm. By the 20th session, LetterWise users achieved an average of 21 wpm with Multitap achieving 15.5 wpm.

Some researchers have explored moving characters to different buttons than found on the standard phone keypad. One option[16] is to retain the alphabetic ordering for ease of learning while moving characters to different buttons, thus changing the number of characters assigned to each button. It is also possible to completely rearrange the character/button mapping. Experiments have shown that the complete remapping is harder for users to learn than the alphabetic form. Though these techniques produce much better disambiguation of words than the standard layout, the KSPC is still only 1.16, which is not a significant advantage over LetterWise.

The previous techniques have all assumed small input devices with small screens. The TNT[17] approach assumes large screens with small controls as one finds with television remotes and game controllers. TNT uses an array of nine keys to select up to 81 characters using two key combinations. The approach is based upon the displayed array shown in Figure 18.5. The user's first key press selects one of the nine regions and the second press selects one of nine characters from that region. This technique has the same KSPC=2 as Multitap, but you can enter many more characters than simple letters or numbers. This is particularly important in European languages with special character modifiers that push the character set beyond the basic 26 letters. Experiments show users reaching 9.52 wpm with some practice.

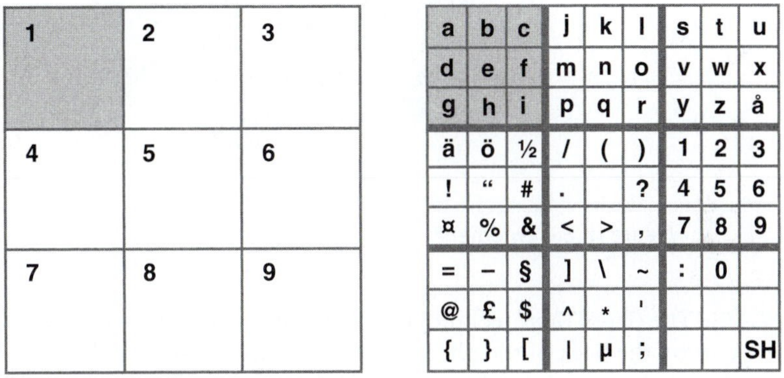

1	2	3
4	5	6
7	8	9

a	b	c	j	k	l	s	t	u
d	e	f	m	n	o	v	w	x
g	h	i	p	q	r	y	z	å
ä	ö	½	/	(	)	1	2	3
!	"	#	.		?	4	5	6
¤	%	&	<	>	,	7	8	9
=	–	§	]	\	~	:	0	
@	£	$	^	*	'			
{	}	[	|	μ	;			SH

Figure 18.5 – TNT character layout

CHORDED TEXT ENTRY

One way to overcome the limited number of keys is to use a chorded input technique. Conrad and Longman[18] were among the first to experiment with this technique. A more recent attempt is the Twiddler[19], shown in Figure 18.6. The arrangement is a row of three keys for each of four fingers so that the device can be operated with one hand. The keys are larger and farther apart than with phone keypads to facilitate one-handed operation. An expert user can achieve 60 wpm, which is comparable to Qwerty keyboard entry. The problem is that the cording is difficult to learn. The Twiddler was compared experimentally with Multitap in a series of sessions. For each session, the user typed for 20 minutes using one technique and then 20 minutes with the other. After eight such sessions, the Twiddler was faster on the average than Multitap and the error rates were below 5 percent.

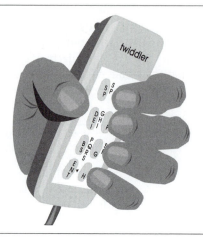

Figure 18.6 – Twiddler[19]

The ChordTap[20] technique uses the phone keypad with the addition of three buttons on the back of the phone. The three buttons select which of the three characters
on the phone pad should be selected. Any two of the chord buttons selects the fourth
character if a key has one. The additional buttons simply accelerate the use of the
Multitap system. By the end of a series of trials, ChordTap achieved an average
16.06 wpm against Multitap's 11 wpm. The error rates for Multitap were 2.6 percent
while those for ChordTap were 3.3 percent. The big advantage of ChordTap over the
Twiddler is the ease with which users can learn how it functions. The direct mapping
between the technique and the key labeling is very helpful.

Scrolling Through Choices

With a very limited number of buttons there are scroll selection techniques as are
found in video games. The most common is the three-key technique where the user
scrolls up or down through the alphabet using two of the keys and then uses the third
key to select a letter. Users achieve 10 wpm after 10 training sessions[21]. A five-key
technique uses four keys to scroll around a matrix of letters and one key to select.
This technique achieved 13 wpm after 10 training sessions[21]. A further variation uses
a game controller joystick to scroll through two different matrices, each with half of
the characters. There are then the left and right selection buttons to indicate which
matrix character to choose. Users achieved 7 wpm with this method[22].

OTHER INPUTS

There are a few techniques for text entry that use other inputs than keys. The TiltType[23] system uses four buttons and an accelerometer to select text. The accelerometer senses one of eight tilt positions while the buttons select from six sets of eight characters. A combination of tilting and a button press creates a text entry technique that fits into the form-factor of a digital watch. There are no speed measurements for this device and indications are that it is not very fast.

A second technique uses a touch wheel[24], which is a round surface that can sense where on the wheel the user's finger is touching. This works somewhat like the scrolling techniques except that the characters are arranged around the wheel. The user can rapidly go near a character by starting at the appropriate location on the wheel and then moving the thumb until the correct character is selected. Using a probabilistic language model, characters that are more likely are easier to select than characters that are less likely, which increases speed. However, this simple language technique causes infrequent characters to be very difficult to select. The authors accommodate this by weighting the language model by the speed of the user's movement. The faster the user is scrolling, the stronger the language model's preference. This corresponds to rapid normal input. As the user slows down, the influence of the language model is diminished making rare characters easier to select. This corresponds to a more careful selection. This technique reports input speeds of 6.2 wpm.

STYLUS

On handheld devices and in other situations, a keyboard is not practical. One option is to use a stylus or pen to input characters. There are four basic techniques in use: soft keyboards, single-character recognition, phrase recognition, and cursive handwriting recognition. This chapter also looks at a novel stylus-based scrolling technique.

Soft Keyboards

A soft keyboard is simply a picture of a keyboard displayed on the screen where users can touch keys with the stylus. Experiments have shown[25] that users reach a speed of about 40 wpm on Qwerty-style soft keyboard layouts. One of the reasons that Qwerty keyboards have remained despite their shortcomings relative to other keyboards is the extensive typing training that people have invested in them. However, such training does not transfer directly to soft keyboards. The "muscle memory" effects that optimize typing do not apply to soft keyboards where very different muscle groups are used. In fact, most touch typists cannot identify the location of a specific key on the Qwerty keyboard without using their hands to simulate typing that key or visually searching the keyboard.

Because key layout for soft keyboards does not have the heavy training associated with physical keyboards, researchers have explored more effective key arrangements. Using Fitts' Law for time to select a target (see Chapter 21), MacKenzie and Zhang developed a metric for measuring the effectiveness of a layout[25]. By using a statistical language model for English, they derived the probability of moving the stylus from one key to another. This probability was used to weight the Fitts' Law prediction of the time to make that movement. A weighted average of such times was used to predict the speed of typing using a particular layout.

Using their metric, they tried a wide variety of layouts and computed the predicted typing speed. They finally focused on the OPTI layout shown in Figure 18.7. Note that because Space is such a common key, they included four separate space keys to make it much easier to enter and made each of them bigger so as to require less time to hit them accurately. Their experiments showed that although users were initially slower with OPTI, they soon reached a speed of 45 wpm that is 10 percent faster than a Qwerty layout.

Figure 18.7 – OPTI soft keyboard layout[25]

Their approach for finding the best layout was to think of a design, then evaluate it with their metric, and then think of another design. To take a more automated approach, Zhai et al[26] modeled their keyboard as a set of circles that could move freely in a 2D plane but could not overlap. They used a digram probability model for sequences of characters and a Metropolis optimization technique to move the keys around seeking a "minimal energy" configuration based on Fitts' Law and the language model. They then translated the "minimal energy" layout using circular keys into a layout of hexagonal keys (hexagons are the most compact shape that completely fills a space), as shown in Figure 18.8. Using a different prediction metric, they reported speeds of 43 wpm on all of the best designs that their algorithms identified.

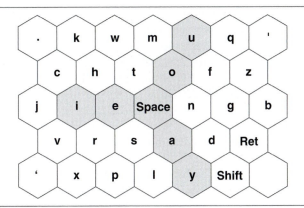

Figure 18.8 – Metropolis keyboard[26]

The primary goal in alternative soft keyboard layouts is to get the most common character pairs close together. Isokoski[27] devised a technique such that when a user selects a character, a menu of the most likely next characters pops up around the selection, as shown in Figure 18.9. The next character can then be selected by a drag movement to the right choice or the stylus can be lifted and the pop-up menu ignored. One of the problems with adapting the pop-up to each letter is that the menu changes from letter to letter. Their solution was to put only the vowels and space key in the pop-up because they are the most frequent. This makes the pop-up stable and less confusing. Experiments showed that users took advantage of the pop-up shortcut 20 percent of the time and users were faster than simple Qwerty layouts after 20 sessions.

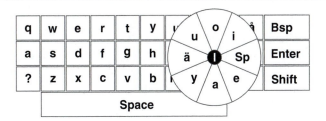

Figure 18.9 – Pop-up keyboard[27]

Masui pushed the notion of pop-ups on soft keyboards even further with his POBox[28] system. His approach uses a language model based on word pairs rather than character pairs. Using the previous word and the characters already typed, he assembles a menu of the most probable words that the user was trying to type. The user could then select a word from this menu or continue typing. If there were not enough high probability words, he adds words that approximately match the characters being typed. A major focus of his work was rapid entry of ideographic characters using a small keyboard. With a menu of 10 words, he is able to present the correct next word 53 percent of the time with only one character. His technique presents the correct word 90 percent of the time after only three characters. In his experiments, he reported people entering text with pen and paper at a rate of 49 char/min. With POBox, his users reached 40 char/min. This compares well with 20 char/min for systems using handwriting recognition. This technique commonly appears on modern handheld computers.

Much of the work on soft keyboards has focused on pen or stylus input. However, new phones and handheld computers are using touch surfaces rather than stylus surfaces that use bare fingers rather than a tool. At the time of this writing, the most notable of these is the Apple iPhone. The text input problem is somewhat different from other soft keyboards in that finger size must be taken into account. The layout issues are all the same as other soft keyboards in that the two-handed touch typing strategies that many people are trained with are not appropriate. However, unlike stylus systems, the user can still use multiple fingers. At present, there is not sufficient research to indicate how multiple touches can or cannot accelerate text input over stylus techniques. Unlike buttons, soft keyboards on a touch surface provide no tactile feedback. Some are trying to remedy this lack of touch feedback by using vibrators to respond to key touches.

Character Input

People have long considered writing with a pen directly on the screen as a natural form of text input. This goal should be tempered by the fact that writing text with pen and paper is much slower and less legible than typing. This means that written character input is not the most efficient means even if it seems more "natural." However, in many physical situations, a keyboard is too large to carry or too awkward to use. It is very difficult to use a keyboard while standing. Two-handed typing requires that the keyboard be supported by a desk or lap. In many of these situations, pen-input of text is more effective.

Character recognition is based on the simple algorithm: collect a digital ink stroke (all points between mouse-down and mouse-up), compute a set of features from the stroke, and match those features against known examples of various characters. The details of these recognition techniques are discussed in more depth in Chapter 20.

Most of the work on pen entry of text has focused on the recognition of individual characters. This has the nice property of only recognizing a few tens of symbols for phonetic writing systems. Ideographic character recognition is much, much more difficult. One of the difficulties with character recognition is the segmentation of characters. If characters are written with one to three strokes of the pen, how do you identify when one character stops and the next stroke belongs to a new character? For example, capital 'A' and a 't' are composed of an initial stroke and a second crossing stroke. The 't' could be mistaken for an 'i' or an 'l' followed by a dash '-'. Various systems were proposed to resolve this, including whether strokes overlapped in the X dimension or whether there was a pause between strokes. These solutions were not satisfactory because users' handwriting styles are never that tidy.

Goldberg and Richardson introduced the idea of not using the true handwritten character as the input but rather using a single, stylized stroke that approximates the character. In their Unistrokes[29] system, the strokes were selected to be easy for character recognizers to identify correctly. By using a single stroke per character, the character segmentation problem is eliminated. The strokes were somewhat shaped like the characters that they represent, but not completely so.

One of the problems with Unistrokes was that users had a hard time remembering the correct stroke. Venolia and Neiberg addressed this problem by using techniques from marking menus (discussed in Chapter 21 on menu systems). Their T-Cube[30] system started with a simple pie diagram with eight starting locations, as shown on the left of Figure 18.10.

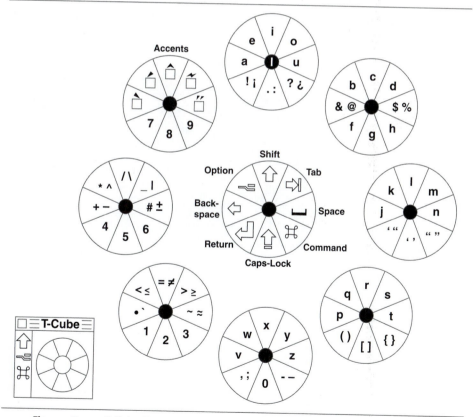

Figure 18.10 – T-Cube Menus[30]

A character is entered by placing the pen down in one of the nine regions of the basic shape. If the user pauses with the pen down, then one of the nine menus shown in Figure 18.10 appears centered on the stylus and the user can select a character by moving in the correct direction before lifting the stylus. If the user does not pause but just makes the stylus movement, the character is selected without popping up the menu. The advantages are that characters are selected by a single flicking stroke and that the system automatically trains the users as to the correct strokes using the pop-up menus.

Pen-based character input achieved commercial success with the Graffiti[31] system that came with Palm Pilot handheld computers. This approach is an alphabet inspired by Unistrokes but with more memorable strokes that looked like the characters they represented. Graffiti also used ideas from T-Cube in that they used two regions separately for letters and numbers rather than a single region for all characters.

The EdgeWrite[32] system addresses the needs of users with impaired motor control. The authors were concerned about people with hand tremors or other aging problems that could not correctly enter Graffiti characters. Their solution was to add a plastic template over the Palm's text entry region, as shown in Figure 18.11. The template provides an edge to guide the strokes. This means that rounded strokes are no longer possible. It also means that strokes are composed by moving from corner to corner rather than freely in the space.

Figure 18.11 – EdgeWrite template[32]

Because all movement is from corner to corner, a character can be recognized by the sequence of corners that the stylus visits. This is a much simpler recognition algorithm. In testing unimpaired users, EdgeWrite was comparable to Graffiti speed. EdgeWrite speed was much better for motor impaired users. A portion of the

EdgeWrite alphabet is shown in Figure 18.12. The alphabet was formed by starting with Graffiti's unistroke stylizations of the characters and then adapting that stylization to corner sequences. The strokes sort of look like the characters they represent, which makes them easier to learn.

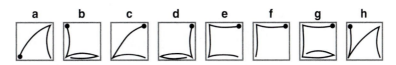

Figure 18.12 – EdgeWrite alphabet[32]

Because the EdgeWrite alphabet is formed by sequences of corner visits, other sensing technologies besides the stylus are possible. Using four keys (one for each corner)[33], you can reproduce an EdgeWrite stroke by pressing the keys in the same sequence as the corners visited using a stylus. After 10 training sessions of five minutes each, users achieved speeds of 17 wpm using the four keys.

You can also view the EdgeWrite alphabet in terms of a sequence of directions rather than corners visited. Based on this observation, the alphabet can be adapted to entry via a trackball[34]. Each direction is sensed as a "pulse stroke" that extends beyond a minimum distance. There are eight possible pulse directions. If you consider the EdgeWrite alphabet and its corner orientation, there are only three possible directions from any given corner. This restriction makes the technique much more stable for those with motor impairments. Unimpaired users achieved speeds of 9.82 wpm and a user with a spinal cord injury achieved 6 wpm, which far exceeded his speed with other techniques.

Stylus Word Input

Several researchers have sought to increase stylus text speed by creating techniques for entering complete words with a single stroke. Two early techniques used a central "resting zone" surrounded by characters. Users begin their stroke in the resting zone and then "visit" the desired characters in the word in sequence. Figure 18.13 shows the stroke for the word "finished" using the Cirrin[35] system. Starting in the resting region, each character is visited in turn. Note that characters that are adjacent both in the word and the key layout can be visited without returning to the resting region. The only data reported with Cirrin is 20 wpm by a single experienced user. The claimed advantage is that a continuous stroke takes less time and effort than a series of tap-and-lift motions. Note that the letters are not arranged in alphabetical order. Instead, they are arranged to minimize the probable distance traveled between characters based on a statistical language model.

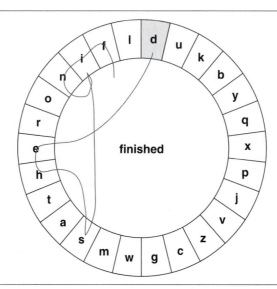

Figure 18.13 – Cirrin stroke for entering the word "finished"[35]

Perlin's Quikwriting[36] takes a similar approach with a different layout and stroke style. His layout consists of eight border zones, rather than one for each character, and a central resting zone. A stroke begins in the resting zone and then moves into one of the character zones. Each character zone is assigned an odd number of characters presented in an order around the periphery of the layout, as shown in Figure 18.14. If the stroke returns to the resting zone, the central character in the zone is selected. If the stroke moves clockwise into another character zone rather than returning to the resting zone, the next character in the clockwise direction is selected. Returning to the resting zone selects a character without lifting the stylus. Figure 18.14 shows the stroke for the word "the."

Figure 18.14 – The word "the" using Quikwriting[36]

No experimental data is reported for Quikwriting, but anecdotal evidence shows much higher speeds than Graffitti after significant practice. The claimed advantage is that users quickly learn the strokes for common words and do not consider individual characters. This allows for the kinds of training speedup that occurs with touch typists. This gesture speedup is less likely to occur with Cirrin because of the greater accuracy required to hit one of 26 zones rather than one of eight. Quikwriting is harder to learn but more tolerant of fast but sloppy gestures.

The notion of a stroke gesture composed by movements among letter zones is carried even farther in Zhai's SHARK system[37]. In SHARK, the idea is that moving among the letters of a word on a soft keyboard, without raising the stylus, creates a gesture with a characteristic shape for each word. In SHARK, these gestures are called *sokgraphs*. The SHARK approach is to compare a given gesture with sample gestures from all of the words in a dictionary. By comparing their shapes rather than their positions, users can become increasingly sloppy about their accuracy while still entering words very rapidly. The idea is that a user begins text entry by tracing words on the keyboard. For common words, the user becomes faster and faster at tracing the stroke. Eventually, the common sokgraphs become a shorthand for words that the user enters very rapidly.

Figure 18.15 shows SHARK's sokgraph for the word "system." The thick, straight line shows the exact sokgraph constructed from key center to key center. The thin, penlike line shows how a user might rapidly draw the sokgraph. The shape that the user draws must be compared against the formal sokgraphs for all of the words in the dictionary. A dictionary of 10,000 is the minimum to be effective and the comparison can be very expensive. To be effective, SHARK must find the correct word in less than one second.

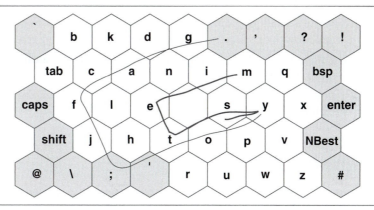

Figure 18.15 – SHARK sokgraph for "system"[37] (see color plate)

The first step in SHARK's recognition is to normalize the strokes so that the largest X, Y dimension is 1.0 and the origin is normalized. This allows for stroke comparison without reference to size or position of the stroke. The positions of the start and end points of the strokes can be compared in normalized coordinates. This allows for very rapid pruning of the set of strokes to be compared. Candidate strokes are compared using "elastic matching" that compares closest points to come up with a distance measure. This measures the shape similarity of the two strokes. The strokes are also compared on the distances between their start and end keys. Even with this effort, there are still words that share the same sokgraph. In Zhai's experiments, the Qwerty keyboard had 537 words with similar gestures. These problems are further reduced using a language model to predict the correct choice. Where confusion among words still remains, a menu of choices is presented for selection. Experiments show "record" speeds of 70 wpm using SHARK.

SUMMARY

Text entry is an important part of any user interface. Keyboards are by far the fastest form of entry, but they are restricted to certain physical situations. For more nomadic text entry, buttons and pens can be used. These are all slower than the keyboard and, in most cases, the input is ambiguous. The input ambiguity is overcome by multiple entries, menu selection from the "best-N" after a preliminary entry, or the use of a statistical digram or trigram language model.

EXERCISES

1. Write a small program that presents phrases to a user to be typed, then measures their speed, total number of keystrokes, and error metrics.

2. Build a soft keyboard implementation using Querty, alphabetic, and OPT1 layouts. Measure user input speed.

3. Collect five handheld computing devices and compare their text entry techniques with the ones described in this chapter.

END NOTES

[1] Hopcroft, J. E., and J. D. Ullman. *Formal Languages and Their Relation to Automata*. Reading, MA: Addison-Wesley, 1969.

[2] Soukoreff, R. W., and I. S. MacKenzie. "Theoretical Upper and Lower Bounds on Typing Speeds Using a Stylus and Soft Keyboard." *Behavior & Information Technology* 14 (1995): 370–379.

[3] Jurafsky, D., and J. H. Martin. *Speech and Language Processing*. New Jersey: Prentice-Hall, 2000.

[4] Darragh, J. J., and I. H. Witten. "The Reactive Keyboard." *Cambridge Series on Human-Computer Interaction*, Cambridge University Press, Cambridge, England, 1992.

[5] Card, S. K., T. P. Moran, and A. Newell. *The Psychology of Human-Computer Interaction*. Hillsdale, NJ: Lawrence-Erlbaum, 1983.

[6] Silfverberg, M., I. S. MacKenzie, and P. Korhonen. "Predicting Text Entry Speed on Mobile Phones." *Proceedings of the ACM Conference on Human Factors in Computing Systems (CHI 2000)* (April 2000): 9–16.

[7] James, C. L., and K. M. Reischel. "Text Input for Mobile Devices: Comparing Model Predictions to Actual Performance." *Proceedings of the ACM Conference on Human Factors in Computing Systems (CHI 2001)* (March 2001): 365–371.

[8] Soukoreff, R. W., and I. S. MacKenzie. "Metrics for Text Entry Research: An Evaluation of MSD and KSPC and a New Unified Error Metric." *Proceedings of the ACM Conference on Human Factors in Computing Systems (CHI 2003)* (April 2003):113–120.

[9] Gong, J., and P. Tarasewich. "A New Error Metric for Text Entry Method Evaluation." *Proceedings of the ACM Conference on Human Factors in Computing Systems (CHI 2006)* (April 2006): 471–474.

[10] MacKenzie, S., and W. Soukoreff. "Phrase Sets for Evaluating Text Entry Techniques." *Extended Abstracts of the ACM Conference on Human Factors in Computing Systems (CHI 2003)* (April 2003): 754–755.

[11] Gong, J., and P. Tarasewich. "Alphabetically Constrained Keypad Designs for Text Entry on Mobile Devices." *Proceedings of the ACM Conference on Human Factors in Computing Systems (CHI 2005)* (April 2005): 211–220.

[12] Guinness Book of World Records.

[13] Matias, E., I. MacKenzie, and W. Buxton. "One-Handed Touch Typing on a QWERTY Keyboard." *Human-Computer Interaction* 11 (1996): 1–27.

[14] MacKenzie, I. S., H. Kober, D. Smith, T. Jones, and E. Skepner. "LetterWise: Prefix-Based Disambiguation for Mobile Text Input." *User Interface Software and Technology (UIST 01)* (November 2001): 111–120.

[15] Pavlovych, A., and W. Stuerzlinger. "Less-Tap: A Fast and Easy-to-Learn Text Input Technique for Phones." *Graphics Interface* (2003).

[16] Gong, J., and P. Tarasewich. "Alphabetically Constrained Keypad Designs for Text Entry on Mobile Devices." *Human Factors in Computing Systems (CHI 2005)* (April 2005): 211–220.

[17] Ingmarsson, M., D. Dinka, and S. Zhai. "TNT—A Numeric Keypad Based Text Input Method." *Human Factors in Computing Systems (CHI 2004)* (April 2004): 639–646.

[18] Conrad, R., and D. Longman. "Standard Typewriter Versus Chord Keyboard: An Experimental Comparison." *Ergonomics* 8 (1965): 77–88.

[19] Lyons, K., T. Starner, D. Plaisted, J. Fusia, A. Lyons, A. Drew, and E. W. Looney. "Twiddler Typing: One-Handed Chording Text Entry for Mobile Phones." *Human Factors in Computing Systems (CHI 2004)* (April 2004): 671–678.

[20] Wigdor, D., and R. Balakrishnan. "A Comparison of Consecutive and Concurrent Input Text Entry Techniques for Mobile Phones." *Human Factors in Computing Systems (CHI 2004)* (April 2004): 81–88.

[21] Wobbrock, J. O., B. A. Myers, and B. Rothrock. "Few-Key Text Entry Revisited: Mnemonic Gestures on Four Keys." *Human Factors in Computing Systems (CHI '06)* (April 2006): 489–492.

[22] Wilson, A. D., and M. Agrawala. "Text Entry Using a Dual Joystick Game Controller." *Human Factors in Computing Systems (CHI '06)* (April 2006): 475–478.

[23] Partridge, K., S. Chatterjee, V. Sazawal, G. Borriello, and R. Want. "TiltType: Accelerometer-Supported Text Entry for Very Small Devices." *User Interface Software and Technology (UIST '02)* (October 2002): 201–204.

[24] Proschowsky, M., N. Schultz, and N. E. Jacobsen. "An Intuitive Text Input Method for Touch Wheels." *Human Factors in Computing Systems (CHI '06)* (April 2006): 467–470.

[25] MacKenzie, I. S., and S. X. Zhang. "The Design and Evaluation of a High-Performance Soft Keyboard." *Human Factors in Computing Systems (CHI '99)* (May 1999): 25–31.

[26] Zhai, S., M. Hunter, and B. A. Smith. "The Metropolis Keyboard—Exploration of Quantitative Techniques for Virtual Keyboard Design." *User Interface Software and Technology (UIST '00)* (November 2000): 119–128.

[27] Isokoski, P. "Performance of Menu-Augmented Soft Keyboards." *Human Factors in Computing Systems (CHI '04)* (April 2004): 423–430.

[28] Masui, T. "An Efficient Text Input Method for Pen-Based Computers." *Human Factors in Computing Systems (CHI '98)* (January 1998): 328–335.

[29] Goldberg, D., and C. Richardson. "Touch-Typing with a Stylus." *InterCHI '93* (May 1993): 80–87.

[30] Venolia, D., and F. Neiberg. "T-Cube: A Fast Self-Disclosing Pen-Based Alphabet." *Human Factors in Computing Systems (CHI '94)* (April 1994): 265–270.

[31] Blinkenstorfer, C. H. "Graffiti." *Pen Computing* (January 1995): 30–31.

[32] Wobbrock, J. O., B. A. Myers, and J. A. Kembel. "EdgeWrite: A Stylus-Based Text Entry Method Designed for High Accuracy and Stability of Motion." *User Interface Software and Technology (UIST '03)* (November 2003): 61–70.

[33] Wobbrock, J. O., B. A. Myers, and B. Rothrock. "Few-Key Text Entry Revisited: Mnemonic Gestures on Four Keys." *Human Factors in Computing Systems (CHI '06)* (April 2006): 489–492.

[34] Wobbrock, J. O., and B. A. Myers. "Trackball Text Entry for People with Motor Impairments." *Human Factors in Computing Systems (CHI '06)* (April 2006): 479–488.

[35] Mankoff, J., and G. D. Abowd. "Cirrin: A Word-Level Unistroke Keyboard for Pen Input." *User Interface Software and Technology (UIST '98)* (November 1998): 213–214.

[36] Perlin, K. "Quikwriting: Continuous Stylus-Based Text Entry." *User Interface Software and Technology (UIST '98)* (November 1998): 215–216.

[37] Kristensson, P., and S. Zhai. "SHARK^2: A Large Vocabulary Shorthand Writing System for Pen-Based Computers." *User Interface Software and Technology (UIST '04)* (October 2004): 43–52.

CHAPTER 19

Digital Ink

Since digital interaction became possible, people have wanted to "draw on the screen." This chapter looks at the technologies of digital ink and the various ways it can be used and processed. For most graphical user interfaces, the mouse is the input device of choice because it is cheap and easy to grasp when moving from the keyboard. However, the mouse is a very poor device when drawing on the screen. The speed and accuracy of human movement generally depends upon the mass of the muscle groups involved and the mass of the body part being manipulated. The mouse is manipulated with the wrist and forearm and, thus, is relatively slow and inaccurate. For drawing on the screen, the pen or stylus is the preferred instrument because it uses only the fingers, which are much more dexterous. A stylus uses the small-mass finger bones manipulated by relatively large-mass muscles in the forearm. Digital ink also exploits user experience with pen and paper. Some systems remove the pen and use the finger itself as the input device.

Digital ink has also been a focal point of new personal computing devices. One of the most influential systems was the Apple Newton. It was a market failure but it broke new ground as to what a personal computer could be. One of its contributions was the focus on a stylus or pen rather than a keyboard and mouse as the key input mechanism. The Palm Pilot took the most usable parts of the Newton vision and produced a cheaper, smaller device that was profoundly successful. Since the Palm, many personal digital assistant (PDA) devices have followed that use digital ink as a fundamental interaction technique. Microsoft's Tablet PC is an example of a device focused on a paper rather than hand-sized form factor. Some systems have tried to dispense entirely with the stylus or pen by using the fingers themselves as an input device. The MERL DiamondTouch targets a tabletop form shared by many people. The Apple iPhone puts finger touch interaction in a hand-sized form factor. Many of the touch-based devices have expanded their interactions to sense and use multiple touch points as an interactive technique. All of these devices use the metaphor of direct sensing of screen location and digital ink. This chapter covers the necessary algorithms for such interaction. The algorithms for digital ink and gesture recognition draw on the graphics and event techniques from Chapters 2 and 3 as well as some of the text input concepts from Chapter 18.

This chapter first discusses various pen/touch input technologies followed by some basic algorithms for processing strokes of digital ink. Gesture recognition is then introduced as a basis for many interactive techniques. Digital ink also has the property of allowing very free-form modes of expression. As such, several systems have been developed that use digital ink as their basic data type. The drawing metaphor of digital ink has led to several systems that exploit it for sketching tools. Lastly, the use of digital ink for annotating existing material in the user interface is discussed.

PEN/TOUCH INPUT DEVICES

Most pen input technologies are either distance, projection-based, or position encoded. The distance techniques use some physical phenomenon to measure the distance between the pen and two or more known points. Knowing the distance between the pen and two different points, you can compute the intersection of two circles to determine a pen position. Note that the intersection between two circles has two solutions. However, in most instances one of the solutions is easily discarded, as shown in Figure 19.1.

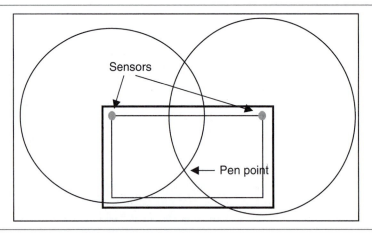

Figure 19.1 – Distance-sensed pen input

One common distance measure is the speed of sound. The pen simultaneously emits an infrared pulse and an ultrasonic pulse. The infrared pulse, traveling at the speed of light, is essentially instantaneous. The sensors each start a timer until the ultrasonic pulse arrives. The time multiplied by the speed of sound yields the distance between the pen and the microphone sensor. The Mimio[1] input device uses two microphones suction-cupped to a white board at a fixed distance apart. The pens are triggered by pressure against the board. This provides an inexpensive input device for a large area. The inputs are accurate to $1/100^{th}$ of an inch up to 8 feet from the sensor pair.

Many PDA stylus pads use a resistive distance technique. A conductive and a resistive layer are placed very close together but separated by flexible spacers. Pressure on the outer layer makes contact between the resistive and conductive layers, as shown in Figure 19.2. Before pressure, no current flows. After pressure, the resistance measured at each edge is proportional to the distance between that edge and the contact point.

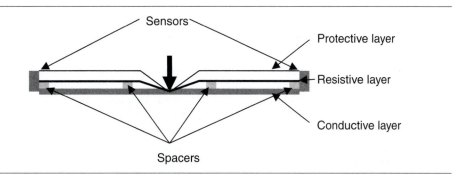

Figure 19.2 – Resistive pen sensing

Projection-based techniques sense each x- and y-coordinate independently to get a projection of the pen or finger point. A simple technique uses light emission and sensing. As shown in Figure 19.3, a set of infrared light emitters is arranged along one side of the touch area. On the opposite edge is a corresponding set of detectors. The control software activates each emitter/detector pair in turn. If a finger or stylus is in the way, no light is detected at the corresponding sensor and you assume that the touch point is somewhere along the line between the emitter and the sensor. The other coordinate is sensed in a similar fashion using the other edges. Together, these provide the x, y coordinates of a single touch point.

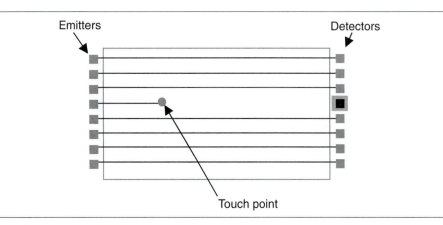

Figure 19.3 – Light interference sensing

Another more common projection-based technique[2] uses two layers of fine wires going in the X and Y directions. Each wire in turn has an AC signal placed on the line. The pen contains an inductor. When the pen is placed close to a wire, the inductor modifies the signal, which can be sensed. The wire with the strongest signal modification is the one that is closest to the pen. The pen tip can also have a pressure sensor designed so that pressure changes the inductance. This change in inductance can also be sensed to provide the tablet with information about the pressure on the tip.

The DiamondTouch[3] technique uses capacitive coupling to sense the position of a finger rather than a pen or stylus. This exploits the fact that the human body is largely water and makes an excellent dielectric. A grid of small antennas is embedded in a tabletop. The user sits on a conductive pad that is grounded to the sensor circuit. When the user's finger is on or very close to an antenna, the user's body forms a capacitive circuit with the sensor. The capacitance difference between touching and not touching can be sensed. If different users sit on different pads, they each form a different circuit that can be independently sensed. The antennas are arranged in a grid so that X and Y projections of a touch position can be independently obtained. Projection-based techniques are challenged when multiple touches occur simultaneously. Two touches will produce two signals in X and two in Y. This essentially defines a rectangle. If a rectangle is all that is required, this works great. If, however, the point positions are needed, you have ambiguous data. Either pair of opposite corners would explain the multiple touches, as shown in Figure 19.4.

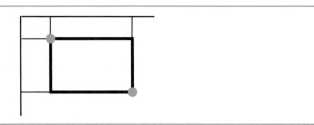

Figure 19.4 – Ambiguous multiple touches in projection sensing

The Anoto[4] pen uses a very different position-encoding technology. The tip of the pen is a small camera that views specially printed paper. On the paper is a pattern of microscopic dots. Each region of the paper has a unique spacing of these dots that can be sensed by the camera. The dots can be preprinted or printed using a laser printer. They give the paper a slightly gray shade. By "reading" the pattern of dots under the camera, the pen can identify where it is located in *dot space*. The Anoto dot pattern can generate enough unique patterns to cover 60,000,000 square kilometers of paper. The Anoto pen is usually coupled with a normal ink pen. This allows users to write on the encoded paper as one would with a normal pen, while the camera digitally logs the same stroke information. By reading the stroke information out of the pen, the digital ink can be recovered as well as a unique identification of the page on which the ink was written.

The previous techniques are among the most common. Others have been developed. Chapter 24 discusses additional camera-based techniques for getting two-dimensional input that can be used for digital ink.

STROKE PROCESSING

The key data type in digital ink is the stroke, which is an array of points in the same sequence as the user entered them. Frequently, the coordinates of each point are accompanied by the time stamp of when the point was received from the input device. The timing of the stroke points is sometimes used in recognition tasks where a particular user's style is important, such as in verifying a signature. For this chapter, you will generally ignore timing information.

Digital ink strokes can be produced by capturing all of the mouse-move events between mouse-down and mouse-up. Pen events are generally passed through the same event mechanism as mouse events. As the pen moves, the stroke is echoed on the screen either as dots at each event point or as lines connecting the event points for a cleaner-looking ink stroke. In modern user interfaces, there is generally a lot of processing associated with input events. In particular, the event/damage/redraw cycle must occur on each input. For digital ink, you want the stroke to be as clean and fluid as possible. For this reason, many tablet software systems handle inking at a very low level and then generate a single stroke event upon pen-up. This allows the ink stroke to be drawn without incurring the whole event/damage/redraw loop. As processors get faster, this will be less of an issue. Regardless of the event-handling technique, the result is a single stroke (array of points) that is passed on to the remainder of the digital ink system.

Several standard steps must be performed in almost every digital ink application:

- Registration and parallax to deal with the relationship between the input device and a display
- Cleaning to remove noise from the stroke that was produced by the input device
- Normalization to make stroke recognition independent of size and location
- Comparing strokes is frequently used in various recognition tasks
- Compare stroke or stroke features to trained classifier

Registration and Parallax

It is common to integrate the pen sensor with a display device. The display is either front projected or rear projected. In either case, there is a difference between the coordinate system of the display and the coordinate system of the pen sensor. Depending on the sensing technique, the input resolution might be much higher or much lower than the display resolution.

These coordinates must be aligned so that the ink appears displayed exactly under the pen. Rear projected displays, where the image comes from under the sensor, can also suffer from parallax. This occurs when there is some visible thickness to the sense/display assembly. Because users rarely look straight down on a surface, this thickness can cause the pen to appear at a different position on the display than where it is actually located, as shown in Figure 19.5. The parallax in Figure 19.5 occurs with right-handed users. The parallax is in the opposite direction for left-handed users and might differ vertically based on whether the device is handheld, resting on a table, or displayed on a wall.

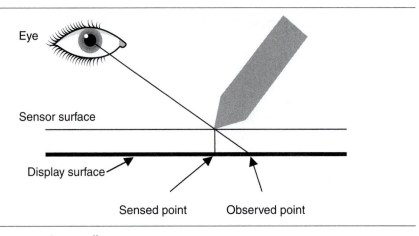

Figure 19.5 – Pen parallax

Both the coordinate alignment problem and the pen parallax problem can be handled with a registration process. In this process, the display shows the users five to eight points in sequence. For each point, the user is asked to click on a spot that appears to the user to be over the displayed point. By having a particular user do this process while in a normal usage configuration, you get information that resolves both problems.

At the end of the user's registration process, you have P_i points in pen coordinates and a corresponding set of D_i points in display coordinates. What you want is a function F such that $F(P_i)=D_i$ for all samples i. The simplest form of F is a pair of linear functions of the form:

$$aP_x + bP_y + c = D_x$$
$$dP_x + eP_y + f = D_y$$

These equations will handle any combination of scaling, skew, rotation, or position misalignment. What you need is a mechanism for reliably getting coefficients a through f from your set of sample points. In the linear system, there are three unknowns for each equation. Collecting five points provides more than enough information to resolve the coefficients using linear least squares. The simple linear function works great on digitizers that are placed directly over flat screens. It does not always account for situations where a projector is producing the displayed image. The projector optics can produce some nonlinear distortions that must be accommodated. For this, functions of the following form handle most situations:

$$aP_x + bP_y + \frac{c}{P_x} + \frac{d}{P_y} + eP_x^2 + fP_y^2 + gP_xP_y + h = D_x$$

$$jP_x + kP_y + \frac{l}{P_x} + \frac{m}{P_y} + nP_x^2 + qP_y^2 + rP_xP_y + s = D_y$$

Because each equation has eight unknowns, 10 or more sample points are needed to resolve the coefficients. Both sets of equations are linear in their coefficients even though the second set of equations has nonlinear terms. This allows you to use a linear least squares approximation to get coefficients that yield a function with the least error. The linear least squares algorithm is found in Appendix A1.2f.

Cleaning

At times, a digitizer produces very erratic points. These are due to momentary noise in the sensing circuit. Where this occurs, you need to remove those extraneous points because they make very ugly ink strokes and can disturb recognition algorithms. In many modern tablet systems, the cleaning step is done before any strokes or input events are sent to the application. However, cleaning is a simple process. What you are looking for are points that are unreasonably far from their neighboring points. For any point P_i, you use the distance between P_i and P_{i-1}. A simple technique is to eliminate any point where this distance is above some threshold. The threshold can be determined from the normal user hand speed and the sampling rate. The threshold can also be determined by sampling a number of strokes and computing the mean and standard deviation of the point distance. The threshold can be set at the mean plus two times the standard deviation.

Normalize

You frequently want to recognize what an ink stroke is without considering the stroke's size or position. For normalization (after cleaning), you compute the maximum and minimum in X and Y of all points in the stroke. You then compute a transform:

$$S = \frac{1}{\max(X_{max} - X_{min}, Y_{max} - Y_{min})}$$
$$T = Scale(S, S) \bullet Translate(-X_{min}, -Y_{min})$$

This translates the upper-left corner of the stroke to the origin, making it position independent and scales the longest axis of the stroke to 1.0, making it scale independent.

Using the same scale factor in X and Y retains the shape of the stroke, which is usually very important. This transformation T is applied to all points in the stroke to compute a new normalized stroke.

Thinning

Many digitizers produce far more points than are useful for recognition. These numerous points also produce low-level noise that can interfere with some recognition algorithms. Low-level noise can also come from user hand tremors. A thinning process can reduce the number of points and remove much of the low-level noise. You always keep the first and last points of the stroke because their locations are frequently important. Starting with point P_i, you collect all succeeding points until you find one that is more than some threshold distance d from P_i. You collect these points and replace them with a single point that is their average. You then move to your new point and continue the process. You end up with a stroke that has points spaced approximately d apart. In normalized strokes, a threshold of 0.01 to 0.1 is appropriate. The larger the threshold, the less noise in the stroke but there are more corner details removed.

Comparing Strokes

It is frequently helpful to measure the difference between two strokes A and B. This comparison usually involves a comparison of pairs of points between two strokes. A simple measure is the average distance between each point and the closest point to it on the other stroke. There is a simple algorithm (see Figure 19.6) for this distance that is linear in the number of points in both strokes. This algorithm assumes that each point's closest point on the other stroke is very near to the previous point's match. Given two points in the sequence that already match, the next matching pair will come from one of the current points and one of the next points in the sequence or from the pair of next points. This assumption allows the search for matching points to be very limited and thus the linear-time algorithm.

```
float strokeDistance(A, B)
{
      int i=0; int j=0;
      float dist = distance(A[i],B[i]);
      int count=1;
      while (i<A.size-1 && j<B.size-1)
      {
            float d1=distance(A[i+1],B[j]);
            float d2=distance(A[i],B[j+1]);
            float d3=distance(A[i+1],B[j+1]);
            if (d1<d2)
            {     if (d1<d3)
                  {     dist+=d1;
                        i++;
                  }
                  else
                  {     dist+=d3;
                        i++;
                        j++;
                  }
            }
            else // d1>=d2
            {     if (d2<d3)
                  {     dist+=d2;
                        j++;
                  }
                  else
                  {     dist+=d3;
                        i++;
                        j++;
                  }
            }
            count++;
      }
      while (i<A.size)
      {     dist+=distance(A[i],B[B.size-1]);
            count++;
            i++;
      }
      while (j<B.size)
      {     dist+=distance(A[A.size-1], B[j]);
            count++;
            j++;
      }
      return dist/count;
}
```

Figure 19.6 – Stroke distance algorithm

The distance used to compare a pair of points is generally the Euclidean distance. However, some researchers have used different distances based on additional features of the points. Consider the two strokes shown in Figure 19.7. It might be desirable for the inflection points in the middle of the strokes to be matched with each other to more accurately characterize the strokes. Because of the way in which these two strokes were drawn, other points might actually be closer. If you modify your distance() function to include other features about the points besides their Euclidean distance, those matches are more likely to occur. Possible features would be the angle formed between A[i-1], A[i], and A[i+1], or A[i-1]-A[i+1]. Comparing features such as these as well as geometric distance produces a match of similar points to similar points.

Figure 19.7 – Two strokes to compare

The algorithm in Figure 19.6 is a greedy algorithm that makes a locally optimal decision on which points to pair with each other. If you start with two points (A[0], B[0]), you can view the problem as a graph search where nodes of the graph are point pairs (A[i],B[j]). From any such pair, the same three choices of next possible match are possible (as in Figure 19.6). However, using the least-cost path algorithm (Appendix A2.2), you can compute the globally minimal matching among points. This distance measure can be more accurate but is more expensive to compute because it is inherently nondeterministic. This *elastic matching* approach using least-cost path was used by Tappert[5] for handwriting recognition and in SHARK[6] for comparison of sokgraphs.

GESTURE/CHARACTER RECOGNITION

One of the goals of pen-based interaction has been to drive user interfaces by user-gesture events rather than by menus or special keystrokes. Gestures have a number of advantages. The most important benefit is that the desired action and the target object for that action are expressed all in one stroke. For example, the gray ink gesture in Figure 19.8 indicates a deletion, and its starting location also indicates the object to be deleted. This combination of action and object can be very efficient. Forsberg et al[7] used this ability to create a music composition tool. Each type of note is recognized from a unique gesture, while the position of the note on the music staff indicates the desired pitch and rhythmic position. This is much more efficient than menu-oriented systems. A very common gesture system is character recognition where each gesture corresponds to a character to be entered.

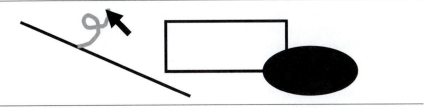

Figure 19.8 – Delete gesture

Use of gestures to interact involves three steps: (1) assembly of strokes into gestures, (2) classification of the strokes into a specific gesture class, and (3) extraction of geometric features from the stroke to use for the rest of the interaction.

Assembly of Strokes

Many gestures are combinations of one or more strokes. Figure 19.9 shows several such gestures. Figure 19.9 also shows a common stroke notation where the beginning of the stroke is indicated by a dot. This is the notation used throughout this chapter.

Figure 19.9 – Multistroke gestures

Deciding which strokes should be combined to form a single gesture can be a messy problem. Many gesture systems get around this problem by defining all gestures to consist of single strokes. This is the technique used by Unistrokes[8] and the original Graffiti[9] character recognizers. Where multistroke gestures are required, strokes are frequently combined when they occur within a very short time. The setting of that time threshold is problematic and the requirement of a time gap between gestures can slow down user input. Another technique is to combine gestures that overlap in the x-coordinate. This would work for the X and the T in Figure 19.9, but not for the K. Another technique is to recognize the strokes as separate gestures and also as a single gesture. This creates multiple hypotheses. A language model or the types of objects where the gesture is used can then be used to resolve the ambiguity.

Classification of Gestures

The gesture classification problem requires a function c(stroke) that will take a cleaned, thinned, and normalized stroke and produce a class from some finite alphabet of possible classes. The classes might be characters for text input, actions such as "bold," "delete," "make thicker," or objects such as a line, circle, rectangle, or musical note. The classification problem is pretty much the same for all of these cases.

Gesture classification is almost always trained rather than hard-coded. One or more strokes are collected from each of the classes of gestures and then one of several classification algorithms is used for training (Appendix A3). Early approaches used sequence classifiers to compare stroke sequences. The elastic matching algorithm or its faster linear variant can be used as a distance metric to drive a nearest neighbor classifier (Appendix A3.1c). However, on many PDAs and on slow computers of any kind, the computational demands of point-by-point matching of a stroke against hundreds of sample strokes is beyond interactive speeds.

The first practical gesture recognizers used patterns like those shown in Figure 19.10 to reduce the point data of the stroke down to a sequence of cell identifiers[10]. Using the grid on the left, the stroke for "C" is reduced to the sequence 3, 2, 1, 4, 7, 8, 9. Using the pattern on the right, the sequence is 2, 1, 3, 4. Recognition uses a minimal edit distance algorithm (Appendix A3.2d) to compare these cell sequences with those stored for the sample strokes. These recognizers were very fast and imposed little burden on the computers of the time. Training was also very fast and many applications provided the ability for users to train gestures for any menu command. However, these recognizers were not very accurate. Frequent misrecognitions occurred.

Figure 19.10 – Character-recognition regions

Most modern gesture recognizers use vector classifiers (Appendix A3.1) rather than sequence classifiers for recognizing gestures. In this approach, a function is programmed that will convert a stroke or set of strokes into a fixed vector of features. These features, rather than the original stroke, are passed to the classifier both for training and for recognition. Any of the vector classifier algorithms can be used. Nearest neighbor, linear perceptron, or Bayesian classifiers are commonly used.

The key to vector classification is the design of the feature function. The set of features very much determines the ability to discriminate among various stroke shapes. A common feature set is one developed by Dean Rubine[11]. The following feature set is based on his work with some simplifications. Starting from this feature set, it is straightforward to invent new features that discriminate in various ways.

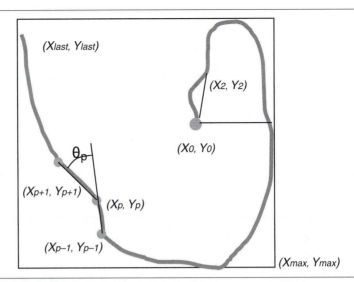

Figure 19.11 – Stroke features

Figure 19.11 shows a cleaned, thinned, and normalized stroke from which you want to compute a set of features. A variety of angles can be computed as part of these features. In most cases, the angles can be replaced by their sines and cosines to provide the same discrimination at lower computational cost. Sample features are as follows:

1. x_0 — The normalized x-coordinate of the start point.

2. y_0 — The normalized y-coordinate of the start point.

3. $\dfrac{x_2 - x_0}{\sqrt{(x_2 - x_0)^2 + (y_2 - y_0)^2}}$ —The cosine of the starting angle. Point 2

   is used to get a good sense of the user's direction and to ignore any starting "wiggles" in the stroke.

4. $\dfrac{y_2 - y_0}{\sqrt{(x_2 - x_0)^2 + (y_2 - y_0)^2}}$ —The sine of the starting angle.

5. x_{max} —This along with y_{max} gives you a measure of the eccentricity of the normalized stroke. For example, the normalized stroke for "I" has a very small x_{max} and a y_{max} of 1.0. The normalized stroke for "-" is the reverse.

6. y_{max} —Also a measure of stroke eccentricity.

7. $\sqrt{(x_{last} - x_0)^2 + (y_{last} - y_0)^2}$ —The distance between the first and last point.

   This distinguishes a "C" (large distance) from an "O" (small distance).

8. $\dfrac{x_{last} - x_0}{\sqrt{(x_{last} - x_0)^2 + (y_{last} - y_0)^2}}$ —The cosine of the angle from first point to last point.

9. $\dfrac{y_{last} - y_0}{\sqrt{(x_{last} - x_0)^2 + (y_{last} - y_0)^2}}$ —The sine of the angle from first point to last point.

10. $\displaystyle\sum_{p=0}^{last-1} \sqrt{(x_p - x_{p+1})^2 + (y_p - y_{p+1})^2}$ —The total summed length of the normalized

stroke. This would distinguish between an "O" and a spiral stroke repeated several times. The end points might be the same but the stroke length would be very different.

11. $\displaystyle\sum_{p=1}^{last-1} \theta_p$ —The sum of all of the point angles in the stroke. Positive and

negative angles cancel each other so that for an "I" stroke that is a little wavy this feature would still come out to be 0.0. For an "O" stroke, this would come out to be 2π radians because one whole turn has been made regardless of any waviness in the stroke. Thinning of a stroke is very important to getting good point angles for these features.

$$\theta_p = \tan^{-1}\left(\frac{(x_{p+1} - x_p)(y_p - y_{p-1}) - (x_p - x_{p-1})(y_{p+1} - y_p)}{(x_{p+1} - x_p)(x_p - x_{p-1}) + (y_{p+1} - y_p)(y_p - y_{p-1})}\right)..$$

12. $\displaystyle\sum_{p=1}^{last-1} |\theta_p|$ —The sum of the absolute values of the point angles. In this case,

positive and negative angles do not cancel each other. Wavy strokes have higher values for this feature than straight strokes.

13. $\displaystyle\sum_{p=1}^{last-1} \theta_p^2$ —The sum of the squares of the point angles. This feature scores higher

for very sharp angles. The square of 180 degrees is very much larger than any sum of 5–10 degree angles.

This feature set is not exhaustive but they are a good start and are easy to calculate. For a given gesture recognition problem where gestures of different classes are not discriminated well, it is helpful to look at the cases and invent a feature that will discriminate. This new feature(s) can be added to the set and exploited by the training algorithm.

Extraction of Geometry

Because you frequently use gestures both for actions and object identification, you need to extract geometry information from the stroke to use as arguments to the action. Geometry extraction is usually performed on the cleaned, thinned, but not normalized stroke. Normalization purposely discards much of the geometry for better recognition. The starting point (x_0, y_0) is normally used to identify the object of an action. When creating objects, such as lines or arcs, the starting and ending points are used to derive the geometry of the object being created. Frequently, the bounding box can be used for rectangle or ellipse gestures. Sometimes sharp corners are used for geometry. These can be identified as point angles (θ_p) whose absolute value is above some threshold.

DIGITAL INK AS A DATA TYPE

One of the advantages of pen and paper is that the medium is completely unstructured. As thoughts and ideas come, you can organize them on the paper any way that you want. Many systems have been developed to mimic this aspect of paper. The model for such an application is a list of stroke objects each containing a sequence of points. Such note-taking applications are trivial to implement. However, the reason for going digital is that the computer is not paper. The computer can erase, move, organize, search, and share information in ways that are not possible with paper. What you want are applications that support the freedom of paper while providing the increased flexibility of digital representation.

Tivoli

One of the most powerful digital ink systems is Tivoli[12] from Xerox PARC. The key insight from Tivoli is the discovery of inherent structure rather than the explicit encoding of structure. Structure in information is critical for a computer to provide leverage to human input. For example, when writing with a word processor, the user can place the cursor between any two letters and begin typing. The word processor automatically moves characters to make room for each new character, rewraps lines of text, and moves subsequent paragraphs out of the way. The word processor can do all of this because it has an encoding of the structure of the document. It has explicitly encoded the concepts of lines, paragraphs, and pages. Using this structure, the program knows how to do many mundane tasks for you. On a piece of paper, you cannot conveniently insert a word into a sentence that has already been written. Part of the problem is the nature of paper and part of the problem is that there is no encoded structure. Imagine trying to build a word processor where the model was a list of characters each with its own X, Y position. Inserting a character would overwrite the character already there. The user would need to move them all around by hand, which is very tedious. Similar structure can be seen in a spreadsheet. You can select, move, highlight, or delete entire rows and columns because their structure is encoded in the model.

The designers of Tivoli recognized that humans can look at a page of text and know what should happen when a new character is typed or a column is moved. You know this simply from what you see, not because of any encoded data structure. As humans, you see only the presented information, not the underlying data structure. If the necessary structure is visually present for humans to see, then it must also be available in the presentation for computers to exploit. In basic Tivoli, the only data type is the digital ink stroke. From this information, Tivoli can infer many structured behaviors.

The original Tivoli paper focused on three types of structure in digital ink: lists, text, and tables. The key tasks that they implemented were selection, deletion, and insertion. For a list, you frequently want to add new things into the list at any point, remove things from the list, and reorder items in the list. The desired help from the computer is to adjust the remaining elements of the list to open or close up sufficient room for these operations. The ink shown in Figure 19.12 is obviously a table in its structure. However, the only encoded information is the ink strokes themselves. The table items are each made up of several ink strokes. Tivoli's approach is to discover structure as it is needed. One approach for structure discovery uses ink histograms. For each row and column, you count the number of ink points, as shown in Figure 19.13. Note that the spaces between rows and columns are indicated by the zero regions in the histograms. This makes it relatively easy to discover these structures from the ink strokes.

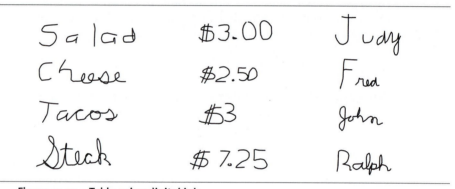

Figure 19.12 – Table using digital ink

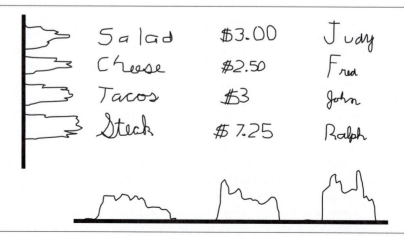

Figure 19.13 – Ink histograms

Tivoli defined several gestures that could be used to manipulate ink. These are shown in Figure 19.14. Row and column insertion (14a and 14c) depend on whether something is already selected. If there is no selected ink, these move ink down or to the right to make room for a new row or column. If there is selected ink, these make room, move the selected ink into the open space, and close up the space where the ink was moved from. The row and column selection gestures (14b and 14d) projection-select all ink in the corresponding row or column (using the ink histograms from Figure 19.13). These selections can then be used with the insertion gestures to move ink around. The deletion gesture (14e) either deletes a single stroke or, if a row or column was selected, it deletes the entire row or column and closes up the empty space. This opening and closing of space and moving ink around to make it happen is far more powerful than simple paper and does not require the user to "create a table object." The necessary structure is discovered on the fly as the user works with the information. The gestures are easily trained for recognition using Rubine's feature set.

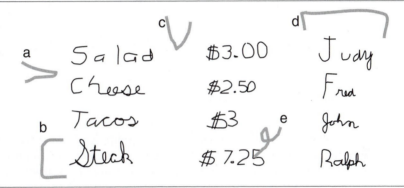

Figure 19.14 – Table manipulation gestures

These gestures can also be interpreted by projecting the gesture coordinates down or across and selecting all strokes for which a majority of their points lie inside of the projected regions, as shown in Figure 19.15. This removes the need for the ink histograms.

Sometimes, it is desirable to work with more than one independent list or table. These can be partitioned using *border strokes*, as shown in Figure 19.15. A border stroke is just another stroke in the ink model. Its presence is detected as a single stroke that is either vertical or horizontal and extends from boundary to boundary. It is treated as just another stroke so that it can be moved and deleted in the same fashion as all of the other strokes. When projecting selection or insertion, the projection stops at any border strokes, as shown in Figure 19.15.

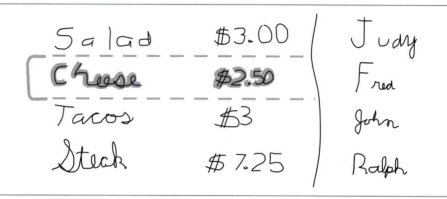

Figure 19.15 – Border strokes

The Tivoli researchers discovered that grouping of ink strokes is a fundamental concept[13]. In the previous discussion, items were implicitly grouped by the selection gestures. Border strokes provided additional structure. In many drawing programs, grouping is defined by explicit group operators to bring items together. Tivoli chose two approaches for defining grouping. The first was a system of explicit border objects. Such border objects are created by gestures that look like border strokes and are then replaced by a movable line that separates groups. This is much like tiled windowing systems.

The second grouping technique was to use enclosing strokes to define groups. Drawing a stroke around a set of other strokes creates a group, as shown in Figure 19.16. This work developed several gestures for modifying enclosures. A wedge gesture cutting across an enclosure would divide it into two enclosures. A gesture that starts and stops on the enclosure stroke would modify its boundary. Any gesture applied to an enclosure could be applied to all strokes in the enclosure. A stroke that started on one enclosure and ended on another created a link stroke. Moving either of the linked enclosures produced a scaling on the link stroke that kept it connected to the original enclosures. This created various dynamic diagrams. A *balloon* gesture when applied to an enclosure as shown in Figure 19.17 would reduce the selected strokes to a single balloon stroke. Clicking on the balloon stroke would pop up the original enclosed strokes for viewing or pasting. This mechanism creates summary diagrams of varying detail.

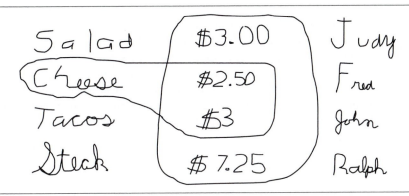

Figure 19.16 – Enclosure strokes

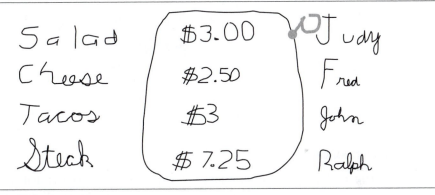

Figure 19.17 – Balloon gesture

Gesture/Ink/Action Segmentation

When working with ink as a data type, there is an ambiguity between what is a gesture and what is a data object. The Tivoli project, as with many others, used a button on the pen to indicate a gesture rather than an ink stroke. The following is a list of ink/gesture discrimination techniques taken from Li et al[14]:

- Press and hold the button on the pen barrel while entering a gesture.
- Press and hold still until gesture feedback appears. This is used in the Microsoft Tablet PC.
- A separate button on the tablet is activated by the nondominant hand.
- Using a pressure-sensing pen, the user presses harder for gestures than for ink strokes.
- Some pens have an *eraser* end that can be separately sensed. The eraser end is used for gestures.

The experiments performed by Li et al noted several trade-offs among these techniques. The use of the nondominant hand was the fastest.

The Scriboli[15] system addressed the problem of segmenting a gesture into a selection of desired strokes and specification of what action should be taken on the selected strokes. In their approach, an enclosing gesture surrounds all of the strokes to be selected. This gesture then ends in a pigtail by crossing over the stroke. When this pigtail is detected, a menu is displayed around the crossover point and the remainder of the gesture selects the correct action from the menu of possibilities. This is shown in Figure 19.18.

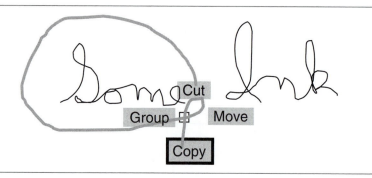

Figure 19.18 – Scriboli gesture menus

PerSketch

One of the advantages of digital ink over scanned images is that the ink stroke itself has more information than a simple map of pixels. As Tivoli demonstrated, dependence upon this information can be a problem. People interact with what they see, not with the order or form in which it was created. In Figure 19.19, object A is perceived as a rectangle even though it is composed of two strokes. Object B is also perceived as a rectangle though it consists of only one stroke. For most users, these are the same kind of shape regardless of how they were drawn.

Object C is composed of just two strokes, each of which is perceived as a rectangle. However, there are nine possible other rectangles such as the one highlighted in gray. None of these nine were explicitly created by the user, but they are perceived by the user. Recognizing the shapes that the user sees rather than the shapes as they were created is important to interacting with them naturally. When only looking at shapes, the user can perceive whatever he or she wants and the software need not be involved. When trying to select objects on the screen, an understanding and support for what users perceive can provide a more intelligent and effective mechanism for selecting the intended shape with minimal effort.

Eric Saund's PerSketch[16] system addresses the perceived shapes that should be discovered from those explicitly created. Rather than trying to recognize shapes from

Figure 19.19 – Perceived shapes from strokes

all of their possible meanings, PerSketch uses selection input from the user to identify the shape that the user intends. In Figure 19.19, the fat gray line represents a selection stroke by the user. This stroke disambiguates the desired shape from all other possible shape interpretations in the figure. The goal of PerSketch is to translate a user's selection gesture into a selection of the most likely shape to be selected regardless of the form of the original strokes.

The PerSketch approach is to divide the ink strokes into a series of *prime objects*. A *prime object* is a stroke with no intersections. Figure 19.20 shows the nine individual prime objects derived from two strokes. These prime objects can be composed to form composite objects, or individual shapes.

As the number of strokes increases, so does the number of prime objects and the exponential number of ways in which prime objects can be composed into shapes. For use in a sketching tool, the algorithms for composing shapes must be very fast.

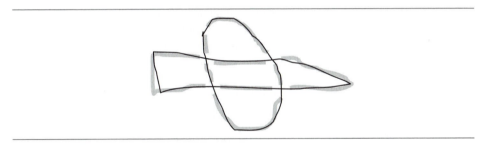

Figure 19.20 – Prime objects

PerSketch uses a *shadow bitmap* as its data structure for rapid discovery of prime objects from ink strokes. A shadow bitmap is an array of pixels that contains pointers to data structures rather than color values. Background pixels have null pointers. Pixels that correspond to a single prime object contain a pointer to that object. Intersection and touching points contain a pointer to a list of prime objects that touch that point. When a new stroke is entered by the user, its pointer is "drawn" into the shadow bitmap. Null pixels are replaced with the stroke's pointer. Pixels that already contain stroke information cause the stroke being entered to be broken apart at that point. The two parts are added to the list of prime objects at the intersection point and the stroke processing proceeds.

Because there are an exponential number of composite shapes in a drawing, you only want to identify a shape when the user actually wants to work with it. Suppose that the user wants to create a propeller shape from the two strokes in Figure 19.21. What is needed is to remove the interior prime objects. These prime objects can be selected by a single gesture, as shown in Figure 19.21. The selected objects can now be easily deleted.

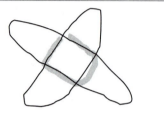

Figure 19.21 – Selecting a composite shape

Given the shadow bitmap and its corresponding connected graph of prime objects, you need an algorithm for selecting the set of prime objects that most closely corresponds to the selection gesture. PerSketch provides two such algorithms: pose matching and path tracing.

Pose Matching

The pose matching algorithm enumerates all of the composite objects that might correspond to the selection gesture. This incurs the exponential cost of enumerating all possibilities. Before enumerating composites, all prime objects that are more than some threshold distant from the selection gesture are discarded as irrelevant. Composite objects are computed from the remaining prime objects by traversing the graph of primes from the shadow bitmap. Each unique cycle in the graph that traverses any prime object at most once is a candidate shape.

From each recognized composite shape, PerSketch computes a *pose model*. The pose model consists of the *x-center*, *y-center*, *orientation-angle*, *length*, and *width*. The center point is computed by averaging all of the points in the strokes. The orientation angle is computed using the algorithm in Appendix A1.3c. This angle is based on the difference in width and height. For square or circular shapes, there is no dominant orientation angle. If the aspect ratio of the object is nearly equal, an orientation angle of zero is used. After the center and orientation are known, you can translate the shape to the origin and rotate the orientation angle to zero. With the stroke points in this normalized coordinate system, the length can be either the average or maximum of the absolute values of X. The width is similarly computed using Y. Note that you are not looking for the actual length and width as much as a feature that represents them.

Using the pose model, you can compare each composite shape to the pose model of the selection gesture. A simple distance metric is not acceptable, however, because of "unoriented" shapes with no distinct direction. PerSketch uses a different distance metric that deemphasizes orientation when the aspect ratio is close to 1.0. The selected prime objects are those that form a composite shape that has the pose model most similar to the selection gesture.

Path Tracing

The pose matching approach is somewhat limited in the kinds of selections that are possible. The selection of prime objects associated with the gesture in Figure 19.22 would not perform well using pose matching. The path tracing algorithm is a variation on the stroke distance algorithm in Figure 19.6. Each point in the selection gesture is compared against the nearest points in the shadow bitmap. You are looking for a sequence of prime objects that are nearest to the stroke. When an intersection point is reached, the algorithm must nondeterministically follow all strokes looking for the least match. This is similar to the elastic matching algorithm described earlier. Path tracing is more expensive than pose matching, but it produces more flexible match possibilities.

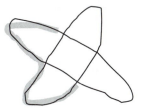

Figure 19.22 – Path traced selection

Flatland

Flatland[17] takes a somewhat different approach for interaction with digital ink. Unlike Tivoli and PerSketch, which focus on selection and intelligent manipulation groups of strokes, Flatland focuses on the interpretation of what strokes mean. In Flatland, structure is specified by the user in the form of *segments*. A segment behaves somewhat like a window in traditional user interfaces except that the associated interactive techniques are different. A segment has boundaries, like a window, except that they are drawn in a "sketchy" style consistent with the digital ink metaphor. The boundaries of a segment are primarily determined by the size of its content. When a segment is selected, the boundary expands to the right and down to make room for the user to draw new content. This is consistent with the way people create lists, notes, drawings, and other items using languages that read left-to-right and top-to-bottom. For other languages, a different convention would be required. When new strokes are entered, the segment automatically resizes to make more room.

The unique contribution of Flatland is in the way that it handles strokes of digital ink. Each segment consists of a boundary, a behavior, and a list of strokes. The only input events are "new stroke" and "move segment." When a new stroke is received, it is passed to the behavior object associated with the segment. The behavior object consults the strokes and other information already associated with the segment and modifies the strokes in the segment's list. This very simple input model provides very powerful features, as shown in Figure 19.23.

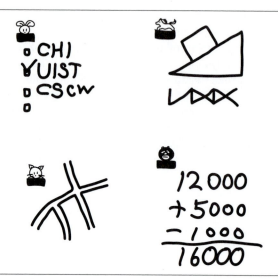

Figure 19.23 – Flatland[17]

The List behavior, shown in the upper left, translates checkmark strokes as gestures and marks a list item as complete. Writing strokes next to the bullet mark at the bottom adds those strokes to the list and makes a new bullet mark. The Pegasus behavior at the upper right uses the Pegasus stroke beautification system to translate strokes into more regular pictures. The lower-left behavior translates single strokes into stroke pairs that resemble streets for easy sketching of maps. The lower-right behavior translates strokes as digits, arithmetic operators, and the answer line. The results of the calculation are shown by the behavior object adding additional strokes to the segment automatically.

Each of these behaviors is independent of the others. However, the user can change a segment's behavior at any time. When behaviors are changed, the strokes remain part of the segment to be interpreted by the new behavior. Thus, a user can slip into Pegasus to draw a tidy drawing, slip into the map behavior to add streets, and then change to the simple ink behavior to write notes on the map. The uniform use of ink strokes as data objects and as input events makes this flexibility possible. The Tivoli system could easily be implemented as a Flatland behavior.

A user moves a segment by dragging one of its edges. When a segment runs into another segment, that encountered segment is moved out of the way. This might cause a cascade of movements of segments bumping into each other to make room. Overlapping segments are not allowed. If there is not enough room to move a segment where it is wanted, other segments are resized. This moving/resizing is performed recursively to automatically make room. If a shrunken segment is selected, it is restored to normal size and other segments are moved/shrunken to make room. This "window management" scheme requires very little effort on the part of the user and makes all information visible simultaneously.

Unlike Tivoli and PerSketch, a Flatland user must pay more attention to the intended structure of what is being drawn. Segments are explicitly created to provide grouping of strokes rather than inferring their structure. Selection of a segment's behavior is required to control how strokes are interpreted. On the other hand, the additional structure simultaneously provides more user control and more sophisticated behaviors.

SKETCHING TOOLS

A second major use of digital ink is in creating drawings or sketches. One of the great advantages of digital ink over pencil and paper is the ability to improve a rough sketch dynamically. An eraser is the only means for correcting pencil drawings and it is not a very satisfying tool. This section looks at two kinds of algorithms for improving sketching techniques. The first is the use of cubic splines to improve strokes and to edit strokes after they are created. Second is a technique for inferring lines and patching together rough strokes to create a cleaner drawing.

Ink to Cubics

An early sketch improvement technique is to smooth a stroke by approximating it with a series of cubic splines. Converting an ink stroke to a cubic has three advantages. The first is that the stroke can be smoothed to remove hand jitter from the line. Second, the cubic curve representation is typically more compact than the ink stroke in that the number of control points is typically much smaller than the number of ink samples. Third, the curve's control points provide handles for editing the curve.

For a given ink stroke represented by a series of points, you want to compute a set of control points for a cubic curve. The easiest curve representation is the Catmull-Rom (see Chapter 12). You can obviously create a curve by using the ink points as Catmull-Rom control points. This, however, would not provide any advantages because the ink points are too dense. What you want is to remove as many of the points as possible while still retaining the shape of the curve. In many situations, the user also provides a *smoothing factor*. The larger the smoothing factor, the more small detail is removed from the ink stroke. A smoothing factor of zero exactly matches the ink stroke. The smoothing factor defines the maximum distance between an ink point and the nearest point on the smoothed curve. This is very similar to the thinning threshold for cleaning up strokes described earlier. Before converting to a curve, the ink should be cleaned and then thinned using a threshold of one-half of the smoothing factor.

One approach to smoothing an ink stroke is to successively remove points that are less than the smoothing factor from the resulting curve until no additional deletions are possible. Figure 19.24 shows an ink stroke consisting of eight points that has been converted to a Catmull-Rom curve. You want to decide if point 6 can be removed while preserving appropriate smoothness. Because of the nature of piecewise cubic curves, you only need to consider the segment defined by points 4, 5, 7, and 8. Using this curve, you find the closest point using the algorithm from Chapter 12. If the distance from point 6 to the closest point is less than the smoothing factor, point 6 can be discarded.

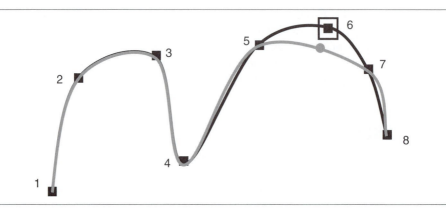

Figure 19.24 – Removing control points

Note that although the curves beyond points 4 and 8 are not affected, the curves between 4 and 5 and between 7 and 8 are changed. This is because the curve between 4 and 5 had its control point changed from 6 to 7. Given the fact that the smoothing factor is typically small, any point that is a candidate for deletion will typically cause very little distortion in neighboring curves. Therefore, you will ignore the effect.

With a criterion for deleting points, you have several strategies for considering which points to remove. You always retain the starting and ending point. You could consider points 2 through 7 in turn. This has problems. Each point N being considered is only half the smoothing distance from point $N+1$. As such, it is very unlikely that point N will be more than the smoothing distance from the curve. This means that point N will almost always be removed. Proceeding in this way, all points but the end points will be removed, which is not a good thing. This is because the removal of prior points discards information about the curve.

A better algorithm is to consider every other point for deletion. This means that points adjacent to the candidate point are original and are retaining information about the curve in that region. After considering every other point, you can repeat the algorithm on the remaining points. The algorithm terminates when there are no points deleted in a given pass. This algorithm is shown in Figure 19.25.

```
Point [] smoothCurve(Point [] inputPoints, float smoothing)
{
    boolean continue=true;
    Point [] curve=inputPoints;
    curve.insertPoint(0,inferFirstPoint(curve)); // provide first control point
    curve.addPoint(inferLastPoint(curve)); // provide last control point
    while (continue)
    {
        int len=curve.getLength();
        Point [] result;
        boolean continue=false;
        result.addPoint(curve[0]); // keep the first point
        for (int i=2;i<len-2; i+=2) // never consider the first two or last two points
        {
            result.addPoint(curve [i-1]); // retain skipped point
            if (closeEnough(i, curve,smoothing))
                continue=true; // another pass will be required
            else
                result.addPoint(curve[i]); // retain point
        }
        result.addPoint(curve[len-2]); // keep second to last point
        result.addPoint(curve[len-1]); // keep last point
        curve=result;
        result=null;
    }
    return curve;
}
boolean closeEnough(int i, Pont [] curve, float smoothing)
{
    Use nearest point on a curve (Chapter 12) to find the distance
    between curve[i] and the Catmull-Rom curve defined by
    curve[i-2], curve[i-1], curve[i+1] and curve[i+2]. The iteration
    can terminate whenever any point is found that is closer than
    the smoothing value or the distance range being considered is
    closer together than smoothing/4.
}
```

Figure 19.25 – Smoothing a curve by point deletion

Note also that the curve between points 1 and 2 in Figure 19.24 needs a control point 0 and the curve between 7 and 8 needs a control point 9. If the curve were closed, this would not be a problem because you could use the other control points. However, you need point 0 and 9 to assist with the tangent of the curve at points 1 and 8. One simple technique is to use the line between the start point and the second point as an approximation of the appropriate tangent. You can add these points using the functions shown in Figure 19.26. You compute a tangent vector, normalize it to length 1, and then add it to the start or end point to infer the extra control point.

```
Point inferFirstPoint( Point [] curve )
{
    float dx=curve[0].x-curve[1].x;
    float dy=curve[0].y-curve[1].y;
    float len = sqrt(dx*dx+dy*dy);
    dx=dx/len;
    dy=dy/len;
    Point result;
    result.x=curve[0].x+dx;
    result.y=curve[0].y+dy;
    return result;
}
Point inferLastPoint( Point [] curve )
{
    int len=curve.getLength();
    float dx=curve[len-1].x-curve[len-2].x;
    float dy=curve[len-1].y-curve[len-2].y;
    float len = sqrt(dx*dx+dy*dy);
    dx=dx/len;
    dy=dy/len;
    Point result;
    result.x=curve[len-1].x+dx;
    result.y=curve[len-1].y+dy;
    return result;
}
```

Figure 19.26 – Inferring starting and ending control points

Sketching Changes to Curves

Even with pencil and paper, artists regularly draw lines that are not quite correct. The control points of cubic curves can be moved and new control points can be inserted by clicking on a point on the curve and adding a control point at that location. Control points can be deleted. These curve editing techniques are not as satisfying as simply resketching the area to be modified. Figure 19.27 shows a curve with an additional gray curve that has been created by the user.

Figure 19.27 – Resketching a curve

A simple mechanism for editing the curve as shown is to insert new control points into the original curve at the start and end points of the editing stroke (gray). Any control points from the original curve (black) that lie between the newly created control points are replaced with the ink points from the *editing stroke*. The inserted region plus two points before and after is then smoothed using the algorithm described in Figure 19.25.

When modifying a curve, it is frequently desirable to "nudge" the curve rather than edit the curve. Figure 19.28 shows a curve (thick black) and an editing stroke (thin gray). The editing stroke is a hint as to how the curve should be modified rather than an explicit edit of the curve. The resulting curve (thick gray) is a blend of the original curve and the editing stroke. This technique was proposed by Baudel[18]. The basic approach is to resample the relevant section of the original curve into points at approximately the same resolution as the thinned edit stroke. The new curve points are computed as an interpolation between the original points and the nearest points on the edit stroke. Nearest points cannot be determined by simple Euclidean distance. Each point can be identified by their proportional distance along the curve. Points are matched by this curve position rather than geometry. Sequence position matching rather than geometry matching allows better ability to change the shape of the curve.

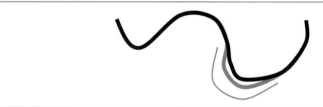

Figure 19.28 – "Nudging" curves

The nudging technique gives more control over curve changes by using several edit strokes to move the curve into the desired shape. The result is more an "averaging" of several strokes than an explicit use of any stroke in particular. This corresponds to common sketching behavior where lines are resketched multiple times to shape them.

Line Sketching

Frequently what is desired is not a sketch but a line drawing. Sketching is the input technique rather than the end result. Recognizing a straight line gesture is relatively easy using Rubine's features. If the arc length (sum of the distance between thinned ink points) is close to the distance between the start and end points, a straight line is inferred between the two end points. Figure 19.29 shows the input strokes (gray) and the resulting lines (thin black). The result is not very satisfying because the diagram is rather messy.

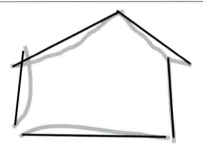

Figure 19.29 – Strokes to lines

The problem is that you expect lines to be vertical, centered, or parallel. You also expect that lines whose end points are touching should actually touch. The Pegasus[19] system takes the lines that were entered and generates multiple constraints that such lines might feasibly satisfy. Figure 19.30 shows several such constraints, including alignment of vertices, snapping to other lines, parallelism, and perpendicular lines. Sometimes there are several conflicting constraints that could be applied to a new stroke. In such cases, they are all presented to the user, who can then select one.

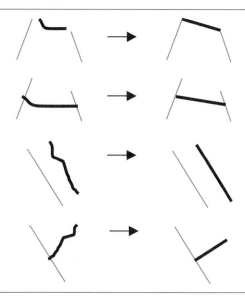

Figure 19.30 – Possible constraints imposed upon lines

ANNOTATION

Previously, you have discussed techniques for intelligently manipulating ink as well as tools for sketching with digital ink. This section now looks at digital ink as an annotation tool. A common use of a pencil is to mark up paper documents. You underline quotes in books, write in the margins, cross out unwanted material, or mark where text should be inserted. Digital pen-based annotation comes in two forms: annotating fully digital documents and annotating paper.

Annotating a fixed document with digital ink is relatively straightforward. A document representation, such as PDF, can be treated as a static image and the ink strokes can be displayed over the top. Ink strokes are stored in the coordinates of the page on which they are to be displayed. This duplicates the behavior of pen and ink, but adds little digital advantage.

XLibris

The XLibris[20] project explored the role of digitally annotated documents by means of a special tablet computing device roughly the shape of an 8 ½ by 11 piece of paper. They were interested in the concept of *active reading* where people annotate, clip, link, and search documents rather than just read them. One of their first contributions was the Reader's Notebook. As the user reads a document, he or she make annotations on it with a digital pen. The annotations and the underlying document materials are excerpted into the notebook to provide a "highlighted" version of the document, as shown in Figure 19.31. This automatically extracts the text that the reader found interesting. In the physical world, this would require the user copying the text in some cumbersome fashion. Looking through the notebook, the user can see the condensed annotated summary and at any time link back to the original context (which is impossible with physical paper).

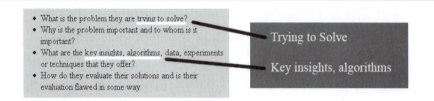

Figure 19.31 – Annotating text (see color plate)

The fact that digital ink is tied to digital text when annotating a document opens other opportunities. The XLibris team extracted the text underlying a user's annotations and used that text to provide focused document searches. In information retrieval, a document is generally represented by a vector of the frequencies of each word in the document. The vector has the length of all words known to the system. The similarity of two documents can be measured by the cosine distance (appendix A1.1e) between two such vectors. This measure can be improved by weighting the importance of various words. A common weighting is dividing the frequency of a word in a document by the frequency in all documents. Very frequent words such as "like" thus get very low scores and infrequent words such as "gastrointestinal" get much higher scores. XLibris augmented these weights by increasing the importance of text annotated by the user. This specifically focuses the comparison on those concepts that the reader felt was important. The retrieval results compared favorably with some of the best relevance-feedback techniques[21].

Annotating HTML Documents

A drawback of the XLibris project was that documents must exist in the XLibris framework and most digital documents do not. One approach is to annotate Web pages. Web pages are not static and are dynamically reformatted when the text size, font, or window width changes. If the underlying text can move and shift, the ink marks on the text quickly get out of sync. What are needed are ink marks that can track and follow the text, as shown in Figure 19.32.

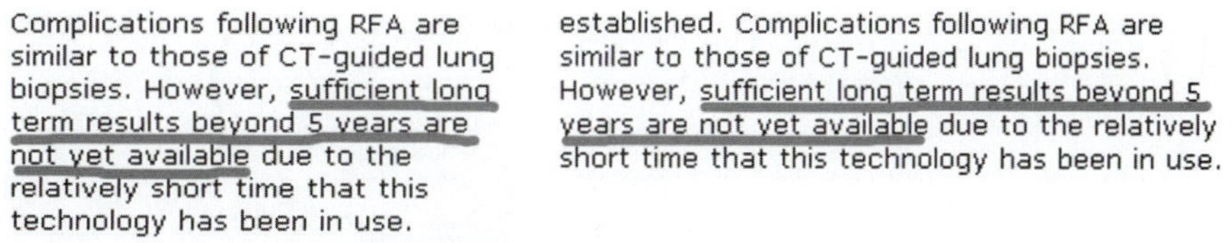

Complications following RFA are similar to those of CT-guided lung biopsies. However, <u>sufficient long term results beyond 5 years are not yet available</u> due to the relatively short time that this technology has been in use.

established. Complications following RFA are similar to those of CT-guided lung biopsies. However, <u>sufficient long term results beyond 5 years are not yet available</u> due to the relatively short time that this technology has been in use.

Figure 19.32 – Moving marks when reformatting

To move marks in the presence of reformatting, the ink must be represented in different coordinates. To accomplish this, marks are classified into three categories: (1) direct text marks (underline or highlight), (2) margin bars and circled passages, and (3) other notes. These classes of strokes can be distinguished using a subset of the Rubine features.

For direct text marks, the ink is broken into overlapping fragments tied to individual words, as shown in Figure 19.33. Each ink fragment is stored with a reference to the word to which it is attached and coordinates that are relative to the bounding box for that word. As the word moves and is resized, the ink stroke is moved and resized accordingly. When words remain together, the overlapping of the individual strokes ties them cleanly in what appears to be a continuous stroke.

Complications following RFA are similar to those of CT-guided lung

Figure 19.33 – Segmented word marks

Margin bars and circled passages are associated with regions of text rather than individual words. The associated words are discovered by projecting the bounding box of the stroke horizontally, as shown in Figure 19.34, and then remembering the first and last word of the selected text. The stroke coordinates are relative to the bounding box of the text. As the text is reformatted, the first and last words identify the associated range of text from which a new bounding box is computed. The stroke is drawn in the coordinates of the new bounding box. If the new region flows across a page boundary, the stroke must be split in a corresponding way.

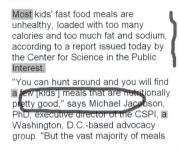

Figure 19.34 – Margin bars and circled text

Other marks, such as comments or little drawn stars to highlight a point, should not be resized along with the text. They only need to be repositioned with the text. These marks are associated with text using the same projection technique as margin bars. These marks are always drawn in the same size with only their position defined by the corresponding text bounding box.

Annotating Screen Shots

The XLibris project confined annotation to documents in a specific format under its own system. This restricts annotation to a small subset of the digital artifacts that people might use. XLibris was extended to Web documents, which further expanded its reach. The ScreenCrayons[22] system went further in supporting annotation of anything that appears on the screen. ScreenCrayons operates by taking an image capture of the screen and then overlaying the screen with a borderless window that contains the captured image. This appears like the original screen except that the underlying applications are no longer active. The image is overlaid by a gray transparent layer. The user annotates the image using the XLibris gesture set. The relevant regions for selection are identified by analyzing the white space. When a region is selected, the gray overlay is removed over that region to fully expose the annotated information. In addition, the user can add typed or pen drawn notes or diagrams on the unannotated gray regions (Figure 19.35).

coverage and services. It has added markets for voice and data coverage, as well as reduced some roaming rates when traveling internationally. Smartphone users can purchase 50MB of data while roaming in 67 specific countries for $60 per month. Laptop card users can purchase 5GB of data in the US, with 200MB of international data, for $230 per month. AT&T has also boosted the number of cruise ships where its customers can roam from 75 to 120, and the number of countries from 145 to 150.

Figure 19.35 – ScreenCrayons Annotations

Annotations are associated with "crayons" that are each associated with some topic of interest to the user. All of the annotations associated with that topic are collected together. ScreenCrayons uses the enclosure hierarchy defined by the annotation (regions within regions) to organize a condensed representation of the annotations. The user can then zoom in for more detail on any region, including expanding to the full screen capture. The advantage of ScreenCrayons is that notes and other information are easily captured but the context is also retained without any additional effort on the part of the user.

Paper Annotation

XLibris and ScreenCrayons support annotation of digital documents on the computer itself. Using the Anoto pen, you can extend annotation to actual paper documents. Paper Augmented Digital Documents (PADD)[23] takes digital documents and prints them on paper with the Anoto pen pattern. The printing system knows which parts of which pages of which documents are printed at every location on the page. When the user writes on the page with the pen, the pen remembers the location of every stroke. These strokes from the pen can then be combined with the original documents to provide many of the advantages offered by XLibris and ScreenCrayons. The PapierCraft[24] system added gestures to the basic system. A user can use pen gestures on an original document to select information and then make gestures on a page of notes to paste in that information and its reference. When the strokes are retrieved from the pen, the notes are reconstructed and the commands interpreted so that the information can be retrieved from the original documents and placed into the digital notes.

This ability to integrate other digital information with notes in a physical notebook is found in the ButterflyNet[25] system that supports field biologists. They write their notes in a field notebook as is traditional, but using the Anoto pen they can integrate digital images and samples into the notes for reconstruction digitally when the contents of the pen are retrieved.

SUMMARY

By rapidly sampling the location of a digital pen, you can simulate the appearance of digital ink. This ink can be recognized as gestures that drive the user interface without menus. The ink can also be used as a free-form data representation that is more flexible than simple pen and paper. The ink strokes can exist on their own or as annotations on existing documents either digital or physical.

EXERCISES

1. Use the Rubine features to implement a gesture recognition system that will create lines, circles, and rectangles as well as deletion of any such objects already in the drawing.

2. Implement Tivoli's row and column selection gestures.

3. Implement a note-taking system that will capture an image from the screen and allow the user to draw highlights over the top with digital ink.

4. Implement a program that will smooth digital ink strokes into Catmull-Rom curves.

END NOTES

[1] www.mimio.com

[2] www.wacom.com

[3] Dietz, P., and D. Leigh. "DiamondTouch: A Multi-User Touch Technology." *User Interface Software and Technology (UIST '01)* (November 2001): 219–226.

[4] www.anoto.com

[5] Tappert, C.C. "Cursive Script Recognition by Elastic Matching." *IBM Journal of Research and Development* 26(6) (1982): 756–771.

[6] Kristensson, P., and S. Zhai. "SHARK²: A Large Vocabulary Shorthand Writing System for Pen-Based Computers." *User Interface Software and Technology (UIST '04)* (October 2004): 43–52.

[7] Forsberg, A., M. Dieterich, and R. Zeleznik. "The Music Notepad." *User Interface Software and Technology (UIST '98)* (November 1998): 203–210.

[8] Goldberg, D., and C. Richardson. "Touch-Typing with a Stylus." *InterCHI '93* (May 1993): 80–87.

[9] Blinkenstorfer, C. H. "Graffiti." *Pen Computing* (January 1995): 30–31.

[10] Newman, W. M. and R. F. Sproull. *Principles of Interactive Computer Graphics*, 1st edition, New York: McGraw-Hill (1973).

[11] Rubine, D. "Specifying Gestures by Example." *ACM Conference on Computer Graphics (SIGGRAPH '91)* (July 1991): 329–337.

[12] Moran, T. P., P. Chiu, W. van Melle, and G. Kurtenbach. "Implicit Structure for Pen-Based Systems Within a Freeform Interaction Paradigm." *Human Factors in Computing Systems (CHI '95)* (May 1995): 487–494.

[13] Moran, T. P., P. Chiu, and W. van Melle. "Pen-Based Interaction Techniques for Organizing Material on an Electronic Whiteboard." *User Interface Software and Technology (UIST '97)* (October 1997): 45–54.

[14] Li, Y., K. Hinckley, Z. Guan, and J. A. Landay. "Experimental Analysis of Mode Switching Techniques in Pen-Based User Interfaces." *Human Factors in Computing Systems (CHI '05)* (April 2005): 461–470.

[15] Hinckley, K., P. Baudisch, G. Ramos, and F. Guimbretiere. "Design and Analysis of Delimiters for Selection-Action Pen Gesture Phrases in Scriboli." *Human Factors in Computing Systems (CHI '05)* (April 2005): 451–460.

[16] Saund, E., and T. P. Moran. "A Perceptually-Supported Sketch Editor." *User Interface Software and Technology (UIST '94)* (November 1994): 175–184.

[17] Mynatt, E. D., T. Igarashi, W. K. Edwards, and A. LaMarca. "Flatland: New Dimensions in Office Whiteboards." *Human Factors in Computing Systems (CHI '99)* (May 1999): 346–353.

[18] Baudel, T. "A Mark-Based Interaction Paradigm for Free-Hand Drawing." *User Interface Software and Technology (UIST '94)* (November 1994): 185–192.

[19] Igarashi, T., S. Matsuoka, S. Kawachiya, and H. Tanaka. "Interactive Beautification: a Technique for Rapid Geometric Design." *User Interface Software and Technology (UIST '97)* (October 1997): 105–114.

[20] Schilit, B. N., G. Golovchinsky, and M. N. Price. "Beyond Paper: Supporting Active Reading with Free Form Digital Ink Annotations." *Human Factors in Computing Systems (CHI '98)* (April 1998): 249–256.

[21] Golovchinsky, G., M. N. Price, and B. N. Schilit. "From Reading to Retrieval: Freeform Ink Annotations as Queries." *SIGIR '99* (August 1999): 19–25.

[22] Olsen, D. R., T. Taufer, and J. A. Fails. "ScreenCrayons: Annotating Anything." *User Interface Software and Technology (UIST '04)* (October 2004): 165–174.

[23] Guimbretiere, F. "Paper Augmented Digital Documents." *User Interface Software and Technology (UIST '03)* (November 2003): 51–60.

[24] Liao, C., F. Guimbretiere, and K. Hinckley. "PapierCraft: A Command System for Interactive Paper." *User Interface Software and Technology (UIST '05)* (October 2005): 241–244.

[25] Yeh, R., C. Liao, S. Klemmer, F. Guimbretiere, B. Lee, B. Kakaradov, J. Stamberger, and A. Paepcke. "ButterflyNet: A Mobile Capture and Access System for Field Biology Research." *Human Factors in Computing Systems (CHI '06)* (April 2006): 571–580.

CHAPTER 20

Selection

One of the fundamental behaviors in graphical user interfaces is the selection of objects or actions for interaction. This selection can be organized in many ways, including pull-down menus, pop-up menus, palettes, toolbars, icons, and semantic objects of various kinds. This chapter looks at the basic theory behind selection and the variety of techniques that have been developed to improve selection performance.

Most of this discussion concentrates on menus because they are the most common form of selection. This chapter begins with a discussion of the theory of selection and how it applies to the more common menu mechanisms and then discusses a variety of improvements that have been proposed for organizing menus. This chapter then examines marking menus, which are a pen-based alternative to the standard menu mechanism. This is followed by stroke-based selection, in which the standard click-and-drag model of selection is replaced by pen strokes to combine several selections. Finally, this chapter looks at distortions of the mouse/cursor relationship to improve selection times and error rates.

SELECTION THEORY

Before launching into various interactive techniques for selecting objects there is some theory of human movement that can focus our discussions. Fitts' Law explains most of what happens when users try to select some target on the screen. The steering law explains many of the things that happen while navigating a path to some location on the screen. There are also some issues in human perception that also help.

Fitts' Law

The foundation of selection theory is Fitts' Law first described by Paul Fitts in 1954[1]. The law can be simply stated as:

$$T = a + b \cdot \log\left(\frac{A}{W} + 1\right)$$

T is the time required to perform a selection. A is the distance from where the user starts to the target to be selected. W is the width of the target. The coefficients a and b are empirically determined for some particular combination of input device and display. Fitts' Law effectively partitions selection theory into two parts that can be considered separately. For a given selection task, the terms A and W are fixed. You can then try a variety of input devices and derive the coefficients a and b. By comparing these coefficients among various input devices, you can make a choice for a given set of tasks. This scenario, however, is not common.

In most cases, the input devices are given (such as screen and mouse) and you must create techniques and designs that will be the most efficient. For this case, ignore a and b, which characterize the devices, and focus on $log(A/W+1)$, which characterizes the selection problem. This is referred to as the *index of difficulty*. The greater this number, the more time the selection requires. Looking at this formula, notice that you can reduce selection time either by bringing the target closer to where the user starts (A) or by increasing the size of the target (W). This is the basis for most selection theory.

Fitts' Law makes several assumptions about the selection task. The first is that any path from the start position to the target is acceptable and the user is free to optimize that path. The second assumption is that the time to visually locate the target is zero. However, in many situations, neither of these assumptions is valid.

Steering Law

Accot and Zhai[2] created the *steering law* to address situations in which the path that the user must take in reaching the target is important. Figure 20.1 shows a normal cascaded menu. Note that to select "Destinations" the user must select "View" and navigate straight down to "Navigation Tabs". If the user tries to cut this corner, the "Document" menu is selected and the user must start over. After reaching "Navigation Tabs," the user must turn right and stay within the menu item while navigating to the right. Any deviation causes a different menu to be selected. Having navigated to the right, the user must turn down and reach "Destinations". Accot and Zhai observed that staying within the "tunnel" slows users down. Their analogy is that when driving on a narrow road, you must slow down so as to not inadvertently steer off the road. With wider roads, you can drive faster because there is a greater margin of error.

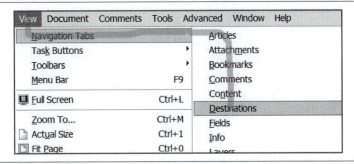

Figure 20.1 – Selection path for a cascaded menu

Their abstraction of the problem was a "tunnel" that is A long and W wide which the user must navigate without bumping into the edges of the tunnel. This is clear from the movement along the "Navigation Tabs" menu but also occurs when navigating down from "View" without cutting the corner. Their paper describes the steering law as an integral along the path. For simple tunnels like that shown in Figure 20.1, the index of difficulty becomes A/W rather than $log(A/W)$. The essence of the result is that narrow paths increase selection times. The tunnel abstraction was further extended by Pastel's[3] analysis of corners in the path. He showed that corners slowed down selection and increasing the path width at the corners would improve selection times.

Perception

The previous theories address the problem of controlling an input device from a starting location to an accurate target selection. They ignore the visual search problem where the user must locate the desired target before navigating to it. Card[4] addressed this question through a series of experiments on menu organization. In his experiments, the structure of the menus was fixed, thus neutralizing the Fitts' Law and steering law effects. What changed was the order in which items appeared in the menu. The three conditions were random order, alphabetical order, and grouping by function. For first-time users of a particular menu, alphabetical was fastest (0.81 sec), followed by functional order (1.28 sec), with random order being the slowest (3.23 sec). The hypothesis is that with a known structure, fewer saccades (eye movements) are required to locate the desired item. The structure optimizes the visual search. However, the same experiments showed that after user training on 800 menu selections there was no difference in performance times among the three conditions. Once users learned the structure (even if random), they no longer needed visual search and the differences disappeared.

STANDARD MENUS

Pull-down menus have been a staple of graphical user interfaces since the Macintosh was introduced. There are two basic strategies. The Macintosh places application menus at the top of the screen. No matter where the application window is placed on the screen, the menu is always across the top. Windows places its application menus at the top of each window. Application of Fitts' Law would indicate that selection time would be lower for the Windows strategy because the menu would generally be nearer to the start point where the user is working. Thus, Windows would have a much smaller average *A* than the Macintosh.

Early experiments showed that this was not so. Users were faster on the Macintosh. The reason is that menus at the top of the screen are backed up by a border beyond which the mouse will not go. Users could rapidly shove the mouse to the top of the screen without having to slow down to hit the menu. In essence, the top-of-screen menu strategy has a very large *W* in mouse control space. This is an important conceptual point. The Macintosh menus are of comparable size to the Windows menus. In terms of screen space, their *W* is virtually identical. However, Fitts' Law and the steering law are about the control system of the hand, not about screen space. Hitting a top-of-screen menu offers a much larger range of mouse positions (control space) than the menu-per-window strategy. These comparison experiments were done on relatively small screens. Modern workstations with multiple high resolution screens might yield different results due to much larger differences in *A*.

Another application of Fitts' Law is the use of pop-up menus. In Windows, these are activated using the right mouse button. Pop-up menus offer two advantages. The first is that the menu is adjacent to the current mouse position and, therefore, *A* is much smaller. The second is that the menu can be tailored to the type object immediately under the mouse location. This greatly simplifies the user's task of finding an appropriate action from the menu. One of the difficulties with pop-up menus is that they obscure the objects underneath. There has been some use of semitransparent menus that allow the objects beneath to show through.

IMPROVING MENUS

A variety of designs have been proposed for improving selection times on menus. Most of these are driven by Fitts' Law and the steering law. An early innovation was the *pie menu*, where the items for selection are arranged in a pie shape around the mouse start position[5]. Figure 20.2 shows a standard linear pop-up menu on the left with a corresponding pie menu on the right. The advantage of the pie menu over the linear menu is that the average distance to each selection is lower for pie menus than for linear menus. The experiments showed that selection time for pie menus is 15 percent less than for linear menus with half the error rate. Most pie menus are arranged closer to the start point than shown in Figure 20.2's early prototype.

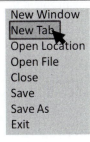
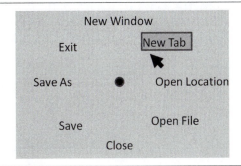

Figure 20.2 – Linear and pie menus

Pie menus have several drawbacks. The first is that they generally consume more screen space than linear menus. They are also limited to about 16 items, whereas linear menus are not. Pie menus can be cascaded, but subsequent levels of the menu must appear over the top of previous levels, creating screen clutter. Screen edges are also a problem. When the start point is very close to the bottom of the screen, a linear menu can appear above the start point. A pie menu, however, derives its advantage from appearing around the start point, which is impossible at the very edges or corners of the screen. Some pie menus adapt by using a larger semicircle to arrange items that otherwise would be invisible.

Walker, Smelcer, and Nilsen[6] proposed an improvement to menus by increasing the size of menu items that are farther away. The idea is to give menu items that are farther away a size that will compensate for the distance. Figure 20.3 shows how such a menu might be laid out. The problem with this strategy is that the size of the menu is an exponential function of the number of menu items. As each menu item gets larger to compensate for the distance, subsequent items are pushed out even farther from the start position.

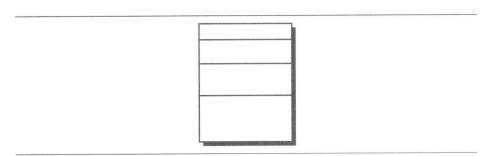

Figure 20.3 – Variable-sized menu items

Subsequent improvements to menu selection focused on the steering law problems of cascading menus, as shown in Figure 20.1. Kobayashi and Igarashi[7] looked at the problem of users cutting corners as they attempt to navigate cascaded menus.

Figure 20.4 shows an example of the steering law problem that they were addressing. When trying to select a submenu, users frequently start down the submenu too soon, causing the selection of the submenu to be canceled.

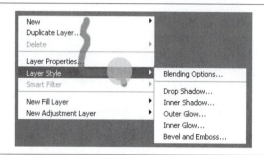

Figure 20.4 – Corner-cutting in cascaded menus

Their solution was to consider the mouse movement direction rather than just the position when activating menus. Moving the mouse up or down moves the menu highlight to match the current mouse position. If the mouse is on submenu node, moving it to the right immediately opens the submenu near the current mouse position, as shown in Figure 20.5. This solves two problems. The extended steering law problem in going all the way to the right is eliminated and the submenu is very near the mouse, reducing the Fitts' Law distance to the next selection. If a submenu is opened inadvertently, moving the mouse to the left closes it. Their experiments showed that selection time was reduced by 12 percent and the total path length traversed by the mouse was reduced by 31 percent. However, some users were confused by the nonstandard behavior of the menu and by the fact that submenus would obscure their parent menus.

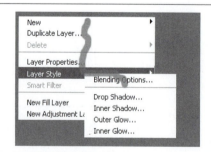

Figure 20.5 – Early opening of submenus

Ahlström[8] proposed that the steering problem be alleviated using a "force field strategy" to guide the mouse toward appropriate selection, rather than interpret gestures. This strategy subtly modifies the menu's control space size without modifying its visual presentation. The force fields are shown in Figure 20.6. When the mouse is inside of a parent menu item, the force field guides the mouse toward the point that will open the submenu. When the mouse is inside of a non-parent item, the mouse is guided toward the center of the item.

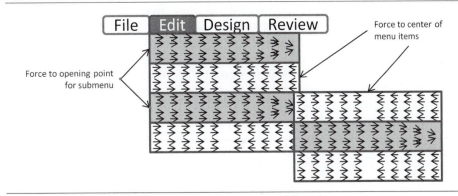

Figure 20.6 – Force field menus

This force field guidance is possible because the connection between mouse movement and cursor position is indirect and can be modified. For each type of menu item, there is a force point f toward which the field is guiding the mouse. For parent items, it is the center of the right edge and for nonparent items, it is the center of the item. Many systems allow the software to "warp" the mouse by setting the cursor to an arbitrary position on the screen. Ahlström's force field formula is:

$$\mathbf{n} = \mathbf{a} + s \cdot \|\mathbf{a} - \mathbf{p}\| \cdot \frac{\mathbf{f} - \mathbf{a}}{\|\mathbf{f} - \mathbf{a}\|}$$

$\mathbf{n}$ = new position to where the cursor should be warped
$\mathbf{a}$ = active position of the mouse from the current mouse-move event
$\mathbf{p}$ = previous mouse position before the current mouse-move event
$\mathbf{f}$ = desired force point
s = strength parameter for the force field that can be adjusted

This technique was tested on several input devices and with novice and expert users. Selection times improved from 11 percent for infrequent track point users up to 30 percent for novice touch pad users. The average of all mouse users was a 17 percent improvement.

These improvements assume that the user is dragging continuously to select a menu. Many users click on parent menus rather than hold down the mouse while navigating to their choices. Ahlström et al[9] modified this click behavior. When a user clicks on a parent item, the submenu is opened and the cursor is "jumped" to the top of the submenu, eliminating the steering task entirely. If after pressing the button the user moves the mouse more than five pixels, the jump is canceled and the submenu is closed. This allows the user to cancel the jump in a natural way. This technique showed an increase in selection errors over standard menus. In selection times, the results were mixed between force menus and jumping menus with no clear advantage.

MARKING MENUS

Pop-up menus tend to obscure the data beneath them. Gestures (Chapter 20) resolve this problem, but tend to be difficult for people to learn and remember. With gesture interaction, a gulf of execution problem occurs because there is no visible menu to help guide the user to the correct gesture. To resolve these issues, Kurtenbach and Buxton[10,11] invented *marking menus*. Figure 20.7 shows the two different modes of operation for marking menus. If the user holds down the mouse button or pen tip switch for one-third of a second, a pie menu appears. By moving the stylus into the desired region, the selection is made. The alternative mode is just to make the same mark without waiting for the menu to appear. Mode (b) behaves like a gesture though it is actually a menu selection. Mode (a) trains the user in the appropriate stroke for each menu selection.

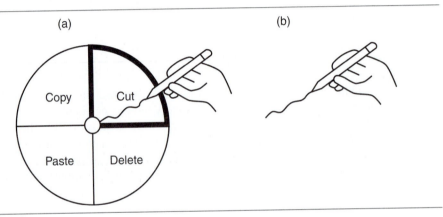

Figure 20.7 – Marking menus

The gesture recognition algorithm for simple marking menus uses only the stroke angle or the differences between the end point and the start point for features. Recognition is trivial.

Initial experiments led to several design principles for using marking menus. The first is that there should be an even number of choices up to a maximum of 12. The second is that the same command should appear in the same position among various marking menus so that the user learns a specific stroke for that command. Experiments also showed that marking menus should be used where the commands are frequent so that users learn to take advantage of the marks. When users were away from an application for a while, they tended to forget the marks. This effect disappears with experience.

An early advance was the introduction of hierarchic marking menus[10]. In this variant, a menu selection could be itself the parent of another menu. The result was that selection becomes a continuous stroke with corners separating the segments for each menu. This was shown to be 3.5 times faster than normal menus and performed better with a pen than a mouse. If each menu has eight choices, a depth of greater than two became inaccurate with too many errors (64 total choices). If each menu had four choices, users could go to four levels without excessive errors (256 choices). These experiments also showed that gesture strokes on the primary x- and y-axes reduced errors.

Tapia and Kurtenbach published several design refinements to make marking menus more effective[12]. These are based on their experience using marking menus in the Alias StudioPaint system. Their first proposal was to discard the pie and use only the menu text. This text was placed in similar positions but without regard for the location of the pie, as shown in Figure 20.8. Removing the pie shows more of the underlying task and frees the text messages to be longer. Boxes behind the text (all of the same size) provide the visual contrast necessary to see the text. Their experience indicates that eight menu items are best and when hierarchic menus are used, previous menus should disappear rather than clutter the screen under the submenu. Figure 20.8 shows only a dot at the bottom and a line leading to the submenu.

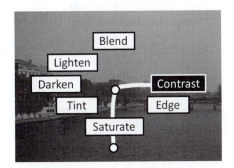 

Figure 20.8 – Removing the pie from marking menus

One of the key causes for problems in deep hierarchies is the steering law effect of drawing the correct stroke without cutting corners. Zhao and Balakrishnan addressed this issue by breaking up the strokes[13]. Rather than carefully turning the corner with the pen down, the user picks up the pen and makes a new stroke in a new direction. This also resolves the ambiguity of two successive menu selections in the same direction. By repeatedly making the marks in the same location, the total screen space requirement is reduced. Selection accuracy (percent correct selections) was significantly higher for separate marks than for long compound strokes. Unlike single stroke techniques, the separate strokes showed very little decline in accuracy as the menu hierarchy got deeper. In terms of total selection time, the separate strokes performed slightly better. This is consistent with Pastel's work on steering through corners[3].

Expanding on the individual stroke concept, Zhao, Agrawala, and Hinckley[14] introduced *zone* and *polygon* menus. The innovation is to allow the starting position of the stroke as well as its direction to serve in selecting the menu choice. Figure 20.9

shows a zone menu. The user first taps the pen and waits for the menu to appear. The tap establishes the menu center. Four menus in each of four zones appear. Each menu has four choices for a total of 16. The start position of the stroke (relative to the center point) selects the zone and the direction makes a choice within that zone. On the left is the learned gesture for the same selection. This technique expands the breadth of the menu to 16, making it faster.

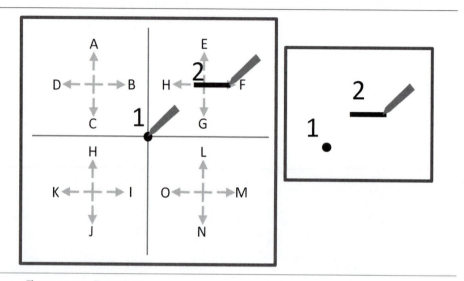

Figure 20.9 – Zone menus

The polygon menu, shown in Figure 20.10, also uses position and direction. The center tap defines an eight-sided polygon. The user is expected to stroke near one of the edges of the polygon. For each stroke direction (out of eight), two possible menu selections exist. By looking at where the stroke is located relative to the center tap, the desired selection can be identified. Selecting the most similar polygon edge plus stroke direction yields 16 choices.

Experiments showed that zone and polygon menus produced similar accuracy and similar speed to previous techniques, but they have twice to four times the breadth of choices at a given level of menu. This results in a sharp decrease in selection time for large numbers of choices.

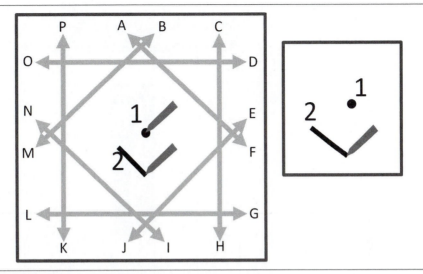

Figure 20.10 – Polygon menus

STROKE SELECTION

As pen devices have become more common, most software has treated the pen as if it were a mouse. This helps the software architecture, but is not necessarily the best interactive solution. The advantage of this strategy is that with a pen, all existing software still works in a familiar way.

The pen creates several difficulties. For example, the double-click, without changing position, is hard to do correctly with a pen. The pen tip switch functions well as the primary button, but the switch on the side of the pen is an awkward substitute for the secondary or menu button. Unlike a mouse, the hand holding the pen can obscure important data and in the case of pop-down menus, it obscures the menu itself.

In addressing the unique characteristics of pens, it is observed that pens are more fluid stroking devices than clicking devices. There have been several proposals for adapting selection tasks to use strokes rather than clicks and drags. The core idea is to perform a selection by crossing a region rather than by clicking on a spot.

One of the first proposals was toggle maps[15]. This is useful when there are many binary selections possible and you want to select large groups of them rapidly. Many problems can be cast as a presentation of a large number of binary choices. Figure 20.11 shows a table of times laid out with days of the week. The task is to select a time to reserve for an activity. Each day/time period is a Boolean value. Selecting "Wednesday from 9:00 to 2:00" is a single stroke down the column. Reserving lunch every day at noon for an hour is two strokes, one for noon and one for 12:30. Performing these tasks by clicking would be painful even with a mouse.

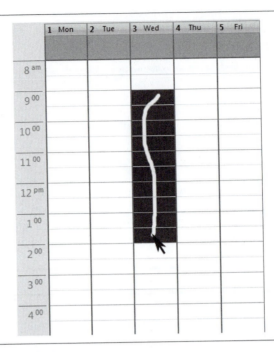

Figure 20.11 – Toggle times

A second stroke selection system is CrossY[16]. Some of the key insights of CrossY are that in many cases the user wants to select several properties at once for a particular task and stroking through a region is easier for a pen than clicking on a spot. Figure 20.12 shows an example of such selections. The pen, its thickness, and its color are all selected in a single stroke rather than by three separate clicks. Note that above and below the centers of each selection are small tick marks. Selection is defined as a stroke that passes between these marks. Only the regions between the marks are selection active. This eliminates problems from the steering law because the user need not steer down the whole box before making a turn. Only the cross regions must be navigated.

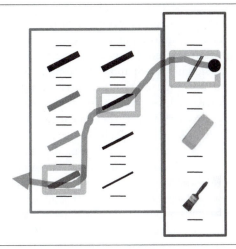

Figure 20.12 – CrossY selection (see color plate)

AREA/CURSOR MODIFICATION FOR ICON SELECTION

Your last topic in selection has to do with distorting the mouse/display relationship. The first distortion is to use a cursor that is an area or region rather than a point and the second is to manipulate the relationship between hand movement and cursor movements.

One of the first problems is the rapid selection of very small targets. For example, trying to hit a point on the screen with a small cursor is very difficult. Kabbash and Buxton introduced *area cursors*. Their idea was to increase the size of the cursor rather than increase the size of the target. Their experiments showed that Fitts' Law holds when the width of the cursor rather than the width of the target is used for such tasks[17]. The problem with area cursors is when there are many targets. The area cursor then has a problem disambiguating among the targets. The only way to disambiguate is to keep the targets farther apart than the size of the area cursor. Usually you have small targets because you want to pack many of them on the screen. This defeats the advantage offered by area cursors.

Keyson[18] introduced the idea of changing the mouse gain. A mouse operates by sending incremental movement signals to the cursor controller whenever a hand movement is detected. By adding up these mouse movements, the controller derives a cursor position. To give users better control over their cursor, most systems use a *mouse gain* control. A common value is 3 to 1 or three mouse move ticks for each pixel movement. If you increase the gain, the mouse must be moved farther to achieve the same amount of cursor movement. This slowing down of the cursor tends to increase control by increasing the size of physical hand movement space. Whenever the cursor approaches a target, the mouse gain is increased. The result is that the size of the target remained the same size on the screen, but became much larger in hand movement space. Because Fitts' Law is a property of hand movement rather than visual search, this has the effect of increasing W without increasing screen space.

Worden, et al[19] noted that when there are many targets on the screen, the cursor will always be slowing down and, thus, tend to increase the hand distance in reaching a particular target if there are many intervening targets. Thus, the A value in Fitts' Law is also increased, negating the advantage. Their insight was that when users begin to move toward a target, they move very quickly. As they approach the target, they slow down to hit it accurately.

Worden, et al used this insight to modify Keyson's increased gain. Initially, their mouse gain is set at normal. As the cursor is moving, they measure its velocity. When the velocity drops below 30 percent of the peak velocity, they raise the gain on the targets. This increase in gain creates *sticky icons* that are only sticky when the user slows down to land on a target. They reported that sticky icons show a 50 percent improvement in speed for elderly users with poor motor control and a 40 percent improvement for young adults.

These ideas were augmented by Blanch, Guiard, and Beaudouin-Lafon in their concept of *semantic pointing*[20]. They propose the notion of a measure of *semantic importance* associated with objects on the screen. Increased semantic importance decreases the mouse gain. This can be exploited in the visual redesign of some widgets. Figure 20.13(a) shows a traditional scroll bar. Figure 20.13(b) shows a redesigned scroll bar that takes less screen space, but is still easy to see. By increasing the semantic importance of the slider and the end buttons, the scroll bar feels like Figure 20.13(c) in motor space.

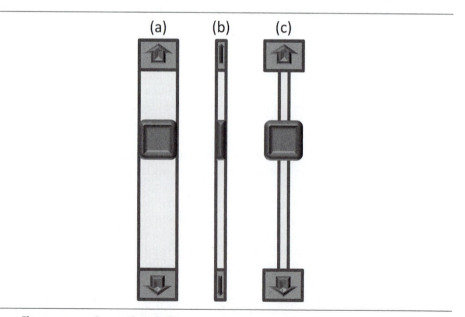

(a)   (b)   (c)

Figure 20.13 – Semantic pointing

Grossman and Balakrishnan's Bubble Cursor[21] addresses the selection problem differently. They stayed with the notion of area cursors, but made them round and made cursor size adaptable to the current selection problem. The cursor changes size so that only one target is inside of the cursor. The idea is that the user need only navigate as close to the target as needed irrespective of the size of the target or its distance. If the target is not completely inside of the bubble, a "bump" on the bubble encloses the selected target so that it is obvious to the user what the current selection will be. Experiments showed a 30 percent decrease in average selection time over normal cursor selection.

SUMMARY

The task of selection is fundamental to graphical user interfaces. Fitts' Law shows that increasing the target size or decreasing the distance can reduce selection times. The steering law showed that small paths that must be navigated as well as careful corners can increase selection time. Various mechanisms have been proposed for overcoming these challenges, including repositioning of selection items, force fields to "nudge" the mouse, larger or adaptable cursors, and distortion of the size of objects in motor space. The special needs of pen users have been addressed by marking menus and stroke selections.

EXERCISES

1. Implement a task where the mouse location is warped to some position and a target is displayed somewhere else. Perform several experiments to determine the device coefficients for this task using Fitts' Law.

2. Modify the experiment in Exercise 1 to draw a narrow track between the mouse position and the target. If the user moves outside of the track, warp the cursor back to the starting location. Perform several experiments to determine new performance measures.

3. Using your favorite toolkit, create a subclass of the check box widget that can be used with the toggle-maps stroking technique. Measure the difference in performance times for techniques that require clicking on each check box.

4. Implement a marking menu that uses multiple strokes to select an item in a hierarchic menu.

END NOTES

[1] Fitts, P. M. "The Information Capacity of the Human Motor System in Controlling the Amplitude of Movement." *Journal of Experimental Psychology* 41 (1954): 381–391.

[2] Accot, J., and S. Zhai. "Beyond Fitt's Law: Models for Trajectory-Based HCI Tasks." *Human Factors in Computing Systems (CHI '97)* (March 1997): 295–302.

[3] Pastel, R. L. "Measuring the Difficulty of Steering Through Corners." *Human Factors in Computing Systems (CHI '06)* (April 2006): 1087–1096.

[4] Card, S. K. "User Perceptual Mechanisms in the Search of Computer Command Menus." *Human Factors in Computing Systems (CHI '82)* (1982): 190–196.

[5] Callahan, J., D. Hopkins, M. Weiser, and B. Shneiderman. "An Empirical Comparison of Pie vs. Linear Menus." *Human Factors in Computing Systems (CHI '88)* (May 1988): 95–100.

[6] Walker, N., J. B. Smelcer, and E. Nilsen. "Optimizing Speed and Accuracy of Menu Selection: A Comparison of Selection Times from Walking and Pull-Down Menus." *International Journal of Man-Machine Studies* 35(6) (1991): 871–890.

[7] Kobayashi, M., and T. Igarashi. "Considering the Direction of Cursor Movement for Efficient Traversal of Cascading Menus." *User Interface Software and Technology (UIST '03)* (November 2003): 91–94.

[8] Ahlström, D. "Modeling and Improving Selection in Cascading Pull-Down Menus Using Fitts' Law, the Steering Law and Force Fields." *Human Factors in Computing Systems (CHI '05)* (April 2005): 61–70.

[9] Ahlström, D., R. Alexandrowicz, and M. Mitz. "Improving Menu Interaction: A Comparison of Standard, Force Enhanced and Jumping Menus." *Human Factors in Computing Systems (CHI '06)* (April 2006): 1067–1076.

[10] Kurtenbach, G., and W. Buxton. "The Limits of Expert Performance Using Hierarchical Marking Menus." *Human Factors in Computing Systems (CHI '93)* (April 1993):482-487.

[11] Kurtenbach, G., and W. Buxton. "User Learning and Performance with Marking Menus." *Human Factors in Computing Systems (CHI '94)* (April 1994): 258–264.

[12] Tapia, M. A., and G. Kurtenbach. "Some Design Refinements and Principles on the Appearance and Behavior of Marking Menus." *User Interface Software and Technology (UIST 95)* (December 1995): 189–195.

[13] Zhao, S., and R. Balakrishnan. "Simple vs. Compound Mark Hierarchical Marking Menus." *User Interface Software and Technology (UIST '04)* (October 2004): 33–42.

[14] Zhao, S., M. Agrawala, and K. Hinckley. "Zone and Polygon Menus: Using Relative Position to Increase the Breadth of Multi-Stroke Marking Menus." *Human Factors in Computing Systems (CHI '06)* (April 2006): 1077–1086.

[15] Baudisch, P. "Don't Click, Paint! Using Toggle Maps to Manipulate Sets of Toggle Switches." *User Interface Software and Technology (UIST '98)* (November 1998): 65–66.

[16] Apitz, G., and F. Guimbretiere. "CrossY: A Crossing-Based Drawing Application." *User Interface Software and Technology (UIST '04)* (October 2004): 3–12.

[17] Kabbash, P., and W. Buxton. "The 'Prince' Technique: Fitts' Law and Selection Using Area Cursors." *Human Factors in Computing Systems (CHI '95)* (May 1995): 273–279.

[18] Keyson, D. V. "Dynamic Cursor Gain and Tactile Feedback in the Capture of Cursor Movements." *Ergonomics* 12 (December 1997): 1287–1298.

[19] Worden, A., N. Walker, K. Bharat, and S. Hudson. "Making Computers Easier for Older Adults to Use: Area Cursors and Sticky Icons." *Human Factors in Computing Systems (CHI '97)* (March 1997): 266–271.

[20] Blanch, R., Y. Guiard, and M. Beaudouin-Lafon. "Semantic Pointing: Improving Target Acquisition with Control-Display Ratio Adaptation." *Human Factors in Computing Systems (CHI '04)* (April 2004): 519–526.

[21] Grossman, T., and R. Balakrishnan. "The Bubble Cursor: Enhancing Target Acquisition by Dynamic Resizing of the Cursor's Activation Area." *Human Factors in Computing Systems (CHI '05)* (April 2005): 281–290.

CHAPTER 21

Display Space Management

Though the Xerox Star[1] in 1981 was not the first instance of a graphical user interface with overlapping windows, it certainly was the most influential. It established in the mind of the research community the concept of rectangular windows scattered around a desktop each behaving like a smart piece of paper. It also established the software architecture ideas of model-view-controller and the operating system/graphics engine being the arbiter of screen space among competing applications.

It is hard to remember how computationally impoverished personal computing was in those days. Computers had 128K to 256K (not megabytes) of memory and 10-MB hard disks. Processing power was 8–10 MHz. Graphical displays generally used one bit per pixel. When the NeXT computer was introduced in 1988, its use of two bits per pixel was considered a little extravagant, though very nice to look at. Though personal computing has come a long way, the rectangular overlapping windows have remained.

This chapter looks at alternative proposals for how to effectively use screen space, which have become feasible with increased computing power. The following sections first address various styles for managing multiple rectangular windows on a screen. The latter sections look at the problems of how to deal with very large spaces that must be displayed in finite-sized windows.

WINDOW STYLES

There have been some studies of the ways in which windows are used and their effectiveness. Bly and Rosenberg[2] challenged the notion that overlapping windows are the most effective way to manage screen space. They predicted that when the relative sizes of window contents are known, a tiled strategy like that shown in Figure 21.1 would reduce the user's window management burden. The ViewPoint system (a descendent of Star) supported both overlapping and tiled windows.

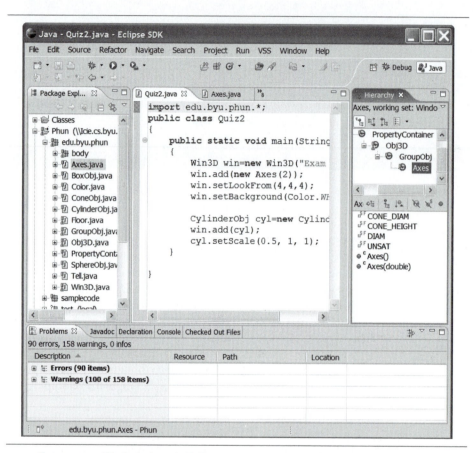

Figure 21.1 – Tiled windows in Eclipse

To evaluate window management schemes, they created two tasks: one highly regular that would seem to conform with the tiled structure and the other irregular that would seem to conform better to the overlapping structure. For the regular task, overlapping windows took 30 percent longer. The activity logs showed that users were performing twice as many window management tasks for overlapping windows than for tiled windows. For the irregular tasks, the subjects fell into two groups. The "fast" group performed in one-third less time with overlapping windows and the "slow" group performed in one-third more time for overlapping windows. The key difference between the two groups was their familiarity with overlapping windows. This indicates that tasks requiring little window manipulation will be much more effective in a tiled arrangement that reduces that burden.

One of the assumptions of desktop window management is that windows will be placed over the top of each other with some windows completely obscured by others. Another assumption is that users will directly control the size of windows. These two assumptions are challenged in the Flatland[3] system for pen-based interaction. In Flatland, regions for drawing are called segments rather than windows. All open segments are visible at once. The currently selected segment is displayed at full size. The full size of a segment is determined by its content. Obviously, not all segments can appear on the screen at full size. Flatland's approach is to shrink segments to make room for other segments. A user moves a segment by dragging one of the borders. Any segments that are in the way are moved to make room or shrunk. At some point, movement and shrinking are not possible and a segment resists further modification. The algorithm is shown in Figure 21.2. The Flatland approach to screen management is to have sizes and positions adjust automatically and predictably in response to movement of the selected window.

```
void move(Segment s, Rectangle newBounds)
{
    move s to newBounds
    foreach (Segment d that overlaps s)
    {  compute a location n for d so that it will move as little as possible and not overlap s
       move(d, n);
    }
    if (s overlaps any other segment or is outside of screen bounds)
    {  try to shrink s so that it will fit
       if (s cannot shrink further and still overlaps a segment or exceeds bounds)
       {   move s back towards its original position so that
           it does not overlap or go outside
       }
    }
}
```

Figure 21.2 – Flatland segment management algorithm

Several researchers have challenged the notion of windows being rectangular and only aligned with the x, y axes. Beaudouin-Lafon[4] proposed that making windows more flexible would actually increase their usability. Figure 21.3 shows windows that can be arranged at various angles and can be folded down. The tilting is controlled by the way in which windows are dragged around. This is modeled roughly on the physics of paper. Every window has a center. When the user grabs a point to drag the paper, the direction of drag and the center of the paper tend to align. This is due to friction between the paper and the surface. The rotation to align, however, is not immediate because friction also inhibits rotation. The result of this simulation is that windows tend to behave much like paper being dragged across a desk with a finger.

Figure 21.3 – Tilted and folded windows

The usability advantage is that overlapping windows no longer align, leaving fragments exposed where they can be more readily seen and selected by the user. Working with hidden windows is also supported in the folding technique. Grabbing the corner of a window and dragging it in toward the interior causes the page to fold down like paper. This naturally reveals what is behind. This also folds any windows on top of the one being folded. This feels like leafing through a stack of papers as you might do on a normal desktop.

Dragicevic expanded on the window folding idea to allow for more effective drag and drop on a crowded screen[5]. The problem is that to drag and drop requires that both source and destination be visible. Dragicevic uses mouse techniques coupled with window folding to simplify this. You can pick up an object to be dragged and move it out of the source window. This causes the edge of the source window that was crossed to fold back temporarily. Crossing back and out again causes the next window to fold, and so on. You can use this "leafing through the pages" technique to reach the desired destination, fold back the windows on top to expose it, and then drop the object. Again, this forms a natural simulation of paper behavior.

Beaudouin-Lafon's windows can also be *zipped* together. This allows a group of windows to be treated as a single entity by the user. When one window (a slave) is brought next to another window (the master), they are zipped together at the common edge. Dragging the master window around drags all of the other windows with it. Dragging the slaves causes them to unzip and, thus, work independently. This allows the user to dynamically group and reattach windows in meaningful ways.

The DiamondSpin[6] system supports people gathered around a table. This means that windows need to be oriented so that people can see them. Figure 21.4 shows this kind of usage. Because straight up and down images are inappropriate, DiamondSpin places windows using a polar coordinate system centered in the middle of the table. In this system, a window's orientation is static in the polar system, but as users drag windows around the screen their Cartesian orientation changes based on where the window is located in polar coordinates. The result is that windows in front of each user end up appearing vertical to them.

Figure 21.4 – DiamondSpin's polar coordinate windows

Agarawala and Balakrishnan[7] pushed the physics-like ideas from Beaudouin-Lafon into increasing realism. Their BumpTop windowing system is supported by a physics simulator and a 3D graphics rendering engine. Windows have weight, friction, and thickness, allowing them to be stacked, tossed, thrown around, folded, and crumpled up. When windows are moved or tossed, they might strike other windows, causing them to move. Their work also included innovative techniques for browsing through "piles" of windows. This included spreading them out like a deck of cards and rummaging or leafing through the pile to examine what is there. BumpTop provides a lot of innovative ideas of how windows might behave. In the future, however, we need data on which of these techniques might actually help users.

The Scalable Fabric[8] system provides natural mechanisms for resizing and grouping windows. The screen space has a central focus area where windows are displayed in their full size and a periphery, as shown in Figure 21.5. When a window is dragged from the focus to the periphery, it is scaled down to a much smaller size. The size is determined by the distance from the center of the screen. Windows are smaller when they are further from the center. Clicking on a window in the periphery causes it to appear full scale at its original position in the central focus. Minimizing the window causes it to return to its peripheral position. In this mechanism, windows never disappear or get obscured—they just get smaller or larger.

Moving two windows close to each other in the periphery forms a task or group, which can be given a name. Moving windows close to an existing task joins that window to the task. This allows users to move related sets of windows around together both in the focus and the periphery.

Figure 21.5 – Scalable Fabric

BIG WORLDS IN SMALL WINDOWS

The solutions described in the previous section all show ways in which the windows can be managed so as to simplify the use of limited screen space. This section looks at the problem of a single window that must view a much larger world space. The common solution to this problem is scrolling. This section examines three alternatives: fisheye views, infinite zooming, and focus + context.

Fisheye

A fisheye view is one where items at the focus of attention appear at full scale while more distant items appear with diminished detail the farther away they are from the focus. This concept was first introduced to user-interface work by Furnas[9]. His work reported many instances of people using this diminishing detail approach when dealing with large amounts of information. When there is a large amount of material to be displayed, a "Degree of Interest" function should be applied to each item or region. His generalized Degree of Interest function was:

$$DOI_{fisheye}(x \mid .=y) = API(x) - D(x,y)$$

$DOI_{fisheye}(x \mid .=y)$ defines the degree of interest in point x given that point y is the current focus of attention. $API(x)$ is the intrinsic global importance of point x and $D(x,y)$ is the distance between x and y. The API function can be many things. It can be uniform across the space, which reflects that all interest is around the focus of attention. Suppose a user is viewing a map and looking at Pendleton, Oregon (y). You might assign $API(x)$ to be the population of each region x. Thus Seattle, Tacoma, and Portland would have high DOI even though they are farther away from Pendleton. You could change $API(x)$ to be the total number of software jobs in the area to produce a somewhat different map.

Though many fisheye views, such as maps, are geometric in their nature, the generalized DOI can be applied to any information structure, including trees, lists, tables, and calendars. The fundamental idea is to allocate display resources where the interest is highest and to allow the user to change that allocation by moving their focus of attention. In a tree, the API of a node might be the sum of the API values of each leaf, and the distance might be the number of graph edges that must be traversed to reach one node from another.

Furnas' seminal work on fisheye viewing has led to many interactive techniques. Carpendale[10] created a space of possible fisheye views of a 2D plane. Her focus was on general techniques for transforming a large 2D space into a fisheye view within a limited space. Figure 21.6 shows the 1D representation of her lens system for viewing. Figure 21.7 shows a sample fisheye view of an image. The lens model has a focus region that is undistorted and presented at full scale. The distortion regions allocate successively less detail as the distance increases and the context regions are a minimal scale and unaffected by the lens.

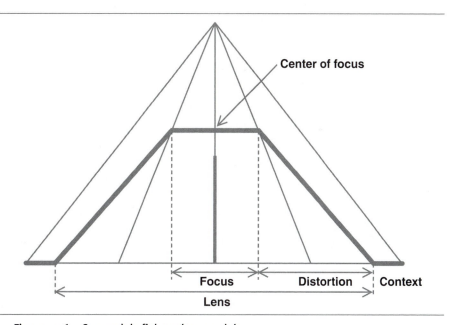

Figure 21.6 – Carpendale fisheye lens model

Figure 21.7 – Fisheye view

This model offers many parameters that can be adjusted to produce many view-ing effects. Expanding the focus shows higher detail at the expense of the context area. The total width of the lens controls the amount of blending region possible between the focus and the context. A narrower lens produces a sharper transition. One of the most interesting effects is in the way that the distortion region drops off from focus to the context.

The actual fisheye viewing algorithm can be thought of as a blending between two transformations, F and C. Transformation F is the viewing transformation that transforms world coordinates into the coordinates of the focus region. This transfor-mation consists of a scaling and a translation. Transformation C transforms world coordinates into the coordinates of the context region. The context transformation also consists of scaling and translation and generally tries to scale the entire world into the available screen or window space. The drop-off function $d(x,y)$ produces val-ues between 0 (context transform) and 1 (focus transform). It is based on the metric for measuring the distance between (x,y) and the focus of attention as well as one of the six drop-off techniques. The idea is that for each point (x,y) in the geometry of our model, we compute a new transformation T using the following function:

$$T= fisheye(x,y)=d(x,y) \; F + (1-d(x,y)) \; C$$

The result is a transformation T that can be applied to the point (x,y) to yield its position on the screen.

Though Carpendale's work focused on fisheye transformations of 2D worlds, Furnas proposed a generalized DOI function to be used in a variety of situations. Bederson used this idea in his fisheye menus[11]. The technique allows very long lists of things to be selected by altering the scale around the mouse pointer. Schaffer, et al[12] reference a large number of fisheye techniques on data structures and propose their own mechanism for viewing large 2D networks of connected nodes. Their idea was to cluster graph nodes using some hierarchic clustering technique and then decide on whether to open or close a cluster based on how close it is to the center of attention.

Fisheye views provide a way to look closely at some part of a large space without losing connection to the context. Gutwin and Skopik[13] studied the problem of interacting with data that is presented in a fisheye view. In particular, they looked at steering tasks where the user must navigate a path that is longer than the focus region. Their experiments show that fisheye performance was as much as two times better than using a traditional panning technique. The reasons for the improved performance were the ability to see the entire path in the fisheye and that you need not manipulate the scrolling while perusing the path.

The fisheye techniques are based on Furnas' idea of focus plus context. The user works in a focus area but needs to retain context for that work. Most implementations of this idea assume that screen resolution is uniform. Baudisch et al[14] provide a novel alternative to this assumption. They created a focus plus context screen that has a high-resolution working area surrounded by a low-resolution context area. This was done by placing a white projection area around a high-resolution screen. The focus information is displayed on the high-resolution focus screen and a projector is used to display low-resolution context information around the periphery, as shown in Figure 21.8.

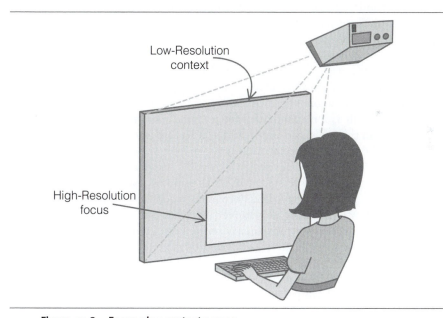

Low-Resolution context

High-Resolution focus

Figure 21.8 – Focus plus context screen

Zooming

User interfaces have long had zooming as a mechanism for dealing with very large spaces. Zooming out provides lots of context. Zooming in provides greater detail. In 1993, Perlin proposed the Pad[15] model for organizing information. In the Pad model, the world consists of an infinite 2D plane. Two kinds of objects exist on this plane: graphics (lines, circles, images, and so on) and portals. What is special in Pad is that this plane is also infinitely zoomable. That is, the user can zoom in on any region to any degree of magnification. A portal is a region of the zoom space that references another region of the zoom space at any magnification or offset. Thus, a portal can be used to link parts of the space together and to explore other parts of the space. Portals can also have filters that allow data to be viewed in a different way.

Pad introduced the concept of *semantic zooming*. This is where objects change their appearance as the user zooms closer. For example, from long range a document is best presented as an icon with squiggles rather than actual text. However, as the user zooms closer, the document should open and its pages should appear. As the user zooms even closer, the actual page layout with editable text should appear. This editing level of detail is wasted when viewed from a great zoom distance.

The advantage of the Pad approach is that opening, closing, arranging, organizing, link following, and many other interactive behaviors are all subsumed into a single model of panning and zooming across an infinite space. Because the space is infinitely zoomable, there is always room for any activity because any region can contain an infinite amount of space when viewed at higher magnification.

The key technical challenge in zoomable interfaces is the representation of the infinite zoom space. In reality, the space is not infinite because of maximum number precision. At the heart of the technique is the Pad *address $A=(x,y,z)$*. This includes x and y as well as a zoom location z. In essence, a Pad address defines a linear transformation $T(u,v)=(x+u2^z, y+v2^z)$. Note that the z component is defined in the $\log_2$ space. This allows a number to reference a very large space of zoom factors. This is one of the keys to Pad's zoom space. A Pad *region* consists of an address and a width and a height. This is a rectangle defined at some zoom magnification. A portal exists at a region in the Pad space and in addition has a *look on region*, which is the region to be viewed through the portal. Changing the look on region of a portal in essence changes the pan/zoom of the information viewed by the portal. At the top level, Pad is viewed through a portal associated with Pad's window. Portals can view other portals and, thus, produce a recursive transformation sequence like those discussed in Chapter 13.

Semantic zooming is achieved by giving every object (graphics or portal) a *visibility range* and a *transparency range*. When objects are rendered through a chain of portal views, they are transformed to some level of magnification. The visibility range defines the range of magnification where that object is visible. If magnification is too low, detail views should disappear. If magnification is too high, summary views should disappear so that detail views can be visible. To create smooth transitions, the transparency range defines magnifications where the object is only partially visible.

Perlin's original Pad implementation had efficiency problems. Many of these were resolved in Pad++[16]. The interesting question is whether pan/zoom techniques like those found in Pad are superior to the fisheye techniques described previously. Nekrasovski et al[17] report extensively on experiments that address this question. Their conclusion was that zooming is 10–15 percent better than fisheye techniques. However, some care must be taken in generalizing their results because they are based on only one type of task.

SUMMARY

Though we are familiar with overlapping rectangular windows, there are many other ways to manage display space. The tiled strategy has all windows visible with the user manipulating the boundaries between them. Flatland also keeps all windows visible but automatically shrinks them as other windows push them out of the way. Metisse provides windows that can be tilted, folded, bent, or shuffled to provide a richer set of mechanisms for arranging work. When multiple people are working together, DiamondSpin provides coordinates that keep windows oriented toward the closest edge of a table.

There are also other ways to manage very large spaces other than just scrolling. Fisheye views distort the presentation so that parts in focus are larger but the context with the rest of the view is retained. The focus+context screen provides a high resolution view immediately in front of the user with lower resolution around the periphery. There are also zooming techniques such as Pad that provide a huge range of zooming with more detail visible as the zoom factor increases.

EXERCISES

1. Take screen captures of a variety of application windows and save them as images. Use these window images to prototype one of the alternative window management techniques described in this chapter. You do not need to implement the applications, but the image-based prototype can provide realistic interaction with such applications.

2. Implement one of Carpendale's fisheye techniques and use it to implement a view of a very large image.

END NOTES

[1] Johnson, J., T. L. Roberts, D. C. Smith, C. H. Irby, M. Beard, and K. Mackey. "The Xerox Star: A Retrospective." *IEEE Computer* 22(9) (September 1989): 11–29.

[2] Bly, S., and J. Rosenberg. "A Comparison of Tiled and Overlapping Windows." *Human Factors in Computing Systems (CHI '86)* (April 1986): 101–106.

[3] Mynatt, E. D., T. Igarashi, W. K. Edwards, and A. LaMarca. "Flatland: New Dimensions in Office Whiteboards." *Human Factors in Computing Systems (CHI '99)* (May 1999): 346–353.

[4] Beaudouin-Lafon, M. "Novel Interaction Techniques for Overlapping Windows." *User Interface Software and Technology (UIST '01)* (November 2001): 153–154.

[5] Dragicevic, P. "Combining Crossing-Based and Paper-Based Interaction Paradigms for Dragging and Dropping Between Overlapping Windows." *User Interface Software and Technology (UIST '04)* (October 2004): 193–196.

[6] Shen, C., F. D. Vernier, C. Forlines, and R. Ringel. "DiamondSpin: An Extensible Toolkit for Around-the-Table Interaction." *Human Factors in Computing Systems (CHI '04)* (April 2004): 167–174.

[7] Agrawala, A., and R. Balakrishnan. "Keepin' It Real: Pushing the Desktop Metaphor with Physics, Piles and the Pen." *Human Factors in Computing Systems (CHI '06)* (April 2006): 1283–1292.

[8] Robertson, G., E. Horvitz, M. Czerwinski, P. Baudisch, D. Hutchings, B. Meyers, D. Robbins, and G. Smith. "Scalable Fabric: Flexible Task Management." *Advanced Visual Interfaces (AVI '04)* (May 2004): 85–89.

[9] Furnas, G. W. "Generalized Fisheye Views." *Human Factors in Computing Systems (CHI '86)* (April 1986): 16–23.

[10] Carpendale, M. S. T., and C. Montagnese. "A Framework for Unifying Presentation Space." *User Interface Software and Technology (UIST '01)* (November 2001): 61–70.

[11] Bederson, B. B. "Fisheye Menus." *User Interface Software and Technology (UIST '00)* (November 2000): 217–225.

[12] Schaffer, D., Z. Zuo, S. Greenberg, L. Bartram, J. Dill, S. Dubs, and M. Roseman. "Navigating Hierarchically Clustered Networks Through Fisheye and Full-Zoom Methods." *ACM Transactions on Computer-Human Interaction* 3(2) (June 1996): 162–188.

[13] Gutwin, C., and A. Skopik. "Fisheye Views Are Good for Large Steering Tasks." *Human Factors in Computing Systems (CHI '03)* (April 2003): 201–208.

[14] Baudisch, P., N. Good, and P. Stewart. "Focus Plus Context Screens: Combining Display Technology with Visualization Techniques." *User Interface Software and Technology (UIST 01)* (November 2001): 31–40.

[15] Perlin, K., and D. Fox. "Pad: An Alternative Approach to the Computer Interface." *International Conference on Computer Graphics and Interactive Techniques (SIGGRAPH '93)* (September 1993): 57–64.

[16] Bederson, B. B., and J. D. Hollan. "Pad++: A Zooming Graphical Interface for Exploring Alternate Interface Physics." *User Interface Software and Technology (UIST 94)* (November 1994): 17–26.

[17] Nekrasovski, D., A. Bodnar, J. McGrenere, F. Guimbretiere, and T. Munzner. "An Evaluation of Pan&Zoom and Rubber Sheet Navigation With and Without an Overview." *Human Factors in Computing Systems (CHI '06)* (April 2006): 11–20.

CHAPTER 22

Presentation Architecture

In Chapter 2, you learned about a presentation model where applications indicate regions of the screen that are out of date by invoking a damage() method on the window. The windowing system can call redraw(Graphics g) on a widget to have it redraw itself for any of a number of reasons. The Graphics object defines the interface to virtually any display surface, including windows, printers, images, or other display devices. This basic presentation architecture is the basis for almost all modern graphical user interfaces.

The damage/redraw architecture has a number of interesting variations that have become the basis for a variety of research systems. Some of these architectures are beginning to move into commercial products. This chapter looks at three such variations. The first is to use the Graphics object interface for very different purposes than its original intent. By creating special subclasses of Graphics, a variety of features can be implemented that work across all applications. The second technique is to render windows onto in-memory images rather than on the screen and then use those images to redirect the interface in new ways. In particular, you can adapt and change the nature of the user interface without requiring the application's cooperation. The last technique is to represent the presentation as a tree or graph of objects. The application modifies this tree and the damage/redraw mechanism becomes invisible to the programmer.

REDIRECTING THE GRAPHICS OBJECT

In an object-oriented architecture, the Graphics object or some similar class provides the universal abstraction of a drawing surface. Application views only know about this class and its methods. The view code is independent of what is actually done with the information in the Graphics object.

Magic Lenses

The first system to exploit the Graphics object was the Magic Lenses of Bier, et al[1]. Magic lenses are special windows that can be dragged over the top of other windows to modify their display. They can do many things, such as produce an achromatic view such as seen by a color-blind person, eliminate the fills from shapes so that shapes behind can be easily selected (Figure 22.1), or magnify the underlying shapes (Figure 22.2).

Figure 22.1 – X-ray magic lens

Figure 22.2 – Magnifying lens

For the achromatic lens, a window is placed over the original view. To implement the lens, you can create the AchromaticLens class, which is a subclass of Graphics. The AchromaticLens class has a constructor that accepts a Graphics object gr. Most of the method calls on AchromaticLens are simply passed on to the gr object. In the case of color-setting methods, the color is modified to its grayscale equivalent before being passed to gr. The result is that any AchromaticLens object behaves just like a Graphics object except that all colors are gray scale.

When the lens window receives a call to redraw(Graphics gDraw), it takes the Graphics object gDraw that it received and creates gLens=new AchromaticLens(gDraw). The lens then calls the redraw() method of the underlying window passing in gLens rather than gDraw. The implementation of gLens passes through any method call to gDraw with the exception of the methods to set colors. The underlying application believes that it is drawing on a normal Graphics object. There is no cooperation required of the underlying application. However, what are actually being drawn are the modified colors. The underlying window still responds to redraw() calls in the same way but the lens window, being over the top, is what the user sees.

For the X-ray lens (Figure 22.1), a modified XRayLens object translates all method calls that draw filled shapes into the corresponding calls for unfilled shapes. Thus, objects behind show through. The magnifying lens (Figure 22.2) simply applies a scaling transformation to all draw calls before passing them on to gDraw. Creating a new type of lens simply involves creating a different wrapper class that is a subclass of Graphics but modifies the calls in some way before passing them on to the Graphics object that the lens received in its own redraw() call.

One of the side effects of this architecture is that lenses can be placed over other lenses in a layering effect. For example, a magnifying lens can be placed over an X-ray lens. When redraw() is called on the magnifying lens, it wraps the Graphics object D in a MagnifyLens object M and calls redraw(M) on the window below. The X-ray lens below takes the drawing object M and wraps it in an XRayLens object X that implements the X-ray transformation and calls redraw(X) on the application window below. When the application window draws a rectangle, it calls X.drawRect(..). The implementation of X strips out the fill information and calls M.drawRect(..) because X is a wrapper for M. The MagnifyLens object M scales the rectangle and calls D.drawRect(..), which draws an unfilled magnified rectangle in the window. All of the lenses and applications know nothing about what each other are doing. All communication is through redraw() and specialized subclasses of Graphics.

Edwards et al[2] added a number of other techniques to the repertoire of graphics object modification. They added drop shadows to objects using a two-pass painting technique. They would first call redraw() with a Graphics subclass whose only color choice was gray and with a transformation down and to the left. This drew a shadow of all objects in the presentation. Then, the original redraw() was called with the unmodified Graphics object so that the real content was drawn over the shadows. They also demonstrated how animation effects such as shimmering can be added by periodically recalling redraw() using an incrementally modified transformation.

Attachments

By definition the redraw() method will reveal all of the user-related information about an application because drawing on the screen is the primary mechanism for communicating to the user. Because all of this information is being passed through the Graphics object, you can exploit that information for other purposes. This is the basis for the Attachments[3] system. Unlike the lens technique above, attachments required additional cooperation from the application in three limited ways. First, the application's redraw() method should generate a drawing for all of the application rather than just the currently visible portion. The Graphics object may have a clip region that could be used to limit the redraw effort, but if the clip region was infinite, all of the information should be drawn. For example, a word processor should be prepared to draw all of its pages in one long vertical presentation if requested.

The second attachment requirement was that the application should reveal its structure through four methods that were added to the Graphics object:

```
groupStart(String name, String type)
groupStart(int index, String type)
groupStart(Interactor toolkitObject)
groupEnd()
```

The idea is that most `redraw()` methods are implemented to tour their model structures as a tree traversal. Whenever the application starts to draw some model object, it calls one of the `groupStart()` methods to identify the object and its type. Objects are identified by name or index. The object types are any names that were meaningful to the application. Identifying an object by interactor supplies both identifier and type information. When an object's drawing is complete, `groupEnd()` is called. When complex objects are drawn, the start/end associations are nested. These methods reveal a tree structure of how objects being drawn on the screen are associated together in meaningful application objects.

The third requirement was that the application reveal its current selection using a path mechanism that used the same names or indices found in the `groupStart()` methods. When the application selects an object, this path representation indicates what is selected. When some attachment wants to modify the selection, it sets the path. When the selection is modified, the application should scroll so as to display that selection.

Based on these three requirements of applications (full world redraw, start/end grouping, and path selection) plus the information normally supplied by calling methods on the `Graphics` object, a variety of attachment tools can be created that augment any application.

The first example is a "bookmark" facility. The bookmark attachment allows a user to save the path of the currently selected object for future reference. A bookmark attachment might name these marks or save them in some other way—the applications do not care. When the user selects a bookmark, the selection is passed back to the application to scroll the selected object into view. A more interesting technique is to create a "radar view"[4] of the bookmarks. A radar view shows where the bookmarks are within the world space of the application. A radar view is generated by invoking the application's `redraw()` with a special `Graphics` object that knows about the bookmarks. By watching the `groupStart/groupEnd` calls, the `Graphics` object knows when one of the bookmarked objects is being drawn. This subclass of `Graphics` does not actually draw anything. Instead it retains the bounding boxes for any drawing of a bookmarked object. From these bounding boxes, a scaled-down version of the application's entire world can be displayed with the bookmarked object locations highlighted. If the user selects one of the bookmarks in this space, the selection of the application is moved to that location. Vertical and horizontal radar views are possible by discarding x or y from the bounding boxes. These radar views can be used to augment scroll bars. This bookmark attachment and its radar views are independent of any particular application.

The bookmark attachment illustrates the need for attachments to highlight objects in an application's presentation to direct the user's attention. This is problematic because there are so many ways that applications can present their data. For example, highlighting an object by drawing a red box around it is a good idea until the application has a red background or many red objects. The generalized pointing[5] technique was developed for attachments. When the `redraw()` of an application is called, a special `Graphics` object that knows about the bookmarks is used. Whenever objects are being drawn that are not part of a bookmark (as indicated by `groupStart/groupEnd`), their colors are blended with a neutral color such as light gray. Objects that are part of bookmarks or other selections are drawn in their normal colors. This technique deemphasizes unselected objects. The more background objects are blended to a neutral color, the more prominent the selected items. The less background blending, the more visible the unselected objects and the more able they are to provide context. Figure 22.3 shows this technique in highlighting a map location without losing context. Again, the application program is unaware of this highlight mechanism because it is just a modification of the Graphics object.

Figure 22.3 – Blended highlighting

Using the previous mechanisms a spell-checker attachment can be written. To spell check any application, the redraw() method is called with a Graphics object that ignores all calls except text-drawing calls. The text is not drawn but is checked against a spelling dictionary. For any text not in the dictionary, the path of groupStart identifiers is added to the bookmarks. When done, all of the objects that contain misspelled words can be highlighted using the previous techniques. A similar technique could be used to provide dictionary lookup or language translation for selected objects. The key is that applications reveal substantial information through redraw()/Graphics objects and that information can be usefully mined.

IMAGE SPACE ARCHITECTURES

All windowing systems must eventually render the application's presentation as an image on the screen. For object-oriented systems, this rendering is encapsulated in the Graphics object. In most windowing systems, the pixel representation is stored in the frame buffer of the display where it can be seen by the user. As computing power and RAM have increased, it has become possible to separate the rendering of an application presentation into pixels and the compositing of those pixels onto the screen. The windowing system can first render the presentation into an image and then in a separate step render that image onto the display. This is the architecture built into Apple's Quartz window compositor[6].

Once the application's presentation is represented as an image, the windowing system can do a variety of things. In Macintosh OS X, windows appear to shrink and "pour" when iconified and then expand out of the icon when opened. This effect is simply a distortion of the window's image. Rendering to an image also allows for redraw of an exposed portion of a window without invoking the application's redraw() method. The exposed segments are simply composited onto the screen from the window's image. This technique was used in the old Blit[7] terminals before the object-oriented damage/redraw architecture was invented. The image representation can also be scaled down to create smaller overviews of a window. This is the basis for Apple's Exposé window management. When desired, the windowing system shrinks all of the window images and moves them apart so that none of them overlap. This gives the user a full view of all of the windows from which the desired window can be selected. A similar technique is behind the thumbnail views in Scalable Fabric[8]. Representing windows as images is behind the VNC collaboration architecture[9]. Once a window is rendered as an image, it becomes a data object that can be used for a variety of purposes and in a variety of ways.

Metisse

These architectural ideas were formalized in the Metisse[10] windowing system. Metisse is implemented as a special X Windows server. The graphics calls are received in the traditional way and then rendered into off-screen images. These images are then passed to the *compositor* that is responsible for rendering the images on the screen. Changes to the compositor allow many different window management techniques to be implemented without requiring the cooperation of the application. This is further simplified by the X Windows approach of separating window management from the windowing system. The compositor is simply a special window manager. Figure 22.4 shows some of the new ways to render windows.

When window images are distorted, modified, and moved around in new ways, input handling becomes an issue. In Metisse, interactive inputs are received by the compositor and the appropriate window is identified to receive the event. The compositor then applies the inverse transform or distortion to the input point before passing the event on to the application through the X Windows server. Thus, the application feels and behaves appropriately without knowing about what has been done to its display on the screen.

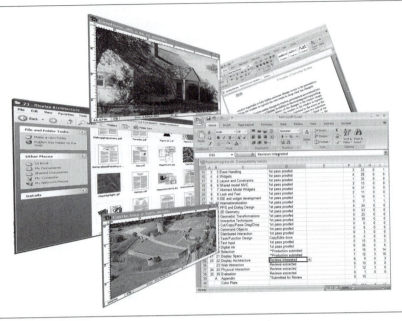

Figure 22.4 – Metisse image-based rendering of windows

Facades

The flexibility of separating image compositing from graphics rendering in Metisse has been used to implement Facades[11]. Facades are a mechanism for adapting a user interface to the needs of a particular user without requiring the application to cooperate. The user can open a special Facade window and then can copy and paste user-interface fragments from existing applications, as shown in Figure 22.5. The fragments included in a façade need not be all from the same application. Using the Metisse architecture, these fragments can be rendered into memory images and then rendered on the screen wherever the fragment has been pasted. When a façade receives user inputs, the events are mapped back to the original locations in the off-screen window images. When a window is damaged and redrawn, the off-screen image of the window is repainted and the façade is then updated from the off-screen image. WinCuts[12] is a similar tool built on top of Microsoft Windows. To the user, the interactive fragments appear to be live parts of the original applications. An application can now provide a large and complex palette of controls and the user can create a façade of only the controls that they use most frequently. The assembled façade can be copied from many different parts of an application's controls.

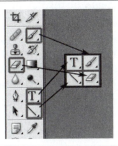

Figure 22.5 – Façade from a tool palette

Though image-based techniques are quite effective in creating facades, the user can be assisted in selecting a specific control. Facades do this by accessing the window tree and specifically the accessibility information for blind users that is stored in the tree. The accessibility information is similar to what Attachments got from `groupStart`/`groupEnd`. The information indicates the bounds and function of regions of the screen. These can be used to simplify selection, copying, and pasting fragments into a façade.

Mnemonic Rendering

A last image-based windowing technique is called Mnemonic Rendering[13]. When a display is very large, such as a 30-foot wall display, the user might not be paying attention when an application on a distant part of the screen makes changes to its presentation. When the user's attention is transferred to that part of the screen, the user needs to be reminded what has happened while they were looking elsewhere. This is a feature that you want to work on all applications, not just those that have been specially modified. A similar situation occurs when a window is partially or fully hidden and some change occurs to its presentation. When the window is exposed, the user wants to recap what has changed.

As an application makes changes to its window, presentations are rendered into an off-screen image, as in Metisse. In addition to the rendering and compositing, the windowing system keeps a history of the changes to the window image. When the user's attention is directed at the window or the window is exposed, depending on the usage scenario, the changes are *restituted* on the screen so the user can see what has happened. Mnemonic Rendering proposes two restitution techniques. The *persistence* technique shows a pixel-by-pixel blend of the historical pixels and the current ones. As the blend moves forward in time, the image shifts from its historical value to the current one. If there has been movement, this appears as *motion trails* across the screen. The *flashback* technique rapidly displays each historical change in fast time so that the user can quickly see all that has happened. These techniques are possible over any set of windows because of the off-screen rendering and use of the window image as a data object to be manipulated by the windowing system.

Triggering the mnemonic display depends on how the technique is being used. If the display is large, tracking the user's attention is important. This can be done by gaze tracking or by head motion tracking. The mouse or other pointer location can be used as a surrogate for the user's attention. For example, touching a new region of the screen can trigger the mnemonic rendering. For smaller displays where mnemonic rendering is used on windows that were previously concealed, the window exposures can be used to trigger a mnemonic rendering.

SCENE GRAPHS

Graphics object and window image techniques work at the outermost levels of the display system and, thus, minimize their entanglement with actual applications. These techniques make it easy for an operating system or windowing system to provide functionality that is independent of any application and impose minimal requirements on the application's implementation. As was seen with the Attachments work, it helps to have additional information about the structure of the application's information. There are a series of architectures that make the structure of the presentation more explicit and, thus, make more information available to external tools.

Most of these techniques revolve around the idea of a scene graph and object-oriented techniques in implementing the nodes of that graph. Scene graphs are sometimes called structured graphics. The ideas are the same. In the very early days of computer graphics, a scene to be drawn was represented as an interconnected set of nodes, each node contained a list of drawing specifications. This was known as the *scene graph*. The old graphics hardware would traverse this structure 30+ times a second to redraw the scene on the display (see Figure 22.6). To modify the display, the application program would modify the contents of the scene graph. The next time the graphics hardware traversed the scene graph, the image would be drawn differently and, thus, would instantly change. There was no damage/redraw. The approach was to change the scene graph and the display would instantly change.

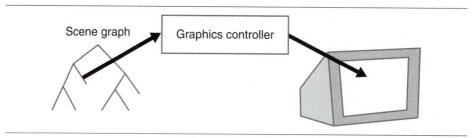

Scene graph — Graphics controller

Figure 22.6 – Scene graph refresh display hardware

Scene graphs disappeared from 2D interface architectures with the advent of frame-buffer graphics where the graphics model is pixel-based rather than stroke-based. The display hardware now refreshed from the frame buffer rather than the scene graph. The damage/redraw architecture took care of getting the frame buffer updated when changes occurred. Scene graphs continued to be used in 3D architectures and animation tools. In 3D architectures, the hidden surface problem made the identification of a damage region quite difficult. The problems of transparency and cast shadows also made it necessary for the rendering tools to have a structure that could be traversed as needed to correctly produce the desired picture. In animation, many changes are going on at the same time. The scene graph architecture allows the animation engine to make needed changes at needed times while leaving the details of screen update to the scene graph. This idea of "change the scene graph and let screen update take care of itself" can greatly simplify application design. The Morphic[14] toolkit used a scene graph architecture to support its animation.

In a 2D pixel-based drawing model, scene graphs work slightly different from the graphics hardware in Figure 22.6. A scene graph is a collection of two kinds of objects. First are the drawing objects that correspond to the drawing methods found in any Graphics object. There are also container objects that contain collections of both draw objects and other containers. Some containers are just a list of draw objects. Other containers can impose attributes such as geometric transformations, default colors, or transparency. Some containers can have rectangular bounds that are checked at redraw time to see if the bounds are actually visible. If not, then the drawing of that subtree can be avoided.

Drawing the Scene Graph

A simple scene graph drawing architecture uses a separate thread and a timer. Whenever the timer goes off (30 times/second), the tree is traversed and the scene redrawn. This mimics the behavior of the old graphics display hardware. If there are lots of changes going on continuously, as in an animation or video game, this architecture works well. If changes are limited or infrequent, as in most applications that only change when an input event occurs, a lot of computing power is wasted on unnecessary redrawing of the same image.

An alternative change propagation architecture can be used. When a change is made to some part of the scene graph, a notification is sent to the parent of the changed object and, thus, propagated up the tree. If a node has multiple parents (scene graphs are directed acyclic graphs), all parents are notified of the change. Whenever a container node receives a change notice, it marks itself as changed. If it is already marked, the change is not propagated up the tree. This makes certain that the root of each tree knows about changes but prevents extensive notification costs when many changes are made.

Periodically (30 times/second), the redraw process checks the root of each tree to see if changes have been made. If a change has been made, a redraw can be initiated. When a tree is redrawn, the change flags are cleared. If there are multiple parents, a count must be maintained so that the change flags are not cleared until the last redraw has occurred. In some architectures, it is possible for the redraw method to check what has changed and, thus, avoid redrawing screen fragments that have not been changed.

Scene Graph/View Relationship

Regardless of the way in which the scene graph gets redrawn, the view manages its presentation by modifying the scene graph rather than through a paint() method. This allows the view to ignore getting the screen updated. A scene graph also helps with essential geometry issues. Because each primitive to be drawn is represented as an object in the graph, those objects can also have geometry methods such as isHit(), distanceToPoint(), or any of the other geometry needs discussed in Chapter 12. Because these methods are defined on scene graph objects, the application does not need to implement them. This architecture also guarantees that the essential geometry exactly corresponds to what is drawn.

To illustrate how this works, consider the tree shown in Figure 22.7 and its corresponding display on the right. When the mouse goes down over the line, the application's view simply asks the tree, "What was hit?" The tree is traversed in front-to-back order (opposite to drawing order) and the geometry of each object in the tree is tested by the scene graph and its code. Finally, it returns the line that is very close to the mouse point.

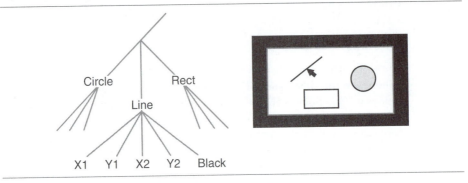

Figure 22.7 – Scene graph for a drawing program

The view responds by adding two new little "handle" objects to the tree (Figure 22.8). These are subclasses of Rectangle and have selection information. Adding the rectangles causes changes to be propagated and the view is redrawn. When the mouse goes down over one of the handle rectangles, the view again asks, "What was hit?" and the scene graph returns the rectangle subclass object. This object contains information about the control point. As further mouse-move events are received, the view need only modify the position of the rectangle and the corresponding end point of the line. All other redraw and screen updating is handled automatically by the scene graph. When the line becomes unselected, the control rectangles are removed from the scene graph and automatically disappear from the display. Once the line is selected, the view can change its color or any other attributes and the display will correspondingly change.

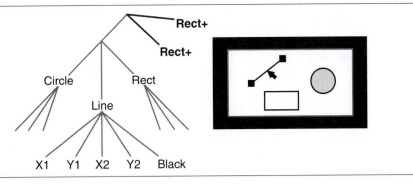

Figure 22.8 – Modified scene graph

One view/scene-graph architecture is for the view objects to maintain pointers to their scene graph objects. When the view receives a model change notification, it follows this pointer and modifies the scene graph to reflect the new model values. However, in an object-oriented world, you can create subclasses of the nodes in the scene graph. Thus, a view can be implemented as a subclass of one of the container node classes. This integrates the view with the scene graph. The view now inherits all of the redraw, change propagation, and essential geometry functionality. This blurring of the view and the scene graph starts to look very much like the widget trees that you worked with before. The difference is that a view object functions by modifying its children in the scene graph rather than by implementing a redraw( ) method.

Bederson et al[15] have defined two basic architectural styles for scene graph systems. They define *polylithic* architectures as ones where the composition of attributes and other information are defined as separate nodes and are composed at run time while traversing the scene graph. They define *monolithic* toolkits as ones where each object is a subclass of some root class and each defines its own attributes. The widget sets in Chapter 4 are of the monolithic variety. Many 3D graphics systems such as OpenGL and Java3D use the polylithic approach. The idea behind the polylithic approach is that there are lots of primitive facilities that can be composed into a scene graph and the composition of these defines the behavior.

Bederson and colleagues compared the Jazz[16] (polylithic) and Piccolo[15] (monolithic) toolkits on a variety of applications. These toolkits have almost identical functionality and differ primarily in their architecture. They found that their execution times were almost identical but that the monolithic Piccolo toolkit was much easier to teach and much easier to debug.

The Fresco[17] toolkit was a very early monolithic, scene graph architecture. Fresco integrated the concepts of variably intrinsic sized layout management with the flexibility of structured graphics. The delegation object-oriented language Self[18] demonstrated how highly flexible dynamic interactions could be built when a scene graph architecture is combined directly with a highly object-oriented language. More recently, the UBit[19] toolkit is resurrecting the polylithic architecture with a more flexible interconnection of components.

The primary advantage of the scene graph architecture is that it simplifies redraw, makes essential geometry much simpler, and also simplifies many basic interactions. For example, drawing a rubberband selection rectangle is as simple as adding the rectangle to the graph and then updating one of its corner points on every mouse move. The redraw issues are all taken care of.

In addition, the scene graph architecture provides the toolkit with a structured representation of the application. This is the kind of information that Attachments were trying to extract by adding groupStart/groupEnd to the Graphics object. In a scene graph, this structure is readily exposed and does not need to be reconstructed from the Graphics object calls.

This scene graph information was exploited by Debugging Lenses[20]. A debugging lens behaves very much like a toolglass except that the information presented inside of the lens is targeted toward debugging user interfaces. A problem in user-interface implementation is that when the display looks wrong it can be very difficult to figure out why. Debugging lenses can show the class of the objects being displayed as well as shrinking them away from each other to show the container relationships. Debugging lenses can display a variety of properties about the view's structure because that structure is directly available to the toolkit.

This object-oriented structure of the scene graph is exploited even further in the C3W system[21]. This system shares the goals of Facades[11] and WinCuts[12] in that it allows portions of the user interface to be extracted and copied elsewhere. The fact that a scene graph is a graph rather than a tree means that the new location can simply reference a portion of the scene graph from the old location. This generates appropriate updates whenever the scene graph changes. This is much less memory intensive than the off-screen image techniques and allows transformations to be performed more efficiently than by image manipulation. The big contribution of C3W, however, is that each node in the graph can have its attributes interconnected much like a spreadsheet. This allows end users to make arbitrary connections between application fragments that they see in the screen. Whenever an attribute changes, the scene graph notification mechanism informs the toolkit and if the changed attribute participates in some formula, then all dependent scene graph fragments can be updated.

SUMMARY

Applications must render all of the information that a user will use through their presentation layer. By capturing and modifying this presentation layer, a whole new set of capabilities can be defined that works across all applications. One simple mechanism is to provide an alternative Graphics object to the redraw() method. This technique allows many toolglasses and attachments to be created. An alternative architecture is to capture all drawing in an off-screen image for each window and then allow many different ways for rendering those images. This provides for new windowing techniques as well as copy and paste of custom user interfaces. Finally, you can represent your presentation as a scene graph rather than in a redraw() method. This simplifies the redraw task, greatly simplifies the computation of essential geometry, and offers new information that can be exploited in new lens and customization techniques.

EXERCISES

1. Use a subclass of the Graphics object to create a magnification lens.

2. Use screen captures and mouse-event redirection to implement a Facade-like user interface.

3. Implement a simple scene graph architecture using rectangles, lines, and ellipses. Demonstrate that the screen gets updated every time the graph is changed.

END NOTES

[1] Bier, E. A., M. C. Stone, K. Pier, W. Buxton, and T. D. DeRose. "Toolglass and Magic Lenses: The See-Through Interface." *Computer Graphics and Interactive Techniques (SIGGRAPH '93)* (September 1993): 73–80.

[2] Edwards, W. K., S. E. Hudson, J. Marinacci, R. Rodenstein, T. Rodriguez, and I. Smith. "Systematic Output Modification in a 2D User Interface Toolkit." *User Interface Software and Technology (UIST '97)* (October 1997): 151–158.

[3] Olsen, D. R., S. E. Hudson, T. Verratti, J. M. Heiner, and M. Phelps. "Implementing Interface Attachments Based on Surface Representations." *Human Factors in Computing Systems (CHI '99)* (May 1999): 191–198.

[4] Gutwin, C., and S. Greenberg. "Workspace Awareness Support with Radar Views." *CHI '96 Conference Companion* (April 1996): 210–211.

[5] Olsen, D. R., D. Boyarski, T. Verratti, M. Phelps, J. L. Moffett, and E. L. Lo. "Generalized Pointing: Enabling Multiagent Interaction." *Human Factors in Computing Systems (CHI '98)* (April 1998): 526–533.

[6] Mac OS X v10.2. "Technologies: Quartz Extreme and Quartz 2D." *Apple Technology Brief* (October 2002).

[7] Pike R. "The Blit: A Multiplexed Graphics Terminal." *AT&T Bell Labs Technical Journal* 63(8) part 2 (1983): 1607–1631.

[8] Robertson, G., E. Horvitz, M. Czerwinski, P. Baudisch, D. Hutchings, B. Meyers, D. Robbins, and G. Smith. "Scalable Fabric: Flexible Task Management." *Advanced Visual Interfaces (AVI '04)* (May 2004): 85–89.

[9] Richardson, T., Q. Stafford-Fraser, K. R. Wood, and A. Hopper. "Virtual Network Computing." *IEEE Internet Computing* Vol. 2, No. 1 (January 1998): 33-38.

[10] Chapuis, O., and N. Roussel. "Metisse Is Not a 3D Desktop!" *User Interface Software and Technology (UIST '05)* (October 2005): 13–22.

[11] Stuerzlinger, W., O. Chapuis, D. Phillips, and N. Roussel. "User Interface Facades: Towards Fully Adaptable User Interfaces." *User Interface Software and Technology (UIST '06)* (October 2006): 309–318.

[12] Tan, D. S., B. Meyers, and M. Czerwinski. "WinCuts: Manipulating Arbitrary Window Regions for More Effective Use of Screen Space." *Late Breaking Results (CHI '04)* (April 2004): 1525–1528.

[13] Bezerianos, A., P. Dragicevic, and R. Balakrishnan. "Mnemonic Rendering: An Image-Based Approach for Exposing Hidden Changes in Dynamic Displays." *User Interface Software and Technology (UIST '06)* (October 2006): 159–168.

[14] Maloney, J. H., and R. B. Smith. "Directness and Liveness in the Morphic User Interface Construction Environment." *User Interface Software and Technology (UIST '95)* (December 1995): 21–28.

[15] Bederson, B. B., J. Grosjean, and J. Meyer. "Toolkit Design for Interactive Structured Graphics." *IEEE Transactions on Software Engineering 30(8)* (August 2004): 1–12.

[16] Bederson, B. B., J. Meyer, and L. Good. "Jazz: An Extensible Zoomable User Interface Graphics Toolkit in Java." *User Interface Software and Technology (UIST '00)* (November 2000): 171–180.

[17] Tang, S. H., and M. A. Linton. "Blending Structured Graphics and Layout." *User Interface Software and Technology (UIST '94)* (November 1994): 167–174.

[18] Smith, R. B., J. Maloney, and D. Ungar. "The Self-4.0 User Interface: Manifesting a System-wide Vision of Concreteness, Uniformity and Flexibility." *Object-Oriented Programming Systems, Languages and Applications (OOPSLA '95)* (October 1995): 47–60.

[19] Lecolinet, E. "A Molecular Architecture for Creating Advanced GUIs." *User Interface Software and Technology (UIST '03)* (November 2003): 135–144.

[20] Hudson, S. E., R. Rodensein, and I. Smith. "Debugging Lenses: A New Class of Transparent Tools for User Interface Debugging." *User Interface Software and Technology (UIST '97)* (October 1997): 179–187.

[21] Fujima, J., A. Lunzer, K. Hornbaek, and Y. Tanaka. "Clip, Connect, Clone: Combining Application Elements to Build Custom Interfaces for Information Access." *User Interface Software and Technology (UIST '04)* (October 2004): 175–184.

CHAPTER 23

Web Interaction

One of the most important changes in interactive systems in the late 1990s and early 2000s was the advent of the World Wide Web (the Web). The Web shifted the center of interactive systems from a personal computer centric model to a distributed user-interface model. A very important problem in creating an interactive application is how it will be distributed and maintained. In the retail model, the application is packaged in a box with one or more CDs containing software and is then sold. Each customer takes out the CD and proceeds to install the software on a personal computer. Because of the diversity of hardware/software platforms, this can be a complicated process. Many users are not prepared to do this well and virtually all users desire to avoid installation as an annoyance.

A second software distribution approach is the corporate strategy. Within the corporation there is an information technology organization whose responsibility it is to manage all of the computers and make the software distribution happen smoothly. This is a time-consuming and expensive effort whose costs can easily outpace hardware costs. In many cases, these costs are reduced by standardization of hardware and software, depriving users of control of their computer.

A third strategy for software deployment is the Web. The heart of the idea lies in three standards: URL, HTTP, and HTML. The URL (Uniform Resource Locator) provides a globally unique method for referencing any piece of information or interactive service in the WWW. This means that any user with an appropriate browser can reach any WWW service for which they have permission. HTTP (Hypertext Transfer Protocol) provides the connection between server and browser. HTML (Hypertext Markup Language) provides a standard way to implement the view/controller of whatever service is being provided.

Any user who installs a Web browser now has access to any interactive resource on the Web. This is in contrast to the retail and corporate deployment models where each installation provides access to one service. Any new service that conforms to HTTP and HTML immediately can function on any of the installed browsers in the world. In the corporate or retail deployment model, each new service could only access users who had that particular software installed. This led to an explosion in browser installations creating a huge, easily reached market and an explosion in new services each reached by a simple mouse click with no installation step.

For our purposes, the Web interaction architecture demonstrates many of the architectural concepts that we have been discussing. Good Web interface programming requires a clear understanding of the model-view-controller architecture (Chapters 1–3). There are many issues in distribution of the user interface (Chapter 17) and how that should be designed. You will see scene graph display architectures (Chapter 22) and command objects (Chapter 16). All of these will come together in interactive Web applications.

Web interaction is also interesting because of its process. Unlike most applications that are created within the closed world of a development group, the Web has grown in the public eye. Standards are defined and then violated for competitive advantage. The Web is a competitive place where conforming is required to function and yet inhibits competitive advantage. The development of the Web is a process of pursuing greatest advantage with minimal upheaval. Architectures are created and then used for very different purposes. This has caused many architecture mechanisms to be bent to serve very different ends than originally intended.

This is not a WWW text and does not cover many of the concepts that have emerged in the Web. That would require a separate text. This chapter first covers enough Web concepts to understand the user-interface architecture and to provide examples. It then looks at how the model-view-controller architecture fits into the Web interaction structure. This chapter then examines how and why to push more of the controller implementation from the server to the browsers and then looks at techniques for automating the restyling of user interfaces. Web interaction is more competitive and dynamic than traditional applications. Users like their Web services to be fresh and interesting. Styling mechanisms help to master this problem. This chapter also looks at the AJAX (Asynchronous Javascript And XML) concepts and how they influence the MVC architecture. Finally, this chapter examines tools for creating Web applications and how they impact the process.

WEB BASICS

Figure 23.1 shows three basic pieces to a Web application: (1) a server, (2) HTTP, and (3) the browser. A Web application is created by extending the functionality of the server by adding new resources that it understands and by extending the functionality of the browser, primarily by giving it an HTML document.

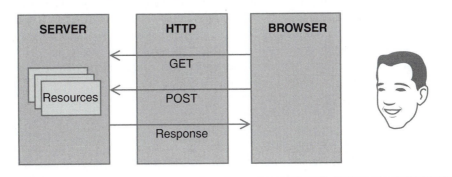

Figure 23.1 – Web structure

URL

A very important part of the Web is the Uniform Resource Locator (URL). This is part of a more general scheme of Uniform Resource Identifiers (URI) that is not addressed here. The key user-interface ideas can be examined within the URL model. Figure 23.2 shows a sample URL with the various pieces identified. The terminology is somewhat different from Web standards but it will help clarify the pieces of the application architecture.

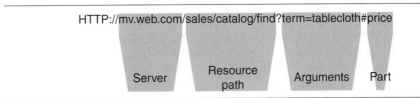

Figure 23.2 – Parts of a URL

- *Server*—This is the reference to the computer(s) and port where the application can be accessed by a browser.
- *Resource path*—This is a pathname that identifies the application, information, or commands that the browser would like the server to provide.
- *Arguments*—These are named pieces of information that are to be provided to any Web application commands so that they can correctly perform the requested function.
- *Part*—There are times when you do not want the entire page; you might want to reference only part of it. This is frequently processed by the browser rather than by the server.

The value of a URL is that it provides a uniform way to make a request of any service that is part of the Web. The original goal of the Web was that the resource path would identify a file and that file would be returned. Depending on the type of the file, the browser would display information to the user. The URL provided a general mechanism for referencing any file on the Web. However, it was quickly recognized that a URL is only a name and that a server is simply a program. Servers could be programmed to do more with a name than simply reference the file system. This conceptual transition from files to services happened very early in the history of the Web and was wildly successful because nothing about HTTP or Web browsers needed to change to support such interactive access to services.

HTTP

Hypertext Transfer Protocol (HTTP) is the basic mechanism of communication between browsers and servers. HTTP is a stateless protocol, which means that the browser makes a request, the server provides a response, and the connection is terminated. The protocol itself has no memory of previous requests and does not support an ongoing series of requests. Each request is independent of all others. This has an impact on how Web applications are structured. In the application architectures discussed previously, the application runs and there is a lot of information saved between each user input. The model, the view, and also the controller state are all saved from input event to input event. This is still true in Web applications, but the server architectures and HTTP do not directly support this.

There are good reasons for the stateless model of HTTP. When there is an ongoing connection, the protocol must deal with problems of setting up, terminating, and recovering from connection failure. In a stateless model, the request succeeded or it did not. This makes for a simple robust protocol but it imposes burdens on application developers.

There are several mechanisms for communicating between a browser and a server. For our purposes here, you only consider two. The GET request is a simple string containing "GET" and the path, arguments, and part portion of the URL. Other information can be included such as authorization keys and information about the browser. A server responds to a GET request either by returning the requested information as HTML, text, image, or any of a variety of file types or it sends a failure message explaining why. Most of the data to be communicated to the server is in the URL. Where additional information must be communicated beyond a simple URL string, the POST request gives the path part of a URL and then includes in the remainder of the request a file of information to be given to the server. This request was intended as a mechanism for changing data on the server. It is now used for many other things. The response from a POST is similar to the response from a GET. These two amazingly simple mechanisms are the heart and soul of Web-based interaction. There are other details about authentication, access, file types, and caching but GET and POST are sufficient to understand Web interaction.

Server Implementation

A server is just a piece of software that listens for requests, generally on port 80. Originally only the path part of the URL was used by the server. This was normally mapped directly to some folder or directory tree on the server machine. Servers were simple programs that looked for GET and POST requests (which are in clear text), found the file that corresponded to the path part of the request, and returned the contents of that file in the response. In the case of a POST, the file was changed to whatever contents were in the POST request. If the response contained HTML, the links could be used to direct the user to other files on other machines and, thus, the WWW was born.

As the WWW grew, servers needed to process multiple simultaneous requests from many browsers. Authorization and access was required. Secure communications were also added to protect commerce and privacy. These all added to the complexity of the server implementation but did not change the way in which users interacted with the Web.

The first serious step toward Web applications came when people wanted to serve data that was stored in databases rather than file systems. HTTP never specified that the model of a Web application must be the file system. The model can be anything. You could build a new server that implements HTTP and uses a database rather than the file system. Many other possible models can be presented through HTTP; however, writing a new server for each such model wastes effort. All the server implementations must still deal with multiple processes, multiple request streams, authentication, security, and so on. You do not want to burden each new Web application with these issues. There are at least three common architectures for sharing server code across many applications.

Common Gateway Interface (CGI)

The first approach to Web applications was the Common Gateway Interface (CGI). The idea is that a program is associated with some path. When a GET or POST containing a URL associated with the path is received, the program is run and the URL and other information is passed to it. The program then writes its response (usually in HTML) to standard out. The URL can contain additional path information as well as arguments and the response part is easy.

Servlets

With the advent of Java on the Web, the *servlet* became a useful mechanism for extending servers. A servlet is a Java class that provides the methods doGet() and/or doPost(). The class is registered with the server and is associated with some path in the server's tree of information. If a GET request is received by the server for that path, the doGet() method is called with a Request object and a Response object as parameters. A POST request works similarly with doPost(). The request object contains information and methods to find out about the received request. The response object is where the servlet puts information about the response to be sent back. Most of the network server implementation issues are masked in the servlet mechanisms. There are other language/server combinations besides Java servlets that provide similar mechanisms.

Looking at a URL, the path has become a reference to a particular object with a particular method on that object. The arguments part of the URL can be thought of as arguments to the method.

Web Services

When people realized that a URL could look very much like a command invocation and that the response information need not be just HTML, the idea of a Web service was born. A Web service uses HTTP and URLs as a protocol for getting services performed over the Internet. There is no requirement that such Web services only support Web browsers. The power of a Web service lies in separating an application's model from its view and controller. Anyone with appropriate permissions can write a view/controller combination on top of a model implemented as a Web service. In the Internet world, this allows basic services to have many faces for many purposes. There are two major approaches for Web services: simple URLs and SOAP.

The simple URL approach basically defines each model command as a URL path/argument combination. The response is generally a data representation rather than HTML. Frequently, the response is XML[1] (eXtensible Markup Language). Other approaches return JSON[2] (JavaScript Object Notation) strings rather than XML. JSON has a much more direct mapping to program data objects than XML with very simple parsers. XML or JSON are used to encode model information rather than a specific view of that information. This model information is then translated by code downloaded into the browser (usually as JavaScript). By returning XML, the command leaves it to the requesting software to generate an appropriate view from the data.

SOAP[4] is a much more formal standard for Web services created by the W3C (World Wide Web Consortium). SOAP is actually a standard for representing requests for service. It includes mechanisms for specifying the desired command as well as providing complex data arguments. One of the problems with the URL approach to Web services is that complex arguments are hard to encode in a simple string. To provide the contact information for a person with their name, company, work phone, home phone, cell phone, e-mail address, instant messaging ID, and fax number, the most appropriate approach is to define a record structure with fields for each of those items. A URL does not provide a mechanism for such structures. Lists of things are also hard in a URL. SOAP defines an encoding for all such information. On the other hand, SOAP is rather complex and difficult to program without a layer of software over the top.

In addition to the basic command functionality, many Web services provide a description of the services that they offer. WSDL[5] (Web Services Description Language) is an XML-based standard for defining such services. The WSDL of a service generally provides both an HTML and an XML description of the commands that a service supports and the arguments that those commands expect. The HTML description allows programmers to explore the available features and to invoke the commands manually so that they can learn what they do. The XML description of a service allows automatic tools to generate program interfaces within some language that will simplify the implementation of the view/controller of the application.

The SOAP/WSDL protocol can be painfully complex to use directly. The simple URL strategy is much easier to learn. However, automated tools can readily exploit a WSDL description to produce a set of methods within a given programming language that very much looks like the model of a local application rather than an Internet protocol. The generated methods hide the networking complexity.

Browser/HTML

From a user's perspective, the Internet browser is the user interface. The user expects a standard set of navigation techniques such as forward and backward navigation buttons, multiple windows or tabs to pursue parallel work, and clicking on links to access new resources. A Web browser is mostly a rendering engine for HTML. HTML is basically a text-based language for defining a display tree or scene graph (Chapter 22). Originally, HTML was defined rather loosely as a text markup language. Its syntax is based on SGML. The basic structure of HTML and SGML were regularized in XML. At the heart of all these languages is the *tag*. A tag defines a tree node. Each tag can have attributes and can have zero or more children. In addition to tag nodes, there are also text nodes.

In XML, there can be any number of kinds of tags and there is no implicit meaning associated with them. This allows XML to describe any tree structure. In HTML, the tags have specific meaning as to how that tag is to be rendered by the browser. XHTML is a variation of XML that has all of the tags of HTML but with the slightly more regular syntax of XML. In XHTML, the structure of the presentation tree is quite explicit, whereas in HTML it is not quite so clear.

When a modern Web browser receives an HTML file, it immediately converts it to a DOM (Document Object Model) tree. Figure 23.3 shows a fragment of HTML and the corresponding DOM.

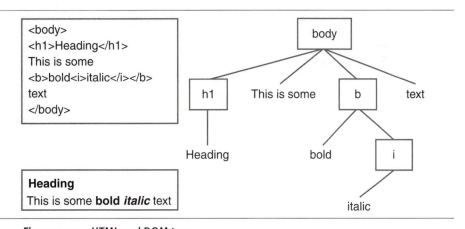

Figure 23.3 – HTML and DOM tree

HTML includes a variety of basic formatting tags for bold and italic, headings of various levels, and control of font and color. Each has a way in which it wants to be drawn. HTML is a mix between the desire to let text be laid out according to its size, length, and the available space while giving the server control over exactly how it appears. The heading tags <h1>, <h2>, and so on simply state that the content is a heading of a specific level and should be rendered appropriately. The <font> tag, however, specifically defines the font to be used and the size of the text. One of the most powerful tags when creating a unique look to a Web page is the image (<img>)

tag. This contains the URL of an image as well as attributes that control the size and placement of the image on the screen. The fact that images can be scaled to various sizes and repetitively tiled across a region allows for the creation of virtually any look to a page.

The general layout of a Web page follows the flowing text strategy where text and other objects are laid out horizontally until there is no more space and then the flow moves to the next line. More sophisticated control is provided by the <table> tag. The table defines a structure of rows and columns with each cell being composed of arbitrary HTML. A table consists of <tr> (table row) tags that each contains <td> (table data) tags for each cell. The width of columns can be defined to layout as the content dictates, a percentage of the width for each column or a fixed width for each column. This provides a wide range of flexible layouts in a relatively simple package. It is closest to the variable intrinsic size layout discussed in Chapter 5. The <div> tag allows separate layouts to appear over the top of others. This is somewhat analogous to overlapping windows.

Interaction

Interaction in HTML was at first primitive. There were only two behaviors: scrolling through pages and clicking on links. One of the great success stories of the Web is that these two interactive behaviors were easy for users to learn, easy for servers to implement, and provided a powerful model for interactively navigating a huge Web of information. The linking mechanism of HTML is based on the *anchor* tag, which is a term derived from hypertext research. Figure 23.4 shows two examples of an anchor tag.

```
<a href="http://my.site.com/here/there/homepage.html">
<a href="wherever/newpage.html">
Link to my home page
</a>
```

Figure 23.4 – Sample anchors

The "href" attribute of the tag identifies the URL to be retrieved when the anchor is selected by the user. The first example shows a complete reference that contains all of the parts of a URL. The second example shows a relative reference. The protocol, site, and path are all omitted. These are retrieved from the URL of the page currently being displayed. The use of relative URLs is essential when creating a collection of pages that should work together. The collection can be put into a folder and the entire folder moved to any location on the Web. Because of relative links, the connections between the files within the folder are not broken. Nonprogrammers, however, frequently misunderstand the correct use of relative links.

Any HTML can appear between the <a href…> and </a>. This content is what the user sees. Selecting any of it causes the browser to follow the anchor's href to a new page. Putting image references into this space creates clickable pictures. However, people soon wanted to create larger images with various spots that could be clicked. The extension was an image map. This simply identified regions of an image with which an anchor was associated. This extends anchors from text to images.

As was shown in Figure 23.2, a URL can contain arguments for a command. Embedding these arguments into an anchor or image map's reference worked but was not really effective. There was no way for the user to specify arguments to the server. The <form> tag was introduced into HTML to satisfy this need.

Figure 23.5 shows the HTML for a simple form that will submit a person's name to a Web server. The form is embedded in normal HTML so that it fits smoothly within the HTML model. The form specification lies between the <form> and </form> tags. User input is provided by the <input> tags. In this example, there are two kinds of input tags: text input and a submit button. The input tags are embedded into normal HTML, which provides the labels and layout.

```
<html>
<h1>Form example</h1>
<form action="http://my.site.edu/personnelApp/enterPerson">
    First Name: <input type="text" name="firstName">
    <p>
    Last Name: <input type="text" name="lastName">
    <p>
    <input type="submit" value="Add Person">
</form>
</html>
```

Figure 23.5 – HTML for a sample form

Figure 23.6 shows what the browser will display for the HTML shown in Figure 23.5. The user has already typed "Dan" into one of the text boxes and "Olsen" into the other text box. There are many attributes that can modify the appearance and behavior of these input tags that we will not discuss here.

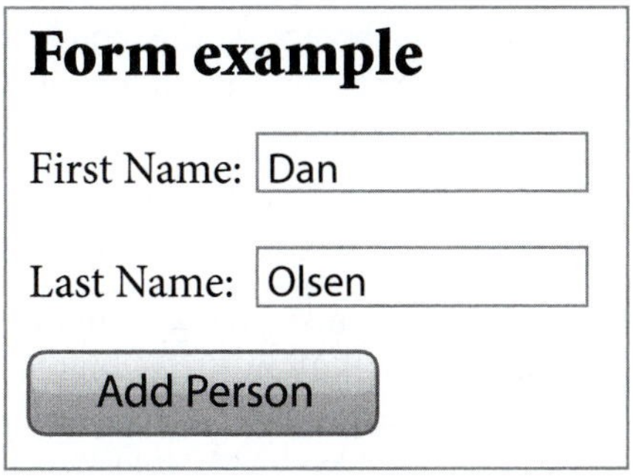

Form example

First Name: Dan

Last Name: Olsen

Add Person

Figure 23.6 – Display of a form

After the user has entered text into the two boxes, the user would then click on the Add Person button. The label for this button was defined by the `value` attribute of the `submit` input object. When a submit button is selected, the browser goes to the `<form>` tag that contains the button and looks for its `action` attribute. This action attribute contains most of the URL that should be retrieved when the form is submitted. The argument part of the URL is formed by using the `name` attribute of each `<input>` tag and whatever value the user has entered for that tag. Given the HTML in Figure 23.5 and the user text shown in Figure 23.6, clicking on the Add Person button will produce the URL shown in Figure 23.7. A complete command URL has been formed from the "action" and from the various input tags found inside the form.

---

http://my.site.edu/personnelApp/enterPerson?firstName=Dan&lastName=Olsen

---

Figure 23.7 – Submitted URL

There are several different types of `<input>` tags, including radio buttons, check boxes, password fields, and text areas. A password field is just a text field where the typed characters are all shown as "*" so that people looking over your shoulder cannot see what was typed. Text areas provide scrolling regions for multiple lines of text. Text areas can get much more data from a user than will fit in a URL. In such situations, the `<form>` can specify that a POST rather than a GET request should be used for the action. A special input type called `hidden` has a name and a value, but does not appear to the user and accepts no input. However, when the action URL is formed, this name and value appear in the arguments. This is one of the ways in which application state information can be embedded in the Web page.

WEB MODEL-VIEW-CONTROLLER

This chapter has skimmed very lightly over the possible facilities of Web browsers and servers. More features are discussed later in this chapter, but most of the information must come from other books. At this point, this chapter has covered enough of the Web architecture so that you can see how it fits with the model-view-controller architecture and how the Web varies from the traditional MVC approach.

Model

The model resides entirely in the server. Within the server, some part of its resource tree is associated with the application. The sample HTML in Figure 23.5 associates "personnelApp" with the application model. When the user clicks "Add Person," the server receives the full URL and extracts "enterPerson?firstName=Dan&lastName=Olsen" as the command that it must process. This would be true using either servlets or CGI.

The first problem for a Web application is to associate the URL with the correct code to process that URL. This is very similar to the event-handling problem of Chapter 3 and can use many of the same solutions. One solution is to create a servlet class for every model command in your application. This is similar to Command objects in Chapter 16. The advantage of this approach is that the Web server handles the command dispatch. The problem is that, like Command objects, the programmer must generate a large number of classes, register them all with the server, and then somehow make sense of them all as they form a complete application.

A second strategy is much like primitive event handling. In a servlet implementation, the code could be structured as shown in Figure 23.8. Each command method receives the request object so that they can retrieve whatever argument values are useful to that command. In a large application, the cascaded if statements can become quite extensive and hard to manage. One approach is to break the application up into meaningful packages with one servlet per package. The if statements then only apply to the commands within each package. Another strategy is to use the fact that only the first part of the path identifies the application. The remainder is still a path and can be used to group commands in meaningful ways. The doGet() method might only sort out the top level and call a method for each one that it finds. Each such method is then responsible for looking further for the actual command implementation.

```
public class PersonnelApp extends Servlet
{
      public void doGet(Request request)
      {    String url = request.getURL();
           String command = extractCommandName(url)
           If (command.equals("enterPerson"))
           {      enterPerson(request); }
           else if (command.equals("deletePerson"))
           {      deletePerson(request); }
           else if (command.equals("findPerson"))
           {      findPerson(request); }
           else
                 . . . . . . .

      }
}
```

Figure 23.8 – Command code binding in a servlet

Another command/code binding model is reflection. You can implement a subclass of Servlet called ReflectServlet that can look at its own Class information to find commands. Each URL command name corresponds to a method name. By creating servlets as subclasses of ReflectServlet, you can give them command methods. When a URL is received by the servlet, the command name is retrieved and used to locate a public method by that name that accepts a Request object as its only argument. That method is then called, passing it the request object. This eliminates the tedious code for binding command names to methods. You should probably use annotation mechanisms (as described in Chapter 9) to label command methods so that hackers cannot use the reflection mechanism to access methods that you did not intend to reveal.

Using servlets or CGI, you can implement a Web application model very much like Chapter 6 with three important differences. In MVC, the model generates change notifications so that various views would update themselves. In the Web architecture we have discussed so far, each model command must generate a complete new view description as its result. The AJAX techniques discussed later in the chapter can improve on this, but given the basic Web architecture, this "new view for every command" is what must be done.

The second difference is that the Web is stateless. The model is not retained between application commands. Some servlet models provide for retained information across a session (a user working with this site at this time) or across a single page, but for the most part the model command gets only its arguments to perform its function. To implement any reasonable application, there must be state preserved between commands. The "hidden" input tags described previously are one technique. These allow the command that generated your current view to store state information in the page where it is returned to the next command as argument values. A second approach is "cookies." These are pieces of information that can be stored with the browser and retrieved at any time in the future. Cookies help to remember things about the user so as to provide better service. They are also notorious for being used to spy on the user.

Finally, there is the file system and/or database. This is the primary form of state shared between commands. Each command stores its changes in the file system or in a database where that information can be retrieved by subsequent commands. This strategy works very well because most Web applications are *read-mostly*. A user interacting with Google or with Google Maps only enters information to help the server find what he or she is looking for. The user never changes Google and only in certain situations will Google add information to the Maps. Shopping sites like Amazon.com are mostly about presenting product information. They implicitly store logs of what users looked at and they do record information when filling a shopping cart or taking orders but mostly they provide information. For the most part, a Web model command does the following:

1. Retrieve arguments from the request

2. Retrieve relevant information from the file system or database

3. Perform the command

4. Save changes (if any) in the file system or database

5. Generate a new view to be returned

The third difference between MVC models and Web models is that Web commands are invoked asynchronously. When the user clicks on Add Person, the Internet might have delays, the server might be clogged, or the message might just fail. To the user, however, nothing has happened. If the user loses patience and clicks on Add Person again, a second request is sent. This might cause two people to be entered as both commands eventually complete. On a shopping site, this might result in two orders being placed for the same thing. Asynchrony and communications failure are important aspects of Web application programming.

View

The view of a Web application is primarily determined by the capabilities of HTML. In servlet and CGI architectures, each command must return the complete new view to be displayed. In the CGI approach, this is accomplished by writing to standard out, which the Web server has connected to the network connection response socket. This is somewhat limited in its ability to report errors and modify header information. The servlet approach provides a `Response` object as a parameter to the `doGet()` and `doPost()` methods. The `Response` object has methods for setting the various forms of information that can appear in a response and also can provide an output stream to which the body of the response is written.

For most Web application commands, the view can be implemented as a method that accepts an output stream and is expected to write HTML to that output stream. The output stream serves the same function as the `Graphics` object parameter on the `paint()` method. Just as the `Graphics` object will render the information from its methods, the browser will render the HTML in a window.

Controller

In a traditional Web application, the controller is completely implemented by the browser. The only possible actions are to scroll and resize the window, follow an anchor or image map link, enter data into one of the `<input>` tag objects, and click on a submit button. By standardizing on these actions, users always know what they can do and deployment of a Web application to a standard browser is quite straightforward.

ENHANCING WEB INTERACTION

The existence of a single browser standard to which many applications can write has enormous power in terms of the kinds of facilities that can be made available. A new Web application can be implemented and delivered without the burden of installing software on the machines of all potential users. A user with a Web browser now has access to millions of services without installing new software. These are great advantages. Two major difficulties with this architecture are latency and interactive style.

Latency

Networks regularly report their bandwidth capacity. Bandwidth is easy to measure for a given physical device and does not vary. Network-based interactive applications are rarely bandwidth limited. Taking all of the pixels in a 1024 $\times$ 1024 screen and shipping them uncompressed takes a maximum of 24M per second. Image compression improves that significantly. X Window's use of drawing calls and distribution of scene graphs generally require less than 100Kbit/sec to deliver a quality interaction. The problem is latency. Latency is the time between the initiation of a message by a sender and the receipt of that message. Latency is introduced primarily by the routers and system software layers that must decide how and where each packet should be sent. Firewalls, junk filters, and other services also introduce network latency. The Web server layers required to launch a CGI program or servlet object and connect it to the network all introduce more latency. For example, dragging a scroll bar up and down only requires a few thousand bits per second of bandwidth to achieve better interactive response than the eye can see. Latency, however, can make that scroll bar feel very sluggish and unresponsive. The only way to reconcile latency and interaction is to (1) perform as much interaction as possible without involving a network round-trip and (2) make network round-trips as asynchronous as possible so that the user is not kept waiting.

Interactive Style

With the need for a standard browser that all Web applications can use, supporting a variety of interactive styles becomes a problem. The <form> and <input> tags provide some additional local interaction. Selection from drop-down lists and editing of scrolling text can all be done in the browser without the network round-trip and, thus, are highly interactive. The introduction of frames allowed Web pages to have various scrolling regions that retrieve pages and work semi-independently.

The fixed set of interactive techniques is fundamentally very limiting. You could add painting widgets, drawing widgets, table widgets, and tree widgets. Such widgets would get increasingly complex with many parameters, descriptors, and other mechanisms for customizing the widget to a particular need. The code base for the browser gets increasingly larger and harder to support. Despite all that is added, there are always new forms of interaction that cannot be supported by the widget set. This is exacerbated by the competitive drive to provide viewers with new Web experiences.

The first strategy to solve the interaction problem is the plug-in. These behave very much like edit-in-place techniques for cut and paste found in OLE (Chapter 15). A plug-in is a separate code library that can register with the browser. In HTML, a screen region can be assigned to the plug-in over which a separate borderless window is laid. The plug-in now has complete interactive control over that window, which appears embedded in the Web page. Being a separate code base, plug-ins do whatever they want. Originally they were designed to play content such as audio, video, 3D animations, or other things that are not built in to HTML. A most notable plug-in is the Java applet. This allows arbitrary Java programs whose code is downloaded as class files to operate within a Web page. In many ways, this solves the interaction problem because the view and controller can now be written in Java and automatically distributed through the Web. This also solves the interactive style problem because now any view/controller combination can be implemented using all of the techniques described in previous chapters. However, there is a problem with download time. Many Java applets can be slow to start because of the time required to download all of the class files for the applet. Caching of class files is a problem because during development they regularly change. All plug-ins have a problem with stepping out of the HTML/Web page interactive paradigm into something completely new. The users might be confused with a nontraditional look and feel embedded in their Web browser. Plug-ins also all require special installation by the user.

JavaScript

The current solution of choice on the Web is based on JavaScript[6]. JavaScript is an interpreted language with syntax like C or Java. It has been implemented in all major browsers (with some variations). It has two key differences from compiled languages in its data model and in how code is created.

JavaScript has the usual primitive data items such as strings and numbers with the usual expressions and functions for manipulating them. Any variable can contain a value of any type; there are no type declarations. A variable is created simply by assigning a value to it. Arrays are created with the syntax "myArray=new Array()". There is no size specified because arrays can grow as needed. The other data structure mechanism is the object. Objects have named fields but the names and number of fields is completely dynamic. Assigning a value to a field of an object will create that field if it did not already exist. This is a highly flexible data model that can represent virtually anything. It does not do system-level bit manipulation but that is not needed for Web interaction.

Code is also created dynamically. Any string can be evaluated as a JavaScript expression. This is very important to event handling. Functions are data objects that can be assigned to values and any value that contains a function can be invoked with parameters. Figure 23.9 shows some sample JavaScript. Lines 1, 2, and 17 are standard HTML for some Web page in which this script is to be used. Lines 3 and 16 specify that the contained region is not HTML but JavaScript code. The function declarations on lines 4 and 11 declare that a function is to be assigned to the variable Room and to the variable squareFeet. Line 14 uses the function Room to create and initialize a new object. Notice that line 9 assigns the function stored in squareFeet as the contents of the sqFt field in the new Room. Line 15 uses sqFt like a method to compute and store the size of the newly created room.

```
1.   <html>
2.   <h1>JavaScript Demo</h1>
3.   <script language="JavaScript">
4.        function Room(name, width, length)
5.        {
6.              this.name=name;
7.              this.width=width;
8.              this.length=length;
9.              this.sqFt=squareFeet;
10.       }
11.       function squareFeet(width,length)
12.       {     return (width*length);
13.       }
14.       room=new Room("living room", 10, 20);
15.       size=room.sqFt();
16.  </script>
17.  </html>
```

Figure 23.9 – Simple JavaScript

The JavaScript in Figure 23.9 has no interactive behavior. Variables are assigned and then nothing happens. The earliest use of JavaScript was to dynamically generate HTML to be displayed by the browser. Figure 23.10 shows a sample JavaScript file.

```
1.    function Room(name, width, length)
2.    {
3.         this.name=name;
4.         this.width=width;
5.         this.length=length;
6.    }
7.    function squareFeet()
8.    {
9.         return (this.width*this.length);
10.   }
11.   Room.prototype.sqFt=squareFeet;
12.   function view()
13.   {
14.        document.write("<p><b>Room</b>: "+this.name);
15.        document.write(" "+this.width+" X "+this.length);
16.        document.write(" sq.ft. "+this.sqFt());
17.   }
18.   Room.prototype.view=view;
```

Figure 23.10 – Declarations in Room.js

Figure 23.10 is a JavaScript file rather than HTML. It contains the same Room function with a few differences. Line 11 attaches the squareFeet() function to sqFt for all Room objects, by assigning it to the prototype that Room objects are built from. The same occurs in line 18. Lines 12–17 define the view() method for rooms. This method uses the document.write() method to dynamically create new HTML that is added to the end of whatever HTML has been processed when this method is invoked. Figure 23.11 shows how your Room.js file can be used to more efficiently generate a presentation for rooms. Line 3 references your Room.js file from Figure 23.10. This is an important technique because Room.js can be cached by the browser rather than reloaded every time you want to display a page with rooms.

```
1.   <html>
2.   <h1>JavaScript Demo</h1>
3.   <script language="JavaScript" src="Room.js"></script>
4.   <script language="JavaScript">
5.        rm=new Room("Living Room", 10, 20);
6.        rm.view();
7.
8.        rm=new Room("Kitchen",10,10);
9.        rm.view();
10.
11.        rm=new Room("Bedroom",7,10);
12.        rm.view();
13.  </script>
14.  </html>
```

Figure 23.11 – Use of Room methods in HTML

Figure 23.11 shows how to use Room() to create new objects and its view() method to generate HTML about those objects. You can define as many different views of a room as desired by creating more methods in Room.js. Your server commands can now use those methods to simplify their view generation and to shorten the size of Web pages so that they download faster. This technique also allows you to change the look of the view by modifying Room.js rather than modifying the server commands. This is not, however, a great restyling solution because the view is still specified in code rather than visually. The resulting display from Figures 23.10 and 23.11 is shown in Figure 23.12.

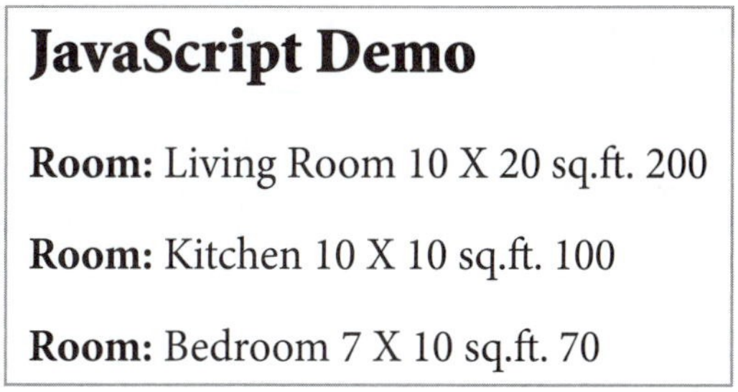

JavaScript Demo

Room: Living Room 10 X 20 sq.ft. 200

Room: Kitchen 10 X 10 sq.ft. 100

Room: Bedroom 7 X 10 sq.ft. 70

Figure 23.12 – Resulting display from JavaScript document.write

JavaScript and the DOM

In Figures 23.10 and 23.11, you used JavaScript to dynamically generate HTML in the browser and, thus, simplify your view generation. This is not yet very interactive. A better solution comes from working directly with the DOM tree. When a browser has entirely parsed the HTML for a page, it creates a DOM tree for presentation (Figure 23.3). After the page is parsed, that DOM tree is placed in JavaScript's document variable. This is the same variable used in lines 14–15 of Figure 23.10. With the DOM as a JavaScript object, you can tour the display tree and make modifications. Any modification made to the DOM tree will be reflected in the display almost immediately. The feature is referred to as DHTML or Dynamic HTML. DHTML coupled with JavaScript gives the power to interactively manipulate the view of an application without requiring a round-trip to the server.

It is possible to access elements of the DOM tree by navigating the tree directly. This can be painful because many of the nodes in the tree are referenced by index. Consider, for example, the HTML and DOM tree in Figure 23.13. Suppose that you have some JavaScript to dynamically change the text input field's value property so that it contains a person's name. Looking at the HTML on the left, you might carefully reconstruct the tree in your mind and deduce that "document[1].value='George';" would be the correct JavaScript to make this change. The DOM tree on the right shows that the browser has inserted a "body" node directly below the "html" node and the JavaScript is, thus, not where expected. This particular DOM tree is quite simple but a real page would be very complex. In addition, while working out the style issues in a page, many nodes will be added, deleted, and moved around, making indexed access to tree elements very brittle.

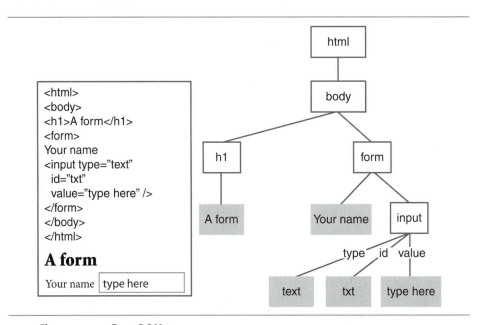

Figure 23.13 – Form DOM tree

A more effective technique is to use the id property. An id can be placed on any HTML tag. In Figure 23.13, the <input> tag has an "id=txt" property. Using this id, the JavaScript "document.**getElementById**('txt').value='George';" will make the desired change. Using ids to reference elements in the DOM tree is much more robust and is used almost exclusively.

Event Handling

You now have JavaScript that can embed code into Web pages and access to the DOM tree so that you can dynamically modify the presentation from JavaScript. The last thing needed is event handling. HTML provides a variety of event-handler attributes that can be attached to virtually any tag node in the DOM. Each type of attribute is associated with some interactive action and they can contain a string. Some of the event attributes are shown in Figure 23.14.

onmousedown	*a mouse button is pressed over the display of this object*
onmouseup	*a mouse button is released over the display of this object*
onmouseover	*a mouse button enters the screen region of this object*
onmouseout	*a mouse button leaves the screen region of this object*
onmousemove	*a mouse move event is received over this object*
onselect	*text has been selected in a text field or text area*
onfocus	*this object just received the key focus*
onblur	*this object just lost key focus*

Figure 23.14 – Some HTML event attributes

Figure 23.15 shows a sample piece of HTML that uses some of these events to add functionality to a Web page. The <script> defines a function that will set the background color for any element for which it receives an id. In this case, rather than use id attributes, you use "this" to pass the actual node itself to the function. The heading "A form" has been set up to turn blue whenever the mouse appears over it and to revert to white when the mouse leaves. The text field has been set up to turn red whenever a user clicks on it.

```
<html>
<script language="JavaScript">
    function setBack(node,color)
    {    node.style.background=color;
    }
</script>
<h1 onmouseover="setBack(this,'blue')"
    onmouseout="setBack(this,'white')">
    A form
</h1>
<form>
Your name
<input type="text"
    color="blue"
    value="type here" onclick="setBack(this,'red')"/>
</form>
</html>
```

Figure 23.15 – Event handlers in HTML

The combination of DHTML that allows instant modifications to the display when the DOM tree is changed, JavaScript to write code, and event-handling properties to create a binding between the DOM and JavaScript form the basis of a great deal of interactive Web programming. Using the DOM tree as the model, whole applications can now be written to run exclusively in the browser. Many effects can be implemented using these techniques. Data can be checked for validity before submission. Images can be changed whenever the mouse goes over them to create better interactive effects.

AJAX

The term AJAX refers to Asynchronous JavaScript And XML. It is not really a tool but a collection of techniques for creating highly interactive Web applications. Given the Web application architecture described so far, three more concepts are required:

- Asynchronous direct access to your model on the server
- A representation of model fragments that can be used in communication with your model
- Better visual representations than document-centric HTML

Asynchronous Server Access

JavaScript, event handlers, and DHTML provide a sufficient mechanism to program a wide range of interactivity directly in the browser. In essence, you have all that you need for a view and a controller implementation. All the notification mechanisms have been eliminated by the single browser view and the automatic redraw offered by DHTML. What is missing is access to the model that is back on the server. Most modern browsers provide JavaScript facilities for contacting a server. The steps are the same for all of them. Figure 23.16 contains some sample JavaScript/HTML for updating the server using the form shown in Figure 23.6.

```
1.    <html>
2.    <h1>Form example</h1>
3.    <script language="JavaScript">
4.    function getHTTPRequest()
5.    {   code to resolve issues with various browser implementations
6.    }
7.    var httpRequest;
8.    var serverURL="http://my.site.edu/personnelApp/enterPerson?";
9.    function findPersonOnServer()
10.   {
11.       var firstName=document.getElementById("fn").value;
12.       firstName=escape(firstName);
13.
14.       var lastName=document.getElementById("ln").value;
15.       lastName=escape(lastName);
16.
17.       httpRequest=getHTTPRequest();
18.       httpRequest.open("GET",
19.          serverURL+"fn="+firstName+"ln="+lastName,true);
20.       httpRequest.onreadystatechange=handleAddPersonResponse;
21.       httpRequest.send(null);
22.   }
23.   function handleAddPersonResponse()
24.   {
25.       if (httpRequest.readyState == 4)
26.       {   var response=httpRequest.responsetext;
27.           code to handle response from server
28.       }
29.   }
30.
31.   </script>
32.   <form>
33.       First Name: <input id="fn" type="text" name="firstName">
34.       <p>
35.       Last Name: <input id="ln" type="text" name="lastName">
36.       <p>
37.       <input type="button" value="Find Person"
38.           onclick="findPersonOnServer()">
39.   </form>
40.   </html>
```

Figure 23.16 – Asynchronous server requests

Lines 32–39 are pretty much the same as in Figure 23.5 except that the submit button is replaced by a normal button that calls findPersonOnServer() whenever it is clicked. Lines 9–22 define this function and demonstrate what is needed to perform a server request. Lines 11–15 retrieve the information from the input fields of the form. You might also verify that both the first and last names have been entered.

Line 17 invokes the getHTTPRequest() function to get a request object and store it in the global variable httpRequest. At the time of this writing, various popular browsers handle the creation of HTTP requests in different ways. Inside the getHTTPRequest() function, line 5 should be replaced by whatever magic incantation is currently required for discovering the type of browser this page is running on and generating a request object in the appropriate way.

Lines 18–19 open the request by specifying "GET" or "POST" and providing the URL for the service to be accessed. The request should be sent asynchronously so that the user is not blocked from doing anything while waiting for the server to respond. This means that when you call the send() method on line 21, it will not wait for an answer from the server. Your code needs to be informed when the server returns with an answer. The function handlePersonResponse() is created and assigned to the request object's onreadystatechange property on line 20. The ready state of the object indicates the progress of the request. Every time this state changes, the handlePersonResponse() function will be called. This function at lines 23–29 checks for the response code that indicates that the request is complete and that the response from the server has been returned. The server's response is found in the request object's responsetext property.

This mechanism for retrieving requests from a server is somewhat cumbersome because you must formulate a URL and deal with asynchrony. Because JavaScript treats functions as special data objects, they can be attached to any object. This gives you a notification mechanism for dealing with asynchrony. There are additional texts on how to handle these server request issues[7].

Response Data

Line 26 of Figure 23.16 retrieves the response text from the request object. You must now address the issue of what should be returned by the server. This directly addresses the relationship between the view/controller on the browser implemented in JavaScript and the model residing on the server. The traditional architecture provides small methods to access all of the pieces of the model. This will not be effective in a Web architecture because there will be too many network requests to maintain interactive speeds. Instead, network requests should return relatively large fragments of the model that can then be manipulated locally on the browser.

A server for the simple application in Figure 23.16 should return all of the relevant information about the named person, or a list of similarly named people, or an error message. This means that simple HTML is not an acceptable response. A common approach is to encode the response in XML (the X in AJAX). Figure 23.17 shows a possible response that describes the requested person. Figure 23.18 shows a possible response that is giving a list of people that might have been intended.

```
<xml>
<person firstName="Fred"
    lastName="Jones"
    age="22"
    homeStreet="1732 Orchard Dr."
    homeCity="Ginsfield"
    homeState="Montana"
    homePhone="892-423-7562"
    />
</xml>
```

Figure 23.17 – XML server response describing a person

```
<xml>
    <alternateNames>
        <person firstName="Fred"
            lastName="Jones"
            homeStreet="1732 Orchard Dr."
            homeCity="Ginsfield"
            homeState="Montana"
            />
        <person firstName="Freda"
            lastName="Jones"
            homeStreet="23 Poinsetta Way"
            homeCity="Poquito"
            homeState="New Mexico"
            />
        <person firstName="Phred"
            lastName="Jensen"
            homeStreet="3345 Apollo Ave."
            homeCity="Athens"
            homeState="Georgia"
            />
    </alternateNames>
</xml>
```

Figure 23.18 – XML server response describing alternate people

Given these possible responses, the usual approach is to parse the XML into a JavaScript object structure. There are several implementations of such parsers and by the time of this reading they may be built in to the browsers. XML has a large standard around it with many encodings and type definitions, which make it somewhat cumbersome. It is also a little painful to parse correctly in its full glory. Because of this, some Web services are starting to encode their response in JSON[2], which is the textual notation for objects in JavaScript. JSON is much less verbose and is trivially parsed by JavaScript.

With the response encoded as a JavaScript object, it is relatively easy to write view code in JavaScript that will translate the model data into an appropriate view or several views of that data. With a model object stored in the browser, many interactions can be performed locally in the browser. In fact, a complete MVC for this application is completely within the browser. Most AJAX implementations do not recognize that with model information in JavaScript objects and most of the interaction in the browser, they need to use MVC techniques in organizing their JavaScript. Consequently the JavaScript is quite entangled. The following architectural points will help.

1. The model needs to be clearly defined and it must be accessed strictly through methods. The access methods need to perform validity checking, notify views of updates and notify the server of important changes.

2. The view needs to be encapsulated in view update methods that translate model objects into appropriate HTML to reflect the view. These should not be buried in event handlers (controller implementation).

3. Asynchronous responses from the server should be treated as events and should access to the model in a similar fashion as other event handlers so that view updates are handled correctly.

Visual Representations

Getting visual representations that go beyond simple text layout is important to the creation of highly interactive Web applications. Unfortunately, this is where the HTML model starts to break down. The approaches supported by current browsers are adaptations of existing facilities rather than really clean designs. The design of HTML and its facilities are being bent rather severely to get them to do things they were never designed to do. However, there is still great value in the server/browser model for distributing applications and the result can be very effective despite the awkwardness.

The first approach for creating striking visual appearance is the use of image fragments. Images can represent anything and piecing them together can create many very nice effects. The use of images to create borders, buttons, and other effects led to a need to more accurately control position of items on the screen. The first step is the addition of the <div> or division tag that encapsulates a complete HTML fragment as an independent entity. The <div> can be given an id and modified independently from other HTML on the page. Within the style attribute of the <div>, you can specify the position on the page for the <div> tag and the Z order or order in which various <div> tags should be painted. The style attribute has its own language for specifying various property values. However, these properties appear in the DOM tree under the style property where they are easily accessed by JavaScript.

These features allow the creation of a great many interesting visual effects. Figure 23.19 shows Google Maps exploiting these image techniques. The map itself is a series of images positioned so that they are adjacent to each other to form the complete map. The user can drag these images around the screen to make the map move. This is implemented by JavaScript changing the position attributes of the map images in coordination with the mouse position. The buttons on the top are images with some transparent pixels that have been positioned in their own <div> so that they "float"

above the map. The pan/zoom control on the left is also composed of images in a
<div>. The little scroll marker to indicate zoom is its own object whose position can
be changed by JavaScript. The combination of images, transparency, and JavaScript
control of position provides for a wide variety of interactive techniques.

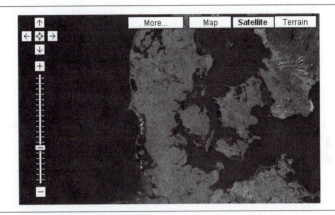

Figure 23.19 – Compositing images in HTML

Though images can represent anything visual, they have interactive limitations.
As discussed in Chapter 2, the stroke and region models provide more interactive flexibility. HTML, however, does not support either stroke or region drawing models. To
resolve this, the SVG[8] (Scalable Vector Graphics) model was developed to encode arbitrary drawing within an XML encoding. This should allow vector graphics to be
embedded in HTML and the DOM tree where it can support interaction through
JavaScript. The problem is that the standards committee designed a very large and
complex standard that, as of this writing, is not implemented in many browsers. The
XAML standard used in Microsoft's Silverlight and JavaFX both provide similar stroke
and region graphics models.

TOOLS

Like many good things, HTML started out small and simple. As the power of the
server/URL/HTTP/HTML model was recognized, increasingly complex systems were
developed in HTML. Where there is complexity there is always a need for tools. Just
as there are IDEs for traditional applications, there are tools for interactively designing
HTML. The same problems in IDEs are found in HTML editors. In addition, underlying HTML representation is open for direct editing by the programmer. The interactive tool must adapt to changes made to the HTML by editors outside of the tool. This
includes adjusting itself to errors that might have been introduced into the HTML.
This is a piece of complexity that most IDEs do not have.

Styling

Because of the size of a Web site and its need for a consistent look, the question of style arises. An entire Web site should share a style in terms of color choices, fonts, icons, and so on. Encoding the common style in every page of a large Web site led to a maintenance nightmare. In Java or C#, you can encapsulate common behavior in classes and functions. No such facilities exist in HTML. The answer was CSS[9] (Cascading Style Sheets). The style property on most HTML tags has many attributes such as color, size, font, position, border width, and so on. The first goal was to control the inheritance of most of these so that they need not be specified on every tag. The next technique was to add a `class` property to every tag. The class property is just a name that specifies the kind of style to be used with this tag. In CSS, there are rules that use tag type and class name to decide what attributes should be applied. Classes can inherit attributes from other classes. CSS provides a mechanism for collecting attributes together where they can be managed and maintained. The interpretation of the style rules is embedded into the browser.

Another approach is to automate the generation of HTML on the server side. The servlets can do this because they are arbitrary code and can be maintained just as other code is maintained. The Web page model leads programmers to want to program mostly in HTML with code inserted only where necessary. PHP[10] is representative of many such tools. PHP processes HTML pages before they are sent out by the server looking for <?php tags.

```
<?php
    PHP processing code goes here.
?>
```

The processor evaluates the code between the tags as PHP code that will dynamically output HTML that is programmatically generated. PHP focuses mostly on retrieving information from databases and formatting that information into HTML. In many respects, this functions like the `<script>` tag in HTML except that it is executed by the server rather than in the browser and it has direct access to the model data. Unlike a general-purpose programming language, PHP focuses its efforts on string processing because its primary output is HTML. Other server-side tools include Microsoft's ASP.NET[11] and Ruby on Rails[12]. All focus on embedding code into HTML that is then evaluated by the server to generate the actual HTML to be sent.

BEYOND THE WEB

Most Web browsers provide the concept of the plug-in. A plug-in is generally a piece of code that behaves much like OLE (Chapter 15) in that it allows for viewing and editing of information formats not supported directly by the browser. The browser essentially creates a window to overlay the desired portion of the Web page and then passes that window, along with the foreign information to the plug-in. One of the earliest plug-ins was Java Applets, which allow arbitrary Java applications to be embedded in Web pages. More recently, Flash has become a very important plug-in. The advantage of Flash is that it incorporates an animation and interaction model that allows for more sophisticated interactive behaviors to be downloaded in the plug-in.

A problem with plug-ins is that they are code that must be downloaded and installed by every user before interaction is possible. This is the problem that the Web helped solve. Plug-ins have two differences from the old installed application model. The first is that browsers provide JavaScript functionality to determine if a particular plug-in is installed. If it has not been installed, the creator of the plug-in can provide JavaScript behavior to help the user get it installed. In addition, the Web provides the file download mechanism that brings the software to the user. Plug-ins do require an installation, but the Web supports simplification of that process. Plug-ins like Flash, Java, and Adobe Acrobat provide such power that almost every browser has them downloaded and installed.

The success of AJAX techniques and its scene-graph approach to drawing on the screen has inspired other techniques for interacting over the Internet. XAML[13] (eXtensible Application Markup Language) is designed as a markup language like HTML only based on Microsoft's .NET drawing model rather than on text. Rather than JavaScript, the language binding is to the .NET languages such as C#. XAML goes beyond SVG in supporting 3D graphics and embedded video playing. XML is used to specify the scene graph for drawing. The .NET languages and in particular C# are class-based languages unlike JavaScript. The XAML notation directly creates objects that can be manipulated by C# and other .NET languages. Modifications to the XAML tree are instantly redrawn similar to the HTML DOM. There is also a XAML Browser Application that performs in a similar fashion to Web browsers except that the presentation model is graphics and video rather than documents.

JavaFX[14] is an approach similar to XAML, yet based on the Java environment rather than .NET. Its notation is distinctly different from XML. Rather than stick to the syntax of document markup languages, JavaFX looks more like JSON with a notation specifically geared toward representation of object trees. Like XAML, it has a direct connection between the notation and the language's object model.

It is clear that new models for describing interaction over the Internet are coming. It is also clear that those models will be based more on drawing models than document models. It is not yet clear what form they will ultimately take.

SUMMARY

Many of the concepts found in other interactive architectures are also found in WWW interaction. However, there are also many differences. The combination of URLs and HTTP provides a generic mechanism for getting information from the model of an application, which resides on a server. One of the powers of the WWW architecture is that the implementation of the server/model information can be quite distinct from the view and the interaction.

The simple, forms-based interaction of HTML is relatively easy to program and quite restricted in what can be done. The introduction of Java and JavaScript into browsers allowed us to distribute code to a remote view. This improves the latency of the interaction but seriously complicates the interconnection between the view on a client and the model on a server. The notifications between controller and model and between model and view are now asynchronous with possibly large delays that must be addressed.

EXERCISES

1. Implement a Web application that will accept the first and last names of people and add them to a list maintained by a Web server. The list of all names should be presented in HTML at the bottom of the page. Set anchor tags around the names so that clicking on a time will request the server to remove the name from the list.

2. Use JavaScript and `<div>` tags to implement an application that will drag images of barnyard animals around a barnyard image.

END NOTES

[1] Benz, B., and J. Durant. *XML Programming Bible*. Hoboken, NJ: Wiley, 2003.

[2] http://www.json.org/

[3] http://www.w3.org/

[4] Seely, S., and K. Sharkey. *SOAP: Cross Platform Web Services Development Using XML*. Upper Saddle River, NJ: Pearson Education, 2001.

[5] Newcomer, E. *Understanding Web Services: XML, WSDL, SOAP, and UDDI*. Upper Saddle River, NJ: Addison-Wesley, 2002.

[6] Flanagan, D. *JavaScript: The Definitive Guide*. Cambridge, MA: O'Reilly Media, 2006.

[7] Gehtland, J., B. Galbraith, and D. Almaer. *Pragmatic Ajax*. Lewisville, TX: Pragmatic Programmers, LLC., 2006.

[8] Cagle, K. *SVG Programming: The Graphical Web*. Berkeley, CA: Apress, 2002.

[9] Meyer, E. *CSS: The Definitive Guide*. Cambridge, MA: O'Reilly Media, 2006.

[10] Sklar, D. *Learning PHP 5*. Cambridge, MA: O'Reilly Media, 2004.

[11] Gibbs, M., and D. Wahlin. *Professional ASP.NET 2.0 AJAX*. Hoboken, NJ: Wrox, 2007.

[12] Black, D. *Ruby for Rails: Ruby Techniques for Rails Developers*. Greenwich, CT: Manning Publications, 2006.

[13] Nathan, A. *Windows Presentation Foundation Unleashed*. Upper Saddle River, NJ: Sams, 2006.

[14] http://www.sun.com/javafx/

CHAPTER 24

Physical Interaction

Most of this book has focused on interaction on a screen. However, much of the living, working, and playing in this world does not occur at a desk or in front of a screen. Computing also needs to be available off the desktop where people live their lives. This is part of Mark Weiser's vision of *ubiquitous computing*[1]. When watching television, a viewer might want to raise or lower the sound with a wave of their hand. By touching a certain spot on their nightstand, they might want to lower the lights. Monitoring a baby or an elderly parent must frequently occur when the caregiver is doing other things. Someone eating dinner might want to see an incoming message without having to get up and go to their computer. A mechanic might need to review repair manuals while her hands are tucked into the engine of a car. These are examples of the ways in which people might want to interact with information and computing from physical settings that are not at a desk. If computing is going to penetrate into much of the rest of your life, you want it to be polite and to not interrupt. These are the kinds of challenges addressed in this chapter.

In moving out into the physical world, you need to revisit the model-view-controller architecture, as shown in Figure 24.1. In the physical world where people are not necessarily working, the information about the user interface is broadcast into physical space rather than presented on a focused screen. You must take into account how the information will make its way into the physical world and how the user might understand it.

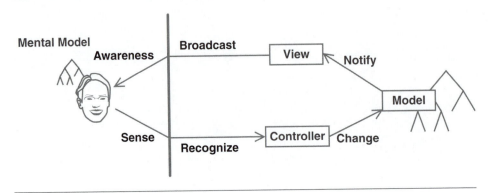

Figure 24.1 – Physical world model-view-controller

One problem that must be addressed in physical interaction is information aware-ness. If the user is not aware of the information being presented, there is no interac-tion. However, if the user does not want to interact right now, a system that demands awareness becomes annoying and will be turned off. Broadcasting of information also involves privacy and politeness issues. People are frequently not alone. Information that others should not see should not be broadcast. Information that others do not want to know can be annoying to them. People who talk loudly to their cell phones in public are generally considered rude. Computers that constantly flash public messages are similarly rude.

Presentation of information in the physical world must first have a channel for communication. The limitations of humans dictate that this channel must be visual, audio, or, to a limited extent, touch. Broadcast of visual information can violate pri-vacy, but if the images are not moving, a lot of the information can be ignored by those who are not interested. For example, stock information projected on a wall can be ignored until someone wants to know. However, if that information is changing very rapidly, it is hard to ignore because of the way your vision system works. Visual information requires the user's attention in order to communicate. The management of awareness and interruptability is key to visual display. There is a fine line between a technology that forces attention when necessary and one that fades into the back-ground until needed by the user.

Interactivity requires that user input and displayed information must be cali-brated to each other. This is more difficult in the physical world than on a screen. Audio allows a user to receive information without paying direct attention. However, audio is very difficult to ignore and has low bandwidth. Broadcasting of audio into a shared space can be very distracting. Tactile information is limited to awareness tasks such as the vibrating of a cell phone.

The largest challenge when interacting in the physical world is sensing what the user is doing and what the user wants done. The user's interactive expressions of intent should not be encumbered by too many devices and be as natural as possible within the user's environment. Avoiding encumbrance poses a sensing problem. You need devices and sensing techniques that fit into the user's environment without making people feel like they have been "instrumented." Naturalness poses the problem of ambiguity. If the gesture is natural to the user, it might be accidentally expressed and inadvertently interpreted by the computer.

Fitting interactive computing into the lives of people poses challenging usability problems. This chapter, however, focuses on the technologies that are available. First, the techniques for presenting information and managing user's awareness are discussed. This includes techniques for detecting when a user can be politely interrupted by new information. Second is an extensive discussion of the technologies and software for sensing what the user is doing and the user's intent. These techniques rely heavily on the machine learning algorithms in Appendix A3. The machine learning algorithms have been placed in the appendix so that readers familiar with them can proceed directly to the physical interaction problems. It is strongly recommended that readers unfamiliar with machine learning read Appendix A3 first.

CONTROLLING LIGHT AND ATTENTION DEMANDS

Hiroshi Ishii introduced the concept of the I/O bulb[2]. The idea is to replace lightbulbs with a digital projector/camera combination. Camera interaction is discussed later in this chapter. What his arguments bring forward is the concept of every physical surface becoming a display and the ability to sense every activity within a space. His approach focuses on projectors and cameras but there are other means for such a pervasive interaction. This chapter uses pervasive display and pervasive sensing as organizing principles for discussing physical interaction.

Projecting Light

The concept of replacing every lightbulb with a projector is an interesting one. Not only can the projector provide normal illumination, but it can also control that illumination in interesting ways to enhance the living/working experience. For your purposes, the projector allows you to present information to the user. Projecting information into a room involves five basic problems. The first is to get enough brightness and contrast so that the information is visible. The problem is that room illumination varies widely and the illumination suitable for comfortable living tends to wash out many projectors. To overcome this, projectors are sold with very high brightness.

Projector brightness is the second problem. Very bright lights generate lots of heat, which must be dissipated. Heat leads to noisy fans. Mitsubishi has introduced a fanless projector using LEDs for the light, but the brightness is not very high. In addition, accidentally looking into a very bright light can be painful. This "sun spot" problem from inadvertently looking into a projector can be addressed by shining down from the ceiling. People rarely look straight up.

The third problem is projector/surface placement. Traditionally, a projector is placed perpendicular to a very flat, specially prepared screen. This works fine for conference rooms but not so fine for use in the general environment. People want their walls where they want them and want the projectors to be unobtrusive. The

Office of the Future[3] project created techniques for sampling the environment and then warping the projected images so that they appeared correct on any light-reflective surface. The problem with their system was that the current position of the user's eyes must be known to correctly compensate for the irregularities of the surface. Instrumenting the user's head seems a little intrusive. GVU-PROCAMS[4] assumes that the projection surface is flat and then provides algorithms to compensate for the distortion caused by a projector that is not perpendicular to the surface.

The fourth problem is user shadowing. If the user is going to live or work in the same environment as the projected information, the user will occlude the projector. This is increasingly likely as the user gets closer to the projection surface. One solution is to project from behind the surface, as with many large-screen televisions. This has the twofold problem of requiring additional space for the projector/mirror and a special translucent surface for projection. Rear-projection surfaces are frequently not robust working surfaces. GVU-PROCAMS uses multiple projectors from oblique angles to eliminate shadowing (Figure 24.2). This is the same as using multiple lights in a workspace to eliminate shadows. Perhaps if Ishii's vision of the cheap I/O bulb becomes a reality, a ceiling might have many small projectors to resolve shadowing. The use of many overlapping projectors might also solve the brightness problem.

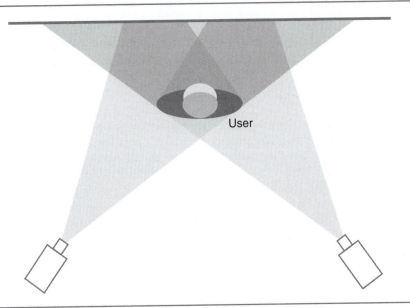

Figure 24.2 – Multiple projectors to eliminate shadowing

The shadowing problem can be mitigated using recently developed short-throw projectors from NEC. A short-throw projector uses a specially machined mirror instead of a lens. This allows for projection at an oblique angle without distortion of the image. For example, an image that is 84 inches across only requires that the projector be 24 inches from the display surface. As shown in Figure 24.3, the user only shadows the display when they are very close. There is also less likelihood that the user will inadvertently look into the projector when it is directly overhead. The heat and fan problems still exist but the occlusion problems are sharply reduced.

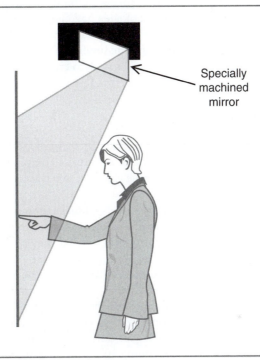

Figure 24.3 – Short-throw projection

The fifth problem is the necessary display size and resolution. The eye does not really have a pixels-per-inch resolution. The resolution of the eye is in *degrees of visual arc*. A readable piece of text needs to be about 0.7 degrees high and at least 10 pixels. The degrees of height relate to the resolution of the retina and the pixel height relates to clear presentation of the text. The actual pixels-per-inch resolution required depends upon the viewing distance. A good rule of thumb for text height is 0.008 times the distance to the screen. When presenting in a physical environment where users are moving around, the viewing distance varies and, thus, the size of displayed objects must vary to maintain the same height in visual arc. There are really only two choices in high-movement situations. The first is to pick an average viewing distance and the second is to track the position of the user.

Luminous Surfaces

The preceding section focused on projection as a means for implementing a pervasive display. However, recent advances in liquid crystal displays (LCDs) and organic light-emitting diodes (OLEDs) have opened an alternative to projection as the mechanism for introducing digitally controlled light into a space. Given a flat lighting technology, it is possible to sidestep many of the occlusion problems discussed with projectors. Each of these technologies also used much less power and does not have the heat dissipation problems. There are still problems with producing such displays with very large dimensions. Most large displays are built by tiling together several displays and existing LCD and OLED technologies have large seams between tiles that are not as evident with projector-based techniques. However, the future might lie with one of these technologies supporting large luminous surfaces that can be inexpensively distributed around work and living spaces to create digitally controlled light.

POLITE PRESENTATION

One of the complaints about computing technology is that it is so intrusive. When moving into the physical world, you want computers that behave more politely. Researchers have addressed these issues in two ways: (1) ambient displays and (2) user interruptability.

An ambient display is one that is readily ignored but can be perceived peripherally. This is similar to a mother monitoring the children in the other room by the noise they make. She is not really listening to what they say, but becomes aware when crying starts or a period of dead silence occurs. Ambient displays can take a variety of physical forms and are not necessarily images. The Live Wire[5] is just a plastic cord attached to an electric motor. The motor speed is controlled by the amount of traffic on a network. As the traffic grows, the motor goes faster, causing the cord to whip around. The cord allows operators to be aware of the traffic without paying direct attention to it. If the network goes down, operators are immediately aware of the fact even though they were not paying attention. A similar technique is to control the rate of water dripping into a pool. The reflection off the water is projected onto the ceiling where the value being presented is seen peripherally as expanding ripples of water. The Bubble Wall[6] presents information by inserting bubbles into columns of water. Because bubbles rise slowly, it is possible to time the bubble generation so that images can be displayed in the rising bubbles. Ambient displays have become the subject of many art installations where information is presented in ways that integrate naturally into the environment.

An interesting variant on the ambient display are the "glance displays" designed by Vertegaal[7]. The idea is that the display only becomes active or generates foreground information when the user is actually looking at it. "Glance" detection exploits the fact that the retina is highly retroreflective in infrared. An infrared camera is surrounded by infrared LEDs. When the user looks at the object on which the camera is mounted, the light from the LEDs is reflected straight back to the camera. In the camera image, the eyes appear as two glowing spots, but only when the eyes are actually looking in the direction of the camera.

Another way to adapt the display of information to the user's life is to understand the interruptability of the user. Polite people do this automatically by checking to see whether someone is busy and only interrupting when something is very important or the other individual appears available. A polite computer would also only interrupt when appropriate. The problem is to provide the computer with a way to determine when it is appropriate to interrupt the user. Fogarty and Hudson, et al[8] performed an experiment to see when it is appropriate to interrupt. They placed cameras in the offices of four subjects and captured everything that was going on for a total of 600+ hours. During this period, the capture hardware would randomly ask the user how interruptible they were on a scale of 1–5. This happened approximately twice per hour. In addition, 40 other people viewed the video and made independent judgments about interruptibility. This annotated the video with evaluations of when the subject could be reasonably interrupted.

Evaluation staff were then assigned to view video segments and carefully code when various activities occurred. Examples of such activities are as follows:

- Is there a guest in the room?

- Are they talking?

- Is the occupant writing or working at the computer?

- Is the door open or closed?

- Is the occupant reading or on the phone?

These coded annotations were intended to simulate a possible sensor that a computer could use to detect interruptibility. The authors then built a machine learning model that could predict interruptibility from the simulated sensors. The surprising result was that interruptibility could be detected 76 percent of the time just by sensing whether anyone was talking. A presentation system that only interrupts when nobody is speaking would be much more polite than current systems.

SENSING THE USER AND THE WORLD

For a system to be polite or for the user to respond to information being presented, you must have mechanisms for sensing what the user is doing and the world around them so that the computer can respond appropriately. Given an appropriate presentation system, the more difficult problem is to sense what is going on in the world and what the user wants the computer to do. You have already seen glance and speech sensors. There are many others. Throughout this chapter, you will follow the general approach of

- Identifying a set of sensors

- Identifying a set of interesting features that you can extract from the sensors

- Identifying the input tokens that you want your controller to receive

- Mapping sensor features to input tokens using machine learning techniques

In this process, the most difficult challenge is identifying a set of useful features that can be extracted from a given sensor. From there, common machine learning techniques generally take care of the rest. The most common cause for the failure of this development strategy is an inadequate feature set that cannot capture the problem. For this reason, much of the discussion in this chapter focuses on possible features and how to compute them.

One of the most powerful sensors for observing the world is the camera. With the advent of CMOS cameras, this sensor has become relatively cheap. Cameras are frequently less obtrusive than other sensors because users generally do not wear anything special and natural objects can be used as input devices. Camera sensor software can be reconfigured so that they can detect many kinds of things. However, cameras do have some disadvantages. One of the most important is privacy. People are uncomfortable having many parts of their lives watched by a digital camera. A second issue is occlusion where people and things get between the camera and the sensing target. Lastly, visible light cameras do not work in the dark.

Image Processing Fundamentals

Before reviewing many of the types of interactive techniques that have been built around cameras, it is useful to present some fundamentals of image processing. For interactive work, you can ignore many of the concepts of image processing. On the other hand, interactive techniques impose rather stringent restrictions on time. For a technique to feel interactive, you must be able to process an image and draw a conclusion within 200 milliseconds. This falls within the saccade of the eye, as described in Chapter 8. That is very quick for many image processing techniques. Throughout this discussion, you will rely heavily on the point algorithms in Appendix A1.3 and the machine learning algorithms in Appendix A3.

Interactive Detection Requirements

Interactive use of cameras generally boils down to three questions:

- Is target T found in region R of the camera image? The region of the image might be the whole image or just a small portion. Are the user's hands on the keyboard? Is there a user in the room? Is the telephone on or off of the hook? Did the user just touch the printer? You might use a toy elf to indicate where your output should go. Therefore, you would want to detect when the "output elf" is placed on the printer. These all involve looking at the pixels in some region of the image (keyboard, phone, printer, screen, projector, or room) and deciding whether the target (user, hands, finger, phone handset, or "output elf") is present. Targets can be people, body parts, or physical objects being moved by the user.

- At what locations (x,y) is target T found in the image? These are tracking questions. Where are the user's hands? Where on the desk are the user's fingers? Where is the user standing in the room? Where is the cell phone that the user is holding? The problem is simpler with only one target. However, there are many cases with multiple targets (two people, 10 fingers, multiple telephones).

- Is movement occurring and if so, in what direction? People frequently interact by movement. You want something to happen when things change and in the physical world change is movement. You might want to know if the user is waving and if so, is he or she waving up and down or side to side?

The remainder of this section discusses a variety of useful features that can be drawn from images and then used to find or track objects in the physical world. Many of the terms here are the same as found in the image processing literature but they are presented here as fast and somewhat "dirty" approximations. In the interactive world, speed is everything and you frequently sacrifice mathematical accuracy to get it.

Pixel Features

Because most of your techniques involve machine learning, you need techniques for extracting features from images. With a vector of features, you can then apply a machine learning algorithm to get the interactive answer that you need. The simplest feature is a grayscale pixel with a value between 0 and 255 or between 0.0 and 1.0. A single gray pixel is generally not very interesting because you cannot detect anything from it. However, even simple pixel features have a number of issues that must be addressed.

Noise and History Blending

For a gray pixel, there is the problem of noise. Many camera sensors will not report the same value for a pixel from frame to frame even though the sensed image has not changed. The extent of this noise varies from camera to camera. The most common solution to this noise is to average the pixel value over f frames. The problem with this average is that you must store f frames and with each new image I_i you throw the image I_{i-f} away and add the new frame I_i to your history. You must also sum up each of the f values for each pixel and divide by f to get the desired average. As f increases, the space required and the computation required at each pixel grows. This is a problem for an interactive system where speed is critical.

Instead of averages, you use the history blend image $H(i,f)$. This is calculated as:

$$H(i, f) = \frac{1}{f} I_i + \left(1 - \frac{1}{f}\right) H(i - 1, f)$$

The history image at frame i is a blend of the current frame image and the previous history image. The contribution of the current frame I_i is still $1/f$ as in the average, but the remaining value comes from the previous history blend. The result is not a true average of f frames but can behave very much like one and with less computation and much less storage. The influence of previous frames falls off exponentially as they become distant in time. Much camera noise can be eliminated by using $H(i,2)$ rather than I_i.

Color and Lighting

Many targets can discriminate based on color. This is a very common technique for detecting skin. (However, it works poorly for very dark skin.) Color is also used for detecting specifically encoded objects in the image. For example, the end of a baton might be painted bright red so that it is very easy to track, provided nobody wears a bright red shirt. Simple color detection uses RGB as the three features.

One of the problems that can arise with pixel features is lighting changes. For example, if a cloud moves in front of the sun, the brightness of everything is diminished. This makes the R, G, and B values for a given pixel quite different even though the object being viewed has not changed. This is frequently resolved by converting

RGB to HSV and throwing away V. Because the value is the brightness, that is the component that will change the most in the presence of lighting changes. Hue and saturation can be very robust features. The RGB to HSV conversion algorithm is found in Appendix A4.1. A final technique is to use all of RGB and HSV with a learning algorithm that selects relevant features (forms of Naïve Bayes, some linear approaches, and decision trees). The learning algorithm keeps what actually works. The caveat is that the training data must include a wide sample of actual usage cases, not just the obvious ones.

An interactive camera system can use infrared light. The first reason is that it is invisible to the user. An infrared light can illuminate a dark scene without disclosing its presence in normal use. Infrared cameras can view a scene without being deceived by RGB light being projected into the scene. Living objects, like people, are generally brighter in infrared than furniture or books. The human retina is highly reflective of infrared light. Cheap CMOS cameras are actually quite sensitive to infrared and must be filtered to work correctly in RGB. Note that sunlight contains lots of infrared and can wash out the image, making it useless.

Edges

The human visual system does most of its interpretation of objects by looking at edges. This is why you can identify a person from a line drawing as well as from a picture. Edge features have the property of being relatively impervious to changes in lighting. Given a pixel at $I(x,y)$, you can measure its "edginess" by the formula:

$$E(x,y) = (I(x+1,y) - I(x,y))^2 + (I(x,y+1) - I(x,y))^2$$

This is actually the square of the magnitude of a gradient vector $G(x,y)$, whose formula is:

$$G(x,y) = [(I(x+1,y) - I(x,y)) \quad (I(x,y+1) - I(x,y))]$$

The gradient vector $G(x,y)$ is an estimate of the normal vector of an edge passing through $I(x,y)$. The gradient vector or its $E(x,y)$ replacement will be used in some shape features.

Region Features

It is rare, in interactive use, that a single pixel is of interest. You usually want features that cover a region of the image. The problem with region features is that their computational cost is not constant as with pixel features. Generally, the cost of a region feature is linear in the number of pixels in the region. Another reason to consider whole regions is you might want to use a "skim and focus" technique to speed the interactive response time of your system. You first want to skim across an image with rather coarse region-based features to find likely places for more focused computing. For the skimming step, you need very efficient region features that can be used to discard areas that are obviously irrelevant to your task.

For example, if you are looking for faces, you can first train a classifier to look for skin using 10 × 10 region features. With this technique, you need only look at every fifth pixel in x and y and, thus, look at $1/25^{th}$ the number of pixels. When you find a region that shows "skin," you can then use pixel-level features to work out whether it is a face or some other skin. This "skim and focus" technique is a very important speedup when using images for interaction.

One very effective tool is the integral image[9]. Integral images impose a onetime cost on the entire image and then provide access to information about arbitrary sized regions in constant time. The definition of an integral image *INT(x,y)* is the sum of all of the pixels above and to the left of *I(x,y)*.

$$INT(x,y) = \sum_{i \leq x} \sum_{j \leq y} I(i,j)$$

This integral can be computed in linear time starting at the upper-left pixel and proceeding left to right, top to bottom. By proceeding in this order, previous integrals will have already been computed and can be used efficiently.

$$INT(x,y) = I(x,y) + INT(x,y-1) + INT(x-1,y) - INT(x-1,y-1)$$

The final subtraction term is essential because those pixels will have been summed twice from the previous two terms.

Once you have the integral image, you can calculate the sum of any rectangular region in constant time, as shown in Figure 24.4. Given a rectangular region whose lower-right corner is at *(x,y)* with a width of *W* pixels and a height of *H*, you can compute the sum of the pixels in the rectangle as:

$$SUM(x,y,W,H) = \frac{INT(x,y) - INT(x-W,y) - INT(x,y-H)}{+ \quad INT(x-W,y-H)}$$

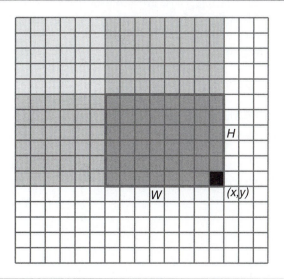

Figure 24.4 – Integral images

A more useful value than the sum is the average (sum / area). Using the average function and an integral image, you can use rectangles of various sizes to compute composite features, such as shown in Figure 24.5.

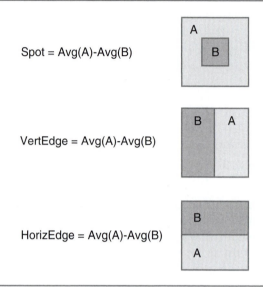

Spot = Avg(A)-Avg(B)

VertEdge = Avg(A)-Avg(B)

HorizEdge = Avg(A)-Avg(B)

Figure 24.5 – Composite features from integral images

A Spot feature can help isolate a hand, a face, or a colored marker from a contrasting background. This would help find laser pointer spots, as discussed later in this chapter. The VertEdge and HorizEdge features can help you find the direction a rod or arm might be pointing. These are also useful in discovering large edge regions within an image such as those used in orientation histograms.

Other integral images can be formed using different base functions to be summed. For example, you can integrate the squares of the pixel values using the formula:

$$INT2(x,y) = I(x,y)^2 + INT2(x, y-1) + INT2(x-1, y) - INT2(x-1, y-1)$$

Using the *INT2* integral image, you can compute the sum of the squares of any rectangular region as:

$$SUM2(x,y,W,H) = \begin{array}{c} INT2(x,y) - INT2(x-W,y) - INT2(x,y-H) \\ + \\ INT2(x-W, y-H) \end{array}$$

With the *INT* and *INT2* images precomputed, you can compute the standard deviation of any rectangular area in constant time using the formula:

$$STDV(x,y,W,H) = \sqrt{\frac{SUM2(x,y,W,H)}{W \cdot H} - \left(\frac{SUM(x,y,W,H)}{W \cdot H}\right)^2}$$

The STDV integral image can help you separate bland areas from regions with lots of variation in the image. You can also measure the amount of "texture" in a rectangular region using the edge function *E(x,y)* to form an "edginess" integral image *INTE*.

$$INTE(x,y) = E(x,y) + INTE(x,y-1) + INTE(x-1,y) - INTE(x-1,y-1)$$

These various forms of integral images provide many different features for many different sized regions for a relatively cheap cost. The recognition or tracking problem can then be handled by a machine learning algorithm.

Shape Recognition

In many cases, it is shape information that identifies the item that you are looking for. The simplest shape technique is *template matching*. This is essentially a nearest neighbor classifier technique (Appendix A3.1c). You take a sample of what you are looking for and compare it with all possible pixel positions in the image looking for the closest match or the set of matches that are closer than some threshold. It is most common to use a rectangular region for the comparisons. Essentially, you are transforming each pixel in the region into a feature in a feature vector (Appendix A3.1). You then use some distance metric to compare your template's features against the sample region of the image. The cosine distance (Appendix A1.1e) is a good choice. The normalization step in the cosine distance tends to diminish the differences due to lighting.

There are two major problems with template matching. The first is that it tends to fail in the presence of rotation. For example, Figure 24.6 shows an image of a finger on the left with a finger search template on the right. The template will never match the finger even though they are both drawn from the same finger image. The only general solution is to use many templates each at a different rotation angle.

Figure 24.6 – Finger with finger search template

The second problem with template matching is the cost of the match. The image fragment and template in Figure 24.6 are each 80 × 80 or 6400 pixels. This makes each match very expensive and it must be applied at every pixel in the image. This match cost can be improved using region features and the "skim and focus" technique described previously.

A third problem with template matching is occlusion. In a cluttered environment, the shape of an object might be obscured by other objects next to it or on top of it. The shape is now slightly different from the template.

A second shape technique is the use of image moments[10]. An image is first converted to gray scale where the shapes you are trying to identify are light and the background is dark. Using image moments, you can compute a variety of features, including the center of mass of the object, its width, height, rotation angle, and many other features. See Appendix 1.3b for details on image moments.

A third shape feature technique is the *orientation histogram*[10]. This technique looks exclusively at edges because they are robust relative to lighting changes and also capture simple information about object shape. For each pixel *(x,y)*, you compute the gradient vector $G(x,y)$. You discard any pixel for which the length of $G(x,y)$ is below threshold as not being an edge. For the edge pixels that remain, you assign them to one of 8 to 16 "buckets" based on the orientation direction of $G(x,y)$. For a given image region, you count the number of pixels that fall into each orientation bucket to produce a histogram of the edge orientations. This orientation histogram forms a feature vector for classifying shapes. Figure 24.7 shows a mock-up of orientation histograms being used to recognize hand gestures. Note that the two gestures show a very different shape signature in the orientation histograms. Orientation histograms are also helpful when rotations are present. A rotation in image space is just a shift in orientation histogram space. Thus with 12 buckets, only 12 shifts and compares are required to capture all possible differences in rotation.

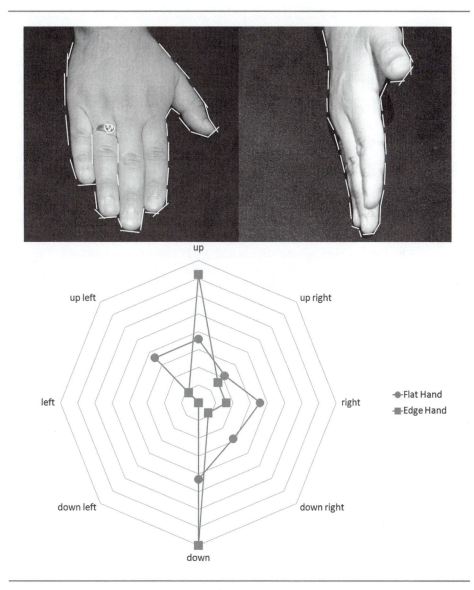

Figure 24.7 – Orientation histograms

You can use integral image techniques to rapidly produce orientation histograms for any image region. If there are 12 orientation buckets, you compute 12 integrals that sum the number of pixels that match the orientation for a given integral. You can then get the sum of the pixels for each orientation for any rectangle in constant time. This can greatly speed the process of finding an object that matches a particular orientation histogram.

Motion Features

A last set of features are those that detect interactive change or movement in an image. The simplest movement algorithm is *background differencing*. For this, you take an image of the space in its quiescent state (no movement or interaction) and subtract it from the current image. If something moves between two frames of a sequence of images, there will usually be strong differences in pixel values where the movement occurred. For example, you could take a picture of an empty office and then use current video images. If there are lots of changed pixels, there is probably someone in the office moving around.

Simple background differencing has two major problems. The first is camera noise. Simple noise will show up as pixel differences, which is inappropriate. The second problem is that the background is never static. If the sun goes behind a cloud, every pixel will change. If the user moves a chair and then leaves, that chair will be permanently different from the original background.

Both of these problems can be reduced by using history blending. You can use a short duration blend to eliminate the camera noise and a long blend to represent the background. The duration of the background blend depends upon the type of motion that you are trying to detect. If you want to detect the presence of a moving person at frame f, you might use a background of $H(f,10*30)$, which will blend across approximately 10 seconds at 30 frames per second. For foreground, you might use $H(f,2)$ to average out camera noise. The difference, $H(f,2)-H(f,60)$, will show basic body movement such as shifting in a chair or hand movement. Lighting changes as the sun goes down or as clouds move will be too slow to cause much of a difference across 10 seconds. If you want to detect rapid motions, you might use $H(f,2)-H(f,10)$. The background is now changing at about one-third of a second and only very rapid changes will show up as strong differences.

Note that integral image techniques can be applied to the history blend images. Computing the blend of the integral image produces a blended integral over time. This gives you the sum of the blends for any rectangle. Using these differences, you can rapidly search an image in large chunks for any movement that has occurred, without checking each pixel individually.

Background differencing can show where changes have occurred but will not give any indication of the direction of movement. Simple approximation of *optical flow*[10] can give you a useful indication of direction of motion. This model assumes that the object(s) being tracked are light and the background is dark. For this simple model of optical flow, three cases can be applied to a pixel $I_f(x,y)$ in frame f.

- $I_f(x,y)>I_{f-1}(x,y)$—In this case, the pixel is growing lighter over time, meaning that the object being tracked is entering the pixel. The direction of movement, therefore, is toward neighboring dark pixels and away from approaching light pixels. The movement vector for this pixel is toward the neighboring pixel $[I_f(x-1,y), I_f(x+1,y), I_f(x,y-1), I_f(x,y+1)]$ that has the <u>lowest</u> value.

- $I_f(x,y) < I_{f-1}(x,y)$—In this case, the pixel is growing darker over time, meaning that the object being tracked is leaving the pixel. The direction of movement, therefore, is toward neighboring light pixels and away from dark pixels. The movement vector for this pixel is toward the neighboring pixel $[I_f(x-1,y), I_f(x+1,y), I_f(x,y-1), I_f(x,y+1)]$ that has the <u>highest</u> value.

- $I_f(x,y) \approx I_{f-1}(x,y)$—In this case, there is no detectable movement at that pixel.

The preceding steps can provide a movement direction estimate for a given pixel but such pixel-sized estimates are not reliable. However, the average movement direction over a region can indicate a general direction of movement.

Summary of Image Features

The previous section has described features for gray values, pixels, and regions of pixels. These are all quite easy to calculate. For shapes, you have cosine matching of image templates, image moment features, and orientation histograms. For movement, you have background differencing and a crude optical flow estimate. These basic features combined with a fast classifier algorithm (Appendix A3) provide the foundation for many interactive techniques in physical space. When creating a new interaction technique using a camera, the common approach is to identify a set of features that can be extracted from the image stream, identify examples of the user action you are trying to sense, and then train a classifier to sense that activity. This approach is seen repeatedly in the sections that follow.

Training Image Classifiers

Many of the techniques described in the following sections use some kind of a classifier either to locate an object in an image or to detect whether an object is present. Because of the prevalence of these tasks in camera-based interaction, Fails et al created Image Processing with Crayons[11]. In many interactive situations, the goal is to classify each pixel in an image as belonging to one of two or more classes. In Crayons, each desired class is associated with a colored "crayon" that the user can use to paint the image. The crayons are semitransparent so that the user can still see the image beneath. In Figure 24.8, the user is painting with a "skin" crayon and a "background" crayon in the left image. After painting some of the pixels, the user requests the system to generate a classifier. The painted pixels are used as the training data. The resulting classification is shown in the image on the right as an additional transparent layer. The transparent layers help the user to understand how successful the classifier has been and where there are errors. The user can continue to paint corrections or move to other images to enter more data. The idea is that anyone who can understand how to paint can create a new image classifier within the limits of the feature set and learning algorithm.

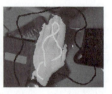

Figure 24.8 – Image Processing with Crayons (see color plate)

Crayons uses 250 features generated from various sizes and combinations of integral image features. A decision tree (Appendix 3.1b) is used to train the classifier because it functions naturally as a feature selector. For a given problem, only 5–10 of the 250 features are actually used. The decision tree algorithm selects those that are most useful. Because a Crayons user can easily produce tens to hundreds of thousands of training examples very quickly, the training time can become slow. The Crayons goal was to never take more than 10 seconds to train a classifier. In most cases, only 1–2 seconds is required. Some modifications to the decision tree algorithm were required to achieve this goal.

Camera as a Pointing Device

The first camera technique is to simulate a mouse or pointing device. In public situations, it is frequently difficult to provide interactive devices that will not be damaged or worn down by the public. However, if potential users bring their own input devices in the form of a cell phone (possibly with a camera), this problem can be eliminated. The Direct Pointer[12] uses a cell phone camera and a wireless network to control the position of a cursor on the display. A cursor is drawn on a screen and the user points the cell phone camera at the cursor. The camera grabs an image and transmits it to the cursor server. The cursor server locates the cursor in the camera image and then moves the cursor on the screen so that it will be closer to the center of the camera image. This feedback loop pushes the cursor in the direction the camera is pointing. When the user moves the camera to the left, the cursor will appear in the right of its image. The cursor server will then move the cursor to the left to compensate. The feedback loop causes the cursor position to converge without knowing the optics of the camera. The advantage of this technique is that anyone with a cell phone can control a cursor on an arbitrarily large screen. Experiments with Direct Pointer showed a performance similar to a track ball.

Another cell phone-based technique is to place a camera above the display screen and use it to detect the display on a cell phone. The C-Blink[13] system puts a unique image on the cell phone and the display on the camera detects where the image is. Moving the cell phone around will change where it appears in the display camera's image and this position can be used to control a cursor. C-Blink can also transmit button press information by flashing the cell phone's display. The display camera detects the flashes and can decode their timing into a binary value indicating which buttons have been pressed. Unlike the Direct Pointer, C-Blink requires much larger physical movements of the user to control the pointer. C-Blink's most important contribution is in signaling information through the visual channel.

The most popular camera-based pointing device is the Nintendo Wii-remote. A sensor bar is placed on top of the television. This bar has 10 infrared LEDs with five in one end and five at the other. The Wii-remote has an IR camera that detects these two collections of LEDs. The average of their positions in the camera's image gives a cursor location. The angle of the vector between the two spots in the camera image gives an angle of rotation. Because the distance between the two ends of the sensor bar is known, the distance between the two points in the camera's image gives an estimate of the distance between the Wii-remote and the sensor bar. When the remote is closer, the points will appear farther apart in the camera image. The use of infrared and known emitters makes the location of the spots a simple image processing task.

A final camera pointing technique uses a simple laser pointer as an input device[14]. The display is projected onto a surface and the user points at the display with a laser pointer. This technique allows anyone in the room who holds a laser pointer to participate in the interaction. This eliminates the one-user restriction found in many interactive approaches. A camera focused on the display surface is used to detect the laser spot, as shown in Figure 24.9. The red arrow shows the laser spot, which is not as easy to detect as you might think. The blue arrow shows where the system believes the laser spot is located. The problem is the time lag of the image processing required to track the laser spot. The problem with detecting laser spots is that their brightness overdrives most cameras. This requires turning the camera gain way down so that only the spot is visible or introducing a very dark filter over the camera.

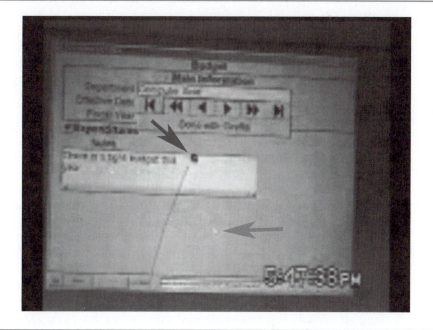

Figure 24.9 – Laser pointer interaction (see color plate)

One of the key reasons for laser pointer interaction is to allow many people to interact with a wall display rather than just one. Anyone with a laser pointer can participate. A variety of "laser widgets" were implemented, including dates, numbers, lists of choices, and Graffiti text, as shown in Figure 24.9. Accuracy with the laser pointer is a problem. Myers et al[15] measured the effectiveness and accuracy of laser pointers and found that hand jitter was a serious issue.

When using a camera to input points, there is the problem of calibration of the camera image to the input space. As Figure 24.9 shows, the camera is frequently off center and viewing the surface at an oblique angle. The most appropriate place to mount a camera to minimize this distortion is also a place where the user's head is likely to be. Therefore, the camera is usually in a location that has inherent distortion in the image. What you need is a mapping from camera image coordinates $[X_c, Y_c]$ to input coordinates $[X_i, Y_i]$. A simple linear mapping is not sufficient because of the perspective and keystone distortions that can occur. The following mapping is sufficient to resolve most problems.

$$X_i = aX_c + bY_c + \frac{c}{X_c} + \frac{d}{Y_c} + eX_c^2 + fY_c^2$$

$$Y_i = gX_c + hY_c + \frac{j}{X_c} + \frac{k}{Y_c} + lX_c^2 + mY_c^2$$

The problem is to determine the coefficients a through m. There are 12 unknowns. If you have 16 points for which you know the mapping, you can use linear least squares (Appendix A1.2f) to approximate the coefficients. This is done by projecting 16 points onto the display surface one at a time and having the camera software find them in the image. You know in input space where you projected the point and you know in camera space where you found it. Doing this in a 4 × 4 grid of points will produce enough data for least squares approximation of the mapping.

Camera Tracking of Objects

A second role for a camera is to track objects in the physical world. The Tangible NURBS system[16] used a rear-projected wall display for its interactive surface. In addition to the projectors, infrared light is also shown on the back of the screen as well as cameras sampling the screen from behind. The user would interact with the system using plastic objects that had been modified so that they were visible in IR and their shape was distinctive. The distinctive shape allowed the object to be identified as well as its orientation. The placement of the user's fingers also could be used as interactive input.

The Illuminating Light[17] project tracked objects on a table using cameras from above as well as projected images from above. The objects were identified by red, green, and blue spots on the objects. These spots were arranged so that the combination of colors yielded the object's identity, location, and orientation. As with the Tangible NURBS, this system allowed users to interact physically with real objects rather than indirectly through a mouse and keyboard.

Frequently, these objects being tracked by the camera are paper with information on them. Not only can the camera find the pieces of paper, but it can also acquire images of what is drawn on the paper. The Designers' Outpost[18] focused on the need for Web designers to rapidly modify designs using physical "sticky notes." The problem with sticky notes alone is that the interconnections between notes are lost when notes are moved. Also the physical notes could not be sent to remote coworkers. In Designers' Outpost, there is a rear camera behind the screen with the projector. This camera can locate the adding, removing, and repositioning of sticky notes on the screen. Because the camera is behind the screen, the user does not obscure this information. Interconnections are drawn digitally using a pen-input device. When sticky notes are moved, the connections are also moved. Once the positions of sticky notes are known, a high-resolution, but slow, camera extracts the information written on the sticky notes from the front. The user interacts by writing on notes, placing them on the screen, and moving them around by hand. The camera system keeps the digital representation synchronized with what the user does with the physical objects.

Continuing in the theme of using physical objects to manipulate digital information, the PaperWindows[19] project uses pieces of paper as window controllers. Each piece of paper is augmented with eight IR reflective markers. These are readily located by an overhead camera. Once the position and orientation of the paper is known, information can be projected from above onto the paper, as shown in Figure 24.10. Moving a window of information around is now as simple as moving the corresponding piece of paper.

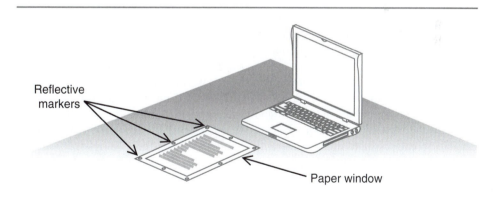

Reflective markers

Paper window

Figure 24.10 – PaperWindows

Not only can the markers be detected in IR, but the user's hands can also be detected. A variety of interactive techniques are possible. Holding a piece of paper makes that window the active window. "Flipping" the top of a piece of paper pages through that document.

Camera tracking of paper can also be used to associate physical objects with their corresponding digital objects. Video-based Document Tracking identifies rectangular objects that enter the camera's view[20]. These can be documents or photographs. These might be printed versions of digital documents. For each rectangle, a set of interesting texture points is identified in the image. The same is done for each digital object. The point pattern for the objects in the camera is matched against those in the database of digital objects to make the association. Using this recognition, digital objects can be sorted into piles or rearranged in many ways. The physical actions with the objects are matched in the digital world.

Person Tracking

The last major camera-tracking approach is to watch people. In particular, you watch their hands and fingers because those are the body parts most frequently used to manipulate the world. Letessier and Berand[21] describe an algorithm for tracking multiple fingertips at 25 Hz, which is more than enough for interactive use. They use background differencing and then apply a threshold to separate the foreground hands from the background. They then successively scan each pixel, applying a series of filters to identify circular fingertips of appropriate width. Once you know where the fingertips are, a variety of interactive techniques can use the information.

Malik and Laszlo[22] describe a tracking technique that uses the whole hand to find the fingers. They also use thresholded background differencing to find the moving hands. They then recognize that fingers are always connected to hands and the hands must enter the image somewhere. They use a flood-fill technique to find the two largest blobs in the thresholded image. If a blob is above a certain size, it is assumed to be a hand. They then look at the contour of each blob to find the sharp turns that indicate fingertips. By knowing where the fingers are attached to the hands, they can recognize a number of gestures such as "grasping" projected objects and moving or rotating them. They then extended this work[23] to define a series of pointing, grasping, selecting, and movement gestures for interacting with objects on a screen.

Most of the hand/finger tracking work uses a camera placed above the work surface. This has problems when users naturally bend over their work. There is also a problem in determining when the user's finger touches the tabletop. Touch is an important part of detecting engagement with the work rather than just passing over it. The PlayAnywhere[24] system addresses both of these problems by using projectors, cameras, and lights at an oblique angle to the surface. Using an NEC WT600 projector that has a very short throw distance, the projection is from front of the user rather than above, which reduces occlusion. The camera and an IR illuminant are also placed at this oblique angle and quite separate from each other. This produces strong shadows of the hands in IR. Normally you try to eliminate shadows, but in this case the shadows are used as the primary detection signal. The shadows have a uniform intensity regardless of the user's hand color and are, therefore, more consistently detected.

The shadows also indicate touching the surface. When a finger is off of a surface, the shadow and the finger image separate because of the oblique angle of the light. When the finger touches, the shadow and the finger image converge with the finger obscuring the shadow. When detecting shadows, this effect appears as a "sharpening" of the shadow fingertip, as shown in Figure 24.11. This shadow sharpening can be detected as a touch on the surface.

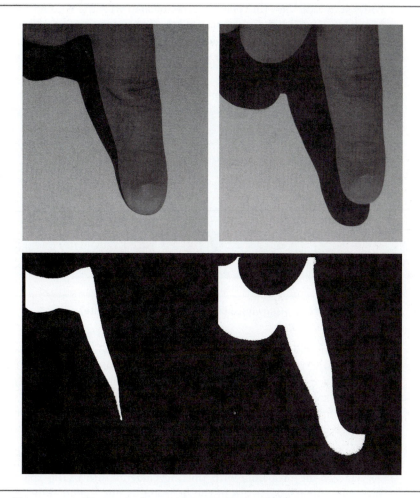

Figure 24.11 – Finger shadows to detect table touching

An interesting technique puts the camera beneath the working surface. Acrylic plastic and glass exhibit the property of *total internal reflection*. That is, when light is projected into the polished edge of a sheet of plastic, it bounces off of its surface edges at an angle that keeps the light inside the sheet. When a finger is pressed against the surface, it frustrates this total internal reflection, causing light to reflect off of the finger and into the region behind the surface[25]. A camera placed behind the surface can easily locate these touch points. By using an IR light source, there is no glow from the surface at all. Working with fingers on the surface shares many interactive techniques with the touch-sensitive tables described in Chapter 19.

The Light Widgets[26] system allows interaction designers to place cameras in a space and then create interactive controls by drawing them on the images. These controls are then sensitive to hands touching those places. Figure 24.12 shows views of a bedroom from two different cameras. A linear light widget has been drawn on the bedpost in each view (in yellow) and associated with the volume control of the room's television. A spot light widget (in red) has been drawn on the nightstand and associated with the television's power switch. A skin classifier has been trained to detect when someone's hand has been placed over one of the light widgets.

Figure 24.12 – Drawing a Light Widget (see color plate)

For spot widgets, only the detection is reported from the camera. For linear widgets, the proportional value (bottom to top) is reported. If the user's hand is actually on the desired spot, both cameras will report the same value. If the user's hand is above the spot, somewhere in the air, the cameras will disagree. This simple agreement mechanism resolves 3D contact without expensive reconstruction of the 3D position of objects in the room. Light Widgets essentially allow a control to be drawn on any surface. A variation using laser spots rather than skin requires only one camera because a laser spot cannot appear in the air and the additional voting is not required.

One of the problems with putting cameras into living spaces is privacy. An Internet-connected camera in the bedroom is not a good thing. By packaging the image processor with the camera, images need never leave the camera device. The device only reports light widget values that can be compared for agreement. Because no images leave the device, privacy is preserved.

A final class of techniques involves mounting the camera on top of a display and watching the user[27]. As the user waves their hands or makes gestures, the interpreted result is echoed on the display. This feedback approach sharply reduces the need for accurate calibration and recognition. The user can move their hand while watching the echo on the screen until the echo matches what is desired. This is very much like visually following a screen cursor while moving a mouse. The position of the mouse is largely irrelevant as long as the cursor reaches the desired location.

Researchers at MERL[10] have used cameras and on-screen feedback in a variety of computer gaming applications. Using image moments to detect the angle of hand gestures, they could fly an avatar through a game. Using image moments on body position, a user could fly a magic carpet by leaning left or right. Magic spells are fired by pointing with the arms. Using orientation histograms, a user can play "paper, rock, scissors" with the computer. Optical flow techniques to detect speed and direction of motion were used in a track and field video game. Speed of motion in the left and right of the screen detected the speed of the user running in place to win a foot race. Running, while lifting the arms to indicate a jump, supported a hurdle race.

PHYSICAL SENSING

Though the camera is a very versatile sensor, there are other means for getting information about user activity. You will briefly look at several alternatives in this section.

Simple Sensors

A very common way to interact with an object is to touch it. Touch is easily sensed using body capacitance. A capacitor consists of two conductors separated by a dielectric. Various materials have various dielectric properties. The greater the dielectric, the more capacitance or ability the circuit has to hold a charge. Air is a rather poor dielectric. Water is a much better dielectric and the human body is mostly water. If some part of a human body establishes a circuit between two conductive surfaces, the capacitance between those surfaces increases sharply. This increase in capacitance can be easily sensed, thus creating a touch sensor.

Sometimes squeezing an object has meaning. The conductive foam in which integrated circuits are packaged has a resistance that can be measured. When the foam is compressed, the resistance lowers because there are more internal contacts within the cells of the foam. Inserting two wires into the foam some distance apart creates a pressure sensor that can be cut to any size or shape.

Proximity of an object to a sensor is easily measured in two ways. IR proximity sensors are relatively cheap. One side is an LED that shines infrared light into the environment. The other side is an IR light detector. The closer a reflective object is to the sensor, the brighter the light on the detector. These generally do not work beyond a few feet but are quite effective at short range. IR sensors do not work if the target object is not reflective in the IR range or if a very bright IR source (such as the sun) is present in the environment.

Another cheap proximity sensor is ultrasonic and behaves much like sonar. The device emits an ultrasonic "chirp" and then times the echo. Short times mean short distances. Soft surfaces tend to absorb the sound, reducing the effectiveness, and changes in humidity can create variations in the echo time. The most annoying attribute from a user-interface perspective is that the ultrasonic "chirp" can frequently be heard as a faint audible click.

MEMS (Micro-Electro-Mechanical Systems) technology has created very cheap accelerometers. A single device will generally sense acceleration along two axes. A second device mounted perpendicular to the other can provide the third axis. These are very cheap and very small. Sensing the acceleration of gravity can create a tilt sensor. These devices generally produce a stream of acceleration values. Using appropriate features on these sensor streams coupled with a good learning algorithm can produce sensors for shaking, walking, running, tipping, and holding still. Many smartphones as well as the Nintendo Wii use accelerometers in their interactions.

Sensor Interaction

As an example, a telephone can have a conductive surface where the user holds the phone and a separate surface where the phone touches the ear. This allows the phone to sense when the user is actually holding the phone to their ear. Conductive paint can be used on any surface for this purpose. Dietz and Yerazunis[28] instrumented such a phone. When the phone is held to the user's ear, it behaves normally. When the user takes the phone from their ear, the phone starts to save the audio being received. When the phone is again placed to the user's ear, the audio is played back at a higher speed, allowing the user to catch up with the conversation.

A similar technology has been used to prototype a wide variety of touch-sensitive controls[29]. In this case, a user sits on a conductive pad to form one pole of the circuit. A processor has several touch-sensitive surfaces wired to it to form the other pole. When the user touches a surface the capacitance between the two poles increases. This can be sensed as a touch. Each surface is tested in turn to see if there is a touch. Any surface that can be made conductive can sense touch and be used as a prototype device. In addition, multiple people can each sit on their own conductive pad. By sampling each circuit combination, the system cannot only sense a touch, but can also identify the user who touched it based on which pad completes the circuit.

Hinckley[30] instrumented a handheld PDA with a touch-sensitive case, an IR proximity sensor, and accelerometers. The PDA knows when someone is holding it by the touch. It knows when it has been put into a pocket because the accelerometer indicates that the device is upright, the proximity is sensed as extremely close, and there is no touch. The accelerometer can tell when the object has been tipped and rotates the display to correspond to the edge that is currently down. The drawing application erases the screen when the PDA is shaken while being held upside down.

Virtual Containers

A large number of techniques can be classified as "virtual containers." A virtual container is a place on some server where data or a program is stored. Physical objects are given an identity that can be sensed and that identity is associated with the container. If the container holds a program or fragment of code, that object represents the execution of that code to perform some service. If the object represents a data value, information can be put into the container or information can be used from the container whenever the associated object is present.

At the heart of this architecture is the ability to associate identifiers with physical objects. You will first look at various techniques for digitally identifying objects and their associated interactive techniques.

Object Properties

One of the simplest techniques is to use the physical properties of the object itself as its identity. Some researchers have used the weight of an object as its identifier[31]. A small scale is placed near a display device and the user places some personal object (cell phone, car keys, watch, and so on) on the scale. The user then drags information on the screen to the location near the scale and the information is "dragged into the object." The user then picks up the object and carries it to a different display and places the object on the scale found there. The information "in" the object pops out onto the screen.

The association between the object and the information is based on the weight. When information is "dragged into" the object, it is actually stored on a server indexed under the object's weight. When the object appears on a new scale, the weight is looked up on the server and the associated information retrieved. Other potential properties are color or width/height.

The problem with most object-property techniques is that the property must remain invariant. The shape of a set of keys varies radically depending on how you set them down. A second problem is that the range of possible values that can be reliably detected is quite small. With the weight technique, only 20–30 separate objects can be recognized.

Bar Codes

A very common labeling technique is the bar code. Most commercial products already have a bar code. However, UPC codes only identify the type of object, not the particular object. Bar codes have several advantages. The first is that they are very easy to print and attach to objects. They are very cheap. A bar code can also be designed to contain an IP address for the server that holds the object's virtual container. This allows such techniques to scale up to millions of codes with millions of differing applications managed by many organizations. The potential interactive techniques can scale to the size of the Internet.

There are two problems with bar-code techniques. The first is that they must be visible despite the fact that they are ugly. Most objects that people use in their environment do not have prominent bar codes because they are not very aesthetically pleasing. The second problem is the readers. Standard UPC codes are intended to be read by a laser scanner. The store-based scanners are too bulky for interactive use. There are handheld scanners, but they are generally about twice the size of a PDA. It is relatively easy to develop a bar-code scheme that can be read by a cell phone camera. The number of bits possible in the identifier is generally reduced, but small cameras attached to a computer are much more widely available than laser-based readers.

Resistor IDs

The mediaBlocks[32] system used simple resistors as identifiers. Each block had a resistor with differing resistance embedded into it. Around the room there were various devices with associated "transfer slots." Inside a transfer slot were two contacts that would engage with any block placed in the slot. Through the contacts the resistance was measured and the block identified.

The blocks were intended to "hold" media content such as images, video, and slide shows. Dragging media materials to a transfer slot would put the media "into" the block. Inserting the block into a printer's slot would print the media on the block. Inserting the block into the slot associated with a camera would place any pictures or video taken by the camera "into" the block for use elsewhere. Each block becomes a physical embodiment of the information that it contains.

In addition to slots, the mediaBlocks system also had *racks*. A rack is basically a printed circuit board on which contacts of various lengths are etched. Putting a media block onto a rack at different positions causes the block to connect to different contacts. A processor can sample each set of contacts and identify each block and where it is on the rack. This position information allowed users to physically sort media information by adjusting the positions and ordering of various blocks on the rack.

There are two key limitations on resistor IDs. As with object properties, the range of possible identifiers is not very high. Additionally, there must be electrical contact for the block to be correctly sensed. The contacts must be kept clean or the resistance changes. In addition, the user must engage directly with the sensing device, unlike camera techniques.

iButtons

The iButton from Dallas Semiconductors is a small microcontroller with a unique identifier encoded in it. This identifier has enough bits to accommodate Internet-sized systems. The microcontroller is encased in a metal shell that provides two contact surfaces. When the iButton is engaged with an appropriate reader, contact is made with the shell, power is supplied, and the iButton can communicate its identifier. This has the same physical contact properties as resistor IDs but has a much more robust range of identifiers. One of the downsides is that solid digital contact must be ensured so that digital information can be reliably transferred. This means that contact between an iButton and a reader is less like touching and more like snapping in place. This is not a physically satisfying solution.

A variation of the iButton has a Java interpreter embedded in it along with a small amount of persistent storage. This means that such a Java button can actually be the container for information without the need for access to a network server. The Join and Capture[33] system used an iButton embedded in a ring so that users could move their interactive work to whatever resources they found in the world. Each location was associated with either a display or some information.

RFID

An emerging technique for digitally labeling objects is RFID tags. The most interesting RFID tags are not powered and essentially static. They are very inexpensive. Inside the tag is a coil antenna. The tag reader contains a much larger antenna and induces a current in the tag's antenna. The induced current in the tag is sufficient to power the circuit that modulates a return signal with the tag's identifier. Identifiers of 96 bits and beyond have been created. This is a great identifier space. RFIDs do not need to be touched to be read. However, the reading distance is dependent upon the size and power applied to the reader's antenna. This means that readers are physically larger than desired.

Want et al[34] have developed a series of prototypical uses for RFIDs in interactive systems. The essence of their idea is that objects should have an interactive meaning associated with what the object actually is. For example, a tagged French-English dictionary can be brushed against a computer equipped with an RFID reader. Having detected the dictionary, any selected text is translated from French to English. Brushing the computer against a poster that advertises the scheduling of a presentation logs that presentation into the user's calendar. Brushing the computer against a tagged book can locate that book on the Internet for purchase. If someone's business card has been tagged, brushing it against the reader causes that person's information to be entered into the contact manager.

The 96 bits of identifier information make RFIDs very flexible. The first 32 bits can contain the IP address of the server that stores the virtual containers. The remaining bits can identify the container. Each of the techniques described previously either delivers some information or a piece of code to be executed. There are some ambiguity problems in these techniques, however. Brushing a book against the reader initiates a purchase request for that book. Brushing the dictionary initiates language translation. Why does it not initiate a purchase of the dictionary? A poster contains much more information than the time and place of the presentation. There are also the presenter and the topic. Why was the schedule determined as the associated meaning? With these ambiguities, the users might be confused.

Fingerprints

One of the problems with associating information and actions with physical objects is that you tend to lose them. One solution is to associate containers with parts of the user's body. An interesting technique is to use fingers[35]. Each finger has a unique print that can be recognized by a reader. The technique is to scan the print and derive a set of features. These features are compared against all known information containers for the closest match. As with the other container systems, the associated information and/or code can be used for a variety of interactive purposes.

The obvious limitation is that people generally have no more than 10 fingers. The toes could be used, but that would be awkward. The fingers also do not have the semantic associations that a dictionary or business card would have. This means that a user can easily become confused about the data/action associated with each finger.

SUMMARY

Interacting in the physical world has the promise of integrating computing into your life. To have interaction, there must be the ability for the computer to present information. If computing is more integrated, it must be more polite. Computers that barge into your life with noise and light at unwanted times are not acceptable.

The second problem is to sense what the user is doing or what the user wants done. One of the most flexible sensors is the camera. For interactive use, you do not necessarily need or want all of image processing. A few simple features and techniques can generate the information you need, from which interactive behaviors can be trained using machine learning.

In addition to the camera, there are a variety of other sensors, including proximity, pressure, touch, orientation, and acceleration. Again, machine learning can be used to translate these inputs into interactive behaviors.

A compelling form of interaction is to associate physical objects with information or behaviors. The key requirement is a technology for identifying the object. A most important question is whether the identifying technology can scale to millions of uses and whether the users will understand what the associated behavior is.

EXERCISES

1. Pick a common room, measure its dimensions, and then calculate how many projectors of a standard resolution will be required to cover the walls of the room with text that can be read from 10 feet away.

2. Given that you have a detector for when a person can or cannot be interrupted, make a list of 10 ways you would modify current application software to take advantage of this sensor. Justify the items in your list.

3. In Figure 24.13, you need to separate sky, buildings, and water. There is a lot of gray in this image and varying amounts of texture. Which of the integral image formulations would you use for features and why?

Figure 24.13 – Sample picture for separation (see color plate)

4. Why would template matching work better for finding windows in the background building of Figure 24.13 than for finding hulls or masts of ships?

5. How would an orientation histogram be used to compare two shapes that are rotated 45 degrees relative to each other?

6. If Figure 24.13 were actually a video, what technique might you use to separate objects on the water from the buildings and sky? Remember that waves affect everything on the water.

7. Use a simple webcam and template matching to implement the Direct Pointer cursor movement technique.

8. Implement "Image Processing with Crayons" and use the resulting classifier to follow the user's hand around using a webcam to capture images of the desktop surface.

END NOTES

[1] Weiser, M. "Some Computer Science Issues in Ubiquitous Computing." *Communications of the ACM 36(7)* (July 1993): 75–84.

[2] Underkoffler, J., and H. Ishii. "Illuminating Light: An Optical Design Tool with a Luminous-Tangible Interface." *Human Factors in Computing Systems (CHI '98)* (January 1998): 542–549.

[3] Raskar, R., G. Welch, M. Cutts, A. Lake, L. Stesin, and H. Fuchs. "The Office of the Future: A Unified Approach to Image-Based Modeling and Spatially Immersive Displays." *Computer Graphics and Interactive Techniques (SIGGRAPH '98)* (July 1998): 179–188.

[4] Summet, J. W., M. Flagg, J. M. Rehg, G. D. Abowd, and N. Weston. "GVU-PROCAMS: Enabling Novel Projected Interfaces." *ACM Multimedia* (October 2006): 141-144.

[5] Ishii, H., and B. Ullmer. "Tangible Bits: Towards Seamless Interfaces Between People, Bits and Atoms." *Human Factors in Computing Systems (CHI '97)* (March 1997): 234–241.

[6] Heiner, J. M., S. E. Hudson, and K. Tanaka. "The Information Percolator: Ambient Information Display in a Decorative Object." *User Interface Software and Technology (UIST '99)* (November 1999): 141–148.

[7] Dickie, C., R. Vertegaal, C. Sohn, and D. Cheng. "eyeLook: Using Attention to Facilitate Mobile Media Consumption." *User Interface Software and Technology (UIST '05)* (October 2005): 103–106.

[8] Fogarty, J., S. E. Hudson, C. G. Atkeson, D. Avrahami, J. Forlizzi, S. Kiesler, J. C. Lee, and J. Yang. "Predicting Human Interruptibility with Sensors." *ACM Transactions on Computer-Human Interaction 12(1)* (March 2005): 119–146.

[9] Viola, P., and M. Jones. "Robust Real-Time Object Detection." *Technical Report 2001/01*, Compaq CRL, February 2001.

[10] Freeman, W. T., D. Anderson, P. Beardsley, C. Dodge, H. Kage, K. Kyuma, Y. Miyake, M. Roth, K. Tanaka, C. Weissman, and W. Yerazunis. "Computer Vision for Interactive Computer Graphics." *IEEE Computer Graphics and Applications* 18(3) (May-June 1998): 42–53.

[11] Fails, J. A., and D. R. Olsen. "A Design Tool for Camera-Based Interaction." *Human Factors in Computing Systems (CHI '03)* (April 2003): 449–456.

[12] Jiang, H., E. Ofek, N. Moraveji, and Y. Shi. "Direct Pointer: Direct Manipulation for Large-Display Interaction Using Handheld Cameras." *Human Factors in Computing Systems (CHI '06)* (April 2006): 1107–1110.

[13] Miyaoku, K., S. Higashino, and Y. Tonomura. "C-Blink: A Hue-Difference-Based Light Signal Marker for Large Screen Interaction via Any Mobile Terminal" *User Interface Software and Technology (UIST '04)* (October 2004): 147–156.

[14] Olsen, D. R., and T. Nielsen. "Laser Pointer Interaction." *Human Factors in Computing Systems (CHI '01)* (March 2001): 17–22.

[15] Myers, B. A., R. Bhatnagar, J. Nichols, C. H. Peck, R. Miller, and C. Long. "Interacting at a Distance: Measuring the Performance of Laser Pointers and Other Devices." *Human Factors in Computing Systems (CHI '02)* (April 2002): 33–40.

[16] Bae, S. H., T. Kobayashi, R. Kijima, and W. W. Kim. "Tangible NURBS-Curve Manipulation Techniques Using Graspable Handles on a Large Display." *User Interface Software and Technology (UIST '04)* (October 2004): 81–90.

[17] Underkoffler, J., and H. Ishii. "Illuminating Light: An Optical Design Tool with a Luminous-Tangible Interface." *Human Factors in Computing Systems (CHI '98)* (April 1998): 542–549.

[18] Klemmer, S. R., M. W. Newman, R. Farrell, M. Bilezikjian, and J. A. Landay. "The Designers' Outpost: A Tangible Interface for Collaborative Web Site Design." *User Interface Software and Technology (UIST '01)* (November 2001): 1–10.

[19] Holman, D., R. Vertegaal, M. Altosaar, N. Troje, and D. Johns. "PaperWindows: Interaction Techniques for Digital Paper." *Human Factors in Computing Systems (CHI '05)* (April 2005): 591–599.

[20] Kim, J., S. M. Seitz, and M. Agrawala. "Video-Based Document Tracking: Unifying Your Physical and Electronic Desktops." *User Interface Software and Technology (UIST '04)* (October 2004): 99–107.

[21] Letessier, J., and F. Berard. "Visual Tracking of Bare Fingers for Interactive Surfaces." *User Interface Software and Technology (UIST '04)* (October 2004): 119–122.

[22] Malik, S., and J. Laszlo. "Visual Touchpad: A Two-Handed Gestural Input Device." *International Conference on Multimodal Interfaces (ICMI '04)* (October 2004): 289–296.

[23] Malik, S., A. Ranjan, and R. Balakrishnan. "Interacting with Large Displays from a Distance with Vision-Tracked Multi-Finger Gestural Input." *User Interface Software and Technology (UIST '05)* (October 2005): 43–52.

[24] Wilson, A. "PlayAnywhere: A Compact Interactive Tabletop Projection-Vision System." *User Interface Software and Technology (UIST '05)* (October 2005): 83–92.

[25] Han, J. Y. "Low-Cost Multi-Touch Sensing Through Frustrated Total Internal Reflection." *User Interface Software and Technology (UIST '05)* (October 2005): 115–118.

26 Fails, J. A., and D. R. Olsen. "Light Widgets: Interacting in Everyday Spaces." *Intelligent User Interfaces (IUI '02)* (January 2002): 63–69.

27 Eisenstien, J., and W. E. Mackay. "Interacting with Communication Appliances: An Evaluation of Two Computer Vision-Based Selection Techniques." *Human Factors in Computing Systems (CHI '06)* (April 2006): 1111–1114.

28 Dietz, P. H., and W. S. Yerazunis. "Real-Time Audio Buffering for Telephone Applications." *User Interface Software and Technology (UIST '01)* (November 2001): 193–194.

29 Dietz, P. H., B. Harsham, C. Forlines, D. Leigh, W. Yerazunis, S. Shipman, B. Schmidt-Nielsen, and K. Ryall. "DT Controls: Adding Identity to Physical Interfaces." *User Interface Software and Technology (UIST '05)* (October 2005): 245–252.

30 Hinckley, K., J. Pierce, M. Sinclair, and E. Horvitz. "Sensing Techniques for Mobile Interaction." *User Interface Software and Technology (UIST '00)* (November 2000): 91–100.

31 Streitz, N. A., J. Geibler, T. Holmer, S. Konomi, C. Muller-Tomfelde, W. Reischl, P. Rexroth, P. Seitz, and R. Steinmetz. "i-LAND: An Interactive Landscape for Creativity and Innovation." *Human Factors in Computing Systems (CHI '99)* (May 1999): 120–127.

32 Ullmer, B., H. Ishii, and D. Glas. "mediaBlocks: Physical Containers, Transports and Controls for Online Media." *Computer Graphics and Interactive Techniques (SIGGRAPH '98)* (May 1998): 379–386.

33 Olsen, D. R., S. T. Nielsen, and D. Parslow. "Join and Capture: A Model for Nomadic Interaction." *User Interface Software and Technology (UIST '01)* (November 2001): 131–140.

34 Want, R., K. P. Fishkin, A. Gujar, and B. L. Harrison. "Bridging Physical and Virtual Worlds with Electronic Tags." *Human Factors in Computing Systems (CHI '99)* (May 1999): 370–377.

35 Sugiura, A., and Y. Koseki. "A User Interface Using Fingerprint Recognition – Holding Commands and Data Objects on Fingers." *User Interface Software and Technology (UIST '98)* (November 1998): 71–79.

CHAPTER 25

Functional Design

Functional design is the process of translating the needs of your users into a task model that represents the work to be done and then into a functional model that represents the model for your user-interface implementation. Creating the model design is a critical part of user-interface development and one that is frequently neglected. In the development of a new interactive application, functional design must come first. In this book, functional design is placed much later to allow students to begin programming projects early in a semester. However, in actual practice, the functional design process is a critical first step before any code is written.

Several years ago, a large software company was losing market share, though they were still the largest producer in their field. Their customers reported that their products were hard to use. This message went throughout the company and a consultant was hired to help improve their user interface. They first presented a document full of screen designs for their new product, which the consultant read and marked up. They then met to discuss the findings and plan remedies.

The consultant began by asking if anyone in the room had actually used their current product. One of their support technicians had been invited and raised his hand. He reported that the most common problem calls he received were about incorrect access privileges. He explained that it was hard to see the implications that a change might have; therefore, people got it wrong and could not figure out why. The consultant suggested that they add a display of the impact of access privilege changes so that users could see results and respond accordingly. At this point, the group manager said, "That API was set by the systems team. It is not part of the user interface. We can't change it." The discussion moved on to font sizes, field names, and other helpful user-interface issues. The product remained hard to use, and the company continued to lose market share and is now a minor player in their field. Usability is not just about putting a pretty face on the interface. It is about clearly serving user needs.

People buy interactive software because there are problems they want to solve. A good user interface must simplify solving those problems. Straightening the widget layouts, upgrading the fonts, and producing a pleasing color scheme are all important to the user interface but as a colleague of mine recently said, "Nicely seasoned, beautifully presented slop still tastes bad."

This chapter discusses the process of understanding what the user needs and translating that understanding into functional designs and model classes. A related visual and usability design process is the design of the various views of our model. This book, however, is primarily for programmers for whom model design is critical. A most instructive text on functional design is *Contextual Design*[1]. This chapter only serves to highlight the issues. To illustrate the functional design process, this chapter uses two examples: programming a VCR to record at a later time and buying basketball tickets over the Internet.

WHY ARE WE DOING THIS?

Every software project has a set of goals. Understanding those goals is critical to a successful user interface. Goals that seem obvious are not necessarily so. The stated goal might be that "anyone can program the VCR to record any show at any time." This sounds like a good goal, but nobody has such a goal. The company building the VCR wants features that (1) sell well in a 15-second demonstration on the showroom floor and (2) present well in any consumer review article. These two goals seem somewhat tawdry but they are the reality of making money building VCRs. The original goal statement is also inappropriate for users. Nobody approaches his or her VCR with the goal of recording a particular channel at a particular time. A more realistic user's goal might be "I want to record Star Trek tomorrow while I am at the school's parents' night." Software developers frequently replace intent (record Star Trek) with mechanism (channel and time). The software you are building is the mechanism, but to correctly design it, you must understand the intent.

A basketball ticket system might have the stated goal of "helping customers buy the tickets they want as easily as possible." The reality might be to produce the same level of ticket sales while spending 60 percent less on personnel. A second goal is to market unused seats by up-selling and cross-selling current customers. Getting at the real goals rather than the surface goals is important to user-interface success.

User-interface designs must function in a context of competing constraints. A project's real goals must reflect those constraints. The altruistic goals of simplicity and ease of use cannot be ignored because they are what attract customers. However, the other goals are just as powerful. A major design challenge is to balance these goals, particularly when some forces lend undue prominence to some goals. For example, every large organization has a financial services group. Their mission is to provide management with a clear picture of budgets and expenditures. In reality, some such organizations are driven by reducing their own costs (financial services should save the company money) or requests of auditors (minimize criticism). Placing too much importance on such goals can produce information systems that enforce static procedures and minimize change. Management, uninformed by auditor-oriented reports, frequently hires additional staff to insulate themselves from financial services software (costing money).

> Clarify why you started this project and identify the desired and implied goals.
> Write them down. Post them where they can clearly be seen. Evaluate design deci-
> sions against them.

As much as you would like to create a compelling solution to all of our organization's problems, this is rarely possible. Sometimes such a global rethinking of all
assumptions is important. It is more common to incrementally improve some aspect of
a system. In such situations, you need to restate the global goals of the system, but
also focus carefully on the specific problem to be solved. Do not bury the project in a
design morass far beyond available resources.

The first step toward a functional design is identifying the users to be served.
Working with representative users leads to understanding their goals (which are not
always what they say they are). In particular, create sample scenarios of how they
accomplish their goals, what information they use, and how they decide when they
are done. Use this information to develop an object model of the entire system and
then winnow that model down to the actual user interface to implement. This leads to
a functional design from which the model of our new interface is built.

A HISTORICAL PERSPECTIVE

This chapter is devoted to the problem of designing exactly what a user interface
should do rather than how it should do it. There is a great temptation to either skip
this step or simply replicate an older design using new technology. A piece of history
is enlightening here.

When Thomas Edison invented the electrical power industry, manufacturing was
primarily powered by steam. Factories were constructed by building a large steam
engine at one end of a factory with a power shaft that ran the length of the factory.
Each machine tool was connected to this shaft by means of a belt that transferred
power from the shaft to the tool. The placement of these tools in the factory was dictated by their proximity to the power shaft. When electricity replaced steam, most
factories replaced their steam engines with very large electric motors to turn the shaft.
Otherwise, the structure of the factory remained the same.

One of the paradoxes was that for the first 20 years of electrical power, there was
no increase in productivity in the economy. Gradually, smaller electric motors were
developed. They soon became small enough to put an individual motor on each power
tool. Power was then transmitted through the factory by wires that could be run anywhere. Factories could be restructured around the workflow rather than the power
shaft. The structure of how the factory worked became more effective. Finally, the
productivity of the economy took a sharp increase. As long as electrical power was
used without restructuring the work, there was little increase in productivity.

The same productivity paradox has been reported for computing[2]. For the first
20 years of computing, the economy did not show an increase in productivity. Personal
computers let secretaries produce nicer looking documents and edit them more
quickly. However, until most of the white-collar workforce learned to type and found
that typing and revising their own letters was faster than multiple drafts through a

secretary, the number of secretaries required per person remained unchanged and there was no net gain. A change of work to reduce staffing was required before benefits were realized. Until businesses like FedEx, Dell, and Wal-Mart changed the way their industry worked to take advantage of the new opportunities provided by computers, the economy did not shift.

As we develop user interfaces, it is most important to remember that the greatest increase in "usability" will come when the work itself becomes simpler, not just beautifying the screens. Beginning with a careful look at the fundamental work being done and then modeling that work in easy-to-understand user interfaces is key to effective design of interactive systems.

With this in mind, this chapter provides a brief sketch of the functional design of an interface. This is only a brief sketch; you should look to software design texts for a more in-depth understanding.

WHO WILL THIS SYSTEM SERVE?

User interfaces are about people interacting with computers. They cannot be effectively designed without knowing who is to be served. The VCR obviously serves home consumers, but things are not quite that simple. The VCR must also serve the salesperson and the magazine writer. If the salesperson is not served, there will be no sale and no consumer use of the system. Fortunately, the salesperson's needs and the consumer's needs are very similar. If the "record" feature can occur in the 15 seconds available for a sales demo and can be readily learned by someone who is selling 25 different models of VCR, then it will probably work well for the consumer. However, a consumer might be willing to spend 15–20 minutes of one-time setup of the system, whereas a salesperson cannot afford such effort. Identify both sets of users and be certain that their needs really are similar. VCR users do not fall in a single uniform lump. There are the elderly with lots of time but poor eyesight, short-term memory, and shaky motor skills. There are the techno-teen boys who joy in mastering new gadgets. There are the elderly retired men who see making the thing work as a nice afternoon hobby. Many consumers want the box to quickly do its job with minimal fuss. We will probably not want to sell our particular VCR to all of these, but rather target a few of them. Knowing which we are targeting is essential.

Basketball sales have a more complex user base. Obviously, there are the people who want to buy tickets. In addition, there is the sales office that must handle problems and coordinate their sales with the new online system. There is the marketing and promotions departments that want to put together packages and cross-selling opportunities. Marketing also wants to track the sales impact of their promotions and advertising. Accounting needs to track income and process credit card information. Auditors need a transaction trail to detect abuse. Lastly, management wants to know sales numbers. Though the customer is king, all of these users must be served. The user interface lives in an organizational context with which it must interact.

Even when working on a project of limited scope, you should still identify all of the users affected by the design and the people that they directly communicate with. You should go one step broader in your circle of users than the actual people who will interact with the user interface in question. The reason for this breadth is to make certain that you have accounted for needs and constraints that might not be obvious to the actual users. Many clerical/data entry people have good knowledge about how they use their current system and its difficulties. However, they rarely have a good feel for the organizational reasons for current practice. Stepping one level beyond them brings in that context.

> Make a list of all of the types of users that will interface with this system. If there are many types, attempt to group them by similarity of needs. Also note the relative importance of each user type.

Each of the types of users has different goals when they interact with the new user-interface design. The VCR salesperson has very different goals from the VCR user. The basketball marketing group has different goals from the sports fan. You need to specifically account for each of these diverse sets of goals.

> Refine the project goals to a set of goals for each group of users. Be specific about what each group is trying to accomplish in using the new system.

Various groups of users have varying skills and their own language or terminology. Accounting departments speak in terms of debits, credits, and encumbrances. These terms are foreign to the sports fan. Management personnel sometimes do not possess typing skills or are reluctant to use them because typing indicates loss of status. Event-planning people talk about venues whereas that term has no meaning for most fans. When designing a VCR for the elderly user, you must remember that their eyesight is poor and they frequently have poor motor skills. Large symbols, numbers, and buttons are required in such a market.

Various groups of users frequently have their own symbols and notations for things. Mathematicians, engineers, medical personnel, and musicians all have well-developed notations for communicating with each other. There are standard symbols on virtually all VCRs for stop, play, pause, fast-forward, and rewind. You need to understand the existence of those symbols and their meaning for various groups of users.

> For each group of users, assemble lists of their skills (or lack of skills), terminology, and symbology.

WHAT ARE WE TRYING TO DO?

Knowing who the users are provides the source for design information. You now need to identify the actual tasks that people are trying to accomplish. These tasks are frequently composed into subtasks. A user might approach their VCR with the task "Record Star Trek tomorrow." The general form of this task is to watch a particular show on a particular day. This task can be broken down into several subtasks, as shown in Figure 25.1.

```
Watch show S on day D
        Find S in a program guide G
                Identify network (ABC, FOX, NICK)
                Find start and end time
        Program VCR
                Indicate that future recording is required
                Enter start and end time
                Translate network into a channel number
                Enter channel number
        Load blank tape
                Put in tape
                Position tape where recording is to start
                Determine if there is enough tape to record the show
```

Figure 25.1 – Task analysis of recording a show on a VCR

It is interesting to compare this task breakdown for a traditional VCR with the new Digital Video Recorders (DVR). In a DVR, the program guide is loaded into the device over a network and the videotape has been replaced by a disk drive. The DVR task structure is as shown in Figure 25.2.

```
Watch show S on day D
        Navigate program guide to find S on day D
        Select record
        Verify that there is sufficient disk space to record the show
```

Figure 25.2 – Task analysis of recording a show on TiVo

By paying attention to the user's actual tasks (find and record a show), a DVR simplifies the process. Start time, end time, and channel are handled automatically. They never were part of the user's goals, only artifacts of the technology. A DVR eliminates the tape start, end, format, and positioning problems by using standard file allocation strategies. No amount of screen, button, or display design can compensate for the fundamentally simpler task structure that a DVR offers over the traditional VCR. Seeing the opportunity to increase system usability involves first considering the tasks to be performed. It cannot be stressed enough that true usability gains almost always come from restructuring the task.

We can perform a similar task analysis for buying basketball tickets. In this analysis, a user might have a variety of tasks, as shown in Figure 25.3.

Order tickets for N people for the game on Friday.
Order tickets for the next time the Lakers come to town.
Change tickets for this Friday's game to the next Blazers game.
The coach of a kiddie basketball team needs to find a game with a cheap promotion
    for 12 tickets on a Wednesday or Thursday night before the end of February.
Tickets for next Tuesday have not yet arrived.

Figure 25.3 – Sports fan high-level tasks

The task of "buying tickets" is not as simple as it might first appear. People approach the system with many different tasks and goals in mind. A particular fan could easily perform all of the listed tasks at various times. This is only the fan's point of view. We also have all of the other potential users. The goals of creating, pricing, presenting, and evaluating special package promotions carries with it a whole different set of tasks that the marketing group must perform.

As you talk with users about their tasks, you need answers to four questions:

- What is the end goal of each task?
- What are the subtasks?
- What information is required to carry out each task or subtask?
- How will the user decide if a task has been successfully accomplished?

We need to keep the goal of the task in mind so that we do not get caught up in our current approach to achieving that goal. A process-centric approach to the VCR recording problem leads us to the subtask of entering a time. A goal-centric approach tells us that time is only a means to an end. In many recording tasks, the user does not care about the time, but only about a particular show or set of shows.

Breaking Down the Tasks

Breaking down the tasks into their component tasks is important for two reasons. First, it helps to understand what the task actually involves. The high-level fan tasks (see Figure 25.3) are not very informative in guiding the user-interface design. More detail is needed. You almost always develop these tasks to reflect a user's currently familiar approaches. This is because users are rarely good at thinking creatively about how they might do something different. You can address the "better idea" later when you have captured the information about their current tasks.

In trying to understand a user's tasks, many researchers have borrowed the techniques of ethnography from the field of anthropology[3]. The idea is to watch and record how users actually do their current work in its current context. These are the same techniques used when sitting in a village observing some tribal society. There is, however, a fundamental difference between user-interface design and anthropology. An anthropologist is trying to understand the observed behavior while influencing that behavior as little as possible. Interference is a major "no-no" in the science of anthropology. User-interface designers hope to change the process to make it better. This is a very different mind-set.

What Information Is Required?

Modern computing is fundamentally about information more than computation. User interfaces communicate information between people and computers. You must know the information required to complete each task and where that information comes from. Simplifying information flow is probably the most important way to increase the usability. Eliminating the copying of channel/start/end information from the program guide to the VCR is a major contribution of DVRs. It simplifies the information flow for the user.

In traditional organizations, information flows on paper. When designing a new user interface, the task analysis should collect copies of every type of form, letter, or other information. Where there are existing user interfaces, screen shots should be collected. Pay particular attention to notes made in the margins or the use of sticky notes. These are indications of information not captured by the current system and yet critical to the process.

How Will the User Know They Have Succeeded in Their Task?

It is very important to note how a user decides that a particular goal has been met. A huge problem when recording on most VCRs is knowing if the recording is set up correctly. In an effort to save display device costs, most VCRs do not show the channel/start/end information for the current recording. At most, a piece of this information is shown overlaid on the same display devices used for other purposes. A VCR user is rarely confident of their settings. A more subtle problem is knowing how much tape is available and whether the show fits. Most VCRs provide no indication of this, leaving the user to guess and make very frustrating mistakes. Most DVRs display a warning if there is not sufficient disk space for a program to be recorded. The user is now informed and can take appropriate action before the recording is lost.

When a person decides to buy basketball tickets, how do they decide when the task has been completed to their satisfaction? If we think about this problem, people care about the game opponent and date, ticket cost, and the quality of the seats. Items like date, time, teams playing, and price are easily displayed. How do people evaluate the quality of their seats? Most people would rather be closer than farther away. Most of us balance good seats with price. Most of us prefer chair seats to bench seats. What a lot of us care about is the view of the court from our seat. Displaying a photo of the court from seat location greatly simplifies seat choice. This approach directly addresses the user's goal of seat quality. Understanding how the user evaluates success tells us a lot about the kinds of information that we should present and how we should present it.

Talk to members of all of the user types and make lists of tasks to be performed along with who performs the task, what information they need to perform the task, and how they will decide that the task has been performed successfully.

Scenarios of Use

While developing a set of tasks, it is very helpful to create and save scenarios of how users will accomplish their tasks. These scenarios should involve a specific user with a specific goal. We then go through their task step-by-step. Many such scenarios can be developed from ethnographic studies of current systems.

These scenarios serve four purposes. First, they force us to be very specific about how the work actually gets done. Second, by working through the scenario, you can carefully identify every function to be performed and every piece of information required to perform that function. Third, these scenarios make the design process real for potential users. Users do not work well with abstract descriptions. Abstraction is a computer science skill that comes with training. Potential users need concrete examples to critique and improve. Lastly, you can use your scenarios to evaluate your functional designs to see if they actually accomplish all that you have planned.

While constructing your scenarios, you need to note the exceptions that can occur. At each step, what are the things that might go wrong? These include missing information, incorrect entry, interruptions, or misunderstandings. Quality systems support all of the work, not just the simple clean portions. Good user interfaces help prevent or highlight errors early rather than later. Understanding these errors is very important.

> For each task, prepare several scenarios of a user accomplishing the task. Note the functions and information required as well as the exceptions that might arise.

OBJECT-BASED TASK/FUNCTION MODELS

User interfaces are primarily designed around information. Even when extensive calculation is involved, the user interface consists of modifying the control information for the calculation, initiating the calculation, and then reviewing the output. Recognizing the info-centric nature of user interfaces, we design models based on the task's information objects.

A variety of representation schemes can be used in model design, such as Entity-Relationship Diagrams[4] or the Unified Modeling Language (UML)[5]. For smaller projects, an abbreviated version of the class definitions of your favorite object-oriented language will serve. What is needed is to clearly capture the types of information objects required, their attributes, and their methods. We do not want to implement them yet; we just want to understand them. In many ways, the approach of this chapter is similar to Shneiderman's Object-Action-Interface model[6].

For the VCR example, the types of information are program guides, days, lists of shows, show times, and VCRs. Figure 25.4 shows a model in C#-like syntax.

```
class ProgramGuide
{      ShowList find(String nameOfShow);
       ShowList find(String nameOfShow, Day whichDay)
}
enum DayOfWeek{Sunday, Monday, Tuesday, Wednesday, Thursday, Friday,
       Saturday}
enum Month(January, February, … December}
class Day
{      Day(DayOfWeek dayThisWeek);
       Day(Month month, int day);
       Day Today();
       Day Tomorrow();
}
class ShowList
{      int numberOfShows(); // how many shows in the list
       Show this[int whichShow]; //index into the show list
       ShowList filter(Day whichDay); // filters a show list to those on a particular day
       ShowList filter(string showName): // filters a show list to a particular show name
}
class Show
{
       string network; //which network is it on
       int channel; //which channel is it on
       string showName; // what is the name of the show
       Time start, end;
       Day dayOfShow;
}
class Time
{      int hour,  minute;
}
class VCR
{      void record(Show whichShow);
       int channel;
       Day recordDay;
       Time start, end;
}
```

Figure 25.4 – Model for VCR programming

This model design does not account for many implementation issues. There are no data structures and none of the view notifications required in MVC. There are fields on the classes without accessor methods to control them. The design is a clean specification of the function of the desired interface.

The model design for the basketball ticket system is much more complex. There are venue calendars, events, classes of seating, promotional packages, group discount packages, advertising material (the HTML promoting each event), transactions, seat availability maps, customers, and credit cards. Great care must be taken in developing this model because it sharply impacts what is possible after it is installed. A simplistic view of ticket sales ignores promotional packages. However, such packages are very important in filling less important games or those high-priced lower bowl seats that are behind the basket. Selling tickets over the Web includes presenting advertising of the games. Simplistic advertising support in the system might jeopardize anticipated cost reductions by increased advertising costs. Capturing all of these interactions before casting the design into code is very, very important.

> Construct an object model by creating classes for each of the types of information extracted from the scenarios. For each class, specify the constructors, fields, and methods required to perform the processes identified in the task analysis. Walk through all scenarios with the object model to make certain it is complete.

Assigning Agency

To this point, the design process has looked broadly at the tasks to be performed. Neighboring tasks, related users, and the rest of the interface's context of use have all been considered. However, at some point, you must decide what will actually be built. It is rarely practical to automate the entire object model. You must pick the key parts of the model and provide those in your system. It is also frequently the case that many parts of the system already exist. The assignment of agency is to determine who or what is responsible for each class of information object in the functional design.

In the VCR example, the traditional VCR design relegates the `ProgramGuide`, `ShowList`, and `Show` to a paper document. The VCR implements only the `Day(DayOfWeek)` and VCR classes. Operations like `Today()` and `Tomorrow()` are done by the user remembering the day of the week and making the right choice. The user is responsible for translating the show information into the required date and time.

A prime reason for casting a wide net during task analysis is the discipline it imposes when assigning agency. Whenever you designate some task step as outside of the system, you must account for how information crosses the boundaries into and out of the system. These information flows across boundaries are extremely important and are a major source of system errors. The information flows between user and system define the functionality of the user interface.

This assignment of agency and communication of information across system boundaries is particularly problematic in business settings. The traditional approach is to use paper to cross boundaries. The process of buying a new laptop illustrates this. In the traditional approach, the following steps occur:

- I decide what kind of laptop I want, write it down, and give it to our department's support staff.
- The support staff <u>types</u> up a purchase order, gets it signed by the chair and dean, and sends it to purchasing.
- Purchasing contacts the vendor and asks for a quote.
- Vendor <u>prints</u> and mails a quote.

- The purchasing office <u>types</u> the quote information into their ordering system.
- The ordering system <u>prints</u> an order that is mailed to the vendor.
- The vendor <u>types</u> the order into their sales system.
- The laptop is built and shipped.
- The invoice is <u>printed</u> and mailed to the purchasing department.

The process actually goes on endlessly through shipping, receiving, and the computing staff. At each stage, paper is used to communicate and information is typed, retyped, and retyped again. Through all of these steps, there is confusion about what is ordered and when it will be delivered. There are many systems with many user interfaces and many phone calls to coordinate and track problems in the process.

The current system is that I get on the vendor's Web site and select the configuration of laptop that I want. The system generates a quote number, which I e-mail to our support staff. They get signed approvals and send the quote number to purchasing, which forwards it directly to the vendor. The vendor builds according to the system that I specified and ships directly to me. At any time, I can check the quote to see the status of when I will receive the system. Invoices and payments happen automatically and digitally. This system is much more usable because information flows have been optimized to meet my task (buying what I want) rather than the cross-organization communication task. Thinking through the functional design of the process rather than fiddling with screen layouts was what provided the great leap in usability.

> Assign agency to all parts of the object model. Who or what is responsible for performing all of the operations and handling all of the information in the model?

> Carefully review information flows between the new implementation and other systems and people.

Functional Design

Having assigned agency to the classes, fields, and methods of our task-based model, we can now produce our functional design. The functional design for the traditional VCR is shown in Figure 25.5. Note that this functional design ignores all of the other functions of a VCR, such as pause and play. To do a real design, you need to account for these other functions.

```
enum DayOfWeek{Sunday, Monday, Tuesday, Wednesday, Thursday, Friday,
    Saturday}
class Time
{    int hour,  minute; }
class VCR
{
    int channel;
    DayOfWeek recordDay;
    Time start, end;
}
```

Figure 25.5 – Traditional functional design for VCR recording

Considering all of your task analysis, object-modeling, and agency, construct a class, constructor, field, and method model for exactly what your user interface must do.

View Sketching to Evaluate Functional Design

A functional design like that shown in Figure 25.5 lays the foundation for model implementation. You now know what you are trying to build. However, the users do not know what you are trying to build. Presenting prospective users with a functional design like that shown in Figure 25.5 will not produce interesting user insight. They have very little idea how this notation relates to their problem or its solution. This functional model needs to be translated into view sketches. View sketches are simply pictures of how the information might appear to the user. Designing the views is not properly part of functional design. However, users cannot evaluate designs any other way. They must see it in concrete terms.

When sketching prospective views of your functional design, it is important that the process be as lightweight as possible. You need to be able to generate and evaluate many designs quite rapidly. If the application can be built out of standard widgets, an interface design tool can rapidly lay out a sample view. This can be prepared in minutes, printed, and shown to prospective users. Using these printed mock-ups, you can work through the scenarios with actual users to see if they can accomplish all of the tasks in a convenient fashion or if some information/capability is missing.

You also need to remember that you are evaluating functional design not presentation design. The question is not how it looks but whether it is easy to accomplish the desired goals. A pitfall in view sketching is getting caught up in issues of color, font selection, layout, and so on. This is the wrong time for such discussions. View sketches should project the functionality of the system in a form the users can understand and evaluate. Having said that, you must not be a purist. You should accept input about screen design, terminology, and layout because you will eventually need such information. The key is to not lose sight of the larger goal, which is to get the functionality right before spending effort on smaller details. This is the time for considering diverse alternatives for modeling the problem, not the time for choosing fonts.

A second pitfall in view sketching is the presumption of "doneness" and the seduction of increased fidelity. When using an interface design tool to present a functional design, the result looks too finished. If users are naïve about software development, the finished look implies that the product is almost done. The finished look of the sketch also creates a mind-set for the way the functionality "must" be implemented. Early rigidity cuts off potentially better alternatives. Some design tools provide a "sketchy" look that purposely makes the design look rough and unfinished[7]. The Silk system allows designs to be drawn as active sketches[8]. It is also tempting when sketching with an interface design tool to keep improving the fidelity of the interface making it more and more real. This produces programmer rigidity. Time investment in a particular design starts to block consideration of alternatives. The goal is functionality, not visual design.

One approach is "paper prototyping"[9]. Software is avoided and paper sketches are used exclusively. With paper designs, there is no implication of "doneness." It is also easy to write on paper designs and, thus, change them on the fly during the design process. This has the additional advantage of being accessible to designers with limited programming skills but good understanding of users and their problems. These are all techniques for getting user feedback on whether our functional designs actually capture the problem we are trying to solve.

> Render the functional design into a series of "view sketches" that show the functional capabilities as a user interface. Use these sketches to evaluate scenarios and do design walk-throughs with prospective users.

Translating to a Model Implementation Interface

The functional design can now be translated into an actual model implementation interface. This is not the functionality of the model but rather the methods that it uses to expose the functionality to view/controllers and to other parts of the system. This design of the interface methods for the functionality allows view/controller development to proceed independently from application functionality development.

The functional model classes translate directly into implementation model classes. Fields must be translated into accessor functions. Methods usually translate directly. In many cases, we need to flesh out our data structures. While doing design, we wave our hands over "lists" and other structures. At this point, you need to design how the views actually access needed information.

Using the view sketches helps to design the view notification strategy. If the views are simple, a single "model changed" method is adequate. If they are more complex, a more specific "this element changed" notification might be required. Detailed view designs are not required, but a general idea of how the information is viewed helps in designing a notification strategy. Now is also the time to make certain that the notification strategy is robust, easily used with the code, and concentrated in a few places.

> Translate functional design into model API by defining all of the classes and methods of the model. This includes accessor methods for data and the view notification strategy.

A Note About Testing

Building a robust testing facility for user interfaces is quite difficult. Regression testing involves the creation of self-checking tests that can be automatically run whenever changes are made. This is extremely important to large development projects. The problem when testing interactive programs is the creation of an "artificial user." How do we test for users having input mouse points at particular locations when layouts allow widgets to shift and move? How do we test for "the display shows the right stuff"? One approach that helps is to carefully develop a model that contains most of the functionality. With such a model and a clean model interface, a series of regression tests can be developed that evaluate the changes, the notifications, and a variety of other properties of the model without incurring the difficulties of simulating a user. Trying to test everything interactively can be frustrating, error-prone, and not very complete.

SUMMARY

Before implementing any user interface you must understand what you are trying to accomplish and what your interface should actually do. This will lead you directly to the design of the model for your user interface. The model is the correct starting place for a good user interface design because it establishes what functionality must be present.

To understand what is needed you must understand the types of users that will be served including their skills, goals, and language. You must then break down the goals into tasks that can be accomplished with the new user interfaces and example scenarios for how this will occur.

From the tasks and the information used in those tasks you can develop a set of object types with fields to contain the information and functions to perform the desired actions. From this object model you can carve out the actual functionality of your user interface by assigning agency to the various object types.

EXERCISES

1. Pick a sample Web-based service and identify the types of users that are impacted by the functions of that interface.

2. Take one type of user from Exercise 1 and identify a list of tasks that the user needs to accomplish relative to this service. Review your list to make certain the tasks reflect user intent rather than current process.

3. Pick one of the tasks and develop a concrete scenario for how that task would be accomplished. Account for every piece of information that the user needs at each step and note anything exceptional that might happen at each step.

4. Take a sample Web-based service and list the object information types, their fields, and their methods. Make certain that all information on the Web page is accounted for in the model and all information that the user brings in making his or her decisions.

END NOTES

[1] Beyer, H., and K. Holtzblatt. *Contextual Design: A Customer-Centered Approach to Systems Designs*. San Mateo, CA: Morgan Kaufmann, 1997.

[2] Landauer, T. K. *The Trouble with Computers: Usefulness, Usability and Productivity*. Cambridge, MA: MIT Press, 1995.

[3] Crabtree, A. *Designing Collaborative Systems: A Practical Guide to Ethnography*. New York: Springer, 2003.

[4] Thalheim, B. *Entity-Relationship Modeling: Foundations of Database Technology*. New York: Springer, 2000.

[5] Larman, C. *Applying UML and Patterns: An Introduction to Object-Oriented Analysis and Design and Iterative Development*. Upper Saddle River, NJ: Prentice Hall, 2004.

[6] Shneiderman, B., and C. Plaisant. *Designing the User Interface: Strategies for Effective Human-Computer Interaction*. New York: Addison-Wesley, 2004.

[7] Hudson, S. E., and K. Tanaka. "Providing Visually Rich Resizable Images for User Interface Components." *User Interface Software and Technology (UIST '00)* (November 2000): 227–235.

[8] Landay, J. A. "SILK: Sketching Interfaces Like Krazy." *Human Factors in Computing Systems (CHI '96)* (April 1996): 398–399.

[9] Snyder, C. *Paper Prototyping: The Fast and Easy Way to Design and Refine User Interfaces*. San Mateo, CA: Morgan Kaufmann, 2003.

CHAPTER 26

Evaluating Interaction

With all of the ways and means for humans to interact with their computers and the creative drive to make new ones, you must decide if any of it is any good. This is actually a challenging question. A direct, valid, and not very satisfying answer is, "It is good if it sells." If your new technique solves a problem in a better way, then capitalism says people should flock to it. In a very global sense, this is true. However, capitalism is driven by costs that once spent are hard to recover. Most people want to believe that a new solution is "good" before they invest money to build it, market it, or buy it and money to convert from whatever they were doing before. If the solution is not "good," little of this money can be recovered. Your first set of questions to ask when evaluating a new user-interface technology has to do with the situation, tasks, and users that the technology is meant to address.

This chapter is not an exhaustive or even very deep treatise on evaluation of user interfaces. There are many books on usability evaluations, experimental methods, and statistics. Much of this chapter is a set of warnings about flawed evaluations. Finding a good set of techniques for really knowing if you are serving your users is hard. This chapter is a guide for avoiding simple but erroneous answers to important questions.

SITUATION/TASK/USER (STU)

It is first important to ask, "Where will this interaction occur?" The answer to this question is the situation for the interaction. The situation imposes constraints on what can be done and how it can be done. Many people prefer text entry with a stylus for handheld devices because standard-sized keyboards are impossible to use while walking around. Pens and mice both point at a location on the screen. If the task involves text entry and pointing in combination, the mouse is superior because it is easier to reach. A pen takes more time to pick up and put into a writing posture than simply laying one's hand on the mouse. Devices and interactive techniques for people sitting in a recliner watching a screen across the room are very different from those used at a desk. Much innovation in interactive techniques occurs to adapt to a situation that is not addressed by previous technology.

You should then ask, "Good for what?" The task to be accomplished also imposes constraints and establishes goals to be accomplished. A gesture recognition system driven by a mouse is a terrible text entry technique, especially if there is a keyboard available. Similarly, the arrow keys on a keyboard can be used to point to a location on the screen, but the mouse is far superior in most cases. The technology should be driven by the task.

Finally, you need to ask, "Who will be interacting?" Users are not all created equal. Children have different input needs from surgeons. Auto mechanics have different needs from secretaries. The elderly or people with motor impairments have needs that are different from the general populace. Technology does not buy technology—people do. User interfaces must serve people.

The most valuable evaluation of a new technique is the importance of the situation/task/user context in which the technique is to be used. In many cases, a new combination of these becomes the most compelling reason for a new interactive technique.

Situation: on the lawn, in the tub, in the grocery store, in the airport

Task: short text messages

Users: just about everyone, but particularly teens and young adults

Technique: MultiTap text entry using 12 keys on a cell phone

Why is MultiTap (pressing a phone key one to four times to select a letter) so popular when it feels so ugly? It addresses the needs of a particular STU context.

Evaluating STU Importance

The very first question before any experiments, prototypes, or user studies are performed is to evaluate whether a proposed technique addresses an important situation/task/user combination. If the STU is not important, there is no point in proceeding with the rest of the evaluation exercise. Too many experiments are performed on questions for which nobody cares to hear the answer.

To begin with, you must have an important user group. Many things make a group important. The group might be all adults in developed countries. That group is important by its size and economic power. A group might be important because of their impact on everyone else, such as doctors, emergency personnel, or teachers. Everyone has a vested interest in these groups performing well. A group might be important for no other reason than they are the customers of your company and that is where your paycheck comes from. For most of you, that is important.

The next question is whether the tasks are important to the users. Better support for fantasy gaming by the elderly is not a real important combination. It would definitely be unique. It would definitely be a challenge, but nobody would care because the elderly are currently not interested in fantasy gaming. That might change, but a change in values must come first. Text entry for toddlers would also not be a great task/user combination.

Lastly, there is the situation. You must be clear about whether the target tasks and users would frequently occur in the proposed situation. Are doctors important? Yes. Do doctors need access to patient information? Yes. Do doctors ski? Yes, many of them do. Do doctors need access to patient information while skiing? Probably not. Techniques for doctors to access patient information while mobile within a hospital or other places would be very important, but the special challenges of patient record interaction while skiing do not seem that important.

Evaluation Challenges in STU

Evaluation studies must reflect the STU that you are targeting. Obviously, the best evaluation studies will be as close as possible to actual practice. However, this is exactly where many user-interface evaluations founder.

Evaluating Situations

The situation in which a technique is to be used is critical to its effectiveness. Some technologies are used in a variety of situations. These are easier to evaluate because you can pick a safe, inexpensive situation for your experiments. The controls for a fighter jet or for digital surgery are not used in safe or inexpensive situations. For each of these interactions, the context of use is absolutely critical. However, the criticality itself makes it hard to perform evaluation experiments. Nobody wants to be the first subject for a user study on laser eye surgery. Such evaluations require many less dangerous evaluations first. If a pilot cannot fly a simulator with the new controls, they will not want to try them in a new airplane. If they cannot fly the plane normally, they will not want to try it in simulated combat. If the controls do not test out in simulated combat, they will not want to actually fight with the plane. A sequence of evaluations successively approaching realistic context is necessary to identify problems with as little risk as possible.

Though you can begin your evaluations in safe, inexpensive situations, you must eventually address your target situation. Real situations are messy. It is hard to control the experiment to eliminate confounding influences. It is very tempting to simplify the experimental situation for cost, safety, and ease of experimental control and then imply that the experiment's results are valid for real situations. Frequently, you have no other choice, but you must be honest about the nature of your assumptions and implications. An experiment performed on five university freshmen in a research lab is frequently better than no data at all, but it is hardly conclusive proof that the technique is usable by rescue workers in the field.

Realistic Tasks for Evaluation

Real tasks are hard and complex. If the tasks were not hard, you generally would not be looking for a computing solution. Tasks are frequently hard because they are embedded within other tasks. Take, for example, the development of a more usable programming language. This is an excellent goal. You all want more usable programming languages. However, serious programming problems take months if not years and teams of many people. Suppose that you want to prove that software development system A is more usable than system B. You could identify 10 development problems and give system A to five teams of five programmers and system B to five other teams of five and ask them to solve all 10 problems. To be realistic, each problem takes six months.

You have just committed 50 programmers to five years of effort at an approximate cost of $25,000,000 in salary alone. In the end, you do not really have a good experiment because you might have picked teams that cannot work together well for five years and their interpersonal issues overshadow the contributions of system A versus system B. At the end of all the time and expense, you really do not know anything about the relative merits of A and B.

One solution is to simplify the task. You select 10 tasks that each take a day to program and assign 30 programmers to solve them in system A and 30 to solve them using system B. Your salary costs are now down to about $300,000 and the number of participants might give you a statistically valid answer. However, the team dynamics of the experiment do not match real team dynamics and the sizes of the problems are no longer realistic. Do you really know how A and B will perform in a realistic scenario? Maybe. Note also that $300,000 is a lot of money to spend on one usability experiment. All is not lost, however, because if a language is not usable at this scale it is probably not usable on a larger scale. You have learned something from this experiment.

A more cost-effective approach is to break down the problem. You can watch software engineers and decide that they do a lot of text entry, a lot of debugging, a lot of test code creation, and hold a lot of design meetings. You can then tackle each of those independently. You might also note that every piece of software they use has a menu. You could decide to improve the usability of the menu. Menu selection looks easy to evaluate. However, if you told the average software engineer that you could make their menus 10 percent more effective, would they care? You also have the problem that debugging and test code creation are themselves very complex and need to be broken down further. Eventually, the tasks get broken down to something you can evaluate, but you are no longer sure that what you have designed works well in the real context.

The point here is not to stop evaluation, but to recognize that real tasks are complex, messy things. You could restrict yourself to developing new text entry techniques or better ways to pop virtual bubbles with a mouse. These are tasks that are easy to evaluate and you might learn something from them, but in the end you must address real tasks in all their messiness.

One approach is to ask users who are experienced with the task to attempt to accomplish it using the new technique and then respond as to whether they think it will help. Another approach is to select interactive problems that experienced users believe need solutions and then ask them whether the proposed solution would actually help. In these approaches, you are relying on the user's judgment about what will and will not help them solve their problem. There are two warnings attached to this strategy. The first is that users are creatures of habit and might respond negatively to a solution that is very different from their habits. The negative response does not mean that the technique is not better—it might just be too different for the limited interest of the test users. Conversely, when presented with a new approach, users frequently will call it "cool," "better," "innovative," and other positive things because they like new stuff and they like you. This does not mean that in the heat of everyday work they will not put your shiny new interaction on the shelf where it will not get in their way. These issues can only be resolved by the evaluator intelligently watching the use and listening carefully to what users are really saying.

Evaluating Users

It has been said that "much of psychology is really about college freshmen." The reason for this is that it is relatively easy to recruit students from introductory classes to be subjects for experiments. Getting a good set of users can be a problem. The two key issues are expertise and motivation.

The expertise problem has two aspects. If the target user set has specialized expertise, it is frequently difficult to find qualified subjects who are willing to devote the time. It is easier to have juniors in computer science evaluate a programming system than it is to use professionals with many years of experience. The first set can be a filter for bad ideas but in the end it is the professionals who select the tools. The medical profession is particularly problematic in obtaining people with expertise to serve as evaluation subjects. Doctors are very busy, very expensive, and somewhat set in their ways.

The second part of the problem is lack of expertise in your new interactive technique. You saw this in your discussion of text input. In many situations, you are willing to invest training in a user interface to help your users be most effective. Frequently, technologies designed to "walk up and use" are not very efficient once users have become proficient. When introducing a new user-interface technology, there are no existing users who are proficient. The lack of proficiency can handicap a new technology in any experiment. This is a serious challenge in very high-expertise disciplines such as medicine or programming where acquiring expertise takes a lot of time. Many experiments cannot afford the time to require expertise and, thus, less realistic experiments are used as substitutes.

User motivation is a challenge in any experiment. Suppose you have a search-and-rescue problem where a single operator is to control many robots searching an area for accident victims. Operating several robots at once is a mentally challenging task. If there is a lost child and it is getting dark, an operator is very focused and trying to get as much searching done as possible. This is the usage that you want to serve and evaluate. However, if the operator is a student who is being paid $25 for an hour of time on the system, he or she frequently will slack off and only operate one robot because it is easier. There is no child's life at stake and they just want the $25 for pizza. The information from such an unmotivated user is not very useful for your search-and-rescue problem. Getting the right set of users with the right expertise and the right motivation is a barrier to good evaluations.

The preceding paragraphs contain several warnings about experiments and how they can fail. This does not mean that you should cast aside evaluation. However, you do need to think carefully about an experiment before collecting 20 users and make certain that the design of the experiment is not suffering from any of the flaws that have been presented. Getting good data is a challenging task. Making design decisions with bad data or no data is much worse. The following sections discuss various evaluation approaches that you might consider.

FORMATIVE EVALUATION

There are two basic approaches to evaluation of user interfaces. In a formative evaluation, you are trying to discover the form or shape of a good user interface for a particular task. In a summative evaluation, you have two or more competing technologies that you want to compare to see which is best. The techniques for formative versus summative evaluations are very different.

In the early stages of the design of a new interaction technique, you are trying to rapidly explore a space of design choices. You have probably identified the situation, task, and users. What you need is a way to winnow down the set of possible design alternatives and to resolve design disputes. This is the domain for formative evaluation. You are not after provable validity of the evaluation. You are trying to identify user problems and understand their nature as rapidly as possible. In a formative evaluation, cheating on situation, task, and user can still be valuable. If a new technique works badly on computer science graduate students working in a lab, it probably will not work in the wild with technically naïve users.

You can also cheat on the number of users to try. Frequently, the very first user reveals problems that the developers had not considered. This is valuable stuff. It is very tempting with a new technique to immediately schedule a 30-subject user experiment to prove the greatness of your new invention. This is probably doomed to failure. The very first user frequently cannot use the technique for some reason. Perhaps you have not trained them correctly or there is a simple flaw that the programmers kept working around. You thank the user for the new insight and prepare for three days of work to fix the problem. However, you have 10 more users scheduled to arrive this afternoon for testing on a system you now know will not work for most of them. Always start with one user, such as the person working next to you. If they do not get it, it is unlikely that anyone else will.

In formative evaluations, you frequently cheat on the fidelity of the implementation. What you want is very early input on the viability of a new technique. In your lab, you have been exploring very small personal computers. You did some sketches of a computer that was a simple cube. These pencil sketches are themselves part of a formative evaluation process. The technique is rapidly sketched and then shown to other people for reactions. Pencil and paper are very cheap and they helped you rapidly explore many approaches. For the cube computer in Figure 26.1, you then bought some two-inch wooden cubes at a local craft store and drew the controls on them in pen. As soon as you tried a simulated use, you discovered that the hand posture was cramped and uncomfortable. Any extended use would be fatiguing. The shape also was very uncomfortable and ugly in a pants pocket. For $1.50 in parts and 30 minutes of testing, you were able to discard this design choice and move on, happy in the thought that no expensive prototypes had been built.

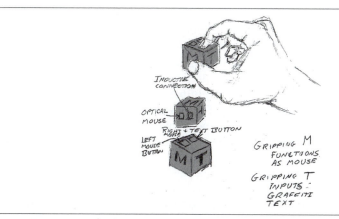

Figure 26.1 – Cube computer sketches

There are many techniques for creating prototypes for rapid formative evaluation. For physical devices, blocks of wood, pieces of paper, and carved high-density foam allow rapid prototyping of the shape and size. For screen-based applications, paper prototypes can be very effective[1]. Acquiring basic drawing skill can be very valuable to an interaction designer. In your lab, you frequently use PowerPoint as a tool for rapidly drawing a design and sequencing through the desired behavior. The designs are crude but they make the discussions very concrete and you can rapidly do many of them. Nielsen[2] and others have developed techniques for rapid evaluation of usability before the expense of a controlled experiment. The goal of formative evaluations is to get information about actual usage into the design process as early as possible to identify what does not work.

SUMMATIVE EVALUATION

A formative evaluation identifies what does not work and guides a design process. It is not necessarily helpful in making progress against other competing solutions. A summative evaluation is good for answering the question, "Is this better?" Summative evaluations are based on experiments and are an attempt to establish verifiable improvements and knowledge about the usability of a new technique. There are many approaches to such an evaluation. One dominant approach is a controlled experiment with appropriate statistical analysis of the results. The second is a comparative analysis of features and capabilities.

Controlled Experiments

In a controlled experiment, there are one or more independent variables that are to be manipulated and one or more dependent variables to be measured. Though a given experiment might measure multiple dependent variables, you generally can separate them from each other in your analysis. In most experiments, the independent variable is the system or interactive technique being used. For example, you might compare keyboard text entry to stylus-based handwriting. Your independent variable would be the entry technique. You might also hypothesize that older people will prefer handwriting while younger people might do better at a keyboard. You can further add the hypothesis that women might have better handwriting than men and, thus, might do better with the stylus. You now have three independent variables (technique, age, gender). Too many independent variables can be a problem because of the possible combinations that must be addressed. If you use these conditions (keyboard/stylus, old/young, male/female), you now have eight possible combinations and need 10 or more subjects in each combination for a total of 80+ subjects. This is quite a large experiment. It is easy to get carried away with conditions that you want to examine. It is usually best to stick with one or two key independent variables and then deal with other questions in separate experiments.

The dependent variables are things that you want to measure. User-interface experiments almost always measure time to complete a task and number of errors in completing a task. You frequently want to measure ease of learning. Sometimes you survey the subject's opinions after the experiment to evaluate their preferences. Opinion data should be used with caution. It is frequently the case that how people think they performed and how they actually performed are different. People also tend to like the novel technique even if they are less efficient in its use.

Secondary dependent variables can be measured to help you understand why the differences in performance might have occurred. For example, you might compare two scroll bars for time to complete a task and at the same time measure the total distance that the mouse traveled. Excessive mouse movement might explain why one technique performed better than another. Because you treat dependent variables separately, you can measure as many of them as you want provided they do not interfere with the actual experiment.

Performance Measures

In most experiments, the dominant measure is time to complete a task. Obviously, a technique that lets the user perform faster should make the user more effective. One of the questions that you must ask, however, is whether the technique makes the difference or the combination of interactive techniques with a specific task. It helps to measure task time on many different tasks so that the technique/task interaction is mitigated.

A second measure is errors. You can measure errors for a particular task or errors per unit of work. For text input, you might measure errors per characters correctly entered. This is a measure that can extend across many tasks. There is frequently a trade-off between errors and speed. Working faster generally causes more errors. This trade-off is sometimes difficult to sort out. One approach is to fold errors into the task performance. For example, you might measure the total time to enter a string of characters correctly. If the string is incorrect, the user must continue to work until it is correct. Error correction becomes part of the task time. This simplifies comparison between interactive techniques. Error rate becomes a secondary measure to better understand results rather than a primary measure of comparison.

A third measure is ease of learning. Learning is defined as improvement in some other measure. There are various ways to evaluate learning. You might offer the user many tasks to do and then plot their speed of performance. Performance will generally rise to some level and flatten out with little improvement after that. The amount of task experience required to reach this plateau is a measure of learning.

There are many other attributes of an input technique to be measured. You might measure fatigue as a decline in performance over long, continuous usage. You might measure attention demand by adding a simple secondary task. Full performance is required on the primary task while the user is also doing as many of the secondary tasks (adding numbers, finding red dots, speaking the largest number from a list, and so on) as possible. The more of the secondary task the user is able to complete, the lower the attention requirements of the primary task.

Two other measures are memorability and satisfaction. Memorability has to do with how easily a system can be used once learned and then not used for a while. An interface might have a few concepts that people must learn (how to pull down a menu) but having learned those they can rapidly come up to speed again just by pulling down a menu and looking at it. Satisfaction can really only be measured by surveys of people who have used the system. One should be aware that polite people tend to like the system they perceive as being yours. They also tend to like novel things that they have not been forced to use extensively in practice. These factors can both skew the results of a satisfaction survey.

It is extremely important to select appropriate performance measures. Suppose that you want to create a new form of interactive television. This would allow users to select what they want to watch and dynamically switch among content. Having created this system, you might perform an experiment where you ask a question that can be answered by using the interactive system to look for the right information. You can then measure the time required to find the answer. This is a good measure that is easily compared and is easily evaluated statistically. You can probably write a nice little paper about the experiment. However, the whole thing is worthless because people rarely watch television as a way to search for information. They watch for enjoyment, to relax, and to socialize. These are much harder to measure. It is difficult to produce the definitive number that demonstrates success. The temptation is to study the measurable rather than what is relevant.

Sampling

In most summative evaluations, you want to know "Is technique A better than technique B?" according to some measure. In every experiment, you cannot measure the entire population of situation, task, user combinations for which your techniques are designed. You must always take a sample and measure the sample rather than the entire population. Your sample must be *representative* of the target conditions for your techniques and it must be *uniform* between the techniques. If your sample is not representative, it is difficult to draw conclusions about the target population. Using computer science students as subjects for a healthcare technology would not be representative. Using males for a task usually performed by females or young people to test a technology for the elderly would not be helpful. Obviously, every test subject is unique in some way. You cannot account for all of the differences between people. It is very important to think about the problem and possible differences in people that might have a bearing on the techniques you are trying to test so that the important differences are represented in the sample of the user population.

If you are going to compare technique A with technique B, you must be certain that the only difference between the two groups of tests is the technique used. If there are other differences, they might confound the result. You want a similar mix of users doing similar tasks in an identical situation. This makes the sample uniform between the techniques being tested.

There are two general approaches for constructing such experiments. The first is a *within subjects* test and the second is *between subjects*. In a within-subjects design, every user will perform tasks using both technique A and technique B. This allows you to factor out the differences in skill because you can compare performance for the same user. The problem with this design is that using technique A for a while might confuse the user when they try technique B. If the same tasks are used for technique A and B (for uniformity), the user's prior experience with the task using technique A might make technique B look very good. The differences might be explained, not by differences in the techniques but by learning on the first technique. You can remove this bias by randomly alternating the technique that is used first for each test subject. The learning effects will occur but they will be balanced out by the mixed ordering of the experiments across many users.

Frequently, the learning conflicts are too great or the tasks too long to perform a within-subjects experiment. Using a between-subjects design, you divide the sample population into two groups that are as uniform as possible. You then assign technique A to one group and technique B to another group. The key here is to be very careful in ensuring uniformity between the two sample groups. The makeup of the two groups must be very similar for the comparisons to be valid.

Comparing Results

Having performed all of your experiments and measured your dependent variables, you must now draw conclusions about the interactive techniques that you are trying to compare. You must differentiate between results that are *significant* and those that are *important*. Suppose you compare two kinds of menus for selection time. You find that the average time in one case is 0.1 percent faster than the other. This difference is not important. Nobody will change menu techniques for that small of an improvement.

Statistical significance is based on sampling theory. If you test one user and technique A is better than technique B, can you conclude that A is better or is it just the case that you picked the one user in the universe who performs better with A? Statistical significance attempts to evaluate the impact of chance on the sampling of a population. Assuming that all of your efforts at being representative and uniform have paid off, you still must randomly select a few subjects from a large population to use in your tests. The question is whether the results of your experiment could be explained by the randomness of selection or do they truly represent something that is true about the population.

Many statistical tests are available for evaluating the quality of your experimental results. Robson's book on experimental design is an excellent resource[3]. The most commonly use statistical test is the *t-test*. This assumes that the populations of groups A and B are similarly distributed (uniformity) and that the distribution is normal. It has been shown that the t-test is quite robust even if the distributions are not normal. You first compute the mean of your measured dependent variable for each group A and B. The question you want answered is, "What is the probability that the difference between these means is due to randomness?" That probability of random explanation is the statistical significance of your results. This probability depends upon the number of users sampled (more is better) and the difference between the means and the standard deviations of the measured values (less is better). Many statistical packages will compute a t-test on your data. Microsoft Excel has a TTEST() function. The result will be the probability that differences in the means is due to chance. When reporting the result of a t-test in a paper, the convention is ($p=0.05$) if the probability from the t-test is 0.05. Lower p is obviously better. The convention is that p must be less than 0.05 for the result to be accepted.

Comparative Analysis

The controlled experiment has served science well, but as discussed earlier it is not suitable for complex situations. In many cases, the tool or system has too many variations in its use. Because of the number of different ways that a user might use the tool, it becomes impossible to ensure uniformity in the experiment.

Even though a controlled experiment might not be appropriate, you still need a mechanism to evaluate progress. In such cases, the comparison can be done by arguing the relative advantages of tools and techniques. Almost always these comparisons are based on differences in situation, tasks, and users. The argument is generally of the form, "In situation S on task T with user population U, it is readily seen that system B is much more difficult than system A." For example, it is very clear to anyone who programs that the 10–50 lines of code required to use a preprogrammed scroll bar widget is much more effective than the 1000+ lines of code required to implement a new scroll bar. A variation on the "clearly better" argument is "system A works for S, T, and U, whereas system B does not." It is easy to make a case for "can be done versus cannot be done." Using a full QWERTY keyboard while skateboarding is simply not possible. Empowering a new user population in a new situation is one of the most powerful of usability claims.

There are other criteria for evaluating complex systems. They include generality, expressive leverage, and expressive match.

Generality
Science generally proceeds from the specific to the general. Observations are made in the world and those observations are then generalized into theories that can explain many of the observations in a uniform way. User-interface tools are similar. After

observing user interfaces to file systems, e-mail boxes, company organizations, and the Internet domain name system, you could conclude that they are all trees. A widget that can support all of these uses is more general than any one of them. A general tool or technique simplifies learning and frequently eliminates repetitive work.

In making a claim for generality, you must show that there are a set of interesting tasks T_i that can all be solved by the new tool or technique. The more diverse the problems are, the more general the tool. When making this claim, it is difficult to demonstrate the use of the tool or technique on all such problems. The more general the tool, the more of these problems need to be tested. The normal approach is to pick a subset of the problems, demonstrate the technique on that subset, and then argue that the technique works on all T_i. The more diverse the subset and the larger the subset, the more persuasive the generality argument.

One pitfall in claiming generality is the work required to specialize the technique to a particular problem. In almost all general tools or techniques, there is some adaptation required to make it work in a specific case. With your scroll bar example, the adaptation is quite straightforward. You simply set the small number of properties and register to listen for changes. In the case of the tree widget, the adaptation can be much more complex. In fact, many implementations of the tree widget are so complicated to configure that it is frequently easier to rewrite the technique for a particular purpose.

To make a generality argument, you must demonstrate the breadth of problems that the tool/technique can be used to solve and that the effort to specialize the general solution to a specific task is not onerous.

Expressive Leverage

The expressive leverage argument says that by using tool/technique X you can accomplish much more work with much less effort than competing techniques. This was the argument used for propositional production systems in Chapter 11. It was shown that for many problems a PPS required a linear number of statements while a state machine required an exponential number. PPS is a special case because it can be shown that any state machine can be encoded in a PPS with no additional work. In many cases, expressive leverage comes with a cost.

The scroll bar again is a good example. Reusing a previously implemented scroll bar takes far less code than implementing a new one. However, there is something lost. Using only previously written widgets limits the kinds of interfaces that can be built. A word processor cannot be built out of the standard widgets. The effort to solve a particular problem is frequently based on the number of choices that the user must make. Expressive leverage generally comes from eliminating many of the choices. Using the standard scroll bar means that many other kinds of scroll bars are not possible. In some cases, the loss of choice is good. A standard widget set with a uniform look and feel creates a better user experience than mixing many different scroll bar behaviors. In many cases, the choices are not lost—they can simply be ignored. Having seven different kinds of scroll bars might not be important. Scrolling is still just scrolling. Custom scroll bars are still possible, but if those choices are not important they can be avoided by using the standard implementation. Avoiding unnecessary choice leads to less effort.

To make the expressive leverage argument, you must show that more work is possible with less effort and that there is either no loss of choice or the loss of choice is worth the gain.

Expressive Match

There are frequently many ways to express a solution to some problem. A technique is more usable if the form of expression is a better match for the problem than competing forms. It is possible to encode colors as RGB constants in a fragment of C code. It is also possible to encode a color in hexadecimal in HTML. However, neither of these is as satisfying as selecting a color using a color-picking widget that actually shows the range of possible colors and the current color selected. Working with actual colors is a better expressive match for the problem than working in hexadecimal. A similar example is the widget layout found in most IDEs (Chapter 9). Placing widgets visually in the layout is a better expressive match than encoding their locations as pixel coordinates in Java.

There are several issues that must be addressed in making the expressive match argument. First, it must be demonstrated that this actually is a better match. If the task is small enough, a usability experiment might make this argument by showing that it is quicker. This can be difficult, however. Color entry in hexadecimal is very fast—the problem is getting the right color. Fast is not always enough. A general technique is to show a desired result and then have users achieve a matching result using competing techniques. The comparison is not necessarily on speed, but effort. For example, people find systems in which they are fast yet make many errors along the way as being less usable than systems that are slower in total task time but more predictable and correct during the process.

Another approach to evaluating expressive match is the "task flaw challenge." Users are shown an incorrect solution to a task and asked to repair it. Systems with greater expressive match will simplify the location and correction of the problem.

A real challenge for expressive match is the integration with other tools. One of the reasons that you still encode colors as RGB constants is that it is a form of expression that fits with programming languages. In many cases, the color is only part of the problem and the color must fit with the rest of the work to be done. Using current tools, it is quite painful to integrate a color-picking widget with a programming language. The great challenge of IDE design is to integrate the visual specifications of the view with the code that implements the controller and the model. When designing a new tool with greater expressive match, you must show that it integrates cleanly with the whole problem and not just one subproblem in isolation.

SUMMARY

Evaluation of user interfaces and interactive technique is important for you to make progress. However, there are many pitfalls in evaluation that must be avoided. Before beginning any user-interface project, you must identify the STU (Situation, Tasks, Users) in which your technology will function. You must then judge if your STU is actually important. When you try out your new technology, you must draw successively closer to the STU for which the technique is intended. This might be complex and you might use other approaches to guide your work, but in the end it is the target STU that must be evaluated.

Formative evaluation is a very important and frequently neglected part of the design process. You need very rapid and lightweight tools to make your designs concrete so that you can talk about them with others, try them out with users, and rapidly make changes. The goal is to rapidly search the design space for ideas before committing substantial resources.

Summative evaluations compare two or more approaches to see which is best. These evaluations are challenged by ensuring uniformity of the user samples and selection of appropriate measures. It is too easy to study the measurable rather than what is really relevant.

For very complex systems, you can use comparative analysis. The most powerful comparison is that technique A functions in a STU and technique B cannot. Generality is a good comparison provided adapting the technique to a particular use is not too awkward. Expressive leverage argues that a new technique can accomplish more with less effort. Frequently, this leverage comes by removing unnecessary choice from the problem. Lastly, you have expressive match where a particular representation of the task is easier for users to understand and compare.

EXERCISES

1. Implement marking menus from Chapter 20 and compare their performance with traditional pull-down menus. Evaluate how long it takes to learn keyboard shortcuts versus marking menus.

2. Suppose you are planning to market a touch-based phone in six months and you want to know if you should use marking menus or traditional pull-down menus as the interaction model. What evaluation would you do to shed light on this question?

3. Do a comparison of edge-anchored layout and variable intrinsic size layout from Chapter 5 in terms of their comparative target STUs.

4. Compare two programming languages for generality and expressive match for a particular STU.

END NOTES

[1] Snyder, C. *Paper Prototyping: The Fast and Easy Way to Design and Refine User Interfaces*. San Francisco: Morgan Kaufmann, 2003.

[2] Nielsen, J. "Enhancing the Explanatory Power of Usability Heuristics." *Human Factors in Computing Systems (CHI '94)* (April 1994): 152–158.

[3] Robson, C. *Experiment, Design and Statistics in Psychology*. New York, NY: Penguin Books, 1994.

APPENDIX A

Mathematics and Algorithms for Interactive Systems

A variety of mathematical concepts and basic algorithms are useful in interactive systems. Most of these concepts are taught in various computer science courses and were developed in areas related to interaction. This appendix collects together many relevant algorithms along with some examples of their use. Many people wanting to work in interactive systems will know many of these concepts already. Because of this, a front-to-back read of this material might not be necessary. It is assumed that readers will dip in and out of this section in various places to find the information that they need. To support such opportunistic reading, each concept is presented in the following format:

- *Prerequisites*—Other concepts that are assumed in the current discussion

- *Overview*—A brief description of the concept and what it is good for

- *Description*—Details of the concept with illustrated examples

- *Implementation*—Pseudocode for implementation of the concept

The pseudocode is in C/C++/Java syntax with some modifications. Because arrays are frequently used, the code uses standard multidimensional array notation ([x,y] rather than [x][y]). In addition, array parameters are specified with their lengths. For example,

```
double dotProduct( double a[n], double b[n])
```

indicates two, one-dimensional array arguments that both have a length of n. The declaration

```
double [r, c] innerProduct( double a[r, n ], double b[n, c] )
```

indicates two, two-dimensional array arguments where the number of columns in A is equal to the number of rows in B and the dimension of the result is r by c. Although nonstandard for C/C++/Java, this notation greatly simplifies the algorithm presentation.

All mathematical concepts are presented both in mathematical notation and as functional expressions or as procedures. Many programmers find the functional/procedural notation easier to read even if it is more verbose.

The concepts are grouped into categories with introductions for each category. The major categories are as follows:

- *Basic mathematics*—Vectors, matrices, linear equations, geometry
- *Basic algorithms*—Priority queues, minimal path searching
- *Classifiers*—Vector classifiers, sequence classifiers

A1 – MATHEMATICS

The mathematics of vectors, matrices, and linear equations form the basis for many of the algorithms in interactive systems. Because so many interfaces are based on graphical images, knowledge of 2D and 3D geometry is also helpful. Because many graphical user interfaces are based on manipulation of points, it is also helpful to compute several properties of a collection of points.

A1.1 – Vectors

Prerequisites
Arithmetic

Overview
A vector is simply a one-dimensional array of real numbers $[x_1, x_2, x_3, \ldots x_n]$. Vectors are used to represent geometric points as well as features of objects. In geometric situations, you use vectors with three or four elements. In other situations, the vectors can be very long. For example, text documents are frequently classified by the count of the number of occurrences of each word in the document. Therefore, a document feature vector has one element for each possible word (a very long vector). Operations on vectors are the basis for a variety of other algorithms. All of the algorithms in this section are $O(N)$, where N is the number of elements in a vector.

Description
The following notational conventions are common for vectors. Names of vectors are generally given with an arrow over the name ($\vec{V}$) and are represented as column vectors. You can think of a column vector as an N by 1 dimensional array (N rows and 1 column). The elements of the vector are represented by the name of the vector and the index of the element as a subscript. By convention, subscripts start with one.

$$\vec{V} = \begin{bmatrix} v_1 \\ v_2 \\ v_3 \\ v_4 \end{bmatrix}$$

The transpose of a vector $\vec{v}^T$ is a row vector (1 by N). When dealing with simple vectors, the row or column nature is not important. However, it does become important when using vectors with matrices.

$$\vec{V}^T = \begin{bmatrix} v_1 & v_2 & v_3 & v_4 \end{bmatrix}$$

A1.1a – Vector Arithmetic

Vectors are added and subtracted by adding and subtracting their components. You can also add or subtract scalar values.

$$\vec{A} + s = \begin{bmatrix} a_1 + s & a_2 + s & a_3 + s & \dots & a_n + s \end{bmatrix}$$
$$\vec{A} - s = \begin{bmatrix} a_1 - s & a_2 - s & a_3 - s & \dots & a_n - s \end{bmatrix}$$

$$\vec{A} + \vec{B} = \begin{bmatrix} a_1 + b_1 & a_2 + b_2 & a_3 + b_3 & \dots & a_n + b_n \end{bmatrix}$$
$$\vec{A} - \vec{B} = \begin{bmatrix} a_1 - b_1 & a_2 - b_2 & a_3 - b_3 & \dots & a_n - b_n \end{bmatrix}$$

Implementation

```
double [n] add(double v[n], double s)
{    double rslt[n];
     for (int i=0; i<n; i++)
     {    rslt[i]=v[i]+s; }
     return rslt;
}

double [n] add(double a[n], double b[n])
{    double rslt[n];
     for (int i=0; i<n; i++)
     {    rslt[i]=a[i]+b[i]; }
     return rslt;
}
```

A1.1b - Vector Length

A vector can be thought of as a line extending from the origin to a point in n-dimensional space. The length of a vector $\vec{v}$ with N elements is represented by $\|\vec{V}\|$.

$$length(\vec{V}) = \|\vec{V}\| = \sqrt{\sum_{i=1}^{N} v_i^2}$$

Implementation

```
double length( double v[n])
{     double dSum=0;
      for (int i=0; i<n; i++)
      {    dSum+=v[i]*v[i]; }
      return squareRoot(dSum);
}
```

A1.1c – Unit Vectors

Unit vectors are vectors whose length is one. For any nonzero vector $\vec{v}$, you can compute a unit vector $\vec{u}$ in the same direction.

$$\vec{U} = unit(\vec{V}) = \frac{\vec{V}}{\left\|\vec{V}\right\|}$$

Implementation

```
double [n] unit ( double v[n] )
{     double rslt[n];
      double len = length(v);
      for (int i=0; i<n; i++)
      {    rslt[i]=v[i]/len; }
      return rslt;
}
```

A1.1d - Dot Product

The dot product of two vectors is found in many applications. Its most common use is to combine a vector of variables with a vector of constant coefficients to produce a linear equation. For example, $\vec{C} \cdot \vec{V} = 10$ would be the same as $c_1 v_1 + c_2 v_2 + c_3 v_3 = 10$. The dot product is defined as:

$$\vec{A} \cdot \vec{B} = \sum_{i=1}^{N} a_i b_i$$

Implementation

```
double dotProduct(double a[n], double b[n])
{     double sum=0;
      for(int i=0; i<n; i++)
      {    sum+=a[i]*b[i]; }
      return sum;
}
```

A1.1e – Comparing Vectors

It is frequently helpful to compare two vectors to see how similar they might be. This section describes three common approaches for comparing two vectors: the

Manhattan distance, the Euclidean distance, and the cosine. Figure A.1 illustrates these three forms of distance between two vectors in a two-dimensional space.

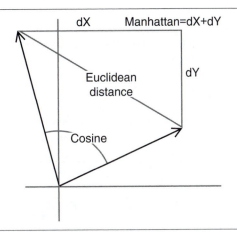

Figure A.1 – Vector distance metrics

Manhattan Distance

It is called the Manhattan distance because it is the distance you would walk between two points in downtown Manhattan. It is not possible to walk directly between two points—you must follow the rectangular streets.

$$manh(\vec{A}, \vec{B}) = \sum_{i=1}^{n} |a_i - b_i|$$

Implementation

```
double manhattan(double a[n], double b[n])
{     double dist=0;
      for (int i=0; i<n; i++)
      {    if (a[i]>b[i])
           {    dist+=a[i]-b[i]; }
           else
           {    dist+=b[i]-a[i]; }
      }
      return dist;
}
```

Euclidean Distance

This is geometrically the shortest distance between two points.

$$dist(\vec{A}, \vec{B}) = \left\| \vec{A} - \vec{B} \right\|$$

Implementation

```
double distance(double a[n], double b[n])
{    return length(subtract(a,b));  }
```

Cosine Distance

The cosine of the angle between any two vectors is the dot product of their unit vectors. The cosine has several interesting properties. If two vectors are parallel to each other, the cosine of their angle is 1. If they are perpendicular (completely unrelated), their cosine is 0. If two vectors are directly opposite of each other, their cosine is −1. The cosine of the angle between two vectors is useful in 2D and 3D geometry, but it is also a useful comparison between two vectors in general. It is sometimes used in text retrieval to compare the word frequency vectors of two documents. One obvious optimization of this computation is to cache the unit vectors rather than the original vectors, so that the cosine can be calculated directly by the dot product.

$$\vec{A} \cdot \vec{B} = \cos(\theta) \cdot \|\vec{A}\| \cdot \|\vec{B}\|$$

where θ is the angle between $\vec{A}$ and $\vec{B}$. Therefore:

$$\cos(\theta) = unit(\vec{A}) \cdot unit(\vec{B})$$

Implementation

```
double cosine(double a[n], double b[n])
{    return dotProduct( unit(a), unit(b) );  }
```

A1.2 – Matrices

Prerequisites
Vectors (A1.1, A1.1d)

Overview
Matrices are used to represent a large variety of linear equations and linear transformations. Matrix multiplication, matrix inverse, and solving systems of linear equations are all quite straightforward using matrices. The key algorithms for these are presented here. A matrix is a two-dimensional array of real values.

$$M = \begin{bmatrix} a_{1,1} & a_{1,2} & a_{1,3} \\ a_{2,1} & a_{2,2} & a_{2,3} \\ a_{3,1} & a_{3,2} & a_{3,3} \end{bmatrix}$$

A1.2a – Transpose

The transpose of a matrix is simply a reversal of rows and columns.

$$M^T = \begin{bmatrix} a_{1,1} & a_{2,1} & a_{3,1} \\ a_{1,2} & a_{2,2} & a_{3,2} \\ a_{1,3} & a_{2,3} & a_{3,3} \end{bmatrix}$$

A1.2b – Matrix Multiply

Matrix multiply combines an $(L{\times}M)$ with an $(M{\times}N)$ matrix to produce an $(L{\times}N)$ matrix. Each element (i, j) of the resulting matrix is the dot product of the ith row of the first matrix and the jth column of the second matrix.

- Matrix multiplication is associative. $(A \cdot B) \cdot C = A \cdot (B \cdot C)$
- Matrix multiplication is **not** commutative. $A \cdot B \neq B \cdot A$ in many cases

Multiplying an $M \times N$ matrix times a column vector of length N produces a new column vector that is a linear transformation of the original vector. Matrix multiplication can, thus, be used to model any linear transformation of a vector of values. Where such transforms occur in sequence, multiplication of their matrices together produces a single matrix that is the concatenation of all the transforms. This is very useful in computer graphics as well as in a variety of other situations requiring the transformation of data.

A most useful matrix is the identity matrix I, which has 1.0 on all diagonal elements and zeroes everywhere else. The identity matrix has the property $I \cdot M = M$.

Implementation

```
double [l,n] matrixMultiply(double a[l,m], double b[m,n])
{     double result[ l, n ];
      for (int r=0;  r<l;  r++)
      {    for (int c=0; c<n; c++)
           {    result[r,c]=0.0;
                for (int i=0; i<m; i++)
                {    result[r,c]+=a[r,i]*b[i,c]; }
           }
      }
      return result;
}
```

A1.2c – Solving Linear Equations

Any system of linear equations can be modeled as the following matrix equation:

$$M\vec{V} = \vec{C}$$

where $\vec{V}$ is a vector of N values, M is an $N \times N$ matrix of coefficients, and $\vec{C}$ is a vector of resultant values. Take, for example, the following system of equations:

$$2x + 3y - 4z = 10$$
$$3x + 2y - z = 4$$
$$x - 7y + 2z = -2$$

This system can be modeled using the following matrix equation where each row of the matrices M and $\vec{C}$ corresponds to an equation and each column of M corresponds to one of the variables.

$$\begin{bmatrix} 2 & 3 & -4 \\ 3 & 2 & -1 \\ 1 & -7 & 2 \end{bmatrix} \cdot \begin{bmatrix} x \\ y \\ z \end{bmatrix} = \begin{bmatrix} 10 \\ 4 \\ -2 \end{bmatrix}$$

The simplest way to solve this system is to use the Gauss-Jordan reduction method. This method is based on two properties of linear equations. The first is that any linear equation can be multiplied or divided by any nonzero value without changing the set of points that satisfy the equation. The second property is that two equations can be subtracted from each other to produce a third equation that is consistent with the system of equations. You use these two properties to transform the matrix M into an identity matrix. You divide a row of the matrix by its diagonal value (which makes the diagonal value a 1) and then you multiply and subtract that equation from all other equations so that every other element in that column becomes a zero. Having done that for all rows, you have $I \cdot \vec{V} = \vec{C}'$, where $\vec{C}'$ is a column vector of the solution values. This algorithm for solving linear equations is $O(N^3)$, where N is the number of variables.

Implementation

Note that this algorithm modifies both M and C in the course of its operation.

```
double [n] solveLinear(double M[n,n], double C[n])
{    for (int r=0; r<n; r++)
     {   if (M[r,r]==0.0)
         {   Exchange row r with a row of a larger index
             for which M[r,r] != 0.0. This code is not included to simplify
             the presentation of the algorithm. However, a correct
             algorithm must include this. If r is the last row, there
             is no solution.
         }

         double div=M[r,r];
         for (int c=0; c<n; c++)
         {   M[r,c]=M[r,c]/div; }
         C[r]=C[r]/div;

         for (int r2=0; r2<n; r2++)
         {   if (r2!=r)
             {   double mul = M[r2,r];
                 for (int c=0; c<n; c++)
                 {   M[r2,c]=M[r2,c]-M[r,c]*mul; }
                 C[r2]=C[r2]-C[r]*mul;
             }
         }
     }
     return C;
}
```

A1.2d – Inverting a Matrix

It is sometimes useful to compute the inverse of a matrix. The inverse of a matrix (M^{-1}) is defined such that $MM^{-1} = I$ and $M^{-1}M = I$. You compute the inverse by replacing the vector $\vec{C}$ with an identity matrix and using the same techniques that you used in solving a set of linear equations. If you can compute the inverse of a matrix, you can use it to solve linear equations. Not all matrices are invertible. This happens when one or more of the equations is some linear combination of the others. The following algorithm detects this condition. Matrix inversion is $O(N^3)$, where N is the number of variables. The inverse matrix can be used to solve a linear system of equations, as discussed in section A1.2c, as shown here:

$$M\vec{V} = \vec{C}$$
$$M^{-1}M\vec{V} = M^{-1}\vec{C}$$
$$I\vec{V} = M^{-1}\vec{C}$$
$$\vec{V} = M^{-1}\vec{C}$$

Implementation

Note that this algorithm modifies the matrix M.

```
double [n,n] invertMatrix(double M[n,n] )
{    double R[ n,n ]=identityMatrix(n);
     for (int r=0; r<n; r++)
     {   if (M[r,r]==0.0)
         {   Exchange row r with a row of a larger index
             for which M[r,r] != 0.0. This code is not included to simplify
             the presentation of the algorithm. However, a correct
             algorithm must include this. If r is the last row, there
             is no inverse.
         }
         double div = M[r,r];
         for (int c=0; c<n; c++)
         {   M[r,c]=M[r,c]/div;
             R[r,c]=R[r,c]/div;
         }

         for (int r2=0; r2<n; r2++)
         {   if (r!=r2)
             {   double mul=M[r2,r];
                 for (int c=0; c<n; c++)
                 {   M[r2,c]=M[r2,c]-M[r,c]*mul;
                     R[r2,c]=R[r2,c]-R[r,c]*mul;
                 }
             }
         }
     }
     return R;
}


double [n,n] identityMatrix(int n)
{    double R[n,n];
     for (int r=0; r<n; r++)
     {   for (int c=0; c<n; c++)
         {   if (r==c)
             {   R[r,c]=1.0; }
             else
             {   R[r,c]=0.0; }
         }
     }
     return R;
}
```

A1.2e – Linear Approximation

Prerequisites

Vectors (A1.1), Matrix Inverse (A1.2d)

Overview

It is sometimes necessary to find a linear function that approximates a set of points. When there are N variables and more than N points, the linear function will, in general, only approximate those points rather than exactly pass through them. To compute the approximation, you compute the linear function and measure its error from the desired outcome. You try to minimize the sum of the squares of these errors (least squares method). Finding an approximation involves creating a matrix of all of the point data. This creation step is $O(V^2P)$, where V is the number of variables and P is the number of sample points. The resulting matrix must then be inverted, which is $O(V^3)$.

Description

In a system of two variables, the linear function that you are trying to discover can take the following form:

$$ax + by + c = d$$

The vector form of this equation would be as follows:

$$[x \quad y \quad 1] \cdot \begin{bmatrix} a \\ b \\ c \end{bmatrix} = d$$

To use this particular form of linear equation, you transform $[x\,y]$ into the homogeneous point $[x\,y\,1]$. The purpose of the additional 1 is to incorporate the offset coefficient c into the vector equation. The general N-dimensional form of the equation is $\vec{P} \cdot \vec{C} = d$, where $\vec{P}$ is a homogenous point, $\vec{C}$ is a vector of coefficients, and d is the desired outcome of the function. The coefficient vector completely characterizes the linear function. For many situations, the desired outcome d is zero.

You can also use this method to approximate nonlinear functions that use only linear coefficients. Suppose you have two coordinates $[x\,y]$, you might use an equation of the form:

$$\left[x \quad y \quad x^2 \quad y^2 \quad xy \quad \frac{1}{x} \quad \sin(y) \quad 1\right] \cdot \begin{bmatrix} e \\ f \\ g \\ h \\ i \\ j \\ k \\ l \end{bmatrix} = d$$

Because the values for x and y are known for any sample point, the nonlinear values are also known. Therefore, the equation is still linear for the coefficients e through l.

You have simply converted the two-dimensional space of x, y into a seven-dimensional space, by computing the new values.

Because the linear function will only approximate the points, each point will have an error. This error is calculated as $\vec{V} \cdot \vec{C} - d = e$ Because e can be positive or negative, you generally use e^2, which is differentiable and always positive. For some set of P points, you want to calculate the vector $\vec{C}$ that minimizes the sum of the squared errors. You set up the error calculation as follows:

$$B = \begin{bmatrix} x_{1,1} & x_{1,2} & \dots & 1 \\ x_{2,1} & x_{2,2} & \dots & 1 \\ \dots & \dots & \dots & 1 \\ x_{P,1} & x_{P,2} & \dots & 1 \end{bmatrix} \text{ where } x_{i,j} \text{ is the } j\text{th coordinate of the } i\text{th point}$$

$$\vec{Y} = \begin{bmatrix} d_1 \\ d_2 \\ \dots \\ d_P \end{bmatrix} \text{ where } d_i \text{ is the desired outcome for the } i\text{th point}$$

The error E is calculated as:

$$E = \vec{Y} - B \cdot \vec{C}$$

Given this matrix formulation for E, you can calculate a vector $\vec{C}$ that will minimize the sum of the squares of E.

$$\vec{C} = (B^T \cdot B)^{-1} \cdot (B^T \cdot \vec{Y})$$

For an N-dimensional space, $(B^T \cdot B)$ is an $(N+1) \times (N+1)$ matrix W of the form:

$$W = (B^T \cdot B) = \begin{bmatrix} \sum_{i=1}^{P} x_{i,1}x_{i,1} & \sum_{i=1}^{P} x_{i,1}x_{i,2} & \dots & \sum_{i=1}^{P} x_{i,1}x_{i,N} & \sum_{i=1}^{P} x_{i,1} \\ \sum_{i=1}^{P} x_{i,2}x_{i,1} & \sum_{i=1}^{P} x_{i,2}x_{i,2} & \dots & \sum_{i=1}^{P} x_{i,2}x_{i,N} & \sum_{i=1}^{P} x_{i,2} \\ \dots & \dots & \dots & \dots & \dots \\ \sum_{i=1}^{P} x_{i,N}x_{i,1} & \sum_{i=1}^{P} x_{i,N}x_{i,2} & \dots & \sum_{i=1}^{P} x_{i,N}x_{i,N} & \sum_{i=1}^{P} x_{i,N} \\ \sum_{i=1}^{P} x_{i,1} & \sum_{i=1}^{P} x_{i,2} & \dots & \sum_{i=1}^{P} x_{i,N} & P \end{bmatrix}$$

For the same space, $(B^T \cdot Y)$ is a vector $\vec{V}$ of length $(N+1)$, which has the form:

$$\vec{V} = (B^T \cdot Y) = \begin{bmatrix} \sum_{i=1}^{P} x_{i,1} d_i \\ \sum_{i=1}^{P} x_{i,2} d_i \\ ... \\ \sum_{i=1}^{P} x_{i,N} d_i \\ \sum_{i=1}^{P} d_i \end{bmatrix}$$

The algorithm, then, is to calculate W and $\vec{V}$, compute W^{-1}, and multiply them together to compute $\vec{C}$.

Implementation

```
double [ ] leastSquares(double B[p,n], double Y[p])
{    double w[ n+1, n+1] ;
     double v[ n+1];

     for (int i=0; i<=n; i++) // initialize w and v
     {    v[i]=0.0;
          for (int j=0; j<=n; j++)
          {    w[i,j]=0.0; }
     }

     for (int i=0; i<p;i++) // compute w = transpose(B)*B
     {
          for (int r=0;r<n;r++)
          {    for (int c=0;c<n;c++)
               {    w[r,c]+=B[i,r]*B[i,c]; }
               w[r,n]+=B[i,r];
          }
          for (int c=0;c<n;c++)
          {    w[n,c]+=B[i,c]; }
     }
     w[n,n]=p;
     for (int i=0; i<p; i++) // compute v = transpose(B)*Y
     {
          for ( int r=0; r<n; r++)
          {    v[r]+=B[i,r]*Y[i];
          }
          v[n]+=Y[i];
     }
     double c[n,n] = matrixMultiply(invertMatrix(w),v);
     return c;

}
```

A1.3 – Clouds of Points

Prerequisites
Vectors (A1.1)

Overview
When working with geometric entities and inputs, you will frequently encounter a collection of points. These points might be all of the points in an ink stroke (Figure A.2), the vertices of a polygon, all of the pixels that make up a shape, or all of the purple pixels in an image. All of these can be modeled as a list of [x y] or [x y z] coordinates.

Figure A.2 – Cloud of ink points

There are a variety of features of such clouds that are helpful. The center of gravity is a useful reference point from which to base these features. The angle of eccentricity (angle of the longest axis on the cloud) is useful when determining orientation of a shape; the size and elongation are also useful features.

A1.3a – Center of Gravity
The simplest feature for a cloud of points is its center of gravity. If you assume that all points have equal weight, this is simply the average of all of the points.

$$C_x = \frac{1}{N}\sum_{i=1}^{N} x_i$$

$$C_y = \frac{1}{N}\sum_{i=1}^{N} y_i$$

Implementation

```
Point center(Point points[n])
{      Point C;
       C.x=0.0;
       C.y=0.0;
       for (int i=0; i<n; i++)
       {    C.x=C.x+points[i].x;
            C.y=C.y+points[i].y;
       }
       C.x=C.x/n;
       C.y=C.y/n;
       return C;
}
```

A1.3b – Moments

The shape of a set of points can be described by a set of moments. The most interesting moments are relative to the center of the shape. Computing the moments relative to the center makes the values of the moments invariant with respect to translation (the position of the object). There is a whole family of these moments that have been defined. This family is parameterized by two integers p and q. These moments were designed for evaluating the shapes of grayscale images. However, for your purposes, the following formula again assumes that the weights of all the points are equal.

$$m_{p,q} = \sum_{i=1}^{N} (x_i - Cx)^p (y_i - Cy)^q$$

Implementation

The following are the more commonly used moments.

```
double moment11(Point points[n],Point center)
{     double sum=0.0;
      for (int i=0; i<n; i++)
      {     sum=sum+(points[i].x-center.x)*(points[i].y-center.y);  }
      return sum;

}
```

```
double moment20(Point points[n], Point center)
{     double sum=0.0;
      for (int=0; i<n; i++)
      {     double diff=points[i].x-center.x;
            sum=sum+diff*diff;
      }
      return sum;

}
```

```
double moment02(Point points[n], Point center)
{     double sum=0.0;
      for (int=0; i<n; i++)
      {     double diff=points[i].y-center.y;
            sum=sum+diff*diff;
      }
      return sum;

}
```

A1.3c – Primary Angle

A very useful measurement is the primary axis of a shape. The primary axis is the angle of the greatest extent of the shape. The shapes in Figure A.3 are examples.

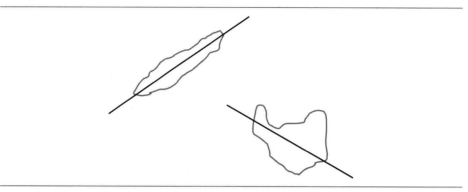

Figure A.3 – Axis of a point cloud

The angle θ of the primary axis can be computed from the first and second degree moments of the shape.

$$\theta = \frac{1}{2} \tan^{-1} \left(\frac{2m_{1,1}}{m_{2,0} - m_{0,2}} \right)$$

Note that the primary axis has two possible primary angles differing by 180 degrees. When comparing two shapes, it is useful to normalize both shapes by rotating the primary angle of each of them to the positive x-axis and then comparing.

Because the tangent function has singularities when the denominator approaches zero, a good implementation will use the ATAN2(dx,dy) function found on most systems. ATAN2() checks all of the various reflections so as to avoid the singularities caused by the normal arctan function.

Implementation

```
double primaryAngle(Point points[n])
{    Point C = center(points);
     return atan2( moment20(points,C)-moment02(points,C),
        2*moment11(points,C) )/2;
}
```

Another approach for determining the primary angle is to use the vector from the center to the point that is farthest from the center. This strategy, however, is more sensitive to outliers than computing that angle from the moments.

A1.3d – Dimensions of a Cloud

It is frequently helpful to determine the "size" of a cloud of points. The simplest computation of size is to use a bounding rectangle. The bounding rectangle can easily be computed by taking the maximums and minimums in X and Y. This is frequently done after the points have been rotated so that the primary angle is on the x-axis. Using maximum and minimum is subject to distortions of outlier points. This frequently does not matter. However, if outliers are of concern, you can use the average distance from the center in X and Y.

$$SizeX = \frac{1}{N}\sum_{i=1}^{N}|x_i - Cx|$$

$$SizeY = \frac{1}{N}\sum_{i=1}^{N}|y_i - Cy|$$

These two size estimates can also be used to compute the elongation or eccentricity of a shape as $\frac{SizeY}{SizeX}$. If the cloud has been rotated so that the primary angle is along the x-axis, this measure of elongation will lie between zero and one. This elongation measure is also size invariant.

A2 – ALGORITHMS

Prerequisites
Basic data structures

Overview
These algorithms are drawn from basic heuristic search methods. They are frequently used in various optimization algorithms to compute a minimal sequence of operations.

A2.1 – Priority Queue

Overview
The priority queue is a simple structure for storing objects that have a priority. A priority is represented as an integer or floating-point number. Items are inserted into the queue in any order. When an item is removed from the queue, it is either the item with the largest or smallest priority, depending on how the queue is designed. For minimization problems, you use a queue that always returns the smallest priority item in the queue. In the discussions, you will return the smallest priority item. The implementation for returning the largest item simply reverses the less than comparisons into greater than.

The implementation of a priority queue uses a structure called a *heap*. A heap is a complete binary tree such that any node in the tree always has less than or equal priority than either of its subnodes. Because the binary tree is complete, you can represent the tree in a simple array and compute the tree relations in the following way.

For any node at index i in the tree:

parent(i)=(i-1)/2
left(i)=i*2+1
right(i)=i*2+2

the root of the tree is at index 0. When you insert a new item, you insert it at the end of the array, at the very bottom of the tree. You then compare it with its parent and if it has lesser priority, you exchange it with its parent. This compare/exchange process continues until either the root of the tree is reached or the inserted object reaches a $\log_2(N)$ point in the tree where its parent has a lesser priority. There will be at most comparisons and exchanges, where N is the number of items currently in the queue.

To remove an item from the queue, you take the root item because by induction the root has a lesser priority than all other items in the queue. You then take the last item in the queue and place it at the root. This item will almost never be the least priority item. This root item is compared with its left and right children. If either is less than the root item, the root is exchanged with the smallest of the two. The original item is now in a new position and is then compared with its children. This compare-and-exchange process continues until the item is less than both of its children, or it has no children. This will take at most $\log_2(N)$ steps.

Implementation

```
interface PriorityObject
{    double priority(); }


class PriorityQueue
{    PriorityObject items[ ];
     int next=0;

     void insert(PriorityObject obj)
     {    items[next]=obj;
          int idx = next;
          next=next+1;
          int parent = (idx-1)/2;
          while (idx>0 && items[idx].priority()<items[parent].priority() )
          {    exchange(parent,idx);
               idx=parent;
               parent = (idx-1)/2;
          }
     }
}
```

```
PriorityObject remove()
{   PriorityObject result;
    PriorityObject temp;
    if (empty())
    {   return null; }
    result=items[0];
    next=next-1;
    items[0]=items[next];
    items[next]=null;
    int idx=0;
    while (true)
    {   left = idx*2+1;
        right=left+1;
        if (left<next && items[left].priority()<items[idx].priority() )
        {   if(right<next && items[right].priority()<items[left].priority())
            {   exchange(idx,right);
                idx=right;
            }
            else
            {   exchange(idx,left);
                idx=left;
            }
        }
        else if (right<next
                && items[right].priority()<items[idx].priority() )
        {   exchange(idx,left);
            idx=left;
        }
        else
        {   return result; }
    }
}
void exchange(int a, int b)
{   PriortyObject temp=items[a];
    items[a]=items[b];
    items[b]=temp;
}
boolean empty()
{   return next==0; }
}
```

A2.2 – Least-Cost Path

Prerequisites
Priority Queue (A2.1)

Overview
Many problems can be cast as a graph searching problem. Such problems are characterized by a state (some set of data values) from which there are several possible

choices. Each choice leads to another state and each choice has a cost. The states and choices constitute the nodes and arcs of a weighted, directed graph. A series of such choices is a path. The cost of a path is the sum of the cost of its choices. What is desired is to make a series of choices that produces the least-cost path from some initial state to some goal state.

Some problems are defined not in terms of cost but in terms of benefit. It would seem in those cases that finding the maximal path would be appropriate. However, in a graph that has cycles, the maximal path is infinite. Such problems, however, can be recast into a minimal cost algorithm by computing *cost=maxBenefit-benefit*. You can now use these costs to compute a minimal cost path, which will be the maximum benefit, acyclic path.

The algorithm works by placing each candidate path on a priority queue weighted by that path's cost so far. You then take the least-cost path off of the queue and expand that path's choices. By always selecting the least-cost path and expanding it, you are guaranteed to find the shortest path if there is one. If there is no path, the priority queue becomes empty before the goal state is located. Each path placed on the queue retains a link to the path it extends. Once the goal state is reached, the least-cost path can be extracted by following these links back to the start state. This algorithm is always expanding the least-cost path, which means it might temporarily pursue paths that are only locally optimal. However, the algorithm terminates with the optimal path if one exists.

Implementation

interface **State**

```
{     boolean matches(State S)
          //returns true if this object and S represent the same state.
      int nChoices() //returns the number of choices leaving this state
      State choice(int N) //returns the next state for choice N
      double choiceCost(int N) //returns the cost of choice N
}
```

class **Path** implements **PriorityObject**

```
{     double pathLength;
      double choiceCost;
      State nextState;
      Path previousPath;
      Path (double cost, Path previous, State next)
      {    if (previous==null)
          {    pathLength=0; }
          else
          {    pathLength = previous.pathLength+cost; }
          choiceCost = cost;
          nextState = next;
          previousPath = previous;
      }
      double priority()
      {    return pathLength; }
}
```

```
Path leastCostPath( State start, State goal )
{    PriorityQueue Q;
     Path startPath = new Path(0,null, start);
     Q.add(startPath)
     while (!Q.empty() )
     {    Path curPath = Q.remove();
          if (goal.matches(curPath.nextState))
          {    return curPath;  }
          for (int c=0; c<curPath.nextState.nChoices();  c++)
          {    if ( notAlreadyVisited(curPath.nextState.choice(c)) )
               {    Path next = new Path(curPath.choiceCost(c),
                                   curPath,
                                   curPath.choice(c) );
                    Q.add(next);
               }
          }
     }
     return null;
}
```

The least-cost path will never have a cycle. Therefore, the call to notAlreadyVisited() can both check to see if the next state has already been visited (in which case a path of equal or lower cost is already under way) and also add the state to the list of visited states. The mechanism for remembering all visited states is unimportant. There are many possibilities depending on how states are represented. Because the number of visited states can be large, this test can be omitted without affecting the correctness of the algorithm. The omission saves storage but in graphs with cycles there might be wasted effort.

A3 – CLASSIFIERS

Prerequisites
Vectors (A1.1), Matrices (A1.2), some of Algorithms (A2).

Overview
As interactive systems move beyond simple point-and-click interfaces, there is an increasing need to recognize what the user has done, to recognize situations in which the user is acting, and to identify the kinds of objects that the user is acting upon. This is particularly true when using cameras, microphones, gestures, and speech as a mechanism for interacting. At the heart of most such advanced interaction techniques is the concept of a classifier. For example, a user might sketch a character using a digital pen. The system might then want to classify that pen stroke as an "a," "b," or "c" or perhaps as "insert," "delete," or "paste." A speech system takes an audio input and attempts to classify it as "help," "save," "run," or "don't know." The range and depth of issues involved in classifier design is quite broad and can be the subject of multiple university courses. However, a small number of quite straightforward classifiers can be readily programmed and applied to a variety of interactive applications.

Description

The goal of a classifier is to take some object O that has a vector of features $\vec{f}$ that are used to characterize the object O. A classifier has two or more classes of objects. By looking at the feature vector, the classifier attempts to identify which class the object O belongs to. Thus, a classifier is a function $C(\vec{f}) \rightarrow class$. A class is simply one of a small finite enumeration of possibilities.

For example, you might take the set of features [hasFeathers, number of legs, color] and attempt to classify animals as one of the set {pig, chicken, dog}. You could write the classifier by saying "if it has feathers and two legs, it is a chicken; otherwise, if it is pink, it is a pig; otherwise, it is a dog." This is a relatively simple classifier. You are generally interested in more complicated classifications.

You are most interested in trainable classifiers. Trainable classifiers are general in nature in that they can compute a wide space of classifications depending upon the parameters. Thus, the classifier becomes $C(\vec{f},P) \rightarrow class$, where P is a parameter structure that controls how the classifier performs its classification. You train a classifier by taking a set of training examples and computing an appropriate parameter P that is consistent with the examples and usable by the classifier. A training example is simply a feature vector for some sample object, with an associated class. The training process attempts to generalize from the training examples to produce a classifier that works well for a wide range of feature vectors. You can categorize classifiers by the kinds of features and feature vectors that they can handle, and by the way in which they compute their parameter from a training set.

One of the biggest differences is between vector classifiers and sequence classifiers. A vector classifier assumes that for a given problem there is a finite set of features and every object has exactly the same number of features. Thus, the classification can work by comparing feature values. The simple animal classifier described previously is a vector classifier. There are exactly three features. Sequence classifiers handle an arbitrary number of features in the feature vector with different objects having different numbers of features. In sequence classifiers, the order or sequence in which values appear greatly determines the classification. String parsing is a sequence classifier. The features are all characters and it is the order of those characters that determines the parse. The algorithms for fixed vectors and sequences are very different.

Feature Selection

It is only possible to cover a small number of the most common classifiers here. There are many possible classifiers [1,2] each with its own strengths and weaknesses. In most interactive situations, the classifiers described here will suffice. Generally, classification performance can be improved more by providing new features or combinations of features than by new classifier algorithms. If a classifier is not performing correctly, it is usually helpful to identify cases where there is confusion and then try to identify some feature or features that would distinguish those cases. Adding the new features can frequently solve the problem.

In expanding the feature set for a problem, you should also recognize the "curse of dimensionality," which means that the more features in a problem, the more training data is required for accurate learning. Adding features increases the number of dimensions in the feature space, and, thus, increases the number of examples required to effectively populate that space. This can be alleviated somewhat by using automatic feature selection to ignore many features. Several of the classifier algorithms can do feature selection.

Types of Features

You categorize features into three types: *real numbers*, *nominal* (enumerated), and *distance comparable*. The real numbers are one of the easiest types of features because you can talk about ranges of numbers, compute the distance between two numbers, and average a set of numbers. All of these are useful when building various types of classifiers. One of the problems with real numbers is that there are infinitely many of them. Even once you have a bound on the set of numbers (for example, between 1.0 and 2.4), there are infinitely many possibilities inside. This is problematic for some types of classifiers.

Nominal or enumerated features have a fixed set of values. For example, hasFeathers is either true or false. A political affiliation feature might be {Republican, Democrat, Libertarian, Other}. The advantage of such features is that they can be used to model a variety of concepts and, for the purposes of your algorithms, the possible values of such a feature can be fully enumerated. It is possible to convert a numeric feature into a nominal one by *quantizing* the values. For example, you could convert weight in pounds into {0-100=light, 100-200=medium, >200 = heavy}. This would allow you to use weight for a classifier that requires nominal attributes. The problem with such quantizing is with the boundaries. The classifier would treat a person weighing 99 pounds very differently from one weighing 101 pounds even though most people could not tell the difference by looking at them.

You can also convert a nominal feature into a numeric one by assigning numeric values to each of the possibilities, for example, {Republican=1, Democrat=2, Libertarian=3, Other=4}. The problem with this conversion is that many numeric algorithms perform generalizations based on numeric values. When nominal features are encoded numerically, these generalizations might not reflect the nature of the features. For example, it is not valid to say that the average of a Republican(1) and a Libertarian(3) is a Democrat(2). It is even worse to place Libertarian between Democrat and Other. You can assign the numeric encodings, but reasoning about them along the real number line is not conceptually valid.

The distance-comparable features are not numeric, but they can be compared and a distance between two values can be assigned. An example might be the set of strings. You can create a "substitution cost" distance for strings. For example, comparing "Heat" with "heat" might produce a very small distance because substituting "H" for "h" is very cheap. The strings "heet" and "heat" might be farther apart because substituting "e" for "a" is not too bad, but they are not as close as "H" and "h." The strings "heap" and "heat" might be even farther apart for similar reasons. Another distance comparable feature might be animal species like {pigs, chickens, cows, elk, . . .}. You can assign a distance between any two species based on differences in their chromosome makeup. Though you can determine a distance between any two values for such a feature, there is no clear ordering of the features, nor can you compute an average. The fact that there is a distance has value in some classifier algorithms, but they cannot be used in as many situations as numeric features. It is possible to take any sequence of nominal values and convert it into one or more distance-comparable features using a distance metric such as minimal edit distance (A3.2d).

A3.1 – Vector Classifiers

Prerequisites
Vectors (A1.1), Matrices (A1.2), Classifiers (A3)

Overview
The vector classifiers are quite general and can solve a variety of problems. Many of them are quite easy to implement and to train. The ability to apply vector classifiers to a problem will greatly enhance the number of options that you have in detecting and responding to interactive human behavior.

In a vector classifier problem, every object has exactly the same number of features and all values for a feature are of the same type. This is in contrast to sequence classifiers that handle varying numbers of features. Sample uses of vector classifiers are as follows:

- Using [hue, saturation] to classify image pixels as human skin or not
- Using [bodyTemperature, pulseRate, bloodPressure] to decide if a patient is healthy or sick
- Using [height, width, strokeLength, startPoint, endPoint] of an ink gesture to decide if it means insert, delete, bold, italic, or justify

Description
There are two broad categories of vector classifiers: those that make a binary decision between two classes (sick/healthy, skin/not skin) and those that can classify any number of classes {insert, delete, bold, italic, justify}. Most binary classifiers return some confidence value of how much they support their conclusions. You can use this to turn a binary classifier into a multiclass classifier. If there are N classes, you can train N separate binary classifiers, each of which decides Yes/No between one class and all of the other classes. You then run the feature vector through all N classifiers and take the class that yields the most confident yes.

Each classifier is trained using a training set. A training set is simply an unordered list of training examples. Each training example is a tuple:

$$[\vec{f}, c]$$

where $\vec{f}$ is a feature vector and c is a class that corresponds to that combination of features.

Classifier algorithms vary in the way in which they *generalize* from training examples. In most realistic situations, the space of possible feature vectors is very large. In many cases, you have far fewer training examples than there are possible points in the feature space. What you want is to generalize from the training examples into neighboring regions of the feature space. Various classifiers generalize in different ways. The way in which a particular type of classifier generalizes is called its inductive bias[2].

Classifier efficiency is measured both in time to train the classifier and in time to classify a particular feature vector, once the classifier is trained. The parameters that control such efficiency are the number of training examples E, the number of features F, and the number of possible classes C.

The classifiers described in this section are as follows:

- *Naïve Bayes*—A relatively simple learning algorithm based primarily on counting and voting. Training is quite simple and the algorithm can learn a large number of patterns. This algorithm is primarily useful when many features must work together to build confidence in a conclusion. The training time is $O(EF)$, and the classification time is $O(F)$.

- *Decision tree*—A larger number of features. All features must be nominal. Decision trees are a little more complicated to train and implement than naïve Bayes. Decision trees can learn arbitrarily complicated decision patterns. Training time is $O(EF)$ and classification time is $O(F)$. Versions of decision trees that use numeric features are possible but more expensive to train.

- *Nearest neighbor*—Any number of features, which must be numeric or distance-comparable. Nearest neighbor can learn arbitrarily complicated decision patterns. Training time is zero because all training examples are used directly by the classifier algorithm. Classification time is $O(EF)$, which is a problem.

- *Clustering*—This is not truly a trainable classifier, but it can be used to reduce the classification time of a nearest neighbor classifier as well as serve other purposes. The goal is to produce a set of classes that separate the data into clusters or classes in an interesting and useful way.

- *Linear classifiers*—These can handle any number of numeric features. They can only be trained on problems where classes are linearly separable (defined later). Training time is variable because the algorithm iterates until it converges or reaches some maximum number of iterations. Classification time is $O(FC)$.

A3.1a – Naïve Bayes

Prerequisites
Arrays, Classifiers (A3)

Overview
This is a relatively simple classifier that assembles evidence from a variety of features to produce a classification. The simplest form of this algorithm uses all of the known features and, thus, can be a little slow to classify. The algorithm is easy to implement and very easy to train. The training time is $O(EF)$, and the classification time is $O(F)$. This algorithm can be augmented with a feature selection step that will improve classification times.

Description
The foundation of this algorithm is Bayes' Law for computing conditional probabilities. The idea is to compute the probability of each class C_i given a feature vector V. The class with the highest probability is the final classification. The approach begins with using Bayes' Law to compute the probability of C_i given a single feature V_f. Bayes' Law is as follows:

$$P(A \mid B) = \frac{P(B \mid A)P(A)}{P(B)}$$

Conditional probability $P(A|B)$ is the probability that A is true given that B is known to be true. In the classification problem, B would be the facts that you know from the feature vector V, and A would be one of the classes to be classified. What you want to know for each class C_i is the probability $P(C_i|V)$ or the probability of C_i being the correct classification given the feature vector V.

The first step that you need is to compute discrete probabilities. Though it is possible to compute exact probabilities for some problems using calculus, you will rarely use that approach in user interfaces. To use calculus to solve the problem, you need continuous functions for the various probabilities. This requires more understanding of the problem and its features than many developers have. The implementation converts the problem to discrete probabilities and uses simple histograms. The output classes are already discrete. If you have nominal features, you are already prepared. However, many problems have real-valued features (naïve Bayes is rarely used with distance-comparable features). To get nominal features from real-valued features, you must *quantize* them in to discrete "buckets." The quantization problem is only briefly discussed here. Once all features are nominal, you can compute the various probabilities using Bayes' Law on each feature. You then combine the probabilities of the various features to produce a final probability for each class.

Quantization

The quantization problem occurs when numeric values are incorrectly quantized into nominal features. Consider a one-feature/two-class problem where the distribution of 224 training examples in two classes (A and B) is shown in Figure A.4.

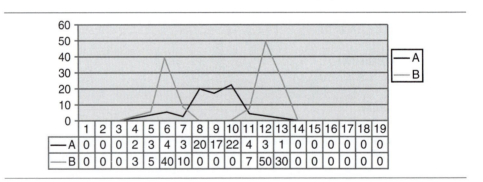

	1	2	3	4	5	6	7	8	9	10	11	12	13	14	15	16	17	18	19
—A	0	0	0	2	3	4	3	20	17	22	4	3	1	0	0	0	0	0	0
—B	0	0	0	3	5	40	10	0	0	0	7	50	30	0	0	0	0	0	0

Figure A.4 – Class feature distribution

Based on this data, values 1-3 and 14-19 will be undecided. Values 4-7 and 11-13 will be class B and values 8-10 will be class A. Suppose, however, to keep the size of the classifier small, you quantized this data into three values. The resulting distribution is shown in Figure A.5.

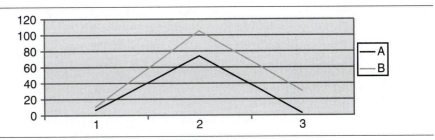

Figure A.5 – Poor quantization of feature values

With this quantization, all values now vote for class B no matter what. The valley in class B where class A resides has been averaged away.

If you quantized to the other extreme with 300 possible values, your training set of 224 examples will guarantee that 76 of the feature values are unsampled and if there are multiple samples per value, an even larger percentage of the feature space will be unaccounted for. The simplest quantization is to pick a "bin" size such that there are many samples per bin, but there is still sufficient information to separate the classes. By quantizing all real-valued features, you now have all nominal features that can be used with simple counting techniques to compute probabilities.

Feature/Class Probabilities

You first use Bayes' Law to compute the probability of a class C_i given a single discrete feature value V_f.

$$P(C_i \mid V_f) = \frac{P(V_f \mid C_i)P(C_i)}{P(V_f)}$$

Remember that the goal is to find the class that has the highest probability. What you want to do is compare $P(C_1 \mid V_f) > P(C_2 \mid V_f)$. Using Bayes' Law, the comparison would be:

$$\frac{P(V_f \mid C_1)P(C_1)}{P(V_f)} > \frac{P(V_f \mid C_2)P(C_2)}{P(V_f)}$$

Notice that $P(V_f)$ appears in the denominator on both sides of the comparison. Because $P(V_f)$ is positive, you can multiply it times both sides of the inequality to produce:

$$P(V_f \mid C_1)P(C_1) > P(V_f \mid C_2)P(C_2)$$

This forms the classification test for a two class case. For multiple classes, you simply compute the argmax across all of the classes. (Argmax is the maximum out of a set of possibilities.)

Computing the probability of a class $P(C_i)$ is simple. You count the number of instances of each class in the training set and divide by the number of items in the training set. The purpose of this term in computing the probability is to account for classes that occur very infrequently. For example, when trying to diagnose a disease (class) from a set of symptoms and test results (features), you would want very strong support from the feature before you published a diagnosis of smallpox because smallpox is almost completely eradicated.

Sometimes the class probability term can cause problems. Suppose that you are trying to create a laser pointer tracker using a camera. You need a classifier that separates laser spots from normal pixels. Many images have a million or more pixels with only three to five of those pixels belonging to the laser spot. This means that the probability of a laser spot as compared with a nonlaser spot is five in a million. It would require a lot of evidence from the features to overcome that hurdle. In many cases, you are using a classifier to find something that is relatively rare in the training set. A good example of such a case is the laser spot detector described in Chapter 24 where pixels with laser spots are very rare in a training image. In those cases, discarding the class probability term produces a better classifier for the task even though it is not a true probability. The classification test becomes:

$$P(V_f \mid C_1) > P(V_f \mid C_2)$$

Regardless of whether you use class probabilities, the key term for classification is $P(V_f \mid C_i)P(C_i)$ rather than $P(V_f \mid C_i)P(C_i)$. This is computed from the training data in a simple two-dimensional matrix Pf, as shown in Figure A.6.

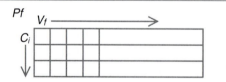

Figure A.6 – Class/feature probability matrix

For each training example, you take the output class and the discrete value of V_f to subscript into the array and increment the count. You then divide each row by the number of training examples for that class to get the probabilities. To compute $P(V_f \mid C_i)$ given feature value V_f, you index the appropriate column in the array for the value of V_f and take the class with the largest probability.

Combined Probabilities

The previous discussion gives you the probability of a class given the value of one feature. What you need is the probability given all of the features. The first step is to compute the matrix Pf for every feature. You then need to combine these feature probabilities into a single composite probability for each class. The approach is to "and" all of the feature probabilities together by multiplying them. This computes the probability of the condition where all of the feature values in the input correspond to a given class. The simple multiplication technique is based on the "naïve" assumption that all features are independent. This is generally not true. For example, the weight and height of a person are not independent features. Taller people generally weigh more than shorter people. However, the "naïve" assumption works just fine in many cases. Hence, you combine evidence from all of the features using the following formula:

$$P(C_i \mid V) = \prod_f P(C_i \mid V_f)$$

In many cases, the probabilities can be small and the number of features large. When this occurs, the product of the probabilities can underflow the floating-point representations of most machines. To resolve this problem, you use the sum of the logarithms of the probabilities rather than the product of the probabilities. This does not change the comparison. You can classify using the following formula:

$$\underset{C_i}{\arg\max} \left(\sum_f \log(P(C_i \mid V_f)) \right)$$

Rather than repeatedly computing the logarithm during classification, you replace the probabilities in the matrices with the logarithm of the probabilities. Classification is simply a matter of summing the matrix values for each feature/class and selecting the class with the largest value. On occasion, some of the probability values will be zero in some bins. The value of $\log(0)$ is negative infinity. To resolve this problem, you initialize Pf to 1 rather than zero before counting. This only very slightly distorts the results and prevents numeric problems.

Implementation

As with all classifiers, there are two algorithms: the training algorithm that produces matrices from the training set and the classification algorithm that takes a feature vector and returns a class. The following code includes the class probabilities. They are easily removed if not desired. It is assumed that the features have already been converted to discrete integer values where needed.

```
class Example
{    int theClass;    // the class that should be the result of this example
     int features[];  // features for the example
}
class NaiveBayes
{    int nClasses;    // number of output classes
     int nFeatures;   // number of features per example
     int nValues;     // maximum number of discrete values per feature
     float logClassProb [nClasses];
         // logarithm of the probability of each class P(C).
     float logFeatureProb [nFeatures, nClasses, nValues];
         // contains the probabilities trained from the sample set P(f,C)
}
```

```
NaiveBayes train( Example examples[nExamples], NaiveBayes data)
{    // Assumes that data already contains nClasses, nFeatures
     // and nValues. Will generate logClassProb and logFeatureProb.
     classProb (examples,data);
     featureProb (examples, data);
     return data;
}
void classProb (Example examples[nExamples], NaiveBayes data)
{    for (int c=0;c<data.nClasses;c++)
     {    data.logClassProb [c]=1; }
     foreach ( e in examples )
     {    data.logClassProb [e.theClass] += 1; }
     for (int c=0;c<data.nClasses;c++)
     {    data.logClassProb [c] =
             log(data.logClassProb [c]/(nExamples+data.nClasses));
     }
}

void featureProb( Example examples[nExamples], NaiveBayes data)
{
     for (int f=0;f<data.nFeatures; f++)
     {    for (int c=0;c<data.nClasses; c++)
          {    for (int v=0;v<data.nValues; v++)
               {    data.logFeatureProb [f,c,v]=1; }
          }
     }
     foreach (e in examples )
     {    for (int f=0;f<data.nFeatures;f++)
          {    data.logFeatureProb [f, e.theClass, e.features[f] ]+=1; }
     }

     int exPerClass[data.nClasses];
     for (int c=0;c<data.nClasses;c++)
     {    exPerClass[c]=1; }
     foreach (e in examples)
     {    exPerClass[e.theClass]++; }

     for (int f=0;f<data.nFeatures; f++)
     {    for (int c=0;c<data.nClasses; c++)
          {    for (int v=0;v<data.nValues; v++)
               {    double prob=
                        data.logFeatureProb[f,c,v]/exPerClass[c];
                    data.logFeatureProb[f,c,v]=log(prob);
               }
          }
     }
}
```

The `train()` algorithm in the preceding code loads a data structure with the computed probabilities from the training data, which can then be used to classify new feature vectors.

```
int classify( int features[nFeatures], NaiveBayes data )
{
    float classLogSum[nClasses];
    for (int c=0;c<nClasses;c++)
    {    classLogSum[c]=0; }
    for (int f=0;f<nFeatures;f++)
    {
        for (int c=0;c<nClasses;c++)
        {    classLogSum[c]+=data.logFeatureProb[f,c,features[f]]; }
    }
    float maxSum=classLogSum[0];
    int maxClass=0;
    for (int c=1;c<nClasses;c++)
    {    if (classLogSum[c]>maxSum)
        {    maxSum=classLogSum[c];
            maxClass=c;
        }
    }
    return c;
}
```

A3.1b – Decision Tree

Prerequisites
Classifier features (A3)

Overview
Decision trees most naturally use nominal features. There are decision tree variations that allow for numeric and distance-comparable features. The time of classification is linear in the number of features for nominal feature trees. The size of the classifier depends upon the complexity of the classification function to be learned. A decision tree for nominal features is never larger than the feature space (product of the ranges of the features) and is frequently very much smaller.

Description
A decision tree works by selecting a feature and using that feature to divide a set of training examples into groups based on the value of that feature. Each such group then recursively forms a subtree. There are two primary strategies for selecting features and doing the decomposition. The first involves strictly nominal features and is the easiest to program. However, there are many cases when numeric features are important. The use of numeric features is discussed after the nominal features

algorithm. To illustrate how the tree is constructed using nominal features, consider the following set of training data.

1 - { tall, heavy, 3, red } → good
2 - { tall, light, 2, red } → good
3 - { medium, veryHeavy, 1, green} → OK
4 - { short, light, 3, green } → OK
5 - { medium, heavy, 3, red } → good
6 - { medium, light, 1, red} → bad
7 - { medium, heavy, 1, red} → bad

Using this data, you can build the top node of the tree using the first feature:

short

4 - { **short**, light, 3, green } → OK

medium

3 - { **medium**, veryHeavy, 1, green} → OK
5 - { **medium**, heavy, 3, red } → good
6 - { **medium**, light, 1, red} → bad
7 - { **medium**, heavy, 1, red} → bad

tall

1 - { **tall**, heavy, 3, red } → good
2 - { **tall**, light, 2, red } → good

Note that the tree under "short" contains only the class "OK" and the tree under "tall" contains only the class "good." These subsets of the training set need no further refinement. Such subsets are considered *pure* because they only contain one class. They can simply report their class. The training examples under "medium" contain all three classes and must be subdivided further. You can continue breaking down the tree using the second feature:

short → OK
medium

    light

6 - { medium, **light**, 1, red} → bad

    heavy

5 - { medium, **heavy**, 3, red } → good
7 - { medium, **heavy**, 1, red} → bad

    veryHeavy

3 - { medium, **veryHeavy**, 1, green} → OK

  tall → good

You can continue this process using the third feature:

short → OK
medium

> **light** → bad
> **heavy**
>
> > 1
> >
> > 7 - { medium, heavy, 1, red} → bad
> >
> > 2
> >
> > 3
> >
> > 5 - { medium, heavy, 3, red } → good
>
> **veryHeavy** → OK

tall → good

You can now produce the final decision tree for the data:

short → OK
medium

> **light** → bad
> **heavy**
>
> > 1 → bad
> > 2 → ?
> > 3 → good
>
> **veryHeavy** → OK

tall → good

Classification Using a Nominal Feature Decision Tree

Each node of a decision tree has the following structure:

```
class DecisionTree
{    int featureIndex;
            // index of the feature for subdividing the tree
            // if this is −1 then there are no subtrees and theClass should be
            // reported
     DecisionTree subtrees[ ];
            // array of decision trees indexed by the values of the
            // feature indicated by featureIndex
     int theClass;
            // if there are no subtrees for this node, then this is the class that
            // corresponds to this part of the tree.

}
```

Using this structure, the classifier algorithm is as follows:

```
int classify(nominalFeatureVector features[n], DecisionTree tree)
{    if (tree.featureIndex== -1)
     {    // this is a leaf of the tree
          return tree.theClass;
     }
     else
     {    featureValue = features[tree.featureIndex];
          return classify( features, tree.subtrees[featureValue]);
     }
}
```

Building the Decision Tree

Building the decision tree is a recursive process. At each step, you select a feature to use to partition the `trainingSet`.

```
decisionTree buildTree( example trainingSet[n])
{    decisionTree result;

     if ( hasOnlyOneClass(trainingSet) )
     {    result.featureIndex = -1;
          result.theClass = trainingSet[0].class;
          return result;
     }
     else
     {
          int feature = pickAFeature(trainingSet);
          if (feature is no feature)
          {    result.featureIndex = -1;
               result.theClass = undecided;
               return result;
          }
          result.featureIndex=feature;
          int nVals = howManyValuesForFeature(feature);
          result.subTrees = new decisionTree[nVals];
          for each value v for feature
          {    result.subTrees[v] = buildTree(
                         matchingExamples( trainingSet, feature, v));
          }
          return result;
     }
}

example [ ] matchingExamples( example trainingSet[n], int feature,
                              nominalFeature Val)
{
     return all examples from trainingSet for which the specified feature
          has the specified value
}
```

The key to the algorithm is the order in which you pick features to break down the training set. This is controlled by how you implement `pickAFeature()`. The simplest implementation is to use the first feature that has more than one value in the training set. Selecting such a feature guarantees that each invocation of `buildTree()` will have a smaller training set to work on and eventually the process will converge. You might, in some cases, reach a training set for which all feature vectors are the same, but the classes are not. You can resolve this by voting (which helps with noisy data) or by reporting no class, which leaves the result undetermined for those cases.

Simply selecting the first usable feature is not a very good approach. It leads to larger tree sizes than necessary and less-effective generalization from training examples. What you want is to select a feature that best divides the training set along the categories that you are ultimately trying to classify. The classic algorithm for decision feature selection is ID3[2].

Evaluating which feature to use is based on a measure of the "impurity" of a set of training examples. A set of training examples is pure (impurity=0) if all training examples in the set have the same class. If there is some mixture of classes in the training set, that set is considered impure. A node of a decision tree should use the feature that will divide its training set into subsets that will reduce impurity as much as possible.

You can compute the impurity of a set of training examples in a variety of ways[1]. The simplest is $imp(T) = 1 - \max_c(P(T_c))$, where T is the training set and $P(T_c)$ is the fraction of T that is in class C.

Given some feature F, you can compute the impurity after splitting the training set on F as follows:

$$imp(F) = \sum_{v=1}^{values(F)} P_v imp(T_v)$$

where P_v is the fraction of the training examples that have value V for feature F and T_v is the set of training examples that have value V for feature F.

This measure of impurity is somewhat of a problem because it favors features that split many ways over features that split a few. Where there are many splits, the probability of each split is somewhat lower than if there are just a few ways to split. This makes $imp(T_v)$ lower for features that split many ways. You can compensate for this by using the following scaling formula:

$$imp_g(F) = \frac{imp(F)}{-\sum_{v=1}^{values(F)} P_v \log_2 P_v}$$

To pick a feature, you compute $imp_g(F)$ for each feature and pick the feature that produces the least impurity.

```
int pickAFeature( example trainingSet[n])
{    int pickedFeature=-1;
     double pickedImpurity = 1.0;
     for each feature f
     {    int nVals = howManyValuesForFeature(f)
          int counts[nVals, nClasses];
          set counts to zero

          for (i=0; i<n; i++)
          {    int val = trainingSet[i].features[f];
               counts[val, trainingSet[i].class]++;
          }

          double impF=0.0;
          double scale=0.0;
          for (v = 0; v<nVals; v++)
          {    int countV = 0;
               int max=0;
               for (c=0; c<nClasses; c++)
               {    countV=countV+counts[v,c];
                    if (counts[v,c]>max)
                    {    max=counts[v,c];  }
               }
               double impTv= 1.0-(max/countV);
               double Pv=countV/n;
               impF=impF+Pv*impTv;
               scale=scale-Pv*log2(Pv);
          }
          impF=impF/scale;

          if (impF<pickedImpurity)
          {    pickedImpurity = impF;
               pickedFeature = F;
          }
     }

     return pickedFeature;
}
```

Decision Trees with Numeric Features

Decision trees with nominal features build a tree where each node is indexed by the value of some feature. This is not acceptable when there are numeric features because there are potentially an infinite number of numeric values for a feature. In describing decision trees with numeric features, you assume that all features are numeric. Algorithms for mixing numeric and nominal features are easily created once the two types are independently understood.

The general approach for creating decision tree nodes for numeric features is to select a feature F and a value V for that feature. You then can divide the training set into two subsets L and G (less and greater) such that:

$L = all\ training\ examples\ T_i\ such\ that\ \ T_i.F < V$

$G = all\ training\ examples\ T_i\ such\ that\ \ T_i.F \geq V$

The class for defining a decision tree can be modified in the following way:

```
class DecisionTree
{    int featureIndex;
            // index of the feature for subdividing the tree
            // if this is –1 then there are no subtrees and theClass should be
            // reported
      float V;
            // the value to be used in partitioning the tree according
            // to the feature
      DecisionTree less;
            // A decision tree for all cases where the feature is less than V
      DecisionTree greater;
            // A decision tree for all cases where the feature is greater
            // than or equal to V
      int theClass;
            // if there are no subtrees for this node, then this is the class that
            // corresponds to this part of the tree.
}
```

The classification algorithm is quite simple. You simply walk the tree comparing feature values as you go until you reach a leaf. You then return the class for that leaf.

```
int classify(float features[n], DecisionTree tree)
{    if (tree.featureIndex== -1)
     {    // this is a leaf of the tree
          return tree.theClass;
     }
     else if (features[tree.featureIndex]<tree.V)
     {    return classify(features,tree.less); }
     else
     {    return classify(features,tree.greater); }
}
```

The challenge lies in building the tree. You not only must select a feature, but you must also select a value for that feature to use as the split value to divide the training set. A very simple approach is to select the mean for each feature. You can then compute the new impurity for each feature division and select the feature that produces the least impurity. Using the mean is easy to compute and tends to divide the training set into roughly equal halves. This means that the decision time will be at worst $n \log(n)$, where n is the number of training examples. The problem is that the mean has little to do with a good division place to produce a good classification. Good feature choices are ignored when their appropriate split point is not near the mean.

The best way to produce such a decision tree is to take each feature and each value in that feature and pick the one that produces the lowest impurity.

```
decisionTree buildTree( example trainingSet[n])
{    decisionTree result;

     if ( hasOnlyOneClass(trainingSet) )
     {    result.featureIndex = -1;
          result.theClass = trainingSet[0].class;
          return result;
     }
     else
     {    int bestFeature = -1;
          float leastImpurity = infinity;
          float bestValue = 0.0;
          example bestL[];
          example bestG[];
          for each feature F
          {    for each value V for feature F
               {    example L[]=empty;
                    example G[]=empty;
                    for each training example T
                    {    if (T[F]< V)
                         {    L.add(T); }
                         else
                         {    G.add(T); }
                    }
                    float splitImpurity = impurity(L) + impurity(G);
                    if (splitImpurity < leastImpurity)
                    {    leastImpurity=splitImpurity;
                         bestFeature=F;
                         bestValue=V;
                         bestL=L;
                         bestG=G;
                    }
               }
          }
          result.featureIndex = bestFeature;
          result.V = bestValue;
          result.less=buildTree(bestL);
          result.greater=buildTree(bestG);
          return result;
     }
}
```

This algorithm can be very slow to build a tree if there are many features and many training examples. This speed can be improved in a number of ways. The simplest improvement is to sample the training examples rather than use all of them. You do not need an exact split value. An approximately good one will do because subsequent layers of the decision tree can correct any inaccuracies. If at each buildTree() you select 100 samples from the training set and consider only their feature values, you have a fixed bound on the number of values to consider. When you actually produce the partitioned sets for building lower nodes in the tree and for calculating impurity, you still use the full training set. This approach can be significantly faster (depending on the sampling size used) and produces very close to the same quality of decision. However, there will frequently be multiple nodes for a feature as multiple layers are used to find the best split point.

When considering a feature for possible split, it can help to first sort the training examples by that feature. The values can then be considered in ascending order. This has several advantages: (1) It is easy to ignore duplicate values. (2) Using the mean between two successive values will in general produce a better split in the presence of sparse data than just using either value. (3) When moving from training example T_i to T_{i+1} in the sorted list, it is simple to increment the counts for the various classes in calculating impurity rather than retest all of the training examples. Because the list is already sorted, only the training example being considered changes subsets with the new value. The two sets L and R are easily represented as two ranges in the training set array rather than building new structures. The sorting approach is more complicated and does not improve the quality of the resulting classifier, but it can significantly increase the speed of the classifier.

A3.1c – Nearest Neighbor

Prerequisites
Classifier features (A3), Vectors (A1.1), Comparing Vectors (A1.1e)

Overview
The nearest neighbor classifier works by storing all of the examples from the training set and comparing a new vector to be classified against all of the stored vectors. It uses any of the vector distance metrics (A1.1e) for comparison. It finds the closest neighbor (least distance) out of the set of examples and returns the class of that example. This algorithm can learn decision functions of any complexity. Its classification time is $O(EF)$, which tends to make the classification slow. This algorithm generally requires features that are distance-comparable or numeric. There are variations of the algorithm that can use purely nominal features.

Description
The nearest neighbor classifier is conceptually quite simple. You store the training set and then compare a feature vector to be classified against all of the examples in the training set, and return the one that is the nearest. Any of the vector distance functions described in A1.1e can be used for the distance.

Implementation

```
class nearestNeighbor( Feature features[n], example trainingSet[nEx] )
{    example E=trainingSet[0];
     double minDist = distance(features, E.features);
     class curClass = E.class;
     for (int i=1; i<nEx; i++)
     {    double tmp = distance(features,trainingSet[i].features);
          if (tmp<minDist)
     {    minDist = tmp;
          curClass = trainingSet[i].class;
     }
     }
     return curClass;
}
```

The following picture shows roughly how nearest neighbor works with two features and three classes (A,B,C). The nearest neighbor surfaces are slightly more complicated than what is shown, but not much. In Figure A.7, Point 1 is closer to an A than anything else and point 2 is closer to a C.

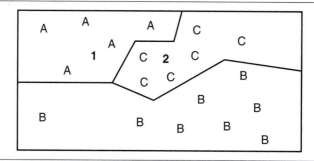

Figure A.7 – Nearest neighbor space partitioning

This simple algorithm is somewhat sensitive to noise. That is, if some of the training examples are incorrect, this algorithm learns those incorrect data. Suppose you had an erroneous C, as shown in Figure A.8. This would create a small pocket of C class space in the middle of B.

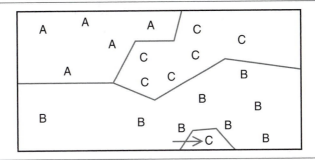

Figure A.8 – Nearest neighbor with erroneous example

The noise problem can be overcome by finding the K nearest neighbors of a feature vector and having them vote on which class would be right. In the example in Figure A.7, using a K of three would eliminate the effect of the spurious C but would also push back some of the corners, as shown in Figure A.9.

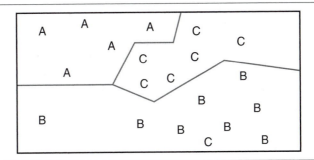

Figure A.9 – Space partition using three nearest neighbors

The averaging effect of using K larger than 1 can be overcome with more training data. Another approach is to weight the influence of each of the K examples by their distance from the point being classified. Thus, closer examples have more influence than those farther away.

Normalizing Features

One of the problems with simple nearest neighbor is that not all features have the same range. Take, for example, a simple character classifier that uses the features StartX, StartY, EndX, EndY, and StrokeLength, as illustrated in Figure A.10.

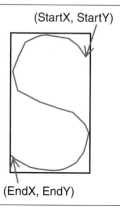

(StartX, StartY)

(EndX, EndY)

Figure A.10 – Character-recognition features

Generally, strokes for recognition are scaled to the unit square before features are computed so that the size of the character does not matter. In such a case, StartX, StartY, EndX, and EndY lie in the range 0.0->1.0. However, StrokeLength can vary much more widely. In the example of an "S", the StrokeLength is closer to 4.0. When computing distances between feature vectors, the StrokeLength has much greater distances and, therefore, separates objects much more widely than the other four features. You would like to eliminate such bias.

One simple normalization is to compute maximum and minimum values for each feature and then normalize the data values into classifier values:

$$classVal = \frac{dataVal}{\max_f - \min_f}$$

where $\max_f$ and $\min_f$ are the maximum and minimum value for feature f. This method is susceptible to outliers. If there were one really extreme example in the training set, it would bias the range. If the values follow a normal distribution (which many do), then 95 percent of all values lie within four times the standard deviation. A more robust normalization is as follows:

$$classVal = \frac{dataVal}{4\sigma_f}$$

where σ_f is the standard deviation of all values of the feature f.

Distance-Comparable Features

Both of these normalizations work for numeric features but not for distance-comparable features. Such features do not have maximum values or standard deviations. However, you can compare all feature values with each other (which is $O(N^2)$ in the number of values) and compute an average distance among values. This average distance is roughly comparable to two times the standard deviation. Thus, you can normalize distance-comparable features by:

$$classVal = \frac{dataVal}{2ad_f}$$

where ad_f is the average distance between values for feature f.

Pruning Examples

One of the big problems with nearest neighbor classifiers is that large numbers of training examples can slow down classification time and take up a lot of space. Both of these factors can be improved by pruning out examples that do not change the outcome of the classifier. In Figure A.11, the gray examples could be removed without changing the result.

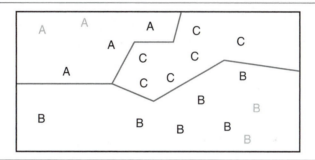

Figure A.11 – Prunable nearest neighbor examples

A variety of algorithms have been developed for performing such pruning. One simple technique is trial deletion. You remove a training example from the set and see if it is still classified correctly when its own example is missing. If it is still classified correctly, remove it; otherwise, keep it. Another approach is trial insertion. You start with an empty set of examples. One by one, you test each new training example to see if it will classify correctly. If it does not classify correctly, you add it to the set of examples. You repeat this process until no new training examples are added.

A3.1d – Clustering – K-Means

Prerequisites

Vector distances (A1.1e), Nearest Neighbor Classifier (A3.1c)

Overview

In many situations, the amount of training data or the number of features is too large or expensive to use directly. One of the ways to deal with this is to break the data into a set of K clusters, with each cluster being represented by a mean vector. For this kind of clustering, all features must be numeric. A feature vector can be classified into one of the *K* clusters by finding which of the K-means has the smallest distance to the feature vector. The key problem is discovering an appropriate set of mean vectors.

Description

The mean vector of a set of vectors is determined by computing the average value for each feature.

$$mean_f = \frac{\sum_{i=1}^{N} items[i]_f}{N}$$

where *f* is a feature, *items* is an array of vectors, and *N* is the number of vectors.

You can use mean vectors as a way to cluster data using a distance metric. If you are initially given a set of *K* vectors, you can cluster a larger set of vectors according to which of the *K* vectors each one is nearest to. You can then compute a new set of *K* vectors by taking the mean of each cluster. You repeat this until the membership in the clusters does not change. You then can retain the *K* mean vectors as the representation of each of the classes.

```
Vector [K] kMeans(Vector items[N], Vector seedMeans[K])
{
     Vector curMeans[K] = seedMeans;
     do
     {    Vector lastMeans=curMeans;
          Cluster clusters[K];
          for (int i=0;i<N;i++)
          {    double dist=distance(items[i],curMeans[0]);
               int clusterIdx=0;
               for (int k=1;k<K;k++)
               {    double d=distance(items[i],curMeans[k]);
                    if (d<dist)
                    {    dist=d;
                         clusterIdx=k;
                    }
               }
               clusters[clusterIdx].add(items[i]);
          }
          for (int k=0;k<K;k++)
          {    curMeans[k]=clusters[k].computeMean(); }
     } until (closeEnough(lastMeans, curMeans))
     return curMeans;
}
```

The ability of this algorithm to produce good clusters depends upon the choice of the seedMeans. One way to produce a good set of *K* vectors is to start with a single mean vector for the entire set. You can divide the cluster by computing a new variant vector where each feature is a very small value different from the original vector. With these two vectors that are very close, but not identical, you can produce two new clusters. These new clusters will converge to their own means. If you have *K* clusters and you want $K+1$ clusters, you can pick the largest cluster, compute a new variant of its mean, and then do K-means again until the clusters converge. Proceeding in this way, you can eventually produce any number of clusters.

Nearest neighbor classifiers suffer from poor classification speed because of the need to compute the distance to each member of the training set. You can improve this performance by replacing the training data with the mean vector for each class. This, however, produces misclassifications in cases where the decision space is more complex than a simple distance. You can handle this by computing the K means starting with the means of each classifier. Any cluster that is impure (has a mixed set of classes in that cluster) is divided into clusters based on the classes in that cluster. Mean vectors are computed for the new clusters and the K-means algorithm is repeated. This splitting process proceeds until every cluster contains training data for only one class. In the worst case, there will be one cluster for every training item, but in many cases, there will be far fewer items than in the original training data.

Vector Quantization

Clustering is also used to produce a "vector quantization" that reduces the feature vector to one of a set of sample classes. The approach is to compute a set of K mean vectors that cluster the vector data into K classes. You can then take a new vector V, compute which of the K means is nearest to it, and then replace that vector with the index of the nearest mean. This, in essence, quantizes V into one of a small set of possibilities. This quantized value can then be used in later stages of a recognition process. This is frequently used to convert a series of vector features into a sequence of quantized values that are then fed to a sequence classifier.

A3.1e – Linear Classifiers

Prerequisites
Vectors (A1.1)

Overview
Linear classifiers use a simple linear function for each class. To classify a point, you compute the function for each class and take the class that produces the largest result. To produce the desired linear function for each class, you use an iterative gradient descent process. At each step, the algorithm finds the direction that will reduce the error of the classifier and moves the coefficients in that direction. Linear classifiers cannot always learn every decision surface. In some cases, the decisions are not linear. This problem can be accommodated by computing additional nonlinear features (see A1.2e).

Description
For the linear functions, you use the same homogenous formulation of a linear function, as discussed in the section on linear approximation (A1.2e). That is, each feature

vector acquires an additional coordinate 1, to accommodate a constant offset in the linear equation. Thus, the linear function for a three-feature system becomes:

$$
\begin{bmatrix} x & y & z & 1 \end{bmatrix} \cdot \begin{bmatrix} p \\ q \\ r \\ s \end{bmatrix} = d
$$

where p through s are the coefficients and d is the desired outcome for the function. The general form of the function is $\vec{V}_T \cdot \vec{C}_c = d_{T,c}$, where $\vec{V}_T$ is the homogeneous feature vector for training example T, $\vec{C}_c$ is the coefficient vector for class c, and $d_{T,c}$ is the desired outcome for training example T for class c.

Linear classifiers can only solve problems that are linearly separable, that is, when a linear hyperplane clearly divides classes from each other. Consider the problem in Figure A.12, which has a two-dimensional feature space and three classes A, B, and C. If the training examples fall into the feature space, as shown in Figure A.12 then each class can have its own hyperplane (line in two dimensions) that separates its examples from all other classes.

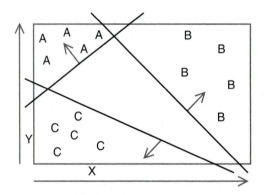

Figure A.12 – Three-class linear classifier

The arrows in Figure A.12 show the direction relative to the hyperplane where positive values of d (the result of the dot product) are found. You can find the class A by using the hyperplane in the upper left and run any feature vector through that equation. If the result is positive, the feature vector belongs to class A. The same can be done with the other two hyperplanes. The classification algorithm then is to run a feature vector through the hyperplane for each class and choose the class whose hyperplane returns the largest value.

Many problems are not linearly separable. Take the distribution of the same three classes shown in Figure A.13. Note that although the classes are clearly clumped together, there is no straight line that will separate class A from all other classes.

Remember that although the diagrams are two-dimensional, the classifier problem is N-dimensional depending on the number of features.

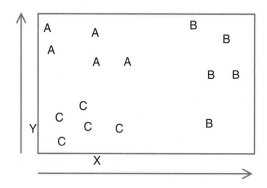

Figure A.13 – Linearly inseparable problem

Although there is no line that will separate the classes, it is possible that a series of parabolas would do the job. You can accommodate this by replacing the $\begin{bmatrix} X & Y \end{bmatrix}$ feature vector with the five-dimensional feature vector $\begin{bmatrix} X & Y & X^2 & Y^2 & XY \end{bmatrix}$.

If the classes are linearly separable, the problem is to come up with an algorithm that will learn the linear coefficients of the necessary hyperplanes from the training data. The perceptron algorithm works by randomly initializing the hyperplanes and then evaluating them against each element of the training set. If a hyperplane gives the wrong answer, you slightly modify the coefficients so that the hyperplane gives a more correct answer. You continue doing this with repeated passes against all of the training data. If the classes are linearly separable, the coefficients will converge. If they are not, you must detect that no progress is being made and stop.

You start the algorithm by initializing all of the coefficients in all of the $\bar{C}_c$ vectors to some small random number. For each training example T, you compute d_c. Given that $T.class$ is the correct class for example T, then $d_{T.class}$ should be the largest outcome. If this is so, the coefficients are left unchanged. If $d_{T.class}$ is not the largest outcome, you must modify the coefficients. Suppose that d_{max} is the largest outcome for a given training example. You want to modify $\bar{C}_{T.class}$ so that it will produce a higher outcome that is larger than d_{max}. You also want to modify the coefficients of all classes with larger outcomes than $T.class$ so that they will produce lower outcomes that are less than $d_{T.class}$. You do this with the following perceptron training rule[2]:

$$\bar{C}_c \leftarrow \bar{C}_c + \eta(t_c - d_c)\bar{V}_T$$

where t_c is the target outcome for class c and η is the learning rate. The learning rate η must be between 0.0 and 1.0 and is usually relatively small (0.1). The learning rate prevents extreme movements of the coefficients that overshoot the desired values.

For class $T.class$, you modify the coefficients to be:

$$\vec{C}_{T.class} = \vec{C}_{T.class} + \eta(d_{max} + 1 - d_{T.class})\vec{V}_T$$

This moves the outcome for $T.class$ toward a value larger than d_{max}. For all classes L such that $d_L \geq d_{T.class}$, you modify the coefficients according to the following rule:

$$\vec{C}_L = \vec{C}_L + \eta(d_{T.class} - 1 - d_L)\vec{V}_T$$

This moves the outcomes for these classes toward a value smaller than $d_{T.class}$. For all classes S such that $d_S < d_{T.class}$, you leave $\vec{C}_S$ unchanged because those functions produce correct outcomes.

This algorithm converges if η is sufficiently small and linear functions can correctly separate the classes. If linear functions are not sufficient, this algorithm does not converge. Nonconvergence is generally detected when some maximum number of iterations has been exceeded.

Implementation

```
int classify( double coef[C,F+1], double features[F])
{     int cls = -1;
      double dMax = smallest possible value;
      for (int c=0; c<C; c++)
      {     double d = coef[c,F];
            for (int f=0; f<F; f++)
            {     d=d+coef[c,f]*features[f]; }
            if (d>dMax)
            {     dMax = d;
                  cls = c;
            }
      }
      return cls;
}
```

```
double [nClasses,nFeatures+1] trainLinear( Example trainingSet[nEx])
{
    double coef[ nClasses,nFeatures+1];
    for (int c=0; c<nClasses; c++)
    {   for (int f=0; f<=nFeatures; f++)
        {   coef[c,f]=a small positive random number; }
    }

    for (int iter=0; iter<maximumIterations; iter++)
    {   int nErrors=0;
        for (int ex=0; ex<nEx; ex++)
        {   nErrors=nErrors+trainExample(trainingSet[ex],coef)
        }
        if (nErrors==0)
        {   return coef; }
    }
    return coef;
}

int trainExample(Example E, double coef[nClasses, nFeatures+1] )
{   double d[ ]=new double[nClasses];
    for (int c=0; c<nClasses; c++) // compute function for each class
    {   d[c]=coef[c,nFeatures];
        for (int f=0; f<nFeatures; f++)
        {   d[c]=d[c]+coef[c,f]*E.features[f]; }
    }

    int errCount=0;
    double L=the desired learning rate;
    double dMax=the smallest possible number;
    double dClass=d[E.class]; // result for the desired class
    for (int c=0; c<nClasses; c++)
    {   if(c!=E.class && d[c]>=dClass) // classification error
        {   double mov = L*(dClass-1-d[c]);
            for (int f=0; f<nFeatures; f++)
            {   coef[c,f]=coef[c,f]+mov*E.features[f]; }
            coef[c,nFeatures]=coef[c,nFeatures]+mov;
            if (d[c]>dMax)
            {   dMax=d[c]; }
            errCount=errCount+1;
        }
    }

    if (errCount>0)
    {   double mov=L*(dMax+1-dClass);
        for (int f=0; f<nFeatures; f++)
        {   coef[E.class,f]=coef[E.class,f]+mov*E.features[f]; }
        coef[E.class,nFeatures]=coef[E.class,nFeatures]+mov;
    }
    return errCount;
}
```

A3.2 – Sequence Classifiers

Sequence classifiers describe objects by a sequence of tokens drawn from some finite alphabet of tokens. Unlike vector classifiers, the number of tokens in the sequence can vary. Generally, sequence classifiers use nominal features with the order carrying much of the information about the object.

In the following discussion of sequence classifiers, you can use strings of characters as sample feature sequences. You also use a simple stroke recognizer as an example. As shown in Figure A.14, you can define nine regions that a stroke of digital ink must pass through and characterize that stroke by the sequence of regions. For example, the character C drawn in Figure A.14 would be encoded as the sequence [3,2,1,4,7,8,9]. In this case, the alphabet of the sequence is the digits 1 through 9. Character strings and stroke sequences can serve as examples for the discussion of sequence classifiers.

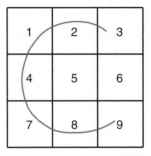

Figure A.14 – Stroke encoding for sequence classification

A3.2a – Simple String Matching

The simplest sequence classifier is simple matching. Suppose, for example, that you want to classify sequences into cats and dogs. The training set would be a set of strings each accompanied by the class that it belongs to. For example:

Chow → Dog
Collie → Dog
Cheetah → Cat
Lion → Cat
Lurcher → Dog
Leopard → Cat
Poodle → Dog
Puma → Cat

You can build a similar training set for the character recognizer. You get multiple sequences mapping to the same characters because of irregularities in user input.

[3,2,1,4,7,8,9] → C
[6,3,2,1,4,7,8,9] → C
[1,4,7,4,1,2,3,6,5,6,9,8,7] → B
[4,7,4,1,2,3,6,5,6,9,8,7] → B
[1,4,7,4,1,2,3,6,5,6,9,8] → B
[1,4,7,4,1,2,3,6,5,4,5,6,9,8,7] → B

The classification algorithm is a simple one. You take the input sequence and compare it against each of the training sequences. If it matches one of them, you return the corresponding class. If it does not match, you return "I don't know."

This algorithm has several problems. The first is that both the classification time and the space requirements are $O(TC)$, where TC is the total number of characters in the training set. The second problem is that the recognition is very brittle. If the user generates an input that is slightly different from any of the training data, the classifier fails. For example, entering "lions" will fail, given the training data. The four instances of B in the character classifier are due to minor variations in user input.

A3.2b – Trie Classification

You can reduce the classification time problem by using a structure called a trie. This structure combines common prefixes of the sequences and, thus, eliminates redundant comparisons. This approach is very similar to decision trees except that inputs are always handled in first-to-last order rather than selecting for minimal impurity. The training data for cats and dogs would produce a tree like that shown in Figure A.15. If a string matches the character in a node, the algorithm moves to the right. If there is a mismatch, you follow the down link. If there is no down link, the match fails. If the algorithm moves to the right and finds a class and the sequence is at the end, there is a match and the class is returned. The classification time is $O(AL)$, where A is the number of tokens in the alphabet and L is the length of the sequence being classified. This is much faster than the simple string match, but still has the same brittleness in that it fails for any sequence not in the training set.

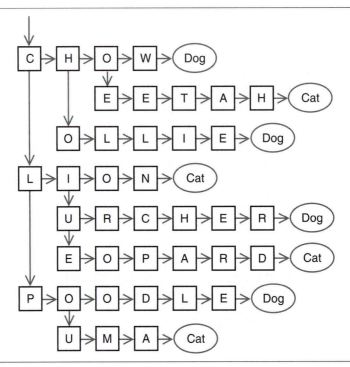

Figure A.15 – Sample trie

Implementation

```
class TrieNode
{    int token, theClass;
     TrieNode matchLink, failLink;

          void addTrainingSequence(int seq[L],int cls)
     {   addTrainingSequence(0,seq,cls }

     private void addTrainingSequence(int tokenIdx, int seq[L], int cls)
     {   if (tokenIdx>=L)
         {   theClass=cls; }
         else if (seq[tokenIdx]==token)
         {   if (matchLink==null)
             {   matchLink=createMatchChain(tokenIdx+1,seq,cls); }
             else
             {   matchLink.addTrainingSequence(tokenIdx+1,seq,cls); }
         }
         else if (failLink==null)
         {   failLink=createMatchChain(tokenIdx,seq,cls); }
         else
         {   failLink.addTrainingSequence(tokenIdx,seq,cls); }
     }
```

```
TrieNode createMatchChain(int tokenIdx, int seq[L], int cls)
{    TrieNode tmp = new TrieNode();
     if (tokenIdx>=L)
     {    tmp.theClass=cls;
          tmp.token=-1;
          tmp.matchLink=null;
          tmp.failLink=null;
          return tmp;
     }
     else
     {    tmp.theClass=-1;
          tmp.token=seq[tokenIdx];
          tmp.matchLink=createMatchChain(tokenIdx+1,seq,cls);
          tmp.failLlnk=null;
          return tmp;
     }
}

int classify(int tokenIdx, int seq[L])
{    if (tokenIdx>=L)
     {    return theClass; }
     else if (seq[tokenIdx]==theToken)
     {    if (matchLink==null)
          {    return −1; }
          else
          {    return matchLink.classify(tokenIdx+1,seq); }
     }
     else if (failLink==null)
     {    return −1; }
     else
     {    return failLink.classify(tokenIdx,seq); }
}
}
```

The implementation can be optimized for speed if each node has an array of matching links that can be indexed by the token number. This consumes more space, but makes the algorithm $O(L)$, where L is the length of the sequence to be classified.

A3.2c – Finite State Machines

The trie is a special case of the more general class of finite state machines. A finite state machine has a start state and zero or more additional states. Each state can have a class that is recognized if a sequence terminates in that state. There are transitions between states. Each transition has one of the alphabet tokens for that transition. Figure A.16 shows a simple state machine that recognizes an opening parenthesis, any number of the letter A, and a closing parenthesis.

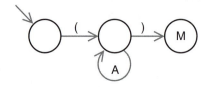

Figure A.16 – Sample state machine

Finite state machines have classification time of $O(L)$, where L is the length of the sequence to be classified. There are deterministic and nondeterministic finite state machines. A deterministic machine has at most one transition leaving a state for a given input token. A nondeterministic machine can have many transitions leaving a state for the same input token. A nondeterministic machine might have a classification time of $O(SL)$, where S is the number of states and L is the length of the sequence. This is much worse than for a deterministic machine.

Finite state machines have many useful algorithmic properties, including the ability to convert any nondeterministic machine into a deterministic machine, to create a new machine that is the union or intersection of any two finite state machines, and to reduce the finite state machine to a unique machine for any recognized set of strings[3]. Finite state machines are widely used for recognizing a variety of input sequences.

A3.2d – Minimal Edit Distance

The introduction of the trie and the finite state machine resolves the classification time problems and the minimal representation problem, but they do not resolve the brittleness problem. All of these classifiers fail if the sequence to be classified is even slightly different from the sequences recognized by the classifier.

What you need is a measure of how close two sequences are to each other. If you have a measure of a distance between two sequences, you can use classification techniques similar to nearest neighbor. This will be much more robust than simple matching. You could compare the two sequences token by token and compute a distance similar to the Manhattan distance [A1.1e]. However, the sequences are frequently not the same length. Simple token-by-token comparison is not adequate.

A common measure of a distance between two sequences is the minimal edit distance. You match two sequences by performing a series of edits on one or both of the sequences until they match. You attach a cost to each editing operation and compute the edit distance as the sum of those costs. The minimal edit distance is the cost for those edits that will produce a match with the least cost.

In most uses, there are three editing operations: substituting one token for another, deleting a token from a sequence, or inserting a token into a sequence. The following are examples of possible edits:

Hat, hat → substitute "H" for "h"
meet, meat → substitute "e" for "a"
hat, heat → either insert an "e" into "hat" or delete "e" from "heat"

The algorithm is driven by three arrays that are indexed by alphabet tokens:

- *sub[a,b]*, which is the cost of substituting token *a* for token *b*; *sub[a,a]* should be zero for all *a*.

- *ins[a]*, which is the cost of inserting token *a* into a sequence.

- *del[a]*, which is the cost of deleting token *a* from a sequence.

In most instances, the array *sub* is symmetric (the cost of substituting "H" for "h" is the same as substituting "h" for "H"). It is also frequently true that the values of *ins* and *del* are identical. This is because inserting a token into one sequence generally produces the same results as deleting that token from the other sequence. The algorithm, however, does not require these symmetries.

In the case of string matching, you might make the same cost of deleting or inserting any character. You might make the cost of substituting an uppercase letter for its lowercase equivalent very low. You might give a medium cost when substituting vowels for another vowel or substituting "c" for "s" because they frequently make the same sound. You might put a higher cost on substituting "t" for "o."

In the case of the gesture classifier that encodes a gesture as a sequence of region crossings, you might assign substitution costs based on adjacency of the regions with insertion and deletion costs being higher still. The cost assignment approach will vary from application to application.

The algorithm works by matching tokens from the two sequences starting at index 0 in both sequences. For a given pair of indices *i* and *j*, you have three choices: substitute, delete, or insert. Note that substitution of matching tokens has zero cost. Thus, using [*i,j*] as the state representation and the choices of editing operations as transitions, the minimal edit distance becomes a least-cost-path problem [A2.2].

Implementation

```
class EditState implements State //see section A2.2
{    int i,j;

     boolean matches(EditState S)
     {    return i==S.i && j==S.j; }

     int nChoices()
     {    return 3; }

     EditState choice(int N)
     {    if (N==0) //a substitution
          {    return new EditState(i+1,j+1); }
          else if (N==1) //delete from seq1
          {    return new EditState(i+1,j); }
          else //insert into seq1
          {    return new EditState(i,j+1); }
     }

     double choiceCost(int N)
     {    if (N==0) //a substitution
          {    return sub[seq1[i], seq2[j] ]; }
          else if (N==1) //a delete from seq1
          {    return del[seq1[i]]; }
          else if (N==2) //an insert into seq1
          {    return ins[seq2[j]]; }
     }
}
```

As described in [A2.2], this algorithm can be optimized by a `notAlreadyVisited()` function so that states are not repeatedly explored. For relatively short sequences, `notAlreadyVisited()` can be implemented with a two-dimensional Boolean array using the indices of the two sequences. The array is initialized to all false and then set to true whenever the combination of two indices is attempted.

A3.2e – Nearest Neighbor Sequence Classifier

You can use minimal edit distance to compare an input sequence against each of the training examples as in the nearest neighbor vector classifier [A3.1c]. However, this can be relatively expensive. If you take the training data and build a trie or a finite state machine, you can adapt the minimal edit distance algorithm. Because a trie is a special case of finite state machines, you use finite state machines for the implementation. Instead of characterizing the match process by the indices of the two strings being compared, you use $[s,i]$, where s is a state in the finite state machine and i is an index into the sequence. You start with the start state of the machine and the index 0.

At a given state, you have several choices. You can take each of the transitions leaving state s using the cost of $sub[seq[i],t]$, where t is the token for that transition. You can stay in state s and increment i using the cost $del[seq[i]]$. You can also take each transition without moving *i*. In this last case, you use the cost *ins*[*t*], where *t* is the token for the transition taken.

Implementation

```
class MatchState implements State //see section A2.2
{    int s; //state in the Finite State Machine
     int i; //index into the sequence being matched

     boolean matches(MatchState S)
     {    return i==S.i && s==S.s; }

     int nChoices()
     {    return 2*nTransitionsLeaving(s)+1; ]

     MatchState choice(int N)
     {    if (N==0) //deleting a token from seq
          {    return new MatchState(s,i+1); }
          else if (N<=nTransitionsLeaving(s))
               //follow transition using substitution
          {    return new MatchState( transition[s,N].next, i+1); }
          else //follow transition by inserting its token into seq
          {    N = N-nTransitionsLeaving(s);
               return new MatchState( transition[s,N].token, i);
          }
     }

     double choiceCost(int N)
     {    if (N==0) //cost of deletion
          {    return del[seq[i]]; }
          else if (N<=nTransitionsLeaving(s)) // cost of substitution
          {    return sub[transition[s,N].token, seq[i]]; }
          else //cost of insertion
          {    N=N-nTransitionsLeaving(s);
               return ins[transition[s,N].token];
          }
     }
}
```

   If you are working with a trie where each node can only be reached in one way, you can assign an index to each trie node and can use that index along with the sequence index to subscript a two-dimensional notAlreadyVisited() array as you did with minimal edit distance. However, because the number of trie nodes might become large and because you might use finite state machines, you need a hash table to take care of the repeated visits. The key to the hash table is composed from the state index and the sequence index. Remember that notAlreadyVisited() is not required for the correct functioning of the least-cost-path algorithm, but if space is not a problem, it can sharply reduce the amount of time required for the match.

A3.3 – Statistical Sequence Classifiers

In the preceding section, you discussed classifiers where the desired sequences were clearly defined and the inputs received were known exactly. In many situations, however, the desired input sequence is not clearly specified. In some systems, the input that the user generates is not known for sure. You use probabilistic methods for dealing with these issues. Statistical recognition is a huge part of pattern recognition and beyond the scope of this work. However, the following three algorithms are quite useful in interactive systems:

- *Probabilistic state machines*—When the desired sequence is modeled as a state machine, but the inputs are uncertain and represented as a vector of probabilities

- *Ngrams*—When the desired sequences are not clearly defined and the inputs might or might not be known exactly

- *Hidden Markov Models*—When you only know sample inputs and must develop a state model that captures those inputs

A3.3a – Probabilistic State Machines

The use of such state machine methods in interactive settings was pioneered by Hudson[4]. These methods apply when you can clearly define the required set of inputs as a state machine, but the input tokens are uncertain. For example, you might have a trie derived from dog and cat breeds, as described in section A3.2, but the inputs come from a character recognizer, which has uncertain results. You might have a state machine of legal command phrases, but the speech recognizer is usually uncertain about which word was actually spoken.

In the dog/cat example, the character recognizer might have a hard time deciding between C and L. You can model this by having the recognizer return a vector of probabilities rather than just a single token. Given the stroke in Figure A.17, the illustrated probabilities might be returned.

Error	0.12
....	
C	0.50
....	
L	0.30
....	
O	0.05
....	
U	0.03
....	

Figure A.17 – Input probabilities for a poorly formed stroke

The recognizer believes that the stroke is a C but is uncertain. This uncertainty is reflected in the probabilities, including the fact that the stroke might be an error. If the state machine is currently in a state that will accept either C, L, or U, you are, therefore, uncertain about the next state as well as whether you should accept the error and remain in the current state. You, therefore, represent the current state not as a specific value but rather as an array of probabilities. You can use the probabilities of the current state, the legal transitions, and the probabilities from the recognizer to work out the uncertainties. The current most probable state might not have a transition on C and, therefore, will only lend its probability to L. The next most probable state might be very close in probability and it might have a transition on C. The high opinion that the recognizer has of C might override. Instead of forcing the recognizer to make the decision, the probabilistic state machine can take past state information, legal inputs, and the recognizer's opinion all into account in choosing a classification result.

You can build a classifier algorithm using these principles. Given a set of states S, you define an array $cur[S]$, which contains the probabilities that the machine is currently in each possible state s. Given an alphabet of inputs I, you can define an array $in[I]$ such that $in[i]$ is the probability that the last input received from the user was i. The key to probabilistic state machines is the algorithm for computing state transitions. You can define the state machine as a set of transitions $t(curState, input, nextState) \in T$. The probability that a transition t will be taken is the probability of $t.input$ times the probability of $t.currentState$. Because there might be many transitions leading into a given state, you need to sum the probabilities of all such transitions.

Implementation

```
class Transition
{     int currentState;
      int input;
      int nextState;
}


double cur[S]; // probabilities for each state
Transition trans[T]; // the set of possible transitions in the state machine

void stateTransition( double in[I] ) // given probabilities for each input
{     double next[S]; // probabilities of all possible next states

      double errorProb=1.0; // probability of incorrect input
      for (int i=0;i<I;i++)
      {     errorProb=errorProb-in[i]; }

      // probability of no transition because of error
      for (int s=0;s<S;s++)
      {     next[s]=cur[s]*errorProb; }

      // transition probabilities
      for (int t=0;t<T;t++)
      {     int curS = trans[t].currentState;
            double inProb = in[ trans[t].input ];
            int nextS = trans[t].nextState;
            next[nextS]=next[nextS]+inProb*cur[curs];
      }

      // normalize cur to sum to 1.0
      double sum=0.0;
      for ( int s=0;s<S;s++)
      { sum=sum+next[s]; }
      for (int s=0;s<S;s++)
      { cur[s]=next[s] / sum; }
}
```

Note that if the input probabilities do not sum to 1.0 (as when the recognizer believes there is an error in the input) or some of the inputs are not acceptable to any of the nonzero states, the total probability in *cur[S]* steadily declines. You accommodate this by dividing every element of *next* by the sum of *next* at the end of each transition.

A3.3b – N-Grams

In some cases, you might not have a state machine that clearly defines the set of legal inputs. For example, it is very difficult to create a state machine or even a context-free grammar that can accurately represent English syntax. Even if you had such a grammar, a syntactically correct sentence might not make any sense or many colloquialisms would be outside of the grammar. You might not want to model all French words by a huge dictionary because new French words would fail or the size might be prohibitive. What you need is a model of valid sequences that does not require that you formulate a state machine.

A common technique for such a model is N-grams. You form N-grams by taking a corpus of valid inputs and finding all input sequences of length N. You count how often each combination of N inputs occurs. Generally, you normalize the N-gram model by dividing each count by the sum of all counts. This gives you a probability for each sequence of length N.

For example, if you use bi-grams (N=2), you can take the last input and use the bi-gram probabilities to predict what the next input should be. If the inputs are from a character recognizer, you can use this information to refine the choice of characters. A "t" never follows a "q" in English. You can be even more accurate if you use tri-grams (N=3). In this case, you use the last two inputs to determine the probabilities for the next input. The N-gram statistics are filling the place of the state machine in helping discriminate among uncertain inputs.

The huge advantage of N-grams over state machines is that you can derive them from examples rather than carefully design them. Rather than build a state machine of possible words, you can compute the letter tri-grams for all words in a dictionary. Rather than build a grammar for English, you can compute word tri-grams for all words in the *New York Times* or from all Web pages indexed by Google.

A major problem with N-grams is their size. If you use letters of the alphabet, there are 676 bi-grams, 17,576 possible tri-grams, and 456,976 quad-grams. These sizes are generally acceptable, except in very small machines. However, if you want to use a 20,000 word dictionary as the set of possible inputs, there are 400 million possible bi-grams and 8 trillion possible tri-grams. In real problems, the N-gram model is quite sparse. There are not 400 million valid word pairs in English. Though this sparseness eliminates a simple array implementation of N-grams, it does make many such problems tractable.

Local Predictors

One use of N-grams is as a local predictor. In this algorithm, the N-grams are used to predict what the next input will be. No history is kept and no future inputs are taken into account. Take, for example, a character recognizer. You can use a tri-gram model of three characters and the last two inputs to predict what the next input should be. If you combine the prediction probabilities with the input probabilities from the recognizer, you can improve the system's ability to select the correct input. This assumes that the history (the last two inputs) is correct and cannot take future inputs into account in making the decision. However, in this example, if the last two inputs were incorrect, the user would have eliminated them and the future inputs do not yet exist.

The following implementation assumes a tri-gram model. It can easily be reduced to bi-grams or extended to larger numbers than three.

Implementation

```
// interface to some previously obtained tri-gram model
interface Trigram()
{
    double getProb(int i1, i2, i3) // probability of the tri-gram (i1,i2,i3)
}

class LocalPredictor
{
    Trigram tg;       // the tri-gram model to be used
    int i2;           // the last input recognized
    int i1;           // the input before last

    // Takes an array of input probabilities that is indexed by
    // the input class number. It uses the tg model and these
    // inputs to predict what the correct input should be.
    int predictInput( double inputProbabilities[nInputs] )
    {
        double maxProb=0.0;
        int selectedInput=-1;
        for (int i=0;i<nInputs;i++)
        {   double prob = inputProbabilities[i]*tg.getProb(i1,i2,i);
            if (prob>maxProb)
            {   selectedInput=i;
                maxProb=prob;
            }
        }
        i1=i2;
        i2=i;
        return i;
    }
}
```

Globally Optimal Input Sequence

N-grams can also be used to evaluate a sequence of uncertain inputs to select the sequence of inputs that is globally optimal relative to some N-gram model. Unlike the local predictor, this approach must have the entire input sequence before starting and takes the entire sequence into account before selecting the most plausible set of inputs.

As with probabilistic state machines and the local predictor, this algorithm models an input as a vector of probabilities indexed by the input class. You use the least-cost-path algorithm to select the most likely sequence of inputs. Each step of the least-cost-path is characterized by the following tuple:

- The index of the input being considered
- The last N-1 inputs that were chosen on this path
- The sum of all costs along this path

The cost of making a particular choice is *(1.0-choiceProbability)* or the probability that the choice was wrong. The *choiceProbability* is the N-gram probability of this choice, times the recognizer probability that this was the input generated by the user. The following algorithm will use tri-grams as the example.

When using N-grams, you have the problem of starting and ending the sequence. For this, you use a special empty input Λ. The sequence always starts with N-1 empty inputs and ends with N-1 empty inputs. In the algorithms, you use input class zero for the empty input. Padding the start and end of the input sequence with empty inputs (class zero) allows the algorithms to ignore the special cases of the start and end.

Implementation

```
// See implementation for leastCostPath (A2.2)

// A RecognizerInput is a vector of probabilities.
// These are the recognizer's opinion
// on which input the user entered.
class RecognizerInput
{    double probs[nInputClasses];  }

// interface to some previously obtained tri-gram model
interface Trigram()
{    double getProb(int i1, i2, i3); // probability of the tri-gram (i1,i2,i3)
}
```

```
class GlobalOptimalSequence
{
      static Trigram tg;
      static RecognizerInput inputs[nUserInputs];

      TrigramState extends State // see LeastCostPath
      {
            int i2;   // the last input selected
            int i1;   // second to the last input selected
            int idx;  // index into inputs for the user input being
                      // considered for this state

            TrigramState( int BeforeLast, Last, CurrentInput)
            {   i1=BeforeLast;
                i2=Last;
                idx=CurrentInput;
            }

            boolean matches(TrigramState S)
            {   if (idx>=nUserInputs && S.idx>=nUserInputs)
                {   return true; }    // this is a goal state
                return (i1==S.i1 && i2==S.i2 && idx==S.idx);
            }

            int nChoices()
            {   return nInputClasses; }

            TrigramState choice(int InputChosen)
            {   return new TrigramState(i2,InputChosen,idx+1); }

            double choiceCost(int InputChosen)
            {   double trigramProb = tg.getProb(i1,i2,InputChosen);
                double inputProb =  inputs[idx].probs[InputChosen];
                double choiceProb = trigramProb * inputProb;
                return 1.0-choiceProb;
            }
      } // end TrigramState

      Path chooseSequence(RecognizerInput in[])
      {   GlobalOptimalSequence.inputs = in;
          TrigramState goal=new TrigramState(0,0,in.length);
          TrigramState start=new TrigramState(0,0,0);
          return leastCostPath(start,goal);
      }
}
```

A4 – COLOR

Color is generally represented by red, green, blue (RGB) because that is what the eye recognizes and what displays generate. However, RGB is difficult for people to work with. A more human-friendly representation is hue, saturation, brightness (HSB). This section contains the algorithms for conversion between these two representations.

A4.1 – RGB to HSB

This algorithm assumes that RGB is represented as three numbers between 0.0 and 1.0. The conversion is to HSB where each component varies from 0.0 to 1.0. The RGB is in the variables red, green, and blue with the result stored in the variables hue, sat, and bright.

Implememementation

```
rgbMin = min( red, green, blue);
rgbMax = max( red, green ,bue);
delta = rgbMax – rgbMin;

bright = rgbMax;
if (delta== 0 )
{    hue = 0;
     sat = 0;
}
else
{    sat = delta/rgbMax;

     dRed=   ( ( ( rgbMax-red ) / 6 ) + ( delta / 2 ) ) / delta;
     dGreen= ( ( ( rgbMax-green) / 6 ) + ( delta / 2 ) ) / delta;
     dBlue = ( ( ( rgbMax-blue ) / 6 ) + (delta / 2 ) ) / delta;

     if ( red == rgbMax )
     {    hue = dBlue-dGreen; }
     else if ( green == rgbMax )
     {    hue = ( 1 / 3 ) + dRed – dBlue; }
     else
     {    hue = ( 2 / 3 ) + dGreen – dRed; }

     if (hue < 0 )
     {    hue = hue+1; }
     if (hue > 1 )
     {    hue = hue-1; }
}
```

A4.2 – HSB to RGB

This algorithm assumes that HSB and RGB are represented by values between 0.0 and 1.0. HSB is stored in the variables hue, sat, and bright, and RGB is stored in the variables red, green, and blue.

Implementation

```
if (sat == 0 )
{    red = bright;
     green = bright;
     blue = bright;
}
else
{    if (hue == 1.0)
          varInt = 0;
     else
          varInt = int(hue*6);
     var1 = bright*(1-sat);
     var2 = bright*( 1 – (sat * (hue*6 – varInt) ) );
     var3 = bright*( 1 – (sat * ( 1 – (hue*6 – varInt) ) ) );

     if (varInt == 0) {red = bright; green = var3; blue = var1; }
     else if ( varInt == 1) { red = var2; green = bright; blue = var1; }
     else if (varInt == 2) { red = var1; green = bright; blue = var3; }
     else if (varInt == 3) { red = var1; green = var2; blue = bright; }
     else if (varInt == 4 ) { red = var3; green = var1; blue = bright; }
     else {red = bright; green = var1; blue = var2;}
}
```

END NOTES

[1] Duda, R. O., P. E. Hart, and D. G. Stork. *Pattern Classification*. New York: John Wiley and Sons, 2001.

[2] Mitchell, T. M. *Machine Learning*. New York: McGraw-Hill, 1997.

[3] Hopcroft, J. E., and J. D. Ullman. *Formal Languages and Their Relation to Automata*. Menlo Park, CA: Addison-Wesley, 1969.

[4] Hudson, S. E., and G. Newell. "Probabilistic State Machines: Dialog Management for Inputs with Uncertainty." *User Interface Software and Technology* (UIST 92) (November 1992): 199–208.

INDEX

redirecting Graphics
object, 450–454

scene graphs, 458–462

primary angle, measuring,
571–572

prime objects, 403

printers, color resolution, 27

printing, and region
models, 28

priority queues, 573–575

probabilistic state machines,
614–620

processMouseEvent()
method, 56, 63, 65, 75,
77, 78

processMouseMotionEven
t() method, 77, 78

programmable API, and user
interface distribution,
351–353

Project Athena, 83

projector light, brightness,
495–496

properties
interface design tools
(IDT), 196–203
table widgets, 163
widget, 85

PropertyEditor
annotation, 197

proportionally spaced fonts,
35, 36

propositional production
systems (PPS)
described, 227–229
translating into code,
235–241

prototypes
paper, 540
and syntax design, 222

pseudocode, 557

pull-down menus, 183

Q

quadratic polynomials, 259

Quartz system, Mac OS, 20

queues, priority, 573–575

query fields, 229, 235–236

Quikwriting input system,
378–379

Qwerty keyboards, 366

R

radians, 273

radio button model (fig.), 11

radio buttons, 89

RadioButton, 203–204

reading scan order, 178

rectangles
selecting, 298
and shape
computation, 258

redraw() method, 18–19,
20, 38, 39, 41, 56, 70,
71, 81, 286,
449–554, 452

redrawing display trees,
38–39

reflection
command/code
binding, 475
described, 65–66, 205
finding widgets, 193–195
and interface design, 188
total internal, 515

region models, 28–30

regions
clipping, described, 20
and draw methods, 33
sensing features, 502–505

registering listeners, 78

Registry, and callbacks, 55

regression testing, 72

Remote Frame Buffer (RFB)
protocol, 346, 347, 349

removeListener()
method, 68

removing
interface items, 180–181
listeners from buttons, 62

rendering speed, and
indexed colors, 26

repaint() method, 70, 193

representing the
history, 337

requestFocus()
method, 48

resistor IDs, 519–520

resolution
of human vision, 175
spatial, of drawn
images, 27

resource bundles, 210

resources
and locales, 209–212
storing for widget design,
198–203

retained graphics, 38, 42

reverse undo
operations, 329

RFB (Remote Frame Buffer)
protocol, 346, 347, 349

RFID tags, 520–521